Fodor's Healthy Escapes

Bernard Burt

Fodor's Travel Publications, Inc.
New York • Toronto • London • Sydney • Auckland
http://www.fodors.com/

Copyright © 1997
by Fodor's Travel Publications, Inc.

Fifth Edition

ISBN 0–679–03229–0

Fodor's Healthy Escapes

Editor: Susan Kleinman
Contributors: Steven K. Amsterdam, Hannah Borgeson, David Low, Linda K. Schmidt
Creative Director: Fabrizio La Rocca
Cartographer: David Lindroth
Illustrator: Karl Tanner
Cover Design: Tigist Getachew
Cover Photograph: Ken Scott/TSW

Design: Vignelli Associates

About the Author

Recognized internationally as an authority on the spa experience, Bernard Burt wrote the original edition of this book in 1987 and has updated five editions in the decade since. A travel industry consultant based in Washington, D.C., Burt has written two guidebooks to that city and contributed articles to *American Health*, *The Washington Flyer*, *Potomac Life*, and *Maturity News Service*. He was founding director of The International Spa & Fitness Association and publishes *SpaGoer* newsletter. Burt was honored by the State of Maryland as Travel Writer of the Year in 1985.

Special Sales

PRINTED IN THE UNITED STATES OF AMERICA
10 9 8 7 6 5 4 3 2 1

Contents

Foreword

The appeal of the fitness vacation—holiday time used for achieving new levels of physical or mental well-being or maintaining health—continues to widen as new facilities, new programs, new technology, and new ideas attract health-conscious individuals.

Where yesterday's working men and women saw vacation time as an opportunity to escape and relax, today's traveler looks for opportunities to expend additional effort in pursuit of a stronger body, a better self-understanding, perhaps a new self-image. Those who invest vacation time to achieve health and fitness goals may groan about getting up before dawn to go on a hike, yet they tend to return home relishing the natural high these activities bring them.

Fodor's Healthy Escapes surveys the entire range of fitness holiday opportunities in North America. In the pages of this guide, the in-depth profiles of more than 240 resorts, facilities, and cruise ships provide the detailed information anyone needs to begin to plan a vacation with a purpose.

The fees and prices quoted in the resort and cruise ship profiles are based on tariffs that were current in 1996 and are subject to change as costs rise and the contents of program and package offerings are reformulated. Where applicable, taxes and gratuities are additional. Deposits must usually be received in advance of the guest's arrival, and a cancellation charge applies to most bookings. Each resort makes its own policy with respect to accepting payment by personal check, traveler's check, money order, or credit card. The following abbreviations are used in the resort profiles in noting credit card acceptance: AE, American Express; D, Discover; DC, Diners Club; MC, MasterCard; V, Visa.

Fees for medical services may be covered by your health insurance and under some circumstances may be tax deductible; consult the resort's program director and/or your tax advisor for further information.

While every care has been taken to assure the accuracy of the information in this guide, the passage of time will always bring change, and consequently the publisher cannot accept responsibility for errors that may occur.

All prices and schedules quoted here are based on information available to us at press time. The availability of programs and facilities is subject to change, however, and the prudent fitness vacationer will confirm the details of resort or cruise line offerings before beginning to make serious plans.

Fodor's wants to hear about your travel experiences, both pleasant and unpleasant. When a resort or hotel fails to live up to its billing, let us know and we will investigate the complaint and revise our entries where the facts warrant it.

Send your letters to the editors of Fodor's Travel Publications, 201 East 50th Street, New York, NY 10022.

Acknowledgments

The author is grateful for the assistance of Naomi Wagman of Custom Spas Worldwide, Jenni Lipa of Spa Trek, Frank van Putten of Spa-Finders Travel Arrangements Ltd., J. J. Reynolds of the Association of Retail Travel Agents cruise ship committee, Judith Singer of Health Fitness Dynamics, Inc., Frank LaFleche of the Canadian Embassy's tourism division, Augustin Ballina of the Mexican Government Tourist Office, and all the concerned professionals who worked out with him and contributed to the research and development of the original concept for this book.

The insights shared by T. George Harris, founding editor of *American Health* and *Psychology Today* magazines, were a constant source of encouragement.

For personal support and advice, the author is indebted to Martha Ashelman, Denise Austin, Jeffrey Burt, Nancy Love, and Duncan Farrell. Travel was facilitated by American Airlines, Continental Airlines, Mexicana Airlines, and USAir.

Additional information on programs and therapies is available from the International Spa and Fitness Association (113 S. West St., Alexandria, VA 22314-2824, tel. 703/838–2930, fax 703/838–2950).

Directory 1: Alphabetical Listing of Resorts

Directory 2: Listing of Resorts by Program

Luxury Pampering

Nonprogram Resort

Nutrition and Diet

Preventive Medicine

Spiritual Awareness

Sports Conditioning

Stress Control

Taking the Waters

Vibrant Maturity

Weight Management

Introduction

By T. George
Harris

Mr. Harris, the
founding editor of
American Health
and Psychology
Today magazines,
is publisher and
editor of Deeper
Health Magazine.

Americans are working harder than ever. In the past 15 years the leisure time of the average adult has shrunk by one-third to just 18 hours a week. The work week has grown longer by 20%, and for many people it now approaches the 50-hour week once condemned in sweatshops.

Indeed, the higher you rise in professional and executive ranks, the longer and harder you work today. Then you labor still more hours learning new things, such as computer uses, that you need to do your job better. For many successful working men and women the stress of overload has become a badge of achievement: It comes with the territory. And those who in a previous generation might have been the idle rich often spend inherited wealth today on opportunities to try harder.

Stress has become the common cold of the busy classes. Fighting it, many strive to get into shape for peak performance. Fitness of body becomes the metaphor for—and means to— fitness of mind. Gallup surveys for *American Health* magazine find that two out of three Americans now aim to do weekly exercise (though we don't always do as much as we intend). One in three of us considers health facilities in planning a vacation trip.

In fact, the short, healthy trips become the turning point in many lives. When you go on vacation, it's foolish not to return in better shape than when you left. Travel is an investment in yourself, your productive capital. More and more people expect to get some good out of their trips. More people now take shorter and shorter vacations, and they vacation more often. Millions look for places where they will get the body back into motion, places where they will learn about fresh, tasty foods that are not larded with fat, sugar, salt, and excessive calories.

This book fills the need for a detailed, easy-to-use guide to hundreds of places that now strive to provide meaningful recreation for the mind as well as the body. Moving far beyond the concept of the old European spa—those Marienbads where the elderly elite went to take the waters and to be attended by doctors—some of the typically North American spots even offer specific programs to tone the brain and the spirit. The Golden Door in California invites a special few into "The Inner Door" to try the meditative lifestyle of serenity. Arizona's Canyon Ranch offers electronic feedback gear to help you tune in on your brain's alpha waves, long associated with meditation and creativity.

The Fodor's guides published by Random House have earned a reputation for providing practical, hard-to-get information. While other publishers bring out exotic volumes on "spas," this book provides the essential facts about healthy travel in a systematic way. *Fodor's Healthy Escapes* not only gives you prices and the details of programs, it provides such down-to-earth specifics as the kind of workout gear available in the exercise room.

The purpose is simple: to help you find the kind of place you want, nearest where you want to be. You will probably be astonished to discover that among the 243 resorts profiled in this book, several are an easy drive from your home or workplace. Then there is the chapter describing cruise ships that sail in Caribbean and Pacific waters.

The resorts described in this guide are grouped by region; if you want to find a facility in a specific area, the *Table of Contents* will tell you where to look. If you already have the name of a resort and want to learn what it has to offer, look for it in the alphabetical listing in *Directory 1*. If you want to find a resort that offers a particular kind of program or treatment, turn to *Directory 2*, which lists resorts under 13 categories of fitness program:

- Holistic health
- Kid fitness
- Life enhancement
- Luxury pampering
- Nonprogram resort facilities
- Nutrition and diet
- Preventive medicine
- Spiritual awareness
- Sports conditioning
- Stress control
- Taking the waters
- Vibrant maturity
- Weight management

In the search for an author, it was clear that this book did not need a health-food zealot, a weight lifter, a spa devotee, or an exotic travel writer who loves only funky or pricey places. We needed someone who could represent the needs of the hardworking woman or man with a limited time to spend on vacation.

The ideal choice turned out to be Bernard Burt, a marketing consultant out of the University of Pennsylvania's Wharton School, a prizewinning travel writer, and a practical-minded executive who had managed programs for Philadelphia's Civic Center. Like many a manager who strives for health, Burt had quite a few naive ideas about health behaviors and healthy food—and found himself totally unprepared, as most executives do, when his doctor told him his life would be shorter than normal if he did not get his weight down. At 58, Burt was ready to study the kinds of places that might help him change his lifestyle, and he signed on to research the new *Fodor's Healthy Escapes*.

As a test run, Burt began with an article on the most innovative places then rising in the U.S. spa world for the April 1988 issue of *American Health*. Eager to discover the ancestry of such places, Burt investigated one of Europe's great spas, Brenner's Park Hotel in Baden-Baden, Germany. The historic Friedrichsbad, the emperor's bathhouse, had just been restored at great expense and was drawing Europe's and Japan's water-takers. Striding into the baths, Bernard paid little attention to the sign *Gemischt* (literally, "mixed"). Only when nude women and men appeared together did he realize the meaning of *Gemischt*. Being a gentleman of poise, he eased into the ancient European customs with hardly a blush.

Back in the United States, Burt's poise underwent a more severe test at the Canyon Ranch in Arizona, one of the most innovative of American health centers. Mel Zuckerman, the founder and owner, has a missionary zeal about providing state-of-the-art programs, seminars, and nutrition. He and Dr.

Bill Day, one of the fitness pioneers out of the national YMCA, have made Canyon Ranch the practical testing site for the fitness education.

Bernard Burt realized a clear break between the European spa tradition and American ideas. In different ways, the American industry strives to serve the individual's strong need for the enhancement of physical and mental resources. For most Americans, health means being the best each of us can be at the things we care about, from work to parenting to spiritual growth.

Burt found that other hardworking people seeking healthy turnarounds make wonderful companions. On his first dawn walks up a mountain, he learned that ordinary city clothes do not keep one warm in the desert. His feet seemed to be freezing until a companion executive dug out and passed on an extra pair of Brooks Brothers wool socks. In the supportive environment of the health resorts, guests as well as staff soon develop more than the customary concern for one another's welfare. The general feeling is, we're all in this together.

The most startling discovery Burt made concerned the cuisine. A gourmet who cares deeply about food, a wine lover and an honorary member of Washington's Sommelier Society, he expected to find tasteless brown things to eat, the bran-and-bean-sprout cuisine of the early health-food restaurants. Not so; in almost every resort he found the food fresh and beautiful.

With help on his personal turnaround, Burt became even more faithful in his daily workouts at the Watergate Health Club in Washington, DC. The grinding work of the writer does not often lead to exercise, but Burt got his cholesterol and his triglycerides under control. He dropped 30 pounds before he finished the first edition of this book, and his doctor no longer threatens him. His single purpose now as a writer is to guide you toward the place you'll choose for your own turnaround.

Glossary

A **Acupressure.** Finger massage intended to release muscle tension by applying pressure to the nerves.

Aikido. Japanese martial art.

Air Dyne Bicycle. See *Schwinn Air Dyne Bicycle.*

Alexander Technique. A massage system created in the 1890s by the Australian actor F. M. Alexander to correct physical habits that cause stress and help improve posture.

Algotherapy. Seaweed bath. See *Thalassotherapy.*

Aquaerobics. Aerobics workouts in a swimming pool; stretch, strength, and stamina exercises that combine water resistance and body movements. Also *aquafit* and *aquacise.*

Aromabath. See *herbal wrap.*

Aromatherapy. Massage with oils from essences of plants and flowers intended to relax the skin's connective tissues and stimulate the natural flow of lymph.

Ayurvedic. 4,000-year-old Indian treatments, based on teachings from the Vedic scriptures, using oils, massage, and herbs.

B **Bach Cures.** Healing with floral essences and oils.

Balneology. Traditional study and practice of water-based treatments using geothermal hot springs, mineral water, or seawater.

Barre. Balance bár or rail used during exercise.

Bindi. Bodywork combining exfoliation, herbal treatment, and light massage.

Bioenergetics. Exchange of energy between persons giving and receiving massage.

Body composition test. Evaluation of lean body mass and percentage of body fat. A computerized system compares personal data with standard percentages to determine whether an individual is overweight.

Body sugaring. Hair-removal process said to date from the time of Cleopatra.

C **Chi Kung.** Chinese energy exercise; breathing and body movements recharge energy.

Circuit training. The combination of aerobics and high-energy workout with weight-resistance equipment.

Circuit weight work. See *Circuit training.*

Cold plunge. Deep pool for the rapid contraction of the capillaries; stimulates circulation after sauna.

Colonic irrigation. Enema to cleanse high into the colon with water.

Contour. Calisthenics for deep toning of muscle groups.

Crystal healing. Healing energy believed to be generated by quartz and other minerals.

Cures. Course of treatments. Also *kur.*

Cybex. Patented equipment for isokinetic strength testing and training.

D David System. Pneumatic weight training units in which air is pumped. See *Circuit training.*

Drinking cure. Medically prescribed regimen of mineral water consumption.

E Ergometer. Exercise machine designed for muscular contraction.

F Fango. A mud pack or body coating intended to promote the release of toxins and relieve muscular and arthritic pain.

Fast. Supervised diet of water, juice, nuts, seeds; intended to produce significant weight loss.

Feldenkrais Method. Developed by Israeli physicist Moshe Feldenkrais in the 1940s to reprogram the nervous system through movement augmented by physical pressure and manipulation.

Free weights. Hand-held dumbbells or barbells.

G Gestalt. Sensory awareness; the inner experience of being.

Guided imagery. Visualization to stimulate the body's immune system.

G5. Percussive hand massage to relax tense muscles.

H Haysack wrap. Kneipp treatment with steamed hay intended to detoxify the body.

Hellerwork. A system of deep tissue bodywork, stress reduction, and movement reeducation developed by Joseph Heller.

Herbal wrap. A treatment in which moisture, heat, and herbal essences penetrate the skin while the body is wrapped in hot linens, plastic sheets, and blankets; it is intended to promote muscle relaxation and the elimination of toxins. Also *aromabath, herbal bath.*

Herbology. The therapeutic use of herbs in treatments and diet.

Hot plunge. Deep pool for the rapid dilation of the capillaries.

Hydromassage. See *hydrotub.*

Hydrotherapy. Underwater massage; alternating hot and cold showers; and other water-oriented treatments.

Hydrotub. Underwater massage in deep tubs equipped with high-pressure jets and hand-manipulated hose. Also *hydromassage.*

I Inhalations. Hot vapors, or steam mixed with eucalyptus oil, inhaled to decongest the respiratory system; breathed through inhalation equipment or in a special steam room.

Interval training. A combination of high-energy exercise followed by a period of low-intensity activity.

Iridology. A theory that links markings in the iris of the eye to the condition of organs of the body.

Iyengar yoga. Exercise system developed in India by B.K.S. Iyengar.

J **Jin Shin Jyutsu.** Ancient Japanese form of body balancing.

K **Keiser Cam II.** A patented system of pneumatic weight-training units. Also *Keiser Cam III.*

Kneipp kur. Treatments combining hydrotherapy, herbology, and a diet of natural foods, developed in Germany in the mid-1800s by Pastor Sebastian Kneipp.

Kur. Course of treatments, as in Kneipp kur, usually associated with baths or drinking mineral water under medical supervision at European thermal spring spas.

L **Lap pool.** A shallow swimming pool with exercise lanes; the standard lap length is 50 feet.

Lifecycle. A computer-programmed exercise bike, made by Bally.

Liferower. A computer-programmed exercise machine that simulates rowing, made by Bally.

Lomi-Lomi. Hawaiian rhythmical rocking massage.

M **Maximal heart rate.** An individual's highest attainable heart rate (the number of heartbeats per minute). It is best determined by means of a graded maximal exercise test, but an estimate can be made by subtracting one's age from 220. See *target heart rate.*

N **Naturopathy.** Natural healing prescriptions that use plants and flowers.

Nautilus. Patented strength training equipment designed to isolate one muscle group for each exercise movement that contracts and lengthens against gravity.

NordicTrack. A patented design of cross-country ski machine.

O **Orthion.** Stretching device for neck, spine.

Ovo-lacto diet. A regimen that includes eggs and dairy products.

P **Parafango.** Combination of mud and paraffin wax. See *fango.*

Parcourse. A trail, usually outdoors, equipped with exercise stations. Also *parcours, vitacourse.*

Pilates Method. Strength training movements developed in Germany by Dr. Joseph Pilates during the 1920s.

Plyometrics. Jumps and push steps to strengthen leg muscles. See *Step aerobics.*

Polarity therapy. Balancing the energy within the body through a combination of massage, meditation, exercise, and diet; created by Dr. Randolph Stone.

Pressotherapy. Pressure cuffs used to improve circulation on feet.

R **Radiance technique.** See *Reiki.*

Rebirthing. A yoga breathing technique combined with guided meditation to relax and clear the mind. Also *reliving the experience of birth.*

Rebounder. A miniature trampoline.

Reflexology. Massage of the pressure points on the feet, hands, and ears; intended to relax the parts of the body.

Reiki. An ancient healing method that teaches universal life energy through the laying on of hands and mental and spiritual balancing. Intended to relieve acute emotional and physical conditions. Also *radiance technique.*

Rolfing. A bodywork system developed by Ida Rolf that improves balance and flexibility through manipulation of rigid muscles, bones, and joints. It is intended to improve energy flow and relieve stress (often related to emotional trauma).

Roman pool. A step-down whirlpool bath, for one or two persons.

Rubenfeld Synergy. A method of integrating body and mind through verbal expression and gentle touch, developed by Ilana Rubenfeld.

Russian bath. Steam bath to flush toxins from the body.

S **Salt glow.** A cleansing treatment, using coarse salt to remove dead skin, similar to the loofah body scrub. Also *salt rub.*

Salt rub. See *salt glow.*

Schwinn Air Dyne Bicycle. A stationary exercise bike that works the upper and lower body simultaneously.

Scotch douche. A showerlike treatment with high-pressure hoses that alternate hot and cold water, intended to improve circulation through rapid contraction and dilation of the capillaries.

Shamanism. Spiritual and natural healing performed by medicine men and women.

Shiatsu. A massage technique developed by Tokujiro Namikoshi that uses finger (*shi*) pressure (*atsu*) to stimulate the body's inner powers of balance and healing.

Sitz bath. Immersion of the hips and lower body in herbal hot water, followed by cold water, to stimulate the immune system. Also a Kneipp treatment for constipation, hemorrhoids, prostate problems, menstrual problems, and digestive upsets.

Spa cuisine. Fresh, natural foods low in saturated fats and cholesterol, with an emphasis on whole grains, low-fat dairy products, lean protein, fresh fruit, fish, and vegetables and an avoidance of added salt and products containing sodium and artificial colorings, flavorings, and preservatives.

StairMaster. A patented exercise machine that simulates climbing stairs.

Step aerobics. Rhythmic stepping on and off a small platform.

Stress management. A program of meditation and deep relaxation intended to reduce the ill effects of stress on the system.

Sweat lodge. Native American body-purification ceremony.

Swedish massage. A treatment that duplicates gymnastics movements with stroking, kneading, friction, vibration, and tapping to relax muscles gently; devised at the University of Stockholm early in the 19th century by Per Heinrik Ling.

Swiss shower. A multijet bath that alternates hot and cold water.

T **Tai chi.** (Sometimes called tai chi chuan.) Movements intended to unite body and mind; an ancient Oriental discipline for exercise and meditation.

Target heart rate. The number of heartbeats per minute an individual tries to attain during exercise; the figure is 60% to 90% of one's maximal heart rate. The American College of Sports Medicine recommends maintaining this rate for 20–30 minutes during exercise three to five days a week. See *maximal heart rate.*

Thalassotherapy. Water-based treatments that use seawater, seaweed, algae, and sea air; an ancient Greek therapy.

Trager massage. A technique developed by Milton Trager that employs a gentle, rhythmic shaking of the body to release tension from the joints.

U **Universal Gym.** A patented weight-training system.

V **VersaClimber.** A patented exercise machine that simulates the climbing of a ladder.

Vodder massage. Manual lymph drainage technique developed by Danish-born Emile Vodder in the 1950s.

W **Watsu.** Underwater shiatsu massage.

Y **Yoga.** A discipline of stretching and toning the body through movements or asana postures, controlled deep breathing, relaxation techniques, and diet. A school of Hindu philosophy that advocates physical and mental discipline for the unity of mind, body, and spirit.

Z **Zen shiatsu.** A Japanese acupressure art intended to relieve tension and balance the body.

1 Health and Fitness Programs

Planning a fitness vacation is a two-part process that involves determining your personal fitness goals and finding the right program or resort. You can begin by setting very specific goals for yourself and then look for the program that best suits your needs. Or you can start by surveying what a number of resorts offer and then decide what you want to achieve from your visit. This chapter will help with both kinds of planning process: It identifies and describes 12 different kinds of fitness programs plus the nonprogram category and explains what each attempts to do and what participants can hope to accomplish.

Never before have there been so many varied and challenging opportunities for exercising the mind, the spirit, and the body in a vacation with a purpose. The range of programs and facilities is wide, both for healthy men and women who want to stay in shape and for those who are determined to address a particular health problem or improve a condition.

Since the first edition of this book was published in 1989, there have been significant changes in spa programs, and several trends are expected to accelerate during the '90s. These include emphasis on preventive medicine and holistic health; less emphasis on weight loss but more education in nutrition and weight management through healthy eating and good exercise habits; and wider use of European hydrotherapy. Hopefully we will see more practical approaches to a total fitness vacation and more vacation spots that can be enjoyed year-round.

Some pleasure seekers may choose to relax amid the luxurious furnishings of a posh resort; others will find gratification in a weeklong hiking adventure or the rugged atmosphere of a ranch, with a rigorous schedule that resembles boot camp. New Age retreats and yoga ashrams, naturopaths and natural healing ranches offer health and healing based on combinations of ancient therapies and the latest concepts in behavior modification. Some establishments preach preventive medicine, taking a holistic approach toward strengthening the body against illness through improved nutrition and an understanding of the relationship between mind and body. Others address such problems as the need to lose weight, to stop smoking, and to deal with stress. These programs educate participants, reinforce motivation, and provide a regimen designed not for quick results but for effective long-term improvement and well-being.

Increasingly sophisticated and often specialized resorts offer programs to help guests change their lifestyles at home. The establishment of new eating and exercise habits is now considered preferable to crash courses and 700-calorie daily diets. Techniques such as biofeedback have advanced to patterning weeks, where people learn how to achieve health goals over the long term. Hydrotherapy equipment from Europe appears alongside mud, seaweed, or algae for body cleansing and accompanies the latest in toning, shaping, and weight-loss techniques.

Crossover programs using European and Asian therapies have resulted in the implementation of new versions of the classic kur—a course of treatments available at spas in the United States. Among the notable programs are those at Marriott's Desert Springs Resort in California, where you'll find hydrotherapy tubs (with underwater jets) filled with Hungarian bath salts. Similar techniques are used at Christina Newburgh's SpaDeus in the Tuscan resort of Chianciano Terme, Italy; and the Trianon Palace Givenchy Spa in Versailles, France. The first Givenchy Spa outside France opened in Palm Springs, California, and a Louison Bobet Institut de Thalassotherapie is now found at Marriott's Camelback Inn in Arizona. Thalassotherapy with fresh seawater and seaweed is added to the tub treatments at the Bobet Institut in the Miramar Hotel on the Brittany seacoast in France, as well as the new Hawaiian Ihilani resort, Georgia's Chateau Elan, and Canada's Auberge du Parc Inn. Bathers at California's Sonoma Mission Inn, Terme di Saturnia in Italy, and the historic Baden-Baden in the Black Forest of Germany relax in thermal water swimming pools and hydrotherapy tubs. At Osmosis Spa in California's wine country you can experience an exhilarating Japanese enzyme bath. Thermal mud baths are featured at Dr. Wilkinson's resort in Calistoga, California, and in ancient Abano near Venice, Italy. In Bangkok's Oriental Hotel Spa, the latest sensation is French thalassotherapy, using the same freeze-dried marine algae as Georgia's Sea Island Spa and the new Broadmoor spa in Colorado. Ayurvedic therapies from India are prescribed at the Raj in Iowa.

Similarly, American-style spa programs, traditionally focused on fitness or weight management, have reached Le Mirador Resort on Lake Geneva, Switzerland; Selma Lagerlof Hotel and Spa in Sunne, Sweden; the stately Hanbury Manor, 25 miles from London, England, which has a golf/spa program that includes a computerized fitness evaluation; and the full-service clubs at London's Meridien Hotel, and Chewton Glen near Southampton, where seaside hikes are followed by aromatherapy massage.

No matter which spa you choose, computer technology is now applied at nearly all levels of fitness training. Interactive exercise machines analyze calories expended, adjust themselves to increase your effort, and calculate at what rate your body best functions. These machines are a valuable aid to staff members in designing health regimens to suit individual goals and physiology, but they don't take the sweat out of conditioning. The results of a fitness vacation remain yours to achieve, with personal training from spa professionals.

Basically, your choices fall into two categories: self-contained spas that focus on wellness, and resorts that feature a spa or health club along with sports and other diversions. In the wellness programs, you'll find group support and camaraderie from like-minded participants who are adhering, as you are, to a structured daily schedule. At the resorts, you may be more self-indulgent, as there are many options and temptations geared toward those who are on nonspa vacations.

The costs of a wellness week or spa holiday vary widely. Where luxury and personal attention are the formula and the staff outnumber the guests, expect to pay premium prices. At the same time, the budget-conscious traveler will find options at $45–$100 a day (including meals) and opportunities to use various resort facilities (without participating in a program) for a small daily fee. Many resorts will offer services (a facial or massage, for instance) at an additional cost, to complement the principal program you have chosen. In some areas the off-season brings markedly reduced rates and bargain packages.

Because rate policies differ widely among resorts, the wise traveler will want to have a clear understanding of precisely what features are included in a program rate and what taxes and tipping will be added to the rate quoted. The prices given in the resort profiles in this book were accurate at the time of writing, but they should be used only as a preliminary guide; they will vary throughout 1997 and 1998 as increases go into effect, new combinations of services are offered, and new programs and packages are formulated.

As this edition was being updated, new trends were becoming apparent. Regions experiencing the greatest growth were Florida, the Southwest, and Mexico. And we've added Carribean resorts with all-inclusive programs; the new California center for mind/body therapies, developed by Dr. Deepak Chopra; and a preventive medicine retreat, directed by Dr. Dean Ornish, head of the Preventive Medicine Research Institute in Oakland, California.

Other new entries to look for in this edition are the grandest spa at sea, aboard Celebrity Cruises' *Century*, which sails to the top of our chapter on cruises; Miraval, the first destination spa in Arizona designed for lifestyle enhancement; and the new Disney Institute in Florida, the first family-oriented resort with programs in fitness, sports, and creativity. In addition to those listed above, alternatives to spas include retreats at The Claremont Resort in California, Duke University's Diet and Fitness Center in North Carolina, the Wellness Program at Dr. Kenneth Cooper's Aerobics Center in Dallas; and Dr. John McDougall's diet and nutrition program in California's Napa Valley at St. Helena Health Center. The growing interest in Complementary Medicine—alternative therapies based on natural health—is reflected in our expanded coverage of hospital health centers that offer structured residential programs.

Among those travel agencies that specialize in arranging spa packages are Custom Spa Vacations (tel. 800/443–7727 or 617/566–5144, fax 617/931–0599); Spa-Finders Travel Arrangements Ltd. (tel. 800/255–7727 or 212/924–6800, fax 212/924–7240), available on the World Wide Web (http://www.spafinders.com); Spa Trek (tel. 212/779–3480 or 800/272–3480, fax 212/779–3471); and the Spa Connection (tel. 303/756–9939, fax 303/758–8862). In Canada, Resort to Fitness (tel. 800/664–5541 or 403/777–0599, fax 403/777–0595) has its catalog on the Internet, handling reservations worldwide (http://www.lexicom.ab.ca/-resort2fitness).

In the following pages, the descriptions of the 13 categories of fitness programs explain in general terms what you can expect to find in different kinds of programs. Each description concludes with Fodor's Choice of resorts that offer that program. Look up the resorts in the alphabetized *Directory 1* and turn to the profiles in the next chapter of this guide for details of the program offerings at each of the resorts. If you want to read about all the resorts offering a particular program, look at *Directory 2*. It gives the complete list of resorts for every program category and indicates the page on which each of the facilities is profiled.

Holistic Health

The premise of holistic health programs is that in order to be truly fit and healthy, you must develop your emotional, intellectual, and spiritual self as well as your body. Nontraditional therapies are used to achieve a sense of wholeness with the world and oneself that will help the body to fend off illness.

Holistic-health training can be vigorous or mellow; it is usually a combination of exercise, nutrition, stress control, and relaxation. Activities include walking, hiking, biking, cross-country skiing, tennis, swimming, and aerobics classes. A wide range of alternative healing therapies stretches from massage to yoga, and the body can be cleansed with herbs, enemas, or psychic diagnoses.

The credo of holistic health retreats is that illness results from a lack of balance within the body, whether caused by stress or physical conditions, and that the balance can be restored without the use of medicine. When one is secluded in places of great natural beauty, the healing process may draw on spiritual sources as well as natural energy to help participants find inner strength.

Holistic Health:
Fodor's Choice
Fit for Life Resort & Spa, Florida
Hawaiian Wellness Holiday, Hawaii
Hollyhock Farm, Vancouver Island, British Columbia, Canada
La Casa de Vida Natural, Puerto Rico
The McDougall Program, St. Helena Health Center, California
New Age Health Spa, New York
Northern Pines Health Resort, Maine
Omega Institute, New York
Pocket Ranch Institute, California
Preventive Medicine Research Institute Retreats at the Claremont, California

Kid Fitness

Programs to motivate children and teenagers to enjoy fitness through fun and exercise are designed to involve youngsters and their parents in a series of health-oriented experiences, complete with nutritious meals, sports, and excursions.

Kid Fitness:
Fodor's Choice
Disney Institute, Florida
Grand Wailea Resort, Hawaii
Green Valley Spa and Tennis Resort, Utah
The Marsh, Minnesota
Omega Institute, New York
The Peaks at Telluride, Colorado
Sea Island Beach Club Spa at The Cloister, Georgia
Sivananda Ashram, Quebec, Canada

Life Enhancement

The life enhancement program aims for long-term physical and psychological benefits. It involves a total assessment of one's condition, with medical tests and personal consultations on nutrition and fitness. Some programs have a spiritual element, while others emphasize an educational approach through exercise, diet, and behavior modification.

Developed in many cases at specialized centers, life enhancement programs usually require complete commitment from participants. The size of the group is generally limited to about two dozen men and women, each working one-on-one with a team of health and behavioral specialists in an intensive experience that little resembles a resort-style program.

Life Enhancement:
Fodor's Choice
Cal-a-Vie Health Resort, California
Canyon Ranch, Arizona
The Cooper Aerobics Center, Texas
Duke University Diet and Fitness Center, North Carolina
Esalen Institute, California
The Greenhouse, Texas
The Heartland Spa, Illinois
La Costa Resort & Spa, California
Lake Austin Spa Resort, Texas
Miraval, Arizona
The Phoenician Centre for Well-Being, Arizona
Rancho La Puerta, Mexico
St. Helena Hospital Health Center, California
Skylonda Fitness Retreat, California

Luxury Pampering

Usually found at resorts where staff outnumber guests, luxury pampering is intended for those who long to be herbal wrapped, massaged, and soaked in bubbling pools fragrant with chamomile. The height of survival chic is lounging in an elegant robe and discussing a delicious spa meal; exercise classes and a weight loss diet can be part of the program, but are usually optional.

An abundance of options makes luxury pampering a highly personalized regimen, designed for men as well as women. The services include exotic body and skin-care treatments and the latest image-enhancers at the beauty salon, among them glycolic acid complexion peels, loofah body scrubs with sea salts and almond oil, aromatherapy massage, and paraffin facial masks for dehydrated skin. Recent advances have joined European spa treatments with American fitness concepts, such as an underwater massage, hydrotherapy with thermal water crystals, and thalassotherapy with seaweed products and seawater.

Deluxe accommodations and lots of amenities are basic to luxury pampering. Some resorts have Sunday-to-Sunday schedules; most offer pampering à la carte. To those who say, "No pain, no gain," the pampered reply, "No frills, no thrills."

Luxury Pampering: Fodor's Choice
Avandaro Golf & Spa Resort, Mexico
Charlie's Spa at the Sans Souci Lido, Jamaica
The Doral Golf Resort and Spa, Florida
The Fontana Spa at the Abbey, Wisconsin
Givenchy Spa, California
The Golden Door, California
Grand Wailea Resort and Spa Grande, Maui, Hawaii
The Greenbrier, West Virginia
The Greenhouse, Texas
Marriott's Spa at Camelback Inn, Arizona
Meadowood Resort, California
Paradise Village Resort, Mexico
The Peaks at Telluride, Colorado

Nonprogram Resort Facilities

Nonprogram resort facilities—often vacation resorts that add fitness elements with a health club—can be just the place for weekend getaways or family vacations. Some fill a gap in areas where fitness resorts are not available; others are close to cultural and historical attractions. Most offer outstanding facilities and special services geared to the fitness-oriented traveler.

Nonprogram Resort Facilities: Fodor's Choice
Banff Springs Hotel, Alberta, Canada
The Broadmoor, Colorado
Cambridge Beaches, Bermuda
The Claremont Resort, California
Marriott's Camelback Inn Spa, Arizona
Ocean Pointe Resort, British Columbia, Canada
Privilege Resort, St. Martin, Caribbean
Scottsdale Princess, Arizona
Spa LXVI at Hyatt Regency Pier 66 Resort, Florida
Spa Internazionale, Florida
Woodstock Inn & Resort, Vermont

Nutrition and Diet

Nutrition and diet programs maintain that well-being begins in the kitchen, that understanding the relationship between nutrition and diet can enhance one's lifestyle and promote sound, healthy habits. Here you may learn to evaluate product labels ("high in fiber," "low in cholesterol") and to cope with the variety of advertising claims.

Participants gain a new perspective on nutrition through lectures and first-hand experience in food preparation. How foods affect your health, how to shop, how to choose from restaurant menus, and how to plan and prepare meals are among the subjects covered. Classes are designed to generate menus and recipes for nutritious dining that participants will then take home with them.

Designed as an educational experience, with no attempt to provide a crash diet plan, the nutrition and diet program provides the fundamentals for following a regimen of eating healthy natural foods. And participants get to enjoy the meals prepared in class.

Nutrition and Diet:
Fodor's Choice

Canyon Ranch, Arizona
Canyon Ranch in the Berkshires, Massachusetts
Doral Golf Resort and Spa, Florida
Duke University Diet and Fitness Center, North Carolina
The Kushi Institute, Massachusetts
New Life Hiking Spa, Vermont
Pritikin Longevity Center, California
Pritikin Longevity Center, Florida
Structure House, North Carolina
Tennessee Fitness Spa, Tennessee

Preventive Medicine

Preventive medicine centers take a scientific approach to health and fitness by combining traditional medical services with advanced concepts for the prevention of illness. Designed for healthy people who want to stay that way, the programs involve medical and fitness testing, counseling on nutrition and stress control, and a range of sports and exercise activities along with massage and bodywork.

Conceived as a regenerative experience for healing and relaxation, the programs can also treat problems associated with obesity, aging, and cardiovascular disease. These programs, usually developed in consultation with your personal physician at home, are carefully structured, supervised at all times, and require full participation.

Participants work with a team of physiotherapists and doctors to learn how to eliminate negative habits and modify a lifestyle for survival. The one-on-one training with fitness instructors, nutritionists, and psychologists can reveal ways of accomplishing personal goals.

Along with hospital-related programs, specialized centers for preventive medicine can now be found at leading fitness resorts and at retreats under the auspices of medical services organizations. They bring together specialists in all fields of health and nutrition to provide a comprehensive prescription for healthy living.

Preventive
Medicine:
Fodor's Choice

Canyon Ranch, Arizona
The Cooper Aerobics Center, Texas
The Greenbrier, West Virginia
Maharishi Ayur-Veda Health Center, Massachusetts
Omega Institute, New York
Poland Spring Health Institute, Maine
Preventive Medicine Research Institute, California
St. Helena Hospital Health Center, California
Weimar Institute, California
Wildwood Lifestyle Center, Georgia

Spiritual Awareness

In celebrating human potential, spiritual awareness programs strive to stretch the individual's limits both mentally and physically. They try to foster a process of personal growth and transformation through workouts that synchronize mind and body and make one aware of one's inner resources. Specializing in alternative education, vegetarian diets, and natural therapies, they offer psychic tools for living.

The experience may draw on any number of Eastern and Western philosophies, and it might focus on yogic training or sensory awareness. Body therapies, visualization, and shamanism are among the healing processes that can be explored. Private counseling and group sessions are usually available for both beginners and advanced meditators.

Retreats rather than resorts, these centers for spiritual training are situated in places where nature's beauty can be enjoyed without distraction or tension.

Spiritual Awareness: Fodor's Choice
Breitenbush Hot Springs and Retreat, Oregon
Feathered Pipe Ranch, Montana
Harbin Hot Springs, California
Hollyhock Farm, British Columbia, Canada
Kripalu Center for Yoga and Health, Massachusetts
Omega Institute, New York
Pocket Ranch Institute, California
The Raj, Iowa
Sivananda Ashram, Quebec, Canada
Sivananda Ashram Yoga Retreat, the Bahamas

Sports Conditioning

For the active vacationer or the athlete seeking new challenges, sports conditioning programs offer advanced training in a variety of sports, workouts with experts, and high-tech training with the latest in exercise equipment.

Most current programs are based on cross-training, alternating sports such as tennis or swimming with exercises such as walking or weight lifting. Mountain hikes, beach runs, and cross-country skiing are programmed to stretch your endurance limits.

Mental training techniques can also be incorporated into sports conditioning programs. Following the lead of Olympic athletes and professional golfers, trainers are offering courses in guided relaxation, affirmations (positive statements), and visualization to improve the competitive edge. These practices are more than morale boosters; the visualization of successful performance may create neural patterns that the brain will use in telling the muscles what to do.

Therapy for sports-related injuries is a feature of some resorts. Others specialize in the mind-body relationship, with disciplines to promote both physical and spiritual development. Martial arts, yoga, and croquet are newly popular vehicles for integrating exercise and mental concentration.

Sports Conditioning: Fodor's Choice
The Aspen Club International, Colorado
Global Fitness Adventures, Colorado
The Hills Health Ranch, British Columbia, Canada
Le Sport, St. Lucia
Loews Santa Monica Beach Hotel, California
The Maui Challenge, Hawaii
The Peaks at Telluride, Colorado
PGA National Resort & Spa, Florida
Swept Away, Jamaica
Topnotch at Stowe, Vermont

Stress Control

Gaining control of the causes of stress is a basic element in the programs of most health and fitness resorts. The approaches to stress control, however, are varied; they include relaxation techniques, behavior modification, biofeedback, and meditation.

As a total experience, with a physical setting and food to lift one's spirits, stress-control programs can create a strong feeling of well-being. Some are offered as an executive retreat within a resort, as an antidote for job burnout, or as a recipe for self-renewal. The opportunity to work one-on-one with advisors, away from the causes of stress, can enhance a person's ability to cope with the stress factors of daily life.

Stress Control:
Fodor's Choice
The Ashram Health Retreat, California
The Claremont Resort, California
Green Valley Spa & Tennis Resort, Utah
Hilton Head Health Institute, South Carolina
The Himalayan Institute, Pennsylvania
The Integral Health Center, Virginia
Lake Austin Spa Resort, Texas
Miraval, Arizona
The Option Institute, Massachusetts
The Raj, Iowa

Taking the Waters

The practice of bathing in hot springs gave rise to the fashionable spas of Europe and America, where people congregated as much for social as for therapeutic purposes. Today taking the waters—which may involve drinking six to eight glasses of mineral water daily—is a practice enjoyed for health and relaxation.

The popularity of water-based therapies and mud baths at American fitness resorts is a recent phenomenon. The cross-fertilization of European and American approaches to maintaining a healthy body and a glowing complexion has revived interest in bathing at grand old resorts where natural waters are available free for the asking. Related treatments that involve seaweed, algae, and seawater are offered at spas that specialize in thalassotherapy.

For the purist, a secluded hot spring promises the best kind of stress-reduction therapy. Others need the added stimulation of body scrubs with sea salts by a masseur armed with a loofah sponge—or a whirlpool bath bubbling with herbal essences.

Taking the Waters:
Fodor's Choice
Alamo Plaza Spa at the Menger Hotel, Texas
Aqua-Mer Center, Quebec, Canada
Berkeley Springs State Park, West Virginia
Calistoga Mud Baths, California
Chateau Elan Bobet Thalassotherapie, Georgia
Glen Ivy Hot Springs, California
Glenwood Hot Springs Lodge & Pool, Colorado
The Greenbrier, West Virginia
Harrison Hot Springs Hotel, British Columbia, Canada
The Homestead, Virginia
Hotel Ixtapan, Mexico
Hot Springs National Park, Arkansas
Ihilani, Hawaii
Safety Harbor Spa and Fitness Center, Florida
Saratoga Spa State Park, New York
Two Bunch Palms, California

Vibrant Maturity

The aging of America has resulted in health and fitness programs designed for specific needs of men and women over age 50. Combining elements of spa vacations with medical services and lifestyle education, these programs can help achieve a healthier way of working, exercising, and eating. The emphasis is on preventing illness by staying fit.

Vibrant Maturity: Canyon Ranch, Arizona
Fodor's Choice   Deerfield Manor, Pennsylvania
Resort Rediscovery at Coolfont, West Virginia
The Cooper Aerobics Center, Texas
Duke University Diet and Fitness Center, North Carolina
Green Valley Spa & Tennis Resort, Utah
The Marsh, Minnesota
St. Helena Hospital Health Center, California
Structure House, North Carolina
The Oaks at Ojai, California
Weimar Institute, California

Weight Management

Learning how to lose weight properly and how to maintain a healthy balance in body mass is the basis of weight management programs. These are not courses for dramatic weight loss; rather, they teach proper eating habits, beginning with what to buy in the supermarket and how to prepare meals.

The weight management resort integrates motivational sessions with exercise, diet, and pampering, reeducation with recreation. Some programs involve fasting on juices and water. Some resorts are residential retreats for the seriously obese; some offer a full range of sports and outdoor activities.

Carefully controlled and supervised, the typical regimen is tailored to the individual's fitness level and health needs. A team of specialists—therapists and nutritionists—coaches you on the basics of beginning and maintaining a personal program. Additional motivation and support arise in the camaraderie of being with a group of like-minded dieters.

Weight   Canyon Ranch, Arizona
Management: Duke University Diet and Fitness Center, North Carolina
Fodor's Choice Green Mountain at Fox Run, Vermont
Hilton Head Health Institute, South Carolina
National Institute of Fitness, Utah
New Age Health Spa, New York
Sans Souci Health Resort, Ohio
Structure House, North Carolina
Tennessee Fitness Spa, Tennessee

2 Health & Fitness Resorts

California

A trendsetter in food, fashion, and fitness, Southern California has been luring health-conscious visitors since the Spanish explorers first landed in San Diego in the 16th century. The 150 miles of coastline between Los Angeles and Mexico boasts more varieties of health spa than any other part of the nation: mud treatments, mineral waters, vegetarian diets, luxury pampering, and spiritual retreats are widespread.

Northern Californians consider themselves residents of a different state, with San Francisco at its center. For them the wine country north of San Francisco is a principal attraction, and taking mud baths at Calistoga ranks with visiting the vineyards of Napa and Sonoma counties. Inland, you have the natural grandeur of Yosemite National Park.

While day spas, providing pampering without a hotel package, have mushroomed throughout California, the new Givenchy Spa & Hotel in Palm Springs offers both. In San Francisco, there is French thalassotherapy at Spa Nordstrom (tel. 415/243–8500), hydrotherapy and facials at Mister Lee's (tel. 415/474–6002 or 800/693–2977), and shiatsu at Kabuki Hot Spring (tel. 415/922–6002). The Los Angeles area has plenty of day spas, but only Beverly Hot Springs (tel. 213/734–7000) in Hollywood has thermal mineral spring water. Celebrity watching at the Regent Beverly Wilshire Hotel Spa and Fitness Center (tel. 310/275–5200) is an added bonus to some of the best treatments anywhere. For pure fun, don't miss Club Mud at Glen Ivy Hot Springs Spa in Corona (tel. 909/277–3529) or the Japanese enzyme bath in dry cedar chips at Osmosis (tel. 707/874–1108), near Bohemian Grove in Freestone. La Jolla is now home to the Chopra Center for Well Being (tel. 619/794–2425). Calistoga's main street is lined with day spas, as is Desert Hot Springs, both budget-priced alternatives to luxury resorts.

The Ashram Health Retreat

Life enhancement
Stress control
Weight management

California
Calabasas

Barbra Streisand called the Ashram "a boot camp without food." Others have found it a rite of passage to a new self-image. Shirley MacLaine described it in *Out on a Limb* as "a spiritually involved health camp."

The Ashram displaces old stresses with new ones. Most of the fairly affluent achievers who come here have high-pressure jobs, and by challenging themselves to a week of enormous physical exertion and minimal meals, they can experience what some speak of as a transcendent, positive change in attitude.

Guests live together in close quarters in groups of about 10, all of them following a routine of mountain hikes, exercise, and yoga. A daily massage and a few hours of relaxation are the only respite. Everyone joins in; participation in every activity is required.

Turning the concept of a retreat (the original meaning of ashram) into the ultimate challenge was an idea tested in a

Guatemalan jungle by the Ashram's owner-chiropractor, Dr. Anne-Marie Bennstrom. A cross-country skiing champion in her native Sweden, she tested her personal limits by spending five months alone in the jungle.

The Ashram has operated at this site since 1975, accepting men and women ages 20–70. The unpaved entrance road winds uphill to a plain, two-story stucco house. Surrounded by towering eucalyptus trees, the garden contains a small heated swimming pool, a solarium for sunbathing, and a geodesic dome where yoga and meditation sessions take place.

Each day begins at 6:30 AM with yoga, stretching, and breathing exercises that help take the kinks out of sore muscles and build energy for a strenuous hike into the hills. Breakfast is a glass of orange juice. The morning schedule usually includes an hour of weight lifting followed by an hour of exercise in the pool and winds down with a game of water volleyball. Calisthenics and at least a two-hour walk complete the day. Bennstrom sets the pace for the hike so the distance varies daily, but some groups have walked more than 90 miles in a week. In the afternoon each guest has a one-hour massage. Program leaders' professionalism and likeable personalities enhance the experience and guarantee that each guest's physical and psychological needs are attended to.

The Ashram Health Retreat
Box 8009, Calabasas, CA 91372
Tel. 818/222–6900

Administration Owner-manager, Dr. Anne-Marie Bennstrom; program director, Catharina Hedberg

Season Year-round, scheduled weeks Sun.–Sat.

Accommodations Guests double up in 5 simply furnished bedrooms in the ranch house with shared bathroom facilities, library, lounge, and weights room. Exercise clothes and robe provided.

Rates $2,200 per week, all-inclusive. V. Gratuities optional.

Meal Plans The 3 lacto-vegetarian meals each day include fruit, vegetables, sprouts, seeds, and nuts. Lunch can be a yogurt-and-cottage-cheese blend with fruit slices, dinner a green salad. Snacks of raw vegetables and juices throughout the day.

Services and Facilities **Exercise Equipment:** Free weights. **Services:** Massage, nutritional counseling, yoga, meditation. **Swimming Facilities:** Outdoor pool. **Recreation Facilities:** Water volleyball. **Evening Programs:** Lectures on developing healthy habits, spirituality, energy centers of the body.

Getting Here *From Los Angeles.* 1 hr by shuttle; not accessible by private car. All guests picked up by van at specified locations in the area. Free pickup from and return to Los Angeles International Airport and local hotels.

Special Notes No smoking.

Cal-a-Vie Health Resort

Life enhancement
Luxury pampering

California Vista Terraced into a Southern California hillside, the 24 country villas of Cal-a-Vie seem lifted from a scene in Provence. There's a lovely outdoor pool, manicured gardens, and wonderful food. The tile-roofed cluster includes an aerobics studio, weights room, bathhouse, and lounge. Each morning the

The Ashram Health Retreat, **15**
Cal-a-Vie Health Resort, **25**
Calistoga Mud Baths, **5**
The Claremont Resort, **10**
Esalen Institute, **12**
Givenchy Spa & Hotel, **22**
Glen Ivy Hot Springs, **19**
The Golden Door, **26**
Green Gulch Farm Zen Center, **9**
Heartwood Institute, **1**
La Costa Resort & Spa, **27**
Loews Santa Monica Beach Hotel, **17**
Marriott's Desert Springs Resort, **24**
Meadowood Resort, **6**
The Oaks at Ojai, **18**
The Palms, **23**
Pocket Ranch Institute, **2**
Post Ranch Inn, **13**
Preventive Medicine Research Institute, **9**
Pritikin Longevity Center, **16**
St. Helena Hospital Health Center, **4**
Sivananda Ashram Yoga Farm, **3**
Skylonda Fitness Retreat, **11**
Sonoma Mission Inn and Spa, **8**
Spa at L'Auberge Del Mar, **28**
Spa Hotel–Casino and Mineral Springs, **21**
Tassajara Zen Monastery, **14**
Two Bunch Palms, **20**
Weimar Institute, **7**

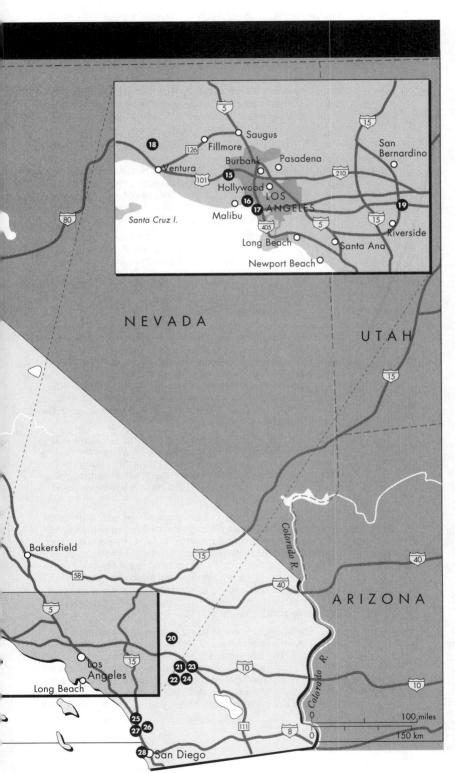

group, usually coed, meets for coffee or tea and a stretch prior to a hike on trails through the property and an adjoining golf course.

For luxury and weight loss, this is the ultimate escape, as confirmed by the high percentage of repeat clients. European hydrotherapy and beauty treatments are the specialty of the house. Seaweed wraps to cleanse the pores, lymphatic massage for detoxification, and underwater-massage tubs are part of the sybaritic experience.

You'll hear the words "detoxify" and "cleanse" frequently here, since the program is designed to heal the body by restoring the balance of mind, body, and spirit. No intrusion from the outside world is allowed to disturb the peace and tranquillity of your week of hikes, aerobics classes, and calorie-controlled meals. Designed as a total environment for health and fitness with personalized attention, the 125-acre resort accepts only 24 guests a week for the Sunday-to-Saturday program.

Guests soon learn to relax as they receive total care. A toothbrush and personal things are all you need to bring; sweat suits, robes, shorts, T-shirts, and rain gear are provided. As you go on to another activity, a fresh set of clothes is supplied. The staff has raised mothering to a fine art, and its members seem to care about clients. With a ratio of four staff members to each guest, little is left to chance.

The first step is your personal fitness evaluation. Your vital statistics and the results of a battery of tests to determine flexibility, cardiovascular capability, and upper and lower body strength are fed into a computer; your personal diet and exercise regimen will be based on the printout. Meals total between 1,200 and 1,400 calories per day on the maintenance diet, though you may opt for the cleansing or reduction programs. Friday evenings, dinner is created while you dine in the kitchen and learn the chef's secrets.

The day begins with a prebreakfast hike into the hills—long or short depending on your preference—followed by cooling down exercises, and group workouts in the swimming pool, or in the gym with a personal trainer. Yoga, tai chi, and aerobics are scheduled. Sparring in the "Boxercise" class helps build finesse and stamina.

During thalassotherapy, you are cocooned in a mixture of micronized algae, coated with Phytomer's French seaweed mix, and gently scrubbed and massaged. Another popular treatment, the aromatherapy massage, is intended to fight tension and its consequences, and is also geared to rid the body of cellulite. Essential oils from flowers and herbs are blended and applied to points of the body in varying combinations. As many as 25 oils can be combined for particular trouble spots. A dry-brush body scrub sloughs off old skin.

While the all-inclusive spa package appeals to many guests, there is a less-expensive California Plan week with limited treatments. The European Plan includes 18 treatments. Being part of a small group helps motivate beginners; returnees, including Hollywood celebrities and corporate CEOs, seek privacy and relief from stress. Retiring to your villa suite reminiscent of a European country home, you enjoy the best of both worlds.

Cal-a-Vie Health Resort
2249 Somerset Rd., Vista, CA 92084
Tel. 619/945–2055
Fax 619/630–0074

Administration Founders-owners, William F. and Marlene Power; manager, Deborah Zie

Season Year-round, except mid-Dec.–Jan. 2

Accommodations 24 private villas with heat; air-conditioning; Country French furnishings; beam ceilings; stone fireplaces; flowered chintzes; carved wooden armoires. Each bedroom has TV, telephone, full bathroom with robes and amenities, and garden entrance. Meals served in main house.

Rates $3,950 per person per week, all-inclusive with meals; California Plan $3,600; summer weeks $3,350. Gratuities included; add taxes. $500 nonrefundable deposit required in advance. AE, MC, V.

Meal Plans 3 meals served to order daily, based on suggested calorie intake. Lunch can include a seafood salad, whole wheat pizza with chèvre cheese, sautéed tofu, and lentils. Dinner entrées can include sautéed free-range chicken with rosemary and roasted garlic, a pilaf of lentils and brown rice, and grilled swordfish. Special diets accommodated.

Services and Facilities **Exercise Equipment:** 2 Startrac treadmills, 2 StairMaster 4000s, 2 Windracer bikes, 5 Bodymaster units, step aerobics, free weights. **Services:** Massage (Swedish, shiatsu, aromatherapy), thalassotherapy, hydrotherapy, water exercise class, Boxercise, dry-brush body scrub, reflexology, pedicure, manicure; facial, hair, and skin care. **Swimming Facilities:** Heated outdoor pool. **Spa Facilities:** Hydrotub, sauna and steam rooms, recessed Roman whirlpool. **Recreation Facilities:** Tennis court, volleyball; golf, horseback riding nearby. **Evening Programs:** Lectures on current topics, fitness, and nutrition; cooking demonstrations; movies.

In the Area San Diego museums, theaters, and waterfront; Sea World; San Diego Zoo and Wild Animal Park; herb farm; Mount Palomar Observatory.

Getting Here *From San Diego.* By car, Rte. 163 to I–15 to Vista (1 hr). Free pickup on Sun. and return to San Diego International Airport. Limousine, taxi, rental car available.

Special Notes No smoking on the property except in designated areas.

Calistoga Mud Baths

Luxury pampering
Taking the waters

California
Napa Valley Calistoga, a tiny town tucked into the vineyards of the Napa Valley, has been blessed with puffing fumerholes and steaming geysers, sources of thermal spring mineral waters and mud that has been tapped by a dozen spas, many of them within walking distance of the town's center, along Lincoln Avenue.

Calistoga is not a secret, however. Day-trippers from San Francisco come here to combat stress; the springs attract families looking for a way to spend some meaningful time together; couples share romantic baths and massages; and people seeking relief from arthritis and rheumatism return regularly for the soothing effects of the mud baths.

The geysers, which were considered sacred to the Wappo tribe of Northern California, also attracted the 17th-century

Spanish explorers who named them *agua caliente,* or hot springs. Later, in 1859, San Franciscan developer Sam Brannan coined the name Calistoga, a contraction of California and Saratoga Springs (the then-fashionable New York spa). Today the town has a mellow, laid-back look that's part Victorian restoration (no building over two stories) and part low-cost housing for workers in the nearby wineries. Adding some spice to Calistoga is the newly opened western branch of the Culinary Institute of America, helping the area to become a rapidly growing mecca for gourmets.

Each of the dozen spas in town offers its own special variation on bathing bliss. Traditionalists head for Dr. Wilkinson's Hot Springs or the Indian Springs resort, where soaking in the volcanic mud is like floating gravity-free. Others prefer the privacy of whirlpool baths mixed with fango mud from Italy, or herbal essences that don't contain sulfurous mineral water. Couples get special treatment at several places designed for duo bathing and massage.

The following is a selection of spas found in Calistoga. Come for a day or a week and try a few; each one has its own distinct personality.

Calistoga Spa Hot Springs. What's unique about this spa hotel is that it has the only exercise facility in town, in addition to four outdoor pools with naturally heated mineral water of varying temperatures. Aerobics classes and use of exercise equipment are complimentary for guests. The pools, mud bath, and massage are available to the public and can be booked by the day if you are not staying on the premises. Admission to the pool is $5 with treatment, $10 without, $7 after 7 PM; towels are not provided. The pool is especially busy on weekends, when families come to visit. Modern and well maintained, the two-story hotel has 52 simply furnished rooms with two twin beds, private bath, cable TV, telephone, air-conditioning; the kichenettes are equipped with hot plate (no oven), refrigerator, dishes, and utensils. *1006 Washington St., 94515, tel. 707/942-6269.* **Facilities:** *4 pools, whirlpools, aerobics classes, rowing machines, exercise bikes, Universal Gym Equipment, free weights.* **Services:** *Mud bath, massage, steam bath, blanket wrap. Reservations for treatments: 8:30–4:30.* **Rates:** *$64–$83 for standard double; $81–$105 for family unit. MC, V.*

Dr. Wilkinson's Hot Springs. Dr. John Wilkinson, still active at age 80, came here as a chiropractor in the mid-1940s. Now run by his children, Mark and Carolyne, the resort encompasses 17 hideaway cottages, a five-bedroom Victorian house, and the 42-unit motel opened in 1952 and featuring the original mud baths. A variety of treatments and packages are offered, including the "Stress Stopper," with spa and salon packages for $106 per person, $169 for two. Another option, "The Works" ($65), begins with a 10- to 15-minute soak in a 105°F mix of volcanic ash, peat, and mineral water. (Between bathers, mud vats are flushed with 212°F water, said to sterilize any residue.) Solicitous attendants swab your face with cool cloths, and offer cups of water. Next, after showering, comes a bathtub soak in bubbling Calistoga water, and a blanket wrap to sweat out any remaining toxins. The finishing touch is a half-hour massage in a private room or alcove. Appointments are available to the public on a day-use basis. Additional salon services, including facials, mud mask, and acupressure face-lift, are in a pretty pink cottage adjoining the motel. Guest rooms are well maintained, and the cottages are decorated with antiques. All rooms have a king-size bed or two twins and are equipped with air-conditioning, TV, phone, and coffeemaker. *1507 Lincoln Ave., 94515, tel. 707/942-4102.* **Facilities:** *Mud* *baths, men's and women's bathhouse, mineral steam room, indoor and outdoor pools.* **Services:** *Facials, cerofango and paraffin treatments for hands and feet, full-body massage. Bath appointments 8:30–3:30; massage appointments 9–4:30.* **Rates:** *Stress Stopper 1-night package (Oct.–June only) $183.92 for double.* **Daily Rates:** *$54–$109 single, $64–$119 for 2 double; bungalows with kitchen, queen-size bed: $69–$89 single, $64–$119 for double; Hideaway cottages with queen-size bed: $67–$150 for double; Victorian house bedroom with queen-size bed: $99–$109 single, $99–$119 for double. Tax included; gratuities optional. AE, MC, V.*

Harbin Hot Springs. Lying 16 miles from Calistoga, this secluded New Age retreat is a bit of a trek, but the holistic health community in the hills offers lodging and good treatments at a modest cost. There is a spiritual quality to bathing in the clothing-optional mineral pools, where the water-supported watsu massage can be experienced. A vegetarian restaurant and community kitchen (meals not included) are available to guests. Accommodations are in frame buildings with rooms (not air-conditioned) that open to a narrow veranda; both private facilities and dormitory space can be reserved. Private rooms are attractively decorated with wicker furniture and country-style bedding. Campsites and dormitory rooms are available also. Reserve well in advance: on summer weekends more than 100 visitors sign up for treatments. *18424 Harbin Springs Rd., Box 82, Middletown, CA 95461, tel. 707/987–2477 or 800/622–2477 in CA; fax 707/987–9638.* **Facilities:** *Mineral pools, restaurant, kitchen, hiking trails, evening lectures, concerts, movies.* **Services:** *Massage, watsu, shiatsu, deep-tissue massage, rebalancing, reflexology, rebirthing, hypnotherapy, chiropractic. Workshops (fee), daily meditation, and full moon ceremony open to guests and members ($5 fee). Day visitor pass $12–$17 per adult, children $10–$12.* **Rates:** *$40–$60 per room for single, $60–$90 for double, without bath; $50–$80 single, $70–$110 for double with half-bath; $80–$125 per couple with full bath; cabin with queen-size bed, bathroom $125–$165 for 2. Dormitory accommodations in rooms with 4–6 beds $23–$35; campsite $14–$23 per adult, $10–$14 per child. Tax included; gratuities optional. MC, V.*

Indian Springs Resort. The attraction here is the spring's all-volcanic ash mud bath, on the site of the town's original spa. For just $65 the seaweed-based Repechage facial is a bargain: Not only is it heavenly, but it's given in the beautiful Mission-style bathhouse. With any spa service, guests can swim free in the naturally heated outdoor Olympic-size mineral water pool and get a discount on glider flights at the adjacent Gliderport. The 16-acre garden complex includes one-bedroom and studio cottages, a small one-bedroom house with full kitchen, and a three-bedroom house. All units have private bath, gas fireplace, TV, air-conditioning. *1712 Lincoln Ave., 94515, tel. 707/942–4913.* **Facilities:** *Mud baths, mineral-water outdoor swimming pool, bicycles, surrey bikes, barbecue equipment.* **Services:** *Facials, mud bath, massage.* **Rates:** *Cottages: $135–$160 for double, $15 each additional guest; studio: $115–$140 for double; single house for 6: $425. MC, V.*

Mount View Hotel. The newest and glitziest spa in town caters to couples looking for attention, luxury, and privacy. In 1993 the hotel was tastefully renovated, but still retains its history, as reflected in period furnishings and suites named for literary figures, Hollywood divas, and First Ladies who once signed the guest register. Six treatment rooms each contain a whirlpool tub and a separate shower with built-in steam bath that can be programmed for a number of soothing effects.

Attendants draw the baths using nonthermal water, adding dehydrated Italian fango mud, salicyl, and an aromatherapy pine oil. The effect is relaxing and analgesic, and the mud does not cling to skin. Additional treatment rooms face the outdoor swimming pool (not heated) and a whirlpool with hot mineral water. An outdoor café serves refreshments in warm weather. You must make reservations for all services, including body and facial treatments, at the reception desk in the hotel lobby. All facilities are clean. All hotel rooms have a private bath with a claw foot tub, air-conditioning, TV, and phone. Suites are decorated with Art Deco and Victorian antiques. Ask for a room in the back; front-facing rooms on the second floor can be noisy. Each cottage has a hot tub and sundeck. The hotel's Catahoula Restaurant (tel. 707/942–2275 for reservations) and saloon are situated in what is now a National Historic landmark, and serve spa and regular cuisine for lunch and dinner. *1457 Lincoln Ave., 94515, tel. 707/942–6877, fax 707/942–6904.* **Facilities:** *Fango mud bath, whirlpools, steam baths, outdoor pool.* **Services:** *Aromatherapy, seaweed toning bath, Swedish-Esalen massage, reflexology, shiatsu, herbal wrap, mini-facial; customized baths with choice of fango, herbal crystals, oils, seaweed, or powdered milk whey. Spa appointments (tel. 707/942–5789) 9 AM–7 PM.* **Rates:** *1-night spa package (no meals) $250 for 2 (available only Nov.–May, Sun.–Thurs.); 33 standard rooms $110–$135; 8 suites $150–$195 for 2. 3 private cottages $198 for 2. AE, MC, V.*

In the Area Sharpsteen Museum and Brannan cottage (Calistoga history), Old Faithful Geyser and geothermal museum, Culinary Institute of America, winery tours, Petrified Forest, state parks, public golf course, tennis, racquetball courts.

Getting Here *From San Francisco.* By bus, Greyhound (3 hr). By car, Rte. 101 to Novato, Rtes. 37, 121 to Napa, Rte. 29/128 to Calistoga (1½ hr). Taxi, rental car, bike rental available.

The Claremont Resort

Luxury pampering
Nonprogram resort facilities

California
Oakland

The San Francisco Bay area's premier urban getaway traces its origins to a romantic 1915 Victorian castle. The white-turreted hotel presides over 22 acres of landscaped grounds in the hills of Oakland and Berkeley. A fitness center with more than 20 scheduled aerobics classes, spa, two large lap pools, full-service salon, and bay-view café offering a low-calorie menu are some of the most noteable features of this resort.

The spa offers a wide range of services, including deep-tissue sports massage, shiatsu, and aromatherapy. There's also a personal trainer on staff to help you restyle your workout routine and improve your tennis technique on 10 day/night tennis courts.

In the hydrotherapy facility, there are rooms with specialized equipment for underwater massage, herbal wraps, and loofah body scrubs. Herbal and floral essences are used in baths, and aromatherapy massage helps detoxify the body. Separate locker rooms for men and women are each equipped with steam room, sauna, and whirlpool; workout clothing is provided daily. The broad range of mind/body fitness classes distinguishes this spa. Among relaxation therapies offered is a one-hour restorative yoga session in which a trainer positions you so that gravity will work to help rejuvenate your whole body.

While your day can be filled with classes, one-on-one training, and treatments, there is no group program. You can get half-day to five-day spa packages, or you can use the facility à la carte. Weekend Adventure packages are scheduled periodically. The Claremont also hosts weeklong retreats of the Preventive Medicine Research Institute (*see below*).

Choice accommodations are in a new wing of spa rooms opened in 1996, or in mini-suites with views of the bay in the original towers, with Art Deco furnishings.

The Claremont Resort
Ashby and Domingo Aves., Box 23363, Oakland, CA 94623
Tel. 510/843-3000 or 800/551-7266; spa reservations
510/549-8583, fax 510/549-8582, guest fax 510/848-6208

Administration Managing director, Henry Feldman; spa director, John DeFontes

Season Year-round

Accommodations 279 spacious rooms with oversize beds (some are four-posters) and sitting areas, marble-walled baths with robes and hair dryers; bay-view rooms and suites command a premium. The 40-room spa wing, opened in 1996, has direct access to the fitness and spa facilities. Fine contemporary art is displayed in the public rooms and halls. Facilities are available for social and business functions.

Rates Daily room rate $175–$245 single, $205–$295 for double; suites to $1,000 for 2. Spa Retreat and overnight accommodations for 2 nights: $550 single, $390 per person double. Prices do not include tax and gratuities. Day packages, including service charge and facility fee, $100–$350. Deposit: 1 night payable in advance or by credit card guarantee. AE, D, DC, MC, V.

Meal Plans Daily meal plan $60 per person for breakfast and dinner. The Pavilion Restaurant features spa choices and traditional favorites in a prix fixe 4-course menu option. Seasonal choices can include mesquite-grilled swordfish with papaya chutney; grilled and steamed vegetables; grilled marinated prawns on linguini; roasted rack of Sonoma lamb; steamed sea bass; buckwheat ravioli with mushrooms, garlic, and tofu ginger in shallot broth.

Services and Facilities **Exercise Equipment:** 2 computerized Lifecycles 9500s, recumbent Lifecycle 9500, Monark bike, Schwinn Air Dyne bike, 2 Concept 2 rowers, 3 Startrac 2000 treadmills, 2 StairMasters 4000 PTs, 4 Climb Max stairclimbers, BioClimber, 13-unit Cybex weight training circuit, dumbbells (3–50 lb), free weights, ankle weights, Physio balls. **Services:** Swedish, sports, underwater massage; shiatsu, acupressure, aromatherapy, thalassotherapy, herbal wrap, loofah body scrub; facials; salon for hair, nail, skin care; nutrition counseling; tennis and swimming lessons. **Swimming Facilities:** Olympic-size outdoor pool, lap pool. **Recreation Facilities:** Water volleyball, 10 tennis courts; golf, horseback riding nearby; hiking, parcourse.

In the Area Oakland's Jack London Square (entertainment, shopping, arts) and The Oakland Museum are about a 10–15-minute drive from the resort. Berkeley and the University of California campus are a short hike from the hotel and include such attractions as a hillside botanical garden, concerts, sports activities, and dining at Chez Panisse. San Francisco, with its museums, beaches, and water sports, is just across the bay; downtown is only a 20-minute ride on the Bay Area Rapid Transit (BART) train. Free shuttle service to the BART station is provided from the hotel. Wine country tours also available.

Getting Here *From San Francisco.* By BART, Rockridge Station (20 mins). By car, Bay Bridge to Hwy. 24, Claremont Ave. exit to Ashley Ave. (30 mins). Limousine, taxi, rental car available. Airport transfers by scheduled van service.

Special Notes Specially equipped rooms, ramps, and elevators provide complete access to the spa for people with disabilities. Tennis and swimming clinics for children. No smoking in the spa or hotel. Spa open Mon.–Sat. 8:30–8:30, Sun. 8:30–6:30.

Esalen Institute

Life enhancement

California The "human potential" movement nurtured in these cliff-top
Big Sur gardens and hot springs is alive and well after more than 25 years. Once considered a hippie haven, the Esalen Institute became an American utopia for seekers of ancient wisdom and new truths. Those goals gave birth to the Esalen style of sensuous massage and turned encounter therapy into an art form. If you're searching for self-awareness, there may be no more beautiful place to experience it than at Esalen Institute. Founded in 1962 by Michael Murphy and the late Richard Price, Esalen remains focused on personal and social transformation. If you enroll in this program, you must be comfortable with nudity, as clothing is optional during soaks at the hot springs.

Seminars and workshops on holistic health, esoteric religions, Gestalt therapy, psychosynthesis, shamanic healing, and neurolinguistics are offered throughout the year. Always popular are Esalen Massage bodywork workshops.

Many who come here simply want to unwind, and accommodations are available at $75 a day (includes lunch) with advance reservation (space permitting). Overnight guests can book a massage, hike in the Ventana Wilderness, and soak in natural rock pools filled by hot mineral springs. The institute also offers a hiking trip to Tassajara Zen Monastery (*see below*).

Esalen Institute
Hwy. 1, Big Sur, CA 93920
Tel. 408/667–3000; reservations 408/667–3005
Fax 408/667–2724

Administration Chairman, Michael Murphy; operations manager, Carol Price

Season Year-round

Accommodations 107 beds in rustic lodges; most rooms for 2, some with bunk beds. Comfortably casual furnishings with ocean views and the sound of the surf. No TV, radio, telephone, air-conditioning. Guests share rooms and baths, make their own beds.

Rates Tuition fee plus standard accommodations: weekend $380, 5-day $740, 7-day $1,110. Daily rate with meals $80–$125; bunk bed weekend $300, daily $75–$80. $100 deposit for weekends, $200–$300 for longer programs. AE, MC, V.

Meal Plans 3 meals daily, served buffet style. Meat, fish, and poultry, salads and fresh vegetables grown organically on the property served at lunch and dinner, with a vegetarian entrée such as spinach lasagna.

Services and **Services:** Massage (Esalen, Heller, Feldenkrais, deep-tissue),
Facilities Rolfing, cranial-sacral work; special studies. **Swimming Facilities:** Heated outdoor pool. **Recreation Facilities:** Hiking, tai chi,

morning exercise class, hot mineral baths. **Evening Programs:** Lectures, concerts.

In the Area Wilderness experiences (5 days or more); Hearst Castle at San Simeon, Mission of San Antonio de Padua (1771), Tassajara Zen Monastery in Los Padres National Forest (May 1–Labor Day), Big Sur State Park.

Getting Here *From San Francisco.* By bus, Greyhound via Monterey connecting in Big Sur with Esalen van (5 hrs) for $30. By car, Hwy. 101 south to Monterey, west to Coastal marker 156, Hwy. 1, south to Esalen road marker (3½ hrs). Esalen van service (for reservations, tel. 408/667–3000) Fri. and Sun. from Monterey airport or bus station ($30).

Special Notes Limited access for people with disabilities. Special activities and dining plan for children; limited child-care facilities. No-smoking cabins, no-smoking areas in dining room.

Givenchy Spa & Hotel

Luxury pampering

California Nestled in the palms and rose gardens of a sun-drenched
Palm Springs desert resort, the new Givenchy Spa & Hotel brings a touch of France to Palm Springs. Conceived as a miniature replica of Versailles, the spa pavilion has treatments with products created under license by famed couturier Hubert de Givenchy. In a 14-acre enclave, with racquet club and swimming pools, the spa building is minutes from the center of Palm Springs, where cultural attractions compete with a small casino. Privacy, however, is a priority for celebrity guests staying in the deluxe villas. Renovated in 1995, standard accommodations are in two-story lodges from the former resort owned by cowboy film star Gene Autry. Each room has the Givenchy monogram on Swisscare cosmetics and soaps, robes, and exercise and jogging outfits.

Forget sweaty workouts. The spa pavilion is a haven of peace and privacy. A beauty salon, under the supervision of Gerard Alexandre, has views of the magnificent gardens. Separate but equal swimming pools for men and women are a central feature of the building, which has spacious treatment rooms and sauna, steam and Turkish baths. Special hydrotherapy tubs are used for bubbling herbal and seaweed baths.

What you won't find at the Givenchy spa is aerobics or a vigorous exercise program. The well-equipped gym is for personal workouts, perhaps with your own trainer. Golfers may play at top-rated courses in the area, and an 18-hole executive course adjoins the hotel. Another option: book a day spa package without hotel accommodations.

The Givenchy offers California's freshest salads and seafood with a French touch. The menu is inspired by Michelin two-star chef Gerard Vie of the Trianon Palace Hotel in Versailles, home of the original Givenchy Spa. The sumptuous combination of food, fashion, and spa services is a refreshing change of pace.

Palm Springs, distinctly geriatric 10 years ago, has become fashionable again. There are plenty of upscale communities nearby—Palm Desert, Indian Wells, Rancho Mirage, La Quinta—as well as Desert Hot Springs, where the main street (Indian Canyon Drive) is lined with budget-priced "spatels" featuring thermal mineral water baths and swimming pools. Local Native American tribes have brought casinos to the Spa Hotel near the center of town, and to Indio off I–10. Hikes in

Joshua Tree National Park, about an hour's drive from town on Hwy. 62, reveal the Mojave Desert in all its glory. There are miles of trails snaking through forests of the park's namesake plant, a member of the lily family, which blooms in late March or early April. Winter is the high season for art and theater, the Bob Hope golf tournament, and an international film festival. Viewing the Coachella Valley from an aerial tramway on Mount San Jacinto, or aboard a hot-air balloon, is a unique experience.

Givenchy Spa & Hotel

4200 East Palm Canyon Dr., Palm Springs, CA 92264-5291
Tel. 619/770–5000 or 800/276–5000
Fax 619/324–6104

Administration Director, Rose Narva

Season Year-round

Accommodations 98 oversized guest rooms, including 12 private single-floor villas. All have separate his-and-hers bathrooms, king-size beds with luxurious bedspreads, heavy window drapes, and floral accents. Le Grand Suite has four bedrooms, duplex living room, and reception salon.

Rates The 6-night/7-day spa package for one person is $3,500, including 3 meals daily, treatments, and spa services. One-day Givenchy Beauté program, without accommodations, $275–$375. Daily rates for room, $225–$250 single, $275–$325 for 2 people; 12 deluxe villas on request, $575. AE, D, MC, V.

Meal Plans Both à la carte and fixed menu served daily in Le Potager restaurant and the spa pavilion's Garden Terrace. Lunch can be a romaine salad in a tulip of parmesan cheese, with a dessert of fresh berries and crème brûlée. Coffee, tea, and wine served. Dinner selections vary with the season: grilled onaga in vegetable broth, pan-seared Norwegian salmon, crispy sea bass in potato slices, Maine lobster, roasted quail, loin of ostrich. Spa package includes 3 meals daily; Day Spa visit includes lunch.

Services and Facilities **Services**: Massage, reflexology, hydrotherapy; facial, mud, or seaweed wrap; salon for hair, nail, and skin care. **Swimming Facilities**: 2 indoor lap pools, 4 heated outdoor swimming pools. **Recreation Facilities**: 18-hole executive golf course, 6 lighted all-weather tennis courts, bicycles.

In the Area The Desert Museum (theater, concerts, art galleries), Living Desert Reserve (botanical gardens), Indian Canyons (Jeep tour, hikes), Polo Club.

Getting Here *From Los Angeles.* Commuter flights by American Airlines and United; VIP Shuttle (tel. 619/328–0222) from LAX or area hotels (2–3 hrs). By car, I–10 to Hwy. 111 in Palm Canyon Drive. Limousine, taxi, rental car available at Palm Springs regional airport. Also direct flights from Minneapolis on Northwest Airlines, from Chicago by United, during winter season.

Special Notes Spa and salon available to day visitors; restaurant open to the public. No smoking in spa pavilion.

Glen Ivy Hot Springs

Taking the waters

California
Corona

Nestled in the foothills of the Santa Ana coastal range, between Los Angeles and San Diego, halfway between the desert and the ocean, is Glen Ivy Hot Springs, a day spa with mud baths, 15 rejuvenating mineral pools, concerts under the stars, and à la carte spa facilities that include massages, facials, and other salon services. The waters here have been known for their healing power, since the Luiseno tribe first built mud saunas around the springs during the 14th Century. (There are no traces of buildings.) The natives used an Aztec word imported by Franciscan missionaries, "temescal," meaning "sweat-house," to name the valley. In 1890, a 10-room adobe house opened as the first hotel to serve the orange ranchers from nearby towns. Artifacts and photos of these early days are on display in the Hot Springs Cafe. In 1912 the springs became popular with city dwellers who flocked from Los Angeles to the waters until 1969, when a flood wiped out the bathhouse and mud bath. With the rebirth of interest in natural therapies came new facilities and gardens. The homey country inn survived as a private residence, and the pools, sundecks, and landscaping were re-created in 1977 when the current management company was formed.

The white stucco buildings and clay-tile roofs counterpoint palm trees and bougainvillea. Warm desert sun, cool mountain breezes, and gardens provide the ambience for a relaxing, indulgent escape. Bathers float in the pools on rented rafts, dozing, reading, meditating. This is about as close to a tropical paradise as you can get for under $20 a day. The mud baths are free, and so is membership into the famous "Club Mud," for those who take a dip in the the vat of soft red clay that's been mined nearby. After you coat your body and hair, sit poolside and let the clay bake until it dries. Then rinse in the mineral water shower; your skin will feel satiny and healthy. The pools are drained and filled with fresh, chlorinated water every day.

Water temperatures vary between 90°F and 110°F at the two wells that supply a constant flow of mineral water to the pools. You'll be cautioned not to stay in the hot water too long, particularly if you're dieting or in poor health. The only organized activity is a 2 PM aquaerobics class held in the big swimming pool. Sign up for massage or salon services when you arrive, or call ahead for appointments. There are 16 massage rooms and well-equipped dressing areas for men and women.

Although sun protection is provided at a covered hot pool, you'll need to bring sunscreen. An old swimsuit and towel are recommended for the mud bath. Food and drink are available at the Spa Cafe, or you can pack a picnic and use shaded tables in a designated area. Perhaps a jog down the road to shop at the farm market will feel invigorating after lazing in the primal ooze. Stay overnight at nearby inns and you get a free admission pass for Club Mud.

Glen Ivy Hot Springs

25000 Glen Ivy Rd., Corona, CA 91719
Tel. 909/277-3529 or 800/454-8772
Fax 909/277-1202

Administration Directors, John and Pamela Gray

Season Year-round; open daily, except Thanksgiving and Christmas

Accommodations **The Mission Inn** (3649 Mission Inn Ave., Riverside, CA 92501, tel. 909/784-0300 or 800/843-7755), in Riverside, provides admission to Glen Ivy Hot Springs and Continental breakfast with overnight accommodations in mission-style lodge: $135 for 2, including tax. AE, MC, V.

Country Side Inn (2260 Griffin Way, Corona, CA 91719, tel. 909/734-2140) has four-poster beds, private bathrooms.

Overnight with full buffet breakfast and admission to Glen Ivy Hot Springs: $77 single, $99 for 2, double occupancy, including tax. AE, MC, V.

Rates Daily admission to the pools, sauna, and mud bath: $19.50 weekdays for adults and children, $18.50 for senior citizens. Children under 2 free. MC, V.

Services and Facilities **Services:** Aromatherapy massage, body polish, facials, anti-cellulite treatment, and nail and hand care. **Swimming Facilities:** Outdoor pool, 14 soaking pools. **Evening Programs:** Concerts (ticketed separately).

In the Area Temecula wineries, Old Town Temecula with its 1890s architecture.

Getting Here *From Los Angeles.* By car, I–10, I–60, or Hwy. 91 eastbound to I–15 south, exit right onto Temescal Canyon Rd., right on Glen Ivy Rd. (1 hr).

Special Notes All facilities accessible for people with disabilities. Bring your own towel and old swimsuit (mud stains some fabrics). Hours: Mar.–Oct., 10–6; Nov.–Feb., 10–5.

The Golden Door

Life enhancement
Luxury pampering
Nutrition and diet
Spiritual awareness

California
Escondido
The grande dame of spas in Southern California, the Golden Door opened in 1959 as a hideaway for Hollywood celebrities, and still attracts a mix of show business and corporate executives. Secluded on 177 acres of canyon and orchards, "The Door" welcomes no more than 39 guests for a minimum one-week stay. While some weeks are designated for men or couples, most of the year this is the private domain of women.

Beyond the ornate brass gate lies an enchanted realm of Oriental gardens and inns. Guests in standard-issue sweat suits step peacefully to aerobics classes; *yukata* robes are supplied for lounging. The setting and the incredibly thoughtful staff create an air of calm order. The experience is restorative and regenerative.

Your transformation from sluggardly to energetic begins on your arrival Sunday afternoon with an interview about your fitness level, diet, and preferences. Do you prefer tennis, instruction in lap-swimming techniques, or a cooking class? A massage with a therapist, who gets to know every muscle in your body, is scheduled every day at the same time. Tipping is not permitted.

On the orientation tour for first-time guests, one can't help but be impressed by the attention to detail and devotion to comfort that have been incorporated into the spa's impressive design, a cross between a first-class resort and a Japanese country inn. The four spacious exercise pavilions have sliding glass walls that open to fresh air and the beauty of the lush gardens. A graceful bathhouse, tiled and topped with gray Oriental carving, contains a modern sauna, steam room, Swiss shower, whirlpool, and body-wrap facility.

Each day begins at 6 AM with a brisk mountain hike led by staff members who, Sherpa-like, supply flasks of cool water and fruit to sustain you until you are served breakfast. During your meal you're presented with a paper fan and schedule for the day. All decisions have been made for you, so all you can do is go with the flow. If you miss an appointment, a kimono-clad staffer will come searching for you.

The 50-minute exercise periods fill most of the morning; afternoons are for pampering and personal pursuits. You can have lunch by the pool, in the dining room, or in the privacy of your room. Massages can be alfresco or in your room, with a choice of shiatsu, traditional Swedish, deep-tissue, or aromatherapy. Daily beauty treatments are included in the program cost.

For fit guests who return whenever they need to recharge, there is an Inner Door program. It is an advanced course for a small group in problem solving, meditation, and body movement. For four days there are two-hour sessions for exploration of spiritual and inner forces, even tai chi, designed for inner serenity. Other weeks are designated for mothers and daughters, or fathers and sons, as a learning and sharing experience.

The Golden Door
Deer Springs Rd.,
Box 463077, Escondido, CA 92046
Tel. 619/744-5777 or 800/414-0777
Fax 619/471-2393

Administration President, Alex Szekely; manager, Rachel Caldwell; program director, Judy Bird

Season Year-round, except Christmas week

Accommodations Single rooms for 39 guests in buildings patterned after old Japanese honjin inns. 1-story ocher stucco buildings have bedrooms with sitting areas opening onto private gardens and decorated with muted colors and Japanese wood-block prints, parquet floors with carpets, sliding shoji screens, and jalousie windows. Private baths are stocked with Golden Door skincare products. Guest units cluster on courtyards, a short walk from the main building. 1 private cottage. All rooms have telephone and air-conditioning, but no TV.

Rates $4,375 weekly; $3,875 during July, Aug., Thanksgiving weekend and New Year's week. Deposit: $500 with reservation. Gratuities included; for tax add $170.19 or $150.76, depending on season. MC, V.

Meal Plans 3 meals plus snacks served daily. Personally planned menu is designed for high-energy meals, low in cholesterol, salt, sugar, and fat, rich in fiber and whole grains, served with oriental flair. Lunch can include miso soup, stir-fry vegetables with tofu, or fresh Pacific shrimp sautéed with orange and ginger. Dinner entrées include boneless breast of chicken with wild mushrooms; whole wheat crepes filled with a mixture of spinach, mushrooms, and ricotta cheese; or cabbage rolls stuffed with bulgur pilaf and vegetables. Special needs accommodated.

Services and Facilities **Exercise Equipment:** 12 Cybex weight training units, 6 Trotter treadmills, 3 Cardioaerobikes, 2 StairMasters, PTS Turbobike, rowing machine, free weights. **Services:** Massage (Swedish, Trager, shiatsu, and others), aromatherapy, herbal wrap, body scrub, daily skin care, facials, manicure, pedicure, hair styling. Instruction in tai chi, yoga, swimming, circuit training; fitness evaluations and submaximal stress test. **Swimming Facilities:** 2 outdoor pools. **Recreation Facilities:** 2 tennis courts, hiking, classes in flower arranging, crafts, gardening. **Evening Programs:** Lectures on nutrition, stress management, sports medicine, other health-related topics; movies.

In the Area California Institute for the Arts, Sea World.

Getting Here *From San Diego.* By car, Hwy. 163 to I–15, north to Deer Springs Rd. exit (40 mins). Free pickup from and return to San Diego Airport.

Special Notes 1-story structures make most facilities accessible to people with disabilities. The entire complex is no-smoking. Remember to bring appropriate shoes for hiking, walking, sports. Minimum age 18.

Green Gulch Farm Zen Center

Spiritual awareness

California Standing amid pines and open fields that stretch to the Pacific,
Sausalito the wooden guest house at Green Gulch Farm seems far removed from the rest of the world, but it is only 25 minutes from San Francisco. A peaceful retreat for study and work, the center is suffused with the spirit of Zen.

Buddhist tradition is experienced here in many ways. You can join classes to study Zen texts on basic teachings and the bodhisattva spirit, practice playing the *shakuhachi* (Japanese bamboo flute), or partake of an ancient meditative tea ceremony. Workshops offer instruction in raku tea-bowl making (using clay dug on the farm), flower arranging, and organic gardening.

Guests are welcome to come and go as they please, joining in communal life and work on the organic farm or quietly meditating on long walks through the nearby woods and on Muir beach. Miles of hiking trails surround the 200-acre Green Gulch, leading to Mount Tamalpais and Mill Valley.

As you enter the Lindisfarne Guest House, you'll gain an immediate sense of ageless serenity. Constructed in the Japanese temple style of handmade woodcraft, it has 12 rooms surrounding a high atrium.

A combination of vacation and partial participation in community work and practice is available from Sunday through Thursday nights. The morning schedule includes meditation, work, classes, and group discussions; afternoons and evenings are free. Called a "Practice Retreat," this program involves a minimum stay of three nights and earns you a modest reduction on the daily rate, plus meals.

Green Gulch Farm Zen Center
Star Rte., Sausalito, CA 94965
Tel. 415/383–3134
Fax 415/383–3128

Administration Spiritual leader, Abbot Norman Fischer; director, Meiya Wender

Season Year-round

Accommodations 12 rooms with shared baths, 1 suite. Simple wooden furniture, 2 beds in each room. Central heat, but no air-conditioning. Each room has outside patio or balcony.

Rates $55–$70 per person in small single room, $90–$105 for 2 persons; weekends, $70–$85 daily, single in large room, $105–$120 for 2 persons. Meals $5 each. Practice Retreat, including meals, $30 per day single, $50 double occupancy (3-night minimum). Beginner's "sitting" $15, includes lunch; no lodging. Weekend workshop: $100 tuition includes all meals and $170 for shared accommodations, $200 for single room; add tax. Deposit: 1 night, plus $10 per person for each additional night. No credit cards.

Meal Plans   3 vegetarian meals daily, served buffet style, include eggs and dairy products. Organically grown vegetables from the farm are steamed, served with brown rice, miso soup.

Services and Facilities   **Services:** Instruction in Japanese arts, Zen, gardening, herbs. **Swimming Facilities:** Ocean beach, outdoor pool. **Evening Programs:** Lectures on Japanese arts in conjunction with scheduled workshops.

In the Area   Muir Woods, Napa Valley, Marin County Civic Center (Frank Lloyd Wright architecture, art galleries, theater), Sausalito waterfront (restaurants, boutiques).

Getting Here   *From San Francisco.* By car, Hwy. 101 to turnoff for Mill Valley, Hwy. 1 (Shoreline Hwy.) toward Muir Beach (25 mins). By ferry, frequent bay crossings from the Embarcadero to Sausalito; then take a taxi.

Special Notes   Scheduled program for workshops/retreats varies weekly.

Heartwood Institute

Life enhancement
Spiritual awareness

California
Garberville

Set on 240 acres in the mountains on California's north coast, this rustic complex serves as a vocational school for practitioners in the healing arts, and also welcomes weekend visitors and participants in wellness retreats. The customized retreat programs are designed for healthy people seeking to become even healthier. A full schedule of classes, exercise, and bodywork is offered during retreats by experts in Hatha Iyengar yoga, transcendental meditation, and nutrition.

The wilderness setting is perfect for walks in the woods, mountain biking, or participating in a group meditation under the wooden dome set in the forest. In the community center, a picturesque log lodge, are eight private treatment rooms, an outdoor hot tub, wood-fired sauna, and bedrooms. Meals are taken in the cozy dining room or on a spacious deck in nice weather. Typically there are 20 participants in a retreat program.

Heartwood Institute
220 Harmony La., Garberville, CA 95440
Tel. 707/923–5000
Fax 707/923–4906

Administration   Owners-managers, Robert Fasic and Roy Grieshaber; retreat coordinator, Susie Yong

Season   Year-round

Accommodations   15 rooms in 3-story dormitory, 36 campsites. Simple amenities include sheets, towels, comforters on beds, and shared bathrooms. No air-conditioning or maid service.

Rates $110 per night for single room and meals, $90 per person for double room and meals; $55 for campsite. $126 tuition for weekend retreat, with $50 advance payment. MC, V.

Meal Plans   3 meals daily, served buffet style. All meals are primarily vegetarian: organic vegetables, grains, fruits, and nuts are supplemented with dairy products and eggs. Fish is served once a week. There is a snack kitchen for personal use in the community center. Special diets are accommodated.

Services and Facilities   **Services:** Yoga classes daily, Swedish/Esalen massage, polarity therapy, hypnotherapy, deep-tissue massage, shiatsu, acupressure, breathwork, Jin Shin Jytsu, transformational therapy, nutritional counseling. **Swimming Facilities:** Outdoor heated swimming pool. **Evening Programs:** Lectures, dances.

In the Area Sinkyone Wilderness State Preserve, redwood forest, Eureka and Arcata (Victorian architecture, museums, galleries).

Getting Here *From San Francisco.* By car, Hwy. 101 north to first Garberville exit (3 hrs). By bus, Greyhound to Garberville (6 hr). By plane, American and United Airlines to Eureka/Arcata Airport. Pickup arranged at airport or bus station (fee). Car rental, taxi available.

La Costa Resort & Spa

Life enhancement
Luxury pampering
Nutrition and diet
Weight management

California
Carlsbad

A mega-resort for the fun and fitness crowd, La Costa Resort & Spa focuses more on pampering than on preventive medicine. When the spa complex was renovated several years ago, the idea was to offer something for every taste. The unfortunate result is overcrowding and lack of privacy in the spa building. The beauty salon, on the other hand, is state of the art.

The Healthy Lifestyles program is a one-week package designed to educate and motivate guests to adopt healthy habits. Each day begins with a brisk walk around the golf course. Power walking has now become the preferred exercise, for the fit and the not so fit, because it does not stress bones and joints like running and jogging. Optional periods allow unlimited golf, tennis, or personal counseling.

Guests are teamed with a personal trainer, nutritionist, and psychologist—you get a full wellness prescription. A computerized exerciser tests your strength, flexibility, and pulmonary function. Nutritional analysis and body composition determine your diet and measure the percentages of fat and muscle in your body. A take-home program is provided.

The Healthy Lifestyles program can begin any day of the week. It's wise to schedule early appointments at the spa, especially when a large group is meeting at the convention center across the way.

La Costa can be enjoyed simply as a luxury getaway or as a structured spa program. Packages are available for two to seven nights, with a choice of eating in any of the dining rooms, all of which serve spa cuisine.

The true luxury of La Costa is the personal attention guests receive, even though the place is crowded. Locker-room attendants remember your name and slipper size and hand out fresh towels and robes without being asked; they deserve handsome tips. The separate facilities for men and women add to the clublike atmosphere. Included are a eucalyptus-scented inhalation room, steam room, sauna, Swiss multihead showers, hot and cold plunge pools, and an outdoor Jacuzzi. The gym and salon are coed.

Currently completing a four-year, $50 million refurbishing of the main facilities, the resort has plans to give the spa a new look. Some regulars say it is long overdue.

La Costa Resort & Spa
Costa del Mar Rd., Carlsbad, CA 92009
Tel. 619/438–9111 or 800/854–5000; spa appointments
800/729–4772
Fax 619/931–7559

Administration	Managing director, John Peto
Season	Year-round
Accommodations	102 spa rooms, 372 golf, tennis, and Courtyard wing deluxe rooms and suites in Spanish-style buildings and a campus-style spa complex. Newer rooms overlook the golf course. Fine furnishings. Fitness- and spa-program guests stay in large, poolside bedrooms with sitting areas, unless they request otherwise. Also private residences.
Rates	Daily single or double occupancy $225–$395, suites $400–$2,100 for 2. Add 10% tax, 1 night payable on booking. AE, D, DC, MC, V.
Meal Plans	No meal plan. Select from daily menus in 4 restaurants offering spa cuisine. Breakfast options include fruit, muffins, an egg-white omelet with salsa, and an energy mix of grains, apple butter, and raisins. For lunch, try cheese blintzes, papaya stuffed with crab, and beef Stroganoff. Chicken stuffed with foie gras, fettucine primavera, salmon fillet with horseradish sauce, and veal with artichoke sauce are dinner entrées, with fresh fruit, sherbet, or custard for dessert.
Services and Facilities	**Exercise Equipment:** Eagle, Nautilus, and Universal weights units; Lifecycles, computerized treadmills, aerobic trainer, rowing machines, free weights, Rebounders. **Services:** Massage (Swedish, shiatsu, reike, aromatherapy, reflexology), Orthion, Myopulse, herbal wraps, loofah body scrub, spot toning, facials. Salon for hair, nail, and skin care. Coed exercise classes $10 (aerobics, Rebounder, yoga). Nutrition counseling, medical and fitness evaluations. Personal trainer for exercise, swimming, golf, and tennis. **Swimming Facilities:** 5 outdoor pools. **Recreation Facilities:** 21 championship tennis courts (8 lighted), 2 18-hole golf courses, driving range, horseback riding, bike rental. **Evening Programs:** Lectures on health and fitness, stress management; movies and resort cabaret.
In the Area	Bus or limousine trips to Sea World, San Diego Zoo, Disneyland; Coronado beaches, San Diego museums, and Horton Plaza shops, Laguna Nigel (the Ritz Carlton); Del Mar Racetrack.
Getting Here	*From San Diego.* By car, I–5 to Carlsbad, La Costa Ave. exit (40 mins). By train, Amtrak to Oceanside (30 mins). Limousine, taxi, rental car available.
Special Notes	Accessible to people with disabilities. Tennis and golf clinics and summer day-camp programs for children. No smoking in the spa building or the dining rooms. Spa open daily 7 AM–8 PM; minimum age 18.

Loews Santa Monica Beach Hotel

Nonprogram resort
Sports conditioning

California *Santa Monica*	If you want a customized fitness program, Hollywood sports trainer Jackson Sousa will give you primo one-on-one training in his own 3,200-square-foot facility, in the Loews Santa Monica Beach Hotel. If he's not motivation enough for you to get into shape, nearby Venice Beach (a.k.a. Surfer's SoHo), with lots of buffed bodies, should give you some impetus to pull in

the waistline. This resort, opened in 1989 and refurbished in 1993, is on the beach and is under an hour's drive from downtown Los Angeles.

Pamper yourself in the airy resort's health club and skin-care salon, and use the glass-dome indoor/outdoor swimming pool and Jacuzzi adjoining the fitness center. Training sessions and massages can be arranged, as can a weekend hiking excursion. An optional package of salon services can be booked for $150, or you can combine fitness and massage services with a $120 day package. Special weekend packages are offered, including high-energy breakfast, personal training, nutritional counseling, and biometric evaluation.

Sousa's fitness center has a full line of state-of-the-art cardiovascular and weight-training machines, plus a studio for aerobics and yoga classes. In addition to scheduled classes in step aerobics, stretch and tone, and water aerobics, physical therapy and orthopedic sports rehabilitation are offered. There are a sauna and a steam room in both the men's and women's locker rooms. Emphasis here is on strengthening, cross training, and prevention of further injury.

Loews Santa Monica Beach Hotel
1700 Ocean Ave., Santa Monica, CA 90401
Tel. 310/458–6700 or 800/235–6397
Fax 310/458–6761

Administration Managing director, Richard Casale; fitness center operator, Jackson Sousa

Season Year-round

Accommodations 350 rooms and 31 suites with ocean view. All have desk, 2 dual-line phones with data ports, phone in bathroom, robes, hair dryer, scale, TV, radio/clock, and air-conditioning. Rooms are refreshed twice daily, and are furnished with pale wood, rattan, and original art. On-site valet and self-parking, concierge service. Suites have marble-wall Jacuzzi, small balcony.

Rates $225–$335 single, $245–$335 for double, suites $500–$2,500. Add tax, gratuities. Credit cards: AE, DC, MC, V.

Meal Plans Healthy options served à la carte or included in weekend package.

Services and Facilities **Exercise Equipment:** Cybex and Keiser weight-training equipment, StairMaster, Lifecycles, Gravitron, bikes, treadmills, free weights. **Swimming Facilities:** 65' x 23' indoor/outdoor pool, ocean beach. **Recreation Facilities:** Bike and skate path, in-line skate rental, public tennis courts all nearby. **Services:** Massage, facial, fitness evaluation, 1-on-1 training, salon. **Evening Programs:** Lobby lounge, nearby Center for the Performing Arts.

In the Area Pritikin Center, Santa Monica Pier (carousel, games, entertainment), Hollywood, J. Paul Getty Museum (art), Pacific Coast Bicentennial Bike Route, Santa Monica Mountains National Recreation Area, Universal Studios, Third Street Promenade (shopping and dining); Huntington Library (art collections and botanical gardens) 1 hr east in San Marino.

Getting Here *From Los Angeles International Airport.* SuperShuttle van (30 mins). By car, Santa Monica Fwy. (I–10) to 4th St. exit, Pico Blvd. to Ocean Ave. (30 mins). Taxi, limousine, rental car available.

Special Notes $10 daily facility fee for Fitness Center. Kid Fitness program on request.

Marriott's Desert Springs Resort

Luxury pampering

California
Palm Desert

The Desert Springs Resort, the elaborate flagship resort created in the desert by the Marriott Corporation, boasts an impressive design: To reach the health spa from the main lobby,
guests step on a boat that glides gracefully to the oasis complex surrounded by lagoons and a golf course.

Guests at this airy 325-acre retreat find its elegance and desert
views relaxing. Escape the midday sun at the juice bar or have
your hair styled at the José Eber salon. Try the dry flotation
unit, a space-age capsule appropriately named Superspace Relaxer that has its own audio, video, and sensory stimulation
unit. When you're working out, enjoy the natural light that
floods the newly expanded weight training gym and aerobics
studios, where yoga, step aerobics, and body sculpting are
among six classes scheduled daily.

Water is involved in many of the treatments and services offered, from hydrotherapy pools to hot and cold plunges, a Turkish steam room, and a vigorous Aquacise workout.
Underwater massage in private tubs is enhanced with crystals from Hungarian mineral springs, developed for the spa's
exclusive Kerstin Florian salon. Stimulating or relaxing aromatherapy oils—depending on your mood—and freeze-dried
seaweed can be added to the bath. Moisturizing creams leave
your skin glowing.

The new European Thermal Kur Program combines a series
of baths and bodywork in a specially priced package. The Spa
Experience package is designed for flexibility, giving you a
choice of services (one hour), unlimited aerobics classes, breakfast or lunch in the spa café, and a body composition test, plus
hotel accommodations on a nightly basis. Or you can pay the
daily admission of $24, which includes workout clothing and
robe, unlimited fitness classes, and use of exercise equipment.
The fee is waived when you book any one-day package that includes lunch, treatments, and exercise classes.

Skin-care products are formulated with natural ingredients
that include lavender, chamomile, vitamins, collagen, seaweed,
thermal mineral water, and glycolic acid. Applied by shiatsu
acupressure technique, the ointments, gels, and sprays are intended to help prevent sun damage and aging. The specialties
here are treatments formulated by Kirsten Florian with European herbal and thermal elements. Treatments can be
booked separately or as part of a half-day pampering package.

Marriott's Desert Springs Resort

74855 Country Club Dr., Palm Desert, CA 92260
Tel. 619/341–1856; spa appointments 800/255–0848; room
reservations 800/228–9290
Fax 619/341–1872

Administration
General Manager, Tim Sullivan; executive spa director, Kim
Cadra

Season
Year-round

Accommodations
892 rooms and executive suites, with oversize beds, private
bath, balcony. All rooms have refrigerator, minibar, 2 phones,
TV, air-conditioning, contemporary Southwestern furnishings. Golf villas available.

Rates
3-night Spa Experience package priced by season, $163–$308
single, $236–$386 for 2, double occupancy. Day packages (no
lodging) $85–$275. Packages include gratuities, tax. Daily

room rates $145–$300 single or double occupancy; suites $375–$2,100. Add 9% tax, gratuities. AE, DC, MC, V.

Meal Plans Spa cuisine is served in 3 of the resort's 10 restaurants, and at the spa café for breakfast and lunch. Meals are à la carte, or part of the Spa Experience package. Lunch can be a salad or cold poached salmon. Main dining room dinner entrées include grilled loin of veal, broiled chicken, pasta primavera. Coffee, herbal tea, dairy products. Special diets on request.

Services and Facilities **Exercise Equipment:** 24-station Bodymaster weight training gym, 4 StairMasters, 6 Lifecycles, 4 Precor treadmills, free weights, including barbells, dumbbells, bench press. **Services:** Massage (Swedish, shiatsu, sports, aromatherapy), full-body masks (aloe, algae, mud), facials, herbal wraps, loofah body scrub, Bindi, reflexology, nutrition counseling, computerized fitness and body-composition analysis, beauty salon. **Swimming Facilities:** Outdoor pool. **Recreation Facilities:** 2 18-hole golf courses, 18-hole putting course, 20 tennis courts, croquet, water volleyball. Bike rental, horseback riding, skiing nearby. **Evening Programs:** Resort entertainment.

In the Area Indian Canyons National Historic Park, sightseeing tours, aerial tramway to Mt. San Jacinto, ballooning, Desert Fashion Plaza (shopping), casinos, Bob Hope Cultural Center, Palm Springs Desert Museum (art, film series, concerts), Living Desert Reserve (nature studies), Polo Club, hot springs, Joshua Tree National Park (hiking trails).

Getting Here *From Los Angeles.* By bus, scheduled shuttle service from LAX and hotels or Greyhound (4 hrs). By car, I–10 to Hwy. 111 (2½ hrs). By train, Amtrak to Indio (2 hrs). By plane, American Airlines and United commuter flights (30 mins). Limousine, taxi, rental car available. Shuttle service by van to airport.

Special Notes Limited access for people with disabilities. Supervised games, movies, tennis lessons for children. No smoking in the spa; no-smoking areas in restaurants. Spa open daily 7:30–7:30. Exercise facilities open daily 5:30 AM–6:30 PM ($6 fee). Minimum age in spa: 16.

Meadowood Resort

Nonprogram resort

California **Napa Valley** Meadowood, nestled in the heart of the wine country 65 miles north of San Francisco, recalls the grand old resorts of the early 1900s with its gabled lodges overlooking the manicured croquet lawn and golf course. Remarkably, most of the buildings are of recent vintage. The health spa was added in 1993 and epitomizes the Napa Valley lifestyle: easy informality and superb taste.

Wine plays an important role in spa treatments and in the dinner menu. Chardonnay cream is used in a body wrap and facial. The cream is exclusively formulated with aromatic essential oils from grape seeds, said to encourage natural revitalization. An extensive selection of massage therapies, body and facial treatments, and fitness classes is available at à la carte prices or as part of a personalized renewal program. (Lodging is not included in spa packages.)

The spa building is airy and sunlit, with an aerobics studio and weight-training room on the upper floor, and a suite of private rooms for massage and facials adjoining the men's and women's locker rooms. A robe is issued when you check in for your appointments, and full amenities are provided. Scheduled classes are open to all guests but rarely crowded: an early morning stretch session is followed by the 90-minute total body work-out. One of the more creative classes offered here includes line-dance steps for country music fans; and aquaerobics, yoga, and step classes are listed on the daily schedule.

Vineyard tours begin right outside the resort. Mountain bikes with helmet and water bottle can be rented at the spa. For groups of four or more, the resident wine tutor, John Thoreen, sets up guided tours and tastings. Guided walks within Mead-owood's grounds are another way to enjoy the rich, natural history of Napa Valley.

Meadowood Resort
900 Meadowood La., St. Helena, CA 94574
Tel. 707/963–3646 or 800/458–8080
Fax 707/963–3532

Administration General manager, Jorg Lippuner; spa directors, Eric and Catherine Chesky

Season Year-round

Accommodations 85 luxury rooms and suites, all in lodges on hillside. French provincial furniture, with king- or queen-size beds trimmed in chintz, covered with down comforter. Most have fieldstone fireplace, high ceilings with fan, and gabled windows. All are air-conditioned, have TV, 2 phones, radiant heating, large tile bathroom. Amenities: coffeemaker, toaster, wet bar, terry-cloth robes, basket of apples. Also under same management, 21-room Inn at Southbridge in St. Helena, 2 miles from resort. Room rate $175–$255 per night, includes use of spa for daily fee ($15).

Rates $305–$445 per night for 2 persons; suites $515–$1,875. Add $295 per person for 3-day Renewal Program with 5 spa services. Add 15% service charge, plus taxes. AE, DC, MC, V.

Meal Plans Meals at Meadowood include a wide range of vegetarian and heart-healthy specialties. Chef Roy Breiman blends cooking techniques from the Provence region of France with the sea-sonal bounty from local farms and California's seacoast. Prix-fixe vegetarian dinner menu ($45) includes salad of couscous with layered zucchini, strudel with wild mushrooms and caramelized artichokes. Spa menu has crispy salmon with mar-inated tomatoes, vegetable spaghettini, fruit sorbet. Lunch se-lections at the Grill include grilled artichoke with crab salad, fettuccine with mushrooms, tomatoes, basil, and garlic. Natu-rally an extensive wine list accompanies meals.

Services and Facilities **Exercise Equipment:** Cybex 12-unit weight training circuit, Lifecycle 9500 recumbent bike, 2 Startrac treadmills, 3 Climb Max units, Monark bike, free weights (3–50 lbs), benches. **Swimming Facilities:** Outdoor heated 25-yd. lap pool, recre-ational pool. **Recreation Facilities:** 7 outdoor tennis courts, 2 croquet courts, 9-hole golf course, bike rental. **Services:** Mas-sage (Swedish, deep tissue, aromatherapy), reflexology, facial, salt-glow body scrub, exercise consultation, personal training, body composition test, nutrition analysis.

In the Area Calistoga mud baths (*see above*), Culinary Institute of Amer-ica, St. Helena (shops, restaurants), ballooning, horseback rid-ing, wineries.

Getting Here *From San Francisco.* By car, Hwy. 101 via the Golden Gate Bridge to Hwy. 80, Hwy. 29 via Napa to St. Helena, Silverado Trail to Hopewell Mtn. Rd. (90 mins). Limousine, taxi, car rental available.

Special Notes Daily charge for spa use $15. Hours: daily 7 AM–8 PM. Minimum age in spa: 16.

The Oaks at Ojai

Nutrition and diet
Vibrant maturity
Weight management

California Built as a country inn in 1918, the dignified wood-and-stone
Ojai structure gained a new lease on life in the 1970s when Sheila
Cluff and her husband became its owners. A former professional ice skater and physical fitness instructor, Sheila Cluff
drew together a team of exercise physiologists. A sister spa
in Palm Springs, the Palms, offers a similar no-frills program.

Ojai is an art center and a favorite of the practitioners of several healing faiths. The Oaks is on the main square of the town,
and appointments can be made with psychics, astrologers,
pyramid enthusiasts, members of the Theosophy movement,
or the Krishnamurti Foundation. All are attracted by the natural beauty of a fertile valley near the Los Padres National
Forest, little more than an hour's drive north of Los Angeles.

At the Oaks at Ojai, fitness and weight-control programs are
the main attractions for men and women who want to unwind
or work out without fancy lodging or physical therapy. When
you stick to the basics—up to 17 exercise classes and activities daily and a diet of fresh, natural foods that total only 1,000
calories—the Oaks helps you lose up to a pound a day safely.

The day begins with a challenging aerobic workout at 6 AM.
Fruits, muffins, and vitamins are set out at the Winners Cir-
cle, a juice bar in the lodge. Lunch can be eaten by the pool or
in the dining room. There is a mid-morning broth break, and
vegetable snacks are served in the afternoon. The program is
aimed at burning calories, conditioning the heart and lungs,
and toning the body. Guests here include young professionals
and grandmothers alike; film industry folk, TV actresses, and
housewives drop in to shape up or relax.

Most activities are held in the main lodge and garden. The complex includes saunas, an aerobics studio, a large swimming
pool, and a cluster of guest bungalows. Classes, rated according to the guests' fitness level, last from 45 minutes to an hour.
A nurse is on staff to help plan each person's schedule. Or you
can work out on weight machines; facilities are open 24 hours.

The program operates on an all-inclusive American plan, and
guests are welcome to stay a few days or weeks and take part
in as many of the activities as they please. A number of special packages are available, including a spa-cooking week and
mother-daughter days.

The Oaks at Ojai
122 E. Ojai Ave., Ojai, CA 93023
Tel. 805/646–5573 or 800/753–6257
Fax 805/640–1504

Administration Owners-directors, Don and Sheila Cluff; fitness director,
Elizabeth Horton

Season Year-round

Accommodations 46 guest rooms in the main lodge and cottages, from small singles to a cottage for 3. Simply furnished with modern beds, all
have private bath, color TV, telephone, air-conditioning.

Rates Daily per person sharing small double lodge room with shower
only; $195–$205 weekdays for single, $135–$175 per person
double. 5-day program (Sun.–Fri. with 1 service) $975–$1,025
single, $675–$795 per person double; 7-day program with 2 services $1,265–$1,435 single, $945–$1,225 double. Spa Day (3

meals, classes; no lodging) $89. Deposit: 1 night payable in advance. Add 14% service charge, 15.25% taxes. AE, D, MC, V.

Meal Plans 3 meals daily. Natural foods, no additives, salt, white flour, or sugar. Lunch can be soup; tuna salad with egg, mushrooms, and cheese; or vegetable crêpes. Dinner entrées: vegetarian lasagna, baked chicken, broiled fish, or pasta salad.

Services and Facilities **Exercise Equipment:** 16-station Paramount weight training system, 2 Trotter treadmills, 2 StairMasters, 2 Lifecycles, hand and ankle weights, stretch bands. **Swimming Facilities:** Outdoor pool. **Recreation Facilities:** Hiking; tennis, golf, and bike rental nearby. **Services:** Massage, facials, reflexology, aromatherapy, hydrotherapy. Salon for hair, skin, and nail care; computerized body analysis. **Evening Programs:** Talks on health and fitness.

In the Area Lake Casitas, annual music and dance festivals, crafts boutiques, Bart's Corners book and sheet-music shop.

Getting Here *From Los Angeles.* By bus, Greyhound to Ventura (2 hrs). By car, Hwy. 101 (Ventura Fwy.) to Ventura, Hwy. 33 to Ojai, Hwy. 150 to center of town (80 mins). Taxi, rental car available.

Special Notes No smoking in rooms or inside hotel. Special seasonal programs. Mother-daughter spa days in Jan. Minimum age: 16.

The Palms

Nutrition and diet
Vibrant maturity
Weight management

California
Palm Springs

Finding an informal place in which to exercise and diet in the center of Palm Springs resort life is quite a feat. The Palms is a "come as you are" place, one with few frills, plenty of options, and no attendance requirements. Goal-oriented guests can have programs tailored to suit their abilities, interests, and needs.

Activity centers on a large swimming pool, and additional classes are held indoors in a small aerobics studio and outdoors under the palms. With up to 16 activities offered daily, guests are encouraged to take part in as many or as few as they please. Special weeks feature high-powered speakers on health, nutrition, and fitness; a seminar on women in management; a 21-day course on quitting smoking; and, in January and May, mother-daughter weeks.

The program operates on an all-inclusive American Plan, regardless of how long you stay (2-day minimum stay required), and guests may arrive on any day (unless a workshop is scheduled). The flexibility allows you to enjoy the attractions of the Palm Springs area, some within walking distance. Spa services also are available without lodging.

The converted manor house and cluster of private bungalows exude a Spanish-colonial ambience and sit handsomely beneath the dramatic starkness of mountains. Although there is no hydrotherapy, a sauna and whirlpool are tucked into the complex.

The Palms
572 N. Indian Canyon Dr., Palm Springs, CA 92262
Tel. 619/325–1111 or 800/753–7256
Fax 619/327–0867

Administration Manager, Bruce Taylor; fitness director, Marilu Rogers Horst

Season Year-round

Accommodations 37 rooms in the manor and bungalows, most on the ground floor with private patio. Motel-style furniture, double beds, generous closets. All rooms with private or shared bath, air-conditioning, TV, telephone.

Rates $169–$179 per person, double occupancy, private bath, on a daily-program basis; $135–$145 with shared bath. Single rooms $199–$209. 7-night package with 2 treatments, $945–$1,183 double, $1,393 single; 5-night midweek package $675–$845 double, $995 single (1 treatment included). Add 15% tax, 15% service charge. Deposit: 1 night's lodging payable in advance. Day Spa package (classes, 3 meals; no lodging) $89. AE, MC, V.

Meal Plans 3 meals totaling 1,000 calories served daily in the dining room. Breakfast is fresh fruit, a diet muffin, and a vitamin supplement. Lunch includes soup, choice of chicken tostada seasoned with chili and cumin, or vegetable crepes. Veal loaf, broiled red snapper in tomato sauce, turkey divan, or vegetarian lasagna for dinner. No salt, sugar, or chemical additives. Coffee and hot or iced herbal tea all day. Mid-morning broth break, afternoon vegetables.

Services and Facilities **Exercise Equipment:** 2 Paramount weight training gym units, 3 Bodyguard treadmills, StairMaster, 2 Lifecycles, hand and ankle weights, stretch bands. **Services:** Massage, body scrub, aromatherapy; salon for hair, nail, and skin care. Consultation on fitness, body composition analysis. **Swimming Facilities:** Outdoor pool. **Recreation Facilities:** Hiking. Bike rental, horseback riding, tennis, and golf all nearby. Downhill and cross-country skiing in the mountains. **Evening Programs:** Talks on dressing for success, the history of Palm Springs, other subjects.

In the Area Local sightseeing tours; aerial tram ride, ballooning, baths at nearby hot springs; Desert Museum, Living Desert Reserve.

Getting Here *From Los Angeles.* By bus, Greyhound (4 hrs). By car, I–10 to Hwy. 111 (2½ hrs). By train, Amtrak to Indio (2 hrs). By air, scheduled service on Continental, American Airlines, and United commuter flights (30 mins). Taxi service and rental car available. Desert City Shuttle bus ($65).

Special Notes Limited access for people with disabilities. No smoking in designated areas. Mother-daughter weeks in Jan. and May. Special seasonal programs. Minimum age: 16.

Pocket Ranch Institute

Life enhancement
Spiritual awareness

California Here is a retreat for people who want to become more self-
Geyserville aware, in a peaceful, wooded setting. Founded in 1986 by Barbara Findeisen, a marriage counselor and specialist working with children and families, the Institute has serious educational programs for caregivers, as well as structured group workshops and personal retreats.

The ranch's spirituality is conveyed in a meditation cottage set on a hilltop, where you may encounter coyotes, horses, and cows roaming the canyons (also snakes in season) during the starry nights. Native American traditions are celebrated the week after Christmas, including a sweat lodge and intention-stick ceremony. Accommodations are available for just 50 participants (including children), which enables the Ranch to maintain an intimate, familylike atmosphere so guests can comfortably "reconnect heads with hearts, and set free the spirit within."

Bodywork is a key element in all programs; for short visits, book a massage to renew your energies. Beyond massage, therapists can work with you on breathing techniques and hypnosis to manage stress, and art as a means of self-expression. Exercise, however, is not emphasized, although you are free to enjoy the large swimming pool or hike on trails into the surrounding hills. The bodywork building has two private rooms, sauna, and showers. For groups, a ropes course teaches team-building exercises.

The focus is a 17-day "STAR" program, which confronts deep-rooted childhood trauma. Although you'll work in a group, you'll be assigned to a therapist for personal consultation, and you can set your own pace. Writing exercises as well as body work are included in the program fee. About half the participants are men, and half are women.

Pocket Ranch Institute
Box 516, Geyserville, CA 95441
Tel. 707/857–3359
Fax 707/857–3764

Administration	Business manager, Diana Barrett
Season	Year-round
Accommodations	25 comfortably furnished bedrooms in 4-unit cabins. Specially designed rustic pine furniture, including desk, hand-crafted bedstead, country fabrics, and built-in lighting. Private bath, air-conditioning; no TV or telephone.
Rates	17-day STAR program $5,200. Tax and gratuities not included. MC, V.
Meal Plans	3 meals daily, plus snacks, included in fee. Vegetarian and non-vegetarian selections. Special diets accommodated.
Services and Facilities	**Exercise Equipment**: None. **Services**: Massage (Swedish, Esalen, shiatsu, deep tissue), hypnotherapy, breathing therapy, personal counseling. **Swimming Facilities**: Outdoor heated pool. **Recreation Facilities**: Hiking trails. **Evening Programs**: Lectures.
In the Area	Harbin Hot Springs, Konocti Lake Resort and Spa.
Getting Here	*From San Francisco.* By car, Golden Gate Bridge, north on Hwy. 101, Hwy. 128, ranch road (unpaved) for 7 mi. The total trip takes about 3 hrs.

Post Ranch Inn

Nonprogram resort

California
Big Sur

Sensuous and environmentally sensitive, the 98-acre Post Ranch Inn blends into the redwoods of Big Sur; with only 30 guest rooms, the grounds still seem pristine. Each guest unit comes with a massage table, whirlpool tub, wood-burning fireplace, and stereo system. Also offered in your room are an herbal facial or body polish and yoga instruction. The ultimate luxury is an hour-long massage in the privacy of your suite.

The ranch's spa is housed in a small cottage and takes advantage of the Ventana Range surrounding the resort. The sea air and refreshing scent of pines will invigorate you during your scheduled sessions of aerobic speed walking and guided nature and wilderness hikes. A personalized program can be arranged by contacting the spa director prior to your arrival. Appointments are scheduled until midnight. Depending on the weather, sessions of yoga and star-gazing are offered outdoors.

There's no tennis or golf; just smashing views of the Pacific Ocean and Ventana Peak. The meals at Sierra Mar Restaurant are as inspiring as the scenery, and Saturday wine tastings are a bonus.

Big Sur has a mystical affect on visitors. Henry Miller and his followers started a back-to-nature cult that still permeates the area. Perched 1,200 feet above the Pacific Ocean, the Post Ranch Inn provides an electric car to transport you to your room, as gas-powered vehicles are banned. Some of the guest units are built on stilts, or hidden under sod roofs. Interiors feature rough-hewn redwood beams and other natural materials.

Post Ranch Inn
Hwy. 1, Box 219, Big Sur, CA 93920
Tel. 408/667–2200 or 800/527–2200
Fax 408/667–2824

Administration General manager, Lawrence Callahan; spa director, Roy Malcom

Season Year-round

Accommodations 30 suites in secluded wooden houses, accented by glass, marble, slate, and granite interiors. All have king-size bed, oversize bathroom with Jacuzzi tub, modern furniture, fireplace, air-conditioning, TV, phone, stereo system. Amenities include terry-cloth robes. View varies in 7 Tree Houses, 12 Post Houses, 5 houses with ocean views, and the 6-suite Butterfly Houses.

Rates $285–$545 daily per suite. Add gratuities, taxes. AE, MC, V.

Meal Plan Continental breakfast buffet included in room cost. Dining room has prix fixe or à la carte menu for lunch (only on weekends) and dinner that includes Atlantic salmon with clams and mussels in dill-shallot broth with corn, peas, and potatoes. Dessert is apricot steamed pudding with ginger ice cream, or coconut crème caramel with orange slices. Specialties include tuna in sesame seed crust with crisp noodle salad flavored by wasabi oil, grilled quail with potato gnocchi, house-cured salmon with corn cakes. Spa selections are low in fat, salt, and calories.

Services and Facilities **Exercise Equipment:** Weight training circuit, treadmills, bikes. **Services:** Massage (Esalen or sports), aromatherapy, herbal wrap, facial, 1-on-1 training, guided hikes. **Spa Facilities:** Cardiovascular exercise room, aerobics studio, outdoor hot tub for 20 persons, sauna, private treatment rooms. **Swimming Facilities:** Outdoor heated lap pool.

In the Area Esalen Institute, Tassajara Zen Monastery and hot springs, tour of Point Sur Lighthouse (ca. 1850).

Getting Here *From Carmel.* By car, Hwy. 1 south to ranch road (40 mins).

Preventive Medicine Research Institute

Life enhancement
Preventive medicine

California
Oakland/Berkeley Changing your lifestyle to reverse the progression of cardiovascular disease is the focus of weeklong retreats held at the Claremont Resort (*see above*) under auspices of the Preventive Medicine Research Institute. Directed by Dean Ornish, M.D., and led by health professionals from the institute, this highly structured program includes lectures and experiential sessions, as well as cooking instruction by celebrity chefs.

Stress management techniques, exercise in the resort's well-equipped fitness center, and group support help you discover how understanding your physical and emotional states can improve your mental health. The finishing touch is a visit to the spa and its salon, but those services are not included in the program cost.

Participation in the retreat is limited to 100 and includes all meals, accommodations, professional staff time, classes, and take-home material. Part of the fee contributes to ongoing programs at the Preventive Medicine Research Institute, a nonprofit public institute associated with the University of California, San Francisco.

Preventive Medicine Research Institute
900 Bridgeway, Suite 2, Sausalito, CA 94965
Tel. 415/331–2323 or 800/775–7674
Fax 415/332–5730

Administration President and director, Dean Ornish, M.D.; administrator, David Liff

Season 7 weeklong programs scheduled throughout the year

Rates $3,600 for primary participant; $2,100 for spouse or companion sharing room.

Meal Plan 3 meals served daily in private dining room. Mainly vegetarian, the meals are low-fat, low-cholesterol.

Facilities *See* Claremont Resort, *above.*

Pritikin Longevity Center

Nutrition and diet
Vibrant maturity
Weight management

California The Pritikin Longevity Center, which occupies an entire
Santa Monica beachfront hotel, is dedicated to the diet and exercise regimen espoused in the 1970s by the late Nathan Pritikin. It is the development center for programs offered elsewhere around the country, and since 1978 it has offered a vacation that presents the elements essential to preventing degenerative disease and improving the quality of one's life.

The medically supervised programs last for 7 or 13 days, with a core curriculum that includes daily exercise, nutrition and health education, and stress-management counseling. A medical examination is performed while you are at the center, and provides guidelines for your regimen, but costs are not included in the program. (Check with your health insurance plan for possible reimbursement.) The two-week program is recommended for weight loss, reducing cholesterol levels, and managing blood pressure.

Healthy people, too, come here to maintain their health, learn to control their diet, cook and eat Pritikin-style, and exercise. A free hot line is included for those who need continuing support after they leave the program.

The daily schedule includes cooking classes, lectures, and three supervised exercise sessions. A full physical examination is a major part of the program; it includes a treadmill stress test and a complete blood-chemistry analysis. Depending on your personal history and fitness level, you will be assigned to a specialist in either cardiology or internal medicine who will monitor your progress on the prescribed diet and exercise program. Restrictions are noted on your identification badge.

Ocean views from the dining room are a pleasure at mealtimes. The chefs cook without added fat, salt, or sugar, and no coffee or tea is served. Meals are largely vegetarian, although fish and chicken are served several times a week; there are many fresh fruits and whole grains. (The Pritikin diet is 5% to 10% fat, 10% to 15% protein, and 80% high complex carbohydrates.) Breakfast and lunch are self-service; dinners are served in the dining room.

This highly regimented program is designed to motivate lifestyle changes. Sharing the experience with a friend or spouse yields savings, and can be the basis for your own support group at home.

Pritikin Longevity Center

1910 Ocean Front Walk, Santa Monica, CA 90405
Tel. 310/450–5433 or 800/421–9911
Fax 310/450–3602

Administration Director, Robert Pritikin; program director, Amy Fates

Season Year-round

Accommodations 128 rooms, from singles to suites, with desk, reading chair, tiled bath, and glass-enclosed shower. Better rooms include a Jacuzzi bathtub and ocean views ($300–$900 supplement for a 13-day program). Air-conditioning, TV, phone in all rooms, and just enough quiet comfort to make it feel like a resort.

Rates One-week program (Sun.–Sat.) $3,480 single, $1,511 for second person sharing room; medical fees $545. Two-week program for first-time visitors $6,409, $2,405 for second person sharing room; medical fees $590. Deposit: $500 in advance. Add gratuities. AE, MC, V.

Meal Plans 3 meals plus 3 snacks daily. Lunches may be vegetarian lasagna, chili relleno, and salad bar. Dinners are mostly vegetarian, but some entrées include fish, such as seafood crêpe or salmon teriyaki.

Services and Facilities **Exercise Equipment:** 51 Trotter treadmills, 9 combi bikes, 7 Schwinn Air Dyne bikes, 3 recumbent bikes, Concept 2 rower, 2 Precor rowers, Climb Max, 3 AeroStep, Schwinn Bow-Flex, 15-station weights system, dumbbells (5–50 lbs.), hand weights. **Services:** Medical, fitness, and nutrition counseling; massage, acupressure in four private rooms; beauty salon appointments. **Swimming Facilities:** Nearby outdoor pool, ocean beach. **Recreation Facilities:** Tennis, golf, fishing nearby. Optional weekend excursions to area attractions. **Evening Programs:** Lectures and films on health-related topics; music and dancing. Concierge service for show and concert tickets.

In the Area Shopping centers, museums, guided food shopping, and restaurant dining; J. Paul Getty Museum, Norton Simon Museum, Venice Beach, Hollywood Park Race Track.

Getting Here *From Los Angeles.* By Bus, Santa Monica Blue Bus from downtown (tel. 213/451–5444) takes about 45 mins. By car, Santa Monica Fwy. (I–10) to 4th St. exit, Pico Blvd. (20 mins). Taxi, limousine, rental car available. Parking on site. SuperShuttle from LAX airport.

Special Notes Elevator connects all floors. No smoking indoors.

St. Helena Hospital Health Center

Life enhancement
Preventive medicine
Spiritual awareness
Vibrant maturity
Weight management

California
Napa Valley Vineyards spread for miles below the hillside perch of the St. Helena Health Center. This is part of a hospital complex run

by the Seventh-Day Adventists, but the center's structured residential programs are nondenominational and nonsectarian. The medically oriented programs are designed to teach self-management. Disease prevention is emphasized here. Following a physical examination and an analysis of your diet, doctors and health professionals prescribe a course of action intended to help you achieve a healthier lifestyle. Their specific recommendations for diet take into account your physical condition, nutritional requirements, and weight-loss goals. Together you devise an exercise schedule and discuss hydrotherapy treatments, massage, and medical tests that are available at an additional charge.

The health center's association with St. Helena Hospital enables it to draw on sophisticated medical facilities, biofeedback, and medical consultants appropriate to your special problems. The center offers programs in smoking cessation, lifestyle change through nutrition, alcohol and chemical recovery, pulmonary rehabilitation, pain rehabilitation, personalized health, and prime-of-life fitness.

The 12-day McDougall Program, dealing with diet and nutrition, includes group therapy and relaxation techniques, vegetarian cooking classes in a teaching kitchen, and bodywork—massage plus use of the steam baths, sauna, and whirlpool. Consultation with Dr. John McDougall, author of four books on the prevention and treatment of disease, focuses on lifestyle changes to lower cholesterol and improve personal health and well-being. The program is scheduled once a month.

Program participants have full use of a gymnasium, running track, and an indoor/outdoor swimming pool. A rest and relaxation program, designed for stress management, and a personalized health program (weekdays), including massages, are available. If you are accompanied by a spouse or family member, there is a special combination rate for the program. Additional weeks are reserved for program alumni.

Taking charge of your health requires a commitment to lifestyle changes, Dr. McDougall advises, and this program provides the tools. Seventy miles north of San Francisco, St. Helena has an inspiring setting, as well as all the comforts of a first-class resort.

St. Helena Hospital Health Center
Deer Park, CA 94576
Tel. 707/963–6200 or 800/358–9195

Administration Program coordinators, Brigitta Karlman, RN, MSN, and Linda Schulz

Season Year-round

Accommodations 54 rooms with private bath, air-conditioning, many with balconies with views of Napa Valley; 2 beds and reading chair, TV, telephone. Furnished in motel-modern style.

Rates 4-day/3-night Personalized Health Program $1,551; 7-day smoking cessation program $2,470 single, $2,295 double; 12-day McDougall program $4,150 single, $3,932 double. Meals included. (Medical insurance may cover part of the cost.) Deposit required for some programs. MC, V.

Meal Plans 3 vegetarian meals daily, buffet style. No tea, coffee, or condiments. Cooking without butter and oil; vegetables sautéed in water. Specialties include vegetarian lasagna with mock cheese topping, baked tofu loaf, and eggplant "Parmesan" without cheese. Whole-grain breads baked without dairy products or eggs, served in the McDougall program. Fresh fruit at all meals.

Services and Facilities	**Exercise Equipment:** Weights room with treadmill, stationary bikes, rowing machines. **Services:** Massage, exercise instruction, private medical counseling, group discussions, group relaxation. **Swimming Facilities:** Outdoor pool (covered in winter). **Recreation Facilities:** Hiking, cycling, tennis, golf, aerobic dancing; horseback riding and glider rides nearby. **Evening Programs:** Informal lectures on health-related topics.
In the Area	St. Helena (boutiques, restaurants), mineral water and mud baths in Calistoga, winery tours, Glen Ellen State Historic Park.
Getting Here	*From San Francisco.* By car, I–80 north past Vallejo to Hwy. 37 going west, Hwy. 29 through St. Helena to Deer Park Rd., cross the Silverado Trail, turn left on Sanitarium Rd. (90 mins). By bus, shuttle service at fixed prices to and from area airports.
Special Notes	No smoking in guest rooms or health center facilities.

Sivananda Ashram Yoga Farm

Spiritual awareness

California
Grass Valley

The Sivananda Ashram Yoga Farm follows the yogic disciplines of Swami Vishnu Devananda. In a peaceful valley north of Sacramento, the simple farmhouse provides lodging and space for two daily sessions of traditional postures (asanas), breathing techniques, and meditation. The intensive regimen of self-discipline is designed to foster a better understanding of the body-mind connection.

Meditation at 6 AM begins the morning session, brunch is served at 10, and then your schedule is open until 4 PM. Attendance at classes and meditations is mandatory.

The teachings of Swami Devananda have been widely documented as promoting both physical and spiritual development. His followers and new students join in practicing the 12 asana positions, from a headstand to a spinal twist, each believed to have specific benefits for the body. Participants learn that the proper breathing (*pranayama*) in each position is essential for energy control.

The 80-acre farm attracts a diverse group, families as well as senior citizens. Guests are asked to share bedrooms and to contribute time to communal activities. You may arrive on any day and stay as long as you wish.

Sivananda Ashram Yoga Farm
14651 Ballantree La., Grass Valley, CA 95949
Tel. 916/272–9322

Administration	Manager, Avoram
Season	Year-round
Accommodations	35 dormitory rooms have 5 beds each, 5 double rooms, minimal furnishings. Showers and toilets shared. Tent space on the grounds. Private rooms on request.
Rates	$35 per person per day includes dormitory lodging, program, meals. Rooms $45 per person double, $55 single; campers pay $25. Supplemental charges for special programs. $25 in advance. No credit cards.
Meal Plans	2 lacto-vegetarian meals daily, buffet style. Morning meal of hot grain cereal, granola, yogurt, fruit. Stir-fry and steamed vegetables, rice, and scrambled tofu for dinner. Homemade soups, whole-wheat breads, green salads.

Services and Facilities	**Services:** Massage. **Swimming Facilities:** None. **Recreation Facilities:** Meditation; skiing at nearby resorts. **Evening Programs:** Lectures on Hindu philosophy; concerts.
In the Area	Lake Tahoe, historic gold-mining towns of Nevada City and Grass Valley, old-town Sacramento.
Getting Here	*From Sacramento.* By bus, Greyhound to Auburn (2 hrs). By car, I–80 to Auburn, Hwy. 49 (1½ hrs). Pickup in the farm van $10 at Auburn, $25 at Sacramento Airport.
Special Notes	Limited access for people with disabilities. Children are welcome to participate with parents. No smoking.

Skylonda Fitness Retreat

Life enhancement
Luxury pampering
Nutrition and diet

California
Woodside

Skylonda Retreat opened in late 1992 on 16 forested acres of coastal hills south of San Francisco. During the five-day retreats and weekend getaways, guests recharge themselves physically, spiritually, and mentally while losing weight. The daily schedule incorporates hikes, yoga, meditation, strength training, aerobics, aquatic exercises, and massage. All meals and services are included in the cost of the program.

Hiking the extensive network of trails surrounding Skylonda is basic to the rigorous program. The forested ridge separating San Francisco and the Silicon Valley from the sea is comprised of a series of microclimates, with tall redwoods, pine, oak, and the reddish madrone tree native to California. On any given day, the trail leader plans two hikes totalling 8–10 miles, with options for those who can't handle some of the more challenging terrain. Although you're expected to traverse vast meadows, sudden ravines, and intensely silent hollows, it's comforting to know that a van awaits at the end of the trail.

Structured to cultivate strength of body and mind, the program allows you to participate in a weekend or full week with 20–30 hikers. Watchful staffers are on hand at all times for assistance. From the 6 AM wake-up call to the 9 PM close of evening programs, there is dynamic interaction with other members of the group. Sessions of yoga and circuit training recharge your energy for the hikes. An hour of silence is included. Evenings are devoted to discussion of stress management, songs in front of a great fireplace, and talks by wellness experts from Stanford University Medical Center.

The spacious log-and-stone lodge, with a view of the forest, has a multipurpose room for aerobics and yoga/stretching classes. Housed on the log-timbered upper floors are a library, dining room, and the main gathering room, which features stained glass windows, Oriental rugs, comfortable sofas, and a VCR/music system. A glass-enclosed swimming pool and outdoor Jacuzzi adjoin the sauna and massage and facial rooms, on the ground floor of the lodge. Exercise clothing is laundered daily, and you pick up outfits as needed. The standard-issue gym suits are worn throughout meals, but warm gear comes in handy some evenings.

Two program options are available: Sunday–Friday, with five nights lodging; and Friday–Sunday, with two nights lodging. As the program progresses, you may experience unexpected physical and emotional reactions to the drastic changes in diet and exercise. Your body will metabolize food faster, as chef Sue Chapman aims for a diet that is 65%–75% carbohydrates,

20%–25% protein, and less than 10% fat. Most guests average about 1,400 calories per day, but the fixed menu does not list caloric content.

Exploring the vast parkland, ridges, ravines, and beaches of the Bay Area is outdoor adventure at its best.

Skylonda Fitness Retreat
16350 Skyline Blvd., Woodside, CA 94062
Tel. 415/851–4500 or 800/851–2222
Fax 415/851–5504

Administration General manager, Larry Callahan

Season Year-round

Accommodations 15 rooms with private bath in 3-story log lodge. Each room contains 2 queen-size beds with down comforters, 2 wooden clothing cabinets. Small bathroom with bath. Rooms have open-beam ceiling, spectacular view of the redwoods, no air-conditioning.

Rates Nightly rates $300–$400 per person for double occupancy, plus 8% tax and gratuities. Two-night minimum. Deposit: 2 days payable in advance. AE, DC, MC, V.

Meal Plans 3 meals daily included in program. Breakfast can be fresh fruit, whole grain muffin, or cereal. Lunch is a self-service salad or soup with whole-grain bread. Dinner includes cioppino, vegetarian lasagna, or halibut baked in parchment, stuffed potato, or grain-stuffed artichoke. Specialties can be roast chicken breast on ragout of corn and black-eyed peas, steamed prawns with Chinese long beans, tart of duck, morels, and roasted shallot. Desserts are seasonal berries with sorbet, peach shortcake, tart of buckwheat, poppyseed, and peaches. Coffee, herbal tea, and decaffeinated coffee available at all times. Energy breaks include a mid-morning drink (orange juice, yeast, nonfat milk) and an afternoon snack of broth, fruit, vegetables, popcorn, or a cookie. Special diets and alternate menu selections are available on request.

Services and Facilities **Exercise Equipment:** 20-unit Cybex weight-training system, 4 stationary bikes, rower, step units. **Services:** Swedish massage, facial, body wrap, manicure, skin care. **Spa Facilities:** Coed sauna, steam room, outdoor whirlpool. **Swimming Facilities:** Indoor 30-ft. pool. **Evening Programs:** Folksingers, movies, talks.

In the Area Jasper Ridge Biological Reserve, Portola Valley, Palo Alto.

Getting Here *From San Francisco.* By car, I–380 west to I–280 south, Hwy. 92W to Scenic Highway 35 (Skyline Blvd.). Complimentary pickup at San Francisco International Airport.

Special Notes No smoking in the lodge. Rain gear provided.

Sonoma Mission Inn and Spa

Luxury pampering

California
Boyes Hot Springs

San Franciscans have been "taking the cure" at the Sonoma Mission Inn since the turn of the century, but fitness training and pampering are more recent attractions. The high-tech spa is a favorite escape for young couples from the city as well as a popular stopover on wine-country tours. Its first consideration is health maintenance rather than weight loss, and a few days here can do wonders for your spirits.

Several wings of deluxe rooms and minisuites have been added to the big pink stucco palace since its new owners restored this grand old hotel in 1980. The resort accepts bookings for corporate conferences and sales meetings and, as a result, can be packed one day, quiet the next. Usually, however, weekends are busy so you'll want to avoid them if you yearn for peace and seclusion.

Midweek spa packages are the best buy; weekend rates are strictly à la carte. All adult guests are charged $10 daily ($20 weekends) for access to the spa (book a service and the fee is waived), which includes two exercise rooms (one with cardiovascular equipment, one for weight training), sauna, steam room, and outdoor and indoor whirlpools beside a flower-bordered outdoor exercise pool. Scheduled daily are coed aerobics classes, aquacize groups, and yoga sessions. Robe and slippers are issued daily, and there are newly expanded locker rooms with full amenities. Despite its compact size, the spa has 10 massage rooms, four facial rooms, and a six-seat beauty salon. All facilities, except locker rooms, are coed and no-smoking. A heated outdoor swimming pool, which is open to all guests free of charge, adjoins the fitness pavilion.

Driving up to the main lobby is like arriving for a party at Jay Gatsby's. The baronial reception hall, awash in pastel pinks and peach against bleached wood, sets the mood of casual elegance. The inn and its fashionable dining room and wine bar seem far removed from the rigors of calorie counting. But the Grille and the Market Café have a spa menu; reservations should be made when you check in.

Down a path through gardens abloom with camellia and jasmine is the fitness pavilion, sandwiched between a conference center and tennis courts. After you check in with the spa director and schedule massage and beauty treatments, you are left pretty much on your own.

An airy, two-story atrium that belies the building's origins as a Quonset hut is the setting for most of the activities. The glass-walled exercise rooms, staffed with trainers, face a sunlit marble fountain. Report for treatments upstairs in a quiet lounge, where you can sip herbal tea and watch TV while you wait to be summoned. Classes are scheduled in the aerobics studio throughout the day, beginning at 7 AM with tai chi, and yoga, which attract a regular group of 10 or so local members. Hikers can sign up for 90-minute morning excursions ($10), which depart from the inn by van at 7 AM, and a wine-country picnic ($25) on Saturday.

Soaking in the natural, hot artesian mineral water is one of the most popular activities at the spa. In 1991 a new well was tapped, bringing to the surface another 135°F mineral-rich spring known for its restorative powers. Examples of the cure are documented in a brochure about the inn's history. The spring feeds into the exercise and swimming pools, and temperatures are regulated and adjusted to achieve maximum benefits from the therapy. Herbal, mud, and seaweed wraps are used to relax muscles, soften the skin, and draw out toxins. Treatments take place in two specially equipped "wet" rooms and include a two-hour Revitalizer ($169–$199) combination that's pure bliss.

Surrounded by 8 acres of eucalyptus-shaded grounds, the Inn is close to trendy shops and wineries in the center of Sonoma— but spa goers may never venture out of this romantic hideaway.

Sonoma Mission Inn and Spa

18140 Sonoma Hwy. 12, Boyes Hot Springs, CA 95416
(Reservations) Box 1447, Sonoma, CA 95476
Tel. 707/938–9000, 800/358–9022, or 800/862–4945 in CA

Administration Manager, Jack Burkham; spa director, Leslie Wilke

Season Year-round

Accommodations 170 rooms in the main building and garden units, all of them renovated in 1994 and 1995. Plantation shutters, canopied beds, and ceiling fans; king, queen, and twin beds. Each of 20 wine country–theme rooms in 3-story unit close to spa features wood-burning fireplace, spacious bathroom with bidet. Amenities include air-conditioning, TV, telephone, robes.

Rates Basic Spa package per night $170–$270 single, $129–$190 per person double; Spa Sampler package with 2 meals daily $240–$380 single, $199–$270 per person double; Deluxe spa package $340–$510 single, $295–$360 double per night with 3 meals. Golf & Spa package for 2 $110–$170 per person. Packages, available Sun.–Thurs. only, include classes, gratuities, tax. Hotel tariff $199–$375 per room. Day Spa packages $180–$350. Deposit: 1 night in advance, $500 for package. AE, DC, MC, V.

Meal Plans Calorie-counted spa menu in the Grille. Choices at 1,000–1,200 calories per day include salmon poached in chardonnay with artichokes, breast of free-range chicken and steamed vegetables, grilled veal loin with leeks, saffron capellini with ratatouille, steamed shellfish. The café offers vegetarian pizza, spa omelette, grilled prawns and scallops with wild rice pilaf. Wine, coffee (regular or decaffeinated), herbal tea, nonfat milk.

Services and Facilities **Exercise Equipment:** Cybex 6-station modular weight training gym, 2 Monark bikes, 2 Cycleplus, 2 Schwinn Air Dyne bikes, Concept 2 rowing machine, 3 Climb Max, 3 Startrac treadmills, Smith press and free weights (5–40 lb). Fitness Pavilion at inn has Trotter and Startrac treadmills, 2 StairMaster 4000s, Lifestep, Lifecycle, Biocycle, Windracer, NordicTrack. **Services:** Massage (Swedish, Esalen), fango clay body pack, herbal and seaweed body wraps, loofah scrub, facials, manicure, pedicure/reflexology combination, shiatsu, aromatherapy, image consultation, personalized meditation, tarot card reading. **Swimming Facilities:** 2 outdoor pools. **Recreation Facilities:** 2 tennis courts, hiking. Horseback riding, golf nearby.

In the Area Sonoma Mission historic area, antiques shops, specialty food shops; Calistoga mud baths, Bodega Bay, winery tours.

Getting Here *From San Francisco.* By bus, Greyhound to Sonoma (90 mins). By car, Golden Gate Bridge, Hwy. 101, Hwy. 37 to Sonoma, Hwy. 12 (45 mins). Public bus at door; Sonoma Airporter scheduled van service to San Francisco airport; limousine, taxi, rental car.

Special Notes Limited access for people with disabilities. Spa Mon.–Thurs. and Sun. 6 AM–9 PM, Fri.–Sat. until 10 PM. Non-registered guest fee: $35 or $20 plus price of beauty treatment.

Spa at L'Auberge Del Mar

Nonprogram resort

California The spa at the beautiful L'Auberge del Mar, which overlooks
Del Mar the Pacific, is a convenient getaway from San Diego. Although facilities are limited, you can exercise, get a massage, or be pampered at the beauty salon. Spa cuisine is served in the resort's Bistro Garden, open to the sunny beach breezes most of the year. The menu changes daily, with the calorie count posted

beside each item. Emphasis is on fresh local ingredients, with low amounts of saturated fat, sodium, and cholesterol.

The original Del Mar Hotel was a legendary gathering place for the rich and famous, especially during the summer season of nearby Del Mar Race Track. The new inn on the same site combines the cozy comfort of a small European auberge with California-casual ambience. Built on several levels, the hotel can provide each guest room with a balcony and ocean view. On the first floor, close to the spa, rooms open onto a terrace surrounding the swimming pool.

Scheduled exercise sessions in the pool and gym, and cardiowalk on the beach, are part of the spa program, open to all guests. Treatments and meals are à la carte, but you can book a spa sampler package.

While upscale La Jolla is only minutes away, the lifestyle in Del Mar is slow-paced and casual; the beach here is broad, uncrowded, and ideal for long morning walks.

Spa at L'Auberge Del Mar

1540 Camino Del Mar, Box 2889, Del Mar, CA 92014
Tel. 619/259–1515 or 800/553–1336
Fax 619/755–4940

Administration General manager, Gordon McMichael; spa manager, Anda Geamva

Season Year-round

Accommodations 123 deluxe rooms and 8 suites with balcony, marble bath and vanity, wooden armoire, minibar, TV. Some have gas fireplaces that ignite at the touch of a button; all are air-conditioned. Amenities include makeup lights in the bathrooms.

Rates $279–$329 for single or double room per night, $560–$950 suites. Add 10% state tax, plus gratuities. 1 night's payment required in advance. AE, MC, V.

Meal Plans Breakfast includes juice, Meuslix cereal, or egg-white omelet. Lunch may be a fruit salad or plate of grilled vegetables (Japanese eggplant, red peppers, zucchini, tomatoes, assorted squash), lightly brushed with extra-virgin olive oil. Dinner entrées include grilled fish or chicken and veal medallions in wine sauce.

Services and Facilities **Exercise Equipment:** Spectrum I weight training units, Sprint bike, Challenger rowing machine. **Services:** Swedish massage, shiatsu, acupressure, aromatherapy, fango, facials; beauty salon for hair, nail, and skin care. **Spa Facilities:** Underwater massage, coed sauna and steam room, 6 massage rooms. **Swimming Facilities:** Outdoor pool (45 ft), ocean beach. **Recreation Facilities:** 2 lighted tennis courts (concrete surface); golf nearby.

In the Area La Jolla (art museum, theater, shopping), Sea World, San Diego (zoo, Balboa Park museums and theaters, Old Town), Del Mar Race Track (July 25–Sept. 15).

Getting Here *From San Diego.* By car, I–5 (San Diego Fwy.) north to Del Mar Hts. Rd., Camino Del Mar to 15th St. (30 mins). By train, Amtrak to Solana Beach (30 mins). By bus, Greyhound. Free transfers on arrival, departure.

Special Notes No smoking in spa. Minimum age 16. Spa open daily 9–8. No-smoking rooms available, some with access for people with disabilities.

Spa Hotel–Casino and Mineral Springs

Taking the waters

California
Palm Springs

The Spa Hotel and Mineral Springs, with lush gardens and spacious rooms, is built on the site of hot mineral springs used by Native Americans for centuries. The Agua Caliente Band of the Cahuillia tribe owns the land and hotel, which was completely renovated in 1993, with the addition of a casino. Although the spa is somewhat dated, it's well maintained and mostly serves as a day retreat (daily fee is charged). The hotel's location, in the center of Palm Springs, is close to shops, restaurants, and recreational attractions.

The fitness program is based on European hydrotherapy methods. Decked out in white slippers and oversize terry-cloth towels, guests attend sessions of eucalyptus inhalation and use the sauna or the steam room. After a shower, they are escorted to sunken marble tubs. The "magical water" of the springs soon dissipates tension.

Herbal tea or ice water is served in the cooling rooms while guests, wrapped in sheets, wait for the masseur or masseuse. After the one-hour treatment guests are free to go for a swim in the Olympic-size outdoor mineral-water pool or a sunbathe in the rooftop solarium (clothes optional).

Day Spa programs are also available nearby, at The Palms and the The Givenchy Hotel (see profiles in this chapter).

Spa Hotel–Casino and Mineral Springs

100 N. Indian Canyon Dr., Palm Springs, CA 92262
Tel. 619/325–1461 or 800/854–1279 (800/472–4371 in CA)
Fax 619/–325–3344

Administration Manager, Ralph Thornton; spa director, Casey Olson

Season Year-round

Accommodations 230 rooms (20 suites) in a completely renovated 5-story hotel. Contemporary Southwestern furnishings, with choice of king-size or double queen-size beds. All have balcony, bathroom, TV, air-conditioning.

Rates Daily European plan per room, single or double: $67–$194 summer, $154–$200 winter, suite $235 for 2 double. Desert Escape 2-night package with spa services $619.85 for 2 double (Sun.–Thurs. only). Deposit: 1 night payable in advance. Tax and gratuities included in package. AE, DC, MC, V.

Meal Plans $75 for 2 breakfasts and dinners with Desert Escape package: fresh fruit and yogurt at breakfast; cold salmon, choice of lamb medallions, whole-wheat pasta, or grilled shrimp and vegetables at dinner. Coffee, tea, and regular menu are available.

Services and Facilities **Exercise Equipment:** 12-station Paramount weight training gym, 3 Lifecycles, Liferower, treadmill, free weights. **Services:** Massage (Swedish, sports, shiatsu), aromatherapy, herbal wrap, body scrub, facial; salon for hair, nail, and skin care. **Bathing Facilities:** 34 private Jacuzzis with mineral water, 2 soaking pools. **Swimming Facilities:** Outdoor pool. **Recreation Facilities:** Tennis, golf, horseback riding, desert hiking, and cross-country skiing all nearby. **Evening Entertainment:** Village Fest street fair Thurs.

In the Area Aerial Tramway, Desert Museum (nature and art exhibits, concerts, live theater), Living Desert Reserve (botanical gardens), Indian Canyons (jeep tour, hikes), Polo Club, Joshua Tree National Park, Agua Caliente Cultural Museum (tribal history).

Getting Here *From Los Angeles.* By VIP Shuttle (tel. 619/328–0222) or Desert City (tel. 619/320–0044) shuttle services from LAX airport, hotels (2–3 hrs); Greyhound (3 hrs). By car, I–10 to Hwy. 111 in Palm Canyon or to Tahquitz Way, turn left one block to hotel. By train, Amtrak to Indio (2 hrs). By plane, American Airlines and United commuter service (30 mins). Limousine, taxi, airport van service, rental car available.

Special Notes No smoking in the spa and in designated areas of the dining room. Casino open 24 hours.

Tassajara Zen Monastery

Nutrition and diet
Spiritual awareness
Taking the waters

California In 1966 the San Francisco Zen Center began welcoming
Jamesburg overnight visitors as well as practitioners of Zen Buddhism to Tassajara. Guests are invited to join in meditation, receive basic instruction, and attend lectures, but no activity is required. Those who wish to participate in a Practice Retreat are required to perform about a half day of work on the buildings and farm. Workshops in yoga, poetry, and sensory awareness are also offered.

This site, surrounded by formidable mountains and overlooking the Pacific Ocean, has been a place of healing and purification for centuries. Native Americans used the hot springs, and Spanish hunters gathered here. Now, among other activities, Tassajara guests bathe in the slightly sulfurous water until parboiled, then stretch out on the rocks to contemplate nature. A clothing-optional policy prevails.

Your day begins at 5:40 AM when a bell ringer awakens you for meditation in the Japanese-style hall, or Zendo, which is the center of the Zen monastery at Tassajara. Students in black garb and with shaved heads join visitors seeking to become familiar with Buddhist practices.

Among the retreat's most popular traditions is its Zen cuisine. Those who know Tassajara primarily through its cookbooks on vegetarian meals and bread baking can begin to experience Zen cooking in a one-week workshop dubbed "Cooking as Meditation," led by Ed Brown, former head chef here and author of *The Tassajara Bread Book.* In addition to actually preparing food, guests learn that cooking embodies many of the elements of spiritual practice: "Working sincerely with the ingredients available, giving more than you ever thought possible, being patient with the fact that everything has a mind of its own, [and] trusting your own sensibilities."

Tassajara Zen Monastery
Jamesburg, CA
Reservations: Zen Center, 300 Page St., San Francisco, CA 94102
Tel. 415/431–3771

Administration Guest manager, Cassandra Bramucci

Season May–Sept.

Accommodations 36 guest rooms in a 1-level structure of stone and pine. Some have 2 beds, others a foam cushion on the floor. Dormitory room has 4 beds. 1 large corner unit, Stone Suite, for 4–6 persons. All rooms open to sundeck, with access to spring-fed pools and stream. No electricity; kerosene lamp provided. Communal bathhouse or shared bathroom. No housekeeping services.

Rates $115–$200 single, $95–$110 per person double occupancy, with 3 meals. Practice Retreat (3-night min.) $40–$45 per day. Dormitory $67 per night; 2-room suite with private bath $130 per person (4–6 beds); add 7.1% tax. Workshop $580–$740. Deposit: $35–$65. No credit cards.

Meal Plans 3 vegetarian meals served daily, buffet style. Breakfast includes oatmeal, tamari-roasted cashew nuts, French toast, yogurt with blackberries. Different breads baked daily. Organically grown vegetables are steamed, served with tofu and brown rice, and baked. Japanese udon and pasta are among entrées.

Services and Facilities **Services:** Meditation retreats, workshops in yoga, cooking, Japanese arts. **Swimming Facilities:** Jr.-Olympic-size outdoor pool. **Recreation Facilities:** Natural rock pools with circulating thermal water (clothing optional), steam room, outdoor swimming pool. **Evening Programs:** Lectures, meditation.

In the Area Big Sur State Park (hiking, beaches), Carmel (art galleries, boutiques), San Simeon State Historic Park (Hearst Castle), Monterey (Spanish colonial historic site, aquarium), Esalen Institute.

Getting Here *From San Francisco.* By car, I–280 south to Hwy. 17, via Monterey to Carmel, Rte. G16 (Carmel Valley Rd.) for 23.2 mi, right on Tassajara Rd. to Jamesburg (3 hrs).

Special Notes Park at Jamesburg for the Tassajara stage ($26 per person round-trip for shuttle from parking to lodge) to avoid steep mountain road. No smoking in compound. Bring bath towel, flashlight, blanket. Day visitors $10–$15.

Two Bunch Palms

Luxury pampering
Taking the waters

California
Desert Hot
Springs

Popular as a hideaway for Hollywood stars and writers, Two Bunch Palms, said to be a long-ago hideaway of Al Capone's, offers privacy (only registered guests get past the guardhouse), intimacy (44 villas and suites), and total relaxation. No spa packages are offered (26 services are à la carte), no gym or golf course exists, and no children are allowed. For those who crave exercise, however, there are stationary bikes, yoga classes, and a jogging trail.

The dry heat of the desert induces a certain lethargy. To avoid the sun, guests indulge inside in the spa's extraordinary repertoire of bodywork and beauty treatments. One innovation is the esoteric massage, "designed to balance and harmonize the physical, emotional, and spiritual bodies." Another specialty is watsu massage (a mix of yoga and reflexology) in the pool: You float in the hot pool on six inner tubes while undergoing hand and foot massage.

An evening soak under the stars is perhaps the best way to appreciate the beauty of this oasis. The original Rock House, where Hollywood stars stayed in the 1930s, has several charming rooms furnished with antiques. The former casino is now a restaurant, the walls dedicated to movie memorabilia.

Geothermal springs on the north slope of the Coachella Valley supply hot mineral water (148°F) for the spa's swimming pool. Cooled a bit for comfort, the water splashes over a rock waterfall into a turquoise grotto framed by tropical shrubbery, and under a canopy of fan palms and tamarisk trees. Moviegoers caught a glimpse of the Two Bunch Palms pool in Robert Altman's satirical film *The Player*.

Total immersion is offered at the Clay Cabana, a palm-shaded mud bath. While you soak in warm, green clay dug from mineral water wells on the property, your muscles relax as toxins are drawn out.

For total bliss follow this with a shower, a soak in the mineral pool, and a massage.

Don't expect entertainment or organized activity. Guests tend to avoid communication with strangers, ordering meals delivered to their villas, or picking up a box lunch. To get in touch with ancient rhythms, go native; the spa's 90-minute Native American treatment stimulates mind, body, and spirit.

Two Bunch Palms

67425 Two Bunch Pkwy., Palms Trail, Desert Hot Springs, CA 92240
Tel. 619/329–8791 or 800/472–4334
Fax 619/329–1317

Administration General manager, Jim Bordycott; spa director, Dana Bass-Smith

Season Year-round

Accommodations 44 guest rooms in villas or motel-like buildings situated near pool. The 2-bedroom suite, No. 14, is popular, at $425 a night, complete with the initials A.C. inscribed in a desktop, plus a bullet hole in a mirror and a lookout tower (with wet bar) that doubles as a tanning deck. Casa Blanca minisuite with Jacuzzi, $375. Villas are spacious, have private garden with whirlpool, kitchen, living room with TV, bedroom with king-size bed. All rooms air-conditioned, with TV, telephone.

Rates $120–$425 for 2 persons, double occupancy, includes Continental breakfast. 2-night minimum. Deposit: 1 night. Add 10% tax, gratuities. AE, DC, MC, V.

Meal Plans 3 meals served daily in the resort dining room. No spa diet, but selections of salads, grilled fish or chicken, and seasonal fresh fruit.

Services and Facilities **Services:** Massage (Swedish, Trager, shiatsu, jin shin do, reflexology, deep-tissue), aromatherapy, 90-min salt-glow body scrub and herbal steam, facials, herbal wraps, mud baths. **Swimming Facilities:** Outdoor mineral-water pool. **Recreation Facilities:** 2 lighted tennis courts, bicycles. **Evening Programs:** Informal entertainment.

In the Area Joshua Tree National Park (desert habitat), Palm Springs (shopping, museums, mountain cable ride).

Getting Here *From Los Angeles.* By car, I–10 to Hwy. 111 (2 hrs). By bus, Greyhound (4 hrs). By train, Amtrak to Indio (2 hrs). Private planes and scheduled air service to Palm Springs (30 mins).

Special Notes Limited access for people with disabilities. No smoking in spa. No children (minimum age 18).

Weimar Institute

Life enhancement
Preventive medicine
Vibrant maturity
Weight management

California
Weimar A diabetic housewife, a stressed-out doctor, and an overweight retiree are representative of the older generation of fitness converts who come to the Weimar Institute, nestled in the Sierra Nevada foothills between Sacramento and Reno, to

learn healthy habits. Medically oriented yet devoted to education and exercise, the 18-day Newstart program teaches guests to help themselves through a combination of physical, mental, and spiritual healing.

Although Weimar is a nondenominational and nonsectarian place, all the doctors and staff are Seventh-Day Adventists, who see prevention as the best medicine. They will accept anyone willing to adhere to a strictly vegetarian diet and exercise regimen at home. The physicians and educators here encourage patients to disconutinue medication as soon as is safely possible. They believe modern technology has overshadowed simple cures for common ailments. Their programs help participants to quit smoking, control weight, and cope with such degenerative diseases as arthritis, diabetes, cancer, and cardiovascular problems. With the help of computers, the staff makes specific recommendations for diet based on assessments of your physical condition, nutritional requirements, and weight-loss goals. After you undergo a complete physical, a physician will create a personal schedule and will continue to monitor your progress throughout the three-week program.

The first activity of the day is calisthenics, after which everyone is encouraged to walk and enjoy the miles of woodland trails, on the 457-acre campus. "Stretchercise" classes that won't strain bodies unaccustomed to exercise are scheduled between cooking classes and private counseling or therapy sessions. Hydrotherapy and massage are also part of the program. Included are a 16-head enclosure of contrasting hot and cold showers, Russian-style steam baths, and whirlpools. Those afflicted with neuromuscular problems learn to relieve themselves of pain.

Newstart shares resources with Weimar College, a training institution for health-related ministries that offers an intensive, outpatient type of program with live-in accommodations. Weekend seminars are often scheduled for those who want a refresher course in healthy cooking or controlling stress. Others come simply to relax at the Weimar Inn, which also has a weights room.

Weimar Institute
Box 486, 20601 W. Paoli La., Weimar, CA 95736
Tel. 916/637–4111 or 800/525–9192

Administration   President, Robert Montague; medical director, Bruce Hyde, M.D.

Season   Newstart program June–mid-Dec.; weekend seminars year-round

Accommodations   29-room no-frills country lodge. Large rooms with sitting area and private bath, single or king-size beds. Informal gatherings around the fireplace in the lobby; self-service laundry. Also 23 rooms with cherry furnishings, quilted bedspreads, mirrored closet doors, and flowered wallpaper at the Weimar Inn.

Rates   18-day live-in Newstart program, including medical fees (some insurance policies will cover fees), $4,450; $3,950 for participating spouse or partner, $2,500 for accommodations only at lodge. Weimar Inn daily rate $45 per night for 2, $39 single, without meals. Newstart program deposit: $500 per person in advance; inn accommodations 50% in advance. Rates include tax, gratuities. AE, D, MC, V.

Meal Plans   3 vegetarian meals daily in the Weimar Country Cafeteria. Specialties include a "haystack" of chili, rice, sprouts, lettuce, and tomato on corn chips; vegetarian lasagna; steamed vegetables on rice with Oriental sauce. Breads baked daily. Whole and sprouted grains. No eggs, cheese, or dairy products.

Services and Facilities **Exercise Equipment:** 3 Exercycles, Schwinn Air Dyne bike, 2 rowing machines, 2 treadmills, cross-country ski machine, tilt-board, free weights, 10-unit hydraulic weight-training system. **Services:** Newstart program includes complete physical and medical history evaluation, blood tests, treadmill stress tests, consultation with physician; hydrotherapy and massage; cooking classes; 24-hr nursing staff. **Swimming Facilities:** River bathing and wading. **Recreation Facilities:** Volleyball; golf course nearby. **Evening Programs:** Music, video presentations, and talks on inspirational and health-related topics.

In the Area Weekend outings to the Empire Mine State Historic Park, the California State Capitol, and the Railroad Museum in Sacramento; sightseeing and shopping in the Lake Tahoe area; Yosemite National Park; the Nevada casinos; Old Sacramento.

Getting Here *From Sacramento.* By car, I–80 north to Weimar, exit on W. Paoli La. (1 hr). By bus, Greyhound to Weimar (1 hr). By train, Amtrak to Colfax (45 mins). Transportation from bus or train station to Weimar Institute provided (fee) on request. Taxi, rental car available.

Special Notes 1 room at the lodge and the inn has access for people with disabilities. No smoking.

The Southwest

Health resorts are the new bonanza in the Old West. Ranches and lodges in the desert offer the latest in diet, nutrition, and exercise programs, and fitness routines can include skiing, mountain biking, and hiking.

The pioneer among fitness resorts in the Southwest is the Canyon Ranch near Tucson, Arizona. Nearby, the upscale Miraval resort opened in 1995. In the Rocky Mountain states, Colorado has the Peaks at Telluride for sports conditioning accented by Southwest traditions, The Broadmoor Spa in Colorado Springs, and a host of rustic, dress-down hot springs.

Summer music festivals in Aspen and Vail add another dimension to holidays for healthy bodies and minds. Scottsdale, Arizona, now offers the recently expanded spa at Marriott's Camelback Inn and The Phoenician Centre for Well-Being. With a dry, warm climate to enhance superb fitness and beauty facilities, these are world-class destination resorts. The area is also optimal for outdoor adventure, family-oriented ranch vacations, and hiking in rugged canyon country.

Stress-control and weight-management courses are the attraction in two modern, palm-studded oases near St. George, two hours north of Las Vegas casinos in an area of intense development commonly referred to as "Utah's Banana Belt" or the "Other Palm Springs." Here amid the red rock hills, the pioneering National Institute of Fitness has expanded and upgraded its facilities, offering one of the best values in weight loss and wellness vacations. Nearby, Green Valley Spa provides the widest range of programs, from tennis camp to native American spiritual traditions, along with deluxe accommodations.

Day spa packages at resorts are another option; you can enjoy a day of pampering without staying in the hotel. Spend a day at hot springs throughout the Southwest, from Arizona, Nevada, and Utah to New Mexico's Ojo Caliente Mineral Springs (tel. 505/583–2233) near Taos, and hot tubs at Ten Thousand Waves overlooking Santa Fe, a new addition to this chapter. Colorado's numerous thermal springs have attracted health seekers since prehistoric times; now there is an Ayurveda Health Retreat (tel. 970/264–9224 or 800/247–9654) near Pagosa Springs and the newly renamed Inn at Zapata Ranch (see review) close to the sand dunes and Valley View Hot Springs. Near Denver, Indian Springs has a modern addition to its Victorian hotel (see review), there's rustic lodging at Mount Princeton Hot Springs Resort (tel. 719/395–2361), and Glenwood Springs (see review) will be easy on your muscles as well as your budget.

The Jimmie Heuga Center (tel. 303/949–7172 or 800/367–3101) in Avon, Colorado, offers outdoor-oriented health enhancement programs for guests using wheelchairs or with other physical disabilities.

Buckhorn Mineral Wells Spa

Taking the waters

Arizona
Mesa

Locals and those with arthritis and skin problems know Buckhorn Mineral Wells Spa, a small resort in the desert near Phoenix that offers treatments on an à la carte basis to overnight guests and day visitors. Bathers enjoy private rooms with tile tubs into which hot mineral water flows continuously; a whirlpool unit enhances the effect, and a licensed massage therapist is on hand from Tuesday through Saturday 9 to 5.

Surrounded by cactus and palm trees, the motel-style lodge looks like a combination of hacienda and gymnasium. Separate men's and women's entrances lead to the cement bathing cubicles. The mineral water, unchlorinated and naturally heated at 106°F, flows at the rate of 7,000 gallons per hour. Cooler water can be added, but the nurse in attendance recommends the high temperature to relieve sore muscles and aching bones. Tubs are drained, cleaned, and refilled after each use.

Built in the 1940s, the Buckhorn Spa was expanded in 1993 by the current owner and operator, and now guests can stay in adobe cottages equipped for cooking. Restaurants and a shopping center adjoin the resort, and there is a small museum on the grounds displaying native birds and animals.

Buckhorn Mineral Wells Spa
5900 E. Main St., Mesa, AZ 85205
Tel. 602/832–1111

Administration Owner-manager, Alice A. Sliger

Season Year-round

Accommodations 15 cottages with twin beds, private bath, kitchenette. Dishes and linens provided. Units have Spanish-colonial furnishings, air-conditioning.

Rates $45 a day for 2, Jan.–Apr.; $295 weekly. Lower rates in summer. 1 night payable in advance. No credit cards.

Services and Facilities **Exercise Equipment:** None available. **Services:** Whirlpool mineral baths ($12), Swedish-type massage with vibrator ($20). Series rates and combination treatments. **Swimming Facilities:** Nearby lake. **Spa Facilities:** Hot mineral well water in 27 private rooms. **Recreation Facilities:** Golf courses, horseback riding, fishing, picnic areas, parks, water sports, all nearby.

In the Area Scottsdale resorts and restaurants, Phoenix, the Heard Museum (Indian art), Paolo Soleri's Arcosanti village.

Getting Here *From Phoenix.* By car, Hwys. 60, 80, 89, Recker Rd. (30 mins). Rental car available.

Special Notes No smoking in the bathhouse.

Canyon Ranch

Holistic heath
Life enhancement
Luxury pampering
Preventive medicine
Vibrant maturity
Weight management

Arizona **Tucson** This 70-acre spread in the foothills of the Santa Catalina Mountains is a high-tech emporium of good health that positively radiates energy. From the moment you are welcomed in the big clubhouse and shown to your casita, you'll encounter good attitudes and a nonstop pursuit of health and well-being. Even the most stressed-out Type A personalities tend to find the extensive schedule of special programs, exercise classes, hiking, bike trips, and bodywork to their liking.

Arizona
Buckhorn Mineral
Wells Spa, **25**
Canyon Ranch, **29**
DesertFarren, **23**
Global Fitness
Adventures in
Sedona, **22**
Marriott's Spa at
Camelback Inn, **26**
Miraval, **28**
The Phoenician Centre
for Well-Being, **27**
Scottsdale
Princess, **24**

Colorado
The Aspen Club, **10**
The Broadmoor, **12**
Eden Valley
Lifestyle Center, **3**
Filhoa Meadows, **9**
Glenwood Hot Springs
Lodge & Pool, **5**
Global Fitness
Adventures, **8**
Indian Springs
Resort, **6**
Inn at Zapata
Ranch, **15**
The Lodge at
Cordillera, **11**
The Peaks at
Telluride, **16**
The Vail Athletic
Club, **7**
The Vail Cascade
Hotel & Club, **4**
Waunita Hot Springs
Ranch, **13**
Wiesbaden Hot
Springs Spa &
Lodgings, **14**

Nevada
Sheraton Desert Inn
Hotel & Casino, **21**
Walley's Hot Springs
Resort, **1**

New Mexico
Ten Thousand
Waves, **31**
Truth or
Consequences, **30**

Utah
Cliff Lodge at
Snowbird, **2**
Green Valley Spa &
Tennis Resort, **19**
The Last Resort, **17**
National Institute of
Fitness, **20**
Pah Tempe Hot
Springs Resort, **18**

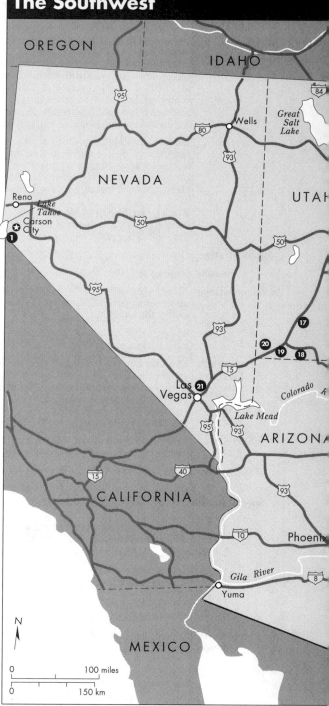

The Southwest

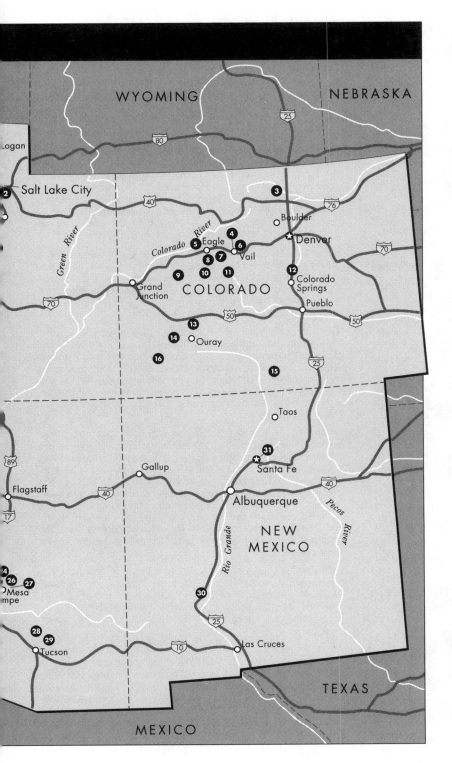

The prebreakfast walk begins at dawn. Typically, about 50 men and women dressed for the chill of early morning warm up on the tennis courts. The fitness instructor sets a brisk pace on paths through the desert landscape of cacti, mesquite, acacia, and palo verde trees. Conversations come naturally with fellow ranchers, and newcomers quickly learn the lay of the land. Later, over a breakfast of Spanish omelet (made of egg whites), orange juice, and freshly brewed coffee (regular or decaf), intense debates on the merits of shiatsu and Swedish massage can develop.

The scope and scale of the sprawling ranch will probably be slightly daunting at first, but you'll soon become familiar with the various centers and residential clusters. Unlike more rigidly programmed resorts, the ranch allows you to select your activities. Many outdoor activities, however, require signing up in advance to reserve a spot; you may find that your appointments clash with other outings or classes. With more than 40 coed fitness activities scheduled daily, you'll want to try more classes than there are hours in the day.

Since its opening in 1979, Canyon Ranch has developed many lifestyle programs that emphasize fitness of mind, body, and spirit. Preventive medicine and spiritual awareness are among the current offerings. Group psychodynamics—a shared experience that builds synergy among the participants—is an important aspect of the ranch's philosophy.

The fully air-conditioned spa complex has seven gyms, aerobics studios, strength and cardio machines, one squash and three racquetball courts; yoga dome; and men's and women's locker rooms with separate sauna, steam, and inhalation rooms, whirlpool baths, and private sunbathing areas. The spa facilities are open 16 hours a day. Also in the spa building are skin-care and beauty salons, and massage, herbal wrap, and hydrotherapy rooms.

Some people return several times a year to combat job burnout or to quit smoking, reduce stress, lose weight, relieve arthritis, and recover from injuries. Preventive medicine is stressed here, especially in the medical/wellness complex. The staff physicians and nurses dress down in sports clothes to complement the ranch ambience, but treat everything from heart disease to hypertension. Routine physical examinations can be scheduled in advance, as can comprehensive medical checkups. The medical team then works with a physiologist and nutritionist to design exercise and diet programs that meet your personal needs.

Periodically Canyon Ranch offers theme weeks: Life Enhancement, Healthy Heart, Arthritis, Asthma, and women's issues. For men and women over 60, ElderCamp ® weeks provide a friendly, supportive environment for exploration of positive approaches to aging.

At the Life Enhancement Center, designed for people who are ready to make a serious commitment to change, you are teamed with specialists on physical and emotional problems. Dealing with anything from diet to healthy aging, in a more structured environment than you'll find in the other centers of the resort, the program is designed to help you make serious lifestyle changes.

Canyon Ranch
8600 E. Rockcliff Rd., Tucson, AZ 85750
Tel. 520/749–9000 or 800/726–9900
Fax 520/749–7755

Administration   Founders-owners, Enid and Mel Zuckerman; general manager, Jona Liebrecht; vice president, Karma Kientzler; fitness director, Linda Marquez; medical director, Philip Eichling, M.D.

Season   Year-round

Accommodations   140 rooms in casitas, suites, and private condominium cottages with kitchen, living room, and laundry. All rooms are decorated in desert colors, with modern, Southwestern furnishings, large beds, TV/radio, private bath, and phone. Year-round air-conditioning.

Rates   5-day/4-night package, standard accommodation $1,895–$1,985. 8-day/7-night package, standard accommodation $3,155–$3,950 single, $2,820–$3,620 per person double occupancy. 8-day/7-night Life Enhancement program (Sun.–Sun.) $3,170–$3,265 single, $2,640–$3,265 per person double occupancy. Add 18% service charge and 6½% tax. 2 days payable in advance. 4-night minimum stay (mid-Sept.–mid-June). AE, MC, V.

Meal Plans   Breakfast selections include sweet potato waffles, breakfast bread pudding, lox, and bagels. Lunch choices may be chicken fajitas, Oriental noodle salad, pasta primavera, hearty vegetarian bean chili. Dinner entrées include roast turkey with garlic mashed potatoes, cioppino, mustard crusted rack of lamb, and fresh fish. Dessert can be cheesecake, fudge brownie, apple pie, fresh fruit. Vegetarian items on menu.

Services and Facilities   **Exercise Equipment:** Full line of Bodymaster weight training machines, 12 stationary bikes, 4 recumbent bikes, 16 treadmills, 11 stair machines, Gravitron, 3 rowing machines, 2 NordicTrack cross-country ski machines, 3-station VersaClimber, free weights. **Services:** 15 types of massage, aromatherapy, herbal wraps, body scrub with crushed pearls; hair salon, nail and skin care. Consultation on nutrition and diet, holistic health, body composition, and fitness level. Biofeedback program, smoking cessation. Cooking class. **Swimming Facilities:** Indoor pool, 3 outdoor pools. **Recreation Facilities:** 8 tennis courts, 3 racquetball courts, squash court, outdoor running track, basketball, volleyball, 21-speed mountain bikes; golf and horseback riding nearby. **Evening Programs:** Talks by psychologists, authors, naturalists, and other specialists.

In the Area   Sabino Canyon; Biosphere 2; Arizona-Sonora Desert Museum, crafts market in Nogales, Mt. Lemmon (pine forest); Tucson's old-town arts district, Mission San Xavier del Bac in Santa Cruz Valley.

Getting Here   *From Tucson.* By car, Speedway Blvd. east to Kolb Rd., Tanque Verde to Sabino Canyon Rd., Snyder Rd. to Rockcliff (30 mins). Free transfer from Tucson airport on arrival and departure. Rental car, taxi service available.

Special Notes   Access for people with disabilities at all facilities. Minimum age of guests is 14. Smoking not permitted indoors or in public areas. Alcoholic beverages not permitted in public areas. Remember to bring completed medical questionnaire, hiking shoes, walking shoes, clothing for warmth, and sun protection. Spa open daily 6 AM–10 PM.

DesertFarren

Life enhancement

Arizona   Nature-oriented DesertFarren lives up to its name, with miles
Carefree   and miles of hiking trails through valleys and mesas, archaeological sites and energy vortexes. Joining a small group of ad-

venturesome fitness buffs, you discover the cleansing effect of desert air, sun, and blue skies. Each day's challenges can include a 15-mile trek. At the end, your reward is a soothing massage.

Tucked into a cliff an hour from Phoenix, the Spanish-style hacienda houses just 12 guests. Soothingly cool, the rooms feature rough-hewn beams, furniture handcrafted in the Arts and Crafts style. In the courtyard, a Jacuzzi lets you meditate with desert views; out back, swim under the stars in a pool cut into a rock hollow. Some days there are sessions of yoga, stretching, and tai chi. On the guided trail hikes, lunch and a waistpack for water bottles are provided.

Don't look for a gym or aerobics classes; this program is for hard-core hikers. While tamer hikes are scheduled for beginners, and team-building exercise is available for executive groups, the focus is on experiencing the desert's outrageous scenery. Some trails (reached by Jeep) lead to Indian burial grounds and Seven Springs, a desert oasis. An evening ramble takes you to a haunted ranch, where Saguaro cacti take on spooky shapes in the moonlight.

Drawing energy from the desert doesn't mean you have to rough it at night. Both the lodging and vegetarian meals are elegant. An hour-long massage is included in the daily program, as well as presentations on wellness, star gazing, and natural history of the Sonoran Desert. Relaxing in the spacious social room, warmed by a double-stone fireplace, you may suddenly discover the beauty of being in touch with nature.

DesertFarren
Box 5550, Carefree, AZ 85377
Tel. 800/783–5550

Administration Owner-director, Larry Farren

Season Year-round

Accommodations 6 contemporary bedrooms with large bathrooms in the main hacienda, which has handmade furniture from the 1930s. Furnished with twin beds, down pillows, and comforter, rooms are air-conditioned as needed. Top-quality mattresses and robes. Midweek laundry service is provided.

Rates 7-day/6-night program $2,795 single, $2,195 per person double occupancy; daily rate $470 single, $365 double. Gratuities included, taxes added. AE, MC, V.

Meal Plans Vegetarian breakfast and dinner served family-style daily, trail lunch packed. Breakfast includes fresh-squeezed juices, homemade breads and granolas, bagels, muffins, and fruit. Dinner offers salad, soup, corn chowder, bean cakes, vegetarian lasagna.

Services and Facilities **Services:** Massage. **Swimming Facilities:** Outdoor pool.

In the Area Phoenix, the Heard Museum (Native American art).

Getting Here *From Phoenix.* Complimentary transfers on arrival and departure at Phoenix Sky Harbor Airport Terminal 2 at 1 PM. Optional pickup at Scottsdale Princess Resort (see seperate entry). No private cars permitted at DesertFarren.

Global Fitness Adventures in Sedona

Holistic health
Spiritual awareness
Sports conditioning

Arizona
Sedona

The weeklong Global Fitness Adventure in Sedona is a journey of self-awareness where guests absorb energy from the canyons, towering rock monoliths, and fire-red buttes of the area; visit four primary vortexes—said to emit positive and negative charges that affect human physiology—and take 8- to 15-mile hikes to the remains of ancient settlements.

Guests begin most mornings with yoga and tai chi on a rock vortex surrounded by incredible views. A purification ceremony in a traditional Native American sweat lodge is optional. The daily schedule also includes a sunset horseback ride, natural healing bodywork, and fitness classes. The group is housed in wooden houses in Oak Creek Canyon, and a private chef cooks organic meals in the main lodge, where evening programs are held.

Global Fitness Adventures in Sedona
Box 1390, Aspen, CO 81612
Tel. 303/927–9593 or 800/488–8747
Fax 303/927–4793

Administration Founder-director, Kristina Hurrell

Season Mar.–May and Oct.

Accommodations 10 wooden houses, each with 2 bedrooms, 2 fireplaces, large living room, kitchen, wood decks. The air-conditioned houses have Southwestern decor, TV, phone, and large modern bathroom for each bedroom.

Rates $2,175 per week includes 3 massages, all meals. $500 check deposit, balance due 30 days prior to arrival. Gratuities suggested ($50–$100). No credit cards.

Meal Plan Organic vegetarian meals served family style. Breakfast can be a power drink made from fruit, soy protein powder, and wheat germ or granola. Lunch is a mixed salad or curry tempeh sprout sandwiches. Dinner is Tex-Mex vegetarian chili with jalapeño corn muffins, mixed greens, or vegetable soup with salad.

Services and Facilities **Services:** Massage, natural healing bodywork, fitness classes. **Recreation Facilities:** Horseback riding. **Evening Programs:** Motivational talks, sweat lodge.

In the Area Jerome (Victorian mining town), Tuzigoot and Montezuma's Castle (prehistoric ruins), the Grand Canyon.

Getting Here *From Phoenix.* By car, I–17N (90 mins). By plane, commuter flights to Sedona airport (20 mins). By bus, shuttle service from Skyharbor International Airport (reservations, tel. 602/282–2066).

Special Notes Programs also in Aspen, CO; Santa Barbara, CA; Dominica in the Caribbean.

Marriott's Spa at Camelback Inn

Life enhancement
Luxury pampering
Nonprogram resort

Arizona
Scottsdale

Within a spectacular hacienda-style structure in the foothills of Mummy Mountain, the Spa at Camelback Inn is a retreat for fitness buffs as well as leisure and business guests. Programs include the latest bodyworks technologies and old-world therapies combined with heart-healthy cuisine. The spa has the most complete facilities in the Phoenix-Scottsdale area, with special packages for men and women. In 1994 it was renovated and expanded, adding state-of-the-art exercise equipment, five massage rooms, and more tables in the restaurant. Ask for accommodations in casitas near the spa; both the desert ambience and spacious rooms are conducive to total relaxation.

Start your day with a 4-mile power walk up the mountainside for grand views of the Phoenix valley and surrounding desert, then through lushly landscaped residential areas. The daily walk at 6:30 AM is open to all resort guests without charge, and if you book at least an hour of services, the daily spa admission charge ($22) is waived. Use of the fitness facility costs $10 daily if you are not on a spa package, or plan a full day at the spa, so you can sample different physical activities and then indulge in a bodywork session and salon services. Workout clothes, robes, and slippers are provided; just bring exercise shoes.

Advancing the art of fitness evaluations, Camelback has linked up with the Institute of Aerobic Research in Texas, where testing procedures are based on those of aerobics pioneer Dr. Kenneth R. Cooper. FITCHECK is a one-hour assessment of body composition, flexibility, cardiovascular endurance, and body strength. For an additional $85, you can enroll in the comprehensive Personalized Aerobics Lifestyle System (PALS), and work one-on-one with an instructor who will prepare a binder with all your customized information, as well as a specific routine that will help you achieve your fitness goals.

There is no question that staffers take their work seriously; many have University of Arizona degrees in physiology and some are trained in esoteric massage techniques at workshops in nearby Sedona or California. What sets the spa apart from others is the wide range of fitness facilities and treatments. Pilates training is a specialty, designed to correct postural alignment, and strengthen the back and abdomen. Specially designed equipment provides overall physical and mental conditioning. New treatments applied here include Kerstin Florian's European Kur using Hungarian crystals and creams, hydrotherapy in whirlpool tubs with marine algae from France's Louison Bobet Thalassotherapie, the Parisian Body Polish with a cream made from crushed pearls, and Jin Shin Jytso stress-reduction massage from Japan. The spa's recent expansion has made it the largest in the Southwest.

Southwestern art and ceramics brighten the locker rooms and lounges, where bottles of water are always at hand to ward off dehydration in the dry Arizona climate. Having a massage outdoors under a crystal-blue sky can be followed by a body scrub with a mixture of sea salts and oils or an herbal wrap. Specially equipped treatment rooms and the sauna and steam room are in an atrium, which has a cold plunge pool and hot whirlpool.

Secluded in this splendid hacienda of health, you may never want to indulge in Camelback Inn's other pleasures. But the choices of golf, tennis, fine dining, and laid-back lodging, plus a service-oriented staff, give vacationers a respite from high-rise hotels.

Marriott's Spa at Camelback Inn

5402 E. Lincoln Dr., Scottsdale, AZ 85253
Tel. 602/948–1700 or 800/242–2635
Fax 602/596–7018

Administration General manager, Wynn Tyner; spa director, John Town

Season Year-round

Accommodations 423 guest casitas on 125 acres. Rooms have king-size bed or large twins, decorated in conservative pastels and earth tones. Some have fireplace, upper bedroom and balcony with extra bathroom. All are air-conditioned, have TV, bath amenities, and phones; parking lot adjoins casita clusters.

Rates Spa Getaway with breakfast or lunch (per night) $188 single, $274 for 2; 3-night/4-day Revitalizer with meals, spa services $908 single, $1,505 for 2; 6-night/7-day Renewal package $1,741 single, $2,875 for 2; Stay & Play package with golf (per night) $138–$210 single, $169–$313 for 2; daily room, spa admission, and breakfast $139–$144 single or double. Packages do not include spa gratuities or tax. Deposit: one night. Spa Day (lodging not included) $75–$235. AE, DC, MC, V.

Meal Plans Choice of spa cuisine in Sprouts Restaurant at the spa building or at the Chaparral Room and the Navajo Room in the main building. Breakfast menu offers egg-white omelet, French toast, cereal, freshly squeezed juices, freshly baked muffins, coffee. Lunch at Sprouts can be a salad, grilled pompano stuffed with crabmeat, or cold skinless breast of chicken. Dinner only in the Chaparral Room offers à la carte choices of pasta bow ties with poppy seeds in tomato-basil sauce, poached loin of lamb, grilled ahi tuna with papaya relish, and roasted breast of capon stuffed with ricotta cheese. The Navajo Room serves three meals a day with Southwestern flair.

Services and Facilities **Exercise Equipment:** Universal multistation weight training gym, 4 Precor treadmills, StairMaster 4000, Gauntlet, 2 Windracer rowers, 2 Windracer bikes, 2 Schwinn Air Dyne bikes, Lifecycle, 2 recumbent PTS-Turbo 400 bikes, free weights. **Services:** Swedish, shiatsu, and sports massage; underwater massage (women only), thalassotherapy, aromatherapy, herbal wrap, loofah body scrub, facial, fitness/wellness evaluations, body-composition analysis, nutritional counseling, one-on-one training; beauty salon for hair, nail, and skin care. **Swimming Facilities:** Outdoor lap pool; 3 resort pools. **Recreation Facilities:** 2 golf courses (36 holes), 9-hole pitch-and-putt course, 10 tennis courts (5 lighted); horseback riding, hiking nearby. **Evening Programs:** Resort entertainment.

In the Area The Heard Museum (Native American art and history), Taliesin West (Frank Lloyd Wright home), Cosanti Foundation sculpture garden, Paolo Soleri's Arcosanti, Sedona spiritual energy tour, Buckhorn hot mineral-water baths, Mexican crafts market in Nogales, Biltmore Fashion Park, Big Surf water theme park, Desert Botanical Gardens, equestrian center, Phoenix Art Museum, and Heritage Square.

Getting Here *From Phoenix.* By car, north on 44th St., Tatum Blvd. to Lincoln Dr. (30 mins). Shuttle bus service from Skyharbor International Airport. Taxi, rental car available.

Special Notes Reciprocal guest privileges at Marriott's Mountain Shadows (tel. 602/948–7111), which has golf, tennis, and a health club. Organized activities for children 5 and older include games, dinner, movies, tennis clinic, tennis day camp. No smoking in the spa. Spa open weekdays 6:15 AM–7:30 PM, weekends 6:15 AM–7 PM.

Miraval

Life enhancement
Luxury pampering
Stress control

Arizona Unexpected things happen at Miraval, a desert resort near
Catalina Tucson where the motto is "Life in Balance." One experienced
spa goer called it a cross between Outward Bound and New
Age. But with all the comforts of a deluxe resort, complete
with 24-hour room service at no extra cost, it's the ultimate
holistic holiday.

Program choices are designed to help you create balance in
your life. That can mean balancing on a 25-foot pole, harnessed
to ropes, and jumping off. Or climbing a custom-designed rock
wall. How about horsing around at a workshop in grooming
horses who interact with you on an emotional level?

The real joy of the Sonoran desert, however, comes on hikes
and trail rides. There's a cool, dry energy, even in the heat of
summer. The desert is supportive without being smothering,
nurturing without being too close. Combined with the exercise classes that can be challenging or mood-enhancing, the effect is invigorating.

Escape desert sun for a workout in the best-equipped fitness
center this side of the Rio Grande. In addition to strength
and cardiovascular training, there are two aerobics studios
(one has a suspended hardwood floor), 6-lane lap pool (25
meter), and locker rooms. The facilities are open 6 AM to 9 PM
daily, and you can schedule a personal trainer as part of your
package.

Miraval's all-inclusive package rates cover everything from
morning tai chi and yoga to body treatments—massage, facial,
scalp treatment, pedicure—and one-on-one training. One personal service per day is included; additional treatments or
training can be scheduled for a fee. No tipping is allowed. Your
choice of activities is planned in advance by a program counselor who arranges airport transfers and fitness evaluation.

Accommodations in spacious stucco-walled casitas are part of
the desert experience. Set amid palm trees, Zenlike meditation gardens, and meandering streams, 106 adobe buildings
accommodate up to 180 guests. Each room is equipped with
minibar and coffeemaker; suites have fireplace. There are five
outdoor swimming pools, including a dedicated lap pool. Water
comes from the resort's own aquifer; fruit and bottles of mineral water are supplied in your room. And two restaurants let
you vary dining each day, with no limit on food.

Set on 135 acres in the foothills of the Santa Catalina Mountains of southern Arizona near Tucson, the resort has evolved
from extensive work in the personal growth fields by the owners. Launched in 1996, Miraval is more than a spa; part ranch,
part self-discovery center, it's an upscale destination for
achievers seeking new challenges or total relaxation.

Miraval
5000 E. Via Estancia Miraval, Catalina, AZ 85739
Tel. 520/825–4000 or 800/232–3969
Fax 520/792–5870

Administration Managing director, Sigi Brauer; program director, Syd Teague

Season Year-round

Accommodations 92 casita-style guest rooms, 14 suites. Southwestern furniture
and carpeting in warm desert tones; choice of queen, king, or

two double beds, with Frette sheets; robes. Most rooms have patio with desert view; suites can have whirlpool tub, fireplace. All with TV and VCR, 2-line phone with voice mail, air-conditioning. Bathrooms are large, with marbled-topped vanity, makeup mirror, hair dryer, dual-spray shower, Saltillo tile floor.

Rates 4-day/3-night package $950–$1,785 per person, double or single occupancy. Daily $300–$595. Suites from $1,365 for 3-night package. Seasonal packages available. Rates include service charges, tax, airport transfers. Deposit: 1 night. AE, DC, MC, V.

Meal Plans 3 meals daily included in package; complimentary in-room refreshments. Breakfast is a buffet of fruits, cereals, juices, and yogurt; choice of wild rice griddle cakes, warm fruit and berry strudel, or omelet. Lunch choices may be vegetarian corn crepe, braised artichokes, grilled swordfish salad. Dinner entrées include braised cactus and baby vegetables with loin of venison, vegetable lasagna, grilled grouper, grape leaves filled with grilled salmon and sea scallops; desserts are fruit, sorbet, chocolate soufflé, baked bread pudding. Coffee and tea served; wine available (extra charge).

Services and Facilities **Exercise Equipment:** Complete line of Cybex VR2 weight training units, free weights (3 lbs.–50 lbs.), 3 Startrac 1200 treadmills, 3 StairMaster 4400, Tectrix bike, 4 Cybex bikes, X100 Cross Conditioner. **Services:** Massage (soothing or hot stone technique), facial, manicure, pedicure, hair and scalp treatment, hydrotherapy, body wrap. Fitness evaluation, one-on-one training, tennis instruction, sand painting and arts instruction, cooking class. **Swimming Facilities:** 5 outdoor pools, some with cascades. **Recreation Facilities:** 4 lighted all-weather tennis courts, horseback riding, croquet lawn. **Evening Programs:** Music, entertainment.

In the Area Arizona-Sonora Desert Museum (indigenous animals and plants), Mission San Xavier del Bac, Sabino Canyon, Colossal Cave, Biosphere 2, Tombstone.

Getting Here *From Tucson.* By car, north on I–10, east on Tangerine Rd., north on Oracle Rd., east on Golder Ranch Rd., north on Lago del Oro Pkwy., right to resort (45 mins). Shuttle from Tucson International Airport.

Special Notes There are 6 specially designed bedrooms for people with disabilities.

The Phoenician Centre for Well-Being

Life enhancement
Luxury pampering
Nutrition and diet

Arizona
Scottsdale Nestled on 250 acres of manicured lawn and desert terrain at the base of Camelback Mountain is The Phoenician, an ITT Sheraton resort that combines elegant accommodations, sports, and a wide range of spa services. Though the hotel caters to conferences and family vacationers, the private-club atmosphere is still maintained. Exceptional service matches the grandeur of the public areas; oversize guest rooms are quiet retreats, with all the amenities of a world-class resort. Completed in 1996 was a makeover that included construction of the 60-room Canyon Building and 9 additional holes of golf.

Inspired by Native American therapeutic traditions, the Centre for Well-Being offers treatments using desert plants and minerals. Jojoba, clay, and aloe-vera preparations appear on the menu along with Kerstin Florian European skin-care products. Special "signature" programs are customized to fit the skin-care needs of men and women: Herbal wraps with muslin sheets soaked in a fragrant blend of sage, juniper, and rosemary are offered as a calming treatment prior to massage; facials both protect your skin from desert sun and combat aging.

The two-level Centre is an escape from the desert, where you can meditate in a secluded atrium, work out on state-of-the-art equipment, or join an aerobics class in glass-walled studios equipped with sprung-wood floors. The exercise facilities, along with beauty salon and barber shop, are on the upper level, enhanced by views of the resort.

While the Phoenician's guest accommodations spread in all directions, spa goers may want to stay in one of the casitas close to the spa. For golfers, top choice would be the 40 new suites in the Canyon Building.

Several restaurants serve "Choices" cuisine selections: Mary Elaine's is formal and French, Windows on the Green at the golf course has both indoor and outdoor dining in a casual Southwestern atmosphere, and the Terrace restaurant is favored for brunch.

Vast spaces, secluded workouts, and attentive service distinguish this spectacular resort.

The Phoenician Centre for Well-Being
6000 E. Camelback Rd., Scottsdale, AZ 85251
Tel. 602/941–8200 or 800/888–8234
Fax 602/947–4311

Administration General manager, Alan Furstman; director, Jill Taylor

Season Year-round

Accommodations 640 guest rooms in the main hotel, Canyon wing, and casitas. Oversize bathrooms in Italian marble, hair dryer, terry-cloth robes, 3 telephones. Desert tones accent wood furniture; suites have hand-carved travertine fireplace. Air-conditioning, TV, daily paper delivery.

Rates Summer: $160–$265, suites $525–$700; winter: $310–$465, suites $950–$1,550. 4-day/3-night Turnaround $1,010–$1,590 single, $1,500–$2,000 per couple. 8-day/7-night Luxury of Choice package $2,110–$3,470 single, $2,920–$4,280 per couple. Twice-as-Nice 4-day/3-night golf/spa package $1,200–$1,910 per couple. 1-day Retreat (no lodging or meals) $95–$160. Daily spa admission ($16; $6 after 5 PM) waived in conjunction with treatments or program. Packages include tax; gratuities extra. AE, DC, MC, V.

Meal Plans Breakfast included in some programs. Choices include seven-grain pancakes with wild berries, egg-white omelet with tomato salsa and herbed goat cheese. Lunch can be grilled vegetable sandwich, or grilled portabello taco with roasted peppers, avocado, and queso anejo cheese. Dinner entrées include grilled salmon with gazpacho relish; penne with grilled chicken, roasted peppers, and eggplant; or pork tenderloin with green corn sauce, roasted vegetables, and white beans.

Services and Facilities **Exercise Equipment:** Eagle Cybex circuit training, 4 Stair-Master 4000 PTs, Concept 2 rower, Liferower, 3 Lifecycle 9500s, 2 Schwinn Air Dynes, PTS Turbo recumbent bike, Stair-Master crossaerobics, 6 Precor treadmills, Olympic free weights, punching bags. **Services:** Massage therapy includes lymphatic drainage, Swedish, shiatsu, sports, reflexology, aromatherapy, jin shin jyutsu; French sea algae body wrap, MoorMud wrap, body scrub; desert clay, herbal, or aloe-vera body wrap; OJA Shirodhara therapy; facial, eye-lifting, back facial; fitness consultation, body composition analysis, cholesterol testing; astrology, herbology, tarot card reading; scheduled classes for self defense, aerobics, tai chi, yoga; salon and barbershop for hair, nail care. **Swimming Facilities:** 7 outdoor pools. **Recreation Facilities:** 27-hole golf course, 12 tennis courts, croquet, lawn bowling, volleyball, badminton, archery, walking, jogging, water basketball and volleyball, bike rental.

In the Area Camelback Mountain hiking, Borgata Mall (shopping), Desert Botanical Garden, Taliesin West (Frank Lloyd Wright Foundation), Heard Museum (Native American art), Sedona arts and spiritual community, Phoenix Art Museum, and Heritage Square.

Getting Here *From Phoenix.* By car, north on 44th St. to Camelback Rd., right to Jokake, left into resort (20 mins). Shuttle bus from Skyharbor International Airport. Taxi, rental car.

Special Notes 10–15 rooms are designed for people with disabilities. Funicians Club for children has daily supervised program. Teenage programs available at certain times of the year. Spa open 6 AM–8 PM. Minimum age in spa: 16.

Scottsdale Princess

Nonprogram resort

Arizona
Scottsdale

The towers of the Scottsdale Princess rise from the Sonoran Desert like a mirage surrounded by a velvet green golf course. The 450-acre resort, member of a hotel chain noted for its upscale facilities in Mexico and Bermuda, was renovated in 1993. It has a king-size spa and fitness center and offers packages as well as daily use ($12) of the exercise equipment and participation in the five daily aerobics classes.

A fitness staff member sets the pace on a 45-minute morning walk in the crisp desert air along the grounds and golf course. The rest of the day is your own to schedule with bodywork and a bit of luxury pampering. Participating in a wide range of outdoor sports is the major attraction for most guests: walleyball, Ping-Pong, a fun run, and desert biking are scheduled daily, in addition to tennis, golf, and water aerobics.

Escape the desert sun in the mirrored aerobics studio, with suspended hardwood floors ideal for step, low-impact, stretch, and body-sculpture classes. Encompassing 10,000 square feet of workout space, the Fitness Center has an array of exercise equipment, and separate men's and women's locker rooms with steam, sauna, and whirlpools. Other options include nearby hiking trails in the McDowell Mountains and a 400-acre equestrian park.

Secluded and self-contained, this is an ideal desert getaway with all the amenities. For extra luxury and privacy, the casitas are choice accommodations, and rates are quoted for two.

Scottsdale Princess
7575 E. Princess Dr., Scottsdale, AZ 85255
Tel. 602/585–4848 or 800/344–4758
Fax 602/585–0086

Administration Manager, Stephen Ast; health club manager, Jill Eisenhut

Season Year-round

Accommodations 600 guest rooms and suites range in style from Mexican colonial to contemporary high-rise. All with living and work areas, terraces, wet bars, and large baths. 75 villas, 125 casitas with wood-burning fireplaces near the tennis courts. All are air-conditioned, have TV, 3 phones with data jacks, bathrooms with double sinks, and separate bath and shower stalls.

Rates $240–$400 single or double occupancy standard rooms, suites $380–$2,000. 2-night Royal Indulgence spa package $267–$843 per person, includes Continental breakfast, services. AE, DC, MC, V.

Meal Plans The Grill (golf clubhouse) and Las Ventanas (garden atrium and golf-course view) feature grilled seafood and chicken, and salads. La Hacienda serves Mexican specialties, and the Marquesa features Catalan cuisine. Vegetarian meals are available.

Services and Facilities **Exercise Equipment:** Full line of Cybex weight training equipment, 3 Quinton treadmills, 4 Lifecycles, Schwinn Air Dyne bike, Concept 2 rower, free weight dumbbells to 65 lbs, 3 Stair-Master 4000s. **Services:** Herbal wrap, shiatsu, loofah body scrub, mud wrap, aloe or algae body mask, massage (Swedish, aromatherapy, therapeutic, reflexology), salt-glow treatment; beauty salon for facials, hair and nail care. **Swimming Facilities:** 3 outdoor pools, 1 (75 ft) for swimming laps and aquatic exercise. **Recreation Facilities:** 9 tennis courts, 2 18-hole golf courses, racquetball and squash courts, indoor/outdoor basketball, croquet, bike rental, walleyball, volleyball, fishing; nearby equestrian center offers riding, shows, and polo. **Evening Programs:** Resort entertainment.

In the Area Desert tours by Jeep, Sedona arts and spiritual center, hiking trails in the McDowell Mountains.

Getting Here *From Phoenix.* By car, north on 44th St. to Camelback Rd., turn right to Scottsdale Rd., then left to Bell Rd. (45 mins). By bus and van service from Skyharbor International Airport.

Special Notes Some rooms equipped for persons with disabilities; ramps and elevators to all areas. No smoking in health club. Spa open weekdays 6 AM–8 PM, weekends 7–7. Kids Klub ($20 per session). Minimum age in spa: 16.

The Aspen Club

Nonprogram resort

Colorado The high-tech workouts at The Aspen Club attract sports
Aspen celebrities as well as vacationers. The schedule on a typical Monday in February includes cross-country and downhill skiing, tennis, and snowshoeing, but it's the personal training and rehabilitation after injury at the Fitness and Sports Medicine Institute that sets this property apart from the others. Planned in 1997 is a new spa building.

The center for therapy and training employs a comprehensive approach to well-being that considers the individual's personal needs and goals in prescribing short-term lifestyle modifications aimed at making significant health improvements.

The fitness program, which is open to nonmembers, is concerned chiefly with weight loss, stress reduction, and sport-specific exercise. Visitors stay a few days or a few weeks, scheduling exercise classes and diagnostic appointments among the activities of a world-class resort.

A complete physical evaluation by a team of physicians, physical therapists, and trainers is the first order of business; you undergo a stress test with EKG readings, pulmonary-function tests, and body-fat, strength, and flexibility measurements. A nutritionist evaluates your eating habits and body chemistry (and schedules blood tests when appropriate) prior to recommending a diet that meets your nutritional needs.

The city of Aspen sits at 7,902 feet above sea level in the heart of the Elk Mountain Range, amid some of the highest peaks in the Rockies. The trembling aspens, the gray-barked trees with fine-toothed leaves that flutter in the wind, are a metaphor for the community, which has shifting moods and trends but is firmly rooted in its ways. Summer is for hiking, the music festival, and the International Design Conference begun in 1951; winter brings dogsledding as well as skiing. Skiers have numerous choices; between Aspen and Snowmass there are four ski slopes with universal lift tickets. Free shuttle buses run between all areas. There are also miles of cross-country ski trails, including a 48-mile course groomed with double-track trails by the Nordic Council.

Restaurants boast about a regional cuisine they call "Rocky Mountain cooking," but most of the featured wild boar, caribou, elk, moose, and quail do not come from the region. For a unique combination of lunch and dogsled ride pulled by yelping Alaskan huskies, make reservations at Krabloonik (tel. 303/923–3953), about 11 miles from town.

Since the Ute Indians established camps here, the area has prospered. Silver magnate and Macy's owner Jerome Wheeler built the opera house on main street in 1889, and it still showcases talented musicians. But all of Aspen is a celebration of the good life, an authentic Rocky Mountain High.

The Aspen Club
Fitness and Sports Medicine Institute
1450 Crystal Lake Rd., Aspen, CO 81611
Tel. 303/925–8900; lodging 303/925–6760, 800/882–2582, or
800/443–2582 in CO
Fax 303/925–9543

Administration General manager, Mark Overstreet

Season Year-round

Accommodations Studios, 4- and 5-bedroom condominiums, private home rentals—all with Jacuzzi, fireplace, sundeck—by arrangement with the Aspen Club Management Company. 91 rooms and suites at the Aspen Club Lodge have oak furnishings, queen-size and twin beds, bath, and kitchen. Maid service, newspaper delivery. Continental breakfast and health-club facilities included.

Rates Lodge rooms $75–$275 Apr. 15–Dec. 19, $325–$365 Dec. 20–Apr. 13; suites $250–$795 per person, double occupancy. AE, MC, V.

Meal Plans Meals are not included in the program. Heart-healthy cuisine is available for breakfast and lunch at the Club dining facility. Recommended restaurants in Aspen include Gordon's, Syzygy, Piñons, Cache Cache, and range from moderate to expensive.

Services and Facilities **Exercise Equipment:** 12-unit David circuit, 4 Keiser Cam IIIs, 3 Nautilus units, Eagle leg press, 2 Polaris units, 7 Stair Masters, 5 Quinton, 1 Precor treadmill, 6 Lifecycles, 2 Life-rowers, Precor rower, 6 Tunturi bikes, 5 Monark bikes, 2 Schwinn bikes, Turbo and Nautilus recumbent bikes, NordicTrack, free weights, dumbbells and barbells (3–100 lbs). **Services:** Swedish massage, nutritional and food-allergy evaluation, strength and flexibility tests, blood-profile analysis, maximal stress test, body-composition analysis, private exercise training, post-injury therapy. **Swimming Facilities:** Indoor lap pool. **Recreation Facilities:** Skiing, 2 indoor and 7 outdoor tennis courts, 3 racquetball courts, 3 squash courts, basketball, volleyball, walleyball, fencing, cycling, aikido; golf and horseback riding nearby. **Evening Programs:** Athletics, tournaments, fitness and nutrition seminar.

In the Area Aspen Center for Environmental Studies (Hallam Lake Wildlife Sanctuary, Northstar Nature Preserve), Aspen Art Museum, Aspen Music Festival and Ballet/Dance Festival (July–Aug.), ballooning, rafting. Crafts shows and classes at the Anderson Ranch at Snowmass. Mineral-water baths at Glenwood Springs.

Getting Here *From Denver.* By train, Amtrak to Glenwood Springs (2 hrs). By bus, Greyhound to Glenwood Springs (3 hrs). By car, I–70 to Dillon, Rte. 91 to Hwy. 24, Rte. 82 via Independence Pass (closed in winter) is scenic route (3½ hrs). By plane, flights on United or Continental Express (40 mins). Free pickup from and return to Aspen airport. Rental car, taxi, limousine available.

Special Notes Full facilities for people with disabilites. Children's athletic programs in swimming, tennis, squash, racquetball, and dance; nursery and toddler swim class by reservation. No smoking in public areas. Some no-smoking apartments and rooms. Spa open daily 6:45 AM–10 PM.

The Broadmoor

Luxury pampering

Colorado
Colorado Springs
Celebrating a 76-year legacy as the premier health and sports resort in the Rocky Mountain region, in 1994 the Broadmoor introduced an exclusive line of body treatments utilizing native Colorado ingredients. The newly constructed spa facilities include hydrotherapy, balneology, and inhalation rooms. Combined with your choice of sports-specific training, bodywork, or fitness activities, the spa offers personalized programs rather than a structured schedule.

The new spa-and-fitness complex overlooks 12 tennis courts and the Dennis Ralston training program, and three championship golf courses. Also housed here are the golf clubhouse and three restaurants.

Set in the heart of 3,000 well-groomed acres, The Broadmoor encompasses a private lake, five swimming pools, and nine hotel buildings. Choice rooms and suites are in the West complex, but the Old World style of the main building and its penthouse Penrose dining room draw devoted visitors. From boating to bike rental, hot-air balloon ascensions, walks around the lake and hikes or trail rides into the foothills of Pikes Peak, the resort offers a wide range of activity. There is a pharmacy, movie theater, nightclub, pub, ice cream parlor, and nine restaurants. Within a few miles are the mineral waters of Manitou Springs and the training center for Olympic athletes; both are worth a visit. Excursions include hikes in the red-rock canyons called Garden of the Gods, riding the original cog railway on Pikes Peak, and touring the U.S. Air Force Academy.

The two-level lakefront spa has an aerobics studio for scheduled classes in step, slide, body sculpting, and box aerobics. There is an indoor swimming pool where aquatics classes are held and a dedicated two-lane outdoor adult lap pool. The weight training and cardio rooms are available to all resort guests for a daily fee or as part of spa packages. Separate locker rooms for men and women have steam room and sauna, and you are issued a robe and slippers on arrival.

Energy and relaxation are well paired here. Conventioneers and club members work out early in the morning, families splash into the indoor pool under a soaring skylit ceiling, and hard-core fitness buffs discover one of the most complete Cybex weight rooms in the west. Having a juice bar alongside the pool is convenient for lunch and snacks, and there are tables on a sunny terrace overlooking the first tee. The spa lounge is an inner sanctum for relaxation, warmed by a log fire, where you sip tea or lemonade while absorbing the changing moods of the mountains from the veranda.

Designed to complement the classic lines of the main Broadmoor building, an Italian Renaissance–style palace opened in 1918, the new spa incorporates 12 state-of-the-art soaking tubs for hydrotherapy, 16 massage rooms (many with windows looking toward Pikes Peak), and special showers built into rock walls. Among sophisticated treatments are facials for men and women, sports massage, and the Rocky Mountain Revitalizer therapeutic bath to acclimate you to the dry climate and sun. Still, this is a pure Colorado experience, infused with scents of spruce and cedar, decorated with the state flower (columbine), and invigorated by mountain air.

Visiting the Broadmoor is like taking a step back to the golden era when Colorado Springs attracted health seekers from around the world. Walking the lake's perimeter, entranced by the view of nearby mountain ranges, you'll be challenged by a resident flock of geese and swans, watched over by groundskeepers who regularly sweep up droppings. It's a minor detail, but typical of traditions that make the Broadmoor unique.

The Broadmoor

Box 1439, Colorado Springs, CO 80901
Tel. 719/577–5777 or 800/634–7711, ext. 5770
Fax 719/577–5700

Administration President, Stephen Bartolin, Jr.; spa director, Marguerite Lykes

Season Year-round

Accommodations 550 rooms, including 67 suites, with full bathroom, porcelain bathtub, sink with brass fixtures. Traditional furniture, air-conditioning, TV, telephones. Choice of king-size or 2 double beds, view of mountains or city. Amenities include clock radio, toiletries, evening turn-down service.

Rates Daily rates per room $245–$365 peak season, $165–$230 off season, suites $260–$1,970. Spa packages including accommodation and spa gratuity (Apr.–Nov.): 4-night Best of the Broadmoor from $1,488 per person, double occupancy; 3-night Spa Spectacular from $770 per person, double occupancy. Add tax and hotel gratuities. AE, D, MC, V.

Meal Plans Cuisine Vivant items on all menus (marked CV) are 20%–25% fat, 50%–55% carbohydrates, 15%–20% protein. Selections are à la carte; breakfast can be low-cholesterol omelet, oatmeal, or fruit plate; lunch entrées include grilled swordfish steak with Mediterranean letscho sauce (pepper-and-tomato sauce), or sautéed Colorado red trout fillet; dinner in the Penrose Room starts with onion soup topped by low-fat mozzarella, or vegetable Napoleon. Dinner entrées include red snapper and halibut, vegetable ravioli with shiitake mushrooms.

Services and Facilities **Exercise Equipment**: 15 Cybex stations, free weights and dumbbells (5–50 lbs) in weight-resistance room, 3 Cybex bikes, 4 Schwinn Pro bikes, 2 Trotter 685 treadmills, 2 Concept 2 rowers, 2 Cross-Conditioning Systems XL180, 4 StairMaster PT4000s in cardiovascular room. **Services**: Swedish and aromatherapy massage, shiatsu, Floraspa herbal body wraps and aromabaths, salt-glow body scrub, mud baths, milk-whey baths, underwater massage tubs, facial room. **Swimming Facilities:** 3 outdoor pools, indoor pool and lap pool. **Recreation Facilities:** 12 tennis courts (Plexi-Plave), 3 golf courses, horseback riding, ice skating, paddleboats, jogging trail, shuffleboard, bike rental; rifle club with skeet, trap, and sporting clays; hot-air balloon ascension; downhill skiing nearby.

In the Area Garden of the Gods (hiking), Pikes Peak (cog railway, hiking), Manitou Springs (historic spa, Indian cliff dwellings), U.S. Olympic Training Center, Air Force Academy, Royal Gorge (white-water rafting), Van Briggle Pottery, Cripple Creek (casinos, Victorian gold rush town), Cheyenne Mountain Zoo (animal habitat).

Getting Here *From Denver.* By car, I–25 to Lake Ave. (90 mins). By air, Colorado Springs Airport has scheduled service to major cities by TWA and regional carriers. Taxi, limousine, rental car available at airport and hotel.

Special Notes Spa hours: daily 6:30 AM–8:30 PM. Minimum age: 16. Daily facilities fee: $10. Facilities are accessible for people with disabilities.

Eden Valley Lifestyle Center

Preventive medicine
Spiritual awareness
Vibrant maturity
Weight management

Colorado
Loveland
This homelike retreat set amid woods, lakes, and streams on 550 acres in the foothills of the Rocky Mountains teaches physical conditioning and nutrition in comprehensive programs lasting 7 to 24 days. The Eden Valley Lifestyle Center's approach emphasizes the pursuit, under medical supervision, of traditional Seventh-Day Adventist philosophies of diet and mental and spiritual health.

Following thorough individual physical evaluations by the medical director, small groups of guests are counseled on health and disease prevention. Cooking demonstrations show how the vegetarian diet can be adapted to one's own kitchen routines.

The doctor monitors each guest's progress and may suggest additional activities. Drinking lots of pure water, walking in the clean mountain air and sunshine, and taking hydrotherapy and whirlpool baths are all part of the program. Optional excursions include horseback riding at a nearby ranch, where trail rides and cookouts are offered for a modest fee.

Personalized strategies for attaining a healthy lifestyle are prepared for those with heart disease, diabetes, degenerative disease, and digestive problems. Chronic fatigue, obesity, arthritis, and high blood pressure are also treated, and there is therapy for those who want to stop smoking.

The Lifestyle program began in 1987 as an extension of services at a nearby home for senior citizens. People of all ages come here to gain new vitality and stamina and to relax in the company of a small supportive group.

Eden Valley Lifestyle Center
6263 N. County Rd. 29, Loveland, CO 80538
Tel. 970/669–7730 or 800/637–9355

Administration Administrator, Daniel McKibben; medical director, Ralph McLure, M.D.

Season	Year-round, with scheduled program 3 weeks per month
Accommodations	5 guest rooms with twin beds in a new ranch-style facility, 3 with private bath; 5 rooms in private homes. Draperies and flowered bedspreads. Private sundeck.
Rates	7-day program $445, 14 days $780, 21 days $1,200, all per person, double occupancy. Medical costs may be covered by health insurance. $300 in advance for the 14- and 21-day programs, $100 for the 7-day program, nonrefundable. MC, V. Companion rates available.
Meal Plans	3 vegetarian meals daily, buffet style. Adventist diet of fruit, raw vegetables, legumes, and grains. No butter, oils, or dairy products. Some olives, nuts, and avocado. Entrées for lunch and dinner include vegetarian lasagna with mock-cheese topping; bean haystack with rice on corn chips, topped with cashew-nut mixture; green salads, steamed vegetables, and baked tofu.
Services and Facilities	**Exercise Equipment:** Stationary bike, treadmill, trampoline. **Services:** Physical examination, blood-chemistry analysis, computerized lifestyle inventory, daily hydrotherapy treatments with massage, Jacuzzi, sauna. **Swimming Facilities:** Community pool and lakes. **Recreation Facilities:** Mountain trail hiking, fishing, boating; downhill and cross-country skiing. Golf course, tennis courts, horseshoe pitch, and picnic facilities; horseback riding nearby.
In the Area	Estes Park (mountain resort), greyhound racetrack, county fair and rodeo, trail rides, ghost towns, antiques shops. Performing-arts and museum exhibitions.
Getting Here	*From Denver.* By car, I–25 north to Loveland, County Rd. 27 to County Rd. 29 (90 mins).
Special Notes	No smoking.

Filhoa Meadows

Holistic health
Preventive medicine
Stress control
Taking the waters
Vibrant maturity

Colorado
White River
National Forest

This family-oriented health retreat close to Aspen is designed to help balance your mental, physical, spiritual, and social selves. Created for the person who is at high risk for lifestyle diseases (cancer, heart problems, arthritis), this is therapy to help change old behavioral habits that are self-defeating and debilitating. For couples with marital problems, founder-owner Robert Durham provides conflict-resolution counseling, with an emphasis on personal communications, family relationships, and Christian values. Sessions can involve children as well as adults.

Coordinated by medical consultants and specialists in physical education and cardiac rehabilitation, the programs are planned on an individual basis to meet the needs and fitness levels of participants. Activities center around a big wooden lodge close to the historic Indian Springs, which provide a constant source of hot mineral water for the indoor and outdoor hydrotherapy pools as well as the hot tubs in the guest cabins.

Guest rooms are in 5 rustic cabins, which have kitchen, bathroom, outdoor deck, and hot tub. In addition to the soothing mineral-water baths, downhill skiing in winter and biking in summer, and the natural scenic beauty at 7,000 feet in the Rockies, you can enjoy a full range of entertainment and sports. Nature-oriented hikes are guided, and you can observe wildlife from a blind at the beaver pond. Camaraderie with fellow guests, never more than 20, and the resident owners and staff is part of the informal appeal that draws many repeat visitors and weekenders.

The health education concentrates on understanding diet, exercise, and how our minds work. No meals are served, so come prepared to do your own cooking as well as participate in discussions on nutrition and a healthy lifestyle. Supervised workouts are scheduled in an indoor pool that is equipped with hydrojets and in a small exercise area that has panoramic views of the Rockies.

Filhoa Meadows
14628 Hwy. 133, Redstone, CO 81623
Tel. 970/963–1989 or 800/227–8906

Administration Director, Robert Durham; seminar coordinator, Melody L. Durham, R.N.; medical consultants, Bernarr Johnson, M.D., F.A.C.S., Claudia and Alan Nelson, M.D., F.A.C.S.

Season Year-round

Accommodations 4 1-bedroom cabins with bathrooms, kitchen; 2-bedroom cabin has full bathroom, kitchen, sundeck, hot tub. Choice of single, queen- or king-size beds. No air-conditioning, TV, or phone.

Rates $85 per night, single or double occupancy; additional persons $10 nightly. Add taxes; gratuities optional. Counseling $45 per hour. Advance payment of 1 night nonrefundable. MC, V.

Meal Plans None. Guests do their own cooking.

Services and Facilities **Exercise Equipment:** Total Gym exercise unit, 2 Schwinn bikes, 2 rowing machines, Sears treadmill, free weights. **Services:** Massage, counseling, cooking demonstration. **Swimming Facilities:** Indoor static lap pool. **Recreation Facilities:** 3 outdoor Jacuzzis, par course, running track; nearby downhill and cross-country skiing, fly casting, hiking, biking, rafting, horseback riding.

In the Area Aspen (summer music and ballet festivals), Glenwood Springs (swimming, golf), jeep tours to the Snowmass Wilderness (ghost towns, nature photography), Colorado River (white-water rafting), Redstone (Victorian mining town).

Getting Here *From Denver.* By car, I–70 to Glenwood Springs, Hwy. 82 to Hwy. 133 (3 hrs). By bus, Trailways to Glenwood Springs (3 hrs). By train, Amtrak to Glenwood Springs (1 hrs). By plane, scheduled flights to Aspen (30 mins). Transportation by prior request to and from Glenwood Springs and Aspen.

Special Notes Limited access for people with disabilities. No smoking indoors.

Glenwood Hot Springs Lodge & Pool

Taking the waters

Colorado
Glenwood Springs This facility has one of the largest natural mineral-water pools in the Rockies and is popular year-round, even in subfreezing temperatures.

In summer and winter the 130°F water is cooled for comfort in the 405-foot-long outdoor swimming pool, fed with naturally hot water. In a smaller therapy pool equipped with underwater jets for massage, the water temperature is 104°F. Together the pools contain 1.1 million gallons of mineral water, changed three times daily. The entire complex, with a 3-story lodge and athletic club, is two blocks long.

Lodge guests use the Hot Springs Athletic Club and can participate in aerobic workouts, use championship racquetball, handball, and walleyball courts, and relax in coed saunas and whirlpools. The club's scheduled fitness classes include water and low-impact aerobics, and Jazzercise.

Nearby are vapor caves (coed), where the hot springs create temperatures that reach 115°F and provide a great sweat. Cold-water hoses are available, but there is no soaking pool. Day visitors are welcome both at the caves and at the pools; lodge guest admission to the caves is $4 adults, $2.75 children.

Dashing from the hotel or locker room into the pool on a winter day is a bracing experience. Shrouded in mist, ice forms on nearby trees. Skiiers and hunters drop by to relax, and families come for fun.

Glenwood Hot Springs Lodge & Pool
Box 308, Glenwood Springs, CO 81601
Tel. 970/945–6571
Fax 970/945–6683

Administration Manager, Kjell Mitchell

Season Year-round

Accommodations 107 modern rooms furnished with 2 queen-size beds (some are king-size), private bath, and double vanity. Deluxe rooms with balcony or patio overlooking the pools, coffeemaker, safe, air-conditioning, geothermal heating.

Rates $56–$89 per day single, $62–$90 for 2, double occupancy; Add 7.75% tax. Daily pool admission $6 adults, $3.75 children. Discount on admission to pools and athletic club for lodge guests. 1 night payable in advance. AE, DC, MC, V.

Meal Plans No meal plan. Meals served at the lodge café.

Services and Facilities **Exercise Equipment:** 10-station Nautilus units, 4 Lifecycles, 2 StairMasters. **Services:** Massage, facials, chiropractic adjustment. **Swimming Facilities:** 4 outdoor pools. **Recreation Facilities:** Hiking, water slide, trout fishing, 4 indoor racquetball courts, 2 handball and walleyball courts.

In the Area Ski resorts, Aspen Music Festival, Wheeler Opera House, Anderson Ranch arts center at Snowmass.

Getting Here *From Denver.* By train, Amtrak twice daily (3 hrs). By bus, Greyhound (4 hrs). By car, I–70 (3 hrs). Rental car available.

Special Notes 2 rooms with access for people with disabilities. No smoking in athletic club or caves.

Global Fitness Adventures

Holistic health
Life enhancement
Spiritual awareness
Stress control
Weight management

Colorado Inspired by the majesty and splendor of the Rockies, former
Aspen fashion model Kristina Hurrell and her husband, Dr. Rob Krakovitz—author and holistic health authority—designed a life-energizing program filled with fun activities for guests of all ages. This Rocky Mountain health retreat accommodates up to 10 participants for its one-week programs.

The picturesque 52-acre ranch is 45 miles from Aspen and is surrounded by 2 million acres of the White River National Forest. Welcomed at the main lodge, you are assigned to a room or private cabin. A variety of natural healing techniques and bodywork are included in the program. Days begin with an hour of yoga and end with dinner by candlelight.

Outdoor recreation is the focus here. Hiking and touring the backcountry fill most days. Horseback riding continues to be a major attraction at this former dude ranch. The seasonal excursions include cross-country skiing, snowshoe hiking, sleigh rides, and downhill skiing (at an additional $45 fee). An optional vision quest, involving a 24-hour ceremony, sweat lodge, and drumming, is often available. A daily massage (1-hour) is included in the program rate.

The combination of healthy eating and extensive daily exercise forms a basis for weight loss. Spa-cuisine meals total 800 calories per day. Vegetarian meals and supervised juice or water regimens are also offered. By adhering to a course of exercise and attending classes on topics ranging from improving communication skills and personal relations to enhancing mental, emotional, and physical energies, you'll achieve a sense of well-being in this magical place that will put you on the road to peak vitality.

Global Fitness Adventures

Box 1390, Aspen, CO 81612
Tel. 970/927–9593 or 800/488–8747
Fax 970/927–4793

Administration Founder-director, Kristina Hurrell; holistic medicine director, Rob Krakovitz, M.D.

Season June–Sept.

Accommodations 18 rooms in main lodge and guest cabins. Rustic charm, ranch-style furnishings, private modern baths. Lodge with high beam ceiling and open fireplace. Jacuzzi on sundeck.

Rates $2,175 per person, double occupancy for 1 week, includes all meals, massages. Deposit: $500, balance due 30 days prior to arrival. $50–$100 per week, gratuity suggested. No credit cards.

Meal Plans 3 meals daily, family style, plus snacks. Breakfast is either pineapple or papaya (high in enzymes that aid digestion), granola, or a power drink made from fruit, soy protein powder, and wheat germ. Lunch is either a salad with tofu, nuts, seeds, and sprouts, or a lemon, garlic, tempeh, and sprout sandwich. Dinner is steamed squash, steamed brown rice with vegetables, grilled trout, or vegetarian lasagna.

Services and Facilities **Services:** Massage, natural healing bodywork, yoga and meditation training, detoxification techniques, diet plan with nutritional supplement. Personal consultation on medical and health problems, with holistic therapies (fee). Horseback riding instruction (fee). **Swimming Facilities:** Nearby lake. **Recreation Facilities:** Horseback riding, trout fishing, rowing, canoeing, snowshoeing, mountain biking; golf and tennis nearby. **Evening Programs:** Informal workshops on health and nutrition.

In the Area Cross-country and downhill skiing, trail rides; shopping, summer arts festival in Aspen; mineral baths at Glenwood Springs; Olympic training center at Colorado Springs.

Getting Here *From Denver.* By car, I–70 to Glenwood Springs, Rte. 82 to Basalt (3 hrs). By air, American, Continental, and United commuter flights to Aspen (40 mins). Free pickup in Aspen on Sun.

Special Notes Laundry service provided. No smoking indoors; smoking discouraged elsewhere. Program also in Sedona, AZ; Kauai, HI; Santa Barbara, CA; and island of Dominica.

Indian Springs Resort

Taking the waters

Colorado At the historic Indian Springs Resort you can swim in mineral
Idaho Springs water surrounded by tropical foliage beneath an arched glass roof. Built in 1869, the Victorian hotel still has its ornate dining room; in 1992 the 20-room inn opened, and in 1995 an additional 20 lodge rooms were completed, providing specially designed facilities for guests with disabilities.

The soaking pools cater to guests who are interested in nude bathing; in fact, no bathing suits are allowed. Separate caves for men and women have walk-in pools hewn into rock. Water flows from three springs at temperatures ranging from 104°F to 112°F. Couples and families may soak together by reserving private tubs (booked by the hour).

Sacred to Native Americans, the hot springs were first developed for prospectors during the local gold rush, and devotees have traveled from around the world to bathe in them ever since.

Chemical analysis of the water has found that it contains trace minerals essential to good health. While no conclusive scientific claims have been made for the waters, experts cite the benefits of bathing for those who suffer from arthritis and rheumatism. Unlike most hot springs, the waters here do not smell of sulfur.

Both day visitors and overnight guests are welcome. On Soda Creek, with a national forest to the west, this bargain getaway is easily reached from Denver.

Indian Springs Resort
Box 1990, Idaho Springs, CO 80452
Tel. 303/567–2191
Fax 303/567–9304

Administration Manager, Jim Maxwell

Season Year-round

Accommodations 74 rooms, single and double. Resort rooms in the original building have only toilet and sink and are furnished with Victorian antiques and brass beds; few modern conveniences. 20 deluxe rooms in the inn with king-size or double beds, color TV, coffeemaker, full modern bath; 20 new lodge rooms have Southwestern furnishings, full bathroom, accommodate those with disabilities.

Rates Rooms $44–$50 for 1 or 2 persons; deluxe inn rooms $55–$59; campsite $14. Bathhouse admission $10. 1 night payable in advance by credit card. MC, V.

Meal Plans No meal plan, but the dining room serves 3 meals daily.

Services and Facilities **Services:** Massage. **Swimming Facilities:** Indoor pool. **Recreation Facilities:** Hiking, horseback riding, fishing, coed Jacuzzi.

In the Area St. Mary's Glacier.

Getting Here *From Denver.* By car, I–70 east to Idaho Springs exit, Hwy. 385.

Special Notes No smoking in pool area or baths. Pool open daily 9 AM–10 PM. Caves open daily 7:30 AM–10:30 PM.

Inn at Zapata Ranch

Nonprogram resort
Spiritual awareness

Colorado
San Luis Valley

Formerly known as the Great Sand Dunes Country Club, The Inn at Zapata Ranch resembles a frontier settlement, with rough-hewn log cabins and 800 head of buffalo roaming the grounds. Don't imagine that you'll have to rough it, however. The native crafts and Western antiques scattered about make the accommodations feel authentic, but all the modern conveniences are present as well. Amenities include a sauna, Jacuzzi, ozone-filtered heated swimming pool, glassed-in gym, and 18-hole golf course.

And you can't beat the scenery: The unique sand dunes, waves of ever-shifting sand lapping at the base of snowcapped mountains, cut a 57-square-mile swath through the valley that is clearly visible from every vantage point on the ranch. The atmosphere is conducive to meditation and contemplation, and you can visit the nearby Zen Center. Children love climbing the sandy slopes, and Nordic skiers often don Arab robes for an outing on a sea of sand.

Rent a mountain bike at the inn to explore the dunes. A visitor center is maintained by the National Park Service. It's like a beach without the ocean.

Inn at Zapata Ranch
5303 Hwy. 150, Mosca, CO 81146
Tel. 719/378–2356 or 800/284–9213

Administration Owner-director, Hisayoshi Ota; general manager, Lyn Brill

Season Mid-Mar.–Jan. 1

Accommodations 15 guest rooms in 3 vintage log buildings. Handmade wooden furniture, some king-size beds. Private bathrooms; no air-conditioning, TV, or telephone. Terry-cloth robes provided.

Rates $75–$180 per room for 2 people, includes full breakfast and afternoon tea. 1-night golf package $190–$250 per person. Add 7.75% tax. AE, D, MC, V.

Meal Plans The restaurant's à la carte menu features local mountain trout and buffalo steaks and burgers (lower in cholesterol and higher in protein than beef). Specialties include Middle Eastern and Italian dishes. Continental breakfast is included daily.

Services and Facilities **Exercise Equipment:** 8-station Universal gym, StairMaster, Lifecycle, Schwinn Air Dyne bike. **Recreation Facilities:** 18-hole golf course, stables for guided 2-hour trail rides, mountain bikes (fee). **Services:** Swedish massage, shiatsu. **Swimming Facilities:** Outdoor pool (heated).

In the Area Rio Grande National Forest, Valley View Hot Springs, Creed (boom town), Haidakhandi Universal Ashram, Tibetan Buddhist Center, Carmelite Hermitage, Taos (skiing, pueblo, Kit Carson Museum).

Getting Here *From Denver.* By car, I–25 south to Hwy. 160, west to Colorado Hwy. 150 to County Rd. 6 east (5 hrs). By air, Continental Express to Alimosa; complimentary pickup at airport with advance request.

The Lodge at Cordillera

Life enhancement
Luxury pampering

Colorado With its small state-of-the-art spa and expansive views of the
Vail Valley Rocky Mountains, the Lodge at Cordillera is an ideal hideaway
for those seeking luxury accommodations along with a workout. Built on 2,000 acres overlooking the ultradeveloped ski
resort of Vail, the lodge is secluded and intimate. There are
just 28 guest rooms in the three-story lodge, and most are quite
large. The architecture is interesting: Walls are made of
stone and stucco and the roof is Chinese slate; downstairs
within the spa, facilities for fitness and body treatments are
the very latest.

The guests (never more than 60 at one time) are an interesting mix of seasoned spa goers, sophisticated travelers, and ex-
acting corporate executives. The staff caters to this upscale
clientele, usually successfully, but still some guests criticize service in the restaurant. The spa lacks camaraderie, but has a
light-filled ambience to relax even the most demanding visitor.

Outdoors are 15 miles of groomed, private trails for hiking,
biking, or cross-country skiing, as well as skating and sledding
areas, a swimming pool, and tennis courts. Activities at the
spa include fitness classes, aerobics, and morning hikes. The
coed exercise room, with an array of high-tech equipment, adjoins a cushion-floored aerobics studio, and atrium. The lap
pool and Jacuzzi offer mountain views. Body treatments feature Decleor products, and there is a complete salon for men
and women. Programs are available for two to five days, or
you can drop in for an afternoon or full-day escape. Plan ahead;
reservations are required.

Adventure-minded guests explore the backcountry on a five-
day hiking program led by staff members several times during the summer. Complete with gourmet picnic lunches and
soothing spa treatments, the itinerary includes parts of the
White River National Forest and the spectacular El Mirador
peak. In winter, ski tours of the area are offered.

After a day on the slopes or in the spa, you're ready for an epi-
curean performance in the Picasso restaurant. First, there are
preliminary samplings in front of a carved limestone fireplace in
the cavernous lobby. The maple-coffered ceilings and plush sofas
might be in the home of an oil-industry executive, which is precisely what managing partner William Clinkenbeard planned
when he retired from Exxon. This is getting away in style.

The Lodge at Cordillera
Box 1110, Edwards, CO 81632
Tel. 970/926–2200 or 800/548–2721
Fax 970/926–2486

Administration General manager, Cary Brent; spa manager, Kail Christensen

Season Year-round

Accommodations 28 rooms and suites, many with fireplace, balcony, or sundeck.
2 queen-size beds or a king-size and a queen-size bed, covered
with European-style duvets. Handcrafted pine furniture,
gemstone-color accents. Spacious bathroom with terry-cloth
robes. TV with VCR, air-conditioning, phones.

Rates $150–$460 per night, single or double occupancy for standard
room; with fireplace, $195–$425. Suites $225–$700 for 2. 2-
night Getaway with spa services and meals, $1,068 for 2. Add
gratuities and tax. Advance payment 1 night. AE, DC, MC, V.

Meal Plans Breakfast buffet included in room rate. Nutritionally balanced menus for guests on a fitness program offer such entrées as salmon fillet wrapped in grape leaves, veal loin Provençale, salad of chicken breast marinated in sherry vinaigrette, and fish of the day steamed with vegetable julienne. Restaurant Picasso has à la carte menus.

Services and Facilities **Exercise Equipment:** 8-unit Keiser Cam II pneumatic weights machines, 3 Trotter treadmills, 3 Lifecycles, StairMaster 4000, PTS Turbo recumbent bike, Precor rowing machine. **Services:** Swedish massage, hydrotherapy, aromatherapy or sea-algae body wrap, body polish, facial, leg-circulation treatment, bust care, waxing, manicure, pedicure, fitness assessment, personal training, endurance testing. **Swimming Facilities:** Indoor 3-lane Olympic (25 m) lap pool, outdoor heated pool. **Spa Facilities:** Separate saunas and steam rooms for men and women, 2 hydrotherapy tubs, lap pool, weights room, aerobics studio, massage rooms. **Recreation Facilities:** 2 outdoor tennis courts, cross-country skiing, ice skating, snowmobiling, dog-sled rides, mountain hiking and biking, bowls, croquet, volleyball, badminton; nearby downhill skiing, golf, trout fishing.

In the Area Vail (cultural center, shopping), Beaver Creek (white-water rafting, skiing), Arrowhead (downhill skiing).

Getting Here *From Denver.* By car, I–70 to Exit 163 at Edwards, Rte. 6 to Squaw Creek Rd., Cordillera Way (2½ hrs). By plane, scheduled flights to Avon Airport (25 mins); private planes land at Eagle County Airport; helicopter landing pad at Cordillera.

The Peaks at Telluride

Kid fitness
Life enhancement
Luxury pampering
Sports conditioning
Weight management

Colorado The $75 million Peaks at Telluride (formerly the Doral Resort)
Telluride opened in 1992 as a luxury retreat catering to both spa lovers and outdoors enthusiasts. Set amid the ski slopes in Southwest Colorado, the 10-story hotel is surrounded by majestic views of the Rocky Mountains and presents a spa program that capitalizes on Southwestern traditions and Native American lore. Options include hiking and trail rides, mountain biking and rock climbing, and skiing. Guests can enjoy morning walks in the crisp mountain air, sunrise yoga in a glass-walled studio, and guided vision quests.

In a hushed enclave atop the hotel's 42,000-square-foot spa and fitness center guests experience the widest range of skin-care treatments and bodywork in the Rockies. The 40-room facility is open to both day visitors and hotel guests. Creams and thermal-mud packs are moisturizing and soothing, especially if you've been on the slopes all day.

The Peaks' Sports Performance package focuses on your sport of choice by working with an exercise physiologist, nutritionist, and the sports psychologist. After an assessment of your current performance level, the team designs an "exercise prescription" to enhance performance, off-season training, and injury prevention. A sport-specific diet is set up for you by the nutritionist. And workouts with a sports performance specialist help you learn to visualize and mentally prepare yourself for performance on the "next level."

The weatherproof facilities include both indoor and outdoor swimming pools, cardiovascular deck with inspiring views, and a weight room packed with the latest Cybex equipment. Rock climbing can be practiced indoors, as well as racquetball, squash, and badminton. For family fun there is KidSpa, a high-tech concept in day camps, and a water slide into the indoor/outdoor swimming pool. Workout clothing is provided in locker rooms.

The Peaks at Telluride

624 Mountain Village Blvd., Box 2702, Telluride, CO 81435
Tel. 970/728–6800 or 800/789–2220; 800/SPA–KIVA for spa
appointments
Fax 970/728–6567; guest fax 970/728–6175

Administration General manager, Kenneth Humes; spa director, Gayle Moeller

Season Year-round

Accommodations 177 rooms surrounding a 4-story atrium. Included are 35 suites with living-dining area. Luxury rooms open to terrace. All have extra-large bathroom with stall shower, Southwestern decor, TV, minibar, air conditioning, 2 phones, hair dryer, magnifying mirror, and full amenities.

Rates 3-day/3-night Alpine Spa Retreat with meals $678–$1,300 single, $996–$1,600 for 2, double occupancy. 5-day/5-night Next Level package with 3 meals daily, $1,733–$3,000 single, $3,000–$4,000 for 2, double occupancy. Daily hotel room tariff for 2 persons in summer, $160–$580; winter $435–$550, suite $235– $850. Other spa packages priced seasonally. 1-day spa packages (no lodging) $120–$400; facility fee $40 for day visitors booking a spa service. Vision Quest excursion $110– $180. Add 12% tax, 15% room gratuity. Deposit of first and last night by credit card. AE, DC, MC, V.

Meal Plans Meals included in some packages. Prepared under specific nutritional guidelines for minimal sodium, fat, and caloric content, the menu might include pizza made with tomatoes, fresh mozzarella, and basil, or a grilled chicken breast sandwich on a whole-wheat pita for lunch. Dinner may be fresh Atlantic salmon, pasta, and mixed salad.

Services and Facilities **Exercise Equipment:** 42-unit Cybex weight training system, 2 Concept 2 rowers, 2 StairMaster Gauntlets, 3 StairMaster 4000PTs, VersaClimber, 6 Precor 9.5 treadmills, 2 NordicTracks, 2 Lifecycle 9500Rs, 4 Lifecycle 9500s, 2 Precor bikes, Pilates, dumbbells (3–100 lbs), free weights. **Services:** Massage (Swedish, shiatsu, aromatherapy, sports), OJA Shirodara therapy, body facial, fango wrap, cellulite treatment, hydrotherapy bath with seaweed; salon for hair, nail, and skin care; personalized training, fitness evaluation, nutrition plan; stress management using biofeedback, respiration, hemi-sync goggles, InnerSea dry float system; kiva with purification bath, sauna, steam room; Ultratone body shaping. **Swimming Facilities:** 25-yard indoor lap pool, heated outdoor/indoor pool. **Recreation Facilities:** 1 indoor racquetball court, 1 squash court, 5 outdoor tennis courts, mountain bike rental, fly-fishing, cross-country and downhill skiing equipment rentals, 18-hole golf course; Preferred Peaks room with climbing wall.

In the Area Crested Butte, Black Canyon National Monument, Million Dollar Hwy. (scenic drive), Mesa Verde National Park (Anasazi cliff dwellings), Durango (historic district, narrow-gauge railroad), Ouray and Pagosa hot springs.

Getting Here *From Denver.* By car, I–70 west to Grand Junction, south on Hwy. 50, west on Hwy. 62, south on Hwy. 145 (7 hrs). By plane, Continental Express and United Express (1 hr). Complimentary shuttle service from Telluride Airport to hotel, and from hotel to town. Car rental, taxi available.

Special Notes KidSpa activities and day care available for half- or full-day ($65–$80). High altitude at hotel (9,490 ft. elevation) will require an initial adjustment. Smoking is permitted in all public areas; some guest rooms and designated tables in dining rooms are no-smoking; no smoking in the spa. All areas are accessible for people with disabilities. Spa hours: daily 6:30 AM–8 PM.

The Vail Athletic Club

Nonprogram resort

Colorado When skiers and hikers come to bustling Vail Village, a replica
Vail of an Alpine town, they get a choice of athletic clubs. All offer spa services and exercise classes, but the best equipped is the Vail Athletic Club, the 3-story modern lodge with indoor swimming pool, squash court, and climbing wall.

The aerobics studio doubles as a basketball court, and from 7:15 AM to noon guests can take step, body sculpting, yoga, and water aerobics. There's more of the same after 5 PM during the winter season. You can also sign up for an hour of cross-training in the fitness room or a consultation with the resident exercise physiologist to help you shape up. To de-stress, there are facials, body scrubs, and mud treatments. Salon services (manicure, pedicure, hair care) and skin treatments with Dr. Hauschka herbal creams, and massage (sports, reflexology, shiatsu) are on an à la carte basis. The facility fee for nonresidents is $20; club residents and members fees are waived.

Vail Athletic Club
352 E. Meadow Dr., Vail, CO 81657
Tel. 970/476–0700 or 800/822–4754
Fax 970/476–7960

Administration General manager, Jeffrey Michaelson; spa director, Lisa de Koster

Accommodations 38 rooms renovated in 1994, including studios with kitchens, and multibedroom penthouses. Some have a fireplace; all are air-conditioned, with TV, phone, full bathroom, down-filled comforters, contemporary furnishings.

Rates Daily tariff per room, single or double occupancy: $275–$735 winter season, $125–$375 spring–fall. Add tax, gratuities. AE, MC, V.

Meal Plans Continental breakfast buffet is complimentary. Terra Bistro specialties include marinated chicken breast with corn salsa and greens, coriander rubbed tuna with tamari vinaigrette, sesame-encrusted salmon, roasted lamb coated with Indian spices, and chickpea tamales. No special spa menu.

Services and Facilities **Exercise Equipment:** Hoggan CamStar weight training equipment, treadmill, 2 StairMasters, 2 Biocycles, 2 Lifecycles, 2 VersaClimbers, rowing machine, NordicTrack ski unit, boxing bags, free weights. **Services:** Sports massage (8–8), bodywork, facial, beauty salon. **Spa Facilities:** Indoor and outdoor Jacuzzis, steam baths, saunas, Swiss showers, lockers. **Swimming Facilities:** Indoor lap pool (20 m), outdoor pool (25 m; summer only). **Recreation Facilities:** 8 outdoor tennis courts, 20-ft indoor climbing wall, racquetball/squash court, skiing.

In the Area Vail Nature Center, Colorado Ski Museum, Dobson Ice Arena (indoor skating), Eagle River (white-water rafting).

Getting Here *From Denver.* By car, I–70 (2 hrs). By plane, commuter flights on Continental, United, and American airlines to Avon Airport (45 mins). Taxi, rental car, limousine available.

Vail Cascade Hotel & Club

Nonprogram resort

Colorado
Cascade Village/
Vail

Upvalley and upscale, the 17-acre Vail Cascade Hotel & Club (formerly the Westin Resort) has a year-round sport and health club that you can enjoy on a daily basis or as part of a ski package. The two-level, 67,000-square-foot Cascade Athletic Club features indoor and outdoor tennis, squash, and racquetball, an indoor running track, workout equipment, bodywork, and over 40 exercise and stretching classes weekly, from yoga to step, 6:15 AM to 6:30 PM daily. Plus there's an outdoor swimming pool with all-weather entrance, whirlpool, herbal steam room, child care center, and juice bar.

Few resorts this side of the Rockies offer such fitness facilities under one roof. Recent additions: an aerobics studio with mountain views and an 11-bike spinning class. Planned: rock climbing wall, ski simulator. Used as a day spa at à la carte prices, it's a bargain. While the club charges a daily admission fee to resort guests ($12), the facilities are open to the public ($16–$25, depending on season). Summer packages, including spa admission and services, are the best value.

Beyond skiing, you can focus on fly-fishing, hiking, biking, riding, and sport shooting. Superbly located on Gore Creek, the resort is close to private sports preserves, where activities are scheduled both for individuals and groups. At the Four Eagle Ranch, a 50-acre spread roamed by prize cattle, you can join a trail ride and participate in a cattle roundup, like in the movie "City Slickers." A few miles down the road, Vail Rod & Gun Club offers instruction for marksmen with sporting clays and fly-fishing on miles of private streams.

You can rent mountain bikes and take off on the path into Vail Village, just over a mile away. Walking is probably your best option, and you can always get a ride back on the hotel's complimentary shuttle bus. Clearly, roughing it is not the style here.

Opened in 1982, the hotel's four-story wings resemble European chateaux and have been decorated in jewel tones as a result of refurbishment in 1994. For skiers, the Cascade Village chairlift provides easy access from the hotel's back door to all of Vail Mountain (3,150-feet incline).

Vail Cascade Hotel & Club

1300 Westhaven Dr., Cascade Village, Vail, CO 81657
Tel. 970/476–7111 or 800/420–2424, Inter-Continental
Hotels 800/327–0200
Fax 970/479–7025

Administration General manager, Dean Manning; Cascade Club manager, Gaye Steinke

Accommodations 300 rooms and suites in 4-story chateau-style lodges. Interiors feature luxurious furniture, wood armoire with TV, air-conditioning, phones, minibar. Some suites and deluxe mountain-view rooms have fireplace, Jacuzzi, and/or sauna. Most rooms have a balcony, with either mountain or courtyard view. Amenities include robes, skin care products.

Rates Daily per room: $200–$500 for double occupancy, suites $300–$1,000. Cascade Club: $12. Summer spa packages $165–$240 single, $225–$340 double occupancy. Add tax, gratuities. Confirmation by credit card. AE, DC, MC, V.

Meal Plans No meal plan. The Heartrate Cafe provides heart-healthy fare such as seasonal salads, Japanese rice noodles, wok-fried vegetables, fruit smoothies, vegetable juice squeezed to order. Alfredo's serves northern Italian and New American cuisine, including heart-healthy items such as grilled mushrooms and spring asparagus, sesame-cured pork loin with salad roll.

Services and Facilities
Exercise Equipment: 17-unit Nautilus circuit, StairMaster 4000, CardioTheater, 2 StairMaster Stepmill, 3 Lifesteps, 3 Tectrix Climb Max, 2 Startrac treadmills, 2 Lifestride 9100 treadmills, 2 Schwinn Air Dyne bikes, UBE ergometer, Concept 2 rower, 6 Lifecycles upright, 4 Lifecycles recumbent, 11 Schwinn spinners, free weights, chip-up and dip machine, speed and heavy bags, indoor running track (⅟₁₅ mile, Mondo flooring). **Services:** Swedish and sports massage, facial, body wrap, body polish, aromatherapy, manicure, pedicure. **Swimming Facilities:** Heated outdoor pool. **Recreation Facilities:** 10 outdoor tennis courts, 4 indoor tennis courts, 4 squash courts, racquetball court, bike rental. Nearby white-water rafting, golf.

In the Area
Gerald Ford Amphitheater (summer concerts), Betty Ford Alpine Gardens, Snowmass Village (crafts), White River National Forest.

Getting Here
From Denver. By car, I–70 to Vail (2 hrs). By plane, commuter flights to Avon Airport on Continental and United Express (25 mins).

Waunita Hot Springs Ranch

Taking the waters

Colorado
Gunnison
National
Forest
This family-oriented dude ranch with a thermal-water swimming pool offers a taste of the Old West but with modern comforts. The 200-acre ranch, family owned and operated since 1962, was among the first settlements in western Colorado. Today horseback riding and outdoor recreation are the main attractions.

Nature lovers and families with children make up most of the 45-person guest list. You can bird-watch, collect rocks, or hike in the national forest. Bring casual clothes, jeans, and boots and discover real Western hospitality.

A log barn houses the riding instruction program, with classes for children and adults. There are corral games and an all-day ride to snowcapped peaks near the Continental Divide. Other activities, scheduled daily, include hayrides and an overnight mountain camp out. Local outfitters offer stream and lake fishing, river floats, and hikes.

Hot mineral water flowing through the swimming pool is cooled to a temperature of 95°F, and is soothing and relaxing after riding or hiking. There are heated dressing rooms, and the area is lit at night.

The weekly program begins on Sunday afternoon and includes riding instruction, trail rides, fishing, and cookouts. As the week progresses, rides become more advanced for those who enjoy this activity, but sightseeing vehicles are available for the others. Anglers need not acquire a fishing license since the private lakes are stocked by the ranch; gear is available from the office.

Meals at the ranch house consist of hearty buffets. A bowl of fresh fruit is always on hand, and you can help yourself to coffee, tea, hot chocolate, or punch. Alcoholic beverages are not permitted, and nondenominational religious services are held on Sunday.

Waunita Hot Springs Ranch
8007 County Rd. 887, Gunnison, CO 81230
Tel. 970/641–1266

Administration	Manager, Junelle Pringle
Season	June–Sept.
Accommodations	22 rooms in the ranch house and a guest lodge, 4 2-room units, all with private bath, wood paneling, leather chair. TV in the library. Thermal-water heating system. Queen-size beds. Laundry facility.
Rates	$990 a week per person, double occupancy, $1,050 single; children's rates on request. $150 deposit per person. No credit cards.
Meal Plans	3 meals daily, buffet style. Cookouts and steak-fry dinners. Home-cooked food to suit any diet. Barbecued chicken and grilled trout specialties.
Services and Facilities	**Swimming Facilities:** 90-ft outdoor pool. **Recreation Facilities:** Hiking, horseshoes, Ping-Pong, corral games, fishing, softball, volleyball. **Evening Programs:** Country-Western Music Hall, movies.
In the Area	Cookout rides, overnight camp out; river raft trip, mountain rides, Jeep trips offered by local outfitters; Continental Divide, ghost towns, mining relics.
Getting Here	*From Denver.* By car, Hwy. 285 to Salida, Hwy. 50 to Doyleville, County Rd. 887 (3 hrs). By air, Continental Express and United Express (40 mins). Complimentary pickup at Gunnison Airport.
Special Notes	No smoking indoors.

Wiesbaden Hot Springs Spa & Lodgings

Taking the waters

Colorado
Ouray

Begun as a mountainside motel with mineral-water baths, the family-owned-and-operated Wiesbaden Hot Springs Lodge has become a well-established, full-fledged health resort. Its facilities include an exercise room with video monitors but no instructors, a weights room, a sauna, and an indoor soaking pool with rock-walled vapor cave.

At an altitude of 7,700 feet, the picturesque old mountain town of Ouray is sheltered from winds by the surrounding forest. Few roads traverse these mountains, which are the source of the Rio Grande and several hot springs. The geothermal water that heats the motel and swimming pool flows from two springs at temperatures of 111°F–134°F. The mineral water is also circulated through soaking pools, avoiding the need for chemical purification.

Scenic canyons in the national forest are a major attraction for hikers. The makings for a picnic can be found in town, a few blocks away (the lodge has no dining room). Dinner at the Bon Ton Restaurant in the nearby St. Elmo Hotel is recommended for a taste of the town's Victorian gold-rush days.

Wiesbaden Hot Springs Spa & Lodgings
625 5th St., Box 349, Ouray, CO 81427
Tel. 970/325–4347 or 970/325–4845
Fax 970/325–4358

Administration	Manager, Linda Wright-Minter
Season	Year-round

Accommodations 20 modern rooms, each with private bath, king-size or twin beds. Private apartments. Glass-walled lounge overlooks the swimming pool and sundeck. Rooms decorated with antiques; some have wood stove. Also, private house with twin beds, bathroom. Complimentary morning coffee and tea.

Rates Daily rate per room for 2 persons $85–$145. Private house for 2, $145. Add 8.2% tax. 1 night payable in advance. MC, V.

Services and Facilities **Exercise Equipment:** Universal weight training gym, stationary bike, NordicTrack. **Services:** Swedish massage, reflexology, acupressure, aromatherapy, facials. **Swimming Facilities:** Outdoor pool. **Recreation Facilities:** Hiking, bike rental.

In the Area Antiques shops, Box Canyon falls, Telluride (historical mining town) film festival, Ute Indian reservation, Durango.

Getting Here *From Denver.* By car, I–70 to Grand Junction, Hwy. 550 (4 hrs). By air, Continental or United Express to Montrose (1 hr). Car rental and taxis available.

Special Notes No smoking on premises. No pets. Thermal pools open daily 8 AM–midnight.

Sheraton Desert Inn Hotel & Casino

Luxury pampering

Nevada **Las Vegas** The combination of a health and fitness club within a country club and casino resort has made the Desert Inn popular. Devoted to exercise and pampering, this well-equipped facility can be enjoyed without entering the casino. Simply pay a daily facilities charge ($18) or sign up for a package plan.

Acquired in 1994 by ITT Sheraton Corporation, they have been undergoing a tremendous expansion. The spa building, however, had not been changed as of press time. A stunning floor-to-ceiling glass-walled rotunda in the men's and women's pavilions leads to therapy pools, hot or cold water plunges, and a big central Jacuzzi. The steam rooms, saunas, and hydrotherapy room are a few steps away.

The water-focused treatments include loofah body scrub with sea salts and herbal wraps. Thalassotherapy consists of varied baths and wraps with seaweed-based products to soothe and cleanse the body.

Given the current building boom along The Strip, there are larger and glitzier spas at The Mirage and MGM Grand resorts. However, the country club atmosphere at Desert Inn will appeal to serious fitness buffs.

Sheraton Desert Inn Hotel & Casino

3145 Las Vegas Blvd. S, Las Vegas, NV 89109
Tel. 702/733–4444 or 800/634–6906, or 800/634–6906 for
room reservations
Fax 702/733–4437

Administration V.P. general manager, John Koster; spa supervisors, Joane Very, Mark Burgett

Season Year-round

Accommodations 821 rooms with a desert theme in original tower. New 1,800-room tower planned, plus 3,000-room Sheraton Desert Kingdom hotel scheduled to open in 1997. Recently refurbished minisuites in the Wimbeldon and Pebble Beach buildings have balconies and are closest to the spa and tennis complex.

Rates $85–$185 a day, single or double; minisuites $135–$215. Spa packages $165 a day, $110 for half-day, plus lodging. Daily facility charge $18 ($10 when services are booked); add 17% gratuities, 7% tax. 1 night payable in advance. AE, DC, MC, V.

Services and Facilities **Exercise Equipment:** 2 Lifecycles, free-weight dumbbells (2–60 lbs), 2 StairMaster 4000, Concept 2 rowing ergometer, 2 Startrac treadmills. **Services:** Massage, paraffin treatment, salt-glow and loofah body scrub, facials, herbal wrap, nail and skin care. **Swimming Facilities:** Lap pool, Olympic-size recreational pool. **Recreation Facilities:** 10 tennis courts, water volleyball, golf. **Evening Programs:** Celebrity shows in casino.

In the Area Waterworld theme park, Lake Mead recreational area and Hoover Dam, the Grand Canyon, Fashion Show shopping mall.

Getting Here *From Los Angeles.* By bus, Greyhound (5 hrs). By car, I–10 (5 hrs). By plane, scheduled flights (1 hr). Limousine on request; rental car, taxi.

Special Notes Ramps and elevators provide access for people with disabilities; all facilities are on 1 level.

Walley's Hot Springs Resort

Taking the waters

Nevada
Genoa A health club and hot mineral baths are the attractions at the charming cluster of Victorian cottages called Walley's Hot Springs Resort. In the foothills of the Sierra Nevada, 12 miles from Lake Tahoe's south shore and 50 miles from Reno, the secluded resort offers a pay-as-you-go treatment plan and free exercise classes.

The main building, a two-story health club, has separate men's and women's sections, each of which contains a sauna, steam bath, and massage rooms. A coed weight-training room is modestly equipped, but there are plans for expansion.

Thermal water is piped from an artesian well into the bathhouse, where it continuously flows through the baths. For an outdoor soak, the 104°F water is collected in six cement pools, where it is cooled for the swimming pool.

Walley's Hot Springs Resort
2001 Foothill La., Box 26, Genoa, NV 89411
Tel. 702/782–8155 or 800/628–7831
Fax 702/782–2103

Administration Owner, Connie Atwood; director, Katherine Vanderbrake

Season Year-round

Accommodations 5 private cabins, 1 with queen-size bed, others with 2 double beds. Private baths, country antiques, turn-of-the-century ambience. All units have TV, telephone, and air-conditioning.

Rates $92.65–$114.45 per day for 2. Tax included; gratuities optional. Deposit: 1 night payable in advance. AE, MC, V.

Services and Facilities **Exercise Equipment:** 7-station Universal weight training gym, treadmill, StairMaster, NordicTrack, free weights, stationary bikes. **Services:** Massage. **Swimming Facilities:** Outdoor pool. **Spa Facilities:** Indoor and outdoor mineral-water pools. **Recreation Facilities:** 2 tennis courts; downhill and cross-country skiing nearby. **Evening Programs:** 2 exercise classes weekly.

In the Area Lake Tahoe resorts and casinos, Reno casinos, historic Carson City.

Getting Here *From Reno.* By car, Hwy. 395 south to Genoa, Genoa La. to Foothill La. (1 hr). By bus, Greyhound to Gardnerville (45 mins). Rental car, taxi available.

Special Notes Limited access for people with disabilities. Children under 12 not permitted in the health club. No smoking in the health club.

Ten Thousand Waves

Taking the waters

New Mexico Perched on a hill overlooking Santa Fe and the spectacular *Santa Fe* Sangre de Cristo Mountains, Ten Thousand Waves brings a bit of Japan to the Southwest.

From the corral-style parking lot you climb a steep path through fragrant cedars, piñon pines, and juniper bushes to the spa and 5-room guest lodge.

Although dozens of people can be soaking in the communal pool, a serene hush pervades the crisp desert air, especially at night.

Sybaritic rather than fitness-oriented, your retreat is planned from an esoteric menu: massage choices include Ayurvedic (hot herbal oils and calamus root powder), deep-tissue, shiatsu, or watsu under a waterfall.

Most bodywork is in breezy, cedar-paneled rooms; options include group sessions and rooms for couples. Soaking tubs are open-air, refilled after every use. Only the lack of thermal mineral spring water separates you from an authentic Japanese *onsen* bath.

Clad in a cotton kimono and sandals issued at check-in, you follow paths from the pools to your room at the Houses of the Moon. Furnished with futons and beds, most rooms accommodate up to 4 persons; one has tatami-mat floor in the style of a Japanese country inn. All are equipped with a fireplace for chilly nights.

Privacy comes with 9 tubs reserved by the hour; some are small and wooden, others accommodate groups. Sheltered from the sun, the tiled Imperial Ofuro holds 10 people and has private bathroom and changing area plus two balconies. The Waterfall has a natural rock deck, warm tub, cold plunge, and holds up to 12 people. New Kojiro has a pebble bottom. All have access to saunas, a steam room, and cold plunge pools. The communal tub is reserved for women only twice daily (except Tuesday), at noon and 5:30 PM; bathing suits are optional at all times.

Cleanliness of the bathhouse and baths is stressed, as the hot tubs are equipped with purification systems using ozone and ultraviolet light rather than chlorine. Forget inhibitions about nudity. The resort's laid-back atmosphere attracts a large number of gay patrons.

Twenty minutes from Santa Fe restaurants, museums, and seasonal attractions, this is a place to meditate and de-stress naturally.

Ten Thousand Waves
Hyde Park Rd., Box 10200, Santa Fe, NM 87504
Tel. 505/982–9304
Fax 505/989–5077

Administration Managing director, Duke Klauck

Season Year-round

Accommodations	5 small suites in adobe-style inn, surrounded by lantern-lit garden. Furnished sparely with queen-size futon bed, sofa bed, Japanese accents. All have private bathroom. No air-conditioning, TV, phone.
Rates	Accommodations without meals, single or double occupancy: $125–$155 per night; additional persons $10 each. Spa packages $100–$120. Bath-only $12–$23 per person. Add tax, gratuities; high-season rates July–Oct. D, MC, V.
Services and Facilities	**Exercise Equipment:** None. **Services:** Massage, watsu, acupuncture, facials, herbal wrap, salt-glow scrub, East Indian cleansing. **Swimming Facilities:** None. **Recreation Facilities:** Hiking trails, nearby downhill skiing, horseback riding.
In The Area	Palace of the Governors (museum of Native American art and history), Mission of San Miguel, St. Francis Cathedral, Loretto Chapel, Taos (Indian Pueblo), Ojo Caliente Mineral Springs, Georgia O'Keeffe house/museum, International Folk Art Museum. Santa Fe Opera (open-air) June 25–mid-Aug.
Special Notes	No smoking inside buildings. Facilities are accessible for people with disabilities. Discount for tubs with New Mexico driver's license, persons 65 and older, children. Last baths Sun.–Thurs. 9:30 PM, Fri.–Sat 11 PM.
Getting Here	*From Santa Fe.* By car, Washington Ave. to Artist Rd., Hyde Park Rd. (20 mins). Taxi, rental car available.

Truth or Consequences

Taking the waters

New Mexico
Truth or Consequences

Many consider the town of Truth or Consequences (named for the popular 1950s radio show) the bargain basement of health spas. Spring water is channeled to bathhouses and guest lodges along Broadway, the main drag, and the adjoining streets. Some properties offer little more than a tub, and most do not accept credit cards, but you also pay blue-light special rates: A 20-minute soak in unchlorinated 110°F mineral water typically costs $5, a 60-minute massage with hand-held massager costs $35.

Naturopathic treatments are offered at some of the older establishments, but a massage is the principal therapy after bathing. Water sports in mile-long Elephant Butte Lake just outside town, hiking, and tubing on the Rio Grande are mentioned in Chamber of Commerce publications. What is not mentioned, however, is the run-down appearance of the town and its once famous baths. Yet local operators say the area is picking up, and there are newer motels on the main road.

At the **Artesia** (312 Marr St., tel. 505/894–2684; open daily 8–8), sunken tubs in three private massage rooms are sanitized and filled with fresh, hot mineral water after each use. The **Indian Springs** (200 Pershing St., tel. 505/894–3823) rely on nature for water circulation, creating a potential for algae buildup.

Bathers at **Ye Olde Hot Springs Bath Haus** (Pershing and Austin Sts., no phone) can exercise in two big pools equipped with metal support bars (for people with disabilities), or soak in three private pools at water temperatures varying from 107°F to 110°F. The **Charles Motel,** in town, has separate facilities for men and women, each with sauna, steam bath, and four individual tubs.

Truth or Consequences
Chamber of Commerce, Drawer 31, Truth or Consequences, NM 87901
Tel. 505/894–3536

Season Year-round

Accommodations Standard motels on the highway, without mineral baths, include Super 8 and the Best Western Motel. Rooms are available in town at the Charles Motel (tel. 505/894–7154).

Rates $49 per room for 2 at the Charles Motel. At Best Western Hot Springs Inn rooms cost $55–$65 for 2. Confirmation by credit card. AE, MC, V.

Services and Facilities **Swimming Facilities:** Nearby lake. **Recreation Facilities:** Hiking, tubing.

Getting Here *From Albuquerque.* By car, I–25 north (2½ hrs).

Cliff Lodge at Snowbird

Luxury pampering
Sports conditioning

Utah
Little Cottonwood Canyon

Alpine views from a penthouse spa, mountaineering courses, and 1,900 acres of groomed ski slopes are the attractions at the sports-oriented Cliff Lodge. Set in Utah's scenic Wasatch Mountains near Salt Lake City, the 11-story lodge hosts university and corporate groups for Life Enrichment workshops, which will be open to the public under a new program.

The Mountaineering Center complements the spa-and-ski program with rock-climbing classes, overnight backpacking trips, bike tours, and guided treks to the peaks of the national forest. Open from July through mid-October, the center attracts outdoors people and climbers of all achievement levels. For golfers, there is helicopter service to the courses in nearby Wasatch National Park and at Jeremy Ranch. Skiers can also be whisked up to powder snow conditions on upper slopes.

The active, youthful vacationers here get into shape at the two-story fitness center on the top floors of the hotel. Sport-specific training, as well as bodywork, are available in the spa on an à la carte basis. There are saunas and steam rooms for men and women and private treatment rooms for sophisticated therapies, such as the French Phytomer process of cleansing and toning the bust with marine products. A skin treatment for the back, popular with men, uses steam, a prep scrub, a Phytomer marine peel, and massage cream to deep-cleanse the pores and moisturize the skin. Beyond the reception area on the 9th floor are 12 cubicles for massages, herbal wraps, and hydrotherapy, a beauty salon with stunning views of the canyon, and locker rooms. Upstairs is the aerobics studio, cardiovascular and weight training rooms, and access to the outdoor swimming pool and whirlpool.

There's plenty for children to do while their parents exercise or pamper themselves. Special skiing (children's lift tickets are free when accompanied by adults) and tennis training are offered for children 5 and older, and kids stay free in their parents' room.

Another spa option is the Canyon Racquet Club, a tennis and fitness complex 10 miles from the ski area. Squash, racquetball, and tennis, plus weight training, cardiovascular exercise, and an Olympic-size pool, are open to guests. Arrangements can be made at the Activities Center near the lodge.

With preparations for the 1998 Winter Olympic Games, this will be a busy area.

Cliff Lodge at Snowbird

Little Cottonwood Canyon Rd., Snowbird, UT 84092
Tel. 801/742–2222 or 800/453–3000
Fax 801/742–3300

Administration Manager, Jack Cole; spa manager, Diana Alexander

Season Year-round

Accommodations 532 rooms and suites with mountain views and/or balconies that open onto the 11-story atrium. Luxury furnishings and baths, king-size beds, cable TV, full service.

Rates Standard rooms $110–$209 for 2 persons per day, deluxe bedroom $160–$309; dormitory beds $32–$53. No spa packages. Mountaineering Center activities charged separately. Deposit: 1 night's rate in summer, 2 nights' rate during winter season. AE, DC, MC, V.

Meal Plans The Aerie's low-fat, low-cholesterol offerings may include vegetarian lasagna or pizza, grilled salmon, broiled chicken, luncheon salads, chicken teriyaki, meatless chili. The Spa Cafe serves fruit smoothies, high-fiber breakfast, and lunch.

Services and Facilities **Exercise Equipment:** 12 Keiser Cam III pneumatic weight-resistance units, Lifecycles, Bodyguard 900 bikes, 2 StairMasters, rowing machine, 2 Trotter treadmills, aerobics studio with suspended wood floor. **Services:** Massage, hydrotherapy, herbal wrap, parafango wrap, Phytomer deep-cleansing treatments, manicure, pedicure, facial, hairstyling. Daily classes in aerobics and stretching. Stress-management course (additional fee). **Swimming Facilities:** Outdoor lap pool, Olympic-size indoor pool. **Recreation Facilities:** 23 tennis courts (10 indoor), 2 squash courts, 2 basketball courts, hiking, skiing, rock climbing, mountain bike rental. Golf and horseback riding nearby. **Evening Programs:** Outdoor adventure films and talks.

In the Area Hidden Peak Tramway; Salt Lake City sports and entertainment centers, Mormon Tabernacle, mineral springs at Heber City, historic Alta (19th-century silver mine).

Getting Here *From Salt Lake City.* By bus, Utah Transit Authority scheduled service from city terminal and airport during winter season (45 mins). By car, I–75, I–80, Rte. 210 to Little Cottonwood Canyon (40 mins). Free pickup on arrival and departure at Salt Lake City airport with package plans. Also, Canyon Transportation (tel. 800/255–1841) provides van service for $32 round-trip. Limousine, taxi, rental car available. Resort parking; valet service and indoor parking at the lodge only.

Special Notes Ski-training course for people with disabilities. Ski and tennis instruction, day-care center for children. No smoking in the spa, the 9th-floor guest rooms, or designated areas of the dining room. Spa facilities accessible to people with disabilities.

Green Valley Spa & Tennis Resort

Kid fitness
Luxury pampering
Nutrition and diet
Vibrant maturity
Weight management

Utah
St. George Discovering a full-service spa along with a concentrated weight-loss and fitness program in the dry desert of southern Utah is reason for many to spend a week or two at the Green Valley resort. Guests can also enjoy full resort facilities plus sophisticated bodywork with locally formulated herbal, mud, and mineral products used exclusively in the spa. There is a relaxation

center, a quiet place to read, nap, and enjoy the view of the herb garden, with wrought-iron tables and a splashing fountain, where guests sunbathe. A certain color will be used to activate the senses each day; for instance, a red day will surround you with red flowers, red-tinted baths, even red dishes. Native American healing traditions are integrated into treatments and services.

The one-week Spa Aerobics program (with bodywork and pampering services), which starts every Saturday, offers you a choice of two electives: hiking or tennis. Beginning with an introduction to how the body's weight-regulating mechanism works, your learning experiences include trips to restaurants and supermarkets, cooking workshops, and discussion groups. The nutritious high-energy meals are a revelation regarding the variety and quantity of food that one can enjoy while losing weight. Even exchanging tips with the Green Valley cook in a dining room–cum–demo kitchen is encouraged.

The fitness training emphasizes correct posture and body movements, shaping and contouring as weight is lost. With a maximum of 52 participants per week, the staff physiologists and nutritionists can maintain personal interaction with guests. Begin your day with the 7 AM group hike, covering up to 8 miles over trails in nearby state parks. Then choose exercise classes, scheduled all day 9:30 AM to 5:30 PM. Tennis lessons can be scheduled instead of treatments; the resort is home to Vic Braden's Tennis College.

Set amid palm-fringed condominiums, the modern spa building is an oasis of health and beauty. Filled with Native American and Southwestern art, the 25,000-square-foot spa draws on indigenous healing traditions and New Age experiences. Colors set the mood, changing daily. Red, you learn, affects a deep spiritual connection to the physical body. Relax in a private Jacuzzi surrounded by lush greenery, brightly lit red candles, and vases of red roses; follow up with a massage or facial. Among specialties are treatments with volcanic clay and herbs.

Hiking amid sandstone ravines, volcanic and red-rock canyons, you come upon 1,000-year-old petroglyphs left by Anasazi Indians. Guided by staffers and a naturalist, these daily outings include a trip by van to Zion National Park, taking in vistas from atop cliffs, where the dry desert air is scented by fresh sage. Camaraderie develops quickly among hikers, some opting for a 12-mile challenge, others taking a beginners' course.

The 10-year-old spa reflects personal attention from the resident owners. They have added a comfortable living room with lofty white arched ceiling, white couches, and rust and blue Navajo rugs. You are housed in a fully furnished apartment rather than standard rooms. While the ambience is upscale, the Native American programs connect you to this special place.

Green Valley Spa & Tennis Resort
1515 W. Canyon View Dr., St. George, UT 84770
Tel. 801/628–8060 or 800/237–1068
Fax 801/673–4084

Administration Owner-director, Alan Coombs; spa director, Carole Coombs; fitness director, Linda Davis

Season Year-round

Accommodations Each guest or couple is housed in one of 50 furnished condominium apartments with spacious contemporary interiors with one or two bedrooms, living room, dining counter, kitchen, private bath, balcony. Some have a Jacuzzi on the deck; all have TV, phone, air-conditioning. Amenities include terry-cloth robe, slippers, sweat suit.

Rates 8-day/7-night Spa Aerobics week $2,350 per person, double oc-
cupancy (Sat.–Sat.), single occupancy add $238. Daily rate is
$350 per night. Tax and gratuities included. Deposit: $500. AE,
D, MC, V.

Meal Plans 3 meals daily. Low-fat diet, no sugar or salt. Breakfast is scrambled eggs, buttermilk biscuits, turkey sausage, assorted fresh
fruit. Lunches include soup, salad, steamed vegetables, a tuna-
salad sandwich on whole-grain bread or turkey salad on pita.
Typical dinner entrées are baked salmon or orange roughy,
stuffed Cornish game hen, beef kebab, or chicken barbecue.
Desserts include banana pudding and apple strudel.

Services and Facilities **Exercise Equipment:** 2 Lifecycle recumbent bikes, 2 Lifestep-
pers, 1 Lifecycle, 13 CamStar weight training units, 2 Trotter
treadmills, 7 punching bags, weight bars (20–55 lbs) with cable
system, Preacher bicep curl bar, free weights (3–60 lbs). **Services:** Swedish massage, hand and foot reflexology, mud and
herbal wraps, facials, powdered-pearl body rub; hair, nail, and
skin care. Personal counseling on tension control, wardrobe,
coloring and makeup, skin care, shopping. **Swimming Facilities:**
Outdoor and enclosed pools, diving pool. **Spa Facilities:** Steam
rooms, saunas, whirlpool. **Recreation Facilities:** 15 outdoor and
4 indoor tennis courts, volleyball, shuffleboard, basketball,
lawn chess, 9-hole executive golf course, putting green, bowling alley, roller skating, 2 racquetball courts. Rental of bicycles. Horseback riding, downhill skiing, water sports nearby.
Evening Programs: Talks on health and nutrition.

In the Area Zion National Park excursion with picnic lunch, Vic Braden
Tennis College (on site), North Rim of Grand Canyon, Snow
Canyon sandstone cliffs, Bryce Canyon National Park, Nevada
casinos, country and western entertainment, river rafting.

Getting Here *From Las Vegas.* By car, I–15 to St. George (2 hrs). By plane,
commuter flights on Skywest and Delta (40 mins). Free pickup
from and return to St. George airport. Van service from/to Las
Vegas on St. George Shuttle (tel. 801/628–8320) costs $30 each
way. Car rental, taxi available.

Special Notes Elevators, oversize bathroom facilities for people with disabilities. Summer fitness/health and tennis camp for children,
with Vic Braden Tennis College. No smoking. Bring a medical
release from your doctor, casual workout clothing, walking
shoes.

The Last Resort

**Nutrition and diet
Spiritual awareness**

Utah
Sunset Cliffs

Yoga studies, meditation, and nature walks are the corner-
stone programs for rejuvenating the body and the mind at the
Last Resort, an informal mountain retreat. In southern Utah
about 40 miles southwest of Bryce Canyon, the two-story log
building 8,700 feet above sea level boasts spectacular mountain views and accommodates up to 10 guests.

Marked trails attract hikers and backpackers in summer and
autumn. In winter the light powder snow makes ideal conditions for cross-country skiing.

Directors Pujari and Abhilasha offer a multidimensional experience, a seven-day retreat that includes Iyengar yoga
workouts twice a day, hiking, and a soak at nearby hot springs.
During year-end retreats, total silence is observed for 10 days.
A five-day natural-foods cooking course in August teaches
meal planning and preparation of tofu, tempeh, whole grains,

beans, fresh vegetables, and other healthy ingredients. Spring is celebrated with a 10-day detoxification and spring cleaning of the body.

The Last Resort
Box 6226, Cedar City, UT 84720
Tel. 801/682–2289 or 619/283–8663

Administration Program directors, Pujari and Abhilasha (Ed and Barbara Keays)

Season Year-round, with retreats scheduled in June, July–Aug., Dec., and Jan.

Accommodations Dormitory beds and private rooms for couples. Simple furnishings, communal bath.

Rates 7-day yoga retreat $695 per person, 5-day cooking course $495, 10-day spring retreat $795; year-end Vipassana meditation, 5 days $295, 10 days $495.

Meal Plans Vegetarian meals prepared by a nutritionist, tea, and juice come with retreats. Menus include steamed fresh vegetables, whole grains, rice, casseroles.

Services and Facilities **Swimming Facilities:** Nearby lakes. **Spa Facilities:** Mineral baths at Pah Tempe Hot Springs. **Recreation Facilities:** Hiking, cross-country skiing. **Programs:** Meditation instruction, rebirthing, Iyengar yoga classes, lectures on lifestyle.

In the Area Bryce Canyon National Park, North Rim of the Grand Canyon, Zion National Park, Cedar Peaks, Shakespeare Festival in Cedar City (mid-July–Aug.).

Getting Here *From Las Vegas.* By car, I–15 to Cedar City, Rte. 14 (3 hrs).

Special Notes No smoking.

National Institute of Fitness

Nutrition and diet
Weight management

Utah
Snow Canyon

Learning time management as well as weight control is the basis of intensive training at the National Institute of Fitness. Founded in 1982 by physiologist Marc Sorenson and his wife Vicki, the no-frills fitness and weight-loss program has been maintained while new and upscale accommodations were added by Franklin Quest Co., owners of the Institute since 1995.

Classes in nutrition, movement, and stress management are combined with a take-home outline of your plan for health and fitness. But the prime attraction is exploring some of the most glorious canyon country in the West. Often called the "Walking Spa," the program includes training with certified coaches on hikes as well as in aerobics classes. The 150–200 participants are divided into groups classified C (most fit), B (average), A (moderate), and Special A (limited fitness).

Vigorous exercise, rather than pampering or bodywork, is central here. On arrival participants are given a fitness evaluation that includes a cardiovascular endurance test. The results-oriented program is designed to get you off diets and drugs and to restore normal cholesterol and sugar levels. Guests with serious weight problems stay a month or more, often shedding 50 pounds. Bodywork and personal services are optional extras.

The program moves along at a fast pace, and instructors concentrate on teaching techniques that guests can practice on their own at home. The indoor facilities include 3 large aerobics studios, weights room, racquetball court, and covered swimming pool for laps and aquaerobics. The Megahealth building, added in 1992, has a 200-seat dining room, lecture hall, and 12 treatment rooms. Choice accommodations are in 2-story lodges, five completed in 1995; budget-priced rooms are in the original dome-shaped structures. Spa services are optional; they are not included in program price.

In the southwest corner of Utah, close to St. George and its active retirement community, as well as national parks, the Institute's outdoor-oriented program is popular with people jump-starting a fitness program or seeking a refresher. At daybreak, before breakfast, guided groups hike more than 30 trails in Snow Canyon State Park, just outside the Institute complex. Along the way are lava caves, ancient Indian petroglyphs, and a variety of desert plants. Mild in winter, the desert climate is dry and invigorating. Camaraderie comes naturally.

National Institute of Fitness
202 N. Snow Canyon Rd., Box 938, Ivins, UT 84738
Tel. 801/673-4905 or 801/628-4338
Fax 801/673-1363

Administration Founder-director, Dr. Marc Sorenson; program director, David Beck

Season Year-round; programs begin on Mon.

Accommodations 227 air-conditioned rooms with 1–4 beds each. Modern furnishings, private bath. Semiprivate rooms have partitions, single beds. New suites and deluxe double rooms are in 2-story lodges. Daily maid service weekdays. No TV or phone.

Rates 1-week program $939–$1,094 per person double occupancy, $1,334–$1,519 single. $100 (nonrefundable) payable in advance. Add gratuities and tax. MC, V.

Meal Plans 3 meals served daily (included in Program fee). Low-fat weight-loss diet, nutritionally balanced, controlled portions. Low in salt, fat, sugar; high in complex carbohydrates. Pritikin-style entrées for lunch are turkey loaf, tuna sandwich on wheat bread; dinner includes vegetarian lasagna, pizza with turkey. Salad bar daily.

Services and Facilities **Exercise Equipment:** 11-station weight training gym, 2 PT 6000 and 6 PG 4000 StairMasters, 6 Cateye Exercycles, 14 Challenger treadmills, NordicTrack cross-country unit, 3 Enduricisers, free weights, Rebounders. **Services:** Massage, aromatherapy, facials, loofah body scrub; hair, nail, and skin care; fitness evaluation; complimentary makeup session and exercise instruction. **Swimming Facilities:** Heated indoor pool. **Recreation Facilities:** Tennis court, indoor racquetball court; horseback riding nearby. **Evening Programs:** Workshops on nutrition and health; line dancing, yoga, cooking class.

In the Area Las Vegas, Salt Lake City, Zion National Park, Cinemax Theater, Tuacahn Amphitheater (summer concerts, musical drama).

Getting Here *From Las Vegas.* By car, I–15 to St. George, Bluff St. north to Santa Clara, Sunset Blvd. to Ivins (2 hrs). By plane, commuter flights on Skywest Airlines or Delta Commuter to St. George (45 mins). Free pickup from and return to St. George Airport. Van service from/to Vegas available on St. George Shuttle (tel. 801/628-8320) for $30 each way. Taxi, rental car available.

Special Notes No smoking. Remember to bring exercise clothing, aerobic and hiking shoes. Spa open daily 6 AM–9:30 PM.

Pah Tempe Hot Springs Resort

Nonprogram resort
Taking the waters

Utah
Hurricane

Deep in a canyon near Zion National Park, hot springs gush from the muddy bottom of the Virgin River to fill a series of pools cut into the rocks surrounding the Pah Tempe resort. Here, bathing is a sybaritic experience for body, mind, and spirit, and conversation comes easily among guests soaking in the warm, sulfur-rich waters or sinking into the mud for a natural body scrub. Swimsuits are required.

Pah Tempe operates as a bed-and-breakfast lodge. The ambience is completely informal, and the inexpensive lodging and camping sites draw many European visitors.

Bodywork is available by prearrangement, and yoga, water aerobics, and health-related workshops are scheduled from time to time; inquiries and advance planning are necessary for those who want to participate. Travelers who are not staying at the lodge may use the pools and showers for a daily fee ($10). Guides for nature walks, bird-watching, and local archaeology are available to introduce guests to the colorful desert and mountain terrain.

Sacred to Paiute Native Americans, the river and its canyon exude healing energy.

Pah Tempe Hot Springs Resort
825 N. 800 East; Box 35–4,
Hurricane, UT 84737
Tel. 801/635–2879
Fax 801/635–2353

Administration Managing partner, Ken Anderson

Season Year-round

Accommodations 4 rooms in the lodge accommodate 14 guests; all are furnished simply (no TV or air-conditioning), all have double bed, some have private bath, fireplace. One cabin for 2. Private lodge (capacity 10) for groups. RV and campsites. No maid service.

Rates $45 per day single, $55–$65 per day for 2, including breakfast; private cabin $65 for 2. Additional person $15, children (age 5 or under) $10. Senior-citizen (63 and older) rates available. RV and camping, $20 single, $10 additional adult. Rates include use of pools, facilities, tax. 1-day pass $10, half-price Wed. and Sat. MC, V.

Meal Plans Vegetarian breakfast included with lodging. Other meals can be picnics or at restaurants in Zion National Park.

Services and Facilities **Services:** Massage, facials, scalp and hair treatments by appointment. **Swimming Facilities:** Outdoor concrete pool with 95°F thermal water. **Spa Facilities:** Natural rock pools with circulating thermal water (103°F–106°F), 2 indoor Jacuzzis.

In the Area Zion National Park, Dixie College Amphitheater, Bit 'n Spur Café for country music, Chums factory outlet for sportswear, St. George Mormon Temple (c. 1877).

Getting Here *From St. George.* By car, I–15 to Rte. 9 (exit 16) via Hurricane; entry road at Virgin River Bridge (25 mins).

Special Notes No smoking in pool areas or restaurant. Bring old swimwear, water sox or old sneakers, beach towel, flashlight.

The Northwest

Native Americans believed long ago that the Great Spirit lived at the earth's center and that steaming hot springs produced "big medicine" waters. Rediscovered by a new generation, the hot springs of the Northwest can be enjoyed in settings of great natural beauty or at large new resort developments. One such sacred spot in Oregon is now the popular resort Kah-Nee-Ta, owned and operated by the Confederated Tribes of the Warm Springs. Wyoming has developed Hot Springs State Park on land near Yellowstone National Park purchased from the Shoshone and Arapahoe Indians. The Sol Duc Hot Springs Resort in Olympic National Park, Washington, is another warm watering spot.

Montana's "big sky" country offers the family-oriented Fairmont Hot Springs Resort and the rustic Chico Hot Springs Lodge, along with 39 ski runs and posh dude ranches. The new Lodge at Potosi Hot Springs in the Tobacco Root Mountains of southwest Montana focuses on hiking, healthy food, and hot springs, with modest cabin accommodations. Alaskan hot springs are simply for soaking: In a verdant valley rich with gold-rush lore outside Fairbanks the sulfur sprites of Chena Hot Springs have welcomed homesteaders and "cheechako" travelers since 1905; isolated Tenakee Springs on Baranof Island offers simple accommodations at the Tenakee Hot Springs Lodge (tel. 907/736–2400).

The region's newest destination resort and conference center, Skamania Lodge, has a fitness center overlooking the Columbia River Gorge in Oregon. Welcome to wilderness adventures with workouts and luxury pampering.

Chena Hot Springs Resort

Taking the waters

Alaska
Fairbanks

A soak at the historic Chena Hot Springs Resort near Fairbanks comes accompanied by reminders of pioneer days. Cabins and pools here were built in the early 1900s, when most visitors were gold miners who had traveled by dogsled and on horseback in search of relief from rheumatism and arthritis in the hot springs. Images of the miners still smile from the photographs of the Victorian era that decorate the dining room and lounge.

The old-time character of the resort has not changed, despite recent renovations. The bathhouse has tile floors and showers in the locker rooms, and expansive use of glass walls in the pool area. The hot mineral water that bubbles to the surface at 156°F is cooled to a tolerable 110°F in the soaking pools, 90°F for swimming. Thermal water also heats the lodge rooms and three whirlpools.

The cluster of cabins around the main lodge has the general appearance of a mining camp. The machinery, carts, and tools that the miners once used now dot the gardens between the steaming ponds where the spring waters run into a creek. Moose have been spotted wandering the grounds, and antlers adorn some of the buildings. Ask for a map of the self-guided history/nature walking tour.

The Northwest

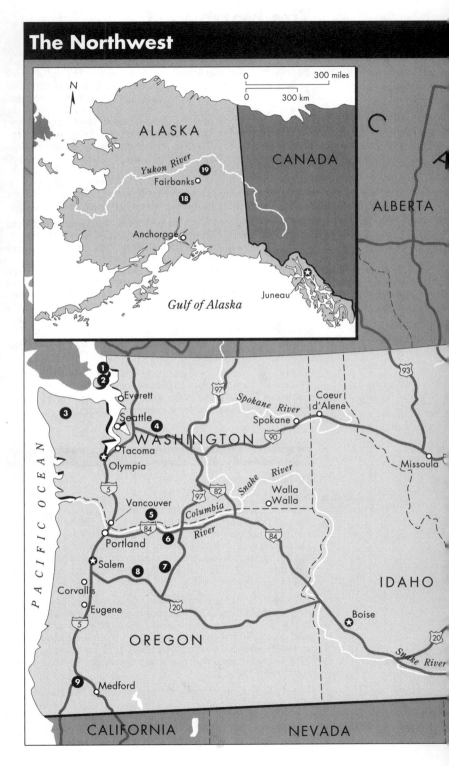

300 miles
300 km

ALASKA

CANADA

ALBERTA

Yukon River
Fairbanks ○ ⑲
⑱
Anchorage ○

Gulf of Alaska

Juneau ★

N

PACIFIC OCEAN

① ②
Everett
97
Spokane River
Coeur d'Alene
Seattle ④
Spokane ○
WASHINGTON
90
③
Tacoma ★
Olympia
5
97   82
Snake River
Walla Walla ○
Missoula ○
93

Vancouver
⑤
Columbia
84
River
⑥
84
Portland
★ Salem
⑧   ⑦
Corvallis ○
Eugene ○
5
20
IDAHO
OREGON
Boise ★
20
Snake River

⑨ ○ Medford

CALIFORNIA   NEVADA

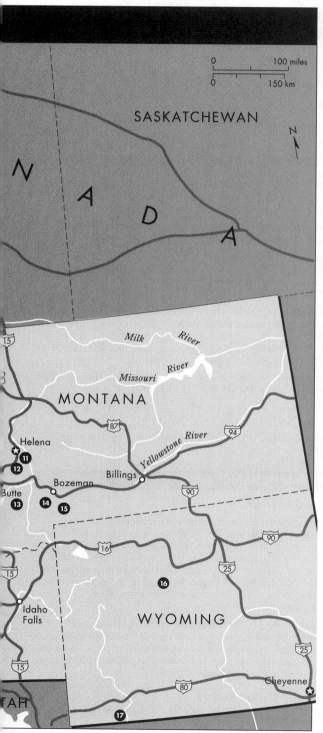

Alaska
Chena Hot Springs
Resort, **19**
McKinley Chalet
Resort, **18**

Montana
Boulder Hot
Springs, **12**
Chico Hot Springs
Lodge, **15**
Fairmont Hot Springs
Resort, **10**
Feathered Pipe
Ranch, **11**
Lodge at Potosi
Hot Springs, **13**
MountainFit, **14**

Oregon
Aesculapia, **9**
Breitenbush Hot
Springs Retreat, **8**
Kah-Nee-Ta Resort, **7**
Skamania Lodge, **6**

Washington
Carson Hot Mineral
Springs Resort, **5**
Doe Bay Village
Resort, **2**
Rosario Resort, **1**
The Salish Lodge, **4**
Sol Duc Hot Springs
Resort, **3**

Wyoming
Antelope Retreat
Center, **17**
Hot Springs State
Park, **16**

A lively crowd from the university in Fairbanks 60 miles down the road comes to ski the nearby slopes and well-marked trails. Don't expect calorie-counted food or any fancy dietetic dishes. Wild blueberry daiquiris are the specialty at the bar.

Chena Hot Springs Resort
57 Chena Hot Springs Rd.
Reservations: Box 73440, Fairbanks, AK 99707
Tel. 907/452–7867
Fax 907/456–3122

Administration	Manager, Kent Walstad
Season	Year-round
Accommodations	44 antiques-furnished lodge rooms, double or single beds, baths private or shared, geothermal hot water, maid service. 7 Trapper Cabins with double and single beds, washbasin, chemical toilet. Some cabins have wood-burning stoves. RV parking/hookup, campsites, laundry, and showers available.
Rates	Lodge rooms $85–$115 per day. Cabins $50–$130 per day for 1–8 persons. AE, DC, MC, V.
Meal Plans	Full menu in historic lodge restaurant; no meal package. Pancakes with berries, hot cereal for breakfast; generous servings of roast beef, ham, roast turkey for lunch and dinner. Fresh produce in season.
Services and Facilities	**Spa Facilities:** 2 indoor whirlpools, swimming pool, outdoor whirlpool. **Recreation Facilities:** Volleyball court, croquet, horseshoe pitch, fishing, hiking, mountain climbing, downhill and cross-country skiing, ice skating, snowmobiling, sledding, dogsled rides, summer horseback riding.
In the Area	Chena River cruise, University of Alaska at Fairbanks Museum (Native cultures, gold rush history).
Getting Here	*From Fairbanks.* By car, Rte. 2 (Steese Hwy.) to Chena Springs Rd. (80 mins). Rental car available.
Special Notes	Limited access for people with disabilities. Pool open 8 AM–10 PM ($8 for nonguests).

McKinley Chalet Resort

Nonprogram resort

Alaska
Denali National Park

Overlooking majestic mountains at a scenic turn in the Nenana River, the McKinley Chalet Resort is a cluster of chalets, rustic cabins, and a modern mountain lodge in an accessible area of the wilderness of Denali National Park. Guests enjoy free use of the only indoor health club and swimming pool this side of Mt. McKinley. Fitness facilities at the resort's Chalet Club include an exercise room with weights, whirlpool, sauna, and an aerobics studio.

Dominated by Mt. McKinley, the Denali experience is a mixture of rugged outdoor treks and guided bus tours. Naturalists and park rangers accompany trips along park roads that are closed to private cars in the summer. River rafting and a scenic float are other possibilities here.

McKinley Chalet Resort
Milepost 239 Parks Hwy. Denali Park, AK 99755
Tel. 907/683–2215
Fax 907/683–2398
Reservations: Box 202516, Anchorage, AK 99520
Tel. 907/279–2653 or 800/276–7234
Fax 907/258–3668

Administration	ARA Resort Management
Season	May–Sept.
Accommodations	288 deluxe 2-room suites in alpine-style chalets, with hotel service. Suites include simply furnished sitting rooms with sofa and reading chair, 2 twin beds (or double with twin), modern bath, wooden balconies and walkways.
Rates	$189.39 for 2 persons, double occupancy, including tax. Daily 7-hour Tundra Wildlife bus tour, $54 per person; 3-hour Denali Natural History tour, $30 per person; rafting $48. Deposit: 1-night's lodging in advance. AE, MC, V.
Meal Plans	À la carte menu offers fresh baked or grilled salmon, salads, poached halibut, roast leg of lamb, pasta, steaks, chicken, pork. For breakfast, home-baked muffins and breads.
Services and Facilities	**Exercise Equipment:** 10-station Universal weight training gym, StairMaster, stationary bikes, rowing machine, free weights. **Services:** Swedish massage. **Swimming Facilities:** Indoor pool. **Recreation Facilities:** River rafting, backcountry hiking. **Evening Programs:** Alaska Cabin Nite buffet $35, children $22.
In the Area	Tundra Wildlife bus tour (6 hrs), air sightseeing, sled-dog demonstration, Vistadome rail excursion to Fairbanks or Anchorage.
Getting Here	*From Anchorage.* By bus, Gray Line of Alaska (5 hrs). By train, McKinley Explorer private car, Alaska Railroad scheduled service daily (6 hrs). By car, Rte. 3 (George Parks Hwy.) to National Park gateway (5 hrs). Free pickup from and return to train station.
Special Notes	Ramps at health club and some lodgings allow access for people with disabilities. Swimming lessons and nature trail hikes for children. No smoking in the Chalet Club, Chalet Center, and designated areas of the dining rooms. Spa open weekdays 11–10, weekends 9 AM–10 PM.

Boulder Hot Springs

Holistic health
Taking the waters

Montana
Boulder

Mineral-spring baths and mountain hikes at the Boulder Hot Springs resort in the foothills of the Elkhorn range of the Rocky Mountains have been an attraction since the early 1800s. Then, in the early 1950s, controversy arose as stories of a radioactive "miracle mine" appeared in the national media.

Operators of the Free Enterprise Radon Mine make no claims of medical benefits. Instead, they point to the documentation of treatments at similar mines near Bad Gastein, Austria, where more than 7,000 patients a year breathe radon under medical supervision.

Those who come to the Free Enterprise mine seeking relief from asthma, arthritis, bursitis, and other forms of chronic, crippling pain bundle up in sweaters and coats and stretch out in deck chairs to breathe the radon gas and drink the radioactive water. Some visitors have claimed to experience improved freedom of movement and relief from pain after a week.

As for the degree of radioactivity involved, the Montana Health Department says that guests are exposed to less than 10% of the maximum legal allowance of radiation to which miners may be exposed. No authoritative medical evaluation of the therapeutic value of the mines has been established.

Three miles from the hotel and 85 feet below ground, the mine is surprisingly dry and comfortable. A large elevator, capable of handling wheelchairs, descends to well-lighted, timbered tunnels equipped with warming lamps. Visits last a maximum of 80 minutes, and a series of up to 32 treatments is suggested. The temperature of the mineral water is 175°F when it reaches ground level. It's pure enough to drink, but it does have the effect of a laxative and diuretic. Call the mine office (tel. 406/225–3383) for more information.

Boulder Hot Springs

Box 1020, Boulder, MT 59632
Tel. 406/225–4339

Administration	Manager, Barbara Reiter
Season	Year-round
Accommodations	7 bedrooms in turn-of-the-century mansion. Furnishings have a well-worn look: heavy wooden pieces, oversize beds, old-fashioned baths. Hostel beds, campsites, RV connections available.
Rates	$40–$60 single, $65–$85 for 2 persons. RV $10. MC, V.
Meal Plans	Breakfast included in lodging rate. Hotel restaurant only serves groups.
Services and Facilities	**Services:** Massage (acupressure, deep-muscle), biofeedback therapy, consultation on nutrition and health. **Swimming Facilities:** Naturally heated outdoor mineral-water pool. **Spa Facilities:** Separate men's and women's bathhouses have hot and cold plunge pools. **Recreation Facilities:** Hiking, fishing, cross-country skiing.
In the Area	Glacier National Park, Lewis and Clark Caverns, Montana State Capitol in Helena, Yellowstone National Park.
Getting Here	*From Helena.* By car, I–15 to Boulder, Hwy. 69 to Boulder Springs (40 mins). Pickup from and return to Helena or Butte (fee). Transportation to the radon mine available (fee). Rental car available.
Special Notes	Limited access for people with disabilities. No smoking in dining room.

Chico Hot Springs Lodge

Taking the waters

Montana
Pray

After a day in the saddle, the prospect of a hot soak makes sore muscles bearable. There's nothing glamorous about the Chico Hot Springs Lodge, but the two hot-springs pools on its 157-acre grounds encourage many visitors to Yellowstone Park to detour. About 30 miles from the park's northern gateway, the resort offers horseback riding and pack trips into the Gallatin National Forest and the Absaroka range of the Rockies.

Surrounded by spectacular mountain scenery, the open-air pools are fed by 110°F untreated mineral water from several springs. Four private areas in the bathhouse have redwood hot tubs large enough for a family of four. Rustic facilities are available for changing; bring a towel if you're not staying at the ranch. The pools are open to the public as well as to registered guests, and as you soak you might even spot deer on the slopes.

Lodging at the ranch includes use of the pools. Construction of a 16-room addition was completed in 1996, providing superior accommodations and 2 suites. Dining options include an outdoor barbecue and homestyle cooking at the lodge.

Chico Hot Springs Lodge
Pray, MT 59065
Tel. 406/333–4933

Administration	Managers, Michael and Eve Art
Season	Year-round
Accommodations	52 rooms in the main lodge, 16 rooms and 2 suites in new wing have full bathroom, contemporary Southwestern furniture. Family-size condominium apartments in A-frame cabins. Lodge rooms have Western furnishings, twin beds, private or shared bath.
Rates	Lodge rooms $45–$79 for 2 persons, double occupancy; new wing $84–$115 for 2 persons per day. 2-bedroom cabin $75–$94 per day. Condominium apartment with kitchen and bath, $119–$295 for 2. Confirmation by credit card. MC, V.
Meal Plans	À la carte lunch menu includes grilled fish, salad, fruit plate; dinner entrées can be roast venison, saddle of lamb, grilled or sautéed trout.
Services and Facilities	**Swimming Facilities:** Mineral-water outdoor pool. **Spa Facilities:** 4 private tubs, 2 outdoor pools, Jacuzzi. **Recreation Facilities:** Boating, trout fishing (private lake), horseback riding; cross-country skiing, snowmobiling, mountain bike rental.
In the Area	Trail rides, Yellowstone National Park, Crow Indian Reservation, river float trips.
Getting Here	*From Bozeman.* By car, I–90 to Hwy. 89 (2 hrs).

Fairmont Hot Springs Resort

Taking the waters

Montana
Anaconda

Big Sky country and big springs come together here. Nestled near the Pintlar Wilderness in an area of boundless views and numerous springs, the Fairmont Hot Springs Resort combines striking modern architecture and Western hospitality. The range of amenities and activities makes it ideal for a family vacation in summer or a skiing holiday in winter.

Native Americans worshiped the "medicine water" of the natural hot springs. The mineral water, 160°F when it surfaces, is treated and cooled for the two Olympic-size swimming pools and the indoor and outdoor soaking pools. Resort facilities include men's and women's steam baths. There are many organized activities to keep children busy.

Accommodations range from rooms at the Fairmont Hot Springs Lodge to a fully furnished condominium apartment.

Fairmont Hot Springs Resort
1500 Fairmont Rd., Anaconda, MT 59711
Tel. 406/797–3241, 800/443–2381, or 800/332–3272 in MT

Administration	Manager, Edward Henrich
Season	Year-round
Accommodations	135 guest rooms in the lodge have double beds, quality furnishings, private bath. Also available: RV hookup, campsites.
Rates	Rooms $74–$89, depending on season; suites $175–$295; condominium $105–$195 for 1 or 2 persons. 1 night payable in advance. AE, D, MC, V.
Meal Plans	Standard American breakfast and dinner in the restaurant.
Services and Facilities	**Swimming Facilities:** Outdoor and indoor Olympic-size pools. **Spa Services:** Massage. **Recreation Facilities:** 2 tennis courts,

18-hole golf course, horseback riding, hayrides, trout fishing, cross-country skiing, sleigh rides.

In the Area Yellowstone National Park, Glacier National Park, Discovery Basin (downhill skiing).

Getting Here *From Butte.* By car, I–90 (15 mins). Complimentary transportation by lodge van. Rental car available.

Special Notes Limited access for people with disabilities. Hayrides, sleigh rides for children. Pools open 24 hours.

Feathered Pipe Ranch

Holistic health
Spiritual awareness

Montana Feathered Pipe Ranch is a magical place that sets spirits soar-
Helena ing, and attracts world-renowned teachers and practitioners. Almost every week from spring to autumn sees an intensive program here on subjects as diverse as astrology, women's studies, shamanism, massage training, and Iyengar yoga. Since 1975 people from many backgrounds, professionals in the healing arts, and novice students have been coming here to gain new ideas and experiences and to attend workshops in yoga and holistic health. The number of participants ranges from 35 to 50, and some families attend with young children.

In the Montana Rockies close to the Continental Divide, the retreat sits on land that was once inhabited by a Native American tribe. Climbing to "sacred rocks" for meditation, you gain a panoramic view of the 110-acre ranch. Miles of hiking trails, a sparkling lake and stream, and the dry, clear air make a heady combination that can generate a tremendous feeling of release.

Log and stone buildings give the impression of a frontier outpost. Beyond the main lodge are Native American teepees and a traditional sweat lodge. Lodging can be in a teepee, Mongolian yurts, cabins (some with bath), and basic tents. A cedar bathhouse holds huge hot tubs, a sauna, and a massage room staffed by professional therapists.

The search for insight is the ranch's principal attraction. Serious concentration is the norm here, with little of the fun-and-fitness holiday atmosphere.

Feathered Pipe Ranch
2409 Colorado Gulch, Helena, MT 59601
Tel. 406/443-0430
Foundation programs: Box 1682, Helena, MT 59624
Tel. 406/442-8196
Fax 406/442-8110

Administration Executive director, India Supera; seminars director, Katherine Smith

Season Late Apr.–Sept.

Accommodations 4 dormitory rooms with bunk beds for 2–6 people in the main lodge. Linens, blankets, towels provided. Tents, yurts, campsites, 6 cabins (3 with bath); teepees sleep 2 persons each.

Rates 1-week program $1,130 in dormitory, $1,280–$1,380 per person in cabin with shared bath. Lodging, meals, instruction included. $300 payable in advance. MC, V.

Meal Plans 3 gourmet vegetarian meals daily, cafeteria style. Organically grown produce. Breakfast includes yogurt, home-baked bread or muffins, fresh fruit; lunch may be tuna-fish salad with pita bread, green salad, or pasta with vegetables; typical dinner selections are baked trout, eggplant and cheese casserole, zucchini baked with tomatoes. Special diets accommodated.

Services and Facilities **Services:** Massage, bodywork. **Swimming Facilities:** Mountain lake. **Recreation Facilities:** Volleyball, hiking. **Evening Programs:** Talks related to study programs; entertainment.

In the Area Helena historical area and shopping; Gates of the Mountains boat tour, hot springs.

Getting Here *From Helena.* By car I–15 (15 mins). Rental car and limo available. Van service ($30 round-trip) is provided by the resort upon request.

Special Notes No smoking indoors. Remember to bring flashlight, sun protection. Lodging only for program participants.

Lodge at Potosi Hot Springs

Sports conditioning
Taking the waters

Montana
Pony Tucked into a canyon in southwest Montana, the new Lodge at Potosi Hot Springs features outdoor adventures and soaks in two natural hot springs. Although horseback riding is available, the daily program orients you to walks and hikes in the Tobacco Root Mountains, which surround the ranch.

Settle into one of the four log cabins that front on South Willow Creek. Each cabin is furnished with modern comforts and a kitchen, and can accommodate up to six people. But most guests elect to have meals family-style in the main lodge, where the chef has won honors as a gourmet.

Hikes in the area range from relatively easy to challenging. A trek to Potosi Peak takes you through mountain meadows to subalpine lakes and rocky ridges overlooking pristine vistas. Each day's outing is planned and escorted by the lodgekeeper, based on the fitness level of participants.

Mountain biking is another option, with equipment provided if you sign up for the all-inclusive rate during summer months. And this being Montana, the fishing is great. The nearby Madison and Jefferson rivers are known for trout, but you may want to try one of the creeks and ponds where private access can be arranged.

After an active day, soaking in the thermal mineral water pools is restorative. Stroll a short distance up a side canyon behind the lodge and you come to natural soaking pools, one 90°F, another 102°F.

The combination of sports and soaks comes at a relatively affordable price.

Lodge at Potosi Hot Springs
Box 688, Pony, MT 59747
Tel. 406/685–3594
Fax (call first) 406/685–3594

Administration Lodgekeepers, Patricia and Dale Trapp

Season Year-round

Accommodations Four log cabins, each with sleeping loft, living room, kitchen, and bathroom. Loft has king- or queen-size bed; sofa bed and river-rock fireplace in living room. Contemporary country furniture, wood stove; no air-conditioning or phone.

Rates $200 per person, double occupancy, including meals and program; without meals or program $250 daily for double occupancy (June–Oct.); lodging and breakfast (Oct.–May) $200 per person, double. Add $50 per additional person in cabin. Tax and gratuities not included. AE, MC, V.

Meal Plans 3 meals daily in optional package during summer months. Prepared to order, served family-style, the seasonal fare includes local fish and game.

Services and Facilities **Services:** Guided hikes and walks, mountain bike trips. **Swimming Facilities:** Pond. **Recreation Facilities:** horseback riding (fee).

In the Area Yellowstone National Park, Grand Teton National Park.

Getting Here *From Bozeman.* By car, I–90 west, Hwy 287 south to Harrison, Pony Rd. (90 mins). Rental car available.

MountainFit

Sports conditioning
Vibrant maturity

Montana The weeklong MountainFit programs in Montana combine
Bozeman strenuous exercise and scenic beauty. (*A River Runs Through It* was filmed nearby.) Hard-core hikers can enjoy challenging treks in Yellowstone National Park, the Absaroka-Beartooth Wilderness, and along the Bridger Range, where the peaks rise above 9,000 feet. Other weeks are designed for persons over 50, and include a variety of outdoor adventures.

Each day's route, selected from among 25 charted hikes, is geared to the average capability of group members (usually guests choose between two destinations), who range in age from 30 to 70 and may include both beginners and experienced hikers. Outfitted with lunch, snacks, and fanny pack, their water bottles refilled and frozen nightly, a group of 6–10 hikers sets off daily with a leader and a guide at the rear. South-central Montana offers forests of tall lodgepole pines, alpine meadows carpeted with rare ferns and bear grass, limestone cliffs with the fossil remains of marine animals, and living deer, moose, mountain goats, elk, bison, golden eagles, and cutthroat trout. Staffers recount local lore and identify plants and wildlife en route.

Safety is a priority: Hikes are registered with park rangers, while the staff carries two-way radio equipment and checks individuals regularly for foot blisters or signs of stress. Transportation to trailheads is provided by van, and the chef prepares a high-fiber lunch for your fanny pack. Bottled water is provided, and you are constantly urged to avoid dehydration.

The six-day Montana Experience includes rock climbing, mountain biking, and horseback riding. Yoga instruction and hiking are major parts of every week, which usually runs from Sunday to Saturday. For hikers over 50, they offer a Big Sky trek in July, and an autumn hiking and fly-fishing week.

Based at either the Gallatin Gateway Inn or an upcountry ranch, you enjoy spa-quality meals specially prepared for the group by local chefs. The inn, opened in 1927 by railroaders, was authentically restored in 1986 (it had been used as an arena for women's mud wrestling) and now offers a heated pool, tennis courts, and a fly-casting pond. The inn's private cottage on the Gallatin River accommodates the hiking group.

Camaraderie develops quickly in this close-knit, small group. Combining awe-inspiring scenery, challenging trails, and outdoor adventure, the program is suited to people of all ages.

MountainFit

Gallatin Gateway Inn, Bozeman, MT 59715
Reservations: Box 6188, Bozeman, MT 59771
Tel. 406/585–3506 or 800/926–5700; inn guest tel.
406/763–4672

Administration Director, Diane Benedict

Season June–Sept.; scheduled weeks

Accommodations 6-room cottage (2 doubles, 4 singles), with brass beds, flowered comforters, and matching curtains; each bedroom has a large, modern bathroom. No air-conditioning, TV, or phone.

Rates $1,795–$2,195 per person in shared room; includes meals, outings. Single supplement $300. Deposit: $300 nonrefundable; balance due 30 days before start of program. AE, MC, V.

Meal Plans Daily menu of 1,200–1,500 calories. Breakfast choices are freshly baked muffins, cereals, fruit, pancakes. Trail lunch consists of cold gazpacho, couscous salad, peanut butter and jelly sandwiches, fruit. A typical dinner, served family style, includes green salad, homemade pasta, salmon poached or baked in phyllo crust, asparagus tips, 4-grain pilaf, and sorbet for dessert.

Services and Facilities **Services:** Massage. **Swimming Facilities:** Outdoor pool. **Recreation Facilities:** 2 tennis courts, Jacuzzi. **Evening Programs:** Lecture-demonstrations, films.

In the Area Lewis & Clark Caverns, Chico Hot Springs Resort, Yellowstone River, Yellowstone and Grand Teton national parks, Museum of the Rockies.

Getting Here *From Bozeman.* Participants' transportation provided on arrival and departure (30 mins). By car, I–90, Hwys. 10/191 (30 mins).

Special Notes No smoking in lodge. Hiking boots required; bathrobe provided. Daily maid service.

Aesculapia

Holistic health
Spiritual awareness

Oregon
Wilderville

Named after the Greek god of healing and ancient dream temples, Aesculapia is a retreat that teaches self-healing. Visitors take part in shamanistic ritual, hike in the woods, or meditate in a sanctuary cabin.

On 80 acres of mountain wilderness in the Siskiyou Mountains of southwest Oregon, Aesculapia fosters the visionary experience of founder-director Graywolf (Fred) Swinney. Dream-healing sessions help participants examine visionary experiences. Among special events scheduled are spring and fall weeks devoted to healing communion, weekend retreats, and a two-week combination of spiritual and outdoor adventure that climaxes with a journey on the Rogue River.

Guided by Graywolf, the wilderness quest begins with 3–4 days of mental and physical training, including a sweat lodge ceremony, drumming, meditation, and discussions of dreams. After a few days on the river, you are challenged by whitewater rapids. There are evening campfires and mornings devoted to sharing dreams before you return to Aesculapia and prepare for the outer world.

Aesculapia
Box 301, Wilderville, OR 97543
Tel. 503/476–0492

Administration Founder-director, Graywolf (Fred) Swinney

Season Year-round

Accommodations Rustic, 4-bedroom house and 4 cabins. Guests bring their own towels, blankets. Campsites and tents available.

Rates 1-week retreat $550, 2-week retreat with Whitewater Wilderness Quest $1,100, 2-day sanctuary $100. 1 night payable in advance. Work-scholarship aid available. No credit cards.

Meal Plans All meals included in retreat price. Vegetarian meals, fresh fruit and produce in season.

Services and Facilities **Services:** Massage, counseling on nutrition and health. **Swimming Facilities:** Lake. **Recreation Facilities:** Hiking. **Evening Programs:** Informal workshops, rituals.

In the Area Ocean beaches, vineyard tours, hot springs, Shakespeare Festival (July–Aug.), Rogue River (white-water rafting), Kalmiopsis Wilderness (hiking).

Getting Here *From Eugene.* By bus, Greyhound to Medford (2 hrs). By car, I–5 south to Grants Pass (90 mins), Hwy. 199. Rental car available.

Breitenbush Hot Springs Retreat

Holistic health
Spiritual awareness
Taking the waters

Oregon
Detroit

The Esalen of the Northwest, the Breitenbush Hot Springs and Retreat is a holistic community for groups and individuals; its rustic cabins cluster on the banks of the Breitenbush River, surrounded by the Willamette National Forest. The daily schedule begins at 7 AM with meditation, then stretching classes. Participation is optional, no charge. Bodywork services at the bathhouse are moderately priced.

The hot mineral waters are a major attraction: Natural springs and artesian wells supply 180°F mineral water for the steam sauna and outdoor pools. At an idyllic spot in the woods, the water flows through four tiled tubs of varying temperatures and a rock-lined pool in the meadow, perfect for a relaxing soak.

Beyond simple, natural pleasures, the community is dedicated to fostering personal health and spiritual growth. Visitors can join daily well-being workshops, rituals and ceremonies in a pyramid-roofed sanctuary and a Native American sweat lodge. Workshops on topics ranging from breathing to botany are scheduled throughout the year.

Cabins are simply furnished, with only a sheet on the bed, and are heated geothermally. Bring your own blankets, sheets, and towels. Nights can get cold during summer, so no air-conditioning is needed.

Breitenbush Hot Springs and Retreat
Box 578, Detroit, OR 97342
Tel. 503/854–3314
Fax 503/854–3819

Administration Manager, Charlotte Carroll

Season Year-round

Accommodations 42 cabins for 2–4 people each, some with bath and toilet; no air-conditioning, TV, or telephone. Sheets and towels can be rented. 20 tents with mattresses, some bare campsites.

Rates $50–$70 a day in shared room includes meals. Private cabin with bathroom $85–$90. Tent $35–$40, campsite $30–$35 with meals. 1 night payable in advance. MC, V.

Meal Plans Lodging includes 3 ovo-lacto vegetarian meals. Breakfast is granola, hot mixed-grain cereal, yogurt, fruit, and home-baked wheat breads. Lunch can be a salad with sprouts or tuna fish, vegetarian pizza. Dinner entrées may include lasagna, Mexican casserole, or vegetarian pizza. Special diets accommodated.

Services and Facilities **Services:** Massage, hydrotherapy, aromatherapy, Reiki, Cranio-Sacral therapy, Lomi-Lomi, Thai massage, emotional release bodywork, herbal wrap. Counseling on health and healing. **Swimming Facilities:** Outdoor, glacial river. **Recreation Facilities:** Hiking, cross-country skiing. **Evening Programs:** Workshops on health and nutrition.

In the Area Native American cultural center at Warm Springs Indian Reservation, Mt. Hood National Forest, Mt. Jefferson Wilderness.

Getting Here *From Portland.* By car, I–5 south to Salem, Hwy. 22 to Detroit, Hwy. 46 to Breitenbush (2 hrs). By bus, Greyhound (3 hrs).

Special Notes Day pass $8–$15; reservation required. Smoking only in designated outdoor areas. Remember to bring a flashlight.

Kah-Nee-Ta Resort

Taking the waters

Oregon
Warm Springs

The Kah-Nee-Ta Resort, owned and managed by a confederation of tribes whose ancestors once worshiped at the springs on their reservation, strikes a delicate balance between tradition and modernity. Guests are invited to tribal ceremonies and festivals and to a salmon-bake feast. Huge swimming pools attract families, and bathhouses offer private soaks and a massage.

The imposing guest lodge and conference center, opened in 1968, sit atop a rocky ridge overlooking the Warm Springs River and a recreation complex. Devastated by a 1996 winter flood, the Indian village, vacation villas, and hot springs bathhouse are scheduled to be rebuilt by early 1997. The Lodge also has a casino, Indianhead, for adult gaming.

Trails for biking, hiking, and horseback riding fan out toward the distant Cascade Mountains on the 60,000-acre reservation. All activities are priced à la carte, and the fees are modest: trail rides $25 ($20 for teenagers) for an hour on horseback, $5 for a 25-minute mineral bath. Arrangements can be made on short notice on any day of the week.

Kah-Nee-Ta Resort
Box K, Warm Springs, OR 97761
Tel. 503/553–1112 or 800/554–4786
Fax 503/553–1071

Administration Manager, Steven Whitaker

Season Year-round

Accommodations 139 luxury rooms in the lodge. Cedar-paneled rooms have balconies with views, oversize beds, full bath, air-conditioning, TV, telephone; 2-bedroom suites have fireplace in living room.

Rates Lodge rooms $95–$160 per day, single or double; suites (2 bedrooms) $190–$200. 1 night payable in advance. AE, DC, MC, V.

Meal Plans No meal plan offered, but guests can dine on a variety of dishes in the lodge dining room.

Services and Facilities **Services:** Massage. **Swimming Facilities:** Olympic-size outdoor pool (village), outdoor pool (lodge). **Spa Facilities:** 5 tiled Roman tubs in men's and women's bathhouses. **Recreation Facilities:** 2 tennis courts, 18-hole golf course, horseback riding, trout fishing, mountain-bike rental. **Evening Programs:** Drumming, ceremonies, rituals, salmon bake.

In the Area Nature walks with resident naturalist, Mt. Hood National Forest, the Dalles recreation area, white-water rafting on the Deschutes River, American Indian Museum.

Getting Here *From Portland.* By car, Hwy. 26 east to Warm Springs (2½ hrs). By air, scheduled commercial service to Redmond (30 mins); private and charter flights land at Madras Airport 25 mi away. Rental car available.

Special Notes Limited access for people with disabilities. No smoking in pool area or designated dining areas. No-smoking rooms in separate wing of lodge.

Skamania Lodge

Nonprogram resort

Oregon
Columbia Gorge

The panoramic sweep of the Cascade Mountains and the mighty Columbia River welcomes visitors to the Skamania Lodge, built on a ridge in the Gorge National Scenic Area, 45 minutes from Portland. This is a dramatic area, well known for the blustery winds that blow through the Gorge and make it a thriving center for sailboarding. But the history of this region long predates the construction of the first Windsurfer: This is Chinook tribe territory, and Skamania Lodge's architecture reflects the past. Creating the casual, calming interior are Native American–style rugs, Pendleton fabrics, and mission-style wood furnishings. A stone fireplace dominates the three-story Great Room. While working out in the spa you enjoy views of the golf course and surrounding forest.

Opened in 1993, this mountain retreat offers big-city comforts. A midweek spa package includes dinner and two treatments, as well as use of the sports facilities. Guests can use a Jacuzzi on the sundeck, indoor whirlpools, and a 60-foot lap pool with its own waterfall.

Don't expect aerobics classes or organized activity; other than trail rides, you plan your own program. Adjoining the men's and women's locker rooms are saunas and two massage rooms. The spa is open 6 AM to 11 PM, and the fitness center has a trainer on staff. The fitness center is open to the public for $6 a day.

Also on the grounds is an 18-hole golf course that winds through the forest. Golfers warm up on a driving range, putting green, and practice bunker before tackling this challenging course. Guided trail rides on horseback ($25 per hour) are reserved through the lodge's guest services desk. In winter trails are groomed for cross-country skiing.

Head out to lush botanical areas and waterfalls within easy reach of the Lodge. For a challenging hike, ask the Forest Service information center in the Lodge about guided treks to the area devastated by the eruption of Mount St. Helens in 1980.

With the Olympic mountain range looming to the north-east, the Columbia Gorge provides a first-class escape in the Cascades.

Skamania Lodge

Box 189, Stevenson, WA 98648
Tel. 509/427–7700 or 800/221–7117
Fax 509/427–2547

Administration General manager, Ian Muirdon; spa manager Shelly Arrowood

Season Year-round

Accommodations 195 rooms, 39 with fireplace. All have contemporary and mission-style wood furniture, full modern bathroom, air-conditioning, TV, phone. Amenities include terry-cloth robes, coffeemaker.

Rates 1-night spa package for 2 (Nov.–Feb.) $149; daily $90–$175 for singles or doubles; suites $280–$360. Add tax, gratuities. AE, DC, MC, V.

Meal Plans No spa menu. The dining room serves fine Pacific Northwest dishes including sea bass with corn and clam sauce, Dungeness crab legs, roast leg of venison with wild berry relish, buffalo fillet.

Services and Facilities **Exercise Equipment:** Apollo multipurpose gym, 3 Lifestride treadmills, 2 Bodyguard stairsteppers, 2 Arrow rowers, 6 Tunturi bikes, Fonda step unit. **Services:** Massage. **Swimming Facilities:** Indoor 60-ft lap pool. **Recreation Facilities:** 2 tennis courts outdoor (unlit), 18-hole golf course with driving range, mountain bike rental, volleyball court, horseback riding, trail hikes.

In the Area Mt. St. Helens Volcanic Monument, Mt. Hood Railroad, sternwheeler river cruise, Bonneville Dam, the Dalles recreation area, Maryhill Museum (European art and fashion).

Getting Here *From Portland.* By car, I–84 east to Bridge of the Gods, or Hwy. 14 (45 mins).

Special Notes Minimum age in spa: 16.

Carson Hot Mineral Springs Resort

Taking the waters

Washington
Carson

The claw-foot enamel tubs are characteristic of the old-fashioned friendliness bathers enjoy at the Carson Hot Mineral Springs Resort. Proud of using "the same bath methods for over 100 years," the management strives to remain unpretentious and comfortable. The rustic cabins, a landmark hotel, and bathhouses on the banks of the Wind River near its junction with the mighty Columbia date from 1876. The oldest remaining structure, a two-story wood hotel, was built in 1897 to accommodate bathers who traveled by steamboat from Portland, Oregon. The cabins were built in the early 1920s.

Taking the waters is a simple, two-step procedure: A tub soak is followed by the traditional sweat wrap, in which an attendant wraps bathers in sheets and heavy blankets to induce a good sweat. Separate bathhouses for men and women offer some privacy.

The 126°F mineral water is piped directly into the tubs (eight for men, six for women), which are drained and refilled after each use. The water is not treated with chemicals; analysis shows it to be high in sodium and calcium, like springs at principal European spas. The crowning touch is the hour-long massage ($26–$32).

Carson Hot Mineral Springs Resort

Box 370, Carson, WA 98610
Tel. 509/427–8292

Administration Manager, Gordon Lee

Season Year-round

Accommodations 9 large hotel rooms, 23 cabins, all simply furnished with double beds. No private bath, TV, or telephone. Cabin rooms have toilet and sink, kitchenette.

Rates Rooms and cabins $35–$50 for 2 persons, $5 each additional person. 1 night payable in advance. MC, V.

Meal Plans No meal plan available. The hotel restaurant serves 3 hearty meals daily, à la carte. Lunch menu includes pasta salad, beef lasagna, vegetarian sandwiches. Dinner entrées are a vegetarian "gardenburger," fruit platter, grilled salmon, steak, ham.

Services and Facilities **Services:** Massage. **Spa Facilities:** Individual tubs in men's and women's bathhouses ($10). **Recreation Facilities:** Hiking, fishing, golf.

In the Area River trips, the Dalles recreation area, Bonneville Dam, Shakespeare Festival (summer), Portland museums and cultural centers, 18-hole golf course.

Getting Here *From Portland.* By car, I–84 east to Bridge of the Gods, Rte. 14 to Carson (70 mins).

Special Notes Limited access for people with disabilities. No smoking in the bathhouses.

Doe Bay Village Resort

Taking the waters

Washington
Orcas Island

The hot tubs at the rustic Doe Bay Village Resort afford spectacular views of the San Juan Islands, and the constant 106°F temperature of the mineral water from nearby springs protects bathers from the chilly mist. Waterfalls, the ocean, hidden beaches, and a sauna with stained-glass windows help to create a special feeling of seclusion and communion.

Native Americans were the first to make a sanctuary here. Loggers and trappers came to enjoy the springs and a tavern in the town, where a general store and post office have operated since the early 1900s. In time the area became an artists' colony and a human-potential center; today the resort is a laid-back haven for people who love bathing in hot springs, hiking, kayaking, and participating in other outdoor activities. A large number of day visitors come here by ferry from the mainland for a soak at the springs.

The open-air hot tubs at the resort are equipped with Jacuzzi jets; two have hot water, one is naturally cold. A wood deck surrounds the bathing complex, which is attached to a big sauna hut in which 20 people can enjoy the wood-fired heat comfortably. The price for eight hours is $6 (including parking if you drove over from the ferry). Bring your own towels.

The paint is peeling and the plumbing doesn't always work, but the prices are reasonable. There are campsites (with communal baths and showers) for those who go for seclusion in the woods. Some sites have a dome of plastic sheeting for protection from the rain. Hostel-style dormitory beds at $14.50, and houses for $56–$86, accommodate groups and individuals.

Doe Bay Village Resort
Star Rte. 86, Olga, WA 98279
Tel. 360/376–2291 or 360/376–4755
Fax 360/376–3637

Administration Manager, John Barnes

Season Year-round

Accommodations Rustic cabins for up to 100 guests range from duplexes to large cottages with private shower, heat, and bedding. Some cabins have private bathroom, and large units have kitchens. Communal bathhouse. No maid service, TV, telephone. Campsites, tents, RV hookups ($16) and dormitory lodging ($14.50) available.

Rates Cabins $40.50–$91.50 a day single or double; $10.50 per additional person. 1 night payable in advance. AE, MC, V.

Meal Plans Vegetarian cuisine, chicken, seafood à la carte.

Services and Facilities **Services:** Massage, kayaking instruction. **Swimming Facilities:** Ocean beach, mountain lake. **Spa Facilities:** 3 outdoor tubs, steam room, Jacuzzi. **Recreation Facilities:** Guided kayak tours, fishing, hiking, golf, tennis, all nearby.

In the Area Ferry trips to nearby islands, whale-watching boat trips, Seattle museums and cultural life, Olympic National Park.

Getting Here *From Seattle.* By car, I–5 to Mt. Vernon, ferry from Anacortes. Drive through Olga to east end of the island (3 hrs).

Rosario Resort

Nonprogram resort

Washington
Orcas Island
Sea-inspired treatments for the body and the seaside setting are the lure of the Rosario Resort, built around the former mansion of the shipbuilder Robert Moran. Many of the guest lodges and public rooms have a nautical look; portholes and other parts salvaged from old ships pop up in the indoor swimming pool and other unexpected places. An organ room with a spectacular cathedral ceiling and stained-glass windows is the setting for concerts and lectures.

The resort has a small indoor spa with whirlpool, coed sauna, aerobics studio, and weights room. The daily schedule includes low-impact and aquatic aerobics, dance exercise, stretching and toning (flexercise) calisthenics, and yoga. Spa services are reserved on an à la carte basis or as part of seasonal packages. Use of the spa is free.

Simple pleasures, such as hunting for driftwood on the 2-mile-long beach, wandering in the pine woods, and relaxing in the sauna, attract most visitors. Families with children, senior citizens, and fitness buffs come for a few days or weeks. Canada, the Rockies, and sophisticated Vancouver are a few hours' drive north; charming Victoria is just 7 miles away by water. Orcas Island is protected by hills on one side, warmed by the Japanese current of the Pacific Ocean on the other. The winters are mild and see no snow accumulation.

Arriving by ferry or floatplane, there's no sign of a hotel. The cottages for guests cluster on a hillside, requiring a short walk to the mansion for meals and the spa. Part of the charm is seclusion and quiet, with long stretches of beach for walking all by yourself. But the spa is being upgraded under new management and will offer a full schedule of indoor activity. Outdoor recreation centers on the marina and its Cascade Bay Cafe.

Bring your hiking boots, or rent a mountain bike to explore the island. Spectacular views and sea air provide instant relaxation.

Rosario Resort
Eastsound, Orcas Island, WA 98245
Tel. 206/376–2222 or 800/562–8820

Administration Manager, Christopher French; spa director, John Baso

Season Year-round

Accommodations 131 rooms in private cottages, all with country antique furnishings, modern beds, private bath, color TV, telephone, air-conditioning, patio; studios have a fireplace. No room service.

Rates Double rooms $80–$220 per couple, additional person $20. Add 7.7% tax. 1 night payable in advance. AE, DC, MC, V.

Meal Plans Menu à la carte in the Orcas Room. Lunch can be a green salad dressed with fresh fruit juice and cayenne pepper or chicken baked in romaine lettuce. Dinner entrées may include grilled salmon with peppercorn, basil, and red-pepper sauce; veal topped with crab and asparagus. The upscale Compass Room menu includes beer-steamed Lopez Island mussels, carpaccio of yellowfin tuna with baby greens and braised Washington lingcod. Special diets on request.

Services and Facilities **Exercise Equipment:** 4-station Marcy weights unit, 4-station Apollo II gym, Precor rower, stepmachine, 2 Lifecycles, NordicTrack, Rebounders, dumbbells (3–50 lbs). **Services:** Massage (Swedish, shiatsu, reflexology), facials, salt-glow body scrub, pedicure, manicure, full-service beauty salon. **Swimming Facilities:** 2 outdoor pools, indoor pool, ocean beach, mountain lake. **Recreation Facilities:** 2 tennis courts, hiking; 9-hole golf course nearby; marina; kayaking center.

In the Area Whale-watching boat trips, kayaking excursions, ferry trips, island crafts and antiques shops in Eastsound, Orcas Island Historical Museum, Seattle, Vancouver, Olympic National Park, Doe Bay Hot Springs.

Getting Here *From Seattle.* By car, I–5 to Mt. Vernon, WA State ferry from Anacortes to Eastsound (½ hr). By plane, scheduled flights to Rosario Resort in Eastsound by Kenmore Airlines (tel. 800/543–9595); by seaplane (1 hr). Van service to the ferry landing provided by Rosano Resort, to and from Eastsound.

Special Notes Limited access for people with disabilities; some ground-floor rooms wheelchair accessible. No smoking in the spa or in designated dining areas.

The Salish Lodge

Nonprogram resort

Washington
Snoqualmie Themed to the Pacific Rim, the new spa at Salish Lodge looks out on the magnificent scenery of the Cascade Mountains. The Oriental touches used to enhance an airy, wood-and-glass pavilion evoke the feeling of a Japanese hot spring *onsen* bathhouse. Seaweed treatments, shiatsu massage, and a spa cuisine menu add to the cross-cultural experience.

Although The Salish Lodge offers no aerobics classes or organized exercise programs, it provides state-of-the-art equipment in a small weights room. The facility's most spectacular features are the two hydrotherapy pools set in natural rock, ideal for soaking—and soaking in the view. The pools, sauna, and steam room are coed. There are four private rooms for massage and bodywork, plus a wet room for body scrubs. The finishing touch comes from trained estheticians who do facials, manicure, and pedicure. The 3-hour Falls Refresher package starts with coating your body in mud with a wrap to remineralize your skin, followed by a rinse in the specially designed Vichy shower, 30-minute aromatherapy massage, and paraffin on your hands and feet prior to nail treatments.

The spa desk can arrange fireside massage in your room. Or, if you prefer to enjoy the fire in public spaces, you can sip complimentary morning coffee, tea, and mineral water by the fireplace in the lodge's library-lounge. Appointments are made for services from 8 AM–9 PM daily; spa facilities are open from 6 AM to 11 PM without charge to lodge guests.

The luxurious lodge, familiar to viewers of the TV series "Twin Peaks," which was filmed here, perches at the crest of a waterfall taller than Niagara, 268 feet, adjoining a state park where you can hike and picnic. Salish Lodge opened in 1988, re-creating an inn built on the site in 1916. The original dining room was restored, using indigenous stone, copper, and wood. Like its sister resort in Oregon, Skamania Lodge, this is a place to celebrate the environment.

The Salish Lodge
U.S. Hwy. 202, Box 1109, Snoqualmie, WA 98065
Tel. 206/831–6500 or 800/826–6124
Fax 206/888–2420

Administration General manager, Loy Helmly; spa director, Kathleen Crews

Season Year-round

Accommodations 91 rooms and 4 suites in 4-story lodge, all with wood-burning stone fireplace, Northwest-designed furniture, king-size or two double beds with down comforters, balcony or window seat. Large bathroom has oversized whirlpool tub, terry-cloth robes. Rooms have color TV with remote control, air-conditioning, modem-capable phone.

Rates $165–$245 per room for 2 people on daily basis; suites $575 for 2. Additional person $25 per night. Spa package with room: Fireside Massage $325–$400 per couple; Salish Falls Refresher $365 single, $566 per couple, including gratuities. Day spa package for lodge guests, $385 including lunch. Add 11% tax. 1-night deposit by credit card. AE, DC, MC, V.

Meal Plans The Dining Room menu highlights calorie-counted spa cuisine. Emphasis is on seafood and Northwest fare. Lunch can start with white bean chili, sweet potato vichyssoise, or corn soup with roasted garlic and apples; entrées include crusted halibut fillet, spinach fusilli, alder-smoked Atlantic salmon. Dinner appetizers are pan-seared black cod, Dungeness crab galette, or pumpkin ginger bisque; entrées can be vegetable terrine with wild rice crepe, spinach fettuccine with sea scallops and prawns. Meals are à la carte.

Services and Facilities **Exercise Equipment:** LifeFitness stepper, treadmill, rower, bike, multistation weight training unit, free weights. **Services:** Swedish massage, aromatherapy, shiatsu, sports massage, body scrub, mud or seaweed wrap, hair pack, body brushing with Vichy shower, reflexology, facial, pedicure, manicure. **Swimming Facilities:** None. **Recreation Facilities:** Sports court, mountain bikes. **Evening Programs:** Entertainment in the Attic Lounge.

In the Area Snoqualmie Falls Park, Seattle.

Getting Here *From Seattle.* By car, I–90 east, exit 27 to Snoqualmie (45 mins). Rental car, limousine service available. Shuttle van from SeaTac Airport ($75 each way), Park Place Limousine (tel. 206/367–7404).

Sol Duc Hot Springs Resort

Taking the waters

Washington
Olympic National Park

Here's the place to bring the family for a soak and a swim after a drive or a hike in Olympic National Park. Within the park, the Sol Duc Hot Springs Resort maintains public and private pools filled with mineral water that flows from springs on federal land.

Piped into a heat exchanger at a temperature of 123°F, the mineral water is cooled for use in the three large outdoor soaking pools. The water's continuous flow into the pools makes chlorination unnecessary.

Swimmers do laps in a 30-meter freshwater pool, heated for year-round use. Operating as a concession of the Department of the Interior, the resort has been updated and expanded in recent years. A visitor center nearby offers trail maps and information on seasonal events.

Sol Duc Hot Springs Resort
Soleduc River Rd., Olympic National Park, WA
Reservations: Box 2169, Port Angeles, WA 98362
Tel. 360/327–3583

Administration Manager, Connie Pons

Season May–Oct.

Accommodations 32 cabins with double bed (or twin beds and sofa bed), 6 with kitchen, all with modern bath. 20 RV sites. No TV, telephone, dresser, or air-conditioning.

Rates Cabin with kitchen $89.91–$100.75 per day, without kitchen $80.46, including tax, for 2 persons. 1 night payable in advance. AE, MC, V.

Meal Plans Vegetarian, fish, and chicken dishes. Granola, yogurt, smoked salmon omelet, buckwheat pancakes with fresh berries for breakfast; burgers and deli selections for lunch; charbroiled chicken, baked cod with mushrooms, steaks, steamed vegetable platter, or zucchini-cheese casserole for dinner.

Services and Facilities **Swimming Facilities:** Large public pool. **Spa Facilities:** 4 indoor whirlpools, outdoor soaking pools. **Recreation Facilities:** Fishing, hiking. **Evening Programs:** Talks by park rangers.

In the Area Nature hikes with park rangers, Seattle museums, cultural centers, Pioneer Square (Klondike Gold Rush museum).

Getting Here *From Seattle.* By car, Hwy. 101 to Fairholm, Soleduc Rd. 11 mi to resort (4 hrs). By car ferry, scheduled service to Winslow, Hwy. 101 to Soleduc Rd. (2 hrs).

Special Notes Ramps at geothermal pools allow access for people with disabilities; rooms are wheelchair accessible. Nature walks for children with park ranger. No smoking in the bathhouse.

Antelope Retreat Center

Holistic health
Spiritual awareness

Wyoming
Savery

An isolated ranch in the foothills of the Continental Divide, the Antelope Retreat Center puts you to work preparing meals, joining in ranch chores, and gardening. Among the special weekly programs are vision quests based on the Native American rite of passage, which include a three-day wilderness fast, and a nature-awareness week devoted to learning survival skills while camping in the Red Desert and Medicine Bow National Forest. Focus programs include gender weeks, with a personal sojourn in the desert; and Sacred Hoop week, which involves exploring Dakota traditions.

John Boyer grew up on the ranch, founding the retreat center in 1986 to share his love of nature and the inner quiet learned from neighboring Native Americans. Guests are initiated at a sweat-lodge ceremony and taught personal awareness exercises. Some even get to help with lambing the small herd of sheep.

Living like a rancher comes naturally here. You have a choice of rooms in the 1890s house, or in outlying yurts built into earthen mounds. Or simply come for a vacation, with no program, and savor Wyoming.

Antelope Retreat Center
Box 166, Savery, WY 82332
Tel. 307/383-2625

Administration General manager, John Boyer; program directors, Gina Lyman and Tom Barnes

Season Year-round

Accommodations 16 guests in the ranch house in 4 bedrooms, plus 2 4-bed native yurts. Shared bathroom; no air-conditioning. Bedrooms have western-style wooden furniture, single or double beds.

Rates $500–$650 weekly with program (Sat.–Sat.), all meals. Vacation week (no program) $375 including meals. Daily $36–$58 per person. Deposit: 50% of fee. No credit cards.

Meal Plans 3 meals served daily, family style. Breakfast can be homemade grain cereal with honey, buckwheat pancakes with fruit, or an omelet. Lunch is soup and salad, sandwiches on homemade bread. Dinner main courses are barbecued chicken, baked or grilled fish, spaghetti, tofu casserole, and vegetable stir-fry. Special diets are accommodated. Vision Quest includes 3-day fast.

Services and Facilities **Swimming Facilities:** Stream. **Recreation Facilities:** Hiking, skiing, outings to rodeos and nearby attractions, gardening, ranching. **Evening Programs:** Sweat lodge.

In the Area Steamboat Springs (downhill skiing, hot springs), Medicine Bow National Forest, Red Desert.

Getting Here *From Denver, CO.* By car, I–70 via Idaho Springs, exit at Dillon, Rte. 9 to Kremmling, Rte. 40 west via Steamboat Springs to Craig, Hwy. 13/789 to Biggs, right on Rte. 70 via Dixon to Savery, left on Creek Rd. (½ hr). By air, scheduled flights to Hayden (40 mins); van transportation Saturday ($50 round-trip) provided on request by Antelope Retreat.

Special Notes Children accompanying program participants charged $75 up to age 4, $200–$362 ages 5–15.

Hot Springs State Park

Taking the waters

Wyoming Long before explorers discovered the Big Spring, it was a
Thermopolis bathing place for the Shoshone and Arapahoe tribes. When

the land was purchased by the federal government in 1896, the deed stipulated that the springs remain open and free to all. Thus there is no charge to bathe in the indoor and outdoor pools maintained by the State of Wyoming. A Holiday Inn, resort apartments, and a rehabilitation center are within the 1-square-mile Hot Springs State Park.

The water wells from the earth at a temperature of 135°F and spills down a series of mineral-glazed terraces on its way to the Big Horn River. Some of the flow is diverted to privately operated bathhouses and swimming pools and into the state-run baths. The sparkling clean and airy facilities are patronized by families en route to Yellowstone and by senior citizens from a nearby retirement home. Park and pools are open daily, 9 AM–10 PM.

The Holiday Inn on the bank of the Horn River offers the most complete facilities. There are separate men's and women's bathhouses for private soaks (coed on request), and an outdoor hydrojet pool is filled with warm mineral water. The outdoor swimming pool contains chlorinated tap water. The Athletic Club facilities are free to inn guests.

In central Wyoming, the town of Thermopolis is surrounded by high buttes and range land where herds of bison still roam free; it's a pleasant stop on the way to Yellowstone from Denver and Cheyenne.

Hot Springs State Park
Thermopolis Chamber of Commerce
220 Park St., Thermopolis, WY 82443
Tel. 307/864–2636

Holiday Inn of the Waters
100 Park St., Box 1323, Thermopolis, WY 82443
Tel. 307/864–3131 or 800/465–4329

Administration Manager, James Mills

Season Year-round

Accommodations 80 rooms with modern furniture, bath, queen-size or twin beds or waterbed. Separate exercise rooms for men and women in the Athletic Club.

Rates $77.40 a day for 2 in twin-bed room, $86–$93 single. Meals à la carte. 1 night payable in advance. Add tax (6%) and gratuities. AE, MC, V.

Meal Plans No meal plan available. The hotel restaurant serves 3 meals daily; special diets accommodated. Western steaks, grilled fish, baked mountain trout, salads in season.

Services and Facilities **Exercise Equipment:** 9-station Universal weight training gym in men's and women's areas, punching bag, stationary bikes, 2 racquetball courts. **Services:** Massage, beauty shop. **Swimming Facilities:** Outdoor heated pool. **Spa Facilities:** 4 private mineral water tubs, outdoor Jacuzzi, sauna, steam bath, men's and women's bathhouses. **Recreation Facilities:** Bicycle rental (tandem, single), golf, fishing, skiing, snowmobiling nearby.

In the Area Outfitters offer hunting and fishing trips, scenic tours, river floats. Yellowstone National Park, Wind River Canyon, County Historical Museum (Hole in the Wall Bar), Jackson winter-sports area, Wind River Indian Reservation.

Getting Here *From Cheyenne.* By car, I–25 to Casper, Hwy. 20 via Moneta (3 hrs). By bus, Powder River Line (4 hrs).

Special Notes   Rooms accommodate up to 5 persons. No smoking in the Athletic Club and designated areas of the dining room; no-smoking rooms available. Club open weekdays noon–8:30, weekends 10–8:30.

The Central States

Dallas has been in the forefront of recent fitness developments in the Central States. Dr. Kenneth Cooper, who did pioneering research in exercise and nutrition in the U.S. Air Force and at the Cooper Clinic, is the guiding spirit for the Aerobics Center's residential program. In the suburbs, the Greenhouse offers luxury pampering and body conditioning for women only. And for golfers or executives on the go, The Four Seasons Resort's full-service spa and health club provide a deluxe retreat for a day or a week.

Texans have taken to European hydrotherapy with the Kneipp herbal baths and Kur Program at the Alamo Plaza Spa in San Antonio and at the Lake Austin Spa Resort near Austin. Close to the heart of Houston, The Houstonian Hotel has a well-equipped health club but no longer operates the Phoenix Spa program.

Day spa packages are an option at many resorts and hotels. Among the best in Dallas (not reviewed here) are those at the Spa at the Crescent Court Hotel and the Wyndham Anatole Hotel.

Akia

Stress control   *Women only*
Weight management

Oklahoma
Chickasaw
National
Recreation Area

Weight loss diet and lots of exercise are the main ingredients of the no-frills weekends and five-day programs at Akia, a fitness retreat for a dozen women. Guests participate in full days of hiking, stretching, and body toning in a rigorous dawn-to-dusk schedule that takes advantage of the scenic Arbuckle Mountains and nearby lakes and forests.

The day begins with exercise on the redwood deck that surrounds the main building. The two-mile hike before breakfast is followed by more stretching and toning in a lakeside pavilion. Aerobics classes, contouring, and relaxation exercises begin the afternoon. Then participants have the option of soaking in the hot tub, getting a massage, walking, bicycling, or swimming in a nearby lake. Private consultation on nutrition with a registered dietitian and one-on-one training with the exercise instructor help you plan a personal fitness program.

Ninety miles south of Oklahoma City and 100 miles north of Dallas, the retreat has a compound ringed by rock cottages, each of which accommodates three women. Participants bring their own linens and towels and help with housekeeping. Meals are prepared by a gourmet spa-cuisine chef. Dinner is served by candlelight and is followed by discussions on health and nutrition.

Akia
Sulphur, OK
Office: 2316 N.W. 45th Place, Oklahoma City, OK 73112
Tel. 405/842–6269

Administration   Founder/director, Wilhelmina Maguire
Season   10-week spring and fall seasons

Accommodations	Stone cottages and wood duplex for 11 guests. Cottages have 3 single beds, shared bathroom, carpeting, wooden deck.
Rates	$450 for 5-day session, $200 for 2-day weekend. Deposit: $150 advance payment. No credit cards.
Meal Plans	3 simple meals daily total 950–1,000 calories, with options at breakfast and lunch; 3-course dinner. Breakfast can be cereal with fruit and juice, lunch a fruit smoothie, pasta salad, or tuna salad on pita bread. Typical dinner entrées are spinach lasagna, baked chicken, eggplant Parmesan, peppers stuffed with lentils and brown rice, Cantonese vegetables stir fry. Dessert is ricotta cheesecake or fruit.
Services and Facilities	**Services:** Massage, facial, personal color analysis, body composition test, nutritional counseling. **Swimming Facilities:** Nearby lake. **Recreation Facilities:** Bicycling. **Evening Programs:** Lectures on nutrition, shopping for health food.
In the Area	Oklahoma City's Kirkpatrick Center (Native American and African art), National Cowboy Hall of Fame, Guthrie (Victorian prairie capital), Cherokee Heritage Center in Tahlequah, Sulphur (antiques shops).
Getting Here	*From Oklahoma City.* By car, I–35 south to Davis, Rte. 12 to Sulphur (2 hrs). By bus, free transfers at Oklahoma City Airport.
Special Notes	No smoking.

Black Hills Health and Education Center

Life enhancement
Spiritual awareness
Stress control
Vibrant maturity

South Dakota
Hermosa

Across three creeks and up a woodland trail, in a lodge that looks like a mountain resort, you'll find the Black Hills Health and Education Center, a Seventh-Day Adventist healing center that offers programs of 13 to 20 days.

Black Hills's medically supervised programs are designed to teach guests healthy habits, and to help those who suffer from diabetes, arthritis, hypertension, heart problems, and obesity. Each person's lifestyle is analyzed and a suitable regimen of exercise and diet prescribed. Rehabilitation therapy is provided for persons who have had cardiac surgery.

The program begins with a complete physical examination, blood tests, and medical counseling. Hydrotherapy (included in the program fee) and massage may be recommended; the lodge is equipped with a whirlpool, a Russian steam cabinet, and a shower that alternates hot and cold water from six sprays. Once or twice a week an excursion takes participants to a fitness center and a swimming pool fed by warm springs.

While the lectures cover stress control and nutrition, the central philosophy is one of learning by doing. Everyone joins in bread-making and cooking classes, and outings to a supermarket and restaurant are led by staff members who demonstrate how to shop for and order nutritious foods.

The health center is in the scenic Banana Belt of the Black Hills, so named for the temperate climate and sunny days that prevail even in winter. Guests explore the canyons, cliffs, and farmlands on daily hikes.

The combined focus on spiritual, mental, and physical health attracts people of all ages to this informal resort, though many

The Central States

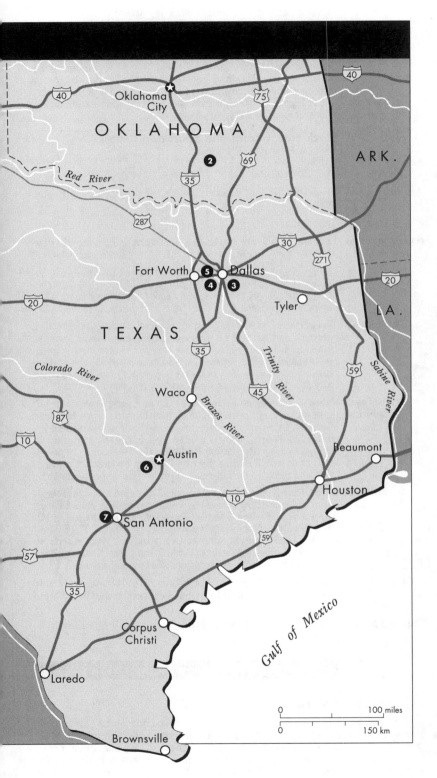

of the participants are over 50. They arrive in motor homes that can be hooked up outside, or they stay in the lodge; some bring children and a baby-sitter. Meals are included in rates.

An affiliate of the Black Hills Missionary College, the health center draws on the campus for services. Friday evening is a time when students and guests traditionally gather around the big stone fireplace in the lounge and join in a music program. Included in the program fee are a physical examination, meals, massage, and hydrotherapy.

Black Hills Health and Education Center
Box 19, Hermosa, SD 57744
Tel. 605/255–4101
Fax 605/255–4622

Administration President, Robert Willard; medical director, Patricia Pagan, M.D.

Season Year-round

Accommodations 12 rooms in a 2-story lodge, modern furnishings, mostly double beds, private and shared baths. Motor-home services.

Rates 13-day program $1,700 single, $2,500 shared by 2 persons; 20-day program $2,500 single, $4,270 shared by 2. $100–$200 reduction for motorhome use. Daily rate $30–$35 per room. $100 per person advance payment. No credit cards.

Meal Plans 3 vegetarian meals daily, buffet style. Fruits, vegetables, legumes, and natural fat sources such as nuts and avocados. Lunch and dinner include salad bar, water-steamed vegetables, entrées such as vegetarian lasagna with mock-cheese topping, baked tofu, cashew chow mein. Whole-grain bread baked daily. No dairy products, eggs, coffee, tea, condiments.

Services and Facilities **Exercise Equipment:** Schwinn Air Dyne bikes, Trotter treadmill, rowing machine, trampoline, multipurpose gym. **Services:** Massage, hydrotherapy, medical consultation. **Swimming Facilities:** At nearby fitness center. **Spa Facilities:** Mineral hot springs nearby. **Recreation Facilities:** Gold panning, rock collecting; downhill skiing nearby. **Evening Programs:** Informal talks and films on health-related topics. Music program Fri.

In the Area Evans Plunge hot springs, a naturally heated indoor mineral-water pool; Custer State Park wildlife preserve; Rapid City's Aka Lakota Museum (Native American art and history); Mt. Rushmore; the Black Hills Passion Play (summer); The Homestead, a working gold mine at Lead; antique train ride from Hill City; Badlands National Park; Wind Cave National Park (caverns); prehistoric excavations, Deadwood casinos.

Getting Here *From Rapid City.* By car, Hwy. 79 south to Hermosa, Hwy. 40 west to entrance road (40 mins). Free pickup to and from Rapid City airport and bus station.

Special Notes Specially equipped rooms, ramps for people with disabilities. No smoking indoors.

Alamo Plaza Spa at the Menger Hotel

Luxury pampering
Taking the waters

Texas
San Antonio
Kneipp herbal baths are the latest addition to the historic Menger Hotel, which has a European hydrotherapy program at its Alamo Plaza Spa. Built on the site of a pioneer beer brewery and Russian-Turkish bathhouse, the hotel taps its own Edwards Aquifer for spring water to fill the big claw-footed Victorian bathtubs in its original 1859 building and the new

spa beneath the fitness center. Directly across from the Alamo, the shrine of Texas independence, this is an urban retreat for body and mind.

Personalized regimens are set up for guests by advance reservation. The spa has five treatments rooms, sauna and steam rooms, and whirlpool. An esthetician is available for facials and treatments on hands and feet. Using Kneipp herbal essences and aromatic oils made in Germany, your *kur* (treatment course) can include water applications, exercise, diet, and combinations of dry heat, wet massage, wet heat, dry massage. Day spa packages ($99–$195), as well as overnight programs, are offered.

Trained at the Kneipp center in Bad Wörishofen, Dr. Jonathan Paul de Vierville adapted these popular European traditions to American lifestyles, opening the Alamo Plaza Spa in 1993 while continuing his state-certified school for bodyworkers. Like the classic spas in Baden-Baden, Karlsbad, and Vichy, the Texans capitalize on the rich cultural resources and natural wonders of their area. Near the hotel is the River Walk, lined with restaurants and strolling musicians. Tour buses and motorized trolley cars take you to museums, galleries, and a performing arts center, as well as to the Alamo Dome.

Alamo Plaza Spa at the Menger Hotel
204 Alamo Plaza, San Antonio, TX 78205
Tel. 210/223-5772; hotel reservations 800/345-9285
Fax 210/228-0022

Administration Director, J. Paul de Vierville, Ph.D, M.S.W.; hotel general manager, Hector Venegas

Season Year-round

Accommodations 320 rooms (23 suites) including the restored 1859 wing with Victorian furnishings. All with private bathroom, air-conditioning, TV, telephone. Many feature ornate balconies overlooking an interior garden that has tropical foliage and a swimming pool. Choice of king-size or twin beds, no-smoking rooms.

Rates Daily room rate for 2 persons $112–$122, double occupancy; suites $182–$546. 3-day/2-night Victorian Kur Spa Holiday $495 per person, double occupancy, $580 single; American Kur Spa Classic 3-day/2-night package including cultural activities $595 per person double occupancy, $690 single. Kur Spa Day (no lodging) $195. Deposit: $50. Add tax, gratuities. AE, D, MC, V.

Meal Plans Breakfast, lunch, and beverage breaks included in spa packages; one dinner only in American Kur Spa Classic. Kneipp Menu choices in hotel dining room include high-protein foods such as cottage cheese, fish, lean meat, whole-grain products, vegetables, fresh fruit.

Services and Facilities **Exercise Equipment:** 2 Tectrix stairclimbers, 2 bikes, Trotter treadmill, stretch board, free weights. **Services:** Hydrotherapy, herbal body scrub, hot linen herbal wrap, facial, inhalation, hand and foot treatment, thalassotherapy, moor, peloid, and fango body treatments, reflexology, classical and sports massage. **Swimming Facilities:** 25-meter outdoor swimming pool (heated) with spring water. **Recreation Facilities:** Whirlpool.

In the Area The Alamo, Spanish colonial missions, Institute of Texas Cultures, San Antonio Art Museum, Witte Museum of Nature History, LBJ Ranch, Sea World, Fiesta Texas, IMAX theater.

Getting Here *From San Antonio Airport.* By bus, Star Shuttle (every 30 mins, $5 for 30-min trip). By car, I–35 south, Commerce St. exit, right on Bowie St., to Crockett, left to Lady Bird Fountain behind the Alamo (20 mins).

Special Notes Spa hours: daily 9–9. Minimum age 18; children under 18 must be accompanied by an adult. No smoking in spa. Facilities accessible for people with disabilities.

The Cooper Aerobics Center

Nutrition and diet
Preventive medicine
Vibrant maturity
Weight management

Texas A recognized leader in the study of the medical value of exer-
Dallas cise, the Aerobics Center has a residential Cooper Wellness Program designed to help participants achieve permanent changes in lifestyle. Programs of 7–13 days and a 4-day wellness weekend teach the adoption and cultivation of healthy habits. Or you can schedule an intensive one-day workout, with optional workshop.

At first look, the guest lodge seems more like a country club than a health center; the stately redbrick mansion is for the exclusive use of guests, members, and visiting professionals. Visitors have meals in the private restaurant and full use of the Aerobics Center.

Four exercise sessions are part of each day's program. You can work out on a treadmill or walk and jog on paved and lighted trails that wind through the 30-acre wooded estate. A gymnasium has basketball and racquetball courts and a three-lane running track. Two heated outdoor lap pools are six lanes wide and 75 feet long. The four outdoor Laykold lighted tennis courts are equipped with automatic ball machines.

Your stay can begin with an optional ($1,100) physical examination. The first day's schedule includes a chest X-ray, a test for pulmonary function, and vision, hearing, and dental exams. A standard skinfold test and weigh-in on an underwater scale determine your ideal body weight. Blood pressure is measured during and after exercise, and an ECG treadmill test measures stress. Before and after the program, 24 blood tests, including HDL and LDL for cholesterol, are administered. (Your health insurance may cover this.) The comprehensive medical report determines the exercise program that will be recommended for you.

Lecture topics include nutrition and health, and you participate in cooking and bread-making demonstrations. Volleyball, aerobics in the swimming pool, and other forms of group exercise are scheduled. The whirlpool, sauna, and steam room are open every night; massage appointments cost extra.

The combination of a supportive environment, state-of-the-art equipment and facilities, and the professional staff creates a disciplined program, and many guests here see significant results in lowering cholesterol and triglyceride levels in only two weeks. Follow-up calls and return visits have confirmed participants' success in lowering blood pressure and increasing vitality and alertness. The center encourages friends and couples to work together on behavior modification, offering a choice of services and workshops in the standard package or more comprehensive premier package. Lodging and a medical evaluation are not included in the program prices, giving you the option of staying at a nearby hotel.

Limited to groups of no more than 20, the program appeals to high-powered executives who have lost control of their health. Here they work with a team of nine full-time physicians, a dentist, nutritionists, and exercise technologists. Guided by Dr. Kenneth H. Cooper, whose pioneering research on aerobics inspired the founding of the center in 1970, these professionals make wellness meaningful to everyday life.

The Cooper Aerobics Center
12230 Preston Rd., Dallas, TX 75230
Tel. 214/386–4777 or 800/444–5192, Fax 214/386–0039
Telex 791578/AEROBICCTR DAL

Administration Program director, Leah K. Gabriel; Founder/president, Kenneth H. Cooper, M.D.

Season Sessions scheduled year-round, except Aug.

Accommodations 63 rooms, including 12 suites, in 2-story air-conditioned lodge. Furniture is heavy mahogany, with king- or queen-size beds, wing chairs. Private bath. A grand staircase dominates the marble lobby.

Rates 13-day program $2,595–$3,190; 7-day $1,995–$2,590; 4-day $1,495–$1,890. Rooms at Guest Lodge $92, single or double occupancy, suites $144–$222. Add 13¼% lodging tax, 8¼% meal tax. AE, MC, V.

Meal Plans 3 calorie-controlled meals daily from planned menu, plus snacks. Breakfast can be whole-grain pancakes with hot blueberry topping, seasonal fresh fruit, low fat milk, decaf tea or coffee. Lunch is tossed salad with low-calorie dressing, Hawaiian chicken with potatoes and baked tomato, fresh fruit tray, mineral water, diet drinks, or decaf coffee or tea. Dinner is beef Burgundy on a bed of pasta, snap peas, spinach salad, skim milk, beverage.

Services and Facilities **Exercise Equipment:** Cybex strength equipment, cardiovascular equipment. **Services:** Personal counseling on fitness, diet, and exercise; medical testing and evaluation. Swedish massage. **Swimming Facilities:** 2 heated outdoor pools. **Recreation Facilities:** 4 25-yd racquetball courts, 4 tennis courts, volleyball, basketball, handball; golf course nearby. **Evening Programs:** Talks on nutrition and health, cooking school, dinner at local restaurant.

In the Area Dallas Baseball Stadium, White Rock Lake, the Omnimax film theater in Fort Worth, Dallas Museum of Art, Kennedy Memorial, Fort Worth Science Center, Dallas Arboretum and Botanical Garden.

Getting Here *From Dallas.* By car, Hwy. 635 (LBJ Freeway), Preston Rd. (20 mins). Limousine, rental car, taxi available.

Special Notes Ramps and elevator provide access to all areas. No smoking indoors. Remember to bring recent medical records, a watch with second hand, a calculator, and exercise clothing.

Four Seasons Resort and Club

Life enhancement
Luxury pampering
Sports conditioning

Texas
Dallas/Irving
Space-age design and Old World architecture meet at Las Colinas, an urban center where the Four Seasons Resort and Club has combined sports and spa programs since 1986. The spa, connected to the hotel and clubhouse by an underground tunnel, offers eight daily exercise classes, weight training, total

fitness regimens, stretch groups, water works, and a range of indoor sports and workout facilities. Sophisticated bodywork here includes Phytomer seaweed and kelp products. The spa offers one-day packages for nonresidents, as well as overnight programs.

Programs can be tailored to suit your needs: You can work out on the advanced Nautilus equipment, do aerobics and body-building exercises, and play a round of golf or team up for tennis. Personal trainers, nutritional counseling, and fitness evaluations are available at an hourly rate that can be combined with any of the resort's special packages.

More than 25 spa treatments and beauty salon services can be booked à la carte. Services range from massage to aromatherapy, herbal wraps, and baths. There are two sets of Jacuzzis, saunas, steam rooms, hydrotherapy tubs, and hot/cold pools in separate wings for men and women. The spa program assures personal attention from the staff and access to a private swimming pool and whirlpool.

Two golf courses, indoor and outdoor tennis, squash, and racquetball courts, and jogging tracks leave little to be desired in the way of sports facilities. While exercising on a vast selection of exercise equipment, you can watch TV with specially designed transmitters that allow sound to be picked up on a headset. The four-level Sports Club is the centerpiece to the 400-acre resort. Choice accommodations are in the villas, set between a free-form swimming pool, the golf course, and the sports club.

Seven miles from Dallas/Fort Worth International Airport, the resort attracts golfers, corporate executives, and local families. You'll have your pick of activities and refreshment, from the heart-healthy menu in the main dining room to the full-service sports bar, and from aerobics classes to the fully equipped cardiovascular and strength-building health club. Set your own pace.

Four Seasons Resort and Club

4150 N. MacArthur Blvd., Irving, TX 75038
Tel. 214/717–0700 or 800/332–3442
Fax 214/717–2550
Telex 735319

Administration	General manager, Jim FitzGibbon; spa director, John Douthitt; Sports Club manager, Mark Herron
Season	Year-round
Accommodations	307 rooms including 26 suites in the 9-story tower, 50 rooms including 6 suites in new 2-story golf villas. Tastefully styled with executive amenities: toiletries, hair dryer, terry robes; comfortable living area, 3 telephones, cable TV, marble bath with separate tub and shower. Private balcony with most rooms; ask for golf course view.
Rates	1-day spa package $340–$410 weekdays, weekend $280–$360, suites to $1,000. Fresh Start spa package 2 nights/3 days $1,380–$1,620 per couple, $950–$1,080 single. Rooms $140–$285. Gratuities included; add 11% tax. AE, DC, MC, V.
Meal Plans	3 meals daily in 2–6 night spa packages. Four Seasons Alternative Cuisine is low in cholesterol, fat, calories, sodium. Menu selections are broiled chicken, Mexican chicken enchilada, grilled salmon, roast quail with fresh berry sauce. Daily caloric intake under 1,000; vegetarian meals available.
Services and Facilities	**Exercise Equipment:** 12-station Nautilus circuit, Universal multigym, stepper, 2 NordicTracks, 6 upright, 2 recumbent

Lifecycles, 2 Windracer cycles, complete line of free weights by Bodymaster and Pacific Gym, machines by Bodymaster, 10 StairMasters, 10 treadmills (Trackmaster, Quinton, Startrac) 2 StairMaster Crossrobics, 2 rowing machines, 5 Schwinn Air Dyne bikes, Tectrix bike, Universal recumbent bike. **Services:** Swedish, shiatsu, reflexology, sports, and aromatherapy massage; herbal and sea-kelp wraps and baths, loofah body scrub, facial, heated mud pack. Beauty salon for hair and nail care. Personal training. Fitness evaluation, Tae Kwon Do course. **Swimming Facilities:** 25-yard indoor lap pool, 25-meter outdoor lap pool, 2 recreational pools. **Recreation Facilities:** 12 outdoor, 4 indoor tennis courts, 4 indoor racquetball courts, 2 squash courts, 1 softball field, 2 handball courts, ½-court basketball gymnasium, 2 18-hole golf courses.

In the Area   Dallas Arts District, West End Historic District, Baseball Stadium, Texas Stadium, Market Center, State Fair Music Hall.

Getting Here   *From Dallas.* By car, Hwy. 35 to Hwy. 183 (Airport Freeway), MacArthur Blvd. exit. (20 mins). Limousine service. Taxi, rental car available.

Special Notes   Access for people with disabilities. Professionally managed child-care center (6 months to 8 years of age). No smoking in the spa or designated dining areas. No-smoking rooms available. Sports Club hours: Weekdays 6 AM–10 PM, weekends 7 AM–9 PM.

The Greenhouse

Life enhancement   *Women only*
Luxury pampering
Stress control

Texas   Privacy and freedom from stress are precious commodities to
Arlington   the harried young career women and the celebrities who check into The Greenhouse for a week of physical and emotional rejuvenation. Completely self-contained, with a staff of more than 160 serving just 39 guests, the retreat specializes in the classic spa tradition of total pampering.

From the airport you'll be whisked in a chauffeured limousine to the Greenhouse, set amid gardens and fitness trails. A special destination for the knowledgeable spa set since 1965, this elegant enclave has maintained its high standard of service and accommodations while expanding programs to appeal to the special needs of guests. Repeat visitors make up 75% of the clientele.

Attention to detail distinguishes a stay here. Each guest is assigned a personal esthetician, hairdresser, manicurist, and masseuse for the week. A resident exercise physiologist, nurse, and other staff members plan a schedule to each individual's needs. Meals are creative, with the executive chef, often joined by visiting chefs, demonstrating spa cuisine that you can make at home. In the dining room, exquisite table settings change nightly to create an elegant dining experience.

Breakfast in bed begins the day at 7 AM. Your daily schedule comes on the tray, and a fresh leotard and robe await you. A brisk guided walk through the garden is followed by exercise classes to energize and tone the body. Choices include aerobics (high and low impact), step classes, yoga, tai chi, strength training, aquatics (Hydrotone, Splashdance, and step), relaxation and breathing, and boxing. Your personal trainer studies your fitness profile (prepared on your arrival) and works with you at your pace.

Lunch is served poolside, followed by a daily massage and serious pampering. Daily schedules are adhered to unless guests request otherwise. Evenings can be dressy or informal, depending on the guests, yet the setting reflects everything you've ever seen on TV about Texan elegance and style.

Airy, bright, and expensively furnished, The Greenhouse has the look of a semitropical sybaritic hideaway. The skylighted, marble-floored atrium for swimming and the luxuriously feminine bedrooms are very much a part of the therapy.

The Greenhouse

Box 1144, Arlington, TX 76004
Tel. 817/640-4000
Fax 817/649-0422

Administration President, Lee Katzoff; Co-director, Shirley Ogle; Program director, Cynthia Lefferts

Season Year-round except early July and Dec. Programs begin and end on Sun.; 3-day miniweeks sometimes available

Accommodations 37 single rooms, 2 suites with queen-size half-canopied beds, matching drapes. Hand-embroidered linens, large dressing area, marble bathroom, sunken tub, air-conditioning, TV, telephone.

Rates From $3,795 to $4,050 per week. Miniweek $2,500. $1,000 deposit. AE, D, MC, V.

Meal Plans Choice of weight loss or maintenance: 1,000–1,200 or 1,500 calories a day. 3 meals plus mid-morning snack and afternoon fruit frappe. Homemade bran muffin, fresh melon and raspberries, coffee or tea for breakfast; vegetarian pizza with baby greens salad, lobster-and-crab salad, cheese soufflé with fruit at lunch; Cornish hens stuffed with shallots and breast meat, broiled lamb chops, grilled salmon at dinner.

Services and Facilities **Exercise Equipment:** Gravitron, Step & Slide, Strongput, 6-station Universal weight training gym, Nautilus units, 4 Trotter treadmills, 8 stationary bikes, cross-country NordicTrack, 2 StairMaster, body-ball weights, hand weights, poles, elastic Thoro-bands. **Services:** Massage (Swedish, shiatsu, reflexology, sports, acupressure, watsu), facials; hair, skin, and nail care; one-on-one workouts. Personal fitness, nutrition, health, beauty, and relaxation programs. Cooking classes. **Swimming Facilities:** Indoor and outdoor pools. **Recreation Facilities:** Tennis court, par course, jogging track. **Evening Programs:** Discussion topics are stress, wellness, makeup, cosmetic surgery; entertainment, feature films, fashion shows.

In the Area Kimbell Art Museum, Dallas Museum of Art, Amon Carter Museum, Dallas Baseball Stadium, State Fair Music Hall, Texas Stadium, shopping malls.

Getting Here *From Dallas.* By car, I-30 to Arlington, Hwy. 360 to Avenue II, left to 107th St. (20 mins). Complimentary limousine service provided by The Greenhouse to and from airport; taxi, rental car available.

Special Notes The entire facility is no-smoking. The Greenhouse at Mar-a-Lago in Palm Beach, Florida, under the same management, is a coed resort for members and guests.

Lake Austin Spa Resort

Life enhancement
Luxury pampering
Weight management

Texas
Austin

Hill-country walks, water aerobics, and a range of body-strengthening exercise classes make up the program at the Lake Austin Spa Resort. The coed retreat provides a great escape in a part of Texas noted for scenic rolling hills and placid lakes.

Although the program offers a wide range of activity choices, you pay a basic daily rate that includes fitness classes, meals, and guided hikes and canoe trips. Also available, for an additional fee, are European facials, mud masque, ayurvedic treatments, and other personal services in the salon. Try the honey mango scrub, a gentle body cleanser that incorporates applications of herbs and aloe vera, followed by a full-body massage.

The day begins at 7 with group walks ranging from 2 to 4 miles. The facilities include an indoor lap pool with resistant jets, a coed Jacuzzi, sauna, and steam room, and outdoor swimming pool. The glass-walled gym and aerobics studio, with suspended wooden floor, overlooks beautiful Lake Austin. Hiking and jogging trails extend into the woods.

The meals are designed to help you maintain a balanced diet, with natural meats, fresh fruit, vegtables, and herbs from an organic garden on the property. Snacks and energy drinks are available throughout the day, and you can request a brown bag lunch for outings.

Close to the city, yet secluded, the resort provides a close-up experience of the nature and ecology of Texas hill country. After an intense uphill climb, hikers enjoy panoramic views. One outing combines a canoe trip with sightings of birds and other wildlife. White tail deer, armadillos, rabbits, squirrels, raccoons, and red fox are frequently spotted by the lakeside. There is also an herb garden where you can learn about organic gardening from the staff horticulturist.

Laid-back and informal, this is a pleasant place to spend a day or a week. Accommodations range from basic cottages to luxury suites. And there is a roommate-matching service for single guests. Special weeks focus on lightening your attitude and improving your self-image, as well as on stress management.

Lake Austin Spa Resort
1705 Quinlan Park Rd., Austin, TX 78732
Tel. 512/266–2444 or 800/847–5637 (Canada 800/338–6651)
Fax 512/266–1572

Administration Executive director, Jeff Wall

Season Year-round

Accommodations 40 rooms in single-level connected cottages facing the lake. Antiques, down comforters on the bed, lots of pillows, create a country B&B feeling. All rooms have TV, phone, air-conditioning, private bath. Some bedrooms have 2 full-size beds or a king-size four-poster. Nightly turndown service is provided.

Rates Daily rate $110–$172 single, $102–$152 per person double. Lighten Up week (Sun.–Sun.) $2,005 single, $1,862 per person double occupancy, $1,718 triple; Refresher week (Sun.–Sun.) $1,972 single, $1,829 double; (Sun.–Thurs.) $1,182 single, $1,100 double. Sampler package (Thurs.–Sun.) $835 single,

$774 double. Add service charge and 6% tax. Deposit: $200 per person. AE, MC, V.

Meal Plans 3 meals daily, plus snacks, high in complex carbohydrates and fiber, low in fat, sugar, and salt, with organic, natural foods and vegetarian choices from menu. Breakfast buffet has muffins, bagels, fresh fruit, coffee, tea, juices, choice of tacos, whole-wheat pancakes, blintzes, French toast, cereals. Lunch and dinner entrées may be enchiladas, lasagna, fajitas, pizza, barbecued chicken, Thai noodle bowl, muffalettas, crawfish creole, pasta. Desserts are frozen peach yogurt, sherbet, cheesecake, or rum soufflé.

Services and Facilities **Exercise Equipment:** Flexmaster weight training equipment, 2 recumbent bikes, StairMaster, 2 Schwinn Air Dyne bikes, treadmill, rowing machine, free weights. **Services:** Massage (Swedish, aromatherapy, shiatsu, reflexology), body scrub, body brushing, polish, herbal wrap, seaweed body masque, moortherapy, ayurveda, facials. Salon for nail care, makeup consultation. Personal consultation on fitness, nutrition, skin analysis, special dietary needs. **Swimming Facilities:** Indoor and outdoor pools. **Recreation Facilities:** Volleyball, badminton, canoes, sculls, paddleboats, 2 tennis courts (lighted), mountain bikes. Golf and horseback riding nearby. **Evening Programs:** Music, comedy, aromatherapy. Talks on health and fitness.

In the Area University of Texas, state capitol, L. B. Johnson Library and Museum, National Wildflower Research Center.

Getting Here *From Austin.* By car, Ranch Rd. 2222, FM 620 to Stone Ranch Rd., Quinlan Park Rd. left to resort sign (45 mins). Free transfers to and from Austin Airport. Taxi, rental car available.

Special Notes Smoking and no-smoking rooms available. Laundry rooms available.

The Middle West

Fitness resorts are a relatively recent phenomenon in the Middle West. Programs in this part of the country tend to be informal and outdoors oriented, focusing on weight loss and general well-being.

Wisconsin offers the widest variety of choices, from the sports-oriented American Club to the sophisticated pampering of the Fontana Spa at the Abbey Resort on Lake Geneva. In Ohio you can work out in a registered historic landmark at the Kerr House, or at Mario's International Spa near Cleveland, with its Americana decor and Victorian antiques. For another kind of spa experience take the thermal waters at French Lick Springs in Indiana and the Elms in Missouri: Both have been popular since the turn of the century with the famous and the infamous.

Destination spas such as Birdwing in Minnesota, and the Heartland near Chicago, offer personal attention and the support of group camaraderie. Perhaps the most unusual example is the Raj in Fairfield, Iowa, devoted to the ancient system of preventive natural medicine known as ayurvedic therapy. The Marsh near Minneapolis is another example of dedicated wellness programs for prevention of illness. At these country retreats you learn to handle stress, manage your diet, and balance mind, body, and spirit.

The Heartland Spa

Life enhancement
Nutrition and diet
Stress control

Illinois
Gilman

Guests are made to feel at home in The Heartland Spa's lakefront mansion, which is rather like an adult camp in the country. The 30-acre estate boasts a guest list limited to 28, and your day can be as structured or unstructured as you please. You don't need to sign up for scheduled exercise classes, but do make appointments for massage and facials. Since bodywork and beauty treatments are included in the package, most guests take advantage of them—and add further pampering services at their own expense.

High-tech workouts with weight machines are held in the barn, an impressive three-level fitness center reached through an underground passage from the house. This barn is unlike anything on the neighboring farms; it has a full complement of cardiovascular workout equipment, pneumatic resistance muscle movers, an indoor swimming pool, whirlpool, sauna, steam room, and private massage rooms.

Personal consultation with staff is included in the five-day and seven-day programs. They advise you to concentrate on activities you enjoy and to continue them when you return home. (Try yoga and race walking!) Scheduled classes include aerobics, aquacise, step aerobics, martial arts, and self-awareness. Try the challenging ropes course, or a winter outing for cross-country skiing.

Secluded and self-contained, The Heartland is less than two hours from Chicago. Weekends are the busiest time; the best deal is a five-day stay, from Sunday to Friday noon. Longer, discounted stays can be arranged to concentrate on weight

Illinois
The Heartland Spa, **8**

Indiana
French Lick Springs
Resort, **12**
Indian Oak Resort, **7**

Iowa
The Raj, **9**

Minnesota
Birdwing Spa, **1**
The Marsh, **2**

Missouri
The Elms Resort, **10**
Marriott's Tan-Tar-A
Resort & Spa, **11**

Ohio
The Kerr House, **14**
Mario's International
Spa, **15**
Sans Souci Health
Resort, **13**

Wisconsin
The American Club, **4**
Aveda Spa Retreat, **3**
The Fontana Spa at
the Abbey, **6**
Holiday Inn
Sunspree Resort, **5**

The Middle West

loss or recuperation from illness. The group spirit here is warm and genuine.

The Heartland Spa

Rte. 1, Box 181, Gilman, IL 60938
Tel. 312/357–6465 in Chicago; 815/683–2182 at spa, or
800/545–4853
Fax 815/683–2144

Administration Founder, Jerry Kaufman; director, Mary Quinn

Season Year-round

Accommodations 14 pine-furnished rooms have country antiques, down-filled comforters, twin beds, private bath with hair dryer, toiletries, large fluffy towels.

Rates 2-day weekend $720 per person double occupancy, $800 single; 5 days $1,260 double, $1,620 single; 8-days/7-nights (Sun.–Sun.) $1,764 double, $2,268 single. Roommate-matching on request. Taxes and gratuities included. 50% deposit. AE, MC, V.

Meal Plans 3 meals daily (table service). Snacks and fruit all day. Breakfast includes freshly baked muffins, hot and cold cereal, coffee on request. Mostly vegetarian menu; dairy products, fish served occasionally. No salt, sugar, or added fats. 1,200 calories a day for women, 1,500 for men. Lunch can include hearty soup, vegetable pâté, or Japanese mushroom salad; typical dinner entrées are grilled swordfish with rosemary, Peruvian fish stew, corn crepes with spinach soufflé, fish and vegetable brochettes.

Services and Facilities **Exercise Equipment:** 8 Keiser Cam II pneumatic resistance units, 3 Cybex exercycles, 2 Schwinn Air Dyne bikes, 2 rowers, 3 treadmills, 3 Tunturi exercycles, free weights, hand weights, StairMaster, soft joggers, NordicTrack, trampolines. **Services:** Massage therapy (sports, relaxation, foot), facial, manicure, pedicure, hair and skin care, personal fitness assessment, nutrition evaluation, underwater body composition test. **Swimming Facilities:** 15-meter indoor pool, 3-acre lake. **Recreation Facilities:** 2 lighted outdoor tennis courts, parcourse, hiking, cross-country skiing (equipment provided), 2-person bike, ¼-mi running track. **Evening Programs:** Informal discussions on health-related topics. Guest speakers on stress management, life enhancement, dependency, financial planning.

In the Area Architecture of Frank Lloyd Wright in Oak Park, Abraham Lincoln's home and tomb in Springfield.

Getting Here *From Chicago.* By car, the Dan Ryan Expwy. south, I–57 to Kankakee Exit 308, Hwy. 52/45 (becomes Hwy. 49) to Rte. 24, R.R. 122 (90 mins). By train, Amtrak to Gilman (1 hr). By bus, Greyhound (2 hrs).

Special Notes No smoking indoors.

French Lick Springs Resort

Nonprogram resort
Taking the waters

Indiana
French Lick Modeled on the great spas of Europe, the French Lick Springs Resort was built in the early 1840s and attracted a wealthy elite who came from all over the country to "take the waters" in as many ways as they could. The sulfurous spring water was bottled and marketed as Pluto Water, and today it is still used in the Pluto Bath in the hotel health club.

Recently restored to its original Victorian elegance in a costly renovation, the hotel has high-ceilinged rooms with ceiling fans, French doors, carved woodwork, and verandas that overlook formal gardens. Its 2,600 acres of lawns and rolling woodland add to the charm and attract families and conventions.

The spa can be enjoyed on a daily-rate basis or with baths and beauty services included in two-night and five-night packages. No formal program of activities is offered; you set your own schedule. The spa director will consult with you on a meal plan, exercise classes, and bodywork. There is an exercise room, sauna, and whirlpools.

French Lick Springs is a place to have fun and enjoy a bit of pampering. With two championship golf courses, tennis courts, and other recreation facilities at hand, the springs are no longer the sole attraction. Yet you can still have a sip from a well beneath a gazebo or take a bath in spring water piped into a claw-foot tub.

French Lick Springs Resort
French Lick, IN 47432
Tel. 812/936–9300 or 800/457–4042

Administration	General manager, Greg James; spa director, Doris Todd
Season	Year-round
Accommodations	502 deluxe suites and large double rooms with king- or queen-size bed, antique furniture, modern private bath, color TV.
Rates	$149 spa day package with lunch. 5-night spa program, $662 per person double occupancy, $860 single; 2-night midweek package $299 per person double, $384 single. Winter rates lower. Gratuities and tax extra. Credit card confirmation or $100 per person deposit for spa packages. AE, DC, MC, V.
Meal Plans	3 meals daily with spa packages. Low-calorie selections include poached salmon for dinner, shrimp shish kebab and teriyaki chicken for lunch. Vegetarian meals on request.
Services and Facilities	**Exercise Equipment:** 10-unit Universal weight training gym, 2 Schwinn Air Dyne bikes, rowing machines, Tredex, Stairobic, AerobiCycle. **Services:** Swedish massage, aromatherapy, reflexology, salt rub, facials, pedicure, manicure, loofah body scrub, makeup lessons, beauty salon for hair and skin care, personal consultation on exercise. **Swimming Facilities:** Indoor and outdoor pools. **Recreation Facilities:** 2 18-hole golf courses, 18 tennis courts (8 indoors), horseback riding, bicycling, bowling, billiards, fishing, sailing, skiing. **Evening Programs:** Resort entertainment.
In the Area	Surrey rides, Evansville historic district (19th-century homes), Old Vanderburgh County Courthouse, New Harmony colony near Vincennes, Amish farms.
Getting Here	*From Louisville.* By bus, Greyhound (2 hrs). By car, I–64 west, Hwy. 150 to Paoli, Rte. 56 west (1 hr). Hotel limousine, rental car available.
Special Notes	Elevators and ramps connect hotel rooms and spa facilities for people with disabilities. Supervised day camp for children during summer; playground, miniature train ride, wading pool. No smoking in the spa.

Indian Oak Resort

Luxury pampering

Indiana
Chesterton

This nonstructured resort offers a variety of spa services in addition to 100 acres of lush, well-maintained grounds, around which many activities—including hiking and water sports—take place. In 1990 the resort was expanded and now offers spa packages that include an extensive selection of personal services such as massages and facials, as well as meal coupons.

There are five rooms for massage, facials, and reflexology, and a newly designed room for wet treatments with mud and seaweed. All guests can use the facilities and participate in exercise classes without charge. Scheduled are aquacize, StepReebok, and Stretch & Tone. While exercising you can enjoy a view of the lake. There is also an indoor lap pool and whirlpool.

Indian Oak Resort
558 Indian Boundry, Chesterton, IN 46304
Tel. 219/926–2200 or 800/552–4232

Administration	Owner-manager, Cathy Chubb; spa manager, Wendy Krantz
Season	Year-round
Accommodations	100 rooms, some with king-size beds; modern furniture, private bath, cable TV, phone, air-conditioning. Lakeside rooms have terraces.
Rates	$60–$118 for 2 persons double occupancy, $55–$113 single; suites $85–$153. 2-night spa package $237–$275 per person double, $292–$358 single; 3-night spa package $338.52–$390.75 per person double, $404.50–$509 single. Taxes included; add gratuities. Deposit for first night by credit card. AE, DC, MC, V.
Meal Plans	Continental breakfast included in all room rates. Spa package includes 2 meals daily, low in fat, salt, and calories.
Services and Facilities	**Exercise Equipment:** Universal gym, 2 StairMasters, 2 treadmills, Schwinn Air Dyne bike, rowing machine, free weights. **Services:** Swedish massage, herbal wrap, facial, shiatsu, body buff; salon for hair, nail, and skin care. **Swimming Facilities:** 50-ft indoor lap pool, private lake. **Recreation Facilities:** Boating, fishing, hiking trails.
In the Area	Lake Michigan, Dunes National Lakeshore, Indiana Dunes State Park.
Getting Here	*From Chicago.* By car, I–80/90 to I–94 (1 hr). By train, South Shore 9 to Chesterton (80 mins). Free shuttle service from train.
Special Notes	Spa open Tues.–Fri. 8–8, Sat. and Mon. 8–5, Sun. 8–1. Minimum age: 16.

The Raj

Life enhancement
Preventive medicine
Spiritual awareness

Iowa
Fairfield

The secluded Raj health center, opened in 1992 in the heart of rolling meadows and woodlands, introduces a new level of luxury to the country's array of destination spas devoted to the ancient system of preventive natural medicine known as ayurvedic therapy. Here, the soothing and refreshing treatments first introduced in America at Massachusetts's Maharishi Ayur-Veda center can be combined with programs incorporating fitness and exercise.

Treatment begins with an assessment of your physiological makeup by a physician concerned with both physical and spiritual health. Maharishi therapies, designed to restore balance in your body, are deeply relaxing. Traditionally known as *panchakarma*, treatments include warm herbal-oil massages, herbal steam baths, and internal cleansing. Aromatic ayurvedic oils are used to enliven energy points (*marmas*) to create a feeling of well-being. For stress reduction and to expand inner awareness, you are introduced to transcendental meditation (TM) and given a mantra.

The Maharishi Ayur-Veda Health Center provides several program options that can be combined with the daily rate for lodging. In the new skin-rejuvenation program, after medical consultation, your daily treatments include mud baths, milk baths, and massage, for 3–7 days. Called the Royal Beauty From Within program, it is a natural evolution of ancient and contemporary philosophies that exemplify the goals of The Raj.

The Raj
1734 Jasmine Ave., Fairfield, IA 52556
Tel. 515/472–9580 or 800/248–9050
Fax 515/472–2496

Administration Owners-directors, Candace and Rodgers Badgett, Jr.; medical director, Christopher Clark, M.D.; fitness director, Barbara McLaughlin

Season Year-round

Accommodations 46 deluxe rooms and suites in 2-story villas and in the Raj Court Hotel. The Spa Wing of the hotel has 19 standard rooms, while the Hotel Wing has 18 larger deluxe rooms. Each private villa has 3 guest suites. All rooms have queen-size beds, carpeting, air-conditioning, and telephone and are decorated with flowered wallpaper, carved-wood furniture, and silk and cotton draperies. Baths are marble-walled with twin vanities, shower and bath (separate in deluxe rooms and suites), and amenities including hair dryer, robes, and slippers.

Rates Royal Beauty From Within program 2 days $1,420, 5 days $2,260, 7 days $3,060. Other programs: 3-day $1,270; 5-day $2,010; 7-day $2,710. TM training not included in program fee. Lodging $85 single per night, $120 for 2, double occupancy; villa apartment $125–$185. Add gratuity and 5% tax. Deposit 50%. AE, MC, V.

Meal Plans 3 gourmet vegetarian meals daily that follow the ayurvedic principles are included in program. Breakfast includes home-baked bread, jam, cereal. Lunch can be fresh organic vegetable soup, eggplant pilaf with basmati rice and cilantro sauce, lemon broccoli or dilled green beans, and dessert. Dinner menus include jade soup, fresh green peas in coconut milk, summer squash sauté, couscous pilaf, asparagus phyllo rolls, and dessert.

Services and Facilities **Exercise Equipment:** 2 treadmills, 2 stairsteppers, 2 stationary bikes, free weights. **Services:** Ayurvedic massage, transcendental meditation, stress management, self-pulse diagnosis, skin care, nutrition and diet counseling, internal cleansing. **Recreation Facilities:** Nearby golf, horseback riding, tennis. **Programs:** Videotapes and lectures on health-related topics.

In the Area Maharishi International University, Pella (Dutch historic settlement), Des Moines.

Getting Here *From Cedar Rapids.* By car, I–380 south, Rte. 1 south to Fairfield airport, right turn on Rural Road 8 (1¼ hrs). Private planes land at Fairfield Airport, where pickup by a Raj car can be arranged upon request (fee). Limousine or hotel car picks up at Cedar Rapids Airport (fee).

Special Notes No smoking. Special accommodations available for people with disabilities. Hotel accommodations and dining open to the public.

Birdwing Spa

Life enhancement
Luxury pampering
Nutrition and diet

Minnesota The first full-service spa in the upper Midwest, Birdwing Spa
Litchfield blends European therapy and Minnesota traditions. The Tudor mansion set on a lakeside estate accommodates up to 25 guests; an exercise studio occupies the former barn, and an outdoor swimming pool and 12 miles of groomed walking and cross-country ski trails are on the grounds.

Oriented to outdoor activity, the spa provides equipment for skiing, canoeing, and biking, in addition to circuit weight training. In two daily "image sessions," guests have a choice of facial, massage, or manicure. Aerobic exercise or an hour of yoga completes the daily schedule in the 3,500-square-foot fitness building.

Birdwing ranks high as a relaxing experience on a 300-acre country estate that preserves the feeling of Old World traditions. In the chaletlike main building, guests relax in a sauna and Jacuzzi, or talk to the chef in the kitchen. Beauty-treatment facilities are housed in an adjacent building. Recent renovation of a large barn on the property added six suites, each with a Jacuzzi bath.

Personalized attention from the owners makes each guest feel at home. They have developed a fitness program to complement a diet regimen of 1,000–1,200 calories daily for women, 1,300–1,500 calories for men, which is tailored to your needs. While group members are friendly, this is a also a good place to enjoy being on your own.

Birdwing Spa
21398 575th Ave., Litchfield, MN 55355
Tel. 612/693–6064

Administration Owner-directors, Richard and Elisabeth Carlson

Season Year-round

Accommodations 9 bedrooms (singles and doubles) with Ethan Allen furnishings, draperies, shared baths. The 7 suites have private Jacuzzi bath, pine armoires, king-size bed. One suite in the main house comes with fireplace and steam bath.

Rates 7-day program with suite accommodation, $1,650 single occupancy, $1,550 per person double; standard rooms in main house, $1,275 single, $1,195 double. 5-day program $1,350 single in suite, $1,250 per person double; standard rooms $1,075 single, $995 double. 2-day retreat $475–$550 per person in suite; $350–$395 in standard rooms. 1-day overnight package $225–$295. Add 15% service charge and tax. $150 in advance for weekends, $300 for other programs. MC, V.

Meal Plans 3 weight-loss meals daily: cinnamon raisin French toast with 3-berry sauce for breakfast, fruit kebabs followed by chicken tacos with salsa or turkey pizza for lunch, chicken asparagus rolls and butterscotch brownies for dinner.

Services and Facilities **Exercise Equipment:** 2 treadmills, 2 Schwinn Air Dyne bikes, StairMaster, free weights. **Services:** Swedish and Esalen massage, facials, hair and nail care, aromatherapy, paraffin therapy, back treatment, nutritional counseling, fitness evaluation, exercise instruction. **Swimming Facilities:** Outdoor pool. **Spa Facilities:** Men's and women's saunas, coed whirlpool, massage room. **Recreation Facilities:** Bicycling, canoeing, cross-country skiing, bird-watching. Tennis and golf nearby. Special weeks for art and nature studies. **Evening Programs:** Guest speakers on stress control, nutrition, cardiac health, and problems of career women. Cooking classes and feature films.

In the Area Minneapolis–St. Paul museums, Mall of America.

Getting Here *From Minneapolis.* By car, I–394, Hwy. 12 west to Litchfield, Rte. 1 and 23 (90 mins). Birdwing makes arrangements for local transportation on request ($50).

Special Notes No smoking in public areas indoors. Minimum age: 16. Ground-floor rooms accessible for people with disabilities.

The Marsh

Kid fitness
Life enhancement
Vibrant maturity
Weight management

Minnesota
Minnetonka

Designed as a center for balance and fitness, the Marsh integrates architecture and aerobics, nutrition and nurturing, to help you balance the mind and body. Begun in 1985 on the edge of marshland near Minneapolis, the dramatic wooden structure seems to grow from the earth: The inside opens to the sky. The spa addition opened in 1993 as part of an expansion that more than doubled the Marsh, providing overnight accommodations for 12 guests in a private wing with lounge area and deck overlooking the natural Minnesota marshlands.

Ruth Stricker practices what she preaches as the founder-director of the Marsh. Despite the onset of crippling lupus, Stricker discovered how meditation and body movements work together to restore health. As the Marsh membership grew, an Over-50 Club was formed to push the envelope in exercise programs for mature bodies. And a KidFitness center serves the community as well as visitors, inspiring teenagers to incorporate fitness regimens with an active lifestyle.

The new, 27,000-square-foot structure includes a climbing wall, a flotation tank, and a silo-shape meditation tower equipped with a computer-controlled "mind gym," with sounds that help guests to meditate. During the day you can sign up for tai chi, yoga, somatics (movements to help manage chronic back pain), centering (exercises for alignment and stretching), flo-motion in the pool, and back therapy with physio-gymnastic balls, among other workouts.

This is the most comprehensive wellness center in the Midwest, with everything under one roof, including cardiovascular and weight-training equipment, a 75-foot lap pool, sauna, and nine treatment rooms. Educational programs, classes, and special services can be part of a retreat program, but there is no package or group activity. Arrangements can be made for a personalized fitness assessment including a 12-lead EKG, nutritional consultation, and physical therapy. Or you can simply join the scheduled activities at the center and reserve time for personal services and meals at the spa.

The Marsh
15000 Minnetonka Blvd., Minnetonka, MN 55345
Tel. 612/935–2202
Fax 612/935–9685

Administration Founder-director, Ruth Stricker; spa director, Jean Sova

Season Year-round

Accommodations 6 bedrooms, each with 2 single beds, private bathroom, chair, bureau. Cozy rather than elegant, the rooms have views of the marsh, are air-conditioned, with TV, phone. Robes are provided.

Rates $90 single, $115 for 2 persons double occupancy, per night. Gratuities and tax not included. AE, MC, V.

Meal Plans Breakfast included with room; lunch and dinner served in restaurant and can be ordered à la carte. Menu choices include fresh grilled salmon, chicken breast with wild mushrooms, pork medallions with salsa, and choice of wine, beer, or herbal tea. Coffee and bottled waters available.

Services and Facilities **Exercise Equipment:** VersaClimber, Cybex, Concept 2 rowers, Combi Ergopower Bicycle, StairMasters, Stretchmate, Equinox 2000, Quinton treadmills, NordicTrack Pro X-C ski machines, Keiser equipment, Nautilus, Pilates. **Services:** Swedish massage, Feldenkrais Method, Alexander Technique, Somatics, herbal wrap. **Swimming Facilities:** 75-ft indoor pool. **Recreation Facilities:** Nature trail, racquetball, squash court, golf, rock-climbing wall.

In the Area Minneapolis/St. Paul museums and theaters, Mall of America.

Getting Here *From Minneapolis.* By car, Hwy. 394 west to Carlson Pkwy., Hwy. 494 south to Minnetonka Blvd., right for ¼ mile (30 mins).

Special Notes All facilities accessible for people with disabilities. No smoking indoors or on decks. Fitness Center open weekdays 5:30 AM–10:30 PM, weekends 7 AM–9 PM. Classes scheduled daily 7–7. Child care and developmental activities for children 6 wks–6 yrs. Minimum age for overnight accommodations is 18.

The Elms Resort

Nonprogram resort
Taking the waters

Missouri
Excelsior Springs

In the 1800s high-living health seekers descended on this sleepy little Missouri town each season to take the mineral waters. The Elms, built to accommodate them in the grand manner, became a tradition that survived two devastating fires; the present limestone and concrete structure was built in 1912 and incorporates the New Leaf Spa.

Ten "environmental rooms" are programmed for jungle rain, wet steam, or dry sauna and equipped with a hot tub for two. The European swim track, which can be mildly claustrophobic, is a one-lane lap pool filled with tap water.

There's a lot of nostalgic charm about the Elms, complete with stories of Harry Truman's visits and all-night parties hosted by Al Capone. Croquet and badminton are played on the lawn, and the tennis court is free to guests. A quaint village of boutiques completes the resort. Popular for conventions and sales meetings, the 23-acre wooded resort is less than an hour from Kansas City.

The Elms Resort
Regent St. and Elms Blvd., Excelsior Springs, MO 64204
Tel. 816/637–2141, spa reservations: 816/637–0752 or
800/843–3567
Fax 816/637–1222

Administration Manager, Douglas Morrison; spa manager, Sandra Kennedy

Season   Year-round

Accommodations   136 rooms furnished with traditional wood dresser and table, desk, ceiling fan, cable TV, old-fashioned tiled bath.

Rates $79–$95 per night for 2, double occupancy; $148.68 summer weekend package for 2; 2-night Escape package for 2 $239–$379; suites $95–$130 for 2; condos $150. Add tax (6.975%) and gratuities. AE, DC, MC, V.

Meal Plans   American and European cuisine. Salads, fresh fish, meat, or chicken for lunch and dinner. Buffet dinners and brunch included in weekend and Escape packages.

Services and Facilities   **Exercise Equipment:** Nautilus circuit gym, Liferower, Lifecycle, treadmill, stationary bike. Indoor running track circles the lap pool (23 circuits=1 mi). **Services:** Swedish massage, facial, cosmetology, beauty salon. **Spa Facilities:** Private mineral baths by appointment ($12.50), hot and cold whirlpools, 3-level spa complex with separate saunas and steam rooms for men and women. **Swimming Facilities:** Outdoor pool, municipal indoor pool. **Recreation Facilities:** Golf, tennis, croquet, badminton, volleyball, horseshoes, shuffleboard; racquetball court nearby; bicycle rental. **Evening Programs:** Resort entertainment.

In the Area   Watkins Woolen Mill (19th-century textile factory) in state park, fishing, swimming, hiking, picnicking, camping, Kansas City Zoo, Country Club Plaza (shopping), Crown Center (Hallmark museum), Nelson Atkins Museum of Art.

Getting Here   *From Kansas City.* By car, I–35 north to Excelsior Springs, Hwy. 69 to Rte. 10 (30 mins). Limo, rental car, taxi available.

Special Notes   No smoking in the spa. Spa open Fri.–Sat. 8 AM–11 PM, Sun.–Thurs. 8 AM–9 PM.

Marriott's Tan-Tar-A Resort & Spa

Nonprogram resort

Missouri
Osage Beach

Outdoor recreation is the principal attraction of Marriott's Tan-Tar-A Resort, surrounded by 400 acres in the Lake of the Ozarks region. The lake, created by a dam in 1931, has countless coves for water sports, boating, and fishing. The hotel caters to conventioneers as well as family vacationers. New in 1992 was the Windjammer Spa, a privately operated facility connected to the resort's indoor swimming pool and fitness center.

Guests enjoy use of an indoor/outdoor fitness center. Aerobics classes are offered three mornings a week, aquatics two mornings. The weights room, staffed by fitness specialists, is open daily, free of charge.

The spa is equipped with a hydrotherapy tub, coed steam room, and whirlpool. Massage and aromatherapy, as well as body scrubs, can be booked à la carte or as part of six packages, priced $50–$216. Programs are individually designed, from after-sports relaxation to stress relief.

Marriott's Tan-Tar-A Resort & Spa
State Road KK, Osage Beach, MO 65065
Tel. 573/348–3131, 800/826–8272, or 800/268–8181 in
Canada; Windjammer Spa: 573/348–3535

Administration   Manager, Leonard Camden; spa manager, Deborah Stanley

Season   Year-round

Accommodations 1,000 rooms in the hotel and cottages have fireplace, kitchenette, bar (in some rooms and suites), coffeemaker, TV, private bath.

Rates Double rooms $110–$165, 1-bedroom suites $225–$255, 2-bedroom suites $214. 2-night golf package for 2, $240 including breakfast and unlimited golf. Day Spa packages $50–$216. Deposit of 1 night's lodging applied to last night reserved (and forfeited on early departure). Rates include tax. AE, DC, MC, V.

Meal Plans The Cliff Room has Continental cuisine and light fare as well as fried catfish. Windrose on the Water serves fish cooked to order (broiled, baked, sautéed, blackened).

Services and Facilities **Exercise Equipment:** 3 Trotter treadmills, 2 Liferowers, 3 Nautilus stationary bikes, 9-station Universal weight training gym, abdominal-muscle exerciser. **Services:** Swedish massage, reflexology, acupressure, facial, body wrap, saltglow scrub, hydrotherapy, paraffin wrap, sea salt bath, aromatherapy; hair, nail, and skin care for men and women. **Swimming Facilities:** 4 outdoor pools, private beach on lake. **Recreation Facilities:** 6 outdoor and 2 indoor tennis courts, 4 indoor racquetball courts, 2 golf courses, 8 bowling lanes, billiards, moped rental, boat rental with fishing guide, trap-shooting range, miniature golf, ice skating. **Evening Programs:** Resort entertainment.

In the Area Trail rides, fishing, Bridal Cave, HaHa Tonka Castle monument and state park, antiques shops, Abraham Lincoln home and tomb in Springfield, IL; Harry Truman home and library in Independence, MO.

Getting Here *From St. Louis.* By car, I–44 to Rte. 65 (70 mins). Limousine service to and from the airport; rental car available.

Special Notes Supervised morning play camp for youngsters, teenage games and indoor activity in summer. No smoking in the weights room. Spa open daily 8–8; $10 facility fee refunded with services.

The Kerr House

**Life enhancement
Luxury pampering**

Ohio
Grand Rapids The Kerr House is an antiques-filled Victorian mansion that functions as a hideaway for men and women who seek privacy and a complete overhaul. With just five to seven guests in residence at a time, the facility takes on the atmosphere of a private club. Some weeks are reserved for men only, women only, or corporate groups.

Yoga, the specialty of the house, is taught in a carpeted exercise room on the top floor. Laurie Hostetler encourages guests by providing her own book of *asanas*, the exercise positions of Hatha yoga. Exercise is limited to low-impact aerobics, walking, and three hours of yoga daily.

Personal counseling makes this spa experience attractive for those who want to learn healthy habits. A good deal of time is spent discussing ways to build self-esteem and to deal with everyday stress. Addictions to smoking, caffeine, and sugar can be addressed. Avoiding temptation, changing one's daily routine, and being in a supportive group often inspire success. During the initial chemical withdrawal, positive support and breathing exercises to cleanse the lungs and flush impurities from the body are prescribed. Drinking lots of water, eating natural foods, and cleansing the colon are also advised. Whirlpool, sauna, and massage sessions are part of the pampering.

The Kerr House

17777 Beaver St., Grand Rapids, OH 43551
Tel. 419/832–1733
Fax 419/832–4303

Administration	Director, Laurie Hostetler
Season	Year-round
Accommodations	5 guest rooms with high ceilings, antiques, lace curtains. The house has massive wood doors, stained-glass windows, a hand-carved staircase.
Rates	5-day program (Sun.–Fri.) $2,150 per person double occupancy, $2,550 single. Tax and services included. Weekends $575 double, $675 single. Gratuities optional. 50% payable in advance. AE, MC, V.
Meal Plans	Diet of 750–1,000 calories per day, mainly vegetarian, with fish and chicken. Low in fat and cholesterol; no salt, sugar, refined flour, additives. Lunch can include a Senegalese carrot soup, lettuce salad, pita bread with couscous stuffing, and herbal tea. Typical dinner entrées are eggplant Parmesan with tomato sauce, baked chicken breast on wild rice, or shrimp and baked potato.
Services and Facilities	**Exercise Equipment:** Rebounders, NordicTrack, backswings. **Services:** Massage, pedicure, facial, hair and skin care, reflexology, polarity, herbal body wraps, mineral baths. **Swimming Facilities:** Community pool nearby. **Recreation Facilities:** Hiking along the Maumee River and the Miami & Erie Canal towpath, paddleboat rides. **Evening Programs:** Speakers.
In the Area	Visit to a glass craftsman's studio, the Ludwig Mill (water-powered saw and grist mill), the restored Fort Meigs, farms and country fairs, hydroplane races (Sept.).
Getting Here	*From Toledo.* By car, Ohio Turnpike (I–75) to Rte. 6, Rte. 65 to Rte. 24 (30 mins). Complimentary pickup and return at Toledo Express Airport.
Special Notes	No smoking indoors.

Mario's International Spa

Luxury pampering

Ohio
Aurora

Clevelanders enjoy formal dinners by candlelight, business executives shift from meetings to massage appointments, and a dozen or so spa guests in terry-cloth robes take tea in a Victorian parlor, all at Mario's International Spa. A few miles from the Ohio Turnpike, this country inn cum spa gives you a sense of having journeyed back to another century; one of the buildings was a stagecoach inn more than 130 years ago.

In addition to the spa building and a conference center, the complex is headquarters for Mario's International, owned and operated by Mario and Joanne Liuzzo, who have combined their experience in the beauty salon business with a love of Victoriana. Their salon outgrew two Victorian houses in eight years. Planned are an Olympic-size pool in the manner of ancient Roman baths, an enclosed jogging track, and 10 new guest rooms.

Fitness is the focus of the programs for corporate members and health-conscious men and women who come here. Aquaerobics, a Dynastic stretch-and-tone class, weight-loss diets, and thalassotherapy are new features. Recreation includes hiking, biking, and other outdoor sports. The spa has widened its selection of exercise equipment and worked on nutrition with Cleveland Clinic. Specialists from the clinic consult on preparation for and recovery from plastic surgery.

Esthetics is what the spa does best: eight facial and throat treatments for men and women, massages, pedicures, manicures, makeup application, and a top-quality salon for hairstyling and dressing. Repechage, a house specialty facial, involves a layered thermal mask with applications of concentrated aloe vera juice, powdered seaweed, and clay. When the hardened clay mask is removed, your complexion feels softer and firmer. The price is $70. Also new is an oxygen treatment to enhance the effect of facials.

Construction of new facilities and an indoor swimming pool is scheduled for completion in 1997. Meanwhile, the spa has added an imported hydrotherapy tub for underwater pressure massage with detoxifying volcanic mud from northern Italy, invigorating pine-needle extract, milk whey protein, or stimulating seaweed. The seaweed, called dulse, is harvested on Grand Manan Island in Canadian waters, where Mario's operates a bed-and-breakfast spa.

Mario's International Spa

35 E. Garfield Rd., Aurora, OH 44202
Tel. 216/562–9171
Fax 216/562–2386

Administration	Director-owner, Joanne Liuzzo
Season	Year-round
Accommodations	14 rooms in the hotel wing and the original mansion, furnished with period pieces and modern comforts: Jacuzzi, large modern bath, hair dryer, terry-cloth robe. Executive suite has fireplace.
Rates	Day at the Spa package with treatments, lunch, and aerobics $225 per person; 3-day/3-night Retreat package $2,050 per couple, $1,999 single. Tax included, add gratuities. One-third of total payable on booking. AE, MC, V.
Meal Plans	3 meals daily with packages. Oatmeal buttermilk pancake topped with fruit sauce (breakfast); shrimp and vegetable kebab, grilled chicken salad, pear and goat cheese salad, or vegetable sub (lunch); ricotta-stuffed zucchini rounds with tomato purée, grilled veal medallions with shiitake mushrooms, and grape mousse made with skim milk (dinner).
Services and Facilities	**Services:** Massage, facials, body scrub with dulse (a nutrient-packed seaweed) and almond oil, manicure, pedicure, parafango muscle treatment with mud/paraffin mix, hydrotherapy tub, Vichy shower, aromatherapy, pressotherapy, hairstyling, makeup consultation, personalized exercise instruction in power walking, aquacise, and other activities, Habitat environmental sauna, health and diet analysis, pre- and post-plastic surgery esthetics treatments. **Recreation Facilities:** Bicycling; golf, tennis, horseback riding nearby; downhill and cross-country skiing. **Evening Programs:** Lectures on health topics.
In the Area	Antiques shops, flea markets, shopping areas, Sea World, Blossom Music Center (Cleveland Orchestra) June–Aug.
Getting Here	*From Cleveland.* By bus, Greyhound (50 mins). By car, I–480 to Rte. 91, Rte. 82 and 306; or the Ohio Turnpike (I–80) to Exit 13 (40 mins). Limousine service from Cleveland Hopkins Airport; rental car available.

Special Notes Limited access for people with disabilities. No-smoking areas designated.

Sans Souci Health Resort

Luxury pampering
Stress control
Vibrant maturity
Weight management

Ohio On a beautiful, secluded 80-acre estate, a small band of health
Bellbrook seekers follows the owner and director of the Sans Souci Health Resort, Susanne Kircher, on a parcourse fitness trail across the immaculate lawn of the country retreat. Birdsong and gentle breezes enhance the outdoor sessions of stretching, breathing, and wake-up exercises. Miles of hiking trails crisscross the woods and meadows of the estate, which borders a 600-acre wildlife preserve.

Kircher, a registered nurse and a former consultant to Olympic athletes, mixes European spa philosophy with no-frills fitness training. The daily agenda is full of aerobics, from dance steps to slimnastics, and water workouts in the swimming pool during warm months. Meals are mainly vegetarian.

The spacious country home where the Romanian-born Kircher began her fitness resort in 1978 reflects her European concept of a healthy lifestyle: spare, clean, and brightened by flowers and art. The organic garden, where guests learn sprouting, supplies fresh vegetables and herbs for the kitchen. Programs are individually tailored, mainly focused on stress management and smoking cessation. Rather than promising a "quick fix," the program helps you plan practical goals. A stern taskmaster, Kircher summons you to join a meditation walk to the pine forest, or race-walking practice. "You will join us for exercise this morning?" is more statement than question. Your answer will be yes.

Sans Souci Health Resort
3745 Rte. 725, Bellbrook, OH 45305
Tel. 937/848-4851

Administration Director, Susanne Kircher, R.N.

Season May–Oct.

Accommodations Spacious, airy rooms furnished English country style, with private bath, dressing area.

Rates 5-night program Sun.–Fri. $1,330 per person double occupancy, $1,580 single; 7-day program $1,910 double, $2,260 single; weekend retreats $650 per person double, $750 single. Daily rate $168 (no room). 30% payable in advance. Tax and gratuity included. MC, V.

Meal Plans 1,000 calorie daily diet includes breakfast (sprouted wheat berries in soy milk or homemade granola), snacks, mineral water, lunch (whole-grain crepe, green salad, and steamed vegetables), and dinner (seafood Divan, fruit-garnished chicken) served by candlelight. Juice fast recommended on day of arrival.

Services and **Exercise Equipment:** Multigym, free weights, stationary bike,
Facilities Rebounder, 18-station par course. **Services:** Massage, aromatherapy, acupressure, loofah scrub, facials, herbal wraps, manicures, pedicures, hair and skin care, cooking demonstrations, personal consultation on nutrition and diet. **Swimming Facilities:** Outdoor pool, lake. **Recreation Facilities:** Horseback riding, badminton, volleyball, croquet; golf, tennis, and fishing

nearby. **Evening Programs:** Workshops on behavior modification, stress management, nutrition; assertiveness training; therapeutic massage and Jacuzzi relaxation. Guest lecturers and films.

In the Area Picnic lunches, tour of Bellbrook, 600-acre Sugarcreek Reserve.

Getting Here *From Dayton.* By car, I–75 to Rte. 725 E (30 mins). Free pickup on arrival at Dayton International Airport; $28 for return to airport.

Special Notes No smoking indoors.

The American Club

Nonprogram resort

Wisconsin In a town dominated by the nation's leading manufacturer of
Kohler plumbing fixtures and bathtubs, it can be no surprise that luxury and bathing are synonymous at the American Club's 237-room hotel owned and operated by the Kohler Company. Part of the club's charm lies in being in a place that looks like a Hollywood vision of middle America yet functions with the precision of a posh resort. The original Tudor-style dormitory, reminiscent of a country inn, has been duplicated across a garden courtyard where a Victorian greenhouse serves as an ice cream parlor.

With a 36-hole golf course designed by Pete Dye, a Sports Core with indoor and outdoor tennis courts and a spa salon, and a 500-acre nature preserve where country gourmet meals are served in a secluded log lodge, the American Club has become an oasis of fitness in the Midwest.

Whirlpools for two are set on glass-covered terraces and in mirrored baths. For the ultimate in hedonism, ask for a suite equipped with the Kohler Shower Tower (similar to Swiss shower) or the Habitat, a master bath with an hour's serenity programmed into it: The sounds of a rain forest, soft breezes, a gentle mist, a steam bath, even desert tanning are simulated.

Wellness programs are tailored to the individual, for stress reduction as much as for aerobics or strength, and to lose weight. Checking in at the Sports Core, you get a locker and towel and the opportunity to schedule herbal wraps, massage, and court times. In addition to racquetball courts (used for handball and walleyball, too), six indoor tennis courts are available for an hourly fee, while the outdoor courts are free. The Peter Burwash International staff offers professional instruction. Exercise rooms, aerobics studio, and health services are downstairs. A glass-walled 60-foot swimming pool, the Lean Bean restaurant (a happy discovery for dieters), and beauty salon are off the lobby.

River Wildlife is a place apart, one where the outdoors and good food are celebrated. Marksmen practice, hikers explore more than 30 miles of woodland trails, and canoeists and fishermen enjoy the winding Sheboygan River. Horseback rides can be solo or escorted. In winter the trails are groomed for cross-country skiing. Lunch is served daily in a rustic lodge, dinner on weekends in front of the huge fireplace. American Club guests need only a $8.25 pass to use the facilities; the trails are open to all.

The American Club
Highland Dr., Kohler, WI 53044
Tel. 414/457–8000 or 800/344–2838
Fax 414/457–0299

Administration Lodging director, James Beley; Sports Core manager, Jean Kolb

Season Year-round

Accommodations 237 rooms with a range of whirlpool baths, 4-poster brass beds with feather comforters and pillows, wood paneling, carved oak doors, sitting areas, glassed-in terrace with hot tub, wet bar, and mirrored bath in some rooms. Suites have fireplace. Rooms in the renovated Carriage House are reached by crossing the parking lot or using an underground walkway. Free transportation between facilities.

Rates $155–$635 for 2 in double room, $125–$635 single. 2-night escape packages for 2 persons, including a bubble massage at the Sports Core and some meals, $345–$580. For golfers, 2 rounds at Blackwolf Run, plus amenities, $830–$1,360 for 2 persons double occupancy. 1-day spa package with services and lunch $315; half-day $160. Deposit: 1 night payable in advance. Tax and gratuity not included. AE, DC, MC, V.

Meal Plans Breakfast buffet in the Wisconsin Room, expanded menu at Sunday brunch. Dinner at the Immigrant is a dress-up affair in small rooms dedicated to the club's original European occupants; specialties are Wisconsin whitefish roe, scallops, shrimp, seafood sausage on spinach pasta, mesquite-roasted loin of Iowa pork, Kohler Purelean beef. The River Wildlife menu, changed every weekend, can feature pheasant pâté, grilled rabbit, broiled fresh brook trout stuffed with vegetables, veal scallops with pesto and 5-cheese sauce. Salad of sprouts and seasonal greens or hamburgers at the Lean Bean or the Horse & Plow pub restaurant for lunch.

Services and Facilities **Exercise Equipment:** 14-station Nautilus circuit, 8 Lifecycles, 3 StairMasters, Liferower; 16-station Universal gym, 6 Schwinn Air Dyne bikes, 2 rowers, Olympic free weights, NordicTrack, 3 step machines. **Services:** Massage, herbal wrap, body wrap, facial, manicure, pedicure, fitness consultation, hydrotherapy. Aerobics classes throughout the day ($7.75 each). Clay marksmanship course, crazy-quail shooting, archery instruction. **Swimming Facilities:** Indoor lap pool, lake with sandy beach. **Recreation Facilities:** 6 indoor and 6 outdoor tennis courts, 2 handball/racquetball courts, fishing, canoeing and boating, bicycle rentals, hiking, cross-country skiing, 2 golf courses.

In the Area Half-day canoe trip, nature walks, charter-boat fishing on Lake Michigan, Kettle Moraine State Forest (Ice Age formations), dunes on Lake Michigan beaches, nature trail at Sheboygan Indian Mound Park, Kohler Arts Center, Kohler Design Center, cheese plant tour, Kohler Company tour, Manitowac Maritime Museum, shops at Woodlake Kohler.

Getting Here *From Milwaukee.* By car, I–43 to Exit 126, Rte. 23 west to Kohler (about 1 hr). By bus, Greyhound to Sheboygan (70 mins). Limousine Service (tel. 800/236–5452) to and from Milwaukee's Mitchell Airport, Amtrak, and bus stations.

Special Notes Elevators link all floors. The Sports Core has supervised activities for children 1½–6. Older children can join weeklong summer-camp programs or sign up for tennis and swimming lessons. No smoking in Sports Core athletic and therapy areas.

Aveda Spa Retreat

Life enhancement
Luxury pampering
Weight management

Wisconsin
Osceola

On the banks of the St. Croix River, about an hour's drive from Minneapolis/St. Paul, is the Aveda Spa Retreat, opened in 1990. A former estate on 80 acres, the prairie-style three-story house dating from 1908 has been rejuvenated with hydrotherapy rooms, European shampoo bed, a few pieces of exercise equipment, and a beauty salon. Five luxury suites and a conference center were added in 1996.

The resort, owned and managed by the Aveda Corporation, a Minneapolis-based producer of natural products for the hair and skin, serves as both a day spa and a country getaway. In summer, you can enjoy walking, running, or biking on scenic trails surrounding the spa, or spend hours canoeing on the placid St. Croix River. In winter, cross-country skiing, snowshoeing, and ice-skating outings are organized. You may also choose to visit their Native American sweat lodge.

Spa treatments, enhanced with flower and plant essences and the pure water of St. Croix Springs, are designed to refresh and relax your body. Advanced cellular skin-care technology has been incorporated into the spa's skin-care treatments, which include aromatherapy.

Much of the decor is retained from the 1920s, along with antiques from the 17th century. A mammoth fireplace fills one end of a living room stripped of furniture for the daily session of yoga. Up the wide oak stairway are six bedrooms with polished wood floors; bright Pakistani, Indian, and Turkish carpets; and antique wooden beds laden with down pillows and duvets.

In the lower level of the house, past the sauna and exercise salon, are areas for treatments plus grottolike single bedrooms. Private rooms for massage, facials, and a hydrotherapy tub are reserved for guest use. Additional treatment and guest rooms are in the carriage house.

Programs are individually tailored to each guest's needs. Organized activity is minimal, as are the meals, but if you want the ultimate in skin care while shedding a few pounds, this is the place.

Aveda Spa Osceola

1015 Cascade St., Osceola, WI 54020
Tel. 715/294–4465 or 800/283–3202
Fax 715/294–2196

Administration

Founder-CEO, Horst Rechelbacher; director, Bootsie Lynch; manager, Peggy Anderson

Season

Year-round

Accommodations

15 guest rooms, including suites. Furniture ranges from Indian to antiques to Art Deco, with wicker chairs, brass beds. Most rooms have private bath, air-conditioning; no TV or telephones.

Rates

A weekend stay with spa services and meals is $675 single, $575 per person double occupancy. 5-day stays are $1,475 single, $1,235 double. Gratuities for meals and taxes included. A 1-day package with lunch is $155–$250 without lodging; overnight $345 single, $395 double. Daily rate $125 single, $62.50 double; suites $200–$300. Deposit: 50% payable in advance. AE, MC, V.

Meal Plans Organic menu includes lunch choices of tomato aspic with gua-
camole, endive, and nasturtium salad. Dinner entrées include
organically raised trout or grilled salmon with jalapeño and
roasted tomato sauce, stuffed baby artichokes, Peruvian potatoes, and steamed green beans. Macrobiotic meals are available.

Services and **Exercise Equipment:** StairMaster, NordicTrack, Windbike, in-
Facilities cline bed. **Services:** Swedish massage, shiatsu, reflexology, aromatherapy, underwater massage; beauty salon for hair, nail,
and skin care. **Swimming Facilities:** Community outdoor pool.
Evening Programs: Speakers on self-management, organic
cooking, stress management, personal success, and the science
of flower and plant essences.

In the Area Antiques shops in the village of Osceola, canoeing, antique
airplane flying (Aug.), Walker Art Center, University of Minnesota Weisman Art Museum, Como Conservatory (horticul-
ture), Taylor's Falls (rock climbing).

Getting Here *From Minneapolis.* Transportation from the Minneapolis/St.
Paul International Airport, $50. By car, I–35 north to Hwy. 97
east, Rte. 95 north to Hwy. 243, east to Rte. 35 north (1 hr).
Rental car available.

Special Notes Minimum age in spa is 18. Limited access for people with disabilities. No smoking in the mansion. Mosquitoes can be an-
noying between June and Sept.

The Fontana Spa at the Abbey

Luxury pampering
Nutrition and diet
Vibrant maturity
Weight management

Wisconsin Surrounded by panoramic views of Lake Geneva and the
Lake Geneva woods, the glass-walled swimming pool and aerobics studio at
the Fontana Spa have an indoor-outdoor feeling that is enhanced by the changing seasons. The spa's opening in 1989
marked a radical innovation for the landmark resort. The ambience here, unlike that of the traditional country inn, is modern with accents in furniture and leaded-glass inspired by
Frank Lloyd Wright's prairie designs.

Unexpected amenities add to the feeling of well-being: pitchers of fresh fruit juices along with muffins and fruit are laid
out in the morning; the spa salon exudes the aroma of herbs
and oils used in the imported French thalassotherapy body
and skin-care products by Phytomer.

The wide range of services in the spa packages (or on an à la
carte basis for resort guests) distinguishes the Fontana as a
destination that will appeal to sophisticated spa goers. Treatments range from loofah scrubs, thalassotherapy, and herbal
wraps to European hand and foot treatments, from mud masks
and aromatherapy facials to massages. In all, 33 different
services are offered in combination with aerobic and aquatic
exercise classes, and one-on-one training with the latest in exercise equipment.

Popular with women who are trying to shed a few pounds, the
spa also has programs geared to the special needs of older
guests. The staff includes a registered nurse who conducts an
initial fitness and health evaluation. Programs are individually tailored to the needs of guests, and maximum enrollment
is 30 participants at one time.

The Fontana Spa at the Abbey

Hwy. 67/Fontana Blvd., Fontana, WI 53125
Tel. 414/275–6811 or 800/772–1000
Fax 414/275–5948

Administration General manager, Maurice Fitzharris; spa director, Vicki Lilla

Season Year-round

Accommodations 358 rooms in modern lodge (24 new spa wing rooms in 1991). Twin double beds, TV, telephone, air-conditioning. Some locations noisy; lodge has direct entrance to spa building.

Rates 2-night spa escape package midweek $389.70 single, $273.68 per person double, weekends $444.95 single, $301.30 per person double; 5-night package $1,513.95–$1,685.23 single, $1,323.34–$1,408.98 per person double. 1-day Spa Spree (including overnight Sun.–Thurs.) $242.06–$270.79 single, $201.73–$216.09 double. Spa packages include gratuities and taxes. 50% advance payment. AE, DC, MC, V.

Meal Plans Menu selections in the spa's dining room are low in calories, saturated fat, and cholesterol. Breakfast can be cinnamon French toast, apple compote, or miniblueberry muffins. 3-course lunch and dinner include barbecued chicken, sea bass wrapped in spinach and served on a bed of saffron couscous.

Services and Facilities **Exercise Equipment:** 10-unit Eagle/Cybex weight training gym, 2 Lifecycles, 2 Turbo bikes, Precor treadmill, Lifestride treadmill, Concept 2 rower, water rower, 2 StairMasters, Schwinn Air Dyne bike, dumbbells (5–50 lbs), benches. **Services:** Swedish massage, shiatsu, acupressure, aromatherapy, fango, herbal wrap, loofah body scrub, facials, body polish, mineral baths, Scotch hose/Swiss shower, 3 underwater massage tubs, aerobics and aquacise classes, fitness evaluation, full-service beauty salon. **Swimming Facilities:** Indoor lap pool (18½ yds), outdoor pool, lake. **Spa Facilities:** Separate men's and women's sauna, steam room, whirlpool; coed Jacuzzis, aerobics studio, pool. **Recreation Facilities:** 6 outdoor tennis courts (lighted), horseback riding, parcourse; golf, boating, racquetball, bike trips nearby; hiking. **Evening Programs:** Cooking demonstration, resort entertainment.

In the Area Live theater and concerts, shopping, antiques shops.

Getting Here *From Chicago.* Limousine service (fee) from O'Hare International Airport. By car, I–94, Routes 50 and 67 (2 hrs). By bus, Wisconsin Limo (tel. 312/427–3100) runs twice daily, takes 2 hrs, and costs $20 each way. By air, Delavan Airport handles private aircraft. Rental car available.

Special Notes No smoking in spa or spa dining room. Ground-floor accommodations for people with disabilities. Minimum age in spa 18; daily charge ($35) for guests not on package plan.

Holiday Inn Sunspree Resort

Nonprogram resort

Wisconsin
Oconomowoc Formerly the Olympia Village, this Holiday Inn Sunspree Resort is a good place to escape for a few days or a week. The spa's aerobics studio, with a cushioned floor, offers a full schedule of classes that includes a workout in the pool.

A three-day spa package includes two lunches and personal services. You're free to exercise in the weight room or work on your appearance. A personalized fitness program and daily diet will be tailored to your needs and physical abilities by the staff director. (Salon services are available in the main lodge, on an à la carte basis.)

Coed whirlpools and sunken Roman baths allow socializing or a private soak. Separate saunas and steam rooms for men and women and private massage rooms are among the extensive facilities for guests and residents of nearby condominiums. Luxuriously tiled and carpeted, the spa combines glamorous atmosphere and gentle discipline.

Holiday Inn Sunspree Resort

1350 Royale Mile Rd., Oconomowoc, WI 53066
Tel. 414/567–0311 or 800/558–9573

Administration	General manager, Ray Wagner; spa manager, Lois Stallman
Season	Year-round
Accommodations	380 modern rooms facing a lake and ski lifts. Fully carpeted and air-conditioned, all rooms have private bath and color TV.
Rates	2-night spa package $369–$399 weekends, $299 midweek, for 2 persons, double occupancy. Suites $75 additional per day. Gratuities and tax included. Advance guarantee by credit card. AE, MC, V.
Meal Plans	Dinner choices include broiled herbed chicken, broiled pike in lemon dill sauce, steamed lobster. Luncheon menu changes daily, features spinach quiche, chef's salad.
Services and Facilities	**Exercise Equipment:** 2 Lifecycles, Biocycle, 2 StairMasters, 12-station Universal weight training gym, rowing machine, dumbbells, 30 free weights, wrist weights. **Services:** Exercise classes, massage, herbal wrap, facial, pedicure, manicure, loofah body scrub, hair and skin care. **Swimming Facilities:** Indoor and outdoor pools, private beach on lake. **Recreation Facilities:** Indoor and outdoor tennis, racquetball courts, golf, horseback riding, bicycle rental, water sports, downhill and cross-country skiing. **Evening Programs:** Resort entertainment, movie theaters.
In the Area	Old World Wisconsin (living history village), Octagon House (historic home), fishing, Milwaukee Brewers baseball.
Getting Here	*From Milwaukee.* By car, I–94 to Rte. 67 (40 mins).
Special Notes	Elevators and ramps connecting all floors provide access for people with disabilities. No smoking in the spa or spa dining room. Spa open daily 6:30 AM–10 PM in summer; winter schedule varies.

The South

From hot-springs spas to holistic mountain retreats, the range of health facilities in the South includes some of the oldest and some of the newest resorts in the nation.

Virginia's venerable Warm Springs spa, The Homestead, is getting a new look as this edition goes to press. And the only national park devoted to taking the waters, Hot Springs National Park in Arkansas, shows how far the pursuit of fitness has come over the last century. Other mineral springs resorts in the South have a long history: Lithia Springs, Georgia (tel. 404/944–3880), once touted as the Piedmont Chatauqua, is undergoing a revival; North Carolina's Hot Springs Spa (tel. 704/622–7676) offers soaks, massage, campgrounds, and an RV park; and Safety Harbor Resort on Old Tampa Bay has new management, a new look, and plans to focus on their historic hot springs.

The Diet and Fitness Center, sponsored by Duke University Medical Center in North Carolina, offers the latest advances in science, nutrition, and exercise. Wildwood Lifestyle Center, a Seventh-Day Adventist medical center in Georgia, and Uchee Pines Lifestyle Center in Alabama, take a holistic approach to the needs of America's aging population. Hilton Head Health Institute, set amid sea pines in South Carolina, provides lifestyle training and weight management programs under medical supervision. Pritikin Longevity Center combines its weight management program with a Miami Beach vacation.

Few resorts can match the combinations of fitness facilities and sports opportunities at PGA National Resort & Spa, Fisher Island's Spa Internazionale, or The Spa at Doral Golf Resort, all in Florida. The recently opened Disney Institute near Orlando is the first family-oriented fitness resort to design programs for adults and teenagers. Also at Walt Disney World, The Grand Floridian Hotel has added a full-service spa. In Virginia, close to Colonial Williamsburg, the Kingsmill Resort now offers a spa along with golf and tennis programs.

The world's only spa at a winery, Georgia's newly expanded Chateau Elan has its own bottled waters and wines, as well as four golf courses, equestrian and tennis centers, and summer concerts in the vineyards, all less than an hour's drive from Atlanta. For a family-oriented resort on an Atlantic beach, The Cloister's Sea Island Spa is the choice of golfers and tennis buffs as well as vacationers combining lifestyle programs and state-of-the-art pampering. And scheduled to open in 1997 on 100 acres of pristine forest land in the North Georgia Mountains, Little Horse Spa for the Spirit (tel. 404/233–9902) will be an upscale holistic retreat with 90 guest suites.

Budget-conscious vacationers get a bonus in weight management programs at the Tennessee Fitness Spa and Miami's Lido Spa Hotel, both of which cater to mature guests. The newly renamed Fit for Life resort in Florida may be the best value on the beach. In the bluegrass country of Kentucky, Foxhollow scheduled holistic retreats too late for this edition (tel. 502/241–8621).

Uchee Pines Lifestyle Center

Preventive medicine
Vibrant maturity
Weight management

Alabama
Seale

This homelike retreat offers health conditioning and special diets in comprehensive 17-day sessions that appeal mostly to people over 50. The medically directed programs at the Uchee Pines Institute treat most degenerative diseases.

The Health Conditioning Center expounds traditional Seventh-Day Adventist (but is nondenominational and nonsectarian) philosophies on nutrition and mental and spiritual health. Led by three physicians, the staff combines medical and natural healing. A nutritional analysis, aided by computers, gives each patient specific diet recommendations and takes into account each individual's physical condition, nutritional needs, and weight loss goals. Following each guest's complete physical examination (some of which may be covered by medical insurance), a physician prescribes a personal schedule and continues to monitor the patient's progress throughout the program. Treatments to stop smoking, drinking, or other lifestyle problems are also offered.

Secluded in a 200-acre woodland preserve near the Chattahoochee River, the center's live-in accommodations for 14 guests provide privacy and comfort. Walks, gardening, exercise, and hydrotherapy balance out daily lectures on preventive medicine, nutrition, and lifestyle change.

The health center is equipped with a heated, full-body whirlpool, steam bath, massage tables, and ultrasound therapy units. Special treatments include fomenation—application of moist heat to the body for relief from congestion or pain—and the use of ice packs to slow down circulation or arrest a physical reaction. Only a few pieces of exercise equipment are available to those who want an active program.

Uchee Pines Lifestyle Center

30 Uchee Pines Rd., Seale, AL 36875
Tel. 334/855–4764
Fax 334/855–4780

Administration Manager-medical director, David Miller, M.D.

Season Year-round

Accommodations 7 twin-bed rooms with modern furniture, flowered bedspreads, ceiling fans, reading lamps, private bath.

Rates $2,595 for a 17-day live-in session, all-inclusive; $2,395 for a spouse as a patient, $1,495 as a nonpatient (includes physical exam and medical consultation). $500 per person advance payment; 5% discount for full payment. MC, V.

Meal Plans 3 vegetarian meals daily, family style. Adventist diet of fruits, vegetables, legumes, and grains. No fats, butter, or oils. Olives, nuts, and avocado in moderate amounts. Entrées include vegetarian lasagna, whole-wheat pizza, baked tofu. Herbal tea served.

Services and Facilities **Exercise Equipment:** Stationary bike, jogger trampoline. **Services:** Massage, hydrotherapy, fomenation hot packs. **Spa Facilities:** Whirlpool, steam bath. **Recreation Facilities:** Nature hiking, bicycling, gardening, orchard work. **Evening Programs:** Informal discussions of health-related topics.

In the Area Group outings to Callaway Gardens; Providence Canyon, Tuskegee Institute Museum (history and agriculture).

The South

Alabama
Uchee Pines Institute
Health Center, **2**

Arkansas
Hot Springs National
Park, **1**

Florida
Disney Institute, **18**
The Don CeSar Beach
Resort, **20**
Doral Golf Resort and
Spa, **32**
Eden Roc
Resort & Spa, **33**

Fisher Island Spa
Internazionale, **28**
Fit for Life Health
Resort & Spa, **25**
Hippocrates Health
Institute, **23**
Lido Spa Hotel, **29**
Palm-Aire Spa
Resort & Spa, **24**
PGA National Resort
& Spa, **22**
The Pier House
Caribbean Spa, **34**
Ponte Vedra Inn &
Club, **17**
Pritikin Longevity
Center, **31**

The Registry Resort &
Spa, **27**
Safety Harbor Spa
Resort, **19**
Sanibel Harbour
Resort & Spa, **21**
Spa LXVI at Hyatt
Regency Pier 66, **26**
Turnberry Isle Resort
and Club, **30**

Georgia
Chateau Elan, **5**
Sea Island Beach Club
Spa at The Cloister, **16**
Wildwood Lifestyle
Center, **4**

North Carolina
Duke University Diet
and Fitness Center, **13**
Structure House, **12**
Westglow Spa, **6**

South Carolina
Hilton Head Health
Institute, **14**
Hilton Head Westin
Resort, **15**

Tennessee
Tennessee Fitness
Spa, **3**

OHIO

WEST VIRGINIA

nkfort
Lexington
KENTUCKY

Knoxville

hattanooga

Atlanta

Augusta

Macon

GEORGIA

Valdosta

Tallahassee

FLORIDA

Orlando

Tampa

Fort Myers

Key West

Washington, D.C.

Richmond

Roanoke

VIRGINIA

Greensboro

Winston-Salem

Raleigh

Charlotte

Greenville

Columbia

SOUTH CAROLINA

Charleston

Savannah R.

Flint River

Chattahoochee River

Savannah

Jacksonville

Daytona Beach

Norfolk

NORTH CAROLINA

Rocky Mount

ATLANTIC OCEAN

N

0   200 miles

0   300 miles

West Palm Beach

Fort Lauderdale

Miami

Virginia
Hartland Wellness Center, **8**
The Homestead, **7**
The Kingsmill Resort, **10**
The Tazewell Club, **11**
Yogaville, **9**

Getting Here *From Atlanta.* By bus, Greyhound to Columbus, GA (5 hrs). By plane, Delta Airlines to Columbus, GA (30 mins). By car, I–185 via Columbus, Rte. 80 to Rte. 431, south to Rtes. 24 and 39 (about 5 hrs). Free pickup to and from airport and bus station.

Special Notes No smoking indoors.

Hot Springs National Park

Taking the waters

Arkansas Hot Springs National Park was once called the Valley of the
Hot Springs Vapors. Native Americans and Spanish conquistadores were attracted by clouds of steam from the 47 springs that bring hot mineral water to the surface in what is now a national park within a resort city. Local lore has it that Hernando de Soto and his explorers relaxed here in 1541. The park rangers tell visitors about the spring water's 4,000-year journey from deep within the earth, where it is heated to 143°F, and its mineral content from which its therapeutic properties derive.

In 1832, the federal government set aside four sections of the springs as a health reservation, the first in the country's history. A partnership evolved with private bathhouse and hotel operators, so the National Park Service now regulates operations and maintains the reservoirs, where the spring water cools down to 100°F for bathing.

Six bathing facilities are open to the public, and plans are under way for renovation and adaptive reuse of several Art Deco buildings on Bathhouse Row. The most splendid of the eight buildings surviving here, The Fordyce, was built in 1915 by a Colonel Fordyce, who credited the spring waters with saving his life. The interior has stained-glass windows and a skylight with scenes of water nymphs, appropriate for the Museum of Bathing, created as part of the building's restoration in 1989.

In the Buckstaff Bathhouse, a stately three-story brick-and-marble edifice, bathers step into a private porcelain tub filled with mineral water heated to 103°F. Plan on about 1½ hours for a soak in the thermal waters, the whirlpools, and a massage. The entire treatment at Buckstaff Baths, including hot packs on sore muscles and a multineedled shower, costs about $35. Reservations are essential.

Vacationing here is like taking a step back in time. Grand old hotels and mansions offer bed and breakfast. Hot Springs is also a modern medical center for advanced therapy of degenerative diseases and rehabilitation treatments for postcardiac or surgery patients. The town has all the charm of a 19th-century European spa—without the exaggerated claims.

Hot Springs National Park
Box 1860, Hot Springs, AR 71902
Tel. 501/624–3383, ext. 640

Hot Springs Convention & Visitors Bureau
Box K, Hot Springs National Park, AR 71902
Tel. 501/321–1705 or 800/772–2489

Administration Superintendent, Roger Giddings

Season Year-round

Accommodations Bathing facilities and 53 rooms with spring water piped into the bathroom at the 488-room Arlington Hotel (tel. 800/643–1502). Other public pools at the Hilton, Downtowner, and Majestic hotels. Guest houses and camping facilities nearby. Rehabilitation therapy and baths at Hot Springs Health Spa, open daily 9–9.

Services and Facilities
Swimming Facilities: Indoor and outdoor pools at hotels; lakes nearby. **Spa Facilities:** 6 bathhouses operate under the auspices of U.S. Department of the Interior. All open Mon.–Sat. 7 AM–11:30 PM, 1:30 PM–4 PM; hotel hours vary. Arlington open Sun. morning. **Services:** Massage, hot packs, baths. **Recreation Facilities:** Hiking trails in Ouachita Mountains, boating, fishing, biking, horseback riding, cross-country skiing. Hotels offer tennis, golf. **Programs:** 12-min slide program scheduled in park headquarters auditorium.

In the Area
Ouachita Lake recreational area, Oaklawn Park (Thoroughbred racing, late Jan.–mid-Apr.), Hot Springs Mountain Tower, Ozark Folk Center at Mountain View (concerts, exhibits), Cowie Wine Cellars in Eureka Springs, Alligator Farm, Toltec Mounds State Park (Indian earthworks).

Getting Here
From Little Rock. By bus, Greyhound (1 hr). By car, I–30 to Hot Springs exit, Rte. 70 West (1 hr).

Special Notes
Ramps and specially equipped rooms in most hotels and Buckstaff Baths. No smoking in bathhouses.

Disney Institute

Kid fitness
Life enhancement
Luxury pampering
Sports conditioning

Florida
Orlando
Conceived as a learning vacation for the '90s, the Disney Institute provides adults and children with a wide range of sports, fitness, and the arts. Here, family members can pursue hobbies, explore nature trails, make a movie, or enjoy the full-service spa. In a separate villagelike community adjoining Disney World, the Institute evokes a spirit of adventure by focusing on carefree comfort in a safe environment.

Forget Mickey Mouse. The cast of characters at Disney World's theme park is notably absent at the Institute. Instructors are professional animators, horticulturists, chefs and sommeliers, broadcasters, and fitness trainers. Active, outdoor classes include a 3-day golf school directed by Gary Player and his son Wayne, and tennis clinics with professionals from Peter Burwash Intnl. Choices range from rock climbing to bird-watching, canoeing, and workouts in an airy 38,000-square-foot Sports and Fitness Center with the latest in Cybex equipment, indoor pool for water exercise class, 2 aerobics studios, and NBA-size basketball court.

Programs are divided into nine general subject areas, some requiring advance sign-up. During the minimum 3-day stay, family members can go their separate ways; teenagers have their own activity center, where they can work with professionals on TV and radio shows and computer animation. Among the activities for adults are garden design, bread baking, food and wine tasting, architecture and interior design. Single adults can meet new people with common interests by joining the small, specialized sessions.

With more than 60 programs offered, your schedule can be structured or relaxed. An Institute scheduler calls prior to your arrival, but popular offerings like the golf experience can be fully booked months in advance; call well ahead of your visit. Arriving at the Welcome Center, you get oriented to the complex and pick up the daily schedule of events. The Seasons dining room is here, as well as the spa, fitness center, theater, and outdoor amphitheater. Nearby, golfers tee-off on the 18-hole championship course, and clay tennis courts can be reserved, as can a class in tennis aerobics. At night there are concerts, films, and lectures, for which free tickets are distributed.

Opened in 1996, the Institute complex is the centerpiece of a residential village, within walking (and noise) distance of Pleasure Island and the newly expanded Disney Marketplace. Accommodations spread out along a lake and the golf course, so you get plenty of exercise walking. (Electric carts can be rented by the day if you prefer to do less walking.)

Lodging options range from one-bedroom apartments to fully equipped bungalows and town houses with one and two bedrooms; daily maid service is provided. The Disney Institute is located on the site of the former Disney Village Resort; the resort's accommodations were all completely renovated during the creation of the Institute. Most units have a kitchen (allowing you to choose the Institute's basic package without meals) and accommodate families of up to six persons. Each of five residential clusters has a swimming pool and laundry facility. Quiet locations face the golf course and lake.

Playing hooky is allowed. To enjoy attractions in the theme park, pick up a free one-day admission pass, and board a shuttle bus that cruises through the Institute grounds all day and into the evening. See sports teams training and in competition at the new 200-acre International Sports Complex. The restaurants at Epcot Center offer heart-healthy selections, and MGM Studios chefs prepare meals to meet your specific health needs with advance notice (call 407/824–4500).

The spa, the smallest part of the Institute, provides an oasis of calm in the midst of all these activities. Its 10 treatment rooms offer massage, a hydrotherapy tub, and skin care, from aromatherapy with Judith Jackson oils to seaweed body masque by Phytomer, Sothys European body treatments. Both men's and women's locker rooms have a large whirlpool, sauna, and steam room, and provide workout clothing and grooming supplies and a lounge where lunch can be ordered from room service. Making an appointment for treatments gets you free access to the spa facilities; charges are added to your account.

While programs at the Institute are only open to registered participants, guests of any of the Walt Disney World Resort hotels can dine there and make spa reservations.

Disney Institute
210 Celebration Place, Celebration, FL 34747
Tel. 407/827–4455 for spa reservations, 800/282–9282 for
registration, 800/496–6337 for information
Fax 407/939–4898

Administration Vice President–director of programming, Richard Hutton; spa and sports/fitness managing instructor, Jeff Kohl

Season Year-round

Accommodations 457 guest rooms in bungalows, apartments, and town houses. Bungalow has sitting room with sofa bed, TV, dining room with patio, kitchen, and powder room on ground floor; bedroom with TV, bathroom on balcony. Air-conditioning, telephone, ceiling fan, are standard.

Rates Basic Plan (no meals) 3-night package $429–$584 per person, double occupancy, Deluxe Plan (with 3 meals daily) 3-night package $576–$730 per person, double. 4-night basic package $559–$765, deluxe $755–$961. 7-night basic package $949–

$1,310, deluxe $1,291–$1,652. Full-day spa programs $170–$200. Tax and gratuities included. Confirmation by credit card. AE, D, MC, V.

Meal Plans 3 meals daily included in deluxe plan. The menu at Seasons dining room offers heart-healthy selections as well as standard favorites. Dinner is prix fixe, with regional offerings that change nightly. Nonalcoholic beverages and all gratuities are included in the package plan; additional dining options in the theme parks available with a World Choice Plan. Wine and alcoholic beverages available.

Services and Facilities **Exercise Equipment:** Full circuit of Cybex VR2 and plate-loaded weight training units, cardiovascular bikes, treadmills, and rowers; interactive Human Performance Center. **Services:** Swedish, aromatherapy, or sports massage, men's facial, seaweed facial, paraffin hand and foot treatment with manicure or pedicure, body masque, seaweed hydro-massage, alpha hydroxy facial, mud pack. **Swimming Facilities:** 5 outdoor pools. **Recreation Facilities:** 4 clay tennis courts (lighted), 18-hole golf course, basketball court, 26-ft. outdoor climbing wall, organic garden and greenhouse. **Evening Programs:** Concerts, feature films, lectures, fireworks.

In the Area Pleasure Island, Magic Kingdom, Universal Studios, Sea World, Orlando Museum of Art (19th–20th-century American art), Leu Botanical Gardens.

Getting Here *From Orlando International Airport.* By car, Beeline Expy. (Toll Rd. 528) to I–4 west, Exit 26 on Bonnet Creek Pkwy. to Community Dr. (45 mins). By public van, shuttle services depart frequently. Taxi, rental car available.

Special Notes Minimum age 10 for Institute programs; day camp half-day (fee) for children 7–9 years old. Facilities accessible for persons with disabilities. Spa open daily.

The Don CeSar Beach Resort

Nonprogram resort
Taking the waters

Florida
St. Petersburg Beach

Thalassotherapy is featured at the new spa facilities of The Don CeSar Beach Resort. This historic hotel's location on the Gulf of Mexico makes it easy to provide a course of treatments using seaweed, marine plant extracts, and spirulina to rejuvenate the body after the ravages of time and sun exposure. Rather than offering a fixed program, the spa, which is the first on Florida's Coast to use such treatments, offers services à la carte and is open to nonguests as well as hotel residents. While facilities are limited (there is no indoor seawater exercise pool), the spa offers a fitness assessment and take-home program.

Reminiscent of the Roaring '20s, this pink palace is affectionately called "The Don" by visitors who relish its stately public rooms trimmed with crystal chandeliers and marble fountains. In 1993 a $14 million face-lift restored its Moorish/Mediterranean ambience. Below the lobby a grand staircase leads to the sleek, cool confines of the spa. Offering daily beachside exercise classes, and the latest in exercise equipment, this can be a welcome retreat from the sun.

Selecting from a menu of eight sea-oriented body treatments, you can set a course to rejuvenate, relax, or restore. Scrubs and polishes are recommended to prepare your skin for the full benefits of body wraps and massage therapies. Seaweed body wraps, using Floraspa products imported from France, are said to revitalize.

Most of these treatments are priced at $60–$70, and the daily spa admission fee ($5–$10) is waived. Issued a robe, slippers, and locker at check-in, you're free to use the Beach Club facilities for the rest of the day, including sauna and whirlpool.

The Don CeSar Beach Resort
3400 Gulf Blvd., St. Petersburg Beach, FL 33706
Tel. 813/360–1881, 800/282–1116, or 800/637–7200
Fax 813/367–3609

Administration General manager, George Fetherston; spa manager, Kris Ruther

Season Year-round

Accommodations 277 rooms including 50 suites and 2 penthouses. All have bathroom with marble walls, traditional bedroom furniture, TV, phone, air-conditioning.

Rates Pink Palace 1-night package for 2 persons $251.86–$406.04. Day spa package (no lodging) $149. Tax and gratuities included. Hotel rooms $175–$215 for 2 during summer. AE, D, MC, V.

Meal Plans Breakfast only included in Pink Palace package. Healthy selections appear on the menus of 4 restaurants and room service.

Services and Facilities **Exercise Equipment**: 5-station Cybex weight training unit, 2 Cybex treadmills, 2 StairMaster 4000PT, 2 Lifecycles, 2 Schwinn Air Dyne bikes, free weights (5–50 lbs), benches. **Services**: Massage, aromatherapy, body wraps, sea scrub, spirulina body masque, reflexology, personal training, fitness assessment. **Swimming Facilities**: 25-yd heated outdoor pool, ocean beach. **Recreation Facilities**: 2 tennis courts with lighted hard surface, beachfront water sports. Nearby 18-hole golf course, deep-sea fishing, sailing.

In the Area Busch Gardens, Disney World, Dali Museum, St. Petersburg Historical Museum, Florida International Museum, Ybor City (historic Tampa), Sarasota Ringling Museum, Asolo State Theater (opera and plays), Ruth Eckerd Hall (concerts), seabird sanctuary, marine mammal center, Florida Suncoast Dome (sports), baseball spring training, Tampa Bay Buccaneers football.

Getting Here *From Tampa.* By car, I–275 (25 mins). By van, scheduled service from Tampa International Airport. Rental car, taxi, and limousine available.

Special Notes Facilities accessible for people with disabilities. Kids Ltd. day care program for ages 5–12. Spa hours Mon.–Sat. 6 AM–9 PM, Sun. and holidays 9–5.

The Doral Golf Resort and Spa

Life enhancement
Luxury pampering
Sports conditioning
Stress control

Florida
Miami
Like a vision of Tuscany, the spa villa's red-tile roof rises above formal gardens, statuary, and cascading fountains at the Doral Golf Resort. The mood inside is modern, without a trace of sweaty workouts to disturb the calm. The spa is self-contained, with a wing of suites, aerobics studios, cardiovascular and weight training room, indoor and outdoor lap pools, and dining atrium.

Around the upper levels of the central atrium are the men's and women's locker rooms, equipped with whirlpool, saunas (dry and steam), sundeck, and lounge; 26 private massage rooms with a selection of treatments; a coed beauty salon and skin-care treatment rooms; and a running track.

The spa at the Doral blends European and American health concepts, but keeps daily regimens flexible. The classes tend to be jazzy, low-impact workouts that appeal to men as well as women. There are one-on-one workouts with state-of-the-art Cybex equipment and cardiovascular machines.

Appointments for personal services begin in the locker room–lounge, where fresh workout clothing is issued. A therapist then escorts you by elevator to private rooms around the lofty rotunda. Serious regimens are planned after consultation with staff specialists who compare your health profile with a computerized model. All this personalized attention comes at a price: about $350 per day, including three meals. A less-expensive option is to stay in the resort's golf lodges and book spa services on a daily basis. Treatments are priced individually or in packages.

Stress management is taught in a seven-day program scheduled at various times throughout the year. Dr. Eric Goldstein, a psychologist at the University of Miami who has worked with Olympic athletes, developed the program with spa trainers and nutritionists. Biofeedback and respiratory training routines and a "Stress Relief" workout teach participants how to control stress in every aspect of their lives.

Beyond beauty, the spa provides tools for taking control of your life. Counselors meet with newcomers to develop a program that can include treatments drawn from several natural sources: marine seaweed body wraps, tropical fruit enzyme facials, herbal ayurvedic hydrotherapy, anti-cellulite treatments, and Kerstin Florian's Kur program using thermal water crystals and mud from springs in Hungary.

Evenings are devoted to new experiences with fellow spa goers: talks by health specialists, an astrologer, and cooking demonstrations. But many guests simply enjoy the luxurious villa suites, refurbished in 1996. You can borrow a feature film from the library for the VCR and prepare for an early morning walk around the golf course.

Golf and tennis are major attractions at Doral, and a number of tournaments and group events are scheduled. Golfers can tee-off on five championship courses, including the legendary Blue Monster, a favorite stop on the PGA tour, and the new Gold Course with water hazards on every hole. Tennis instruction is with professionals from Peter Burwash International.

The Spa at Doral has become increasingly popular since its opening in 1987. Since changing ownership in 1994, programming is less rigid, and the spa is open to all guests at the newly renovated 650-acre resort, as well offering day spa packages to nonresidents. Complete with Olympic swimming pools, day or night tennis at the Arthur Ashe Tennis Center, easy access to South Beach and all that Miami has to offer, it is the most complete resort in South Florida.

Doral Golf Resort and Spa
8755 N.W. 36th St., Miami, FL 33178
Tel. 305/593–6030 or 800/331–7768
Fax 305/591–8266

Administration General manager, Joel Paige; spa director, Josie Feria

Season Year-round

Accommodations 694 rooms and suites. In spa villa, 48 extra-large suites with twin baths, Jacuzzi, wet bar and refrigerator, VCR, 2 dressing areas, hair dryer, queen- or king-size bed. Suites with private terrace or balcony overlook golf courses or garden.

Rates Spa plan includes suite accommodations, 3 meals daily, and choice of services. 2 nights $800–$1,150 single, $600–$850 per person double occupancy; 4 nights $1,250–$1,700 single or double (includes extra services and limo); 7-night package $2,500–$3,475 per person double or single. 7-night weight management plan $2,950–$3,925 single, $2,400–$3,000 double. Flexi-Plan 1-night suite package $275–$850 single or double. Add tax and 18% service charge. $500 advance payment within 7 days after booking 7-night plan, balance 14 days before arrival. Full payment within 7 days after booking short stays. Refundable (less $50) up to 14 days prior to arrival date. AE, DC, MC, V.

Meal Plans Spa packages include 3 meals daily, snacks, and fruit smoothie drinks. Specialties include buckwheat waffles with fruit topping or 1-egg omelet with spinach (breakfast), small pizza topped with turkey sausage (lunch), steamed lobster with mussel sauce or grilled honey basil chicken with rice and fresh vegetables or polenta lasagna with layers of smoked chicken, spinach, sliced tomato, or pork loin sautéed with mushroom and marsala sauce (dinner). Seafood is offered nightly; special diets accommodated.

Services and Facilities **Exercise Equipment:** Complete Cybex system, free weights (3–65 lbs), VersaClimber, 2 StairMasters, 2 Lifecycles, 2 Liferowers, 2 StairMaster cross aerobics units, 3 Schwinn Air Dyne bikes, 5 Trotter treadmills, barbells (10–50 lbs), aquacise with resistance buoys. **Services:** Fango mud facial and body treatments, facials, herbal wraps, underwater massage, body cream cleansing, hand and foot therapy, Swedish, aromatherapy, acupressure massage; beauty salon; cooking class; tai chi. **Swimming Facilities:** Large outdoor pool with cascades, separate Olympic-length lap pool, indoor pool for aquatics. **Recreation Facilities:** 5 golf courses, 15 tennis courts, horseback riding, hiking trail. **Evening Programs:** Lecture and discussion group daily.

In the Area Complimentary use of beach club at Doral Hotel On-the-Ocean; shopping at Bal Harbour, Coral Gables; performing-arts seasons and festivals in Miami and Miami Beach; museums and Vizcaya mansion; Orange Bowl games and concerts; jai alai and racetracks; sailing and deep-sea fishing, major-league baseball and basketball.

Getting Here *From Miami International Airport.* 15 mins away, served by major airlines. Amtrak station in Miami. Airport transfers by Doral limousine service included in the spa villa plan (4-day minimum). Taxi, rental car, limo arranged by concierge. Free scheduled shuttle bus to Miami Beach. Free parking, restricted to spa guests.

Special Notes Barrier-free facilities and dining rooms for people with disabilities; elevators throughout the spa center and villa. No smoking indoors. Spa open daily 8–6.

Eden Roc Resort & Spa

Nonprogram resort

Florida
Miami Beach Oceanview workouts at the Spa of Eden are a bonus when you stay at the Eden Roc Resort. Created in 1994 as part of a $30-million face-lift lavished on one of Miami Beach's distinctive

Art Deco hotels, the spa and sports complex are now the best value on the beach for fitness buffs. Combining a weight room full of Cybex equipment, a cardiovascular theater with computerized treadmills, cycles, and stairclimbers plugged into an audio/visual system, and a variety of aerobics classes, the spa can keep you busy and out of the sun. But the surprise is an indoor court complex on the beach terrace, featuring a full-size regulation basketball court, squash and racquetball courts, and South Florida's only rock climbing wall—all in air-conditioned comfort—at no charge for spa plan guests.

On the hotel's mezzanine, the spa offers a wide range of pampering and body treatments, available in day spa packages as well as 3–7 day escapes. The daily admission fee ($10) is waived when you book services. Also included in packages are spa cuisine meals at two restaurants: Fresco Cafe, which has Mediterranean specialties, and Jimmy Johnson's sports bar and grill overlooking the beach.

The boardwalk is ideal for morning jogs and walks, and offers easy access to lively South Beach and the convention center.

Eden Roc Resort & Spa

4525 Collins Ave., Miami Beach, FL 33140
Tel. 305/531–0000 or 800/327–8337
Spa res. 305/538–6604
Fax 305/531–6955

Administration   General manager, Michael Furcht; spa director, Cynthia Bell

Season   Year-round

Accommodations   350 rooms, including 49 suites, in 14-story oceanfront hotel. Most rooms have balcony, sitting area, double or king-size beds. Decorated with Art Deco furniture and tropical colors, rooms are air-conditioned, have TV, phone.

Rates   3-night Escape to Eden package $966–$1,116 single, $769–$861 per person, double occupancy. 7-night Week of Luxury $2,263–$2,693 single, $1,918–$2,097 double. Day spa package $205; half-day $120. Tax and service charges included. AE, D, MC, V.

Meal Plans   Week of Luxury includes 3 meals daily; Escape to Eden, breakfast and dinner daily. Breakfast choices include poached egg with turkey sausage on spinach/tomato concasse, buckwheat pancakes, tropical fruit and juices, 7-grain toast. Lunch entrées at Fresco are spiced eggplant and spinach salad, grilled chicken breast on spinach, vegetable lasagna, grape leaves filled with couscous, grilled vegetable platter. Dinner can begin with smoked pheasant and bean salad, turkey sausage with wilted arugula, or grilled vegetables; entrées include spa burger, stir-fried mahimahi, steamed halibut in lettuce leaf, pizza with vegetables. Coffee, tea, skim milk, and smoothies available.

Services and Facilities   **Exercise Equipment:** Full circuit of Cybex weight training units, including VR2, cardiovascular theater with bikes, treadmills, stair climber, free weights. **Services:** Massage (Swedish, sports, deep tissue, aromatherapy), shiatsu, reflexology, algae body masque, herbal or Dead Sea mud wrap, body polish. Salon for hair and nail care. **Swimming Facilities:** Olympic-size lap pool, ocean beach. **Recreation Facilities:** Indoor basketball court, 3 squash courts, racquetball court, rock climbing wall; beach concession with parasailing, kayaks, Hobie Cat sailboats, SCUBA; yacht marina.

In the Area   Lincoln Road (boutiques, theaters), Gusman Performing Arts Center, Miami Dolphins stadium, South Beach.

Getting Here *From Miami International Airport.* By car, MacArthur Causeway to Hwy. A1A, Collins Ave (25 mins). By van, Super Shuttle departs frequently. Taxi, rental car, and limousine available.

Special Notes Spa open weekdays 6:30 AM–10:30 PM, weekends 8–7. Minimum age: 16.

Fisher Island Spa Internazionale

Luxury pampering

Florida
Biscayne Bay Secluded on Fisher Island off the southern tip of Miami, the Spa Internazionale welcomes a limited number of guests to experience a very private world of luxury amid gardens ablaze with tropical flowers. The concierge can explain the island's development from the 1925 hideaway built by William K. Vanderbilt to the 1990s condominium community complete with beach club and marina.

Beyond the swimming pool with underwater jets, you discover a patio pool and open-air massage rooms, where a waterfall cascades refreshingly cool water into a heated Jacuzzi. Nero never had it so good.

The spa also has 15 beautifully decorated treatment rooms, one VIP Suite for private services, a salon, two aerobics studios, and a cardio/weight-training room. Separate men's and women's saunas, steam rooms, and lounges stocked with fruit and juices add to the clublike atmosphere. Among your choices of treatments are Gunot skin care, Yonka's European back facial and alpha/beta hydroxy fruit acid skin peel, Kerstin Florian's thermal mineral kur from Hungary, and aromatherapy hydromassage in a French tub fitted with 47 underwater jets. Don't miss the Parisian hydradermie facial, to cleanse and moisturizing your face to combat Miami's subtropical climate.

With a maximum of 20 guests padding about, the spa staff is available to lavish attention on you. For beginners, this eliminates problems during yoga and aerobics. The daily schedule lists six classes, from Reebok Bodywalk to step, waterworks, spinning, Boxercise™, and body-toning. Cross-training is organized with a full line of Keiser equipment. Don't expect to interact with a group; programs are tailored to your time and needs. Club members who work out at the spa are a mix of hip Europeans and island or Miami residents, and there isn't much socializing with outsiders, who are charged a daily membership fee ($25) and facility fee ($20) as part of the spa packages.

The 216-acre private island has a variety of accommodations, from cottages to casitas and oceanfront apartments, including original Vanderbilt cottages. Five restaurants, an informal beach club with yellow umbrellas accenting the seascape, and access to tennis and golf clubs come with membership. An electric cart facilitates getting around and making ferry connections. The Vanderbilt mansion, now a restaurant, is not on the spa plan, but you can enjoy its big swimming pool set in a lush garden. Relaxation, rather than diet and exercise, distinguishes this island escape.

Fisher Island Spa Internazionale
1 Fisher Island Dr., Fisher Island, FL 33109
Tel. 305/535–6020 or 800/537–3708
Fax 305/535–6032

Administration Fisher Island Club managing director, Thomas Wicky; Spa Internazionale director, Deborah A. Smith

Season	Year-round
Accommodations	60 suites, guest rooms in cottages, 2-story villas, and condominium apartments. Vanderbilt cottages (3) and seaside contemporary suites have kitchen and living room with period furniture, full bathroom, 1–3 bedrooms, each with bathroom. All accommodations are air-conditioned, with TV, telephone. Casitas have king-size bed, upholstered sofa, TV in armoire, polished marble floors, ceiling fan, large bathroom with whirlpool tub. Terraced for ocean views, some suites have whirlpool outdoors; cottages have private patio and whirlpool.
Rates	3-night/4-day spa package $1,945–$2,365 single, $1,420–$1,655 per person double occupancy; 7-night/8-day spa package $4,175–$4,695 single, $3,020–$3,455 double. Guest rooms, villas, cottages, and suites $330–$1,400 daily for 2 persons. Add 9.5% tax, 17% service charge. $25 daily club membership fee per couple. Perfect Spa Day package for island residents $195 plus service charge. AE, DC, MC, V.
Meal Plans	Spa packages include 3 meals daily. Spa cuisine selections for breakfast include oat bran pancakes with banana and yogurt, or fresh fruit plate. Lunch choices include grilled mahimahi pita sandwich, Southwestern shrimp grilled with red pepper relish. Dinner entrées include grilled fillet of salmon on spinach with sorrel sauce, whole wheat pasta with fresh vegetables.
Services and Facilities	**Exercise Equipment:** Cardio-weight room with 17 Keiser units, 4 Stair climbers (Tectrix Climb Max, StairMaster Gauntlet, 4000 PT Climber), 5 treadmills, Unisen Startrac 2000, 3 Bikes (Schwinn Air Dyne, Cybex, Tectrix), Gravitron, Liferower, Cybex UBE, 2 recumbent bikes, 12 free weight stations with overhead and underhand cable, Smith machine, dumbbells (3–50 lbs), barbells (15–65 lbs). **Services:** Massage, shiatsu, aromatherapy, body polish, reflexology, hydrotub, herbal wrap, algae body masque, facials. Salon for manicure, pedicure, hair treatment, paraffin hand/foot treatment. **Swimming Facilities:** Indoor lap pool, outdoor recreation pools, ocean beach. **Recreation Facilities:** 18 tennis courts (grass, clay, hard surface; lit for night play), 18-hole golf course, bike rental, marina for deep-sea fishing and yacht charter.
In the Area	Miami Beach and South Beach, Theatre of the Performing Arts, Bayside Mall (free ferry at scheduled times from and to island), Vizcaya museum.
Getting Here	*From Miami.* MacArthur Causeway to Fisher Island ferry terminal. Complimentary airport transfers for spa package guests. Rental car, taxi, limousine available. Helicopter and seaplane base nearby.
Special Notes	Facilities accessible for people with disabilities. Spa open weekdays 7–8, weekends 8–7. Minimum age in spa is 18.

Fit for Life Health Resort & Spa

Holistic health
Life enhancement
Luxury pampering
Weight management

Florida *Pompano Beach*	Based on the book *"Fit for Life,"* co-authored by Harvey Diamond, this resort's all-inclusive program was introduced in 1995 at the former Royal Atlantic Spa. It's a no-frills place to veg-out, de-stress, and shed pounds. Guided by the resident health director, you learn to cope with emotional problems through exercise, meditation, and nutritious meals.

Structured for group camaraderie, the daily schedule allows you to be as active or relaxed as you choose. Exercise classes are held in a large gym that adjoins the poolside dining room. Cooking classes in gourmet vegetarian cuisine are held most evenings, with lessons in how fruits, vegetables, and starches can eliminate cravings and reduce the fats and proteins that contribute to weight problems, heart disease, diabetes, cancer, and aging.

Each day begins with a walk along the beach, followed by stretching, step, and other low-impact classes. To improve body awareness and flexibility you can join a session of yoga or tai chi held under the palm trees, or aqua conditioning in the swimming pool. The spa treatment rooms, sauna, and beauty salon are in the U-shape hotel complex surrounding a private garden with open-air pool and Jacuzzi.

Directly on the beach, the informal resort provides comfortable accommodations but aims to be affordable. Designed as an eight-day shape-up (minimum stay is four days), the program includes all the basics and meals. There are eight massage rooms where optional treatments can be scheduled at an additional cost. Participants in the program mingle like a family, ranging in age from teenagers to octogenarians, as friendly staff members encourage real lifestyle changes. Author Diamond occasionally joins daily lectures that cover all aspects of health and nutrition, with practical guidelines to take home.

Vegetarian buffet meals vary daily. A juicing program, supervised by the health director and nurse, based on an evaluation of your physical and nutritional needs, is available as well. After three days of this liquid diet of fresh fruit, or simply water, you are expected to feel cleaner and more energetic.

Fit for Life Health Resort & Spa

1460 S. Ocean Blvd., Pompano Beach, FL 33062
Tel. 954/941–6688 or 800/583–3500
Fax 954/943–1219

Administration Directors, Morton Pine, Harold LeBovic; health director, Robert Sniadach, D.C.

Season Year-round

Accommodations 70 guest rooms in 3-story court with swimming pool. Renovated in 1993, rooms are furnished motel-style, with 2 queen-size beds, private bathroom, air-conditioning, TV, telephone. Garden-level rooms have private patio open to pool and beach; ocean-view rooms have balcony.

Rates 1-week program with meals and accommodations $899–$1,199 single, $699–$999 per person double. Add tax and gratuities. $100 advance payment. AE, MC, V.

Meal Plans 3 low-cal vegetarian meals daily. Breakfast is all fresh fruit. Lunch buffet of salads, baked potato, and fruit. Dinner served by candlelight may include vegetarian lasagna or stuffed pepper with salad. Juice and water diets optional.

Services and Facilities **Exercise Equipment:** Universal weight training gym, 3 Challenger treadmills, 2 Preference stationary bikes, step machine, free weights, bench. **Services:** Facial, herbal body wrap, massage, mud or seaweed wrap, anti-cellulite wraps, aromatherapy, reflexology, manicure, pedicure. **Swimming Facilities:** Outdoor pool, ocean beach. **Recreation Facilities:** Tennis; golf nearby. Bicycles, snorkeling, and fishing gear can be rented. **Evening Programs:** Informal discussion groups.

In the Area Disney World, Morikami Museum, Fort Lauderdale Performing Arts Center, art museums.

Getting Here *From Fort Lauderdale International Airport.* By car, I–95 to Commercial Blvd., east to Hwy. A1A (35 mins). Rental car, taxi, limousine available.

Special Notes No smoking in rooms or on premises. All facilities accessible for people with disabilties. Minimum age: 18.

Hippocrates Health Institute

Holistic health
Weight management

Florida
West Palm Beach

A vegetarian diet, medical consultation, chiropractic therapy, and psychological consultation are central to the health-renewal program at the Hippocrates Health Institute. Sessions are planned on an individual basis; about half of the 15 to 20 participants have cancer, heart disease, or other serious illnesses. Highly structured, the program includes nutritional education, regular exercise, massage, reflexology, detoxification, and relaxation techniques to aid in prevention of illness.

Guests stay in a spacious hacienda or at private cottages on the 30-acre wooded estate. A peaceful, healing serenity pervades the grounds, where walkways wind through tropical surroundings to a dry sauna and ozonated swimming pool. Expansion in 1995 included a hydrotherapy building. Planned is an adjoining residential community.

The Hippocrates lifestyle involves learning to be self-sufficient in matters of food and medicine. A typical day begins at 8 AM with light exercise before breakfast, then a blood-pressure check and discussion session on health and diet. Guests learn and practice how to sprout and grow greens and wheatgrass for home use. The emphasis is on detoxifying the body by consuming only "live foods"—unprocessed, organically grown fruits and vegetables, all eaten raw.

Personal counseling comes with the program. A psychologist and an M.D. work closely with the medical director to monitor your progress and advise you on personal problems. Deep-relaxation techniques are taught to enhance healing, creativity, and inspiration. Focus programs provide intensive training in fitness and other health-related issues.

The detox diet is a drastic change for the first few days. Wheatgrass is said to have great healing properties. The institute's chefs prepare meals composed of 60% green vegetables and the sprouts of such plants as sunflower, buckwheat, alfalfa, clover, cress, dill, garlic, peas, radish, and spinach. Vegetables such as carrots, squash, radishes, and corn make up 15% of the diet, all eaten raw to preserve nutrients. Cooked foods are limited to no more than 20% of the diet.

Hippocrates Health Institute
1443 Palmdale Ct., West Palm Beach, FL 33411
Tel. 407/471–8876 or 800/842–2125
Fax 407/471–9464

Administration Co-directors, Brian R. Clement and Anna Maria Gahns

Season Year-round; scheduled programs

Accommodations 25 guest rooms, from 3 luxury suites in Spanish-style hacienda to garden apartments and 2 cottages, some with marble-walled bath and whirlpools. Southwestern-style furnishings in most rooms. Some share bathroom and are off premises.

Rates 1-week Health Encounter $1,900–$3,500 with private room, $1,500–$1,900 in shared accommodations with up to 2 persons.

2 weeks in private bedroom $3,500–$6,500, sharing $2,500–$3,500 per person; 3 weeks in private bedroom $4,500–$7,500, sharing $3,250–$4,500. 50% of room rate required as a nonrefundable deposit by certified check or major credit card. AE, MC, V.

Meal Plans 3 meals daily, buffet style, with days designated for juice fasting. Live Food diet of unprocessed organic raw vegetables, fruits, nuts, seeds, sprouts, sea plants and algae, and herbs. Raw juices and legumes in enzyme-rich menu, including combination of red pepper stuffed with mix of nuts and seeds or sauerkraut and seed loaf.

Services and Facilities **Exercise Equipment:** Lifecycle, NordicTrack, stepper, Rebounder, Hoist 880 multipurpose weight trainer. **Services:** Massage (Swedish, lymphatic drainage, neuromuscular, deep tissue, cranial-sacral, Thai), reflexology, shiatsu, energy work, yoga therapy, colon irrigation, hydrotherapy, personal training, health consultations. **Swimming Facilities:** Outdoor pool, ocean beach nearby. **Recreation Facilities:** 2 tennis courts, golf and boating nearby. **Evening Programs:** Lectures and discussions nightly.

In the Area Trips to the beach, local museums, shopping excursions.

Getting Here *From Miami.* By bus, Greyhound to West Palm Beach (90 mins). By car, Florida Turnpike (I–75) to Palm Beach Exit 40, Okeechobee Blvd. to Skees Rd. (1 hr). Free service to and from West Palm Beach airport and bus station. Taxi, rental car available.

Special Notes Ramps provided for people with disabilities; 1 specially equipped guest room. No smoking.

Lido Spa Hotel

Vibrant maturity
Weight management

Florida
Miami Beach An all-inclusive daily rate that covers massage, exercise classes, and nutritional guidance makes the Lido Spa Hotel a good alternative to luxury spas. It's really more a residential hotel than a resort. Occupying choice frontage on Biscayne Bay, it is linked to Miami Beach by the scenic Venetian Causeway, a toll road for Miami commuters.

Family-owned-and-operated, the Lido has a comfortable, lived-in look, but shows its age. The main building opened in 1962 and is flanked by two-level wings of motel-like accommodations. Garden-level rooms are popular with older guests, who make up the majority of the Lido's regular clientele; they are a friendly community of mature adults, and many return year after year. The managers of the men's and women's spas provide a limited amount of guidance but, at the same time, are responsive to guests' personal needs and interests. If you are self-motivated and can set your own schedule, this could be a pleasant, relaxed vacation.

The daily schedule includes two low-impact exercise classes in the air-conditioned gym and occasional workouts in the swimming pool. Otherwise you're on your own to schedule massage appointments, swim in the two outdoor pools (one contains filtered saltwater), or sunbathe in private cabanas.

Lido Spa Hotel
40 Island Ave., Miami Beach, FL 33139
Tel. 305/538–4621 or 800/327–8363.

Administration	Director, Aaron "Chuck" Edelstein
Season	Nov.–May
Accommodations	106 rooms, mostly in 1- or 2-story garden wings. Fully equipped apartments (15) nearby. Furniture has plastic, 1960s look, well maintained and serviced daily. TV, telephone, air-conditioning; extra charge for refrigerator.
Rates	Varies with season, $70–$128 single, $60–$100 per person, double occupancy. Daily rate includes massage (30 min), 3 meals, exercise classes, outings. Add 9.5% tax, gratuities. Deposit $100 per room. AE, MC, V.
Meal Plans	Selections from menu include grilled snapper, pasta salad, baked chicken. Eggs, dairy products; coffee and tea available. Kosher food on request.
Services and Facilities	**Exercise Equipment:** 6 treadmills (Precor, Trotter, Lane), 10 stationary bikes (Tuntori, Monark, Schwinn), StairMaster, 3 Lifecycles, Universal multistation gym, free weights, pulleys, barbells, tiltboard, Rebounder. **Swimming Facilities:** Outdoor lap pool, recreational pool. **Spa Facilities:** Steam room, private whirlpools, Swedish massage, loofah body scrub, facial for women only, beauty salon. **Evening Programs:** Musicals or movies.
In the Area	Bass Museum of Art, Lincoln Road (arts district), Theater of the Performing Arts (concerts, opera, ballet, musicals), Dade County Cultural Center, Art Deco hotels and cafés, Bayside shops.
Getting Here	*From Miami.* By car, Biscayne Blvd. to Venetian Causeway. Free transfer to airport or Amtrak station on departure.
Special Notes	No smoking in spa or special areas of dining room.

Palm-Aire Resort & Spa

Life enhancement
Luxury pampering
Weight management

Florida
Pompano Beach

Surrounded by five 18-hole championship golf courses, 37 clay and hard-surface tennis courts, and condominium apartment buildings, the spa at Palm-Aire Resort has built a clientele of local residents and "snowbird" winter visitors for 25 years.

Since the days when Elizabeth Taylor hid out here to lose weight, the spa has changed focus. No structured program is available, and spa packages have been dropped in favor of services tailored to your time and interests, more like a day spa. In the spacious spa building, separate men's and women's pavilions have private sunken Roman baths, Swiss showers (17 nozzles that alternate warm and cool water), and some of the most experienced hands in the massage business. Each side has sauna, cold plunge, steam room, and outdoor exercise pool (try aquaerobics in the buff). There's a well-equipped coed gym, racquetball courts, and junior-Olympic-size outdoor swimming pool. Ocean swimming, however, is about a 20-minute ride away.

A typical day begins with a brisk walk on a half-mile outdoor track. An instructor monitors your pulse rate on every lap. In the locker room you are issued a robe and slippers, invited to relax in the lounge while waiting for your next appointment or aerobics class. There's a clublike atmosphere as resident members and regular guests swap gossip and watch the stock market reports. Staff members are attentive and accustomed to gratuities.

Calories count in the hotel's private spa dining room; the food is portion controlled, high in carbohydrates, and low in fat. The 1,000-calorie-per-day plan is sufficient, but second helpings are available. A regular, "fattening" menu is served in the adjoining dining room.

The newly renovated hotel has spacious room and suites, some with full kitchen. With the full-day and half-day spa packages you get use of all the facilities, even if you're not staying at the hotel.

Palm-Aire Resort & Spa
2601 Palm-Aire Dr. N, Pompano Beach, FL 33069
Tel. 954/972–3300 or 800/272–5624
Fax 954/968–2711

Administration General manager, Philip E. Deery; spa director, Kathy Eggleston

Season Year-round

Accommodations 88 spacious rooms in 4-story hotel, renovated in 1996, all with separate dressing rooms. Also available, deluxe efficiency studio and luxury suites with 1 or 2 bedrooms, kitchen, private terraces, about half overlooking golf course. King-size beds and sofas, remote-control TV, built-in wet bar, air-conditioning, telephone in all rooms.

Rates Daily rate for standard room, single or double occupancy, $109–$159, studio $139–$179, suite $169–$199. Add taxes, gratuities. 2-night minimum. Ultimate Day (no room) spa packages $200–$270, half-day $125–$225 includes tax and gratuity. Golf and tennis packages available. Deposit: 1 night's advance payment by credit card. AE, DC, MC, V.

Meal Plans Spa Day packages include lunch; other meals à la carte. Breakfast can include poached egg on wheat bread or cottage cheese and a bran muffin. Lunch choices include spinach-mushroom salad followed by baked potato stuffed with cottage and Jarlsberg cheeses or Spanish omelet made with egg whites. Broiled or poached snapper, chicken cacciatore, and vegetable lasagna for dinner.

Services and Facilities **Exercise Equipment:** 2 Trotter treadmills, 4 Precor treadmills, 2 StepMasters, 2 Liferowers, 4 Lifecycles, 2 StairMasters, Heartmate bike, 2 Bodyguard ergometer bikes, 3 Schwinn Air Dyne bikes, 2 recumbent bikes, 16-unit Bodymaster strength-conditioning system, complete Olympic free-weight gym, barbells (1–100 lbs). **Services:** Body massage (Swedish, deep muscle), thalassotherapy, facial treatments, loofah body scrub, herbal wrap, hand and foot paraffin. Separate men's and women's salons for hair, nail, and skin care. Golf and tennis clinics, personal conditioning. **Swimming Facilities:** 25-yd outdoor lap pool; separate men's and women's contrast (hot/cold) pools. **Recreation Facilities:** 37 tennis courts, 3 18-hole golf courses, 2 racquetball courts, indoor squash court. **Evening Programs:** None.

In the Area The Everglades, Fort Lauderdale Museum of the Arts, performing arts center, Parker Playhouse, 1-day Bahamas cruise, Pompano Harness Track, Dania Fronton (jai alai), dog and thoroughbred racing, deep-sea fishing charters, canal cruises, Yankee spring training games.

Getting Here *From Miami.* By car, I–95 north to Exit 34, Atlantic Blvd., 27th Ave. to second entrance road (45 mins). Limousine service (fixed fee) available to and from Fort Lauderdale International Airport and Miami. Rental car, taxi available. Valet service at hotel.

Special Notes Spa facilities on ground level and elevators make this hotel accessible for people with disabilities. No smoking in the spa, the spa dining room, or the lounge.

The Pier House Caribbean Spa

Nonprogram resort

Florida
Key West
The Caribbean Spa is a special enclave within the popular Pier House resort. Working out here is both liberating and seductive, mirroring the laissez-faire attitude of Old Town Key West itself. While for most guests the big event of the day is watching the spectacular sunset with beer in hand, you can also indulge in a sybaritic escape.

Decorated in tropical color schemes, the spa building has 22 guest rooms and a boutique spa on the ground floor, where a professional trainer or esthetician will develop your personalized program. Facilities include men's and women's locker rooms with steam room and sauna, outdoor whirlpool, complete exercise circuit, and salon for hair styling, facials, manicures and pedicures.

The salon's specialty is Prescription Plus creams and lotions formulated for your skin type by the esthetician doing your facial. Try the "Coma," a 90-minute combination of massage, reflexology, and paraffin treatment on your hands and feet. Services are available à la carte or as part of packages with hotel accommodations.

Workouts with a harbor view are a bonus when you join one of the daily aerobics classes held in the resort's waterside disco. Options include step and low-impact aerobics. All hotel guests can join the water aerobics session held in the swimming pool.

The convenient, fun location in the heart of a sometimes boisterous town gives you plenty of opportunity to stroll to shops and tourist attractions—all the while knowing you can retreat to the spa's hushed quarters. The resort's beach is not up to the quality of the accommodations. Really a small, rocky cove, it does offer some attraction, if you enjoy nude bathing; local rules are tolerant. With all the temptations in Key West, the Caribbean Spa offers a healthy alternative.

The Pier House Caribbean Spa
1 Duval St., Key West, FL 33040
Tel. 305/296–4600 or 800/327–8340
Fax 305/296–4600

Administration General manager, Joyce Matt; spa director, Michele Herald

Season Year-round

Accommodations 22 spa rooms; corner minisuite with fireplace, some have Habitat baths with steam/sauna, some have bathrooms with marble-topped double vanity, whirlpool tub. White wicker furnishings, sitting area, king-size bed, ceiling fans, French doors opening into a private patio or balcony. Amenities include color TV with VCR, CD players, AM/FM radio, air-conditioning, telephones. The main buildings have 123 guest rooms, including 13 suites.

Rates 2-night Stress Breaker package $659–$850 per couple. Full-day package with lunch (no lodging) $184, half-day $120.75. Packages include tax, service charge. Other rooms $195–$300 single or double, suites $325–$700. Add tax and service charge. Daily facility charge for resort guests ($10–$15) is waived when services are booked. Advance payment for 1 night (longer during holidays). AE, DC, MC, V.

Meal Plans Breakfast included in spa package; other spa cuisine selections on à la carte menu. Breakfast can be tropical fruit with yogurt or egg-white omelet with spinach, onions, and cottage cheese, cereal with skim milk. Lunch choices are grilled seafood, chicken salad, flank steak. Dinner can begin with conch bisque or conch egg roll, salad of field greens in vinaigrette; entrées include Key West shrimp with pasilla chili barbecue sauce, sautéed yellowtail with Key lime sauce, papaya, and avocado.

Services and Facilities **Exercise Equipment:** 9-unit Keiser weight training gym, 2 StairMasters, 2 Precor treadmills, 2 Lifecycles, "Wave Webb" gloves, dumbbells (5–45 lbs), bench press. **Services:** Massage (sports, therapeutic, aromatherapy, combination), deep pore cleansing, loofah scrub, facial with Key West aloe; salon for hair styling, waxing, manicure, pedicure; 1-on-1 training. **Swimming Facilities:** 2 outdoor pools, saltwater beach.

In the Area Audubon House and studio, Sloppy Joe's, Hemingway's house, Conch Train tour of historic district, Sunken Treasure Museum, Harry Truman Little White House Museum.

Getting Here *From Miami.* By bus, Greyhound (3 hrs). By car, Hwy. 1 (Overseas Highway) via Seven-Mile Bridge (3 hrs). By air, scheduled service on USAir, American Eagle commuter. Rental car, taxi available; bike and moped rental.

Special Notes Spa open weekdays 7 AM–9 PM, weekends 8–8. No smoking in spa.

Pritikin Longevity Center

Nutrition and diet
Weight management

Florida
Miami Beach

Dieting at the Pritikin Longevity Center may be the healthiest part of a holiday on Miami Beach. Everyone, from the doctors on staff to the exercise instructors, eats Pritikin-style.

The revolutionary diet introduced by the late Nathan Pritikin in 1974 is the foundation of 1- to 4-week programs designed to treat and control medical problems. The medically supervised live-in program here provides the support many people need in changing their lifestyles.

The regimen demands discipline, so don't expect a fun-in-the-sun holiday. Along with 50 other participants, you work out in the gym or pool and walk on the beach. If you enjoy ocean swimming, it can be part of your exercise plan. The staff doctor decides what's best for you.

Exercise, nutrition, stress management, health education, and medical services are the core curriculum. The 2-week program is recommended for sufferers of heart disease, insulin-dependent diabetes, obesity, or uncontrolled high blood pressure. Doctors have found that people with angina have much less pain within two weeks of beginning the Pritikin program; people with diabetes need much less insulin. Some participants who arrive with canes leave with improved mobility.

The full course offers individual attention, counseling, and close supervision. Healthy people come to learn how to safeguard their health, and to gain knowledge and self-assurance in the face of temptation. The daily schedule includes cooking demonstrations, lectures, and three exercise sessions. A full physical examination is a major feature of the program and includes a treadmill stress test and complete blood chemistry analysis. Depending on your personal history and fitness level, you are assigned to a specialist in cardiology or internal medicine who monitors your progress on the prescribed diet and exercise program.

Like the original Pritikin center in California, this beachfront property is both a resort and a lifestyle learning center. After your first visit, there are refresher courses and seasonal programs at substantial discounts. Companions or spouses may opt to participate in the program and medical tests (health insurance reimbursement may be available). Housed in a refurbished hotel, the Pritikin program provides motivation along with relaxation.

Pritikin Longevity Center
5875 Collins Ave., Miami Beach, FL 33140
Tel. 305/866–2237 or 800/327–4914 (Flamingo Hotel,
305/865–8645)
Fax 305/866–1872

Administration Executive director, Joan Mikus

Season Year-round, scheduled dates

Accommodations 100 rooms in beachfront hotel, some facing traffic on Collins Ave., others with an ocean view on penthouse floor, and suites. Smaller rooms included in program with single or double beds, private baths, and comfortable furniture. All with air-conditioning, color TV, telephone, maid service.

Rates 1-week program $3,727 single, $2,028 spouse or companion; 2-week program $6,472 single, $2,967 spouse or companion; 4 weeks $10,794 single, $5,679 with companion. Tax included, gratuities optional. $500–$1,000 advance payment. AE, MC, V (for deposit only). Discount for repeat visitors.

Meal Plans 3 meals plus 3 snacks daily. Buffet-style breakfast and lunch, table service and menu choices at dinner. Lunch and dinner salad bar. Lunch includes Pritikin vegetarian pizza, eggplant patties with marinara sauce, and rice-tofu moo goo gai pan; chicken teriyaki or poached salmon in dill sauce for dinner.

Services and Facilities **Exercise Equipment:** 23 Trotter treadmills, Trotter multistation gym, 8 Schwinn Air Dyne bikes, 2 rowing machines, StairMaster, bench press, hand weights. **Services:** Private counseling on nutrition and health, complete medical and physical examination, including blood tests. Massage, acupressure appointments by request. **Swimming Facilities:** Olympic-size outdoor pool for aerobics, direct access to beach. **Recreation Facilities:** Nearby tennis courts and golf course, boardwalk. **Evening Programs:** Nightly entertainment by local talent, exercises.

In the Area Group trips to shows and jai alai games, Miami museums and sightseeing, deep-sea fishing.

Getting Here *From Miami.* By car, I–95 to Rte. 195 exit, Arthur Godrey Causeway to 41st St., left on Collins Ave. (15 mins). Public bus, airport shuttle service, taxi, rental car available. Private parking on site.

Special Notes Ramps and elevators provide access for people with disabilities. No smoking on the premises. Spa open daily 6:30 AM–10:30 PM.

PGA National Resort & Spa

Luxury pampering
Sports conditioning
Vibrant maturity
Weight management

Florida
Palm Beach
Gardens

Golf and tennis champions exercise here during tournaments, but the spa at the PGA National Resort can be enjoyed as a sybaritic getaway combined with sports conditioning year-round. Since 1981 the 2,340-acre PGA community has expanded to include five golf courses, five croquet courts, a state-of-the-art spa building, Health & Racquet Club, and six restaurants. While there is no group program, you can plan a comprehensive health and fitness regimen, or combine spa packages with sports, with or without lodging.

At the Health & Racquet Club, instructors recommend a varied workout program to develop specific muscle groups and cardiovascular strength. Skiers might train on a cross-country exercise machine, a stair-climbing machine, and alternate 20-minute sessions on Nautilus equipment. For the tennis player, there's the treadmill, selected Trotter strength training units. Schedule sessions with a personal trainer by calling well in advance of your arrival date. Advanced workouts are in a private training room, from 6:30 AM weekdays. Scheduled aerobics classes every morning, from step to cardio intervals and water workouts, are open to all resort guests for a small charge or as part of a spa package.

The European philosophy of cleansing the body of impurities and toxins is carried through at the spa building. Hydrotherapy treatments, thalassotherapy, and body masks with natural plants and sea extracts are offered à la carte or in spa packages. The spa is connected to the main resort building by a garden with an outdoor pool complex called "Waters of the World." You can soak in imported salts and mineral crystals from the Dead Sea and the French Pyrénées, enjoy a hot tub, take a cold plunge, or just swim.

Golf, however, is the principal recreation here. The home of the Professional Golfers' Association of America, the five courses challenge professional golfers and Sunday duffers alike. Getting in shape for the ultimate golfing experience, a round on the General (a course designed by Arnold Palmer), could be the goal of a fitness regime devised by a team of golf pros and fitness instructors. Try the daily clinics, private lessons, or the advanced PGA National Golf Academy (2–3 days).

The nutritional needs of a sports regimen are the specialty of resident Registered Dietician Cheryl Hartsough. Personal consultation on diet, meals, and fitness training are included in the four-night Healthy Weight program. To learn the secrets of counteracting the aging process, guests are now offered a four-night Ageless Beauty Retreat. The full-service spa salon is open to the public.

Opened in 1992, the spa building has separate locker rooms for men and women, where you are issued a robe and slippers. There are 25 coed treatment rooms, 6 facial rooms, 4 wet rooms, 2 hydrotub rooms. With more than 140 services offered, spa packages are tailored to your needs daily. Advance consultation with a planner may result in a manual lymph drainage massage using the Vodder technique, followed by a cooling soak rather than heat treatment. Thalassotherapy tubs are advised to relax you for a massage or seaweed wrap.

Both advanced training for bodywork professionals at the new Bramham Institute, and the busy schedule of Pro/Am golf tournaments, make this a popular destination for active vacationers and area residents.

PGA National Resort & Spa
400 Ave. of the Champions, Palm Beach Gardens, FL 33418
Tel. 407/627–2000 or 800/633–9150, spa reservations 800/843–7725
Fax 407/622–0261

Administration Vice President–managing director, David Bagwell; spa director, Nancy Soccorso; fitness director, Randy Myers; Health & Racquet Club director, Ruth Barnett

Season Year-round

Accommodations 339 spacious guest rooms, including 60 suites, with tile floors and Mediterranean Revival fabrics and furniture, and 80 cottage units along golf courses, each with 2 bedrooms, 2 baths, and kitchen. Renovated in 1992, all rooms have balcony or terrace, private bath, and walk-in closet.

Rates Daily: $109–$325 single or double, suites $195–$995, cottage suites $245–$380. Spa plan, per day with deluxe accommodations and meals, $509 single, $395 per person double occupancy. Full-day spa package with spa cuisine lunch (no lodging) $249, half-day escapes $168–$195. Tax and service charges included in spa packages. 1 night advance payment. AE, DC, MC, V.

Meal Plans Spa cuisine breakfast and lunch daily on spa plan, dinner choices à la carte at Italian and seafood dining rooms. At the Citrus Tree restaurant, lunch menu starters can be Chesapeake Bay crab cakes, baked mushroom and artichoke in crispy tortilla cone, quesadilla with smoked turkey; entrées can be crab-avocado salad, Florida red snapper or grouper grilled over mesquite wood, Cajun blackened beef, grilled chicken, pizza with chicken sausage and fresh tomato marinara, steamed yellowtail snapper in an eggplant boat, chilled fruit soup served in coconut shell, or mixed seafood with Asian noodles and stir-fry vegetables. CrabCatcher dinner choices include Pacific Rim sushi plate, Siam squid salad, Ceasar salad, grilled lemon sole, steamed King Crab legs, broiled snapper over cappellini pasta, tuna tempura. Arezzo antipasti are grilled eggplant with ricotta cheese, or homemade mozzarella with red and yellow tomatoes; entrée can be sauteed salmon, grilled fillet of beef with portabello mushrooms, or whole wheat pizza.

Services and Facilities **Exercise Equipment:** Member/guest training center has 2 18-station Nautilus circuits, 12 Trotter treadmills, 4 recumbent Lifecycles, 5 Lifecycles, 9 StairMasters, NordicTrack cross-country ski machine, UBE ergometer, 3 Liferowers, 2 Concept 2 rowing ergometers, 4 Cybex weight training units, 8 Trotter resistrance units, free weights (5–50 lbs). Personal training center with 17 Trotter resistance units, Cybex cable cross-over, leg press, squat, lat pulldown, 12 Nautilus units, bench and overhead press, 510 lbs Olympic free weights (2- to 45-lb bars), dumbells (1–50 lbs), Smith machine, 3 Trotter treadmills, StairMaster 400PT, Concept 2 rowing ergometer, Crossaerobics machine, 2 Monark bikes. **Services:** Massage (Swedish, sports, shiatsu, aromatherapy, reflexology, lymphatic, cellulite), salt-glow marine algae body wrap, seaweed body polish, aromatherapy wraps, hydrotherapy tubs with sea salts, essential oils, Vichy shower, facials. **Swimming Facilities:** Family pool at hotel, 5-lane lap pool at health club, outdoor pool and Jacuzzi at the spa. **Recreation Facilities:** 5 golf courses,

19 Har-Tru outdoor tennis courts (12 lighted), 3 indoor racquetball courts, 5 croquet lawns, 26-acre lake with sailboats and aquacycles; horseback riding nearby. **Evening Programs:** Resort entertainment, lectures during scheduled weight management, golf and tennis programs.

In the Area Palm Beach Worth Avenue shops, Flagler Museum (Whitehall), Golf Hall of Fame, the Gardens (shopping), Burt Reynolds Dinner Theater, Palm Beach Symphony Orchestra, opera and pops concerts at Kravis Center, Polo Club, Morikami Museum and gardens (Japanese arts).

Getting Here *From West Palm Beach.* By car, I–95 to Exit 57, PGA Blvd. west to resort entrance; Florida Turnpike to Exit 44, PGA Blvd. (20 mins). Limousine and van service (fixed fee) to and from airport. Taxi, car rental available.

Special Notes Ramps, elevators, and specially equipped rooms provide access for people with disabilities. Daily baby-sitting; golf and tennis clinics or private instruction for children. Spa hours daily 8:30–7; fitness room Mon.–Thurs. 6:30 AM–9 PM, to 8 PM Fri., weekends 8–5:30. Daily facility fee ($25) included in spa; $12 per day for fitness/aerobics packages.

Ponte Vedra Inn & Club

Nonprogram resort

Florida
Ponte Vedra
Beach

It hasn't always been all golf, tennis, and pampering on the 300-acre stretch of northeastern Florida coastline occupied by the 69-year-old Ponte Vedra Inn & Club. At the turn of the century, minerals were mined here, but beginning in 1928 alumni of Princeton University developed the club facilities. With the opening of a full-service spa in 1996, the resort offers an outstanding combination of sports, fitness, and exercise programs.

Clublike atmosphere prevails in the main building, with its formal dining room and conference center, and guests are treated like members. Dining options include the beachfront Seafoam Dining Room atop the Surf Club, which has light cuisine selections on the menu, and lunch on the spa patio. Lodging is in two-story beach houses that cluster along a pristine Atlantic Ocean beach or the golf courses.

The new 10,000-square-foot spa building adjoins the fitness center and two 18-hole championship golf courses, with a big Jacuzzi on the patio overlooking fairways and Lake Guana. Designed to complement the style of the 1940s beach houses, the one-story building features whitewashed and pickled-pine furnishings, muted tones of cream, blue, and taupe, and terra-cotta tile roof topped by a lighted cupola. Facilities include five massage rooms, five facial rooms, wet room with Jacuzzi tub and Vichy shower beds, and salon. Services are scheduled à la carte or as part of Day Spa packages for men and women. The ground-floor fitness center has more than 50 pieces of exercise equipment that can be used for a daily fee ($8) or with a personal trainer. Aerobics classes open to all resort guests are held here daily, including aquacize sessions in the outdoor lap pool.

While there are no health-oriented programs, the spa can schedule fitness evaluations and physical examinations at a nearby branch of the Mayo Clinic.

Following a regimen recommended by the medical staff, your special diet needs and exercise can be combined with a relaxing stay. This family-oriented resort has a distinctly Southern ambience and a feeling of privacy.

Ponte Vedra Inn & Club

200 Ponte Vedra Blvd., Ponte Vedra Beach, FL 32082
Tel. 904/285-1111 or 800/234-7842
Fax 904/285-2111

Administration General manager, Dale Henry; spa director, Jeanette Chesney

Season Year-round

Accommodations 202 spacious oceanside rooms, including 20 suites, in 8 cottage-style buildings. All with 2 queen-size beds, TV, coffeemaker, ironing board and iron, air-conditioning, balcony. Bathroom has upscale amenities, robes, hair dryer.

Rates Daily per room (1–5 persons), $135–$240. Day spa packages $85–$215, including tax and gratuities.

Meal Plans Spa lunch included in full-day packages. Choices include seafood, seasonal salads, herbal tea or coffee. Light cuisine selections are on à la carte menu at resort restaurants.

Services and Facilities **Exercise Equipment:** 16-unit Cybex modular strength system, VersaClimber, 5 StairMasters, 4 treadmills, 4 recumbent bikes, 3 Schwinn Air Dyne bikes, NordicTrack, free weights (2½–45 lbs). **Services:** Swedish or Bio-Energy massage, facials, loofah body polish, herbal wrap, paraffin hand and foot treatment, fango wrap, hydro-shower, waxing, glycolic peel; salon for hair, nail, and skin care. **Swimming Facilities:** Outdoor lap pool, recreational pool, ocean beach. **Recreation Facilities:** 15 Har-Tru tennis courts, 2 18-hole golf courses, putting green, pedal boats, bikes.

In the Area Jacksonville, St. Augustine, Association of Tennis Professionals (ATP) international headquarters (play on grass, red clay, cushioned hard courts), deep-sea or lagoon fishing.

Getting Here *From Jacksonville.* By car, I-95 to Butler Blvd., east to Hwy A1A, Ponte Vedra Blvd. (40 mins). Limousine, taxi, rental car available.

Special Notes Spa open daily 8–7. Minimum age: 16. Fitness Center open weekdays 5:30 AM–9 PM, Sat. 7–6, Sun. 8–6. Facilities for persons with disabilities available.

The Registry Resort & Spa

Luxury pampering
Nonprogram resort
Weight management

Florida
Fort Lauderdale

If you want to go first class on a tight budget, consider a holiday at the Registry Resort & Spa, where you can arrange first-rate services à la carte or as a package. The difference between the two is in quantity of services, not quality. You can stay a weekend, four days, or a full week; take unlimited exercise classes and enjoy expert bodywork and beauty treatments; or orient your visit around sports—tennis, golf, and horseback riding. But beware adding too many extras to your spa schedule, as your bill will quickly run up.

Sybaritic pleasures aside, management takes a serious approach to fitness here. A staff nurse interviews you on arrival and may suggest consultation on a diet plan. Guests can opt for calorie-controlled meals or dine in the gourmet dining room.

A typical day begins with a walk or jog around the golf course before breakfast, then an hour-long aerobics class. Three levels of conditioning are offered in a dozen different classes that range from easy stretches and yoga to deep toning calisthenics and energizing routines. Workouts in the water are popular, especially for people with orthopedic problems; there's support for joints and the back while doing aquatics in the pool. There are cardiovascular exercises for men only, as well as a thermal mineral water body scrub and massage to condition the male physique.

What sets this spa apart from others is the wide range of body and skin-care treatments. Always on the cutting edge, the Registry recently introduced the European Kur program developed by Kerstin Florian with thermal-water crystals from Hungary. Adding to its repertoire of hydrotherapy, the kur includes bodywork with an imported line of essential oils used in the aromatherapy massage.

Although the spa is popular with single guests and couples, there is no group camaraderie. Privacy is one of the best features of the building's separate wings for men and women, each with a lap pool and sundeck. An international array of pleaures, equal on both sides, includes Turkish steam rooms, Swiss showers, and Finnish saunas, hot and cold plunge pools, and individual whirlpools. Families with children have the extra advantage of the sports program for teenagers and day camp for youngsters. Ocean beaches are 30 minutes away by car, making outings a reasonable alternative to staying on resort grounds throughout your vacation.

The Registry Resort & Spa

250 Racquet Club Rd., Fort Lauderdale, FL 33326
Tel. 954/389–3300 or 800/327–8090
Fax 954/384–6157

Administration Managing director, Greg Horeth; spa director, Tanya Lee

Season Year-round

Accommodations 493 luxury guest rooms and suites in 9 4-story buildings; spacious rooms with balconies overlook lake or golf course with 2 beds (queen-size or twin) or 1 extra-large king-size. Rattan seating and tropical colors. Oversize bath with dressing area.

Rates $105–$175 daily single, $165–$255 for 2 persons; Perfect Day package at spa $195 per person (lodging not included), plus tax and gratuity. Spa Sampler 2-night package $474–$654 single, $399–$489 per person double; 4-night Spa Experience $1,031–$1,391 single, $881–$1,061 double; 7-night Spa Retreat 1,797–$2,427 single, $1,535–$1,850 double. Nightly Boot Camp package (2-night min.) $167–$257 single, $130–$175 double. Packages include tax, service charges. Additional bodywork and beauty treatments, golf and tennis packages available. 1 night's advance payment 7 days after booking or credit card confirmation. AE, D, MC, V.

Meal Plans 3 meals with calorie-counted selections served daily in private Spa Dining Room included in packages. 1,200 calories suggested for those not on weight-loss diet. Lunch specialties include pasta primavera, curried chicken soup, baked vegetables marinara with tofu, and fresh fruit. Dinner entrées include Maine lobster with asparagus spears, stir-fried chicken and vegetables on cellophane noodles, dessert crepe with blueberry and cheese filling.

Services and Facilities **Exercise Equipment:** 10-station Keiser gym, 3 Lifecycles, 5 Quinton treadmills, 3 stationary bikes, 2 StairMasters, Gravitron, 2 Lifesteps, Liferower, free weights (5–50 lbs). **Services:** Massage (Swedish, shiatsu, aromatherapy, reflexology), aromatherapy bath, loofah body scrub, herbal wrap, seakelp body wrap, thermal back treatment, baths, and facials. Men's and women's salons for skin and nail care, hairstyling.

Private exercise, golf, tennis, and horseback-riding instruction. Individualized fitness profile, nutrition profile, and body composition analysis. **Swimming Facilities:** Outdoor pools; ocean beach nearby. **Spa Facilities:** 3½-foot exercise pool, outdoor Jacuzzi, Finnish sauna, Turkish steam bath, hot and cold plunge baths. **Recreation Facilities:** 24 tennis courts, 2 18-hole golf courses, 6 racquetball and squash courts, horseback riding, bicycle rental. **Evening Programs:** None.

In the Area   Shopping trip to Sawgrass Mill Mall, beach shuttle; local sightseeing on request. Everglades tour by airboat, jai-alai fronton, Bahamas cruises, dog-and horse-racing tracks, Seminole Indian village, Fort Lauderdale museums and performing arts center.

Getting Here   *From Miami.* By car, I–75 to Fort Lauderdale, Arvida Parkway Exit, State Rd. 84 (40 mins). By plane, scheduled service (15 mins). Taxi, rental car available.

Special Notes   Ramps, elevators, and specially equipped rooms for guests with disabilities. No smoking in spa building or in designated areas of the dining room. Spa open daily 7–7 winter season, summer hours vary.

Safety Harbor Spa Resort

Life enhancement
Luxury pampering
Taking the waters
Weight management

Florida
Safety Harbor
(Tampa Bay)

Walking along Bayshore Drive in the morning, swimming laps under swaying palms, and soaking in mineral spring water are among the pleasures of a vacation at Safety Harbor Resort. Focused on fitness, this long-popular spa emerged from a series of renovations and management changes begun in 1955 with a fresh, slim look. The 52-year-old hotel has new furniture, an enlarged dining room and café, and a Clarins salon for skin care.

With renewed interest in mineral water springs on the property (four are located under the dining room), once touted as a cure for just about anything that ails you, hydrotherapy has become a feature of the spa. Modern chemical analysis shows that each spring has a different proportion of calcium, magnesium, sodium, potassium, and other minerals. This water is used for filling two coed Jacuzzis and a chlorinated indoor pool.

Aquatics is a strong feature of the health-oriented program. Private hydrotherapy tubs in the men's and women's bathhouses are enhanced with blends of herbs and marine algae for stress reduction, relief of muscular tension, and toning treatments. Exercising in the specially designed shallow indoor and outdoor pools burns calories efficiently without straining the body. Even out of the water, though, exercise instructors promote low-impact routines, and the shock-absorbing floors are specially constructed to help avoid tendonitis and shin splints. The instructors here specialize in a variety of routines, from gentle to active, to keep you from getting bored.

A member of the fitness staff will check your overall physical condition, monitor your heart rate, and analyze your body-fat-to-muscle ratio. Based on a computer analysis, a specific combination of exercise and diet will be recommended.

Bodywork appointments are made through a guest coordinator and charged on an à la carte basis or as part of seasonal packages, 2–8 days. Men's and women's locker rooms have sauna, steam room, and direct access to the exercise pool, but it's a good idea to bring footwear, even aquatic socks for water aerobics. Robe and slippers are provided daily, along with locker room amenities.

Don't expect group interaction; you're pretty much on your own until meeting kindred souls in the dining room or the nightly excursions to cultural events, movies, and shopping. Beach trips are scheduled several times a week. The spa's laid-back feeling may be just the restorative you need. For more active pursuits, there's Phil Green's Tennis Academy, where two hours of instruction daily can be combined with fitness classes. The tennis pros conduct classes at beginner, intermediate, and advanced levels. Unlimited use of the tennis courts for daytime play, a golf driving range, and transportation to a nearby golf course are other options.

Unpretentious and informal, the resort has won legions of loyal friends by providing tools for looking and feeling good. The average guest's age is 40, with a smattering of older clients (often snowbirds taking an extended vacation) and the occasional twentysomething fitness fanatic.

Safety Harbor Spa Resort
105 N. Bayshore Dr., Safety Harbor, FL 34695
Tel. 813/726–1161 or 800/237–0155
Fax 813/726–4268

Administration General manager, Brett Smith; spa director, Hugh Jones

Season Year-round

Accommodations 172 spacious bedrooms and suites, all with balcony, sitting area, and dressing room. Standard rattan furniture, floral-print fabrics, 2 queen-size beds, TV, air-conditioning, phone, toiletries. Carafe of mineral water daily on request.

Rates 2-day/1-night package, full American plan with lodging, $286.81–$400 single, $317.26–$450 for 2 double occupancy; 5-day/4-night package $1,228.80–$1,606.80 single, $1,086.72–$1,335.52 per person double occupancy. 8-day/7-night package $2,142–$3,449 single, $1,885–$2,830 double. 3-night Tennis Academy/Spa package $743.76–$919.47 single, $640.41–$730.83 double. Gratuities and tax included. Deposit: 1 night advance payment. AE, DC, MC, V.

Meal Plans Spa packages include 3 meals daily from menu in dining room. Breakfast choices can be fresh-baked pumpkin muffins, whole-wheat pancakes with raspberry puree, and egg-white omelet with farmer cheese. Lunch includes vegetable chili with white or brown rice, vegetable lasagna, pizza with whole-wheat crust, and breast of chicken with herbed ricotta cheese. Special dinner salads, such as romaine lettuce with Parmesan dressing, then entrées of broiled lobster, crab Mornay, shrimp with linguini. Coffee and herbal tea available; wine à la carte.

Services and Facilities **Exercise Equipment:** Paramount sports trainer system with adductor, abductor, abdominal pullover, pull-down, butterfly back press, lateral raise, leg-kick pulley, bicep/tricep machine. Nautilus hip/back, leg curl, lower back, and abdominal machines. 12 Precor treadmills, 3 StairMasters, Lifestep, Lifecycle, 2 Windracers, 2 Heartmate TV bikes, 2 Schwinn Air Dyne bikes, VersaClimber, 2 Concept 2 rowing machines, upper body ergometer, 4 trampolines, Hydra-Fitness Total Power machine, Roman Chair abdominal unit. Free weights (1¼–45 lbs) and dumbbells (3–40 lbs) with bench press, incline bench, Uniflex unit. 2 speed bags for boxers. **Services:** Fitness evaluation, massage, herbal wraps, salt-glow loofah body scrub, facials, haircuts and styling, makeup consultation, manicure, pedicure, tennis instruction. **Swimming Facilities:** Outdoor and indoor pools, lap pool. Mineral spring water in all swimming pools and Jacuzzis. **Recreation Facilities:** 7 Har-Tru tennis courts, 2 hard courts, putting green, free use of bikes, basketball, water volleyball. Golf and horseback riding nearby (fee). **Evening Programs:** Lectures on stress management and health-related topics, cooking demonstrations, cultural programs, lounge dancing on weekends.

In the Area Clearwater Beach, Tampa, Ybor City (Tampa's colorful Cuban quarter), 1-day Bahamas cruise, Busch Gardens (family theme park and wildlife preserve), history museums, Tarpon Springs sponge harvest and sales center, Disney World.

Getting Here *From Tampa.* By bus, scheduled van service every 20 mins ($20) by Airport Limo Connection (tel. 800/282–6817) from Tampa International Airport. By car, I–275 south to Exit 20, Rte. 60 toward Clearwater, exit on Bayshore Blvd. (20 mins). Hotel van to the airport. Taxi, rental car available.

Special Notes Elevators but no specially equipped rooms for people with disabilities. No smoking in the spa and in designated dining areas. Arrival can be any day. Minimum age: 16.

Sanibel Harbour Resort & Spa

Luxury pampering
Sports conditioning

Florida On 80 wooded acres overlooking island-studded San Carlos
Fort Myers Bay, the resort is memorable for its easy access to Sanibel and Captiva islands and its top-quality tennis courts and fitness facilities. A private beach, marina, and bayfront swimming pool add to recreation options.

More than 40 aerobics classes a week are taught at variable impact levels in a plush studio with carpeted floor. New on the schedule are yoga fitness and line dancing. The spa's indoor lap pool is used for an energizing aquafit class. For more active pursuits, four air-conditioned racquetball courts can be booked by the hour. The Racquet Club offers daylong tennis workouts.

Set in lush tropical gardens, the spa is tucked under a tennis stadium. In addition to a full line of Cybex weight training equipment, a surprising range of body treatments is offered: Swiss showers, aromatherapy, salt-glow body scrub, herbal and seaweed wraps, and a salon for hair, nail, and skin care. Both men's and women's sections have sauna, steam room, 5 whirlpools, and hot and cold plunge pools. For a sonic massage, relax on the BETAR bed, a combination of stress-releasing musical energy impulses.

Day Spa packages, priced without lodging so that you can visit just from morning to evening, provide a sampling of services and full use of the facilities. Resort/spa packages range from three to eight days and include a honeymoon getaway. Otherwise, you pay the daily facility fee ($15) and use services à la carte.

Sanibel Harbour Resort & Spa
17260 Harbour Pointe Dr., Ft. Meyers, FL 33908
Tel. 941/466–2157 (spa), 941/466–4000 (resort), or
800/767–7777
Fax 941/466–3633

Administration Managing director, Robert Moceri; spa director, Thor Alan Holm

Season   Year-round

Accommodations   340-room hotel in resort complex with 100 2-bedroom luxury condominium apartments facing San Carlos Bay. Hotel rooms offer private balcony, king- or queen-size beds, cable TV, Florida furniture, bath with robes, hair dryer, air-conditioning, telephone, nightly turndown service. Condominiums in 2 12-story towers have bath with each bedroom, full kitchen, washer/dryer, dining room. Suites available in hotel.

Rates $130–$300 daily per room for 2 persons, suites $175–$325; condominium for 4 persons $169–$599. 3-day/2-night Spa Discovery package without meals $440–$758 single in hotel, $313–$472 per person double in hotel, $356–$589 double in condominium; 5-day/4-night Spa Escape $872–$1,508 single in hotel, $618–$936 double, $703–$1,169 double in condominium; 8-day/7-night Spa Pursuit $1,337–$2,449 single in hotel, $893–$1,449 double, $1,041–$1,856 double in condominium. Spa gratuities included in packages, 9% tax added. Day Spa packages $199–$229 include lunch, 17% service charge added. Meal plan $61 per person daily (breakfast, lunch, dinner), including taxes and gratuities. Deposit: 1 night advance payment by credit card. AE, DC, MC, V.

Meal Plans   Breakfast can be buckwheat pancakes or yogurt with fresh fruit, coffee or herbal tea. Light gourmet specials at lunch include chicken terrine appetizer or marinated tuna and grouper carpaccio with baby mixed greens. Entrées are chilled Floridian grouper with lightly spiced papaya coulis, whole-wheat pizza with goat cheese, grilled lamb chop, steamed chicken breast stuffed with mushrooms. "Cuisine of the Sun" nightly special menu uses all natural ingredients.

Services and Facilities   **Exercise Equipment:** 15-unit Cybex circuit, Smith machine, tricep bar, Preacher curl, 4 Schwinn Air Dyne bikes, 6 Trotter treadmills, 4 Lifecycles, Liferower, 4 StairMasters. **Services:** Massage (Swedish, reflexology, sports, aromatherapy), fango, salt-glow body scrub, herbal or seaweed wrap, facial with paraffin, Repechage seaweed facial, algae masque, apricot scrub, Biodroga milk and honey body wrap. Salon for hair, nail, skin care. Fitness evaluation, nutritional counseling, personal training, tennis instruction. **Swimming Facilities:** Indoor lap pool, outdoor resort pool, bay beach. **Recreation Facilities:** 12 lighted tennis courts (8 clay, 4 Spin-flex), center court stadium, fitness trail, 4 racquetball courts at spa, marina for sailing and fishing charters; golf, horseback riding nearby. Fishing pier, water sports, canoe rental.

In the Area   Everglades National Park (sightseeing boat, overnight canoe trip from Everglades City), Corkscrew Swamp Sanctuary (Audubon Society boardwalk tour), J.N. Ding Darling Wildlife Refuge (naturalist tour), baseball spring training camps, Thomas Alva Edison winter home and laboratory, Henry Ford estate, Burroughs Home (19th-century Georgian Revival mansion), Bonita Springs Dog Track, Seminole Gulf Railway, Sanibel Island, Captiva Island (shelling), Florida International Museum.

Getting Here   *From Fort Myers or Southwest Florida Regional Airport.* By car, I–75 to Daniels Rd., left at Six Mile Cypress, which becomes Gladiolus Rd., left on Summerlin Rd. to Sanibel Island causeway entrance, right on Harbour Pointe Dr. (20 mins). Airport shuttle service on request ($17 per person). Taxi, limousine, and rental car available.

Special Notes   Supervised children's program (ages 5–12) daily. No smoking in spa. Spa open Mon.–Sat. 7 AM–9 PM, Sun. and holidays 9–5. Daily spa admission fee ($15) included in packages, waived with services. Minimum age: 16.

Spa LXVI at Hyatt Regency Pier 66 Resort

Nonprogram resort

Florida
Ft. Lauderdale

The landmark Pier 66 Tower Hotel underwent changes in 1996, with Hyatt management upgrading the spa as well as the hotel rooms. Directly on the Intracoastal Waterway, the resort's 22-acre tropical gardens and 142-slip marina contrast with the busy beach scene just down the road. When you want to swim in the ocean, hail the water taxi at the resort's dock for a three-minute trip to the beach.

Spa LXVI is refreshingly tucked away in gardens and has a full-service salon for body, skin, and hair treatments. Owned and managed by MCM Hospitality, Inc., this indulgent hideaway has indoor and outdoor heated whirlpools, private massage rooms, and a room full of exercise equipment. Aerobics classes are offered poolside, and all guests can join an exercise session in the swimming pool.

A convenient place to escape from business at the nearby convention center, or to relax before boarding a cruise ship, the spa offers day packages, personal training, and locker rooms equipped with sauna, steam rooms, and Swiss showers.

Spa LXVI at Hyatt Regency Pier 66 Resort
2301 S.E. 17th St. Causeway, Ft. Lauderdale, FL 33316
Tel. 954/525–6666 or 800/327–3796
Fax 954/728–3541

Administration General manager, James R. Allmand

Season Year-round

Rates Daily room rate single or double occupancy $119–$249, jr. suite $189–$279. Add 11% tax. AE, DC, MC, V.

Accommodations 380 deluxe rooms with ocean, Intracoastal, or pool view in 17-story tower and garden lanais. All have private bathroom, air-conditioning, TV, and telephone.

Services and Facilities **Exercise Equipment:** 6 Nautilus units of "Next Generation" weight training equipment, 3 StairMasters, 2 Precor treadmills, 5 Lifecycles, rower, free weights. **Services:** Swedish and sports massage, aromatherapy, seaweed wrap, facial, pineapple or salt-glow body scrub; salon for hair, nail, and skin care; fitness evaluation, personal training, aerobics and aquatics classes. **Swimming Facilities:** 2 outdoor pools. **Recreation Facilities:** 2 Har-Tru clay tennis courts (lighted), snorkeling, scuba, parasailing, deep-sea fishing, marina with pleasure craft charter. Golf privileges at nearby course. **Evening Programs:** None.

In the Area Everglades National Park, International Swimming Hall of Fame (Olympic training center), Riverwalk (nightlife, aquarium), Brickell Station (vintage train station, multiscreen cinema), Sawgrass Mills Outlet Mall, Las Olas Blvd. (boutiques), Galleria Mall, jai alai fronton, horse racing tracks, Fort Lauderdale Museum of Art, Broward County Performing Arts Center.

Getting Here *From Ft. Lauderdale International Airport.* By car, east on 17th St. Causeway to bridge (15 mins). Rental car, taxi, limousine available.

Special Notes Specially equipped rooms for people with disabilities. Minimum age in spa is 16. No smoking in spa.

Turnberry Isle Resort & Club

Luxury pampering

Florida
Aventura (North Miami)

Here's a luxury hideaway for the executive who wants to shape up in privacy. Turnberry Isle Resort & Club accepts guests to share the members' spa and sports privileges, including spacious accommodations on the Intracoastal Waterway, and two Robert Trent Jones championship golf courses. A well-guarded secret, the 300 tropical acres and waterfront resort is overseen by the Rafael Group, international hoteliers who know how to maintain a very private club atmosphere.

Rarely crowded, the club has two air-conditioned racquetball courts, indoor and outdoor whirlpools, and lounges with sundecks. Scheduled aerobics classes in the sprung-wood-floor studio are attended by club members and attract some of the area's best instructors. Yoga also is popular as an afternoon unwinder. Exercise clothing and robe come with your locker, and the lounge is stocked with fruit, juice, newspapers, and a TV.

The focus of Turnberry's sport facilities is golf. Designed by Robert Trent Jones, the splashy South Course has a famous 18th hole "Island Green." Jones's challenging North Course provides smooth, consistent greens. The club hosts many prestigious tournaments.

For a break in the sports routine, try the beach. There are cabanas, a swimming pool, and light fare for lunch at the members-only Ocean Club. Relax in a Turkish steam bath and Swedish sauna, or get one-on-one cardiovascular training in the weights room, complete with large-screen TV. The entire array of equipment is top-of-the-line.

Overlooking yachts on the Intracoastal waterway, the spa building and adjoining swimming pool are a self-contained island of relaxation and wellness. The spa plans let you choose accommodations at the yacht club or country club, with free transportation throughout the resort and to Aventura Mall's upscale shops.

Turnberry Isle Resort & Club
19999 W. Country Club Dr., Aventura, North Miami, FL 33180
Tel. 305/932–6200 or 800/327–7028
Fax 305/933–3811

Administration General manager, Jens Grafe; spa director, Frederick Benke

Season Year-round

Rates 2-night minispa plan $439–$899 single, $319–$539 per person double occupancy; 4-night Spa Indulgence plan $1,339–$2,269 single, $1,119–$1,579 double; 7-night plan, $2,109–$3,729 single, $1,719–$2,529 double. Includes taxes, service charge. Daily room rates $150–$445, suites $295–$2,100, plus taxes and service charge. Deposit: 1 night's advance payment with credit card. AE, DC, MC, V.

Accommodations 340 deluxe rooms and suites in Mediterranean-style country club and hotel complex, all air-conditioned, with king-size beds, marble bath with hair dryer, whirlpool tub, 3 phones (2 lines), cable TV with VCR. Also 60 spacious rooms in 5-story Yacht Club hotel adjoining spa; 27 1-and 2-bedroom villas. Additional 100 rooms at country club scheduled for completion in 1998.

Meal Plans Spa plan includes full American breakfast daily. Spa cuisine selections on menu: luncheon includes grilled swordfish, pasta primavera, and cold shrimp plate. Typical dinner entrées are steamed lobster tail, tenderloin brochette, eggplant Parmesan, mesquite-grilled redfish with scallions.

Services and Facilities **Exercise Equipment:** 20-unit Nautilus circuit, Plus II Cybex units, 2 Liferowers, 5 StairMasters, VersaClimber, 5 Lifecycles, 9 Precor treadmills, Precor 3-D bike, Biocycle, recumbent bike, 2 Cybex ergometers, 2 Bally Lifesteps, hand weights. Dumbbells (3–80 lbs). **Services:** Therapeutic massage, Swedish massage, shiatsu, reflexology, aromatherapy; back cleansing and heat treatment, Phytomer marine mask, herbal wrap, loofah body scrub, Swiss shower, hydrotherapy tub, Breton sea kelp bath, Dead Sea mineral bath, mud pack. Computerized body-composition analysis, nutrition consultation, blood cholesterol test, medical consultation. Spa salon for hair, nail, and skin care. **Swimming Facilities:** 2 pools at spa, Ocean Club, Country Club. **Recreation Facilities:** 2 championship golf courses, 24 tennis courts (18 lighted), 2 indoor racquetball courts, walleyball, basketball, yacht charter.

In the Area Aventura Mall, Thoroughbred races at Gulfstream Park, Disney World, Miami and Fort Lauderdale museums, Pro Player Stadium (Miami Dolphins), Dania Fronton (Jai Alai), Biscayne Dog Race Track, baseball.

Getting Here *From Miami.* By car, I–95 to Exit 20, Ives Dairy Rd., U.S. Rte. 1, Biscayne Blvd. (25 mins). By boat, Intracoastal Waterway to Turnberry Isle Marina. Taxi, limousine, rental car available.

Special Notes No smoking in the spa and in designated areas. Spa open daily 7 AM–9 PM. Shuttle bus to beach, mall, country club, and spa.

Chateau Elan

Life enhancement
Luxury pampering
Stress control

Georgia A new and unique addition to the Atlanta area in 1992, the spa
Braselton at Chateau Elan is a restful retreat within a 3,400-acre gated resort community. The chateau is, in fact, a working winery, complete with vineyards and a reproduction of a 16th-century French manor house. Follow the woodland trails to a private lake and discover the elegant spa building where beautiful bodies and skin are complemented by luxury accommodations.

Decor in the 14 theme rooms at the spa range from high-tech to Georgian crafts, Greek, French, Western, and Great Gatsby themes, with matching T-shirts presented upon your arrival. There's a VCR and CD player in each room, where you might choose to watch "Gone With The Wind" from the library offerings, or bring your own entertainment. Tea is served every afternoon in the library; dinner can be ordered in.

After a welcome session with a scheduler, you're left to your own devices. Recently expanded, the spa has 20 private rooms for personal services, including thalassotherapy treatments with seaweed developed at the Institut Louison Bobet in France. The professional staff at the spa is supplemented by Atlanta area medical consultants, and specialists in nutrition and smoking-cessation.

Dining options are numerous. The concierge will make dinner reservations in the winery's Le Clos, which has a classic French menu for those not counting calories. The spa has its own dining room where breakfast and lunch are served as part of packages for 2–8 days. The menus blend European and American cuisine by Executive French Master Chef Bernard

Groupy, along with Georgia wine and water bottled by Chateau Elan.

The complex houses the South's largest equestrian center, three all-weather arenas, riding trails, and Grand Prix show facility, a 7-court tennis center by Stan Smith, four golf courses and country club, 274-room inn and conference center managed by Marriott, and vineyards where summer concerts and picnic dinners are an added attraction. The winery offers tours and tastings daily, and houses shops and a café as well as Le Clos restaurant.

A quiet, warm, and friendly atmosphere prevails. Mornings begin with easy stretches, then a guided hike on nature trails winding through the resort. In addition to aerobics classes, you can include horseback riding and golf along with one-on-one training and beauty salon services. All of these options come in a variety of packages; make appointments prior to your arrival to assure availability. You can also stay in a golf villa or at the inn, which has a small health club, and sample spa services à la carte.

Don't expect lots of exercise equipment and group programs. In this vision of Southern comfort, there's no place for regimentation.

Chateau Elan
Haven Harbour Dr., Braselton, GA 30517
Tel. 770/932–0900 or 800/233–9463
Fax 770/271–6005

Administration President, Nancy C. Panoz; spa director, Kyle Covington

Season Year-round

Accommodations The spa building has 14 rooms, individually decorated in themes ranging from Oriental to Greek, Western, Art Deco, and Victorian. Antiques and high-tech amenities, queen-size or twin beds, lavish bathroom fixtures. 2 Loft suites feature upper level bedroom with 4-poster bed, 2 bathrooms. All air-conditioned, with VCR, phone, concierge service. Nearby is the 274-room French-style inn, and 18 small villas bordering the golf fairways.

Rates Daily rate for spa rooms $145–$225 single or double occupancy. Spa Getaway (2-night/3-day) $1,206 per couple, $850 single. Luxury week (7-night/8-day) $3,845 per couple. Day Spa package, including lunch, services, no lodging, $175–$245. Inn rooms $79–$95 daily, single or double. Villas on request. Add 9% tax, optional gratuities. Deposit: $1,000 for a week's stay, $500 for other packages. AE, MC, V.

Meal Plans Spa plans include some meals, afternoon tea, evening snack. Breakfast specials are blue corn pancakes with fresh berries, egg-white omelet with steamed spinach and mushroom or cheese, gravlax, and cereals, muffins, croissants. Lunch begins with salad or Belgian endive, choice of 2 soups, entrée choice such as duckling breast, salmon supreme on black noodles, vegetarian goulash. Dinner main course can be petit fillet of beef or grilled chicken. Desserts include yogurt fruit ice, fresh fruit, and berry cocktail.

Services and Facilities **Exercise Equipment:** Landice treadmill, 2 Alpine stairclimbers, Preference stationary bike, Bodyguard ergometer, hand weights (complete cardiovascular circuit at the Inn). **Services:** Massage (Swedish, shiatsu, therapeutic, sports, aromatherapy), reflexology, body wrap, loofah, body gommage, collagen masque, facials, glycolic acid series, thalassotherapy, paraffin hand and foot moisturizing, mineral bath; salon for hair, nail, and makeup; tanning bed; fitness evaluation, skin analysis, makeup instruction. **Spa Facilities:** Coed sauna, steam bath, whirlpool. **Swimming Facilities:** Outdoor heated pool with resistance jets; nearby health club's indoor/outdoor pool. **Recreation Facilities:** Bicycles, horseback riding (extra charge), 3 18-hole golf courses, 9-hole executive course (greens fee), 7 tennis courts. **Evening Programs:** Concerts.

In the Area Atlanta museums, Buckhead Mall, Atlanta Underground, Olympic stadiums.

Getting Here *From Atlanta.* By car, I–85 north, Exit 48, turn left on Old Winder Hwy. 211 (45 mins). Airport transfer by limousine through Chateau Elan transportation service, taxi, rental car.

Special Notes Minimum age: 16.

Sea Island Spa at the Cloister

Life enhancement
Luxury pampering

Georgia
Sea Island

After more than 60 years as the grande dame of southern seashore resorts, The Cloister opened its Sea Island Spa at the Beach Club in 1989. Group activity, plus programs tailored to each guest's fitness level and personal goals, provides a flexible schedule. You can join a morning beach walk and stretch class, exercise in air-conditioned comfort, and enjoy sophisticated pampering in the privacy of spa suites.

Thalassotherapy by the sea is a major attraction here. Treatments include French seaweed masks and salt scrubs to nourish and cleanse the skin. In the hands of a licensed esthetician, the facial treatment becomes a succession of cleansing and soothing experiences as four layers of aloe, seaweed, and Repechage creams are applied. While your complexion is being detoxified and moisturized to combat the ravages of time and sun, your feet are softened with paraffin wax. The final touch may be a reflexology massage, one of 18 different techniques offered by staff therapists. There are nine treatment rooms, hydrotub, and consultation rooms for fitness evaluations or makeup consultation.

The aerobics studio and exercise rooms attached to the spa are open to all resort guests for modest daily fees. In the locker rooms, you are issued a robe and slippers, then relax in a lounge where coffee and juices are served while you await your appointments. Spa programs include these services, as well as a hospital-affiliated fitness evaluation, and seminars on women's health issues.

Sports add a special dimension to this seaside escape. The Cloister offers 54 holes of golf at two clubs, plus an acclaimed golf learning center with indoor and outdoor training by professionals. Water sports, a tennis club with 17 courts, a cycling center with 300 bikes for rent, stables with 60 horses, a skeet and gun club, and docks for boat rental and fishing expeditions on the Intracoastal Waterway are also available to guests.

Tradition clings to The Cloister as attractively as the Spanish moss dangling from great old trees shading the roads. The main building, a 1928 Spanish-Mediterranean palazzo designed by Addison Mizner, is the setting for dress-up dinners with dancing and a multicourse menu. The family-oriented Beach Club bustles with breakfast and luncheon buffets, heavy on Southern specialties but also offering light fare. Romantic carriage rides meander amid oaks along the 5-mile stretch of private beach on the Atlantic seafront.

Sea Island Spa at The Cloister
Sea Island, GA 31561
Tel. 916/638–3611 or 800/732–4752
Fax 912/638–5814

Administration Managing director, Ted Wright; spa director, Jane Segerberg

Season Year-round

Accommodations 262 guest rooms in spacious, modern lodges overlooking the beach and waterway, plus private cottage rental. Choice of twin or king-size bed, patio or balcony. Air-conditioned, with TV, sitting area, walk-in closet, full bathroom, telephone and desk.

Rates Spa package priced per day (minimum stay 3 nights), $396–$682 single, $309–$452 per person double occupancy. For cottage renters: 3-day spa retreat (without lodging) $480, 5-day Signature Spa Experience $800. Add tax, service charge, spa gratuities. Deposit: $300. No credit cards.

Meal Plans Full American Plan, 3 meals daily, included in spa package with lodging. Limited selection of spa cuisine on menu in main dining room; lunch and breakfast buffet at the Beach Club. Seafood buffet, fresh fish featured daily at the club's beachside restaurant. Formal dinner menu and dancing nightly in main building.

Services and Facilities **Exercise Equipment:** 12-unit Eagle Cybex weight training circuit, 2 StairMasters, Liferower, Cycleplus bike, 2 Quinton treadmills, dynabands, Resist-a-Balls, dumbbells. **Services:** Massage including acupressure, deep-muscle therapy, aromatherapy, facial, paraffin hand and foot treatment, herbal or seaweed wrap, body scrub. Fitness evaluation, nutrition consultation, exercise program, personal training and exercise video. **Swimming Facilities:** Diving pool, heated freshwater recreational pool, ocean beach. **Recreation Facilities:** Horseback trail rides with lunch or evening cookout, 17 tennis courts, 2 18-hole golf courses, skeet range, bike and boat rental, sea kayak tour of marshes, Windsurfer rental.

In the Area Ft. Frederica (British colonial village, ca. 1740); St. Simons Island (historic church); Jacksonville, FL; Savannah, GA.

Getting Here *From Jacksonville.* By car, I–95 north, Exit 6, east on Hwy. 17 (70 mi). Van service scheduled by The Cloister transportation desk from Jacksonville Airport ($30). By plane, Delta Express to Brunswick, GA; hotel van on request ($24 for two persons). Limousine, car rental, taxi available.

Special Notes Teenage skin care and makeup classes and kids' fitness classes during holidays. Teenage golf clinic. Supervised program for children 3–11 daily and evenings during spring, summer, and holidays.

Wildwood Lifestyle Center

Life enhancement
Preventive medicine
Vibrant maturity

Georgia
Wildwood

Converts to fitness come here to learn a healthier way of life. Up to 26 middle-aged professionals and housewives participate in each session of the Wildwood Lifestyle Program. Medically oriented and devoted to education and exercise, the program provides a basis for self-help.

Set amid 550 acres of southern pine forest, Wildwood has been devoted to preventive medicine for more than 40 years. Attached to a hospital, the Lifestyle Center is staffed by medical doctors, nurses, and other personnel, all Seventh-Day

Adventists (programs are nondenominational and nonsectarian), who see diet as a means of disease prevention. Their nutritional computer analysis makes specific recommendations for diet and takes into account your physical condition, nutritional requirements, and weight-loss goals. After a complete medical examination a physician—who monitors your progress—prescribes a program for you.

Group support and camaraderie help participants achieve significant lifestyle change. You are encouraged to walk daily on 25 miles of trails that wind through the grounds. For those seeking motivation to stop smoking, special weeks are scheduled at various times during the year.

The philosophy at Wildwood is to treat the causes of disease rather than the symptoms. High blood pressure, coronary heart disease, angina, arteriosclerosis, diabetes, stress, constipation, arthritis, and obesity are addressed in lectures and private counseling sessions during the 10-day and 18-day programs. The focus is on the special needs of mature adults, providing tools for healthy living.

Wildwood Lifestyle Center

Box 129, Wildwood, GA 30757
Tel. 706/820–1490 or 800/634–9355
Fax 706/820–1474

Administration Director, Wilbur Atwood; Lifestyle Program director, Mary Fisher; medical director, Scott Grivas, M.D.

Season Year-round

Accommodations 26 mountain lodge bedrooms with twin beds, private patio; some share large bath. Woodland views. Lounge for informal lectures around fireplace, laundry facility.

Rates 18-day program $2,575, 10-day program $1,640–$1,800 sharing accommodation. Private rooms when available. 20% discount for spouses participating in nonmedical parts of program. Transportation included certain times of year. 3-day/2-night Get Acquainted program, $100 per person. Deposit: $150–$250 per person, refundable up to 2 weeks before program begins. MC, V (4% surcharge).

Meal Plans Fruits, vegetables, legumes, and grains. No butter or oil, but nuts, olives, and avocados available. 3 daily buffets without dairy products, fish, or meat. Specialties include vegetarian lasagna with melted "cheese" topping of tahini, pimiento, and tomato; oat-burger roll; steamed vegetables with rice; 7-grain bread.

Services and Facilities **Exercise Equipment:** 2 Lifecycles, 2 trampolines, rowing machines. **Services:** Swedish massage, hydrotherapy showers, medical treatment. **Swimming Facilities:** Lake on property. **Spa Facilities:** Sauna and steam room. **Recreation Facilities:** Hiking, boating. **Evening Programs:** Lectures on health-related and spiritual topics.

In the Area Picnics, outings to historical sites and Civil War memorials, Atlanta museums, shopping, Chattanooga museums.

Getting Here *From Atlanta.* By bus, Trailways to Chattanooga (2 hrs). By plane, scheduled flights to Chattanooga metropolitan airport. By car, I–24 past Chattanooga, Exit 169 (about 2 hrs). Free service to and from Chattanooga airport and bus station. Rental car available.

Special Notes All rooms on ground level; patients who use wheelchairs are accepted when accompanied by companion. No smoking indoors. Remember to bring an alarm clock, laundry detergent, umbrella, rain gear.

Duke University Diet and Fitness Center

Life enhancement
Nutrition and diet
Vibrant maturity
Weight management

North Carolina
Durham

Durham has been known as a hub of the diet and fitness industry for more than 40 years. During 28 of those years, the Duke Diet and Fitness Center (DFC) has provided an on-campus program for weight and health management that resembles a college course in healthy living. Four-week stays are typical, although two-week and longer programs are offered, and there is a new one-week crash course for beginners and returnees.

Classes, consultation, and meals take place in the DFC building, which has a fully equipped gym with cardiovascular and weight training machines. Starting with a physical examination Monday morning (including testing, treadmill exercise, and body-composition evaluation) and personal assessments, the specialized faculty of physicians, dieticians, and psychologists set up a schedule based on your fitness level and personal interests. Choices range from workshops on stress management to cooking classes, fitness training to psychological counseling. The daily schedule keeps you busy from around 8 AM through dinner. There is some free time on weekends and evenings to explore the area, taking in sports events and entertainment. Throughout the week you work out on fitness equipment, take stretch and aerobics classes, and exercise in the pool and gym.

Learning strategies for lifestyle change and long-term success keeps you busy in classrooms, on local supermarket tours, and on dining out at local restaurants. The DFC encourages family members or close friends to accompany program participants, to make it easier when you bring home new, healthy habits. (After receiving medical clearance, support persons can participate in most of the daily activities offered at the DFC.) There is a special program to help smokers kick the habit.

Homework reinforces lessons in integrating exercise and good nutrition into your daily life. Program graduates are encouraged to return periodically for continuing education and reinforcing healthy goals.

Duke University Diet and Fitness Center
804 W. Trinity Ave., Durham, NC 27701
Tel. 919/684–6331 or 800/362–8446
Fax 919/682–8869

Administration
Director, Michael A. Hamilton, M.D.; administrative director, Michele Hudgins, R.D.

Season
Year-round

Accommodations
Local inns cater to dieters. Duke Tower, across the street from the center, has furnished apartments with bedroom, living room, kitchen, from $59 per night. Rooms in private homes $75–$110 per week.

Rates
1-week program $2,400, 4-week program $5,195, 2-week program $3,895. $500 refundable deposit required. AE, MC, V.

Meal Plans
3 low-calorie, portion-controlled meals daily at center provide 800- to 1,200-calorie diet high in complex carbohydrates, moderate in protein, low in sodium, fat, and cholesterol. Vegetarian and kosher diets accommodated. Lunch entrées include seafood gumbo with rice, lamb stew, and eggplant Parmesan.

Italian baked fish, barbecued chicken, sirloin steak, and black bean tortillas for dinner. Menu published weekly, with calorie counts.

Services and Facilities
Exercise Equipment: 5 Precor 962 treadmills, 4 Schwinn Air Dyne bikes, 4 Lifecycle recumbent bikes, Tectrix virtual reality bike, Precor Transport, 4 Concept 2 rowers, NordicTrack, Tectrix stairclimber, 8 Paramount weight machines, free weights, benches, dumbbells, seated cable row, Smith machine, cable crossover, prone leg curl. **Services:** Massage, personal fitness training, swimming instruction, body composition testing, individual psychotherapy, career counseling, on-site medical clinic. **Swimming Facilities:** 25-meter indoor pool. **Recreation Facilities:** Basketball and volleyball in DFC gymnasium. University campus and city parks provide full range of sports, including tennis, golf, fishing. **Evening Programs:** Lectures by outside specialists, such as image consultant, dance instructor, Overeaters Anonymous member. Duke University performing arts and cultural programs.

In the Area
Atlantic Ocean beaches, Blue Ridge Mountains, outlet shopping, furniture shopping in High Point and Charlotte, Brevard Music Center concerts late June–mid-Aug., Asheville folk arts, Biltmore Estate near Asheville.

Getting Here
From Raleigh-Durham Airport. By car, I–40 to Durham Fwy. (Rte. 147), exit at Duke St., right on Trinity Ave. (20 mins). Taxi, rental car available.

Special Notes
Ramps in most buildings provide access for people with disabilities; all facilities at DFC on 1 floor. Theater, arts, recreational outings for children through community organizations. No smoking indoors and in patio area. Remember to bring casual seasonal clothing, exercise and swimming outfits, jogging or walking shoes, notebooks and pens, wristwatch, alarm clock, padlock for gym lockers.

Structure House

Vibrant maturity
Weight management

North Carolina
Durham
Founded in 1977, Structure House specializes in serious weight problems. Most first-time visitors stay a month or more to learn long-term weight control, and find the new environment helpful, particularly if they have failed to lose weight at home or in other programs. Alumni often come for one-week reinforcement visits; many members of both groups bring their spouses. Over 40 qualified professionals help you to understand the reasons behind unhealthy lifestyles and to practice problem solving.

The cluster of residential units around the new Life Extension Center and the large Georgian-style Structure House, where one goes for meals, classes, and professional services, convey a college campus atmosphere. A healthy lifestyle, in fact, is what you learn here.

The medically managed program involves mental and physical conditioning. A full physical examination and diagnosis precedes the planning of an individual diet and exercise regimen. To better serve the elderly, those with disabilities, and those with health problems, the medical staff consults with patients' private physicians in order to monitor and continue health services.

The integration of medical and psychological aspects of weight loss with dietary and exercise programs makes this program work for people who need a structured environment. The exercise facilities and classes at the Life Extension Center are the equal of those at many leading spa resorts. Classes are varied: step aerobics, aquacise, and dynaband. The gymnasium has cardiovascular and strength training equipment.

Structure House

3017 Pickett Rd., Durham, NC 27705
Tel. 919/493–4205 or 800/553–0052
Fax 919/490–0191

Administration Program director, Gerard J. Musante; medical director, Steven Hirsch, M.D.; fitness director, Ann Archer

Season Year-round; sessions begin Mon. 8 AM., new arrivals on Sun.

Accommodations 76 1- and 2-bedroom apartments in 10 2-story houses on campus. New modern units, sliding glass door opens onto porch. Washer/dryer, linens, telephone, color TV with HBO, weekly maid service.

Rates 1 week $1,599 single, $1,445 per person double occupancy, for all-inclusive program and apartment. 2 weeks $3,198 single, $2,870 sharing; 4 weeks $6,396 single, $5,780 sharing. Returnee 1-week program $903 single, $749 sharing. Tax included, gratuities optional. (Health insurance may cover some services.) $500 per person advance deposit. MC, V.

Meal Plans Selections from weekly menus that individuals plan for themselves. Suggested 1,000-calorie menu includes 3-cheese quiche, chef's salad, bean chowder, and French toast. Friday lunch is a potato bar with toppings. Dinner entrées include sea scallops in wine, baked chicken, and filet mignon. Vegetarian and special diets accommodated.

Services and Facilities **Exercise Equipment:** 6 Paramount strength training units, 5 Precor treadmills, Quinton treadmill, Lifecycle treadmill, 5 Schwinn Air Dyne bikes, Lifestep, Lifecycle recumbent bike, Cybex leg press, abdominal crunch, free weights, benches. **Services:** Massage (Swedish, Trager, deep-muscle, polarity), medical consultation and testing, consultation with clinical psychologist, dietary reeducation workshops. **Swimming Facilities:** Indoor and outdoor pool; lakes nearby. **Recreation Facilities:** Nature trails, basketball, badminton, Ping-Pong, tennis; golf, horseback riding nearby. **Evening Programs:** Occasional parties.

In the Area Eastern Piedmont mountains and lakes, plus numerous historic sites; minor-league baseball at *Bull Durham* park.

Getting Here *From Raleigh-Durham Airport.* By car, I–40 west (20 mins to Structure House). Shuttle service prearranged by Structure House, $30. Taxi, rental car available.

Special Notes Ramps for wheelchairs; some apartments equipped for people with disabilities. No smoking indoors or in designated dining areas. Remember to bring recent medical records, exercise clothing, wristwatch with second hand, walking or jogging shoes.

Westglow Spa

Life enhancement
Weight management

North Carolina
Blowing Rock
This historic 20-acre mountain retreat overlooking Grandfather Mountain in the Blue Ridge was converted into North Carolina's first European-style spa resort in 1991. The graceful Colonial-style mansion built in 1916 now houses six guest

In case you want to be welcomed there.

We're here to see that you're always welcomed at establishments everywhere. That's why millions of people carry the American Express® Card – for peace of mind, confidence, and security, around the world or just around the corner.

do more

In case you're running low.

We're here to help with more than 118,000 Express Cash locations around the world. In order to enroll, just call American Express before you start your vacation.

do more

Express Cash

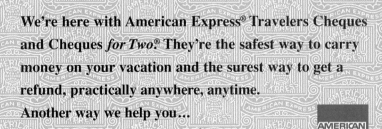

And just in case.

We're here with American Express® Travelers Cheques
and Cheques *for Two.*® They're the safest way to carry
money on your vacation and the surest way to get a
refund, practically anywhere, anytime.
Another way we help you...

do more®

AMERICAN
EXPRESS

Travelers
Cheques

rooms and the spa's main dining facility. Additional accommodations are found in two new guest cottages equipped with kitchen, fireplace, TV, and phone.

The Life Enhancement Center has an indoor swimming pool, men's and women's whirlpools, dry sauna, six body treatment rooms, beauty salon, weights room, aerobics studio, and poolside café. Health and beauty services range from fitness and nutrition training to massage and body therapy; a daily schedule of classes is posted, though the staff will also do training and aquatics on request. Personal services are included in day spa packages as well as overnight programs and can be alternated with hiking excursions.

The miles of forest surrounding the resort provide vacationers with the opportunity to hike, take rafting trips in nearby white-water rapids, or go canoeing. Arrangements can be made nearby for horseback riding, golf, and in winter, downhill skiing.

Westglow Spa
Hwy. 221 S, Box 1083, Blowing Rock, NC 28605
Tel. 704/295–4463 or 800/562–0807
Fax 704/295–5115

Administration Founder-director, Glynda McPheters; general manager, Jean Teague

Season Year-round

Accommodations 6 guest rooms in main house, 2 cottages with 1–2 bedrooms. Vintage furnishings, Oriental rugs, large library retain mansion's original elegance. Modern bathrooms and amenities added in 1989. Cottages have fireplace, air-conditioning, phone, TV, and kitchenette.

Rates 2-night package $630–$784 single, $540–$620 per person double occupancy; 7-night package $2,075–$2,520 single, $1,600–$1,746 double; day spa package with lunch (no lodging) $110–$220. Tax, gratuities included. Deposit: 50% in advance. AE, MC, V.

Meal Plans 3 meals daily included in 2- to 7-night packages. Breakfast can be cereal, blueberry pancakes, with herbal tea, decaffeinated or regular coffee, low-fat milk, yogurt. Lunch choices include Oriental pasta, vegetarian sandwich, or sliced pork tenderloin on wheat bread, garden salad, soup. Dinner entrées are mountain trout, mixed grill, vegetarian platter, and baked chicken.

Services and Facilities **Exercise Equipment:** 15-unit Cybex weight training circuit, 12 Cybex Fitron bikes, 4 Lifecycles, 2 Challenger treadmills, 2 Cybex Lifesteps, dumbbells. **Services:** Swedish or deep-muscle massage, aromatherapy, herbal wrap, reflexology, body scrub, facial, cellulite/lymphatic drainage, fitness assessment, exercise, nutrition and diet consultation, personal trainer, salon for hair and nail care. **Swimming Facilities:** Indoor lap pool. **Recreation Facilities:** Outdoor tennis court (composition surface), croquet court, walking trails; horseback riding, 18-hole golf course nearby.

In the Area Tweetsie Railroad and theme park (vintage trains, country music), Blue Ridge Parkway, Great Smoky Mountains National Park.

Getting Here *From Charlotte.* By car, I–77 north, I–40 west to exit 123, Hwy. 321 north to Blowing Rock Bypass exit for Sunset Blvd., Main St. to Hwy. 221 south (2½ hrs). By air, USAir Express to Hickory (45 mins). Airport transfers $80 round-trip by Blowing Rock Taxi (tel. 704/295–7032). Rental car available.

Special Notes No smoking indoors.

Hilton Head Health Institute

Life enhancement
Nutrition and diet
Stress control
Vibrant maturity

South Carolina The concentrated courses held here since 1976 are concerned
Hilton Head with modifying behavior in order to achieve practical results:
Island changes in your daily life and work habits, nutritional education for weight maintenance, smoking cessation, and managing stress. The highly structured program has a maximum of 40 participants; you can stay as many weeks as needed to gain control of problems, but the program and facilities are not designed for vacations.

Health education begins with an understanding of your body. Lectures, workshops, exercise classes, and meals designed to advance that understanding are scheduled in the institute's main building, a short walk from your living quarters. The effect of nutrition and exercise on the body's metabolism and the effect of stress on productivity and health are taught by a team of psychologists, nutritionists, and physical fitness specialists.

The delightful climate, 12 miles of white, sandy beach, and ample walking and biking trails through local nature preserves go far to enhance and renew the spirit. Other activities center in a campuslike cluster of Low Country cottages. Participants share apartments, fully equipped for laundry or cooking. The medically supervised programs are suited for individuals and couples who have reached a point in their lives where change is necessary and they need a boost to get started.

Hilton Head Health Institute
Box 7138, Hilton Head Island, SC 29938
Tel. 803/785–7292 or 800/292–2440; 800/348–2039 in Canada
Fax 803/686–5659

Administration Executive director, Peter M. Miller, Ph.D.; medical consultant, Robert Trotter, M.D.; fitness director, Francis Gertadffer

Season Scheduled programs year-round; closed during Christmas week

Accommodations Cottages in Shipyard Plantation have traditional furniture, fine fabrics, color TV. Each participant has a private bedroom and bath, sharing the living room and fully equipped apartment and laundry facilities with another person in the program. Private porch, parking space, pedestrian walkways.

Rates 8-day/7-night program (Sun.–Sun.) $1,200–$1,600; for returnees, $600 per week. MC, V.

Meal Plans 3 meals and "Metabo" fruit snack daily. Weekday diet totals approximately 800 calories daily, more on weekends, when outdoor activity increases. Food high in complex carbohydrates, moderate protein, low fat, no sugar or salt. Lunch can feature pasta primavera with raw vegetables, dinner entrées include chicken enchilada with salsa and brown rice.

Services and **Exercise Equipment:** 8-station Paramount weight system, 5
Facilities Schwinn Air Dyne stationary bikes, 2 rowing machines, 3 treadmills. **Services:** private massage therapist on request; beauty salon nearby. **Swimming Facilities:** Outdoor pool, ocean beach. **Recreation Facilities:** 24 tennis courts and 3 golf courses

within walking distance, for a fee. Nature preserve of sub-tropical marshes for hiking. Horseback riding, bicycling, wind-surfing, sailing, deep-sea fishing available through resort.

In the Area Community theater, cinema, shopping mall. Nature tours by boat; Historic Savannah, GA (1 hr), Beaufort, Charleston (antebellum homes and gardens, 2 hrs north).

Getting Here *From Savannah.* By car, I–95 to Rte. 278 (50 mins). By plane, Hilton Head Island airport has scheduled service on USAir (via Charlotte) and American Eagle (via Raleigh/Durham). Limousine service hourly from Savannah airport. Taxi, rental car available.

Special Notes Programs for children at community centers. No smoking indoors. Bring an alarm clock, flashlight, medical records. Group size limited to 40.

Hilton Head Westin Resort

Nonprogram resort

South Carolina
Hilton Head Island Port Royal Plantation's health facilities at the posh Westin Resort are a happy addition to an island noted for golf, tennis, and fishing. Equipment, classes, and outdoor recreation on 24 acres of landscaped, subtropical beach are available for a fee; guests in the hotel get complimentary health-club privileges.

Mornings may begin with a beach walk, led by a trainer at the Spectrum Health Club. Invigorated by sun, sea, and air, you can join an exercise class or have a personal program planned for you. The club's full-time fitness pro is available for consultation and cardiovascular testing.

The sprawling, five-story hotel has big-city airs and a breezy, Southern Low Country ambience. Enjoy the view of the grand courtyard and three swimming pools from the mirrored weights room. One of the pools is glass-enclosed for year-round swimming and water aerobics classes. Scheduled daily are three or four aerobics classes ($5 each), including step and low-impact, held in a studio with suspended wooden floor that has room for 10–12. Other facilities include a steam room with Swiss shower, a sauna misted with eucalyptus oils, three outdoor whirlpools, and private rooms for massage appointments. Although no spa package is available, staying at the hotel's Royal Beach Club earns you extra amenities.

Hilton Head Westin Resort
2 Grasslawn Ave., Hilton Head Island, SC 29928
Tel. 803/681–4000 or 800/228–3000
Fax 803/681–1087

Administration General manager, Anthony Cherone

Season Year-round

Accommodations 410 luxury rooms (including 38 suites), with separate dressing areas, hair dryers, large baths. Furnishings and architecture are reminiscent of grand southern homes. All have balcony.

Rates $240–$320 for 2 people in summer; Royal Beach Club $340 per couple. Suites $390–$2,000. Add 7% tax and daily service charge. Golf and tennis packages available. Deposit: 1 night by credit card. AE, DC, MC, V.

Meal Plans Carolina Cafe buffet serves breakfast, lunch, dinner. Barony Restaurant's low-cholesterol and sodium menu includes free-range chicken with black-pepper pasta and chanterelle mushroom sauce, sautéed shrimp Provençale over angel-hair pasta, and broiled fish of the day. All meals à la carte; dinner in the Barony about $50 per person, including tip, tax, and wine.

Services and Facilities

Exercise Equipment: Weights room with 14 Universal units, free-weight dumbbells (3–50 lbs), Lifecycle, rowing machine, 2 StairMasters, treadmill, NordicTrack, Schwinn Air Dyne bike, bilateral board equipment, Nautilus abdominal machine. **Services:** Fitness testing, personal instruction on exercise equipment, classes and beach activity, massage by appointment (fee), golf and tennis clinics. **Swimming Facilities:** Indoor pool, 2 outdoor pools (1 with lap lanes), ocean beach. **Recreation Facilities:** Beach runs and walks, volleyball, water polo, 3 golf courses, 16 tennis courts (clay, hard, and grass, 6 lighted), croquet lawn; horseback riding, windsurfing, sailing, and fishing nearby. **Evening Programs:** Resort entertainment.

In the Area

Historic Savannah (1 hr), Beaufort, and Charleston (antebellum homes and gardens, 2 hrs north).

Getting Here

From Savannah. By car, I–95 to Hardeeville, Rte. 278 (50 min). By plane, Hilton Head Island airport has scheduled service on USAir Express (via Charlotte). Also, private aircraft facilities. Hourly limousine service from Savannah airport. Taxi, rental car available.

Special Notes

Ramps, specially equipped rooms, elevators to all floors provide access for people with disabilities; beach wheelchair with dune buggy wheels available. The Kids Korner for children has arts and crafts, games, pool and water activities morning and evening May–Sept., Nov.–Apr. Health club open Mon.–Sat. 7 AM–8 PM, Sun. 9:30–6. No smoking in the health club.

Tennessee Fitness Spa

Nutrition and diet
Weight management

Tennessee
Natural Bridge

At this mountain camp for healthy living, guests get back to nature and back in shape at the same time. The Tennessee Fitness Spa organizes hikes, swimnastics, canoeing, bike rides, and walks through the area's scenic surroundings for fitness and to aid in weight management.

Regularly scheduled classes on nutrition are held in the natural stone dining hall, where the spa chef demonstrates how to cook meals that are low in fat, sodium, and sugar. Most guests are concerned with weight management, and some come for several months to develop a workable weight-loss regimen that they can continue at home.

Guests, who range in age from 20 to 70, join a group leader for a 7 AM hill walk, a 2½-mile warmup followed by stretch class and aerobics. The daily schedule rotates among step aerobics, line dancing, aquacise, floor work, and lectures. Cross-training can be followed by a volleyball game or a soak in the big hot tub. Personal services, such as massages and facials, are optional extras.

Housing choices include standard rooms in two-story wooden lodges and new lake-view cottages that have four-bedroom apartments. Casual and friendly staff are noted for creating group support and camaraderie, which adds to the fun as you shed pounds together.

Tennessee Fitness Spa
Rte. 3, Box 411, Waynesboro, TN 38485
Tel. 615/722–5589 or 800/235–8365
Fax 615/722–7441

Administration General manager, Richard May; fitness director, John Alexander

Season Mid-Feb.–mid-Dec

Accommodations 33 double rooms, 2 with 4 beds, in 6 2-story wooden chalets. Simply furnished, with private bathrooms, choice of queen-size bed or twins, shower for every 2 guests, heat. No air-conditioning, TV, or telephone. New deluxe rooms in lake-view cottages and penthouse apartment have bathtub, phone connection.

Rates $899 per week for private room including meals and program, $579 per person double; $499 per person for 4 sharing room and bath. Deposit is $100, gratuities optional. Local tax added. MC, V (4% surcharge).

Meal Plans 3 meals daily included in program are low in fat, sodium, and sugar. Breakfast can be pancakes, apple spice cake, French toast, or cereal with skim milk. Herbal tea, fruit juices available all day; no coffee. Lunch choices are pizza or black beans and rice, salad bar. Dinner entrées include chicken enchiladas, turkey burgers, Friday night seafood, salad bar.

Services and Facilities **Exercise Equipment:** 4 Nautilus units, 3 StairMasters, 3 Precor treadmills, 2 Windracer bikes, free weights. **Services:** Massage, facial, hair styling, manicure/pedicure. **Swimming Facilities:** Covered, heated pool. **Recreation Facilities:** Bicycles, canoes (charge), racquetball court, fishing. **Evening Programs:** Cooking class, cross training, volleyball, pool games, movies, entertainment.

In the Area Natural Bridge (world's only double-span natural rock bridge formation), Natchez Trace (scenic highway), Nashville (country music).

Getting Here *From Nashville.* By car, I–65 south, Exit 46 (Columbia), Hwy. 412 via Hohewald, Rd. 20 to Hwy. 99 southwest (2 hrs). By bus chartered by the spa: Sunday pickup at 1 PM in Nashville ($45 round-trip). Rental car available.

Special Notes Roommate matching service and 4-person rooms with 2 bathrooms available.

Hartland Wellness Center

Preventive medicine
Vibrant maturity
Weight management

Virginia The 10- to 18-day program incorporating health, education,
Rapidan and exercise at Hartland Wellness teaches you how to help yourself. The core program consists of practical nutritional instruction, private and group counseling, and physical therapy guided by a team of physicians, dietitians, educators, chaplains, and therapists.

The doctors and staff, all Seventh-Day Adventists (although the program is nondenominational and nonsectarian), focus on disease prevention. Their specific recommendations for diet take into account your physical condition, nutritional requirements, and personal goals. Heart disease, arthritis, cancer, diabetes, obesity, addictions, and digestive disorders are among the diseases addressed by a team of specialists.

On a 760-acre estate in the foothills of the Blue Ridge Mountains, the Hartland has extensive nature trails where you are encouraged to walk daily. There is an indoor swimming pool and limited exercise equipment for your free time. Spouses are encouraged to participate at a reduced fee.

Your personalized schedule begins with a daily check of vital signs and weight, which is followed by breakfast. Group exercises and lectures, aquatic therapy in the pool, individual counseling sessions, cooking class, hydrotherapy, and massage fill out the balance of the day. This intensive live-in program is offered in an elegant, hotel-style building near Hartland College, with all amenities provided in the same building.

Hartland Wellness Center
Box 1, Rapidan, VA 22733
Tel. 540/672–3100 or 800/763–9355
Fax 540/672–2584

Administration Director, William Evert

Season Sessions monthly

Accommodations 15 rooms in a 2-story residential-treatment building. Furnished with antiques, cherry-wood dresser and bed, individual temperature control, scenic view. 10 rooms have 2 queen-size beds, 5 have 1 queen-size bed. All have private bath.

Rates 10-day program $1,500, spouse $1,350; 18-day program $2,500, spouse $2,250; Deposit 50% of program fee. MC, V (3% surcharge).

Meal Plans 3 vegan meals daily. Lunch may include baked tofu loaf, water-steamed vegetables, green salad, baked potato, and homemade bread. Fruit and vegetables are plentiful, along with grains, cereals, and legumes. No dairy products, cheese, eggs, meat, fish, butter, margarine, or oils. Emphasis is on whole, natural foods.

Services and Facilities **Exercise Equipment:** 2 stationary bikes, treadmill, Bowflex, Easy Rider bike, Universal Gym, minitrampoline. **Services:** Hydrotherapy, massage, stress-management classes, exercise counseling, smoking-cessation program, cardiac and cancer rehabilitation, medical tests, body-composition evaluation, physician and nurse counseling, hands-on vegetarian cooking instruction, weight-control counseling, spiritual guidance. **Swimming Facilities:** Indoor pool. **Recreation Facilities:** Hiking, jogging trails. **Evening Programs:** Social events.

In the Area Scheduled tours to Monticello (estate of Thomas Jefferson), Montpelier (home of James Madison), Shenandoah National Park and the Skyline Drive, historic Fredericksburg, Civil War sites.

Getting Here *From Washington, DC.* By train, Amtrak to Culpeper (80 mins). By bus, Trailways to Culpeper (90 mins). By car, I–66 to Lee Highway (Rte. 29 South to 3rd Culpeper exit, Rte. 15 toward Orange, to Rte. 614 West (about 2 hrs). By plane, Dulles International and National airports, commuter service to Charlottesville. Pickup arranged at airports, bus and train stations for fixed fee. Rental car available.

Special Notes No smoking on premises. All facilities accessible for people with disabilities.

The Homestead

Nonprogram resort
Taking the waters

Virginia
Hot Springs Style accounts for the enduring popularity of this historic spa. The mineral springs that made the Homestead famous as long ago as 1766 still gush in front of the Bath House (built 1892, renovated 1994–97). Furnished with 1920s-style wicker furniture and flowered chintz draperies, the spa still has huge

marble tubs for mineral-water soaks, plus an Olympic-size indoor swimming pool, built in 1903. Daily aerobics and aquacise classes are scheduled at the spa's new fitness center, which has an array of cardiovascular and weight resistance conditioning equipment and a spectacular view of the grounds. Admission is free of charge for resort guests. Nonresidents can book services and use the facilities.

Relaxation therapy begins with a private soak in one of the marble tubs. The naturally heated thermal water, high in sulfur, magnesium, and 16 other minerals, reaches your tub at 104°F and overflows to keep the temperature constant. After a few minutes in the sauna or steam room (the men's side has a Turkish bath), you're led to a marble slab for a rubdown with coarse salt, then hosed off in the Scotch spray (hot and cold shower). After cooling down, you're treated to a massage by a real pro. The treatment, which originated here more than 100 years ago, is called Dr. Goode's Spout Bath and costs $22. Other spa services, aromatherapy to hairstyling, are available in the fourth-floor health and beauty salon.

Three golf courses and 12 tennis courts, playable most of the year, are big outdoor attractions. For sports, there's horseback riding, mountain trout fishing, archery, skiing, and trap shooting. Surrounded by a 15,000-acre mountain preserve, the Homestead has miles of hiking trails. Winter attractions include snowmaking equipment on the slopes and groomed trails for cross-country skiing. Despite its rambling size, the Homestead makes you feel at home, even as it caters to conventions. The East wing and tower rooms, renovated in 1994, have dramatic views of the surrounding mountains. Each season, from blossoming spring dogwood to blazing fall foliage, has special appeal.

Legendary for its Southern hospitality, the hotel looks like a set for "Brigadoon," its redbrick castle with tower trimmed in white, framed by the deep green-blue colors of the Blue Ridge Mountains. Arriving in the Great Hall, flanked by 16 stately Corinthian columns, guests are treated to afternoon tea as a trio entertains with music of a quieter, gentler era.

The Homestead

Box 2000, Hot Springs, VA 24445
Tel. 540/839–1776 or 800/838–1776
Fax 540/839–7670

Administration President, Gary Rosenberg; spa managers, Donna Keyser and Hugh Hite

Season Year-round

Accommodations 521 guest rooms including 81 parlor suites in main section and tower, built 1902–1929, and South Wing, added with conference center in 1973. Choice rooms and best views in the tower. Mahogany bedsteads, writing tables, lounge chairs, lacy white curtains, damask draperies. Some rooms with French doors that open onto private balconies or screened porches have fireplace, walk-in closet. All are air-conditioned, with TV, telephone, large tiled bathroom.

Rates MAP (2 meals daily) per person double occupancy, $117–$157; single $184–$262. Children with adults free through age 12, $29 age 5–12, $50 age 13–18. Packages for golf and tennis. $250 advance payment. Add 4% tax, 15% service charge. AE, MC, V.

Meal Plans The Modified American Plan includes breakfast and dinner. Country breakfasts include grits, omelets, steak, mountain trout. Dinner features Virginia ham stuffed with greens, roast beef, broiled chicken, farm produce, sautéed whole trout or smoked fish appetizer.

Services and Facilities
Exercise Equipment: 12-unit Cybex circuit with leg extension, chest press, shoulder press, hip and arm units; Startrac 2000 treadmill, StairWalker treadmill, Liferower, Tunturi 702 Air Group cycle, CalGym free weights, abdominal board. Exercise room open daily 6 AM–10 PM. **Services:** Mineral tub, therapeutic whirlpool, aromatherapy bath and massage, Swedish massage loofah body scrub, herbal wrap; salon for facials, manicure, pedicure, and hair styling. **Swimming Facilities:** Large indoor pool with mix of mineral and well water, 2 outdoor pools. Indoor pool open daily 6 AM–10 PM. **Recreation Facilities:** 3 golf courses (54 holes), 12 tennis courts (Har-Tru and Gras-Tex), horseback riding, hiking, skeet and trap shooting, archery, fishing, lawn bowling, carriage rides, bowling alley, downhill skiing, ice-skating, cross-country skiing (equipment rental). **Evening Programs:** Movies, dancing.

In the Area
Mineral baths at Warm Springs (Jeffersonian structure), chamber music concerts at Garth Newel, historic Lexington (Washington and Lee University), Virginia Military Institute (George Marshall Library).

Getting Here
From Washington, DC. By train, Amtrak from Union Station or Alexandria, VA, to Clifton Forge (4 hrs). By car, I–66 west to I–81, at Mt. Crawford Exit, Rtes. 257 and 42 to Goshen, Rte. 39 to Warm Springs, Rte. 220 south to Hot Springs (about 6 hrs). By plane, USAir to Roanoke, VA (1 hr). Private aircraft land at the Bath County Airport. Limousine meets train or plane by arrangement (fixed fee). Rental car available.

Special Notes
Ramps and elevators in all buildings and some specially equipped rooms provide access for people with disabilities. Swimming, tennis, and skiing lessons for children; supervised playroom (summer only) and outdoor activity at the spa building (fee). No smoking in the spa and designated areas of the dining room. Spa services available Mon.–Thurs. 9–6, Fri. and Sat. until 7, Sun. until 5.

The Kingsmill Resort

Nonprogram resort

Virginia
Williamsburg
Nestled amid lush, green woodlands on the banks of the historic James River, Kingsmill Resort combines sports and spa in a newly expanded facility that serves as the focal point for family recreation but also has a serious side in its fitness program. Resort villas provide an ideal base from which to explore Busch Gardens, Colonial Williamsburg, the scenic Tidewater area, and Atlantic beaches. Built and managed by Anheuser-Busch, the 2,900-acre resort is part of a gated residential community, complete with marina. Golfers play the new Woods Course, designed by Tom Clark and Curtis Strange; the River Course, designed by Pete Dye; the Plantation Course, designed by Arnold Palmer; or a 9-hole course.

The Sports Club was expanded in 1996 to provide a dedicated fitness environment. Workouts on state-of-the-art cardiovascular and weight training equipment, one-on-one training, and indoor and outdoor swimming pools are available to all resort guests at no additional charge. There are racquetball courts, saunas, steam rooms, whirlpools, and a game room. Spa services are scheduled à la carte.

In southeastern Virginia's rolling hills and forests, Kingsmill Resort possesses both cosmopolitan sophistication and Colonial gentility. It's big enough so corporate conferences and vacationers needn't mix. Dining ranges from formal at the river-view Bray Dining Room to casual at the sports club grille and a tavern at the country club. In addition to Virginia's largest golf resort, you can explore area attractions with the complimentary shuttle service. The atmosphere is more residential than resort, and if you enjoy planning your own program, the elements are all here.

The Kingsmill Resort
100 Kingsmill Rd., Williamsburg, VA 23185
Tel. 804/253–1703 or 800/832–5665

Administration General manager, Terri A. Haack; Sports Club manager, Beverly Cutchins

Season Year-round

Accommodations 400 rooms in villas overlooking river or golf course. 1–3 bedrooms, some complete kitchens, living rooms with fireplace. Residential furnishings, daily maid service. Air-conditioning, king- or queen-size beds, color cable TV.

Rates Seasonal pricing. $140–$215 per day single/double occupancy for guest room, $470–$705 for up to 6 adults in 3-bedroom suite in Riverview Rooms. 3-day Golf Academy package with accommodations $795 per person, double. 5-day package with admission to Colonial Williamsburg and other attractions $752–$992 for 2 in room, $992–$1,232 in suite. Add 8½% tax, gratuities optional. AE, MC, V.

Meal Plans Sports Club bistro-style restaurant serves light fare, including grilled chicken breast on brioche, pasta salad, and individual pizzas 11–10. Fruit dishes, nut breads, and whipped drinks of yogurt, honey, and fruit prepared daily. Peyton spa specials at dinner (4–9:30) are sautéed chicken breast over pasta and grilled pork tenderloin with a spicy mango sauce.

Services and Facilities **Exercise Equipment:** 15-station Nautilus circuit, 2 treadmills, 2 stationary bikes, 2 Schwinn Air Dyne bikes, 2 rowing machines, 2 StairMasters, NordicTrack, power rack incline bench, bench press, free weights. **Services:** Aerobics classes and water aerobics ($5 per class), instruction on exercise equipment. **Swimming Facilities:** Indoor 56-ft lap pool, outdoor recreational pool. **Recreation Facilities:** 3 golf courses, 13 clay tennis courts, 2 Deco Turf hard courts (lighted), 2 racquetball courts, game lounge with billiards, table-top shuffleboard. **Evening Programs:** Summer season of pop and rock concerts.

In the Area Colonial Williamsburg (88 restored 18th-century buildings, shops, and residences), James River plantation tour, Jamestown Festival Park (replicas of 3 historic ships), Yorktown (Revolutionary War battlefield), Williamsburg Pottery (outlet shops and boutiques), Virginia Beach, Mariner's Museum, Nature Museum and park.

Getting Here *From Washington, DC.* By train, Amtrak from Union Station or Alexandria, VA, to Williamsburg (all seats reserved, 3 hrs). By bus, Greyhound (3 hrs). By car, I–95 south to I–64 east, Exit 242-A to Rte. 199W (3 hrs). By air, commuter service to Norfolk and Newport News on USAir and American Eagle.

Special Notes Kamper summer program for children age 5–12, with interpretive tours at historic sites ($18 half day, $26 per day). No smoking in sports club. Facilities accessible to persons with disabilities.

The Tazewell Club

Nonprogram resort

Virginia
Colonial
Williamsburg

The first health club in the old Colonial capital opened in 1988. A part of the Williamsburg Lodge and Conference Center complex, facing a golf course, the Tazewell Club is minutes from the 173-acre historic area. It's an escape to the latest in pampering and exercise after immersing in 18th-century life.

Though designed for newcomers to fitness, the club also challenges fitness buffs. Low-impact aerobics classes are taught on weekdays, aqauaerobics morning and night three times a week. The swimming pool is popular with families, but certain hours are reserved for lap swimmers. Pool hours are extended to 10 PM Friday and Sunday, allowing you to spend a full day touring the historic area or enjoying golf and tennis.

The workout area has views of the surrounding valley, once part of the Tazewell estate. The swimming pool opens onto a sundeck. The spa, with separate saunas, steam rooms, whirlpools for men and women, and private massage areas, is on the same floor. Try a loofah body scrub or massage.

Admission to the club is complimentary if you stay in any of the five hotels operated by the Colonial Williamsburg Foundation. Nearby are two Robert Trent Jones golf courses, eight tennis courts, croquet court, bowling green, and two outdoor swimming pools. Personal services, court time, and greens fees are extra.

The Tazewell Club
Williamsburg Lodge
Box C, Williamsburg, VA 23187
Tel. 804/229-1000 or 800/447-8679
Fax 804/221-8797

Administration   Club manager, Robert Sweel

Season   Year-round

Accommodations   25 Tazewell Club guest rooms in the Williamsburg Lodge, color TV, spacious baths. Also 5 hotels and group of Colonial houses, plus 2 deluxe suites with Jacuzzi, fireplace, wet bar, and private balcony on penthouse level of club. 235 guest rooms in the Williamsburg Inn, a short walk from the health club and 85 rooms in restored homes with Colonial atmosphere. All air-conditioned, with TV, telephone, private bath.

Rates   Double or single occupancy in Tazewell wing $145–$235; regular lodge rooms $105–$149; suites $450 for 1–4 persons. Williamsburg Inn room $260–$395, suites $525–$750 for 2 persons. Colonial House rooms $129–$650. Variable deposits, about $90–$100 per room. Add 8½% tax, gratuities optional. AE, MC, V.

Meal Plans   No meals at the Tazewell Club, but guests can charge meals at historic area restaurants to their room. In Regency Dining Room (jacket and tie required) at the Williamsburg Inn, specialties include Chesapeake crabmeat sautéed in wine, picatta of shrimp and veal, and scaloppine of lamb with garlic. Traditional Virginia recipes in the town's taverns—King's Arms, Christiana Campbell's, Josiah Chowning's—run the gamut from peanut soup to stuffed trout. Chesapeake Bay specialties are available at the Friday seafood buffet at the Williamsburg Lodge.

Services and Facilities
Exercise Equipment: 11 Keiser Cam II stations, 3 treadmills, 2 Lifecycles, 2 Liferowers. **Services:** Massage, loofah scrub, herbal wrap, facial, manicure, pedicure, nonsurgical face-lift, hair/skin care, individual instruction on exercise equipment. **Swimming Facilities:** 60′ 4-lane lap pool, large outdoor pool. **Recreation Facilities:** 18- and 9-hole golf courses, 8 tennis courts, lawn bowling and croquet, jogging trail, bicycle rentals; badminton, volleyball, and water aerobics on request. Miniature golf. **Evening Programs:** 18th-century concerts, tavern entertainment. Shakespeare productions.

In the Area
Busch Gardens (family-oriented theme park), James River plantation tour, Jamestown Festival Park (replicas of 3 historic ships), Yorktown (Revolutionary War battlefield), Virginia Beach, Mariner's Museum, Nature Museum and park.

Getting Here
From Washington, DC. By train, Amtrak from Union Station or Alexandria, VA, to Williamsburg (all seats reserved, 3 hrs). By bus, Gold Line (tel. 301/386–8300) or Trailways (3 hrs). By car, I–95 south to I–64 east (3 hrs). By plane, scheduled flights to Norfolk or Richmond, VA (30 mins). Taxi, car rental available; limousine on request. Scheduled van service to airports from Williamsburg hotels.

Special Notes
Elevator to all floors, some specially equipped rooms provide access for people with disabilities. Tours of historic sites and golf lessons for children. No smoking in club. Remember to bring fitness shoes (white-soled aerobics), workout clothing, leotards. Tazewell Club open weekdays 6 AM–8 PM, weekends 8–7 (until 10 Fri. and Sat.). Minimum age: 16, or with parent.

Yogaville

Holistic health
Spiritual awareness
Vibrant maturity

Virginia
Buckingham
The body-mind connection is strengthened at Yogaville through in-depth workshops in three essential yoga practices: *asana* (physical postures), meditation, and *pranayama* (breathing techniques). A permanent community in the beautiful James River valley near Charlottesville, the ashram welcomes people of all faiths and backgrounds to study and practice the teachings of Integral Yoga under the guidance of the Rev. Sri Swami Satchidananda. Guests are free to participate or observe, and special training in Hatha Yoga is available for beginners. Classes begin at 6:30 AM, alternating with meals and meditation until 6 PM. Meditation techniques and an understanding of karma also are taught, and guided nature walks provide an introduction to the valley's ecology.

Guest accommodations range from a two-story wooden lodge, the Lotus Inn, which has a health food café and offers private rooms, to dormitory or tent space. Motor homes can be parked on the grounds of the 750-acre retreat. The main meal is lunch, served in a communal hall. Those who volunteer for work in the organic garden, kitchen, or other areas of the community may earn free meals.

The ashram offers a variety of 2- to 5-day workshops, retreats, and yoga-training programs. Chiropractic care and therapeutic massage are available at the Intergral Health Center.

Yogaville
Rte. 604, Buckingham, VA 23921
Tel. 804/969–3121 or 800/858–9642
Fax 804/969–1303

Administration Founder, Rev. Swami Satchidananda; program director, Ram Wiener

Season Year-round

Accommodations The Lotus Inn has 6 private rooms with kitchenette, full bath, 1 double bed and a sofa bed, individually controlled heat and air-conditioning. 15 dormitory rooms (4–6 beds) have air-conditioning, communal bath, in a 2-story building that includes classrooms. 8 campsites are in a wooded area, some with platforms, near the dormitory, with shower and laundry facilities.

Rates $80–$90 daily for 2 in private room, $45–$48 per person in dormitory, $60 single room including meals, program. Lotus Inn rooms with private bath $85–$95 for 2. 4-day Hatha yoga program $175 dormitory, $245 in private room, $470 for 2; 4-day silent retreat $250. Campers $25–$30 single, $45–$50 couples per day. Motor home $50 per couple daily, $300 per week. Special rates for children. Advance deposit for visits of 2 weeks or more, $100. Add tax. MC, V.

Meal Plans 3 meals daily included in guest rate. The lactovegetarian diet includes whole grains, protein sources such as tofu and legumes, fresh fruit, and vegetables. Lunch is the main meal of the day; breakfast and supper are light buffets with cereals, herbal tea, yogurt, low-fat milk. Dinner favorites are brown rice pasta or baked tofu. The Lotus Cafe offers coffee and snacks throughout the day, plus yogurt drinks.

Services and Facilities **Services:** Instruction in meditation, Hatha Yoga, daily schedule of classes. **Swimming Facilities:** Private beach on 16-acre lake, river. **Recreation Facilities:** Nature walk, gardening, sauna, hot tub. **Evening Programs:** Classes or spiritual concert.

In the Area Charlottesville (University of Virginia), Monticello (Jefferson's Palladian villa and orchards), Richmond (Confederacy museum, historic mansions), Shenandoah National Park, Skyline Drive (scenic highway).

Getting Here *From Washington, DC.* By train, Amtrak to Charlottesville (3 hrs). By bus, Greyhound to Charlottesville (4 hrs). By car, I–66 west to Rte. 29, I–64 west (toward Lynchburg), 29 Bypass to I–64 east (toward Richmond), Rte. 20 south, Rte. 655 into Rte. 601, left on Rte. 604 (5 hrs). By plane, USAir, United Express, or Delta, (45 mins). Pickup from airport, train, or bus, $15. Rental car available.

Special Notes Elderhostel for senior citizens, Oct. Cleaning and linen service provided twice weekly for guests staying 1 week or more at Lotus Inn. Specially equipped facilities for people with disabilities. No smoking, alcohol, illegal drugs, or pets allowed.

The Middle Atlantic States

George Washington made taking the waters in West Virginia fashionable at about the same time that Europeans discovered a place called Spa in Belgium. Health resorts flourished over the years in the Poconos, the Alleghenies, and the southern Appalachians. These resorts tend to be small-scale and conservative, emphasizing service and personal attention, and oriented to golf and tennis rather than to high-energy workouts. While the renowned Greenbrier Resort in White Sulphur Springs, West Virginia, made the great leap from traditional to contemporary in its health spa, Berkeley Springs—where George Washington bathed—remains a sleepy country town with modest accommodations for spa goers in a West Virginia state park. The Coolfont Resort, secluded in a valley near Berkeley Springs, brings together the past and present with its own blend of holistic health programs and luxury pampering. The introduction of snow-making equipment has added a new dimension to resorts throughout the area, with downhill and cross-country skiing now complementing indoor exercise.

In building the nation's first boardwalk, Atlantic City touched off a development boom along the New Jersey shore. The introduction of casino gambling in 1978 brought the town out of a long decline, and when the manufacturer of Lifecycles and other exercise equipment became a Bally company, the shore gained its first full-scale fitness center at Bally's Park Place Hotel. Like most spas in the area, it offers exercise as an amenity rather than a comprehensive health vacation program.

Diversity makes the Middle Atlantic states a rewarding destination for the fitness-oriented traveler. Your choices range from charming Deerfield Manor in the Poconos to the most sophisticated facilities this side of the Alleghenies at Nemacolin Woodlands in the Laurel Highlands of Pennsylvania. Affordability also distinguishes spa programs in the Mid-Atlantic region. Midweek packages offer full services at substantial savings. Weekend packages near New York City are featured at two New Jersey Hiltons, in Short Hills and Long Branch.

The Hilton at Short Hills

Luxury pampering

New Jersey
Short Hills

The combination of a luxurious hotel and deluxe European health spa has made the Hilton at Short Hills a popular hideaway for Manhattanites as well as corporate executives visiting the Newark area. With full-service spa facilities—from a Roman-style pool to hydrotherapy and fango treatments—and a fitness center and calorie-conscious cuisine, this Hilton offers all the amenities of many fitness resorts. Even complimentary workout attire is provided.

Expansion of the day spa program, completed in 1996, added a second floor to the fitness facilities, plus additional rooms for massage and body wraps. Two aerobics studios are in use daily, with scheduled classes from morning to night. Access for hotel guests is free of charge. The salon at the spa provides a wide range of face and body programs. Under the direction of Pierre Pellaton, the therapists use European techniques and products for facials, skin rejuvenation treatments, and mud baths. Along with gentle underwater hydromassage, they

The Middle Atlantic States

Lake Erie

Allegheny River

OHIO

Pittsburgh

Ohio River

Wheeling

West

Morgantown

Parkersburg

Clarksburg

Potomac River

WEST VIRGINIA

Charleston

0   50 miles

0   75 km

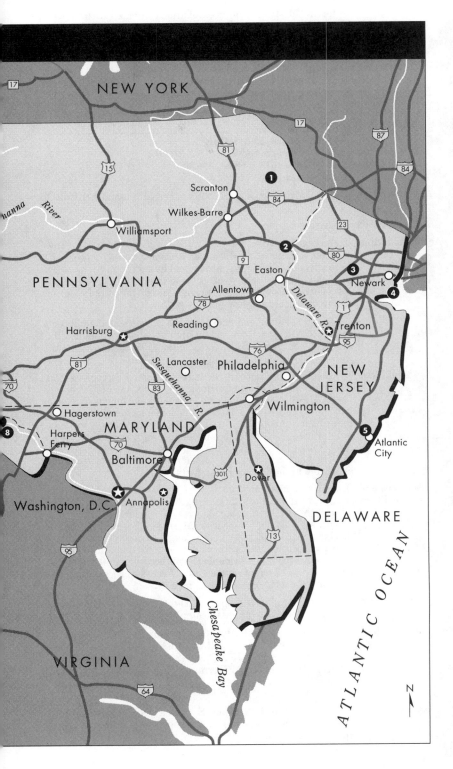

offer an herbal wrap or an exfoliation combined with seaweed wrap. Completing your new look are hair and nail services, and waxing.

All salon services are à la carte, and it's wise to call ahead for a schedule on busy weekends. The hotel offers a Spa Sampler package with a Friday or Saturday night stay that includes health consultation, half-hour massage, aquacise and exercise classes, use of equipment and brunch. A shuttle carries guests to the elegant Short Hills Shopping Mall.

The Hilton at Short Hills

41 JFK Pkwy., Short Hills, NJ 07078
Tel. 201/379–0100 or 800/455–8667
Fax 201/376–0481

Administration General manager, Gary Schweikert; spa director, Christine De Maio

Season Year-round

Accommodations 300 rooms in a 10-story glass-walled office complex. The Towers has additional amenities in 70 rooms and 37 suites with French doors dividing bedroom and living room. All have TV, 2 phones, marble bathroom with hair dryer, scale, and an array of toiletries. Concierge and private lounge for complimentary breakfast, cocktails, and dessert buffet.

Rates Spa Sampler weekend package $150 per person, double occupancy, $200 single. Rooms daily single/double per person $145–$266; Towers rooms $175–$301; suites $195–$355. Add 6% tax plus gratuities. Deposit: 1 night. AE, DC, MC, V.

Meal Plans No meal plan. Spa cuisine served in the casual Terrace Restaurant. Breakfast choices include egg substitute omelet with salsa, Mueslix cereal, steamed Irish oatmeal; lunch entrées include vegetable frittata, chilled poached salmon with cucumber/onion compote, lobster/angel-hair pasta with mushrooms; dinner menu has shellfish consommé, crispy red snapper with lime-salsa glaze, seared tuna with ratatouille and crisp leeks, grilled chicken breast with pink lentils. Dinner selections also available in the Dining Room (prix fixe).

Services and Facilities **Exercise Equipment:** Full line of Cybex cardiovascular and weight training units, 2 Concept 2 rowing machines, 3 Bodyguard treadmills, 2 StairMasters, 4 stationary bikes, free weights (3–50 lbs). **Services:** Massage (Swedish, shiatsu), herbal wrap, facial, body polish, fango, salon for hair, nail, and skin care. Fitness assessment, computerized nutritional analysis, 1-on-1 training. **Swimming Facilities:** Indoor 50-ft lap pool, outdoor pool. **Recreation Facilities:** Access to racquetball and squash courts (fee); golf, tennis nearby.

In the Area Short Hills Mall (150 shops and boutiques), the Meadowlands (baseball and entertainment complex).

Getting Here *From New York City.* By car, New Jersey Turnpike to Rte. 78N, or Garden State Parkway to Exit 142, Rte. 78 west in local traffic lane to JFK Pkwy (20 mins). By bus, NJ Transit from Port Authority Terminal (45 mins). By air, complimentary shuttle service to Newark International Airport (15 mins).

Special Notes No-smoking rooms available. Spa open weekdays 6 AM–10 PM, weekends 8–8. No smoking in spa; poolside lunch service. Business Center open Mon.–Sat.

Ocean Place Hilton Resort & Spa

Luxury pampering

New Jersey
Long Branch

Within commuting distance of Manhattan, the Ocean Place Hilton's seafront spa is a popular weekend escape for young executives. Skin care to repair damage wrought by the climate and sun is a specialty here. The French moor therapy mud, a black organic natural product by Remy Laure, is used in facials and underwater massage. This is preceded by a vigorous scrubbing with mineral salts and body oils to stimulate circulation, remove dead skin cells, and unclog pores. For those who prefer a more soothing experience, aromatherapy wraps, facials, or massages are suggested. All treatments can be booked à la carte or as part of one- to three-day packages, with or without hotel accommodations.

Fitness classes in the aerobics studio and the indoor pool can be charged to your bill individually, or you may arrange a program package with spa meals. Over 25 hours of classes are scheduled weekly on the studio's cushioned floor, from step to stretch-and-tone. The spa guests enjoy an oceanfront promenade and a nearby state park beach.

Ocean Place Hilton Resort & Spa
1 Ocean Blvd., Long Branch, NJ 07740
Tel. 908/571–4000 or 800/445–8667
Fax 908/571–3314

Administration General manager, Frank Gaynor; spa manager, Lisa Ryan

Season Year-round

Accommodations 254 rooms, all air-conditioned, with balcony, TV, phone, modern bath. Contemporary furniture includes desk in oceanfront rooms. Direct access to spa and beach promenade.

Rates Daily room rate $195 single, $190–$215 double for 2 persons. 2-night Spa Getaway $230–$294 single, $395–$466 for 2, double occupancy. 3-night Getaway $760–$896 single, $1,340–$1,418 for 2, double occupancy. Full-day Stressbuster package with lunch, no lodging $277. Packages include tax, gratuities. Daily spa fee $15, class $15. AE, DC, MC, V.

Meal Plans Hilton Food For Life lunch (choice of salads, fruit platters, seafood) included in spa packages. Spa cuisine dinner includes choice of grilled catch of the day, broiled chicken with local vegetables in season, salad bar, fresh fruit.

Services and Facilities **Exercise Equipment:** 11-unit Maxicam circuit, 2 Lifecycles, 2 Stairobic machines, 3 Startrac 2000 treadmills, dumbbells (3–55 lbs), 2 benches. **Services:** Massage, MoorMud hydromassage or wrap, aromatherapy, herbal wrap, French body polish with Vichy shower, salt-glow loofah scrub, facials, reflexology, seaweed body masque or facial. Personal goal training, body-fat analysis, fitness assessment, circuit training, swimming and tennis lessons. **Swimming Facilities:** Indoor lap pool, outdoor resort pool on sundeck, ocean beach. **Evening Programs:** Dancing.

In the Area Monmouth Park Race Track, Garden State Arts Center, Presidents' Park (beach dunes).

Getting Here *From New York City.* By car, I–95 (New Jersey Turnpike) south to Garden State Pkwy., Exit 105 to Rte. 36 (1 hr). By train, NJ Transit commuter services from Penn Station via Newark (2 hrs). Taxi, rental car available.

Special Notes Children's day camp Memorial Day–Labor Day. Bike rental available. Specially equipped rooms for guests with disabilities. Spa open weekdays 7 AM–9 PM, Sat. 8 AM–10 PM, Sun. 8–6. Beach conditions posted at Presidents' Park.

The Spa at Bally's Park Place Casino Hotel

Luxury pampering

New Jersey
Atlantic City

Amid the glitz and glamour of the beachfront casinos, the Spa at Bally's Park Place Hotel & Tower is a health and fitness oasis. The spacious facilities and top-of-the-line equipment would be the pride of any fitness resort, though here they serve as a complement to gambling and entertainment. It's possible not to set foot in the casino, but most of the people working out in the weights room also exercise the one-armed bandits.

The pool, saunas, whirlpools, and treatment rooms are open to hotel guests and members. Terraced gardens dotted with whirlpools, showers, and a coed glass-walled sauna flank the swimming pool. Upstairs are men's and women's locker rooms with Turkish bath, treatment rooms, and exercise equipment. The ultimate relaxer here is a private session in the MVP Suite, which boasts a marble whirlpool and steam shower. Also try aromatherapy, Swedish, or shiatsu massage.

The midweek spa package includes a meal plan that allows you to dine in the hotel's restaurants on a fixed menu. Among the services included in the package are salon treatments that feature Sothys products, and daily exercise classes, such as slimnastics, low-impact aerobics, stretch and tone, and aquafit, scheduled from 11 to 3 in the aerobics studio.

The spa's exotic gardens and waterfalls dramatically terrace into the indoor swimming pool. Steps away is a deck overlooking the Atlantic, giving you the sensation of being on an ocean liner. Actually on a barrier island, Atlantic City is putting on a new face with the opening of its convention center, linked to the Boardwalk by a landscaped boulevard. The wooden walkway flanking the ocean dates from 1870, and has been the scene of the Miss America Pageant parade since the 1920s. During pageant week in September, many contestants are seen working out at the spa.

Starting your day with a walk or jog on the Boardwalk is the best antidote for an evening at the casinos. Bikes can be rented at several points; an excursion to Margate and Ventnor reveals the residential side of the gaming resort. The beach and ocean bathing, among the finest on the East Coast, assure a healthy glow.

The Spa at Bally's Park Place Casino Hotel

Bally's Park Place Casino Hotel & Tower
Boardwalk and Park Pl., Atlantic City, NJ 08401
Tel. 609/340–4600, 800/772–7777, or 800/225–5977

Administration General manager, Ronald Mann

Season Year-round

Accommodations 1,260 rooms with private bath; 110 suites; 9 restaurants. Art Deco touches in the original building; luxury rooms with sitting area in the 48-story Tower are decorated in mauve with lots of woodwork, have marble-walled bathroom, hair dryer, lighted makeup mirror, robes.

Rates Rooms $135–$215 per day, suites $310–$350 for 2 double occupancy. Spa admission $10 for hotel guests. Treatments priced individually. 1-day spa package $99, 3-day/2-night spa package $395 per person double, $475 single. Add tax, gratuities. (Saturday night is not included in any package plan.) AE, DC, MC, V.

Meal Plans Spa packages include 3 meals daily. Breakfast can be an egg-substitute omelet or French toast, fresh fruit with yogurt. Buffet lunch in the Spa Cafe includes salads, soup, fruit. Spa cuisine in the hotel dining rooms features fresh fish, lean meats. Dinner choices include pan-seared scallops with saffron rice, steamed salmon with onions in balsamic vinegar sauce, lobster and shrimp casserole, and scallops Newburg with lemon-dill rice. Daily diet has 55% carbohydrates, 15% protein, 30% fat.

Services and Facilities **Exercise Equipment:** 10 computerized Lifecycle bikes, Pyramid weight training equipment room, 3 Quinton treadmills, 10-unit Cybex weight training circuit, 5 Trotter treadmills, 2 Lifesteps, 5 StairMasters with video, cross-country ski machine, 2 Nautilus recumbent bikes. **Services:** Massage, herbal wrap, aromatherapy, algae body masque, loofah body scrub, facial; salon for hair, nail, skin care. **Swimming Facilities:** Indoor pool, ocean beach. **Recreation Facilities:** 4 indoor racquetball courts, bike rental on the Boardwalk; golf and tennis nearby. **Evening Programs:** Cabaret and celebrity shows.

In the Area Brigantine National Wildlife Refuge, Farley State Marina, the Noyes Museum (contemporary art), Historic Town of Smithville, Atlantic City Race Track.

Getting Here *From Philadelphia and New York.* Atlantic City is served by daily casino bus from points throughout the region. By plane, USAir commuter flights. By train, Amtrak or commuter service via Philadelphia offers daily service. By car, the Garden State Pkwy. From points north and south, the Atlantic City Expressway from Philadelphia (1 hr). Taxi, rental car, minibus available locally.

Special Notes Facilities for treatments and hotel accommodations available for people with disabilities. Spa open Mon.–Sat. 7:30 AM–9 PM, Sun. 8–7. No smoking.

Deerfield Manor

Life enhancement
Vibrant maturity
Weight management

Pennsylvania
East Stroudsburg

The program at Deerfield Manor takes an individualized approach to diet and nutrition and encourages you to achieve a healthy lifestyle. Participation is limited to 33 men and women who want to unwind and shape up. The daily activities include guided walks, exercise classes, aerobics, yoga, and calisthenics in the heated outdoor pool. Surrounded by mountains, the 12-acre spa retreat encourages moderate exercise and diet amid lots of country charm. Weekend as well as Sunday-to-Sunday packages are offered.

Hiking trails in the Poconos are explored daily by the spa group. Transportation to trail heads is provided, and destinations can include the Pocono Mountains Environmental Center as well as parts of the Appalachian Trail. Led by naturalists, these outings are an excellent introduction to the ecology of the mountain area. Bird-watching areas are especially popular.

The attractive white clapboard farmhouse, dating from the 1930s, has a warm, supportive environment nurtured by a 16-member staff, with occasional visits from lecturers and health professionals. A familylike feeling tends to develop among guests, many of whom are repeat visitors in the over-50 age bracket.

Guests make informed nutritional choices when following the "Total Fitness" program: Each guest selects a menu plan according to personal need and based on the consumption of about 1,000 calories per day. In some cases guests opt for a day of freshly squeezed fruit and vegetable juices. Meals are served in a bright, spacious dining room.

Structuring your daily schedule of spa appointments may be the most rigorous exercise. Workout equipment is minimal and no activity required. Energy comes from a caring staff and the splendor of the mountains.

Deerfield Manor

R.D. 1, Rte. 402N, East Stroudsburg, PA 18301
Tel. 717/223–0160 or 800/852–4494
Fax 717/223–8270

Administration Owner-manager, Frieda Eisenkraft; fitness director, Susan Lipkin

Season Apr.–mid-Nov.

Accommodations 22 single and double rooms in main country house and deluxe annex rooms with private bath. Furnished with wicker furniture, antiques. Informal lounge with VCR, records. Sauna.

Rates Weekend $210–$340 per person double occupancy, $350–$390 single. Weekly (Sun.–Sun.) $699–$935 per person double occupancy, $924–$1,125 single. Add gratuities (15%), taxes (6%). $200 payable in advance. MC, V.

Meal Plans 3 meals daily; fish and chicken, locally grown produce, fresh fruit. Vegetarian meals optional.

Services and Facilities **Exercise Equipment:** StairMaster, treadmill, Universal recumbent bike, VersaClimber, NordicTrack, free weights (3–15 lbs). **Services:** Massage (Swedish, shiatsu, reflexology), facial, wrap. **Swimming Facilities:** Heated outdoor pool. **Recreation Facilities:** 2 tennis courts, golf, roller skating, ice skating, horseback riding, all nearby. **Evening Programs:** Guest lecturers on health-related topics, handwriting analysis, concerts.

In the Area Pocono Mountains Environmental Center (bird-watching), shopping tours, summer theater, antiques markets.

Getting Here *From Philadelphia and New York.* By car, I–80 from New York, I–84 from New England, I–83 from the Baltimore–Washington area connect with Rte. 402. By plane, major airlines serve Allentown, PA. By bus, Martz Lines to Stroudsburg. Taxi, rental car, and limousine service available locally.

Special Notes No smoking indoors. Ramps and accommodations for people with disabilities.

The Himalayan Institute

Holistic health
Spiritual awareness
Stress control

Pennsylvania
Honesdale

Physicians and psychologists at the 400-acre international headquarters of the Himalayan Institute of Yoga Science and Philosophy of the USA offer a wide variety of programs in holistic health, hatha yoga, meditation; the science of breath, diet, and nutrition; Eastern philosophy and other subjects. The Institute founder is Sri Swami Rama, who was born in northern India and served as a research consultant to the Menninger

Foundation Project on Voluntary Control of Internal States in 1970. His demonstrations there, under laboratory conditions, of his precise control of his own autonomic functioning (stopping his heart from pumping blood for 17 seconds), changed scientists' understanding of the human ability to control the body.

Individuals come to this Pocono Mountain estate to learn to control the mind and body, overcome illness, accelerate healing, and prevent illness. Therapies include homeopathy, detoxification, and ayurvedic treatments. Biofeedback, a technique that uses machines to teach regulation of the nervous system, is linked with the practice of Eastern philosophy and yoga exercises to form the institute's holistic approach to living. Meditation and relaxation can enable one to gain control of the body and the mind, according to Swami Rama, and the serene atmosphere at this mountaintop retreat provides the appropriate setting for exploring the mind and exercising the body.

Guests are asked to maintain quiet from 10 PM until 8 AM, and 5 to 6 PM, seeking external silence and inner tranquillity.

The Himalayan Institute
R.R. 1, Box 400, Honesdale, PA 18431
Tel. 717/253-5551 or 800/822-4547

Administration President, Deborah Willoughby, M.A.

Season Year-round

Accommodations 100 guests are housed in the main building, a 3-story brick structure with austerely furnished rooms. Each room has 1 or 2 beds and a sink. Sheets and towels provided; no lock on the door. Communal toilets.

Rates Weekend seminar tuition $85–$95; shared room $100–$110 per person double. Personal retreat with meals on request. Deposit for all programs ($25 per person for programs costing as much as $300, $50 per person for programs more than $300). MC, V.

Meal Plans 3 vegetarian meals daily, cafeteria style, and herbal tea included in program rate. Breakfast is oatmeal with apples, fresh banana, whole-grain bread with butter, herbal tea. Lunch can be minestrone soup, hummus, and green salad, or steamed rice with raisins. Dinner includes soup (butternut squash or potato), homemade bread, graham crackers, apples, or tofu-and-lentil casserole. Vegetables from organic garden. Nondairy options available.

Services and Facilities **Exercise Equipment:** Stationary bikes, rowing machine, Stair-Master. **Services:** Biofeedback training, hatha yoga class, vegetarian cooking classes, massage, ayurvedic body therapies, medical and psychological consultations. Massage and body therapies not available. **Swimming Facilities:** Pond on property, with sandy beach. **Recreation Facilities:** Tennis, basketball, handball courts, hiking trails, cross-country skiing, ice skating. **Evening Programs:** Lectures or practica.

In the Area Pocono Mountains sightseeing, Lake Wallenpaupack, downhill skiing.

Getting Here *From New York City.* By bus, Short Line from Port Authority Terminal (3 hrs). By car, via Lincoln Tunnel to I–80 W to Exit 34B (Rte. 15 N) through Milford, Rte. 6 W/191 N through Honesdale to Rte. 670 N (3 hrs). By air, scheduled flights to Scranton. Airport transfer service (tel. 717/252–3070). Taxi, rental car available.

Special Notes Preschool, kindergarten, and elementary school programs (ages 3–9) combine Eastern and Western educational concepts, Montessori methods, and yoga philosophies. No smoking indoors. Pets, radios, alcohol, and illicit drugs are not allowed on the grounds.

Nemacolin Woodlands

Luxury pampering
Stress control
Weight management

Pennsylvania
Farmington

Atop a scenic bluff in the Laurel Highlands of southwestern Pennsylvania stands the Woodlands Spa, a $6 million centerpiece of the Nemacolin Woodlands resort and conference center. Despite its name, this is no rustic retreat. The four-level building of native stone, buff brick, and glass is the best-equipped spa this side of the Allegheny Mountains.

The range of bodywork available is exceptional—scrubs and wraps using sea salts, oils, mud, and herbal mixtures; aromatherapy or Swedish massage; foot reflexology. After a session in the steam room or the sauna, you can relax in a glass-walled whirlpool and enjoy the view of woods and distant mountains. Downstairs is devoted to exercise: an array of Keiser pneumatic weight training machines, plus bikes, treadmills, and a StairMaster with video monitors to help you meet your goals; a four-lane indoor lap pool 65 feet long that's also used for water aerobics; and a mirrored aerobics studio with spring-cushioned wood floor that can hold groups of 40 or more.

Upstairs are the beauty salon and 20 treatment rooms, spacious and airy and warmed in winter by a fireplace. Dermalogica skin-care system treatments are offered to retard aging, control blemishes, and rejuvenate your complexion. Body care includes a detoxifying masque of moor mud, followed by a scrub and moisturizer. One room is specially designed for hydrating pedicures and manicures, a process in which your hands and feet are dipped in liquid paraffin, a coating that helps moisture penetrate outer layers of skin, leaving a smooth, soft finish. Lunch and snacks are offered in the reception area, allowing you to spend the whole day indoors or at the pool.

At the Woodlands Spa you set your own pace. Treatments and optional spa meals are included in packages of one to six days, or booked à la carte. Fitness classes range from high-impact aerobics to step, body sculpting, and tai chi. Personal training, as well as fitness evaluation with biofeedback analysis of body composition, can be part of your program. Nonprogram guests pay a daily fee ($15), refunded if you book a service.

The 1,000-acre resort features a wide range of sports. Two golf courses, indoor Equestrian Center with dressage training as well as trail rides, outdoor tennis courts, championship croquet, horseshoes, biking, and trout fishing in a stocked lake are among the options. In winter, trails are groomed for cross-country skiing and snowmobiles, and the lake is filled with ice skaters. Downhill skiing on a gentle 325-ft slope with three runs, lifts, and a snow-making system, became available in 1995. Equipment can be borrowed from the Activities Center.

Golfers are challenged by Pete Dye's new par-72 6,832 yard course, and the original 6,600-yard par-70 course. Instruction and video analysis of your form are offered at the Golf

Academy, which has scheduled classes and private instruction year-round.

Your appetite sharpened by the mountain air and exercise, you can sample spa cuisine at six restaurants, including the country club grill. The elegant Golden Trout dining room reserved for spa package guests serves a menu low in fat and cholesterol, and has a no-smoking policy.

Once a private hunting reserve, this sprawling resort has grown and changed during the years since it was acquired in 1987 by Joseph Hardy, founder of the nationwide 84 Lumber Co. Expansion begun in 1995 linked the spa with an outdoor swimming pool with sunken bar, and an enclosed arcade to the English country-style lodge. A second hotel, styled as a replica of The Ritz in Paris, opened in 1997. Art and antiques from the Hardy collection decorate all the buildings, ranging from Tiffany glass to contemporary prints, carved carousel animals and lifelike sculptures by Philip Johnson.

Nemacolin Woodlands
Box 188, Farmington, PA 15437
Tel. 412/329–8555 or 800/422–2736
Fax 412/329–6177

Administration President, Maggie Hardy Magerko; spa director, Tammy Pahel

Season Year-round

Accommodations 98-room lodge is closest to spa building; new 125-room hotel has spacious bedrooms and terrace suites. Choice of room style includes traditional English, French, or Art Deco. 2 queen-size beds are standard, some have four-posters. Separate bathroom and commode, some with whirlpool bathtub, balcony; TV, 3 telephones, air-conditioning. Also, 40 furnished condominiums and cottages with kitchens.

Rates Day Spa packages without lodging $107–$248. Hotel rooms daily, double or single, without meals $109–$215, suites $159–$295, penthouse $189–$395. 2-day/2-night Weekend Discovery package with meals $384 single, $282 double. 1-night Spa Retreat with 2 meals (Sun.–Thurs.) $340 single, $254 double. Sport/Spa summer package $438–$495 single, $338–$371 double daily with 3 meals. Add tax, gratuities. Golf and tennis packages available. Deposit $150. AE, MC, V.

Meal Plans Spa packages include 2–3 meals daily. Spa dining room in lodge has breakfast buffet with muffins, hot and cold cereals, juices, yogurt, fruit, choice of egg-white omelet, honey-oat waffle, 10-grain cereal. Lunch, served at spa or in café, can be salad with chef's award-winning New England clam chowder. Dinner selections include brook trout stuffed with scallops, shrimp, grilled chicken breast, veal scallops. Menu on 14-day cycle, special diets accommodated.

Services and Facilities **Exercise Equipment:** 11 Keiser pneumatic weight training machines, Lifecycle, StairMaster, 2 Trotter treadmills, 3 VersaClimbers, 2 Monark bikes, free weight dumbbells (1–50 lbs) Lifestep, Tectrix stepper. **Services:** Massage (Swedish, sports, aromatherapy, reflexology), facials, back cleansing, body wrap, loofah body polish; hair, nail, and skin treatments. Personalized fitness-assessment, stress-management program, body-composition evaluation, 1-on-1 training. Scheduled walks and group exercise. **Swimming Facilities:** Indoor lap pool, outdoor recreational pool. **Spa Facilities:** Coed weights room, aerobics studio with Reo-Flex floor, treatment rooms, beauty salon, men's and women's saunas, whirlpools, workout shorts and robes provided in locker room, juice bar, boutique.

Recreation Facilities: 4 tennis courts (Omni surface, lighted), bicycle rental, Equestrian Center, 2 18-hole golf courses, miniature golf, Golf Academy, croquet, boating, trout fishing, badminton, shuffleboard, winter skating, cross-country and downhill skiing, snowmobiles. Racquetball nearby. Greenhouse, table tennis. **Evening Programs:** Spa lectures and training sessions, music weekends, chess, sports bar.

In the Area White-water rafting at Ohiopyle State Park, Fallingwater (Frank Lloyd Wright architecture), Laurel Caverns, Fort Necessity (French & Indian War), Antietam Battlefield (Civil War), Western Maryland Scenic Railroad (June–Oct.).

Getting Here *From Washington, DC.* By car, Capital Beltway (I–495), I–270 north to Frederick, MD, I–70 west to I–68, Uniontown exit to Rte. 40 (Old National Road) to Farmington, PA (3 hrs). By air, USAir to Pittsburgh (45 mins). Transfers on request, private airstrip, rental car.

Special Notes No smoking in spa or spa dining room. Children's playground, petting zoo, and Family Activities Center open year-round. Plants sold in greenhouse. Pony ride, canoe rental, golf instruction available.

Berkeley Springs State Park

Taking the waters

West Virginia
Berkeley Springs

Berkeley Springs State Park has been called the Kmart of spas: An hour-long "tub and rub" treatment costs $40, and in the summer you can swim in the big outdoor pool. All the mineral water you care to drink or take home is free. Although no larger than a town square, the tiny park wins high marks for cleanliness and no-frills treatments: Bring your jeans and a sense of humor.

Spartan and a bit old-fashioned by today's standards, the state-run facilities offer a down-home Blue Ridge brand of healing. In the original 1815 Roman bath building, step-down tubs rent for $10 an hour per person. Filled with 750 gallons of spring water heated to 102°F, the recently renovated pools hold several people—coed company is fine—in privacy. The eight pools can be rented by the hour and can hold up to four people at a time. No reservations are taken; the policy is first come, first served.

Both the main bathhouse and the Country Inn hotel across the street date from the 1920s. In the women's bath, heated mineral water spurts from enormous pipes into two 3-foot-deep tiled plunge pools where patrons soak in privacy. The men's masseurs operate in open cubicles, steam cabinets line yellow brick walls, and bathtubs provide a relaxing soak. Adjoining the park is the Country Inn (tel. 800/822–6630) and its hillside Renaissance Spa, which provides limited beauty salon treatments and private mineral water whirlpools open to the public.

Ever since George and Martha Washington took the waters here, Berkeley Springs has attracted healers and promoters. A museum atop the Roman baths documents the area's development. Recently the town has been a mecca for body-workers and therapists, and a bottling plant exports the spring water. At the Bath House massage and health center on Fairfax Street facing the state park, you can shop for health products and spa guides, make appointments for therapeutic treatments, take yoga and tai chi classes. Nearby is a full-service homeopathic pharmacy where medicinal tinctures are available, and educational classes and exhibits trace develop-

ment of homeopathy by a German physician, Samuel Hahne-
mann, 200 years ago. Tari's Premier Cafe on Washington
Street, next door to the venerable Star Theatre, serves vegetable burgers, and Washington's Birthday is celebrated with
an international waters tasting.

The park also preserves a spring where you can fill jugs with
free, cold drinking water, deeded to the people of Virginia by
Lord Fairfax under a grant from King George III of England
in the 18th century. Bring your own jugs.

Berkeley Springs sits at the upper end of a three-state
region, taking in parts of Pennsylvania, Maryland, and West
Virginia along upper reaches of the Potomac River. Surrounded by the Allegheny Mountains, the area remains relatively undeveloped.

Berkeley Springs State Park
Washington St., Berkeley Springs, WV 25411
Tel. 304/258–2711 or 800/225–5982

Administration	Superintendent, Robert Ebert
Season	Year-round
Accommodations	The adjacent Country Inn (tel. 800/822–6630) has rooms with shared bath for $37 for 2, $60–$105 with private bathroom, choice of king-size or twin beds. The inn's 2-night Ultimate Spa package is $470 (Sun.–Thurs.) for 2. There are several bed-and-breakfasts in town or nearby. The Highlawn Inn (tel. 304/258–5700), a hilltop Victorian mansion, has antiques-filled rooms and a carriage house suite, each with modern bath or shower, and full breakfast for $85–$235 for 2. Add 9% taxes. Also, Coolfont Resort (*see below*) has tent sites, RV hookups, and a wide range of accommodations, with or without spa packages. Cacapon State Park (tel. 304/258–1022 or 800/225–5982), 10 mi south of town, offers cabins, lodge rooms, restaurant, and golf course. AE, MC, V.
Rates	Bath and massage $40 (1 hr), thermal water bath $15 (1 hr).
Services and Facilities	**Services:** Massage (30 min), private bath, Roman plunge pool, steam cabinet. **Swimming Facilities:** Outdoor pool open May 30–Sept. 1 ($5 adults, $2 children).
In the Area	Cacapon State Park, Berkeley Castle mansion (1887), Harpers Ferry National Historical Park, Charles Town racetrack, Antietam Battlefield (Civil War), Blue Ridge Outlet Center (shopping), C&O Canal, Prospect Peak Overlook (3-state view), Winchester (apple orchards, festivals), Whitetail Resort (downhill skiing), Shepherdstown (summer theater festival).
Getting Here	*From Washington, DC.* By car, I–270 to Frederick, MD, I–70 west to Hancock, MD, cross Potomac River on Rte. 522 (90 mins). By train, Amtrak to Martinsburg, WV.
Special Notes	Facilities accessible to people with physical disabilities. Discount on bathhouse admission and services for senior citizens. No smoking in bathhouses. Spa open Apr.–Oct., Sat.–Thurs. 10–6, Fri. 10–9; Nov.–Mar., daily 10–6. Old Roman Bathhouse open weekends only Columbus Day–Memorial Day. Summer concerts at bandstand, Sat. 5 PM.

Coolfont Resort

Holistic health
Life enhancement
Vibrant maturity
Weight management

West Virginia
Berkeley Springs

A relaxed, informal, budget-priced mountain retreat occupying 1,300 acres in the foothills of the Appalachian Mountains, Coolfont has the laid-back look of a summer camp for adults. With the opening of the Spectrum Spa in 1992, the resident owners culminated 20 years devoted to creating an environment for healthy vacations. In addition to a fitness center with indoor spring-water swimming pool, the spa has 21 private rooms for a wide range of bodywork, a full-service salon, demonstration kitchen, and aerobics studio with sprung-wood floor. In the Swim and Fitness Club are a coed whirlpool and sauna, weights training room with exercise bikes, and Cybex equipment. The daily schedule of classes is open to all resort guests, and ranges from morning stretch to aquatics, body sculpting, and yoga.

Members of the resident staff combine expertise in physical fitness, nutrition, massage, and holistic health. In addition to regularly scheduled programs, guest instructors lead workshops on natural nutrition, creative problem solving, and stress reduction. Also offered regularly is a weekend of massage instruction for couples, and a weeklong Breathe-Free program for smoking cessation.

The emphasis here is on health awareness, exploring the area's hiking trails, and sharing the experience with a motivated group of spa goers. Camaraderie develops among program participants, and they enjoy a private dining room where nutritionally balanced meals are served. For those 40 and older, Camp Rediscovery weeks, modeled after the Adult Health and Development Program at the University of Maryland, are scheduled during August and January, and Elderhostel weeks in December are conducted in cooperation with a state university. Also based here are corporate team-building programs and adventures conducted by Outward Bound.

While the main building has a large restaurant catering to families and convention groups, as well as a woodsy cocktail lounge, Coolfont also has a cultural dimension: Folk singers, chamber music ensembles, and storytelling recitals are presented on weekends; art classes bring out amateur watercolor painters; and there are occasional celebrity sightings among guests from Washington, DC.

The lack of big-resort amenities is perhaps what draws so many guests back each season. Outings include a highly rated golf course run by the state at rock-bottom prices, historic Berkeley Springs and its bargain baths, and bargain shopping at the Blue Ridge Outlets. In winter, downhill skiing is nearby. Yet this is a country place with its own style, a blend of holistic health and down-home comfort.

Coolfont Resort
Cold Run Valley Rd., Rte. 1, Box 710, Berkeley
Springs, WV 25411
Tel. 304/258–4500 or 800/888–8768
Fax 304/258–5499

Administration Owner-managers, Martha and Sam Ashelman

Season Year-round

Accommodations 150 rooms in lodges and chalets. The modern 3-story Woodland Lodge has 23 rooms with twin or queen-size beds, bathroom, patio or balcony, some with wood-burning stove. All are air-conditioned, with phone. Set on a hillside, 23 deluxe chalets have 2 bedrooms with double beds, 2 bathrooms with large whirlpool tub, large living room with wood-burning stove. Chalets can be shared or used as 2 private units. All are air-conditioned, with telephone, TV, coffeemaker, wet bar, daily maid service. Also guest rooms in the historic Manor House (no smoking); RV hookups and log cabins available.

Rates Daily Modified American Plan $84–$120 per person double occupancy, $112–$150 single, includes admission to Swim & Fitness Center; 2-night Spa & Fitness package $360–$400 per person double occupancy, $400–$450 single; 2-night Massage Workshop $750 per couple; 5-night Healthy Me package $975–$1,250 per person double. Breathe-Free program $1,395 single. Spa for a Day (no lodging) $125. Add taxes, optional gratuities. Deposit: 50% payable in advance (refund when canceled at least 48 hr before start of program). AE, DC, MC, V.

Meal Plans 3 meals daily included in spa packages, 2 meals daily in MAP rate. Breakfast in spa dining room can be omelet, hot cereal, fruits. Lunch menu has lentil stew, pita sandwich with turkey, vegetarian pizza, tempeh burger. Dinner may be salmon baked in parchment, chicken dijon, cajun beans and rice. Salad bar, fruit bowl, herbal teas, decaffeinated coffee available. Juice and fruit snacks. Vegetarian meals available; special diets accommodated.

Services and Facilities **Exercise Equipment:** 15-unit Cybex weight training system, 2 Trotter treadmills, StairMaster, Tunturi ergometer, Precor rowing machine, Schwinn Air Dyne bike, free weights (3–20 lbs), hand weights. **Services:** Massage (neuromuscular, cranial/sacral, sports, deep-tissue therapy, Swedish), herbal wrap, loofah body scrub, facials; salon for hair, nail, and skin care. Fitness evaluation, nutrition consultation. **Swimming Facilities:** Indoor pool; beach on private lake. **Recreation Facilities:** 8 tennis courts, boating, hiking, horseback riding, team sports, cross-country skiing, ice skating, 18-hole golf course nearby. **Evening Programs:** Concerts, health lectures, line dancing.

In the Area *See* Berkeley Springs State Park, *above.*

Getting Here *From Washington, DC.* By car, I–270/70 to Hancock, MD, Rte. 522 (2 hrs); or the Pennsylvania Turnpike (I–76) at the Breezewood exit. By air, USAir has scheduled service to Hagerstown, MD; private planes use Potomac Airport. By bus, Greyhound to Hagerstown, MD. By train, Amtrak or MARC to Martinsburg, WV. Rental car, taxi available.

Special Notes Special accommodations for people with disabilities. Supervised camp for children, July–Aug. and seasonal weekends. No smoking in the dining room or designated accommodations. Swim and Fitness Club open weekdays 10–8, weekends 8 AM–9 PM. Elderhostel in Dec., Jan.; Camp Rediscovery (tel. 301/431–3733) Aug., Jan.

The Greenbrier

Luxury pampering
Preventive medicine
Taking the waters
Weight management

West Virginia
White Sulphur
Springs

The legendary Greenbrier resort blends old-fashioned comfort with high-tech spa treatments. The spa wing was opened in 1987 and has separate soaking pools and therapy rooms for men and women, a mirrored aerobics studio, and interactive exercise equipment. Hydrotherapy comes with mineral water—your choice of sulfur soak or bubbly herbal foam. Sports, riding, and hiking in the foothills of the Allegheny Mountains are significant attractions within the 6,500-acre resort, which includes three golf courses and a rifle club.

While the hotel is a busy scene of conferences and afternoon teas in vast halls filled with Oriental decor, the spa is serene and small, awash in pinks and greens, with sprigs of rhododendron painted on tiles. The staff includes both old hands and university-trained physiology specialists; they make newcomers feel comfortable about trying some of the exotic-sounding treatments. Seaweed body wraps, aromatherapy, and facials with European floral products are among the à la carte offerings.

The Greenbrier Clinic, established in 1948, occupies a separate building that is completely equipped for diagnostic and preventive medicine. Health examinations can now be combined with spa therapy. Checking in with the resident medical staff, the participant undergoes a two-day diagnostic assessment plus advanced fitness evaluation. A doctor will confer with the spa nutritionist and physiologist to plan a personalized diet and exercise regimen.

Spa cuisine is available to guests in a five-day package that includes breakfast, lunch, and dinner, unlimited exercise classes, luxury pampering, and individual nutrition consultation. The meals contain 30% fat or less, are moderate in cholesterol and sodium, and include high-fiber selections. Presented with classic Greenbrier flair, the menu capitalizes on fresh, natural foods from nearby farms.

Frequently refurbished, guest suites are huge, with parlor and walk-in closet, traditional furniture, and Greenbrier green carpet. There is a Greenbrier look and style, an aspect of artistic rightness and service that starts at the white brick gateway. The great white neoclassical hotel rises from beds of flowers. Its lobbies have flooring of black and white marble squares, Dorothy Draper decor, flowers massed on tables, and a full-length Gilbert Stuart portrait of George Washington.

The Greenbrier
White Sulphur Springs, WV 24986
Tel. 304/536–1110 or 800/624–6070
Fax 304/536–7854

Administration President, Ted J. Kleisner; General manager, Gil Patrick; spa director, Judy Stell

Season Year-round

Accommodations 650 rooms in main building, deluxe cottages, and guest houses.

Rates Daily rate $164–$208 per person double occupancy, $187–$490 single, including breakfast and dinner. Suites from $290 per person, cottages $198–$255 per person. Daily service charge $16 plus 6% tax per person. 5-night/6-day spa package $2,400 per person double or single, 2-day spa package $1,150 per person double or single, including 3 meals daily. 5-day Spa and Clinic program (Sun.–Fri.) $3,055 per person double or single. Deposit: $300 per room payable in advance. Tax and gratuities included in spa packages. AE, DC, MC, V.

Meal Plans American fare plus low-calorie alternatives at breakfast and dinner in the main dining room. Dinner can begin with smoked-duck salad, mushroom consommé, an entrée of grilled swordfish or mountain trout with lentil ragout, braised spinach leaves, followed by a salad of red-oak leaf lettuce with tomatoes in yogurt dressing. Dessert is pear strudel in fresh berry sauce. Café service for lunch. Tea daily.

Services and Facilities **Exercise Equipment:** 7-unit Nautilus weight training circuit, 3 Trotter treadmills, 3 Schwinn Dynavit bikes, UBE ergometer, 2 StairMasters, dumbbells (4–40 lbs); $10 facility fee includes use of sauna/steam room. **Services:** Full-body massage, back facial, pressure-point facial, herbal wrap, scalp massage, mineral or herbal bath, paraffin hand treatment, aromatherapy; hair, nail, and skin care in salon; 1-on-1 training, fitness evaluation, personal exercise program. Aerobics class $6. **Swimming Facilities:** Indoor Olympic-size pool, outdoor pool. **Recreation Facilities:** 15 outdoor and 5 indoor tennis courts, platform tennis, 3 golf courses, fishing, skeet- and trapshooting, bowling, croquet, horseback riding, carriage rides, jogging and hiking trails, par course, bicycle rental. **Evening Programs:** Feature films, food and wine weekends, dancing.

In the Area Presidents' Cottage Museum (displays memorabilia of famous visitors), crafts studios, mineral water springhouse.

Getting Here *From Washington, DC.* By car, I–95 or Skyline Drive, I–64 (6 hrs) to Richmond. By plane, Lewisburg Airport has scheduled flights by USAir nonstop from National Airport, also New York LaGuardia (45 mins). By train, Amtrak's Cardinal between New York City, Washington, and Cincinnati stops at the Greenbrier Fri., Sun., and Tues. Private limousine connects with flights at Lewisburg. Rental cars, taxis available.

Special Notes Special accommodations provided for people with disabilities. Sports school for children June–Labor Day. No smoking in the spa and areas of the dining room. Spa open daily 7–7. Daily facility fee $10.60, classes $6.

Lakeview Resort

Nonprogram resort

West Virginia
Morgantown
The fitness and sports center of the Lakeview Resort complements an executive conference center and two championship golf courses. Surrounded by woodland and a scenic lake, it's a place for both rigorous workouts and simple relaxation.

The action is continuous in the fitness center (a separate facility), and registered guests enjoy unlimited access to facilities at no extra cost. Inside is a 50-foot lap pool, jogging track (22 laps equals a mile), and aerobics studio with 20 classes scheduled during the week. Indoor and outdoor tennis facilities are available, too.

A personal fitness evaluation is offered when you arrive, and the only extra fees are for massage, use of the racquet-sport courts, and aerobics classes. A nursery will take care of the kids while parents work out. Lunch and snacks are available at the spa juice bar.

Lakeview Resort
Rte. 6, Box 88A, Morgantown, WV 26505
Tel. 304/594–1111 or 800/624–8300

Administration Manager, W. G. Menihan; fitness director, Greg Orner

Season Year-round

Accommodations 2-story inn with 187 well-appointed rooms and 55 2-bedroom condominium units with maid service.

Rates Daily rate per room $89–$199 for 2 double occupancy, $135–$145 single. Condominium apartments (up to 6 persons)

$280 per day. Credit card guarantee for 1 night. AE, DC, MC, V.

Meal Plans   Light fare in the lakeview restaurant, juice bar and snacks in the fitness center.

Services and Facilities   **Exercise Equipment:** 10-station Nautilus circuit, Marcy weight-resistance gym and recumbent bike, 4 StairMasters, 2 Life-cycles, Selectrix treadmill, 3 Schwinn Air Dyne bikes, Liferower, free weights. **Swimming Facilities:** Indoor lap pool and outdoor pool, lake. **Spa Facilities:** Coed whirlpool, separate saunas. **Recreation Facilities:** Racquetball and walleyball courts, 2 indoor and 4 outdoor tennis courts, fishing, boat rentals, horseback riding, waterskiing, 2 18-hole golf courses. **Evening Programs:** Dancing, cabaret.

In the Area   Lakeview Theater (summer stock), Cheat River Gorge (white-water rafting), Star City (glassmaking), Cooper's Park State Forest (hiking trails).

Getting Here   *From Pittsburgh.* Located 75 mi south of Pittsburgh, the resort is accessible by interstate routes and commuter airlines. By car, Rtes. 48 and 79 (90 mins). Morgantown's Hart Field is served by USAir. Courtesy car pickup to and from airport.

Special Notes   No smoking in the fitness center, some guest rooms, designated areas of the dining room. Fitness & Sports Center open weekdays 6:30 AM–10 PM, weekends 7–5. Minimum age in center is 16.

New England and New York

A return to elegance marked a decade of intensive development throughout the northeastern states. Grand old estates have been rejuvenated, and hotels have updated their fitness facilities and introduced European therapies. The result has been a broader range of vacation options for both luxury-minded and budget-conscious travelers.

Tradition blends with the latest concepts in nutrition and bodywork at the Norwich Inn & Spa, a Connecticut landmark. In the Berkshires, the famed Canyon Ranch offers innovative health programs only minutes away from the Boston Symphony Orchestra's popular summer home at Tanglewood. The facilities at this first destination spa and fitness resort in the northeast are among the most comprehensive in America. Nearby, the modestly priced Kripalu Center for Yoga and Health exercises your body and mind in a sanctuary unlike traditional ashrams in its size and scope of programs.

Advancing the concept of preventive medicine, spas are teaming up with doctors, nutritionists, and psychologists in new programs that address stress control, aging, and lifestyle. In Vermont, Green Mountain at Fox Run has a Liquid Diet Recovery program. At the New Age Health Spa in New York, you can participate in a challenge course designed by experts from Outward Bound, or luxuriate in the newly expanded spa building. In the Hudson Valley, Omega Institute has been at the forefront of personal and professional development in holistic health since 1977.

Norwich Inn & Spa

Luxury pampering

Connecticut
Norwich
Combine a 1920s country inn with a contemporary spa, and you have a perfect escape for city dwellers. Two hours north of New York City, the imposing Georgian-style Norwich establishment took on a new life in 1987 with the addition of the spa. Development of lakeside villas expanded the resort accommodations. Today the inn blends sophisticated cuisine and beauty treatments with New England tradition, and is linked to a nearby casino operated by Native Americans.

Nurturing and unadulterated pampering, rather than intensive workouts, are the spa's hallmarks. From flowered chintz and hand-rubbed pine in the old-fashioned bedrooms to high-tech workouts in the gym, the comfort and regimentation complement each other. Services and classes are offered à la carte, but daily and overnight packages provide the best value. Join the daily guided walk at 7 AM, free of charge, and get an orientation to the resort complex.

The spa building's focus is a 35-foot swimming pool, flanked by glass-walled aerobics and exercise rooms. The weight training facility features Keiser Cam II pneumatic resistance units. You can sign up for one-on-one training, join scheduled classes, or set up a series of skin and beauty treatments. The range of treatments makes this spa special. Choices include polarity therapy, acupressure, thalassotherapy, body wraps with Canadian glacial clay or algae imported from France, facials, and hydrotherapy in a deep tub with a 60-jet water massage

New England and New York

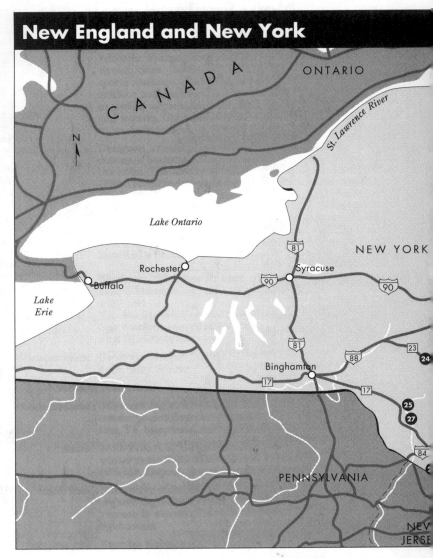

Connecticut
Norwich Inn & Spa, **21**

Maine
Northern Pines Health Resort, **1**
Poland Spring Health Institute, **2**

Massachusetts
Canyon Ranch in the Berkshires, **17**

Kripalu Center for Yoga and Health, **18**
The Kushi Institute of the Berkshires, **19**
Maharishi Ayur-Veda Health Center, **16**
The Option Institute, **20**
Rowe Conference Center, **14**
Smith College Adult Camp, **15**

New Hampshire
Waterville Valley Resort, **3**

New York
Aegis, **13**
Gurney's Inn, **30**
Living Springs Lifestyle Center, **29**
Mohonk Mountain House, **26**
New Age Health Spa, **25**

Omega Institute, **22**
Sagamore Resort & Spa, **10**
Saratoga Spa State Park, **12**
Sivananda Ashram Yoga Ranch, **27**
Tai Chi Farm, **28**
Vatra Mountain Valley Lodge & Spa, **23**
Zen Mountain Monastery, **24**

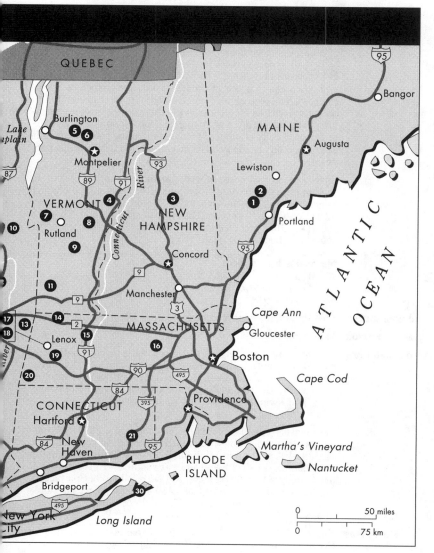

Vermont
The Equinox, **11**
Four Seasons
Healing, **4**
Golden Eagle, **6**
Green Mountain at
Fox Run, **9**
New Life, **7**
Topnotch at Stowe, **5**
Woodstock Inn &
Resort, **8**

followed by a body scrub with Hungarian mineral salts. The Personal Escape Plan lets you tailor a spa package to your daily needs.

Introduced into the recent renovation here was an abundance of country chic comfort, but standard inn rooms are small. Antiques, four-poster beds, ceiling fans, handwoven rugs, and lace curtains enhance the bedrooms. A 6-foot birdhouse in the lobby is home to a pair of finches. Public areas include a taproom with a large stone fireplace and a quiet sunroom full of palms and wicker. An alternative is staying in one of the charming villas that border a pond near the inn. Complete with four-poster bed, fully equipped kitchen, and living room, each unit can be rented on a daily basis in conjunction with the spa program.

Surrounded by 37 acres of woodland and a public golf course, the inn offers numerous diversions after workouts, including casino gaming. The Mashantucket Pequot Indian tribe, which owns Foxwoods Resort and Casino in nearby Ledyard, bought the inn in 1994 and changed the slightly faded look of public rooms and bedrooms.

Norwich Inn & Spa

607 W. Thames (Rte. 32), Norwich, CT 06360
Tel. 203/886–2401 or 800/275–4772
Fax 203/886–9483

Administration Vice President–general manager, Mark Vinchesi

Season Year-round

Accommodations 65 inn rooms including 16 suites, all with private bath, furnished with antiques and reproductions. The 44 villa suites come with fireplace, deck, Ralph Lauren prints, and kitchen serviced by the inn and have access to a private clubhouse, gym, and swimming pool. All rooms have TV, phones, air-conditioning.

Rates Personal Escape Plan per day $355–$455 single, $310–$470 per person double, includes accommodations, spa services, meals, gratuities, tax (2-night minimum midweek, 3-night minimum weekends; deposit $250). Getaway Country Retreat with 2 meals daily, $170–$260 single, $115–$165 double. Spa facility fee $10 per day, exercise class $10–$15. Day Spa packages $150–$300. Inn room $115–$185, single or double occupany; villa $200–$285. Add 12% tax. AE, DC, MC, V.

Meal Plans Three meals daily in Escape plan; breakfast and dinner in Country Retreat package. Breakfast choices include spa omelet or buffet with fruit, scrambled egg substitute, pancakes, cereals. Lunch includes butternut squash chowder, choice of grilled chicken salad or crab cakes, white bean and tuna salad or chicken fajita, spinach salad or spa pizza. Dinner entrées can be sole Florentine, roulade of veal, scallops on pasta, vegetable plate, Polynesian shrimp. Desserts include pear-cranberry parfait, baked apple, brown-rice pudding.

Services and Facilities **Exercise Equipment:** 5 Keiser Cam II pneumatic resistance units, 4-station Universal gym, Liferower, 5 Lifecycles, 4 Challenger treadmills, 3 StairMasters, free weights. **Services:** Facials, body massage, loofah scrub, hydrotherapy, herbal or clay wrap, fango bath, cellulite massage, thalassotherapy, aromatherapy massage, skin-care salon. **Swimming Facilities:** Indoor exercise pool, outdoor recreational pool. **Spa Facilities:** Men's and women's sauna and steam room, whirlpool, aerobics classes, private workouts. **Recreation Facilities:** 2 Har-Tru tennis courts (lighted). Bicycle rental, Norwich Golf Course.

Evening Programs: Cooking demonstrations, fitness lectures, color analysis.

In the Area Mystic Seaport Maritime Museum, General Dynamics submarine base in Groton, Old Lyme art center and historic homes. Cathedral of St. Patrick in Old Norwich, Essex summer beach colony, Eugene O'Neill Theater Center, Goodspeed Opera House in Haddam, Fort Shantok State Park, Gilette Castle.

Getting Here *From New York City.* By train, Amtrak from Grand Central Station to New London (90 mins). By air, scheduled flights to New London by American Airlines and USAir. By car, I–95 to I–395, Rte. 32 to Norwich (3 hrs). Hotel limousine service to the airport and Amtrak station in New London ($21 each way). Taxi and rental car available in Norwich and New London. Ample free parking.

Special Notes No smoking in the spa and dining room. Spa open Sun.–Thurs. 8–8, Fri.–Sat. 8 AM–9 PM. Minimum age in spa: 18.

Northern Pines Health Resort

Holistic health
Preventive medicine
Stress control
Weight management

Maine
Raymond Getting back to nature can be a healthy experience on the 68-acre lakefront Northern Pines Health Resort. The diet and fitness programs, based on a holistic approach, are designed to help participants develop a positive attitude toward weight loss and stress control; the transition is a gradual process, not a quick fix. Lifestyle management, rather than exercise, is emphasized.

Essentially a year-round self-help camp with a limited number of optional services, Northern Pines offers a program designed for men and women who want to take control of their lives. Campers range widely in age, but many are over 40. The affordable rates make it popular with singles. About 50 guests are resident in summer, 30 during the ski season, allowing for a friendly mix with lots of personal attention from the staff. At other times, cabins are rented for private retreats.

Each day begins with stretching exercises and a brisk walk through the woods, followed by a choice of focus sessions or aerobics. Instruction is available in transcendental meditation, art, and music. Morning and afternoon yoga are optional. Evenings offer more learning activities, from cooking classes to massage demonstrations. Fasting regimens are offered, and about 20% of the guests opt to go on a weeklong juice fast.

The camp's lakeside log cabins date from the 1920s and provide total seclusion for couples. New lodge rooms and cabins with two bedrooms are on the hillside amid towering pines, spruce, and hemlock. There are also two-person yurts (earth-covered cabins) that have carpeting and modern conveniences.

The informality and laid-back pace appeal to stressed-out professionals who come here to rejuvenate and relax.

Northern Pines Health Resort
Rte. 85, R.R. 1, Box 279, Raymond, ME 04071
Tel. 207/655–7624

Administration Owner-director, Marlee Turner; manager, John Baldwin

Season Year-round

Accommodations Private cabins and lodge rooms for 50. Some share a bathroom, others a communal facility; most have private toilet and shower. Well-worn wood furniture and buildings. Self-service laundry.

Rates 1-week program (Sun.–Sun.) $654.35–$1,18.43 single, $490.76–$838.82 per person double occupancy. Daily rate $109.06–$186.66 single, $81.79–$140 double. Tax included, add gratuities. 50% deposit per person. AE, MC, V.

Meal Plans Vegetarian diet. 3 daily buffets include pasta, salads with home-grown sprouts. Supervised fasts begin with 2 days of raw fruit, vegetables, followed by 3 days of juices and broth.

Services and Facilities **Exercise Equipment:** NordicTrack cross-country ski machine, 2 stationary bikes, Solaflex unit, slant board, Rebounders, free weights. **Services:** Massage, shiatsu, reflexology, aromatherapy, facials, hair treatment, herbal wrap, float tank sessions, Clearlight therapy. **Swimming Facilities:** Lake with sandy beach. **Recreation Facilities:** Hiking, canoeing, sailing; jogging trails. **Evening Programs:** Cooking demonstrations, massage techniques, sauna baths, salt rubs, videos, storytelling.

In the Area L. L. Bean store, ocean beaches, White Mountain Range, Acadia National Park, ferry trips to Nova Scotia, Portland's restored Old Port, summer theater, Portland Museum of Art, factory outlets in Freeport.

Getting Here *From Portland.* By car, I–95 to Exit 8, Rte. 302 northwest to Rte. 83 (45 mins). Rental car, taxi available.

Special Notes Summer camp for children, 3½ or 7 weeks. No smoking in public areas. 2 rooms accessible for people with disabilities.

Poland Spring Health Institute

Preventive medicine
Vibrant maturity

Maine
Poland Spring
An extended visit to Poland Spring Health Institute is more like taking a holiday in the country than being at a clinic. Poland Spring has been synonymous with healthy water for more than a century, largely due to a commercial bottling plant near the institute. Everything here that has to do with water—from drinking 8–10 glasses a day to soaking to steaming in a room where you receive body wraps preceding a massage—uses the Poland Spring. Additionally, following a vegetarian diet and participating in rigorous outdoor exercise are requirements of the program.

Just 10 guests are accommodated in old-fashioned comfort in the big New England farmhouse, where the average stay is two weeks. A special program for smoking cessation (14 days) is offered, as well as five-day nutrition and health seminar.

Guests work closely with specialists on diabetes and stress related ailments. A series of exercises and hydrotherapy treatments is prescribed that is appropriate for their physical condition. Testing by the medical office, when needed, carries an additional charge; everything else is included in the weekly fee.

This nonprofit, private wellness center was founded in 1979 and emphasizes Christian prayer. The 260-acre property is bounded by a 2-mile-long lake, with hiking and biking trails and a parcourse, and in winter guests can cross-country ski and ice skate.

Poland Spring Health Institute

R.F.D. 1, Box 4300, Summit Spring Rd., Poland Spring,
ME 04274
Tel. 207/998–2894; clinic 207/998–2795
Fax 207/998–2164

Administration Medical director, Richard A. Hansen, M.D.; program director, Ulla Hansen

Season Year-round

Accommodations 5 large rooms, most sharing a bath.

Rates Semiprivate room $745 a week with meals, private room $950, tax and service charge included. $200 nonrefundable reservation fee. No credit cards.

Meal Plans Salads and steamed vegetables, fresh fruit, and home-baked bread make up the diet rich in complex carbohydrates. Lunch buffet may consist of gluten roast, baked potato, green beans, salad. Dinner is fruit, salad, toast. No eggs, dairy products, fish, or meat is served.

Services and Facilities **Exercise Equipment:** Stationary and outdoor bikes. **Swimming Facilities:** Lake, steambath, whirlpool. **Recreation Facilities:** Boating, canoeing, biking, horseback riding; golf nearby. **Evening Programs:** Lectures on health-related subjects.

In the Area Shopping and sightseeing trips, Shaker village at Sabbathday Lake.

Getting Here *From Boston.* By air, Portland International Airport (40 mins). By car, I–95 to Rte. 302 (2 hrs). Courtesy transfers.

Special Notes No smoking indoors. Remember to bring sturdy walking shoes, rain gear, and personal medical records as requested. Special attention is paid to people with disabilities and heart patients.

Canyon Ranch in the Berkshires

Holistic health
Life enhancement
Luxury pampering
Preventive medicine
Vibrant maturity
Weight management

Massachusetts Canyon Ranch has a mind-and-body approach to fitness that
Lenox focuses on improving your lifestyle. Skiers can get in shape before tackling cross-country trails, and executives can use the latest biofeedback systems to de-stress. Attuned to the seasons in its outdoor activity, the ranch has an indoor fitness center like no other in the Northeast, complete with cardiovascular and weight training gymnasiums, racquetball, squash, and tennis courts, running track, 75-foot swimming pool, and separate locker rooms for men and women with saunas, steam rooms, inhalation rooms, and Jacuzzis.

The Arizona Canyon Ranch's guided hiking and biking programs have been adapted to the Berkshire terrain, but the specialty in the Berkshires is a regimen that nurtures both body and soul. Options include cutting-edge treatments, possibly daunting to a novice, which the schedulers can discuss if you call in advance of arrival. Instead of standard Swedish massage, consider the cranial-sacral, an osteopathic technique that releases tension in the neck, cranium, and spine. Services included with a spa program are based on the length of stay; other treatments can be booked à la carte. Also included is a health and fitness assessment with brief medical evaluation, to determine your exercise and nutrition needs. After a blood pressure check and body measurements, you're pretty much on your own.

The centerpiece of this 120-acre woodlands retreat is a mansion that dates from 1897—Bellefontaine—reminiscent of the Petit Trianon in Versailles. Dining at the mansion is a pleasant surprise; while the menu is annotated with calorie counts, you can sample many items. Uniformly tasty and satisfying, selections make staying within recommended guidelines easy. A daily Lunch and Learn demonstration cooking class provides ideas on how to prepare healthy fare at home. For single guests who want company, there is a Captain's Table.

Glass-walled walkways connect the inn, mansion, and fitness center. With more than 40 fitness classes daily, from yoga to line dancing, you might get frustrated if you try to fit it all in with treatments. For longer stays, you receive increasing price breaks for the health and healing services.

Opened in 1989, this northern outpost of Canyon Ranch has gained a high percentage of repeat visitors. The winning combination of having fun, learning something new, and feeling good can be addictive.

Canyon Ranch in the Berkshires
165 Kemble St. (Rte. 7A), Lenox, MA 01240
Tel. 413/637–4100 or 800/726–9900
Fax 413/637–0057

Administration Manager, Mary Ellen St. John

Season Year-round

Accommodations 120 rooms and suites, with New England–style functional furnishings. Rooms are air-conditioned and have telephone, TV with VCR, humidifier, digital clock radio with alarm. Terrycloth robe and thongs supplied; hair dryer and makeup mirror in bathrooms. Self-service laundry.

Rates 8-day/7-night package $1,860–$2,950 per person double occupancy, $2,394–$3,250 single. 3-night minimum package (arrival Sun.–Tues.) $829.50–$1,160 double, $1,008–$1,360 single. Service charge (18%) and tax added. 2 nights' deposit in advance. AE, MC, V.

Meal Plans Menu for à la carte choices at 3 meals daily. Also salad bar and breakfast buffet (fruit, cereals, breads). Selections include New England lobster with Burgundy sauce and scalloped potatoes, roasted turkey breast with garlic potatoes, breakfast items like blueberry pancakes, bread pudding with fruit coulis, sweet potato waffle, lox and bagel. Lunch choices include kiwi-cantaloupe soup, salmon with lemon-lime yogurt dressing, pasta with lobster-fennel sauce. Dinner entrées are Cantonese tempeh stir-fry, grilled vegetable strudel with bean ragout, tuna in pepper crust, osso bucco. Dessert can be nonfat frozen yogurt with chocolate sauce, apple empanada with cinnamon yogurt, chocolate mocha mousse, blackberry-orange cobbler. Vegetarian meals and special diets available. Coffee (decaf and regular), herbal tea, low-fat milk served; no alcohol.

Services and Facilities **Exercise Equipment:** State-of-the-art treadmills, stair climbers, stationary bikes, rowing machines, free weights, 2 Gravitrons, 2 NordicTracks, complete circuit of Keiser CAM 300 pneumatic units, 15 spinning bikes. **Services:** Herbal wraps, 9 types of massage, aromatherapy, hydrotherapy, acupuncture. Salon for hair, nail, skin care; holistic health counseling, biofeedback training; medical checkup and fitness evaluation; cooking class. **Swimming Facilities:** Indoor and 50-ft heated outdoor pool. **Spa Facilities:** Separate wings for men and women with sauna, steam room, Jacuzzi; studios for aerobics, yoga. **Recreation Facilities:** Cross-country skiing, hiking, bicycles for daily group outings, 3 indoor tennis courts (hard surface), 3 outdoor courts (Har-Tru), 2 racquetball courts, squash court, indoor track, canoeing, kayaking. **Evening Programs:** Visiting specialists speak on health and lifestyle topics.

In the Area Tanglewood Music Festival, Jacob's Pillow Dance Festival, the Sterling and Francine Clark Art Institute in Williamstown (summer theater), Hancock (Shaker Village), Appalachian Trail.

Getting Here *From Boston and New York City.* By car, Massachusetts Turnpike (I–90) (3 hrs). By train, daily Amtrak service to Rensselaer, NY, or Pittsfield, MA; complimentary transfer. By air, scheduled flights to Albany Airport or Bradley International at Hartford/Springfield. Taxi, rental car, limousine available. Complimentary transfers to/from airports.

Special Notes Minimum age of guests is 14. Smoking not permitted indoors or in public areas. Alcohol not permitted in public areas. Ramp entry to all buildings and facilities. Some bedrooms specially equipped for people with disabilities. Fitness Center open daily 6:30 AM–10 PM.

Kripalu Center for Yoga and Health

Kid fitness
Life enhancement
Preventive medicine
Spiritual awareness

Massachusetts
Lenox

Kripalu synthesizes the ancient science of yoga with modern approaches to holistic health and personal growth in a series of programs designed to fight stress and increase well-being. The Kripalu Center occupies a former Jesuit seminary (built in 1957) on a 300-acre wooded site adjacent to the Tanglewood Music Festival grounds. The four-story brick building has spartan accommodations, without daily maid service, in dormitories and small private rooms. But the spectacular views and gardens laid out by Frederick Law Olmsted, designer of New York's Central Park, provide a suitably expansive setting to experience spiritual balance.

On a typical day you have a choice of lectures, workshops, bodywork, and several yoga sessions. Mornings begin at 5:45 with chanting by members of the resident community; a yoga session from 6:45 to 8 AM followed by breakfast eaten in silence. Most of the guests, who can number over 300 at a time, start their day walking about the grounds, and join evening sessions of chanting.

In addition to the daily schedule, there are weeklong programs with such names as DansKinetics™, Men and Yoga, Life After 50, Self-Esteem, and Meditation Retreat. Women's issues are addressed in weeklong programs where practicing the gentle movements of Kripalu yoga becomes a metaphor for taking control of one's life. Options include all-juice fasting, an inner quest intensive, and outdoor treks.

Drawing on anatomy, psychology, and Sanskrit philosophy, these programs teach energy balancing techniques that can be used to develop a healthy lifestyle. An understanding of love is the basis for optional weekend programs, another is devoted to transforming stress by using meditation and yoga techniques. Each day is structured to involve you in a new awakening to your personal needs and powers.

Kripalu is family oriented and offers supervised programs for teenagers and children, encouraging noncompetitive and loving friendships. Teenagers can participate in the one-week "Coming of Age" outdoor camping program, which mixes yoga and sports, take leadership training, and learn communications skills. Creative exercise for children ages 9 to 13 is scheduled during summer. Sessions for boys and girls include a ropes course, shamanic journey, sweat lodge, and vision quest. Parents can enroll younger children on a daily fee basis in the supervised sessions of yoga, dance, and sports.

Getting oriented to the daily yoga regimen, you learn about optional classes such as "The Dance of Tennis," and can sign up for Kripalu bodywork, including soothing, meditative massage, and Phoenix Rising yoga therapy based on body posture training. Also available are large tiled whirlpool baths and wooden saunas, in separate facilities for men and women. In summer, there is swimming at a lake on the property, but no pool.

Kripalu teaches peace of mind, vibrant health, and spiritual attunement. Participants range in age from 16 to 80 and work together to rediscover themselves through a variety of inner-attunement techniques. Some come for a few days of rest and renewal; others seek compassion and healing through private consultation.

Kripalu Center for Yoga and Health
Box 793, Lenox, MA 01240
Tel. 413/448-3152 or 800/741-7353
Fax 413/448-3196

Administration Executive Director, Belinda Bothwick

Season Year-round

Accommodations 300 modest rooms in two categories: standard dormitory with 10–24 bunk beds (upper/lower), sheets, blankets, and towels provided; standard rooms for 2 with low twin beds or queen/double bed, access to hall bath; Standard Plus larger rooms with double, queen, or twin beds, have either private bath or access to hall bathroom, pre-made beds. No daily maid service; linens replaced weekly, towels daily. Lake-view rooms (2 beds) at extra cost.

Rates 2-night programs $340–$480 single, $200–$350 per person double, $180–$250 dormitory; 6-night workshop $1,035–$1,320 single, $570—$1,100 double, $495–$690 dormitory. Nightly rate $140–$195 single, $80–$155 double, dormitory $70–$80. Children's Program $45 per day; 6-day youth program $465. Deposit: 25% in advance. No refunds, but deposit can be applied to future programs. MC, V.

Meal Plans Program rate includes 3 vegetarian meals daily, buffet style, with whole grains and vegetables, dairy products. Full salad bar, several entrées, fresh-baked bread, variety of condiments. Hot or cold tea served at noon. Food is low in fat and sweeteners. Special diets accommodated by advance request. Silence is maintained during breakfast and lunch.

Services and Facilities **Services**: Kripalu massage, polarity, shiatsu, reflexology, Phoenix Rising yoga therapy. **Swimming Facilities**: Private lake. **Spa Facilities**: Saunas for men and women, whirlpools. **Recreation Facilities**: Skiing at Jimmy Peak (tel. 413/738-5500), bikes. **Evening Programs**: Communal meditation and chanting, Indian dancing and concerts.

In the Area Tanglewood Music Festival (July–Aug.), Jacob's Pillow (dance), Sterling and Francine Clark Art Institute in Williamstown, Hancock (Shaker Village Museum).

Getting Here *From Boston.* By car, Massachusetts Turnpike (I–90) to Exit B-3, Rte. 22 south, Rte. 102 east via West Stockbridge, Rte. 183 (2 hrs). By air, scheduled service to Albany or Bradley International Airport at Hartford/Springfield. By train, Amtrak has 1 train daily from Boston to Pittsfield, with connections to Lenox by Bonanza Bus (tel. 800/556–3815). Taxi, limousine service, and car rentals available in Lenox, Albany and Bradley airports. By bus, Peter Pan Lines (tel. 800/237–8747) to Lenox (3 hrs).

Special Notes Facilities and rooms specially equipped for people with disabilities. No smoking in or near the center. Remember to bring mat or cushion for meditation and yoga. Similar program offered near Philadelphia, PA, at Kripalu Yoga Ashram, Sumneytown.

The Kushi Institute of the Berkshires

Nutrition and diet
Spiritual awareness

Massachusetts Since 1978, the Kushi Institute has been in the forefront of
Becket macrobiotic research and education. The center offers an intensive seminar in cooking, plus four or five days of instruction on preventing cancer and heart disease. For newcomers to macrobiotics, there is a weeklong introductory course that includes exercise and massage.

Secluded on 600 acres of woodlands and meadows, the Berkshire center provides a peaceful, natural environment for study and relaxation. In a former Franciscan abbey, the bedrooms and working kitchen accommodate up to 15 participants in year-round programs. Several of these seminars are taught by founders Aveline and Michio Kushi.

The daily activities begin with a session of *do-in*, stretching exercises that are simple and easy to learn. Periods of meditation alternate with lectures and workshops in food preparation. Individuals, couples, and families often participate together.

The Kushi Institute of the Berkshires
308 Leland Rd., Box 7, Becket, MA 01223
Tel. 413/623–5742
Fax 413/623–8827

Administration Manager, Maria Pencke; program directors, Charles Millman, Christine Lefevre

Season Year-round. Macrobiotic residential seminar is offered twice a month, beginning on a Sun. and running through lunch the following Sat. Cooking intensives and topical seminars run 4–5 days. Multipart spiritual training seminar scheduled at various times of the year.

Accommodations 10 guest rooms in main lodge, simply furnished with 1 or 2 beds; 3 rooms have private bath or shower facility. New building scheduled for completion in 1997 has 12 large rooms with private bath.

Rates 6-day Way to Health seminar (Sun.–Sat.) with meals and a shared bedroom, $1,250 for first participant, $1,145 accompanying person. 1-month Dynamics of Macrobiotics program $2,900 per person double occupancy. 6-day cooking program $985 per person double. 3-day/2-night weekend $350 double. $100 advance deposit per person. AE, MC, V.

Meal Plans 3 meals daily, family style. Brown rice, miso soup, beans, and cooked vegetables with salads, natural desserts. Specialties include tofu and seitan dishes, sushi, noodles and pasta, amasake pudding.

Services and Facilities **Services:** Shiatsu massage, acupressure. **Swimming Facilities:** Nearby lake. **Evening Programs:** Workshops and discussions on diet and nutrition, informal entertainment.

In the Area Tanglewood Music Festival at Lenox (35 mins), summer theater and the Sterling and Francine Clark Art Institute in Williamstown (90 mins), Jacob's Pillow Dance Festival in Becket.

Getting Here *From Boston.* By car, Massachusetts Turnpike (I–90), exit for Lee (2½ hr). By bus, Peter Pan Bus Lines (tel. 800/237–8747) or Bonanza Bus Lines (tel. 800/556–3815) to Lee (3 hr). By air, Bradley International Airport at Hartford/Springfield. Free pickup at bus station in Lee; taxi, car rental available.

Special Notes No smoking on premises except in smoking lounge. 6-day macrobiotic summer conference held at nearby facility, $575 plus $220 lodging.

Maharishi Ayur-Veda Health Center

Holistic health
Nutrition and diet
Preventive medicine
Spiritual awareness
Stress control

Massachusetts Ancient Indian healing techniques and modern biofeedback
Lancaster technology are the means to relaxation and good health in the elegant mansion of the Maharishi Ayur-Veda Health Center. Ayurvedic medical treatments are based on an analysis of one's *dosha,* or physical and emotional type. The therapy includes a special diet related to body type, massage with warm oil and herbal essences, and total relaxation.

The healing process of *panchakarma* begins with a physical examination, pulse measurement, and a thorough questionnaire to determine whether you are *vata* (quick, energetic, movement prone), *pitta* (enterprising and sharp), or *kapha* (tranquil and steady). Therapy and diet are prescribed accordingly.

The medically supervised program is based on ayurvedic principles, as practiced in Asia. The center's doctors and registered nurses are trained in both Eastern and Western medicine. People with cancer and other diseases frequently come for treatment.

A daily two-hour session to rid the body of impurities includes massage, heat application, and a gentle laxative. Neuromuscular training may be recommended through yoga exercises. Aromatherapy is also available, and a course in transcendental meditation is taught for an extra fee. The combination of these treatments and meditation is said to be effective in stress reduction, encouraging balance at the most fundamental level of holistic health.

Furnished with large beds and heavy but comfortable chairs, the high-ceiling rooms retain a look of luxury from the 1920s, when this was the country cottage of a shipping magnate involved with the *Titanic.*

Maharishi Ayur-Veda Health Center
679 George Hill Rd.,
Box 344, Lancaster, MA 01523
Tel. 508/365–4549
Fax 508/368–0674

Administration Director, Jay Glaser

Season Year-round

Accommodations 14 bedrooms and several suites. Some small single rooms share a bath. All rooms air-conditioned.

Rates 1-week program $3,190–$4,190 single or double occupancy. Weeklong Ayur-Veda Rejuvenation program with suite $3,190–$4,190 single, $2,790–$3,790 per person double occupancy. Tax included, gratuities optional. MC, V.

Meal Plans 3 vegetarian meals daily in the formal dining room or guests' rooms. Indian rice and dal with cooked vegetables, herb seasoning, and cooked fruit. Specialties include vegetable pâté. Bland diet with few fats and no dairy products other than milk. Herbal teas and lassa as recommended by the doctor.

Services and Facilities **Services:** Transcendental meditation (TM) instruction in stress-management techniques, psychophysiological audio program, self-pulse diagnosis, aromatherapy. Most programs include massages, herbal steam bath, heat treatments, and internal cleansing. **Evening Programs:** Videotapes and lectures on health-related topics.

Getting Here *From Boston.* By car, Massachusetts Turnpike (I–90) west to Rte. 495 north, exit on Rte. 117 West to Rte. 70. Entrance is on George Hill Rd. (about 3 hrs). Limousine (tel. 800/666–4252), rental car available.

Special Notes No smoking.

The Option Institute

Holistic health
Life enhancement
Spiritual awareness
Stress control

Massachusetts
Sheffield

The goal at the Option Institute, a mountain retreat, is to nurture healthy attitudes toward life rather than emphasize physical fitness. Personal attitudes, beliefs, and feelings are examined to develop a fuller understanding of how to improve one's physical and mental health. Working in group sessions and private consultations, participants are taught to be more accepting of themselves, to learn to find alternatives, and to form more loving relationships.

Founded in 1983 by Barry Neil Kaufman and Samahira Kaufman, who have written and lectured on interpersonal relationships, the Option Institute sets out to provide a stimulating environment for people from all walks of life. Young professionals as well as families of children with special needs come for weekends and intensive programs of up to eight weeks. A participant is expected to gain a profound sense of energy and vigor from the release of tensions.

The Kaufmans lead problem-solving sessions on the lawn or in the living room of the main house. The 85-acre campus set amid grassy meadows, forests, and streams provides the setting that can inspire a fresh attitude toward life. The title of Kaufman's latest book sums up his philosophy: "Happiness is the Choice."

The Option Institute
2080 Undermountain Rd., Sheffield, MA 01257
Tel. 413/229–2100
Fax 413/229–8931

Administration	Program director, Susan Abrams
Season	Year-round
Accommodations	28 bedrooms in 2-story lodges, each with 2 beds, shared bath, and shower. The simply furnished buildings use natural wood and lots of windows for an open, rustic feeling.
Rates	3-day weekends (Thurs.–Sun.) $465 per person double occupancy, meals included. 1-week intensives exploring the impact of attitude on body and health $995 per person, double. Specially designed programs, about $150 per day. Some kitchen-equipped cottages for families with autistic or learning-impaired children. 50% deposit. MC, V.
Meal Plans	Vegetarian meals 3 times daily, buffet style. Specialties include vegetarian lasagna, whole-grain casseroles, legumes, seasonal vegetables, Greek salad, pasta. Limited amounts of eggs, cheese, milk.
Services and Facilities	**Services:** Swedish massage; private counseling. **Swimming Facilities:** Pond. **Recreation Facilities:** Hiking the Appalachian Trail; downhill skiing at Butternut and Catamount, cross-country skiing. **Evening Programs:** Workshops and group discussions on health, personal relationships, communication.
In the Area	Tanglewood Music Festival at Lenox, summer theater, the Sterling and Francine Clark Art Institute in Williamstown, Jacob's Pillow Dance Festival in Lee.
Getting Here	*From New York City.* By car, I–95 to the Massachusetts Turnpike, exit for Sheffield (3 hrs). By bus, Bonanza Bus Line (tel. 800/556–3815) from Port Authority Terminal to Sheffield (3 hrs). By air, Bradley International Airport at Hartford/Springfield. Free pickup at bus station in Sheffield; private limousine service from airport.
Special Notes	Limited access for people with disabilities. Special training for children who have mental disabilities, autism, or learning problems. No smoking indoors.

Rowe Conference Center

Spiritual awareness

Massachusetts
Rowe

Weekend programs to stimulate the mind on spiritual and health topics are the specialty of the Rowe Conference Center, a mountain retreat affiliated with the Unitarian Universalist Association. The white clapboard farmhouse and a pair of three-story lodges host a small, nondenominational community that offers a warm, uncompetitive atmosphere for personal and spiritual growth.

Surrounded by 1,400 acres of forest in western Massachusetts, Rowe provides a quiet place to discuss current health issues. Topics include clinical and spiritual healing, mastering the mind-body connection, and shamanism. Special weeks are devoted to adult recovery from alcohol problems, gender issues, and issues concerning single parenting.

The center is operated like a camp, but offers no organized fitness program and lets visitors take advantage of natural attractions on their own schedule. Recently expanded guest accommodations provide basic comforts, including a coed sauna. Guests do their own housekeeping; in the dormitory, bring your own bedding (linens available at extra charge).

Rowe Conference Center
Kings Highway Rd., Rowe, MA 01367
Tel. 413/339–4216

Administration	Administrative assistant, Judith Brink
Season	Year-round
Accommodations	13 private bedrooms, all with semiprivate bath and 2 beds, linens, and towels. Also dormitory rooms for 6–8 people.
Rates	Weekend program $125–$185 (depending on guests' financial situation). $100 dormitory. All require $100 deposit. MC, V.
Meal Plans	Meals from Fri. dinner to Sun. lunch. Vegetarian food served family style, including homemade bread, lentil loaf, squash casserole, and pasta primavera. Eggs and dairy products served, meat on request; special diets accommodated.
Services and Facilities	**Services:** Swedish massage. **Swimming Facilities:** Lake. **Recreation Facilities:** Hiking, cross-country and downhill skiing. **Evening Programs:** Discussion groups, sweat lodge.
Getting Here	*From Boston.* By car, Mass. Turnpike or Rte. 2 to Hwy. 91 in Greenfield, MA, then west on Rte. 2 (the Mohawk Trail) 19 mi to Rowe (3 hrs). By bus, Peter Pan Line (tel. 413/781–2900) to Greenfield (2¾ hrs). Pickup by Rowe on request.
Special Notes	Guest house accessible for people using wheelchairs. Summer camp for children; weeks for 4th graders to high school seniors. No smoking indoors. Bring sheets and blanket for dormitory rooms.

Smith College Adult Camp

Sports conditioning
Vibrant maturity

Massachusetts
Northampton

Based on the campus of Smith College in the scenic Berkshire Mountains, this one-week program offers cross-training with professionals and faculty members in a variety of sports. In addition to tennis, squash, swimming, and track there is a fully equipped gym.

Scheduled activities include aerobics classes, yoga, tai chi, and group hikes. Organized bike trips and outings to nearby attractions are available at no additional charge. Also offered is an introduction to stress control using biofeedback equipment.

Nutrition and dietary consultations with the staff nutritionist helps those concerned with weight loss. Meals are served cafeteria style in the college dining hall; vegetarian meals can be provided with advance request.

Limited to 35 participants, the program attracts a mix of men and women. Average age, 50; minimum age, 22.

Smith College Adult Camp
Northampton, MA 01063
Tel. 413/585-3975
Fax 413/585-2712

Administration	Manager, Donald Segal
Season	June
Accommodations	Dormitory rooms with 2 beds, shared bathroom. Laundry room.
Rates	$750 for 6-day program (Sun.–Sat.), includes room, meals, activities, 50% advance payment. No credit cards.
Meal Plan	3 meals daily.
Services and Facilities	**Services:** Massage. **Exercise Equipment:** Eagle weight training gym, indoor and outdoor running tracks. **Swimming Facilities:** 25-yd indoor pool, lake. **Recreation Facilities:** 12 indoor tennis

courts (lighted, Mondo surface), 4 outdoor tennis courts, 6 squash courts. **Evening Programs:** Orienteering, panel discussions, dances, cookouts.

Getting Here *From Boston.* By car, Mass. Turnpike (I–90) to Hwy. 91, Northampton exit (2½ hrs). By bus, Peter Pan Lines (tel. 413/781–2900) to Northampton (3 hrs). Rental car available.

Waterville Valley Resort

Nonprogram resort

New Hampshire
Waterville Valley

Surrounded by mountain peaks and forests of green fir and silver birch, this 500-acre recreational complex became a four-season resort in 1987 with the opening of a $2-million sports center. The use of the facilities is a bonus for guests at the deluxe lodges and condominiums of the Waterville Valley Resort. In warm weather, you can play tennis on one of 18 clay courts, use mountain bikes or in-line skates, or play golf with a $20 recreation pass sold daily at your lodge. In winter, world-class downhill and cross-country skiing covers 225 acres. Services and classes at the center are offered à la carte.

A full-service ski shop at the foot of Mt. Tecumseh rents equipment and offers instruction. Thirty-five downhill trails are ranked for beginner, intermediate, and advanced skiers. Snow-making equipment assures good snow conditions from mid-November through mid-April. The Cross Country Ski Center at one end of the valley is another attraction. Fourteen trails lead into the heart of the forest.

The Sports Center, open every day of the year, offers indoor and outdoor tennis and swimming, racquetball, squash, and a weights room. A coed sauna and Jacuzzi are available in addition to separate facilities and steam rooms for men and women.

The range of activities makes Waterville Valley a good choice for family vacations. A community bus service provides free transportation all day.

Waterville Valley Resort
Box 417, Waterville Valley, NH 03215

Tel. 603/236–8303; reservations 800/468–2553

Administration Sports center manager, Ralph Trinque

Season Year-round

Accommodations 4,000 beds in quarters that range in variety from deluxe chalet-style inns to modest condominium apartments. Leading choices are Snowy Owl Inn, Black Bear Lodge, and fully equipped 2-story houses. Bookings through the lodging bureau.

Rates 1-bedroom apartments at the Black Bear $98–$281 daily for 1 to 2 persons. Add 8% tax. 50% advance payment. AE, DC, MC, V.

Meal Plans No meals in ski or spa packages. Spa food at 2 restaurants: O'-Keefe's has vegetarian burgers, fitness salads; Chili Peppers has light fare such as broiled fish, fruit plate with cottage cheese, roast chicken.

Services and Facilities **Exercise Equipment:** 4 Nautilus, 1 lats unit, Lifecycle, Alpine stairclimber, rowing machine, free weights. **Services:** Swedish massage, aerobics classes, aquacise. **Swimming Facilities:** Indoor and outdoor 25-m pools, pond. **Recreation Facilities:** 2 indoor tennis courts, 2 racquetball courts, squash court, indoor running track, golf, canoeing, horseback riding, skiing, ice

skating, hiking, sailing, biking. **Evening Programs:** Seasonal
entertainment.

In the Area Mt. Washington cog railway.

Getting Here *From Boston.* By car, Rte. 3 to I–93, exit for Waterville (28),
then 11 mi on Rte. 49 (2½ hrs). By bus, Greyhound to North
Conway, NH (3 hrs). By air, scheduled flights to Manchester,
NH. Rental car, Valley shuttle bus available.

Special Notes Ramps and elevator in Sports Center will accommodate
wheelchairs. Sports Center open daily 8 AM–9:30 PM. Ski
camps, tennis camps, and outdoor wading pool for children. No
smoking in Sports Center.

Aegis

Spiritual awareness

New York A philosophy of the interrelatedness of all spiritual traditions
New Lebanon is at the heart of the study programs offered by Aegis in historic Shaker buildings on the grounds of a 430-acre mountaintop compound. Life is celebrated here in all its diversity
with topics ranging from Taoist healing to Zen dance. A visit
is an experience in living together harmoniously and learning
how to share life's bounty.

Founded in 1975 as an esoteric school for the Sufi Order in the
West, the permanent community here is known as the "Abode
of the Message." The teachings of their spiritual leaders, notably Pir Vilayat Inayat Khan, focus on the nature of healing.
The Sufi path is explored at weekend retreats and in a summer series of workshops and retreats, which attract about 75
participants.

Aegis brings together people from diverse walks of life in a
common quest for self-fulfillment and inner growth. You can
pitch a tent or work in the kitchen at the Abode as part of a
personal retreat. The program office provides rooms in the
Shaker buildings for seekers of rest and relaxation. For those
in need of guidance, private retreat huts are available, and
meals are delivered.

Aegis
R.D. 1, Box 1030D, New Lebanon, NY 12125
Tel. 518/794–8095 or 518/794–8090

Administration Director, Donald Halley

Season Year-round

Accommodations 30 rooms in Shaker village wooden buildings, 20 personal retreat huts, 25 dormitory rooms with 2–4 beds, camping space
in the woods. Buildings have no electricity or heat. Wash-
houses have hot showers and toilets for men and women. Bedding and towels not provided.

Rates 2-day weekend tuition $125 plus lodging. Rooms for two $30,
single $40 per night, including meals. Tent space $20 with
meals. 50% advance payment. Credit cards: MC, V.

Meal Plans 3 vegetarian meals a day, with dairy and nondairy choices.

Services and **Services:** Massage, Reiki, shiatsu, reflexology, Jin Shin Jyutsu.
Facilities **Swimming Facilities:** Nearby lakes. **Recreation Facilities:** Hiking, cross-country skiing.

Getting Here Between Albany, NY, and Pittsfield, MA, the Abode provides
pickup service at Bonanza Bus Lines (tel. 800/556–3815)
station, and at Albany airport. *By train*, Amtrak to Albany

(2 hrs). *From New York City.* By car, Taconic Pkwy. north to Rte. 295, Rte. 22 to Rte. 20 in New Lebanon.

Special Notes No smoking in communal areas. Remember to bring sleeping bag or bedding, warm clothing, insect repellent. No children.

Gurney's Inn

Luxury pampering

New York
Montauk
At the International Health and Beauty Spa the specialty is seaside seawater therapy. On the tip of Long Island, the spa at Gurney's Inn offers all the amenities of a big beach resort and draws on the ocean for inspiration. The sybarite can revel in seaweed baths, swim in a 60-foot indoor seawater pool, have a seaweed facial, and dine on seafood while enjoying a view of the sea. Modeled after European spas where ocean water is an integral part of advanced hydrotherapy, Gurney's adds aerobics, stress control, diet programs, and beauty salon services. For cardiovascular and strength training, a sea-view exercise room offers a full line of equipment, plus personal trainers.

Sea air and miles of white sandy beach come with your room at the inn. Brisk morning walks along the shore start the daily program. Add to that a 14-station parcourse, with instruction twice daily, for exercise at your own pace. Invigorated by the ocean, you can join an aquatics exercise class in the pool, relax in a sunken Roman bath, or swim in the surf.

The diversity of the seawater treatments makes Gurney's special among spas on this side of the Atlantic. Filtered and heated water from the ocean is pumped into whirlpools designed for underwater massage. Mixed with Argilite mud, micronized seaweed is applied to your body in a mineral-rich gel as part of a wrap treatment that helps promote balance and healing in the body while relieving many symptoms of arthritis and stress. Then there are body scrubs with salt from the Dead Sea. Treatments are scheduled 8 AM–10 PM. Spa-plan guests receive priority.

Anti-aging programs are offered October through April. Working with a professional team to develop a personal health strategy, your sessions can include an exercise physiologist, nutritionist, biofeedback therapist, and certified nurse. The spa building is a world apart from the convention and time-share vacation crowds that keep Gurney's Inn busy much of the year. The pool and classes are open to all guests, however, and this puts a strain on the facilities during the peak summer season. For peace and quiet, schedule your visit when the beach crowd goes home or during the winter.

Montauk offers special attraction for anglers: Charter boats offer deep-sea fishing excursions, and fly-fishing guides, lessons, and gear can be booked (tel. 616/324–7979 or 800/773–6427).

Gurney's Inn
Old Montauk Hwy., Montauk, NY 11954
Tel. 516/668–2345 or 800/848–7639,
spa 516/668–2509

Administration Innkeepers, Lola and Nick Monte; spa director, Margaret McNeill-Byrnes

Season Year-round

Accommodations 126 bedrooms in time-share rentals, including suites and cottages. None connect to the spa. All are air-conditioned, have full modern bathroom, TV, telephone; some with sea view from balcony.

Rates 3-day Escape package without room $556; lodging $145–$180 per person, double occupancy, $235–$280 single. Autumn-Winter 5-day Health and Beauty Plan with lodging and meals $1,400 per person, double occupancy. Daily facility fee for non-package visit $20; 1-day package $196.50. Add 15% service charge, 8.25% tax. 25% payable in advance. AE, DC, MC, V.

Meal Plans 3 spa meals daily included in packages. Spa cuisine in a private room and the main dining room. Calorie-controlled meals (1,000–1,200 calories per day) low in salt and sugar. Lunch can begin with tortellini en brodo or egg-drop soup, 3-bean salad; entrée choice of manicotti, grilled salmon, steak stir-fry, or whole-wheat pasta. Dinner entrées include seafood brochette, paella, vegetarian lasagna, chicken breast with asparagus. Herbal teas and espresso are available, as are vegetarian meals on request.

Services and Facilities **Exercise Equipment:** 10-unit HammerStrength weight training circuit, 2 Lifesteps, 2 Lifecycles, Maxicam, 2 treadmills, dumbbells (3–75 lbs), Olympic plates (2½–45 lbs). **Services:** Massage, (Swedish, cranial-sacral), Reiki, shiatsu, acupressure, reflexology, loofah scrub, herbal or seaweed wrap, facial, fango pack, Agrilite mud pack, aromatherapy, seawater private bath, health/fitness profile, biofeedback, private training, full-service salon. **Swimming Facilities:** Indoor pool, ocean beach. **Recreation Facilities:** Hiking, jogging, disco dancing, yoga; tennis, horseback riding, and fishing nearby; golf at Montauk Downs public course. **Evening Programs:** Lectures on health and nutrition; dancing and entertainment.

In the Area Historic homes, art galleries, whale-watching, museum, wineries, and boutiques in Montauk; summer theater; bird-watching.

Getting Here *From Connecticut and New England.* By ferry, at New London and Bridgeport. *From New York City.* By bus, Hampton Jitney and Montauk Express. By car, Long Island Expressway to Sunrise Highway (Rte. 27). By train, from Grand Central Station, the Long Island Railroad (tel. 212/526–0900) has daily round-trip schedules. By air, USAir has scheduled flights to MacArthur Airport at Islip, private planes land at Montauk and East Hampton airports. Courtesy car meets trains and private planes. Rental car, taxi available.

Special Notes Children's swimming at midday and after 6 PM; under 18 not permitted in spa treatment areas. No smoking in the spa.

Living Springs Lifestyle Center

Preventive medicine
Vibrant maturity

New York
Putnam Valley A budget-priced alternative to health resorts, the Living Springs Lifestyle Center, run by the Seventh-Day Adventists, is a residential retreat where you can improve your life and tone your body with spa-quality treatments. The center is non-denominational and open to persons of all faiths, particularly to people over 50 who want to recharge their lives holistically. The educational and conditioning programs focus on disease prevention, stress control, nutrition, weight management, and quitting smoking.

Set on 68 acres at the edge of a clear lake in the Taconic Mountains, the retreat, which was founded in 1977 as a non-profit corporation, offers a homelike atmosphere that can be conducive to establishing lasting new habits. Healthy cooking is taught, and methods for preventing heart and other diseases are discussed. Daily exercise is geared to your level of fitness and personal goals.

The holistic approach teaches you to coordinate mind and body, addressing weight management, smoking cessation, and lifestyle enhancement. Following a consultation, you can schedule hydrotherapy treatments to promote healing or focus on relaxation. Saunas, alternating hot and cold showers, and exercise are also prescribed.

Natural foods and lots of spring water are key nutritional features, and the retreat specializes in vegetarian meals that are high in complex carbohydrates and fiber and free of fats and oil. (Also note that the kitchen is kosher.)

Living Springs Lifestyle Center
136 Bryant Pond Rd., Putnam Valley, NY 10579
Tel. 914/526–2800 or 800/729–9355

Administration	Manager, Wesley Rozelle, M.D.
Season	Year-round
Accommodations	2-level modern lodge with 5 semiprivate rooms, 3 private rooms.
Rates	7-day program $1,095 in private room, $795 semiprivate. $100 payable in advance. AE, MC, V.
Meal Plans	3 meals a day, buffet style. Lunch can include steamed vegetables, cashew chow mein, salad, fruit. No coffee or spices.
Services and Facilities	**Exercise Equipment:** Treadmill, rowing ergometer, 2 stationary bikes, outdoor par course. **Swimming Facilities:** Spring-fed lake. **Recreation Facilities:** Hiking and nature trails, boating, cross-country skiing, biking. **Evening Programs:** Lectures and films on health-related topics.
In the Area	West Point, Bear Mountain.
Getting Here	*From New York City.* By car, Taconic Pkwy. to Rte. 6 exit. By train, from Grand Central Station, Metro-North Commuter to Peekskill (free transfers). Pickup at airports on request. Courtesy car available.
Special Notes	No smoking.

Mohonk Mountain House

Life enhancement
Sports conditioning

New York
New Paltz

Nature walks have been a way of life at Mohonk Mountain House in the Hudson River Valley since 1869, and members of the founding family of Quakers are still active in organizing health and fitness weeks. Here at the spa where "The Road To Wellville" was filmed, hikers, runners, and cross-country skiers choose from more than 100 miles of trails, paths, and carriage roads that link scenic sites within the 2,500 acres of private woodland. Others ride horseback or enjoy the crystal-clear lake.

In the hotel, a turreted and gabled Victorian castle that rambles an eighth of a mile and accommodates up to 500 guests, 19th-century manners and ambience are preserved. Choice rooms in the towers have original Victorian woodwork, working fireplace, balcony. There is no bar or smoking in public rooms, and a dress code is in effect for dinner.

Golfers are challenged by a nine-hole par-35 course designed along Scottish lines, complete with driving net, and there is a lighted 18-hole putting green. Equestrians can join guided trail rides (English or Western) at the resort's stables. In winter, the riding trails are groomed for cross-country skiing. Indoors, the fitness center has exercise equipment, an aerobics studio with ballet bar, and saunas and showers. Low-impact aerobics and stretch classes are scheduled regularly, as are classes in nutrition and back care. Physiologists, sports trainers, and fitness buffs get together at Mohonk for exercise workshops and lectures. Programs range from designing a personal fitness plan to nutrition and walking. Weeks are devoted to quitting smoking, stress management, women's issues, and the holistic way.

Mohonk Mountain House
Lake Mohonk, New Paltz, NY 12561
Tel. 914/255–1000, 914/255–4500, or 800/772–6646
Fax 914/256–2161

Administration	President, Bert Smiley; general manager, Gillian Murphy; fitness director, Geri Owens
Season	Year-round
Accommodations	273 rooms, many with balcony and working fireplace, some with washbasin only, some sharing an adjoining bath. Rooms and bed-sitting rooms with private bath, double or twin beds.
Rates	Rooms and 3 meals daily $109–$291 single occupancy, $229–$391 for 2 persons; tower room with fireplace $391–$475 for 2 persons. Add 15% service charge, taxes. Deposit: 1 night payable in advance. AE, DC, MC, V.
Meal Plans	3 meals and afternoon tea included with room. The menu follows the American resort tradition, with some light selections. Buffet-style lunch.
Services and Facilities	**Exercise Equipment:** 6-station Universal gym, 2 Schwinn Air Dyne bikes, 2 Monark bikes, StairMaster, Lifecycle, NordicTrack cross-country unit, hand weights. **Services:** Massage. **Swimming Facilities:** Mohonk Lake, ½-mi-long 60-ft-deep freshwater lake with swimming and diving areas. **Spa Facilities:** Separate saunas for men and women. **Recreation Facilities:** 6 tennis courts (4 clay, 2 Har-Tru), platform tennis courts, 9-hole golf course, ice skating and downhill skiing, croquet. **Evening Programs:** Concerts, films, dancing, speakers on health and fitness.
In the Area	Carriage rides, trail rides, hayrides.
Getting Here	*From New York City.* By car, New York State Thruway (I–87) to New Paltz (Exit 18). By train, Amtrak to Poughkeepsie. By bus, from Port Authority Terminal. (Other cities served by Adirondack Trailways.) Hotel transfer service to bus or train station and New York City and airports.
Special Notes	Weekday outdoor adventures and walks for children. No smoking in public areas indoors.

New Age Health Spa

Holistic health
Life enhancement
Nutrition and diet
Sports conditioning
Weight management

New York
Neversink

Committed to a holistic lifestyle, the New Age Health Spa offers a wide range of physical treatments. The tranquil, 160-

acre farm estate in the Catskill Mountains is an ideal setting in which to balance body, soul, and mind.

The farm is a full-fledged spa whose owners live on the grounds, join the hiking groups, and are active in all the decision-making. They have added sophisticated bodywork as well as stress management, yoga, and preventive medicine therapies since the spa opened in 1986. Challenging outdoor activities include an Outward Bound type of ropes course on a 45-foot alpine tower, used for building corporate teamwork and teaching self-reliance. Excursions are scheduled to nearby state parks for rock climbing, hiking, and cross-country skiing.

No one goes hungry here, but diet options are offered at a dedicated table in the dining room. The daily menu is planned along guidelines set by the American Heart Association (high carbohydrates; low protein, fats, and salt; no sugar). For determined dieters, "juicing" is the recommended program for fast weight loss, and supervised participants are advised to sign up for an accompanying colonic cleansing, a water treatment that serves to speed up "detoxification" of the body. Other food plans include Spartan (700- to 800-calorie vegetarian) and Rotation (900- to 1,100-calorie plan consisting of vegetarian meals alternating with a fish, turkey, or chicken meal). Much of the salad fixings and fresh vegetables come from the spa's organic greenhouse, where lessons in growing sprouts are offered.

The programs allow you to set your own pace; opt for exercises in Zen meditation, a tai chi class, or a 3- to 5-mile aerobic walk before breakfast. Move on to a yoga class or weight-management lecture followed by a series of innovative low-impact aerobics and floor-work classes that enable you to match activities to your energy level.

With the expansion of the spa building in 1996, there are 14 massage rooms and two wet rooms, and separate saunas and steambaths for men and women. Optional treatments include ayurvedic botanical exfoliation, body wraps with Austrian moor mud or French sea algae, reflexology, and a combination with paraffin coating of hands and feet.

The New Age Health Spa offers proven alternative healing therapies and consultation with experts in dealing with stress, diet, and personal communication. One of the most popular speakers charts your astrological cycles in a private session. Seminars and workshops provide working models for preventive medicine programs that can complement your personal health regimen.

Popular with young Manhattanites and knowledgable spa goers from all over, the spa has a no-frills attitude but provides comprehensive programs at budget prices.

New Age Health Spa
Rte. 55, Neversink, NY 12765
Tel. 914/985–7601 or 800/682–4348
Fax 914/985–2467

Administration Owner-directors, Stephanie Paradise and Werner Mendel; fitness director, Rhoda Goldstein

Season Year-round

Accommodations 39 rooms in 2-story cottages, each with "country charm" decor, air-conditioning, private bath. TV and phone in main house lounge.

Rates 1-week package, including diet and exercise program, $854.48–$1,151.92 per person double occupancy, $1,224.08–$1,521.52 single. Miniweek package (Sun.–Fri.) with 2 spa services

$665–$935 per person double, $965–$1,235 single. Daily rate $133–$187 double, $193–$247 single. Add 17% service charge, 8% tax. 25% payable in advance. AE, MC, V.

Meal Plans 3 meals daily included in rates. Salad bar and fresh vegetarian diet available at all times. Dinner entrées include vegetarian lasagna, poached fish, pasta, baked chicken. Special dietary requests accommodated. Juice fast available with staff consultation.

Services and Facilities **Exercise Equipment:** 2 StairMasters, 3 Trotter 645 treadmills, Cat's Eye rowing machine, NordicTrack, 3 Tectrix bikes, free weights, Smith machine, 11-unit Trotter Galileo strength training circuit. **Services:** Massage (Swedish, shiatsu, therapeutic), reflexology, paraffin wrap or hand/foot treatment, herbal wrap, loofah scrub, colonic, mud or algae body mask, paraffin body waxing, aromatherapy. Salon for hair, nail, skin care, ayurveda facial, Shirodhara hair and scalp treatment, glycolic exfoliation. **Swimming Facilities:** Indoor lap pool (30´), outdoor pool. **Recreation Facilities:** Volleyball; cross-country skiing and snowshoeing. **Evening Programs:** Talks on healthy living and personal growth; workshops in astrology, psychology, awareness; movies, disco.

In the Area Grossinger resort (golf), Lake Minnewaska (nature preserve), Hudson Valley (historic homes, wineries).

Getting Here *From New York City.* By New Age van, express service Fri. and Sun. morning and return ($40 each way) at 72nd St. and Madison Ave. By bus, Greyhound from Port Authority (2 hrs). By car, New York State Thruway (I–87) to the Catskills, Rte. 17 to Liberty, Rte. 52 and 55E to Neversink (2 hrs). Local taxi available.

Special Notes No children under 16; no alcohol, smoking, or drugs. Bring clock, flashlight, and personal radio with earphones.

Omega Institute

Holistic health
Life enhancement
Preventive medicine
Spiritual awareness
Stress control

New York
Rhinebeck

Call it a New Age mecca or a quest for higher consciousness; it's chiefly an adult summer camp where you can strive to develop physical and mental balance alongside people on the leading edge of preventive medicine and holistic health.

Sometimes referred to as Esalen East, the Omega Institute brings together people of different backgrounds—doctors, lawyers, housewives, college students—who want to function more positively as individuals and as members of society. More than 250 educational workshops, from Native American studies to wellness and stress control, last two to five days each. The classes, including diet workshops and "Shamanic Journey, Power and Healing," are led by faculty and guest lecturers comprising a veritable *Who's Who* of the human potential movement.

About 100 miles north of Manhattan, the rustic, 80-acre campus hasn't changed much since the Institute took over a former summer camp in 1977. A recent addition is the Wellness Center, complete with sauna, massage rooms, flotation tanks, nutrition and stress-reduction counseling, and holistic medical consultations. On campus are a theater, gift shop and bookstore, and café. Yet there's not a Nautilus gym in sight.

A Wellness Week integrates study and practice of a healthy lifestyle. Omega's core faculty offers a sound medical understanding of the roles that diet, nutrition, exercise, and fitness play in the ongoing development of health. Through experiential sessions in massage, yoga, tai chi, group support, and games, each participant forms a positive attitude toward wellness.

On a typical morning, when as many as 350 people are camping out or living in the dormitories and cottages, groups assemble before breakfast for optional yoga, meditation, and tai chi sessions. For first-timers there are introductory weekends full of experiential learning, as well as workshops in self-discovery, health, and wellness. It's an easy way to join a vibrant community, make new friends, and learn a lot about yourself.

Omega Institute
260 Lake Dr., Rhinebeck, NY 12572
Tel. 914/266–4444 or 800/944–1001
Fax 914/266–4828

Administration Program director, Thomas Valente; general manager, Skip Backus; president and cofounder, Stephan Rechtschaffen, M.D.

Season June–mid-Oct. Winter programs in the Caribbean, New Mexico, and New England.

Accommodations Rooms in cottages, dormitory beds, camping facilities. Private rooms with shared bath. No rooms have TV, phone, or air-conditioning.

Rates 5-day Omega Wellness Program tuition $285–$305 plus lodging. Accommodations in dormitory for 5-day program $210; cabin rooms for 5-day program $295–$365 per person, double occupancy (limited number of single rooms available). 2-day lodging $105 dormitory, $150–$185 in cabin; Introductory weekend $90. Campsites $43 per person, per day. Meals and tax included in lodging fee. 50% payment in advance. MC, V.

Meal Plans Cafeteria service of 3 meals daily included in lodging. Mainly vegetarian, with some fish and dairy products. Many locally grown fresh fruits and vegetables. Whole grains, beans, and bean products. No artificial sweeteners.

Services and Facilities **Swimming Facilities:** Private lake. **Services:** Massage, aromatherapy, counseling in nutrition, antistress, wellness. **Recreation Facilities:** Basketball, canoeing, jogging, tennis, volleyball. **Evening Programs:** Concerts, films, lectures.

In the Area The historic village of Rhinebeck, Old Rhinebeck Aerodrome.

Getting Here *From New York City.* By car, New York State Thruway (I–87) or the Saw Mill River Parkway north to the Taconic Parkway, Bull's Head Rd. west to Lake Dr. (2 hrs); By train, Amtrak from Grand Central Station stops at Rhinecliff, where Omega vans pick up guests (for train schedules, tel. 800/872–7245). By bus, Bonanza Bus Line (tel. 800/556–3815) from Port Authority Terminal to Rhinebeck (2 hrs). Omega vans pick up in Rhinebeck at Beekman Arms Hotel.

Special Notes Some cottages and facilities equipped for people with disabilities. Family Week in Aug. includes nature studies and creative games for children. No smoking indoors.

Sagamore Resort & Spa

Luxury pampering

New York Surrounded by the Adirondack Mountains and set on a 70-acre
Bolton Landing private island, the huge white clapboard Sagamore Resort &

Spa suggests an escape to the quiet pleasures of a bygone era. Rejuvenated by private owners, the resort now includes a modern health club, indoor swimming pool, and indoor tennis and racquetball courts. Fitness classes are scheduled throughout the day, from walks and low-impact aerobics to water exercise, at no charge to hotel guests who book one or more spa treatments and services.

The health club has separate sauna, whirlpool, and steam-room facilities for men and women. There is a coed exercise area, with sunlit, airy space to accommodate the equipment, and a wet area specially equipped for body scrubs. Appointments are made for treatment on an à la carte basis, which includes the daily charge for club facilities and workout clothing. A flexible spa plan is available for two days or more.

In addition to massage, facials, and beauty makeovers, the specialty here is moormud therapy using natural healing mud in body wraps, facial and scalp treatments, and packs for sports injuries. You can wind down your treatment with a full-body rubdown using a mixture of sea salt and massage oil that leaves your skin tingling. After the scrub with loofah sponges, the salt mixture is hosed off. Next, a coating of Adirondack herbal and floral creams leaves you with a glowing feeling. The cost: $35–$80 for each treatment; or this could be included as part of a two-day spa package. (A 17% gratuity is added to the cost of services.)

The classic 1930 hotel is on the site of the original Sagamore, opened in 1893. Recent additions include seven lakeside lodges. At the fitness center you can work out and enjoy an unbroken vista of Adirondack State Park. Don't miss the par-70 Donald Rose golf course, full of bobsledders in winter, even if just for dinner at the clubhouse.

Sagamore Resort & Spa

Box 450, Bolton Landing, NY 12814
Tel. 518/644–9400 or 800/358–3585
Fax 518/644–3033

Administration	Manager, Robert MacIntosh; spa director, Damian Alessi
Season	Year-round
Accommodations	350 rooms, including 178 deluxe suites, and lodges. The main hotel's 100 rooms embody history and contemporary comfort. Condominium-style suites in lodges were refurbished in 1996.
Rates	Weekend Spa Sampler $289 plus lodging. Spa Day $99–$199 (accommodations not included). Rooms $89–$300 per night in main hotel. Deposit: 1 night payable in advance. Add $4 daily service charge, tax. Spa gratuity and tax included in package rate. AE, MC, V.
Meal Plans	Meals not included in spa plan. Choices from Trillium restaurant's dinner menu include as appetizers seafood terrine or fresh berries, spinach consommé, green salad. Entrée choices include poached salmon, grilled chicken breast, linguine. Desserts are apple strudel or blueberry cake, Grand Marnier Bavarian. 5 restaurants provide low-calorie options, emphasizing fish and local produce.
Services and Facilities	**Exercise Equipment:** 10-station Keiser training circuit, 3 StairMasters, 2 Lifecycles, 4 Trotter treadmills, 3 Concept 2 rowers, Windracer, NordicTrack, dumbbells (3–50 lbs). **Services:** Massage (Swedish, shiatsu, sports), loofah salt glow, reflexology, facials, herbal wrap, seaweed or mud wrap, aromatherapy, Jurlique botanical facial; beauty salon for hair, nail, and skin care. **Swimming Facilities:** Indoor pool, lakeside docks.

Recreation Facilities: 18-hole golf course, 4 outdoor lighted and 2 indoor tennis courts, jogging trails, hiking, boating, water sports, snowsledding, ice skating, cross-country and downhill skiing, tobogganing, horseback riding and horse-drawn sleigh rides. **Evening Programs:** Dancing, jazz club, scheduled entertainment.

In the Area Cruises on Lake George aboard a classic 72-foot Morgan wooden yacht, the Adirondack Museum (history and art), Fort Ticonderoga (circa 1755 war memorabilia), the Hyde Collection (European and American art), Saratoga Springs' Victorian area, summer season of concerts, ballet, and horse races (Saratoga Springs), Colonial Fort William Henry (setting for *Last of the Mohicans*), Lake George Village.

Getting Here *From New York City.* By car, 4-hr drive on the New York State Thruway (I–87) to Exit 24 (Bolton Landing). By air, Albany is served by Eastern, USAir, and Continental airlines, among others. By train, Amtrak to Fort Edward, from Boston or New York City. A hotel car meets guests at Albany or the train station ($50 round-trip).

Special Notes No smoking in the spa. Facilities charge ($15) includes shorts, T-shirts, robe, slippers.

Saratoga Spa State Park

Taking the waters

New York
Saratoga Springs

Once a rival of Europe's glamorous spas, Saratoga is better known today for thoroughbred racing and the arts. But the mineral springs at Saratoga Spa State Park remain a major attraction, and plans are underway to develop a complete health and fitness center in some of the original buildings. The Roosevelt Bath is undergoing renovations through mid-1997; meanwhile the Lincoln Baths has expanded the list of services offered, from mineral bath to herbal wrap and sea mud packs.

The mineral-rich water bubbles up all around the town, but at the park you can drink for free; in town you pay for the bottled water. Pick up a map from the Old Drink Hall, downtown, or at the spa visitor center operated by the State of New York. If you park at the Geyser Picnic Area lot and follow the path, you will encounter three of the best-known springs, all of the saline-alkaline variety. First is the Hayes Well, which has a breathing port at one side for inhaling carbon dioxide—said to be good for the lungs and sinuses. The gas also carbonates the water and powers geysers that spout up 10 feet or higher at this spot.

For a diuretic effect, try Hathorn Spring No. 1, a block east of Broadway on Spring Street. This water contains large amounts of sulfur, iron, lime, and other minerals. Dense, green-tinted, and faintly malodorous, it has been prescribed for everything from sinus troubles to complexion problems.

More palatable is the 90-minute relaxer offered spa visitors: a 15- to 25-minute mineral bath followed by a half-hour massage, then a 30-minute rest. Your float in the salty, effervescent warm mineral water induces relaxation by slowing breathing; studies have shown that some carbon dioxide is absorbed through the skin, where it dilates the blood vessels, improves circulation, and aids the flow of blood. Wrapped in warm sheets, you cool down before enjoying a relaxing massage. The cost of this treatment varies according to season; it is $36–$50 in July and August.

In the middle of the spa park, the Gideon Putnam Hotel offers a two-night package (Nov.–Apr. only) that includes the mineral baths and a taste of the resort's bygone glory. The sprawling, neo-Georgian hotel has old-fashioned country-club charm. Built during the New Deal era and refurbished in 1992, it is the only hotel in the spa park, and operates the bathhouses under contract with the state. The Lincoln Baths, opened in 1911, moved into the present building in 1930, said to have been the largest bath building in the world, able to treat 4,500 visitors a day.

Get a full taste of the town and its Victorian landmarks. A stroll along Broadway, the main shopping and eating street, includes the Urban Cultural Park (tel. 518/587–3241), where walking tours are guided by knowledgeable local residents. After an excess of gingerbread mansions, browse the Lyrical Ballad Bookstore at 7 Philadelphia Street, or feed the ducks on Congress Park ponds. Among the park's sculptures is "The Spirit of Life" by Daniel Chester French, whose other works include the statue in the Lincoln Memorial in Washington. Saratoga's historic district is chockablock with charming houses that offer bed-and-breakfast accommodations, as well as the grand old Adelphi Hotel on Broadway (tel. 800/860–4086), built in 1870 and lovingly restored by the current owners. In summer, the big draws are concerts at the performing arts center and the race track.

Saratoga Spa State Park

The Gideon Putnam
Box 476, Ave. of the Pines, Saratoga Springs, NY 12866
Tel. 518/584–3000 or 800/1732–1560
Fax 518/584–1354

Administration Manager, Robert Gigliotti

Season Year-round

Accommodations 132 rooms, 12 suites, with traditional furnishings, modern bathroom. All have phone, flowered drapery, TV, air-conditioning.

Rates Daily rate $140–$450 per room for 2. Spa Park 2-night package $122–$175 for 2, double occupancy (Nov.–Apr.) includes mineral baths, meals, raceway pass, gratuities, taxes. 1 night payable in advance. AE, DC, MC, V.

Meal Plans Salads and light cuisine on the spa menu.

Services and Facilities **Services:** Swedish massage, baths, hot pack, aromatherapy, body polish, reflexology, algae or herbal wrap, sea mud body mask, paraffin hand treatment. **Swimming Facilities:** Victoria Pool in the spa park ($8), Great Scandaga Lake in nearby Adirondack State Park. **Spa Facilities:** Mineral-water baths in semiprivate tubs at the spartan facilities of the Lincoln Baths (tel. 518/583–2880), Roosevelt Bath (518/584–2011). Days and times of operation vary with season; call for reservations. **Recreation Facilities:** 8 free public tennis courts and 2 golf courses in the spa park, hiking trails at Spruce Mountain near town, guided history walks, jogging in Congress Park. **Evening Programs:** Saratoga Performing Arts Center (tel. 518/587–3330) in Spa State Park presents the New York City Ballet in July, the Philadelphia Orchestra in Aug., and popular and jazz artists. Dance companies perform at the Little Theater (tel. 518/587–3330).

In the Area 900 buildings on the National Register of Historic Places; tours include the rose garden at the Yaddo artists' colony and the 1864 gable-roof clubhouse at the track. Polo matches and a harness-racing track nearby. Saratoga Battlefield National

Historical Park has a scenic 9.5-mi drive open to bicyclists. Museums in former spa buildings are devoted to dance, racing, and local history.

Getting Here *From New York City.* By car, New York Thruway (I–87), Exit 13N to Rte. 9 (3½ hrs). By train, Amtrak from Montreal (3 hrs), Boston, and New York City. By air, USAir flights to Albany. By bus, Adirondack Trailways (tel. 800/858–8555). Rental car at airport, taxi in town. Park admission: $5 per car, free for Gideon Putnam hotel guests.

Special Notes Specially equipped baths and rooms for people with disabilities. Remember to bring drinking cups.

Sivananda Ashram Yoga Ranch

Spiritual awareness

New York When stressed-out urbanites join members of the farm community to exercise and meditate or to jog through 80 acres of woods and fields, the effect is spiritual as well as physical. Guests from diverse social and professional backgrounds around the world meet at Sivananda Ashram Yoga Ranch to share their interest in yoga.
Woodbourne

Morning and evening, everyone participates in classes devoted to traditional yogic exercise and breathing techniques. The dozen asana positions range from a headstand to a spinal twist, and each has specific benefits for the body. You will be taught that proper breathing, *pranayama*, is essential for energy control.

The daily schedule includes meditation and chanting at 6 AM and 8 PM, yogic posture and breathing exercise classes at 8 AM and 4 PM, and vegetarian meals served at 10 AM and 6 PM. Participation in program activities is mandatory, including karma yoga classes and various talks on yogic practice and philosophy. The ideal is to become harmoniously balanced; the discipline can provide physical, psychological, and spiritual benefits.

Sivananda Ashram Yoga Ranch
Box 195, Woodbourne, NY 12788
Tel. 914/434–9242
Fax 914/434–1032

Administration Director, Sri Nivasan; director, Swami Sankarananda

Season Year-round

Accommodations 50 small rooms: singles, doubles, apartments in the turn-of-the-century farmhouse and cottages. Apartments have private bath. Tent space available.

Rates Room $35–$40 daily per person, including meals; 1-month work-study program $100. $25 payable in advance. No credit cards.

Meal Plans 2 meals daily, buffet style. Lacto-vegetarian diet with fresh vegetables grown on the ranch and dairy products. No coffee, eggs, alcohol.

Services and Facilities **Swimming Facilities:** Pond. **Spa Facilities:** Communal sweat lodge and sauna. **Recreation Facilities:** Woodland trail hiking. **Evening Programs:** Meditation, chanting, lectures.

Getting Here *From New York City.* By bus, Short Line (Port Authority Terminal) to Woodbourne, then arrange for pickup; during the summer, van service operated by Sivananda provided every weekend (from 243 W. 24th St., $20 round-trip). By car, Rte. 17N to Exit 105B, Rte. 42 to Woodbourne (2 hrs).

Special Notes No smoking. Remember to bring towels and meditation mat.

Tai Chi Farm

Spiritual awareness
Sports conditioning

New York
Warwick

Martial arts and inner discovery bring harmony to participants in workshops at the Tai Chi Farm. Founded and led by Master Jou Tsung Hwa, the farm has a summer schedule devoted to understanding and perfecting the tai chi postures and meditations. Specialists teach such exercises as Swimming Dragon Chi Kung, a complete muscle and organ toner that makes your body seem to flow like a swimming dragon. From the Creative Being Centre in England, a master teaches how to transform stress into self-discovery using Dragon Breath Energy.

The Chinese have been studying chi for 4,000 years. Here the concepts of leading, sticking, neutralizing, and attacking are discussed and practiced with experts in many specialized forms of tai chi. Characterized by a spirited give-and-take, San Shou is an ingeniously choreographed set of 88 matched movements that refine your form and sensitivity. In the body mechanics of tai chi, you discover how to root and balance the yin of letting go with the yang of connecting and projecting energy.

Tai Chi Farm
Box 828, Warwick, NY 10990
Tel. 914/986–9233

Administration Master, Jou Tsung Hwa; manager, David Pancarician

Season May–Oct.

Accommodations 10 wooden cabins with cots or mattresses for 2–10 persons. Bedding not supplied. No electricity or running water. Outhouse shared by campers. Campsites available.

Rates $30 per person for weekend lodging, $95 tuition; $50 per person for 5-day workshop lodging, $170 tuition. Campsites $10–$20.

Meal Plans No meal service. Participants prepare their own meals.

Services and Facilities **Services:** Individual and group instruction. **Exercise Facilities:** Indoor studio. **Swimming Facilities:** Pond.

Getting Here *From New York City.* By bus, NJ Transit from Port Authority Terminal to Warwick (2 hrs). By car, Rte. 80W, 23N to I–94N, exit 1 mi past NJ-NY state line in New Milford.

Vatra Mountain Valley Lodge & Spa

Luxury pampering
Nutrition and diet
Weight management

New York
Hunter Mountain

Shedding 7–10 pounds per week is the goal of most guests at the Vatra Mountain Valley Lodge & Spa, which opened here in 1992. Set on 23 acres at the base of Hunter Mountain, the resort displays the backdrop and foreground of the majestic Catskill mountain range. Hiking trails lead into the Catskill State Park, and the Hunter Mountain Ski Center is only a mile away.

A brief medical background check and orientation is given for new arrivals. The spa director determines your level of fitness and your nutritional needs. A computerized body-composition analysis (additional fee) may be recommended. The program includes massage sessions (depending on length of stay), full fitness program with low-impact aerobics, step aerobics, abdominal and back clinic, stretching, toning, yoga, and guided walks. There is no mandatory schedule or arrival day.

Aquatics classes take advantage of the indoor swimming pool. Gloves and tubes are supplied to enhance your workout in the water exercise circuit. But the best part of the day is spent outdoors on the miles of private trails that encircle the lodge.

Don't expect luxury accommodations. Basically a ski lodge, the spa recently changed ownership and has links with the Polish Vatra health resort. The fitness staff's serious approach to weight loss, and the group camaraderie, add up to a well-focused program without frills.

Vatra Mountain Valley Lodge & Spa
Rte. 214, Box F, Hunter, NY 12442
Tel. 518/263-4919 or 800/232-2772
Fax 518/263-4994

Administration Director, George Borkacki; fitness director, Francesca Ortolano

Season Year-round

Accommodations 32 rooms, each with private bath, color TV (with cable and satellite), telephone. Some rooms are lofts with skylights, 2 have whirlpool bath.

Rates Weekly (7 nights) package rates $1,295–$1,450 single, $995–$1,095 per person, double occupancy. 4-night midweek package $850–$950 single, $650–$725 double. Weekend packages (3 nights) $650–$695 single, $495–$550 double. Add 8% tax and 15% service charge. Deposit $200–$300. AE, D, MC, V.

Meal Plans 3 meals daily based on a 750-calorie weight loss diet; optional juice fast, vegetarian meals, and special dietary requests. Breakfasts feature egg-white omelet, hearty grain cereals, and fresh fruit. Lunches include tomato bisque, zucchini lasagne, spinach frittata. Dining-room service, candlelight dinners include Cornish game hen with apple glaze, chicken Parmesan, flounder Florentine, haddock with Creole sauce, chocolate mousse.

Services and Facilities **Exercise Equipment:** 3 treadmills, 2 StairMasters, 2 stairclimbers, 2 recumbant bicycles, free weights, aquacize tubes and gloves. **Services:** Therapeutic massage, reflexology, shiatsu, facial, seaweed and cellulite body wraps, exfoliating body polish, body waxing, manicure, pedicure. Individual nutritional fitness and stress counseling available. Body-composition analysis, cholesterol testing, Innerquest behavior-modification technology. **Swimming Facilities:** Indoor pool and heated outdoor pool. **Recreation Facilities:** 2 tennis courts, basketball and volleyball courts, hiking trails, cross-country skiing.

Getting Here *From New York City.* New York Thruway to Exit 19 (Kingston), Rte. 28 west to Phoenicia, follow signs to Exit 214 north (Pine Hill, 2 hrs away). Vatra Mountain Valley Lodge & Spa will be 15 mins farther on the left.

Special Notes Ramps and some ground-floor rooms offer access to people with disabilities. No smoking in public areas, but smoking and no-smoking rooms are available.

Zen Mountain Monastery

Spiritual awareness

New York
Mt. Tremper

Joining a group of Buddhist monks as they work in silence, meditate, and celebrate Zen rituals and arts is the unique experience at the Zen Mountain Monastery. You can sip green tea at a Zen tea ceremony, hear the broken notes of a Shakuhachi bamboo flute, learn ink painting or traditional wood carving, and explore the subtleties of Ikenobo flower arranging. There are weekends devoted to Taoist martial arts, poetry, and Zen photography.

Founded in 1980 by Zen priest John Daido Loori, who is addressed as *sensei* (teacher), it is the only monastery in America that offers concerts and programs for visitors throughout the year. Scheduled monthly retreats attract 60–100 participants.

The day's activities move to a measured cadence, sometimes with chanting, often in silence. Everyone does caretaking, an hour of giving back to the buildings and land some of the benefits received from them. Periods of *zazen* (meditation) provide concentration during intensive *sesshin* silent retreat weeks.

In a state forest preserve, a 10-minute drive from Woodstock, the monastery seems to be of another time and world. It was, in fact, built at the turn of the century by Catholic monks and Norwegian craftsmen. There are endless mountain trails, ponds, and streams for hiking and recreation, and the atmosphere of peace and solitude is conducive to introspection.

Zen Mountain Monastery
Box 197PC, S. Plank Rd., Mt. Tremper, NY 12457
Tel. 914/688–2228

Administration Director, John Daido Loori; program director, Geoffrey Arnold; coordinator, Kathy Nolan; registrar, Jimon

Season Year-round; weekend programs scheduled in summer, retreats in fall and winter

Accommodations 4-story stone monastery with 175-bed dormitory. Main hall, classrooms, dining hall, library. All facilities shared on a communal basis. Rustic cabins available for couples.

Rates Weekend programs $125–$185, retreats of 3–7 days (Tues.–Sun.) $185–$325 per person, including 3 meals daily. Advance payment of $50. MC, V.

Meal Plans Vegetarian meals and some fish or meat, served buffet style 3 times a day. Weekends begin with Fri. dinner (steamed fish with rice and vegetables) and end with Sun. lunch. Dairy products served. Much of the food from the monastery garden.

Services and Facilities **Services:** Zen training, intensive meditation, artist retreats. **Swimming Facilities:** Nearby mountain lakes. **Recreation Facilities:** Hiking; tubing on creek, skiing at Hunter Mountain. **Evening Programs:** Occasional concerts of contemporary and Oriental music, an introduction to Zen.

In the Area Woodstock artists' colony, Catskill Mountain Forest Preserve, Beaverkill River scenic area.

Getting Here *From New York City.* By bus, Adirondack Trailways (tel. 800/858–8555) from Port Authority via Kingston to Mt. Tremper (about 3 hrs). By car, New York State Thruway (I–87) to the Catskills, Rte. 28 and 212 to Mt. Tremper (2½ hrs).

Special Notes No smoking.

The Equinox

Life enhancement
Luxury pampering
Sports conditioning

Vermont
Manchester
Village

Falconry as well as golf, tennis, and spa programs are featured at the 2,300-acre historic Equinox resort. In the heart of a picturesque valley, the resort has an 18-hole par 71 golf course, three tennis courts, and spa facilities that include a coed Turkish steam bath, indoor and outdoor swimming pools, whirlpools, and a Swedish sauna. Skiing at Mt. Equinox is a major attraction, but if you are injured, it's comforting to know that the spa has the area's first physiotherapy center.

The comprehensive fitness facilities are complimentary to all hotel guests, and specialized spa programs are available à la carte. A three-night spa package includes three spa meals daily and treatments or salon services. There is also a two-night Fun and Fitness package, with breakfast and dinner. Before you begin your regime, a staff member will give you a computerized body-composition analysis, which will be used to tailor your exercise schedule, and you'll participate in an informal discussion on exercise physiology, nutrition, and stress management. Advance planning with the spa director will help you focus on weight loss, stress management, or behavior modification.

Workout options include brisk walks and personalized training with weights, and programs are limited to 16 participants, so early reservations and travel plans are suggested. The sports focus comes with several spa packages; falconry training costs $45 per 45-minute lesson, including equipment, or you can enroll for a four-day course. Practicing the handling and flying of native birds of prey—Harris hawks—takes place in fields near the hotel, which have been dedicated as a nature preserve by the resort's owners, Guiness Brewing Co.

The Equinox houses many participants, and recently converted an early 19th-century residence, called Orvis Inn, with luxury suites. After fishing season, the inn houses participants in the Orvis marksmanship courses. When you're not working out with the birds, you can try fly-fishing at the long-established Orvis school just down the road.

The hotel and golf course were refurbished in 1992, but the 1800s charm has been retained, especially in the dining room, which dates back to 1769 when it was a tavern. Guest rooms have a fresh but historic style, with Audubon prints and Vermont country charm. All bathrooms have been reconstructed with 18th-century tile, pedestal sinks, and natural finish beaded pine-paneled ceilings.

If your idea of exercise is shopping til you drop, just stroll into Manchester Village.

The Equinox
Rte. 7A, Manchester Village, VT 05254
Tel. 802/362–4700 or 800/362–4747
Fax 802/362–1595

Administration General manager, S. Lee Bowden; fitness director, Susan Wheeler

Season Year-round

Accommodations 163 bedrooms and 10 suites, furnished in classic New England inn with pine beds and dressers, flowered chintz fabrics, modern conveniences. Beds turned down at night; *New York Times*

delivered. All with large modern bathroom, TV, phone, air-conditioning. Also available, 9 town houses with 1- to 3-bedroom suites, 9 suites at Orvis Inn.

Rates Daily rate $159–$289 single, $169–$280 for 2, double occupancy. Orvis Inn suite $569–$899 for 2, 1-bedroom parlor suite for 2 $559, town house suite $369–$669 for two. 3-night/4-day spa package $1,057 single, $833.50 per person double, $779 triple. 3-night/4-day Fun & Fitness package $919 single, $620.50 double, $541 triple. Add 7% tax, gratuity. Deposit of 1 night. AE, DC, MC, V.

Meal Plans Meals included in spa packages. Spa breakfast offers choice of fruit, buttermilk pancakes with blueberry coulis, hot oatmeal or bran cereal with skim milk; lunch can be ceviche of sole with cilantro, grilled medallion of beef with shallots, or chilled asparagus with seasoned wild rice; dinner choices include herbed pasta with mushrooms, poached salmon, or veal medallion.

Services and Facilities **Exercise Equipment:** 8-station Nautilus circuit, free weights, 2 Lifecycles, 3 AMF semirecumbent bikes, NordicTrack, stairclimber, computerized rowing machine. **Services:** Massage, Reiki, reflexology, herbal wrap, honey-almond and sea salt, Bobet sea algae body masque, body scrub, pedicure, essential oil treatments, hair and skin care. **Swimming Facilities:** 47′ indoor and 75′ outdoor heated pools. **Recreation Facilities:** 3 Har-Tru tennis courts, golf course, hiking trails, bicycle rental, nearby downhill and cross-country skiing, horseback riding, canoeing, horse-drawn carriage rides. **Evening Programs:** Resort entertainment.

In the Area Antiques shops, shopping at factory outlets, summer theater, jazz concerts, Marlboro Music Festival, Brattleboro Museum, Norman Rockwell Museum, Bennington crafts center, Hildene (Robert Todd Lincoln's estate).

Getting Here *From New York City.* By car, New England Thruway (I–95) north to I—91, exit at second Brattleboro turnoff for Rte. 9 to Rte. 30 (4 hrs). By bus, Greyhound from Port Authority Terminal (4½ hrs). By air, scheduled flights to Albany, NY; bus service to Manchester by Vermont Transit (tel. 800/451–3292). Taxis and rental cars available.

Special Notes No smoking in the spa. Spa open weekdays 7–7, weekends 8–7:30. No minimum age until 6 PM; 15 years after 6 PM.

Four Seasons Healing

Holistic health
Spiritual awareness

Vermont
Norwich

The Four Seasons Healing, a private retreat, was founded 15 years ago as a nonprofit organization in southern New England, and in 1994 it moved to a 20-acre site in the Upper Connecticut River Valley of Vermont. Action-oriented healing practices, drawn from psychodrama, shamanism, depth, existential, humanistic, and transpersonal psychologies are practiced. Groups are limited to eight people for the six-day Vision Quest; and 20 people at the Breakthrough Weekends devoted to gender reconciliation for individuals and couples.

The mountain lodge is the base for wilderness programs and workshops that encourage personal health and exploration. Counseling comes from a team of doctors, psychologists, psychotherapists, and Vision Quest guides. Among the relaxing activities that weekend-program guests can participate in are lounging in front of a fire, hiking through the woods, and meditating by a stream with other visitors.

Programs can be customized for individuals, couples, or a group that wants a private retreat. The scheduled events, held during summer and the fall leaf-changing season, include an 8-day Wilderness Awakening, weekend gatherings for men or women, and a one-day introduction to shamanic journeying. Bring your own tent or use equipment supplied for overnight wilderness experiences. The philosophy of the nature-oriented activities is that spending time alone can enable you to face the cycles of life and death and facilitate a spiritual rebirth.

The communal attitude at the lodge helps participants share problems and connect with their deeper selves. Meals are vegetarian, with lots of grains and steamed vegetables, served family style. This is a very informal place, where guests share the outhouse and communal shower facilities.

Four Seasons Healing
961 New Boston Rd., Norwich, VT 05055
Tel. 802/649–5104

Administration	Director, Israel Helfand, M.S., Ph.D.
Season	July–Oct.
Accommodations	Shared rooms in rustic lodge with communal shower and outhouse.
Rates	Weekend program $85, Breakthrough Weekend $250, 8-day Wilderness Awakening $825.
Meal Plans	2 meals daily, served family style, included in program. Vegetarian main dish for dinner can be tofu casserole or spinach lasagna. Breakfast is hot cereal, lunch a pita sandwich, salad, fruit. Herbal tea, decaf coffee available.
Services and Facilities	**Services:** Counseling, guided hikes and backpacking treks, lifework planning, couples relationships.
In the Area	Marlboro Music Festival, Brattleboro, Woodstock Dartmouth College Hopkins Center (performing arts), Saint-Gaudens Studio (sculpture), Manchester Village.
Getting Here	*From New York City.* By car, I–95 north to I–91, exit at Norwich to New Boston Rd. (4 hrs). By air, scheduled commuter flights to Lebanon, NH (1 hr). Car pools arranged; taxi, rental car available.
Special Notes	Additional weekend retreats planned in Virginia/Maryland.

Golden Eagle

Nonprogram resort

Vermont
Stowe

Toning and body shaping are what this budget spa does best, and it draws a mixed crowd of singles and families mostly between 30 and 60. The traditional mountain lodge has winter and summer activities, and a health spa open to guests.

Set on 80 acres near the center of Stowe, the resort has well-developed nature trails. A self-guided tour brochure includes descriptions of local flora and fauna. Staff members accompany guests on walks if requested in advance. For longer hikes and bike rides, try the Stowe Recreation Path, a 5½-mile scenic route through the valley, close to the entrance to Golden Eagle and out toward Mt. Mansfield ski area.

This nonstructured program is a good vacation base for families. A nature trail winds through the property, and two ponds are stocked for fishing (poles can be rented). Mountain bikes are available from the activities desk, which also lends tennis

Use your MCI Card®

for the easy way to

call when traveling.

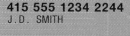

MCI ★   Calling Card

415 555 1234 2244
J.D. SMITH

Convenience on the road

- Your MCI Card® number is your home number, guaranteed.

- Pre-programmed to speed dial to your home.

- Call from any phone in the U.S.

MCI.

1 - 8 0 0 - 7 5 4 - 8 9 4 1

http://www.mci.com

rackets for free play on two Har-Tru courts. For relaxation, try the coed whirlpool and sauna.

Golden Eagle

Box 1110B, Mountain Rd. (Rte. 108), Stowe, VT 05672
Tel. 802/253–4811 or 800/626–1010

Administration	Manager, Neil Van Dyke; spa director, Vicki Demeritt
Season	Year-round
Accommodations	71 rooms with private bath; suites, cottages, apartments with cooking facilities, color TV, air-conditioning, oversize beds. Some rooms with Jacuzzi and fireplace. Also a Bavarian-style chalet.
Rates	$79–$159 daily per room for 2, single occupancy $10 less. 1-night deposit on booking. AE, DC, MC, V.
Meal Plans	Heart-healthy selections on breakfast and dinner menus. Dinner may include veal marsala, fish rolled with vegetables, or broiled scrod. Special diets are accommodated.
Services and Facilities	**Exercise Equipment:** 8 Universal gym stations, 2 Trotter treadmills, Stairclimber, 2 Schwinn Air Dyne bikes, Concept 2 rowing machines, free weights. **Services:** Massage, reflexology. **Swimming Facilities:** Indoor lap pool, 2 outdoor pools. **Recreation Facilities:** 2 clay tennis courts, bicycles, scenic path for jogging. **Evening Programs:** Resort activities.
In the Area	Shelburne Museum, Cold Hollow Cider Mill, Trapp Family Lodge, Ben & Jerry's Ice Cream Factory.
Getting Here	*From Boston and New York City.* By train, Amtrak to Waterbury, VT (10 mi from Stowe). By car, I–91, I–89 to Stowe exit (3 hrs from Boston, 6½ hrs from NYC). By air, scheduled flights to Burlington, VT. Hotel limousine arranged on request to meet trains and planes; taxi, rental car in area.
Special Notes	Ground-floor rooms for people with disabilities. No smoking in the spa and sections of the dining rooms. Spa open daily 9–9.

Green Mountain at Fox Run

Life enhancement   *Women only*
Weight management

Vermont
Ludlow

On more than 20 acres of private land in the Green Mountain National Forest, overlooking the Okemo Valley and ski area, this is the country's oldest all-women program devoted to developing a self-directed plan for eating and exercise that can be integrated into your life at home. Participants range in age from 17 to over 80.

For women with a serious weight problem, coming to Green Mountain at Fox Run is a commitment to change. The difference is not just a new diet or vigorous exercise, but a new lifestyle based on healthy habits. The program provides a practical approach to eating, exercise, and stress management that can ensure long-term success.

One of the first lessons you learn here is that diets don't work. Instead of deprivation, moderation becomes the key. Eating three balanced meals a day is required, and you are encouraged to give in, ever so slightly, to an occasional yearning for sweets. Guests learn to cope with food fads and are shown that being more active can be as pleasant as taking a walk down a country lane. For women who have unsuccessfully attempted to manage their weight with liquid diets, there is a special program to overcome negative effects and resume a livable and enjoyable approach to eating. Professional workshops for nurses and social workers are also offered.

Working with a team of registered dietitians, exercise physiologists, and behavioral therapists with specialties in weight, health, and addiction, you develop a personalized weight and health program that becomes part of your daily routine. A follow-up program helps you to maintain this routine at home. Tuition costs cover individual nutrition/dietary counseling, exercise prescription and modification, and private behavioral counseling sessions. The only extra expense is for massage therapy.

Owner-operated since 1973, this is a homey place. There is some high-tech gym equipment and an outdoor, heated pool, but otherwise the facilities are quite simple. Pampering services are à la carte. Exercise classes, running, walking, hiking, biking, and cross-country skiing in winter fill most of the day. Aerobic dance and body-conditioning sessions teach that exercise can be fun, something that fits easily into everyday life.

Green Mountain at Fox Run
Fox La., Box 164, Ludlow, VT 05149
Tel. 802/228–8885 or 800/448–8106
Fax 802/228–8887

Administration	Program directors, Alan H. Wayler, Ph.D., and Marsha J. Hudnell, M.S., R.D.; fitness director, Kelly Wright
Season	Year-round. Special seminars scheduled weekends.
Accommodations	26 rooms: singles, doubles, and triples (2–3 persons), all with modern bath. Lounge with fireplace, TV; high-ceiling, raftered dining room. Bedrooms redecorated in 1996 with mission-style wooden furniture, Vermont country accents.
Rates	1-week session $750–$1,950; 2-week $1,425–$3,705; 4-week $2,400–$6,240. Season rates based on type of accommodation, single–triple occupancy (roommates matched on request). Tax and gratuities included. $500 deposit with application. MC, V.
Meal Plans	1,200-calorie-a-day diet low in fat and sodium, high in complex carbohydrates. Menus include a salad plate, pasta, eggplant Parmesan, tortilla dishes, liver and onions, baked potato with trimmings, even ice cream. Coffee and tea are available throughout the day.
Services and Facilities	**Exercise Equipment:** 2 Trotter treadmills, 2 Schwinn Air Dyne bikes, NordicTrack, Concept 2 rower, Ross stepper, Nautilus recumbent bike, free weights, 5-station CalGym. **Services:** Swedish massage, facial, manicure, pedicure, sports instruction. **Swimming Facilities:** Olympic-size heated outdoor pool, nearby indoor pool and Jacuzzi. **Spa Facilities:** Sauna. **Recreation Facilities:** 2 tennis courts, outdoor track, nearby golf course, downhill and cross-country skiing, snowshoeing, mountain bikes. **Evening Programs:** Cooking classes, movies, group discussions, lectures.
In the Area	Trips into town for shopping (including antiques shops), scenic mountain drives, summer stock theaters.
Getting Here	*From New York City.* By car, I–95 north to I–91, Exit 6 in Vermont (Rte. 103 North) to Ludlow (4½ hrs). By bus, Vermont Transit (tel. 800/451–3292) from Port Authority Terminal to Ludlow. By air, scheduled flights to Lebanon, NH, on Delta, Northwest Airlines. By train, Amtrak's Vermonter to White River Jctn. (4 hrs). Complimentary pickup from airports, train and bus station. Transfers upon departure included in tuition.

Special Notes Smoking only in specified areas. Remember to bring recent physical report, walking and aerobics shoes.

New Life

Holistic health
Life enhancement
Nutrition and diet

Vermont Two vacations rolled into one is the concept of New Life fit-
Killington ness guru Jimmy LeSage: His program mostly attracts hikers who want to get in shape and enjoy the outdoors. The Inn
of the Six Mountains, where New Life is housed, is set in a picturesque alpine valley, and operates from mid-May through
autumn (dates depend on when the leaves stop turning).

A former professional cook and hotel manager, LeSage caters
to his guests' needs while exhorting them to learn ways to improve their habits. His philosophy on food and eating is published in a book given to each guest and experienced firsthand
in a cheery dining room. Fresh fruit, herbal teas, decaffeinated
coffee, and spring water are always on hand in the hospitality
lounge.

Exercise classes are held in a tent with specially designed floor,
and are scheduled around outdoor activities. Sivananda-style
yogic movements gently stretch muscles and prepare the body
for vigorous outdoor activity; the afternoon program relaxes
the body and works off fatigue. Other options are offered at
the indoor complex with swimming, steam room, and heated
whirlpool that guests can use at any time.

Dubbed "The Hiking Spa," the program capitalizes on the
natural beauty of the Green Mountains. Hiking the lush
valleys and slopes is a great way to strengthen your heart
and muscles. Guided by New Life staff members, groups hike
daily. The treks become more challenging as your stamina increases. The climax is an all-day hike that includes a picnic
lunch.

New Life
The Inn of the Six Mountains, Killington Rd.,
Killington, VT 05751
Tel. 802/422–4302 or 800/545–9407
Fax 802/422–4321

Administration Founder-director, Jimmy LeSage

Season Mid-May through Oct.

Accommodations 100 rooms with double beds, private baths, color TV, and
phone. Pine-paneled lobby, lounge with fireplaces and comfy
chairs.

Rates 3-day sampler (Thurs.–Sun.) $599 single, $540 per person
double; 6-day/5-night program (Sun.–Fri.) $999 single, $899
double. $200 advance payment per person. Add 15% service
charge, 7% tax. MC, V.

Meal Plans 3 meals served daily. Modified Pritikin diet (1,200–1,500 calories per day) low in fats and high in complex carbohydrates.
Chicken, fish, vegetables, and fruit among the choices. Specialties include lentil loaf, chicken curry salad, sandwich with
spicy tofu filling. Special diets accommodated.

Services and **Exercise Equipment:** Cardiovascular power circuit with Life-
Facilities cycle rowing ergometer, Rebounders, NordicTrack ski machine, StairMaster, Precor rower, Cybex multigym, Mohawk
stationary bike. **Services:** Swedish massage, shiatsu, facials;

classes in aerobics, yoga, tai chi; aquacise. **Swimming Facilities:** Indoor lap pool, heated outdoor pool. **Recreation Facilities:** Outdoor tennis, racquetball courts; golf course and horseback riding nearby; mountain-bike rentals. **Evening Programs:** Discussions on healthy living, talks on beauty, lectures on nutrition and stress.

In the Area Antiques shops, summer theater, jazz concerts, Marlboro Music Festival.

Getting Here *From New York City.* By car, New England Thruway (I–95) north to Exit 24, Northway to Exit 120 (Fort Anne/Rutland), Hwy. 4 east via Rutland to Killington Rd., Rte. 100 (5 hrs). By train, Amtrak to White River Jct. (4 hrs). By bus, Vermont Transit to White River Jct. (5 hrs). Complimentary pickup at bus station. By air, Delta Business Express or Northwest Link to Lebanon, NH (1 hr). Limousine, car rental available.

Special Notes No smoking in public areas. Remember to bring warm clothing, hats, walking shoes. Spa open daily 8 AM–10 PM.

Topnotch at Stowe

Luxury pampering
Nutrition and diet
Sports conditioning
Stress control

Vermont Perched in Vermont's Green Mountains, Topnotch is a classic
Stowe country inn that caters to sports enthusiasts and weary urbanites seeking escape from civilization. Complementing its four-season outdoor activity, the resort opened a full-service spa in 1989.

Topnotch emphasizes health education by putting each guest through a "Fitness Profile" analysis. Based on your body composition, strength and flexibility, cardiovascular and blood tests, an exercise program is planned. Outfitted with a daily issue of shorts, T-shirt, robe and slippers, you have a choice of classes, one-on-one workouts, and circuit weight training. There are coed sauna, steam room, and Jacuzzi.

Sport-specific fitness and conditioning classes get you in shape for tennis and skiing. The program for three to seven days includes instruction as well as time on the courts and slopes. The resort has an indoor tennis center with four lighted courts (Deco Turf II), and transports guests to nearby Mount Mansfield, Vermont's highest peak, top-rated for downhill skiing. Also, there are 30 kilometers of groomed cross-country trails winding through the 120-acre resort, which link with the Catamount Trail along the ridge of the Green Mountains. For the riding enthusiast, the Topnotch Equestrian Center provides horses, trail rides, riding rings, lessons, and a gallop across the meadows and backwoods.

Golfers get guest privileges at the Stowe Country Club. A popular focal point for swimmers is the cascading waterfalls alongside the 60-foot heated indoor swimming pool. Tennis clinics and an Orvis school for fishermen are scheduled throughout summer.

While the spa is sophisticated, the inn is comfortable and homey. Its 92 guest rooms are spacious, many with views of the mountains. A massive fireplace warms the main lounge, and there is a cushy sofa for reading by the fire. If you're not too sleepy after a day of sports and spa followed by evening fitness rap sessions, there's a well-stocked library in your room for bedtime reading.

Topnotch at Stowe

Mountain Rd., Box 1458, Stowe, VT 05672
Tel. 802/253-8585 or 800/451-8686
Fax 802/253-9263

Administration General manager, Robert Boyle; spa director, Kathy Berry

Season Year-round

Accommodations 100 rooms furnished with antiques, fine wooden beds, some with canopy, and library. Modern bathroom with imported soaps and bath gels, plush towels. All have air-conditioning, cable TV. Also suites, condominiums, town houses.

Rates Daily without meals $176–$236 per person double occupancy, $186–$226 single. 4-day/3-night Tennis/Spa package $267 single, $376 for 2, double. Add 17% service charge, 5% taxes. AE, DC, MC, V.

Meal Plans Breakfast included in spa packages; daily meal plans $48–$55 per person. Menu choices for breakfast are tofu omelet, buckwheat pancakes with fruit topping, hot or cold whole-grain cereals. Lunch selections include mushroom-barley soup, salad of asparagus and roasted red peppers, whole-wheat pizza, chicken breast in cilantro-mint sauce. Dinner entrées can be seafood pasta in creamy 3-mustard sauce, or grilled chicken. Vegetarian meals, snacks available. Coffee, tea, milk served.

Services and Facilities **Exercise Equipment:** 9-station Cybex weight training unit, 2 Schwinn Air Dyne bikes, 4 Precor treadmills, pulley machine, ProTec PT5-1000 recumbent bike, Liferower, 3 StairMasters, 2 Lifecycles, Gravitron, free weights. **Services:** 2 aerobics studios with 13 scheduled classes, aquacise, yoga; massage (Swedish, shiatsu, reflexology), acupressure, aromatherapy, hydrotherapy, herbal wrap, loofah body scrub, facials; beauty salon for hair, nail, and skin care; instruction in tennis, skiing, riding. **Swimming Facilities:** Indoor 60´ lap pool, outdoor pool. **Recreation Facilities:** 12 tennis courts (4 indoor), equestrian center, putting green, lawn croquet, bikes, table tennis, billiards, art studio, spa sauna, steam room, coed Jacuzzi. Nearby golf, downhill skiing, squash, and racquetball. **Evening Programs:** Bike rides and walks, nutrition seminars, scheduled events 5 nights per week.

In the Area Stowe Village (antiques shops), Trapp Family Lodge (concerts), Shelburne Museum (Americana), Cold Hollow Cider Mill, Ben & Jerry's Ice Cream Factory, Smuggler's Notch, Bingham Falls (swimming, picnics).

Getting Here *From Boston.* By train, Amtrak to Waterbury, VT (4 hrs). By bus, Greyhound and Vermont Transit (tel. 800/451-3292) (5 hrs). By air, scheduled flights on USAir to Burlington, VT (1 hr), private-plane airport at Stowe. By car, I-93 to Concord, NH, I-89 north to Exit 10 (Stowe/Waterbury), Rte. 100N to Stowe, left on Rte. 108 (Mountain Rd.) 4 mi (4 hrs). Taxi, car rental available; town trolley service, hotel limo.

Special Notes No smoking in spa or spa dining room. No-smoking guest rooms available. Limited access for people with disabilities. Spa open weekdays 8–6, weekends 8–7. Daily facility fee ($10–$20) included in spa packages.

Woodstock Inn & Resort

Nonprogram resort

Vermont
Woodstock

Picture the perfect New England town: the county courthouse and library facing an oval green, a covered bridge leading to immaculate farms, a cluster of fancy boutiques, and a Colonial inn. Add a $5-million sports center, 50 miles of cross-country ski trails, nearby mountains with more than 200 downhill trails, and you have the Woodstock Inn & Resort.

The current inn, the fourth on the site, spreads from the historic town center to the sports center. Included are a golf course and croquet lawn, outdoor and indoor swimming pools, tennis courts, and a 69-station parcourse. The weight equipment and aerobics studio are luxury-spa caliber, and they can be used for a nominal fee. Classes cost $5 each. A winter ski package includes lift tickets and equipment rental.

Traditions are alive at the inn from the dress code to the hearty New England menu. The nearby Billings Farm Museum has exhibits of early New England farm life, and offers visits to a prize-winning dairy barn. Phone and power lines were buried with a grant from a neighbor, Laurence Rockefeller, to preserve the view of the town green.

Woodstock Inn & Resort
14 The Green, Woodstock, VT 05091
Tel. 802/457–1100 or 800/448–7900

Administration
General manager, Chet Williamson; sports directors, Tom Avalino, Chuck Vanderstreet

Season
Year-round

Accommodations
121 bedrooms with patchwork quilts, cable TV, air-conditioning, clock radio, modern baths.

Rates
In summer, $149–$499 for 2 persons. Meals not included. Health & Fitness Center sports package (3 days, 2 nights) $374 single, $562 for 2 persons double occupancy, includes racquetball or tennis, massage. Add 7% tax, and gratuities. Deposit: 2 nights. AE, DC, MC, V.

Meal Plans
Modified American plan (breakfast and dinner) $46 per person per day. Courtside Restaurant in Sports Center serves a chicken salad plate or assorted melon slices with cottage cheese, sherbet, or yogurt sauce for lunch. The main dining room offers poached chicken, roast young pheasant, and sea scallops for dinner.

Services and Facilities
Exercise Equipment: 11 Nautilus units, 2 Concept 2 rowing ergometers, 2 Monark bikes, Trotter treadmill, incline station, hyperextension station, free weights. **Services:** Swedish and deep-tissue massage, sports instruction, yoga and aerobics classes, aquatics for arthritics, personal trainer. **Swimming Facilities:** Indoor and outdoor pools. **Spa Facilities:** Coed steam room, separate men's and women's saunas, whirlpools in the Sports Center. **Recreation Facilities:** 10 outdoor and 2 indoor tennis courts, 2 indoor racquetball courts, 2 indoor squash courts; cross-country skiing, downhill skiing at Suicide Six, Killington, Ascutney Mountain, Okemo Mountain; volleyball, horseshoes, croquet; horseback-riding center nearby, sleigh rides, and nature walks. **Evening Programs:** Resort entertainment.

In the Area
Quechee Village (crafts), Dartmouth College Hopkins Center (performing arts), Saint-Gaudens Studio (sculpture), Marlboro Music Festival (chamber music), walking tours of historic Woodstock.

Getting Here *From Boston.* By car, I–90 to I–91 (100 mi). By air, scheduled flights to Lebanon, NH. Taxi, rental car available.

Special Notes Ramps and specially equipped rooms for people with disabilities. Tennis camp for children June–Aug. No smoking in the sports center.

Hawaii

Polynesian culture has given new dimensions to the pursuit of fitness. On the volcanic island of Hawaii, guests at Kalani Honua live in traditional lodges made of cedar logs or camp out among the palm trees. On Maui you can join a quest for spiritual renewal at a residence designed by Frank Lloyd Wright that houses the Millenium Institute. Throughout the island state there has been a redicovery of native healing traditions, experienced in sacred mud treatments at Hyatt's ANARA Spa on Kauai, herbs and plants used for body wraps at Ihilani Resort and Spa on Oahu, and exfoliating salt glows at Spa Grande on Maui.

At the same time, developers of luxury resorts have competed for the distinction of having the most opulent health club on the island. On Maui, you can indulge in a combination of Japanese, Hawaiian, European, and American fitness fantasies at the Grand Wailea Resort, where the Spa Grande has a two-level cardiovascular-fitness and weight-training center, or retreat to the Polynesian spirit of Hotel Hana-Maui. On Oahu, close to Pearl Harbor, the Ihilani Resort has a spa with "Hawaiian Thalasso" seawater treatments. Hawaii is a golfer's paradise, and many of the islands' resort courses rate among the world's best. But while golf and water sports of Hawaii are famous, the islands are full of more unexpected fitness opportunities, such as bicycle rides down the slope of Maui's extinct volcano, Mt. Haleakala. Local outfitters will drive you to the top of the 10,023-foot slope to see the sunrise and provide bikes for the leisurely ride down. Or you can cruise the islands on one of the twin liners of American Hawaii Cruises and make use of the on-board spa.

Home of the strenuous Iron Man Triathalon, Hawaii offers a full range of sports ventures for every taste—from horseback riding on ranches to kayaking up the Huleia River on Kauai through a wildlife refuge. Polo matches abound on Oahu and the Big Island; the Hawaii Polo Club even offers five-day training programs. The waters off the Kohala coast are legendary for deep-sea fishing, and the Kona coast has spectacular sites for scuba diving—Napoopoo Beach Park and Keei Beach are favored spots. In the winter, you can go skiing on the Big Island. From December through May, the upper slopes of Mauna Kea, 13,796 feet above the sea, frequently have enough snow for sun-baked skiing.

Waikiki Beach hotels have some of the smallest fitness facilities and encourage guests to take part in water sports or use private clubs. Anyone can join the daily 8:30 AM aerobics class on the beach in front of the Pacific Beach Hotel with staffers from Gold's Gym. At Fort DeRussy, a military club, you can work out in the fully equipped health club, The Point, at Hale Koa Hotel (tel. 808/955–9155) for a daily fee, and join a beach adventure trip with locals on Thursday ($70). There's even a free clinic at the local YMCA to prepare runners for the Honolulu Marathon.

Island parks give hikers the opportunity to enjoy the real Hawaiian paradise. For information on organized treks, contact clubs such as Hawaii Ike Travel Society (tel. 808/326–5775) and the Waikiki Community Center (tel. 808/923–1808). Leeward Community College (tel. 808/956–8946) publishes a statewide *Eco-Tourism Directory*. The comprehensive *Hawaii Health and Fitness Guide* is available from Aurora

Productions (4400-4 Kalanianaole Hwy., Honolulu, HI 96821, tel. 808/988–7975).

One word of caution, however: When venturing into secluded areas on any of the islands alone, be sure you aren't wandering onto a farm or other private property, as there have been shooting incidents in the past. Check with local park-service officials before you start out on a hike or ride.

Grand Wailea Resort and Spa

Luxury pampering
Nutrition and diet
Preventive medicine
Stress control

Wailea, Maui   Amid the splendor of the $600 million Grand Wailea Resort, the 50,000-square-foot Spa Grande offers the most extensive health and fitness facilities in Hawaii. In addition to 10 individual and private Jacuzzi areas, there are Roman-style whirlpools 20 feet in diameter in the atriums of the men's and women's pavilions as well as 42 individual treatment rooms for everything from facials and loofah scrubs to mud treatments and massage.

Water sets the mood for the entire 40-acre resort. On Maui's south shore, 25 minutes from Kahului Airport, the eight-story hotel and two-level beachfront spa overlook formal gardens and placid surf.

Hydrotherapy comes with the spa's daily admission fee or as part of half-day and full-day packages. The Terme Wailea circuit begins with a choice of two treatments designed to exfoliate and cleanse the skin: a loofah scrub or Japanese goshi-goshi scrub, sitting shower, and soak in a furo tub. Next you have a choice from five specialty baths in marble and gold mosaic tubs: aromatherapy for relaxation, Maui mud to remineralize, limu (Hawaiian seaweed) for detoxification, herbal for rejuvenation, and tropical enzyme bath for toning and softening the skin. To stimulate circulation there are saunas, steam rooms, and cold-water plunges. Upstairs are private, oceanfront treatment rooms where seven types of massage and five different facials are offered. A scalp treatment combines limu, ginger, kelp, papaya, kuki nuts, and other native Hawaiian plants. The body wraps include ti tree leaves. Ayurvedic treatments are also available.

Aerobics classes are held several times daily. An air-conditioned racquetball court (convertible for squash) and weight-training rooms are also available. Water sports on the hotel beach include catamaran cruises, canoe rentals, snorkeling, windsurfing, and scuba diving. The Wailea resort area contains two 18-hole golf courses in its limits, and a tennis club with 14 courts, three of which are grass. Guests at the neighboring Four Seasons resort also have access to Spa Grande.

Grand Wailea Resort and Spa
3850 Wailea Alanui Dr., Wailea, Maui, HI 96753
Tel. 808/875–1234 or 800/888–6100
Fax 808/874–2442

Administration   Manager, Gregory Koestering; spa director, Darryll Leiman

Season   Year-round

Accommodations   787 rooms in an 8-story tower, all with ocean view, private lanai, modern bath. Included are 53 suites and 100 rooms of

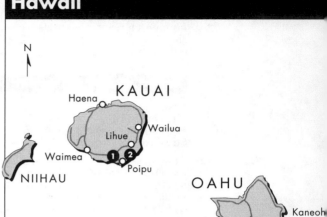

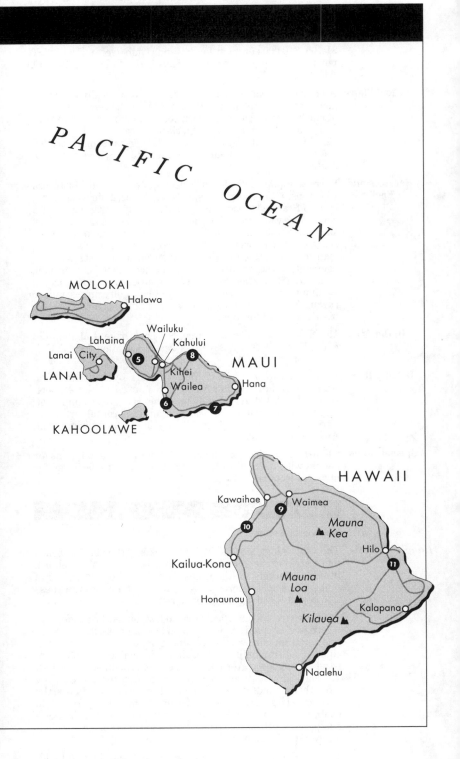

PACIFIC OCEAN

MOLOKAI
Halawa

Wailuku
Kahului
Lahaina
Lanai City
Kihei
Wailea
Hana
LANAI
MAUI

KAHOOLAWE

HAWAII

Kawaihae
Waimea
Mauna
Kea
Hilo
Kailua-Kona
Mauna
Loa
Honaunau
Kalapana
Kilauea

Naalehu

Napua Club floors. Air-conditioned, telephones, TV, and full amenities.

Rates Oceanfront Grande room for 2 or 1 $495 per night; Garden $445 per night; Mountain View Terrace room $380 per night; Suites $1,100–$10,000 per night for 2; Napua Club–Ocean Front $580 per night. Day Spa packages (half- and full-day) $209–$349. AE, DC, MC, V.

Meal Plans All meals à la carte. Spa lunch features organically grown island food with Italian and Provençale touches: grilled breast of chicken with mango chili sauce, mahimahi with snap peas and roasted red peppers, black-bean salad with cilantro. Breakfast typically is buffet of cereals, egg-white omelet, tropical fruit. Optional Italian, Japanese, and Polynesian restaurants.

Services and Facilities **Exercise Equipment:** 14-unit Keiser system, 3 StairMasters, 4 Lifesteps, 4 Windracer bikes, 2 Cybex cycles, 2 Biocycles, 2 Accufit, 5 Startrac treadmills, Gravitron, Liferower, Concept 2 rower, free weights, and barbells. **Services:** Massage (Swedish, shiatsu, lomi-lomi, aromatherapy, sports, reflexology), facial, seaweed body pack, loofah scrub, wraps, herbal baths, ayurvedic treatments. Consultation on health, stress management, nutrition, fitness. Full-service salon for hair, nail, skin care. **Recreation Facilities:** Ocean beach water sports, 2 swimming pools (1 Olympic size), 2 18-hole golf courses, indoor racquetball/squash courts, billiards, 14 tennis courts, 8,000 sq. ft. "Keiki"-land for kids.

In the Area Mt. Haleakala (volcano crater), Skyline Drive, Lahaina (old port), Hana Highway, Seven Sacred Pools, Maui Arts & Cultural Center.

Getting Here *From the U.S. mainland.* Direct flights by United, Delta, American, and Hawaiian Airlines to Maui's Kahului Airport. By car, Hwy. 380 to Hwy. 350 via Kihei Hwy. 31. Complimentary transfers included in Grande Plan. Taxi, rental car, limousine available. *From Honolulu.* By interisland airlines and American Hawaii cruises.

Special Notes Children's activities and lunch, $35 daily. Accommodations for people with disabilities available. Separate spa facilities for men and women.

Halekulani Hotel

Nonprogram resort

Honolulu, Oahu Three mornings a week, at 7:30, guests gather on the beach for stretching exercises and a morning jaunt with Max Telford, fitness consultant for the Halekulani Hotel. Telford, holder of numerous world records for distance running, offers fitness tips as you jog along his favorite route.

The Halekulani fitness facility is modest, but is like a hideaway where you can plan a workout with free weights, multiple-exercise Paramount weight-training gym, bicycles, rowing machines, and treadmills. The facility is available free of charge to all hotel guests. Aerobics classes are scheduled at 7:30 AM Tuesday, Thursday, and Saturday, although there are rarely more than a handful of participants. For serious workouts, the hotel concierge arranges admission to the nearby Honolulu Club, where for a modest fee you can enjoy one of the best-equipped health clubs in the world, and salon services including Kerstin Florian facials.

The Halekulani is a small, private enclave, and the five-building complex and lush gardens meticulously maintain island traditions. The newly heated outdoor swimming pool, tiled with orchid motifs, and Charlie Chan's "House Without a Key" lounge, are enduring landmarks amid a sea of mass-tourism hotels.

Halekulani Hotel

2199 Kalia Rd., Honolulu, HI 96815
Tel. 808/923–2311 or 800/367–2343
Fax 808/926–8004

Administration	Manager, Patricia Tam; fitness-program director, Max Telford
Season	Year-round
Accommodations	456-room luxury hotel, 5 wings (1930s building and new additions). Rated best hotel in Hawaii. Rooms have sitting area, full bathroom with deep-soaking tub, glassed-in shower, marble vanity. Most have views of the beach and Diamond Head. 3 telephones, nightly turndown service, cable TV (CNN), work desk.
Rates	Rooms for 1 or 2 persons $265–$430 daily, suites $580–$3,500 single or double. Confirmation by credit card. AE, DC, MC, V.
Meal Plans	Orchids Restaurant specializes in Pacific seafood and contemporary American cuisine. La Mer specialties include Lanai venison in a black pepper sauce, Norwegian salmon smoked over kiawe wood, onaga fish baked in herbed salt crust. Meals are à la carte.
Services and Facilities	**Exercise Equipment:** Paramount weight-training multigym, 2 Lifecycles, 2 Precor treadmills, Lifestep, Precor rower, dumbbells (3–35 lbs), bench press. **Services:** Shiatsu massage, aerobics class. **Swimming Facilities:** Outdoor pool, ocean. **Recreation Facilities:** At Honolulu Club: racquetball, volleyball, golf driving range; nearby tennis and golf. Water sports equipment on beach. **Evening Programs:** Resort entertainment.
In the Area	Honolulu Museum of Art, Pearl Harbor, Ihilani Resort and Spa
Getting Here	*From Honolulu International Airport.* Limousine, shuttle service, rental car, or taxi available (20 mins).
Special Notes	For people with disabilities, elevators, ground-floor lanai suites, and 14 specially equipped rooms are barrier free. Supervised activities and excursions for children. No smoking in designated dining areas; some no-smoking rooms. Fitness room open daily 7 AM–10 PM.

Hawaiian Wellness Holiday

Holistic health
Life enhancement

Kauai   Combine a holistic approach to health and nutrition with a beach condominium resort, add therapeutic massage and chiropractic treatments, and you have Dr. Grady Deal's prescription for a fitness holiday. Dr. Deal—a psychologist, licensed massage therapist, gourmet cook, and practicing chiropractor—and his wife, Roberleigh, have created a warm, homelike atmosphere for their guests. Using facilities at the Sheraton Beach Resort, the Hawaiian Wellness Holiday is tailored to individual needs and interests. By keeping the group small—an average of 10 per week—the Deals aim for a high level of success in meeting each person's goals.

Yoga, aerobics, and aquacise in the swimming pool are part of the daily program. Included in the program cost are three massages or chiropractic therapy. Detoxification, weight loss, and body toning are the primary objectives. Invigorating exercise and a cleansing diet are supplemented by natural therapies.

Spending most of the day outdoors, on scenic hikes and walks as well as at aerobics classes, guests quickly discover the natural healing effect of the island. Excursions included in the basic fee take the group to such scenic places as Waimea Canyon; the NaPali coast; Lumahai beach, where *South Pacific* was filmed; and the Seven Sacred Pools. Kauai is said to have a rare energy vortex, a metaphysical natural beauty that relaxes the mind and body. Exploring the island with a like-minded group of health seekers adds a special quality to the fitness holiday. Each person is encouraged to search for inner energy.

Rounding out the program are cooking demonstrations based on the macrobiotic and vegetarian meals that are served, workshops on nutrition and health, meditation, and deep-breathing exercises for relaxation. At the end of the day, you can unwind in the steam room, sauna, or Jacuzzi while awaiting yet another memorable sunset.

Hawaiian Wellness Holiday
Box 279, Koloa, HI 96756
Tel. 808/332–9244 or 800/338–6977

Administration Program director, Roberleigh Deal; medical director, Grady A. Deal, Ph.D., D.C.

Season Year-round

Accommodations Deluxe room or suite at Sheraton Kauai Beach Resort, with king- or queen-size beds, full bathroom, balcony, TV, telephone, air-conditioning, ceiling fans; choice of oceanfront or garden view.

Rates All-inclusive week $2,095 single, $3,295 for 2 double occupancy in ocean-view room; $1,795 single, $2,895 for 2 in garden-view room. Add 7% tax; gratuities optional. (5% discount for 2-week program.) Deposit: $500 on booking, balance due 30 days prior to arrival. AE, MC, V (5% surcharge).

Meal Plans Vegetarian, cleansing, or macrobiotic meals with whole grains, raw and cooked vegetables, fruit, juices, legumes, and fish. Breakfast can be wheatless waffles with berries; lunch, a vegetable stew or baked macaroni with cashew-pimiento cheese-less topping. Dinner includes green salad with oil-free dressing, brown rice cooked with sesame seeds, and herb tea. Special dietary needs accommodated.

Services and Facilities **Exercise Equipment:** Cybex circuit with 10 variable resistance units, 3 Stairsteps, 2 Aerobicycles, 2 Monark bikes, computerized rower, Olympic free weights, dumbbells. **Services:** Massage (Swedish, shiatsu, deep tissue), reflexology, G-5 vibrator massage, chiropractic, physical therapy; hair, nail, and skin care (added fee). Nutritional counseling, cooking classes. Detoxification/colonic program ($250 additional). **Swimming Facilities:** 2 outdoor pools, ocean beach. **Recreation Facilities:** 2 tennis courts, water sports, hiking. Golf, horseback riding, bicycle rental nearby. **Evening Programs:** Talks and slide shows on health-related topics, Hawaiian cultural performances.

In the Area Scheduled group hiking and sightseeing trips to various parts of the island; botanical garden, fern grotto, Spouting Horn blowhole, Kokee State Park, Waimea Canyon. Optional: helicopter tour, scuba dives, day cruises.

Getting Here *From Koloa.* By car, Poipu Rd. to Poipu Beach (15 mins). Transfers on arrival/departure at airport (and for all excursions) included in program fee. Taxi, rental car available.

Special Notes Accommodations for people with disabilities. Full program for children over 12; resort activity available. No smoking in program areas. Remember to bring medical or chiropractic records.

Hilton Waikoloa Village

Luxury pampering
Nonprogram resort

Hawaii Created on a mammoth scale, the Hilton Waikoloa Village has the secluded Kohala Spa, which serves as an escape from the beach scene. Opened in 1988 by Hyatt and managed since 1993 by Hilton, the spa is part of a 1,352-acre resort that includes ancient fishponds and petroglyph fields. Guests sign up to swim with dolphins, take horse-drawn carriage rides into the countryside, and go surfing in catamarans. Instead of walking to your room, you ride a canal boat or the "tubular tram." There is also a spiritual walk with guided meditation recalling the ancient kahunas.

The spa offers European thalassotherapy in baths, herbal wraps, body masks, and loofah scrubs. Seaweed-based cosmetics and natural oils nourish the body and prevent sun damage to winter-weary complexions. Participants are provided with workout clothing and robes. In one of the spa's posh, private massage rooms you can experience a traditional Hawaiian Lomi-Lomi massage, a form of lymphatic cleansing. With rhythmic rocking, the therapist chants while relaxing your muscles and stimulating circulation. Services are billed to your room on an à la carte basis, plus $15 for daily use of spa facilities; $10 after 4 PM if you include a massage or treatment.

Pleasures in Paradise 4- or 7-day packages combine a spa program and outdoor adventure. In addition to three spa cuisine meals daily, unlimited fitness classes and use of spa facilities, and a personal training session, you receive a medical screening, relaxation session with hydrosonics, and a choice of kayak trip or ocean sail. An ocean-view room and airport transfers are included.

Extensive facilities are at your disposal. In separate sections for men and women are Turkish steam rooms, Finnish sauna, outdoor whirlpool, showers and locker room with full amenities. A beauty salon, a gym for aerobics classes, and a weights room are all part of the freestanding spa building.

The spa's combination of Eastern and Western health philosophies includes daily tai chi chuan and yoga classes as well as stress reduction, water aerobics, and meditation. The ancient Chinese tai chi chuan movements are demonstrated on the beach at 8 and 9:45 AM. All guests are invited to join a power walk around the property, called the Sunrise Pacer (3–5 mi). Classes are complimentary with the spa's daily fee.

From the mile-long museum walkway filled with $3.5 million of Oriental and Pacific art to the acre-size swimming pool with its waterfalls, hidden grotto bar, and twisting water slide, nonstop fantasy rather than fitness is the reason for vacationing here.

Hilton Waikoloa Village

69-425 Waikoloa Beach Resort, Waikoloa, HI 96743
Tel. 808/885–1234 or 800/445–8667
Fax 808/885–2901

Administration General manager, Dieter H. Seeger; spa manager, Susan Bordeaux-Johlfs

Season   Year-round

Accommodations   1,241 guest rooms in 3 low-rise towers. Contemporary furnishings include king-size or 2 queen-size beds, marble-floored bathroom, full amenities. 75% of rooms have ocean view.

Rates   Daily $280–$330 per room, single or double occupancy. Spa sampler $99 (includes service charge and gratuity). 4-night Pleasures in Paradise package $1,782 single, $2,420 for 2, double occupancy; 7-night package $3,119 single, $4,488 for 2 double. Add 4.167% state sales tax. Deposit: Confirmation by credit card. AE, MC, V.

Meal Plans   3 spa cusines meals daily in Pleasures in Paradise package. Lunch at the spa can include chili chicken salad with confetti of marinated rice and vegetables in cilantro vinaigrette, poached salmon with cucumber and tomato on Bibb lettuce with dill couli, vegetable antipasto with tuna. Dinner entrées include grilled mahimahi, vegetarian platter.

Services and Facilities   **Exercise Equipment:** 10-unit Keiser weight-training gym, 2 StairMaster 4000 PT, Gravitron, 4 PTS Turbo recumbent bikes, 2 Biocycles, 2 Precor treadmills, Concept 2 rowing machine, dumbbells (2½–50 lbs). **Services:** Massage (lomi-lomi, aromatherapy, shiatsu, sports, Swedish), reflexology, seaweed pack, body facial, body mask, loofah buff, herbal wrap, herbal or aroma bath, hydrating facial. Beauty salon with French Phytomer products for hair, nail, and skin care. **Swimming Facilities:** Outdoor freshwater pools, seawater lagoon, ocean beach. **Recreation Facilities:** 8 tennis courts (2 clay, 6 plexi), 2 championship 18-hole golf courses plus 2 courses nearby, horseback riding, windsurfing, snorkeling, scuba diving, sailing.

In the Area   Hawaii Volcanoes National Park (2 active volcanoes, Kilauea and Mauna Loa), Kona coffee plantations, Captain Cook (fishing port), Hilo (shopping), Mookini Heiau (royal palace), Puukohola Heiau (temple), Lyman House Museum (missionary home), downhill skiing (Jan.–Mar.).

Getting Here   *From Honolulu.* Interisland air services to Keahole Kona Airport (45 mins), transfer by hotel van ($17.50 each way) or rental car (20 mins).

Special Notes   Specially equipped rooms for people with disabilities. Children's day camp with lunch ($35). No smoking in spa. Spa open daily 6 AM–8 PM.

Hyatt Regency Kauai

Nonprogram resort

Poipu Beach Kauai   Secluded within the Hyatt Regency Kauai resort is the full-service ANARA Spa, which stands for "A New Age Restorative Approach." But what's new here are old Hawaiian healing treatments: a sacred red clay called alaea (Kapu Kai' Alaea is the treatment's name) used as a skin softener in a sea salt body scrub, followed by a soak in an herbal botanical bath while sipping Hawaiian hibiscus tea; lomi-lomi massage—reputed to imitate the wind-and-sea rhythms of the islands in its quick strokes—starts with chants once performed by the kahuna high priests. Skin treatments with honey-mango or papaya blossom oil, and facial cleansing with gardenia-scented coconut oil, are among the specialties.

An open-air courtyard encloses the lap pool and the lava-rock rinsing showers, creating a quiet place to awaken the senses. Then you can work out in an air-conditioned fitness facility, including steam room, sauna, whirlpool, and aerobics studio with impact-absorbing wooden floor. Scheduled daily are aerobics classes, weight training clinics, and aqua-trim water exercise.

Services worth noting include the Ti Leaf Cool Wrap, designed to alleviate the discomfort of sunburn and elevated body temperature. Guests are spread on a bed of the cooling leaves, covered with a gel made from aloe vera and comfrey, then covered with more heat-absorbing leaves and wrapped in a sheet for 20 minutes to sweat out any toxins. Another treatment is the Sacred Bath of Hawaiian elders or kapunas: red colloidal clay from the base of Kauai's Mt. Waialeale is mixed with sea salts and spread on the body after a session in the steam room. This treatment is followed with a botanical bath with a limu or seaweed and salt mixture, which simulates thalassotherapy in helping to stimulate blood circulation.

This plantation-style resort, set on 18 acres of lush beachfront, has long and rambling low-rise wings. From your patio or lanai there are views of a junglelike lagoon. Public areas are decorated with museum-quality Asian and Pacific art. Joggers can enjoy a 2-mile course on the beach. Family-oriented programs include an introduction to island archaeology. Surrounding the grottoes, waterfalls, and swimming pools is a Robert Trent Jones, Jr.–designed golf course. For relaxation, try Stevenson's Library (named for island-lover Robert Louis), with its books, billiards, and cheery bar.

Nature lovers and hikers who want to explore the island can schedule a tour of Limahuli Garden in a lush, green valley dedicated to preserving Hawaiian plants. A botanical paradise set between mountains, sky, and sea, the gardens have been cultivated since 1940, but include a Polynesian settlement believed to have been built 1,000 years ago. On the Na Pali coast near Haena, the preserve is part of the National Tropical Botanical Garden.

Hyatt Regency Kauai

1571 Poipu Rd., Koloa, Kauai, HI 96756
Tel. 808/742–1234 or 800/228–9000
Fax 808/742–1557

Administration	General manager, Mark Heinzelman; spa director, Shelly Widen-Hall
Season	Year-round
Accommodations	Spread out on 3 floors, the 600-room resort includes concierge service floors in the Regency Club, closest to the spa. Spacious, contemporary rooms, full bath, lanais, balconies, luxury amenities, air-conditioning, TV, telephone.
Rates	$275–$395 per day for 1 or 2 persons; Regency Club $465. 1-day spa package $245, plus room. Credit-card confirmation. AE, DC, MC, V.
Meal Plans	No special meal plan. Selected low-calorie, low-fat items for heart-healthy dining available daily.
Services and Facilities	**Exercise Equipment:** Nautilus weight-training units (6 stations), Lifecycle, treadmill, free weights. **Services:** Massage (shiatsu, lomi-lomi, Swedish, Esalen), facials, body scrub; beauty salon for hair, nail, and skin care; tennis clinics, private lessons, scuba course. **Swimming Facilities:** Free-form ½-acre pool, ocean beach. **Recreation Facilities:** 18-hole golf course, 5 tennis courts, hiking, bicycle rental. **Evening Programs:** Resort entertainment.
In the Area	Hanalei National Wildlife Refuge (kayak tour), Kokee State Park (mountain lodge), Waimea Canyon (scenic drive), Waimea (Capt. Cook landed here in 1778), Na Pali Coast State

Park (hiking trails), National Tropical Botanical Garden, Fern Grotto.

Getting Here *From Lihue.* By car, Hwy. 50 to Poipu Beach Rd. (20 mins). Rental car, taxi, airport shuttle van available.

Special Notes Crafts programs and Camp Hyatt ($34) day camp for children. Ground-floor rooms for people with disabilities. Daily spa admission $10. Open daily 6 AM–8 PM; salon services by appointment, 9–6.

Ihilani Resort and Spa

Luxury pampering
Taking the waters

Oahu Inspired by the sea and ancient Hawaiian healing therapies, the spa program at the Ihilani Resort provides revitalization and relaxation. On Oahu's western coast, 25 minutes from Honolulu International Airport, the 640-acre resort opened late in 1993. Designed for upscale travelers and members of the Ko' Olina Golf Club, the luxury hotel is set amid thousands of coconut palm trees, banyans, monkeypods, and silver buttonwood trees, as well as flowering bougainvillea, firecracker plants, and fragrant plumeria. Surrounded by four tranquil lagoons and the Waianae mountains, this property may be the ultimate Hawaiian escape.

Aerobics classes are scheduled in a coed studio on the top floor of the three-level spa, where there is also a weights room. Jacuzzi and locker rooms are on the second floor, where you enter from the hotel. An ocean environment is created with French thalassotherapy technology and fresh saltwater piped directly from the Pacific. Specially designed treatment rooms have a hydrotherapy tub by Doyer, a Vichy-style shower massage table, and a Needle Shower Pavilion with 12 shower heads for water massage. The treatments involve Hawaiian seaweed packs and wraps, salt scrubs, and facial masques with marine algae.

Four program packages are offered, including three spa cuisine meals daily. The Hawaiian Revitalization Program, and a Health and Vitality Program, both seven days, can begin on any day, but a Sunday welcome is suggested by the spa director who prepares a personal program for each guest. Postural and body alignment sessions may be included, as well as Swedish and shiatsu massage, or a more challenging fitness component. The four-day Energy Booster package allows you to sample therapies Tuesday through Saturday, or you can shed pounds on a four-day Getaway package for weight loss or maintenance. If you simply want a day of pampering, hotel guests can book the Ali'i For a Day package.

The spa's selection of treatments includes Hawaiian herbs and medicinal plants such as ti leaves. In addition, Essensa and Nina Ricci skin care products are used. Workout clothing is supplied daily, as well as cotton robes, slippers, and personal grooming items. Complete your day with a lomi-lomi massage, the traditional rhythmic strokes accompanied by chanting, and perhaps dancing the hula.

After being wrapped and steamed in herb-soaked raw linen, you can drink the same herbs in tea, or taste them in spa meals made with local seafood, seaweed, and fruits. With five restaurants, including a dedicated spa café, a splendid beach cove, golf, and tennis, this hideaway lives up to its name, "heavenly splendor."

Ihilani Resort and Spa

92-1001 O'lani St., Kapolei, Oahu, HI 96707
Tel. 808/679–0079 or 800/626–4446
Fax 808/679–3387

Administration General manager, Charles Park; spa director, Ann Emich

Season Year-round

Accommodations 387 guest rooms and 42 luxury suites in a Japan Air Lines hotel dominated by a 15-story, glass-dome atrium. Oceanfront guest rooms include 7 with private garden terrace lanais and access to outdoor spa. All rooms have ceiling fan, air-conditioning, TV, 3 telephones, oversize marble bathroom with deep-soak tub, glass-enclosed shower stall, double vanities, lighted mirror, and private lanai with cushioned teak furnishings, a dining table, and reclining "Queen Mary" lounge chair. Amenities include robes, custom toiletries, hair dryer.

Rates 7-day Revitalization program $3,646 single, $2,834 per person, double occupancy. 7-day Vitality package $3,554 single, $2,749 double. 4-day Energy Booster package $2,021 single, $1,530 double. 4-day Getaway $2,098 single, $1,618 double. Prices include tax, gratuity, and airport transfers. Spa Day packages (no lodging) $140–$295. Daily room tariff $275–$550 for 1 or 2 persons, plus taxes; suites $700–$5,000. Deposit: $300–$800. AE, DC, MC, V.

Meal Plans 3 spa cuisine meals daily included in program packages. Meals are served in the main dining room or spa café: daily salad, fish entrée, fresh tropical fruit. Breakfast may be egg-white omelet or banana whole-wheat pancakes with yogurt. Lunch selections include vegetarian pizza or lasagna, seafood Mediterranean style.

Services and Facilities **Exercise Equipment:** Fitness Master cross-country skier, 2 rowing machines, Vigor 10-station training equipment, including 3 Quinton treadmills, 2 Cateye bikes, and 3 StairMasters. **Services:** Swedish massage, shiatsu, hydrotherapy, thalassotherapy, body scrub, herbal wrap, marine masque, aromatherapy, loofah body wrap, Vichy shower, facial, personal training, health and fitness evaluation. Beauty salon for hair, nail, and skin care. **Swimming Facilities:** Outdoor lap and exercise pools, ocean beach. **Recreation Facilities:** 6 tennis courts (Kramer Sports Surface), 18-hole golf course, water sports, complimentary snorkling equipment, croquet, boccie balls.

In the Area Pearl Harbor Memorial, Waikiki Beach, Honolulu Museum of Art, Bishop Museum (Hawaiian cultures), Iolani Palace.

Getting Here *From Honolulu.* By car, Hwy. 1 west, past Honolulu International Airport, to Ko'Olina exit (30 mins). Limousine transfers included with spa program; rental car at hotel and airport, taxi available.

Special Notes Spa open daily 7–7. Minimum age is 16. Supervised child-care facility available.

Kalani Honua Eco-Resort

Holistic health
Life enhancement
Taking the waters
Weight management

Kehena Beach, Hawaii—The Big Island Kalani Honua Eco-Resort puts you in close touch with the spectacular natural environment of the Big Island. This rough-edged budget-priced retreat offers health-oriented activities, and an intercultural program, with yoga and hula, complements workshops scheduled throughout the year. Subjects covered by workshop retreats include men's health, organic gardening, and the body-mind-spirit connection. Visitors can participate or venture off to explore on their own.

Founded in 1982, the center attracts an interesting mix of robust, healthy men and women, families hiking the volcano trails, and professional bodyworkers attending seminars on holistic health and preventive medicine, but there is no fixed program. Of special interest are presentations on native Hawaiian cleansing rituals by islanders.

In keeping with the spirit of old Hawaii, guests are housed in *hales*, wood lodges made of cedar logs. Each hexagonal lodge has its own kitchen and ocean-view studio space, with dormitory rooms, but mostly private accommodations. Campers can sleep under the stars at 25 sites among the palm trees.

Therapeutic services and exercise classes are the focus of a Japanese-style spa. The wooden bathhouse has a communal hot tub, sauna heated by wood-burning stove, and private massage rooms. Four pavilions with suspended wooden floors are used for yoga, aerobics, and dance performances. Nearby are a 25-foot swimming pool and a Jacuzzi, plus a fitness center.

New Agers mix easily with visitors on the Big Island—at 4,038 square miles it's the biggest island in the Hawaiian chain— and there are numerous "clothing optional" beaches as well as shops offering natural foods, crystals, tarot cards, and books. Hawaii Volcanoes National Park provides a close-up look at rivers of red-hot lava flow from Mt. Kilauea. On the Puna Coast, just south of Hilo, the resort is 5 miles from the lava flow.

Kalani Honua Eco-Resort

Box 4500, R.R. 2, Pahoa, HI 96778
Tel. 808/965–7828 or 800/800–6886
Fax 808/965–9613

Administration Director, Richard Koob; program director, Delton Johnson

Season Year-round

Accommodations 4 2-story lodges, 37 rooms double or multiple occupancy. Cedar walls and floors, minimal furniture, many windows; Hawaiian prints and fabrics, fresh flowers. Baths shared, except for 2 private suites in each lodge. No maid service; communal kitchen. Also available: private cottages, 25 tent sites. Amenities: coin-operated laundry, rental of water sports gear. No air-conditioning.

Rates Lodge room $75–$95 per night with private bath ($110–$145 with meals) for 2 persons; 18 share-bath lodge rooms $60–$70 ($85–$120 with meals); 3-bed rooms, $45 per person ($70 with meals). 7 cottages with private baths $85–$95 (with meals $110–$145) for 2; house with kitchen, 2 baths, $165. Dormitory bed $45 (with meals $70). Tent site $20. Deposit: 1 night. AE, DC, MC, V.

Meal Plans Primarily vegetarian, meals at Cafe Cashew are à la carte. Hawaiian-style breakfast includes papaya, passion fruit, banana smoothies, buffet of tropical fruits, brown rice, French toast. Lunch can be sautéed vegetables with tempeh and tahini sauce, broiled mahimahi, or spinach lasagna. Dinner choices can be grilled chicken or mahimahi baked with mushrooms in lemon and garlic sauce, cream of papaya cashew soup, and a salad bar. Beer, wine, coffee, tea available. Special diet requests (Pritikin, macrobiotic) accommodated. Daily meal plan $29; breakfast $7, lunch $9, dinner $13.

Services and Facilities **Exercise Equipment:** Weight-training units, stationary bike, treadmill, free weights. **Services:** Massage (shiatsu, Swedish, Esalen), acupressure, acupuncture, watsu, chiropractic, Kripalu yoga. Counseling on weight loss, diet, nutrition. **Swimming Facilities:** Outdoor pool, ocean beaches. **Spa Facilities:** 2 Jacuzzi whirlpools, steam baths. **Recreation Facilities:** Bicycle rental, tennis court, horseback riding, hiking, volleyball; golf course, ski slopes nearby. **Evening Programs:** Workshops on health, hula, sports conditioning, yoga; cultural performances, traditional Hawaiian feasts.

In the Area Volcanoes National Park, Jaggar Museum (Volcanoes Park history), Kilauea caldera, lava tubes at Wahaula Visitor Center, Hawaii Tropical Botanical Garden, Parker Ranch resort area, Pahoa (plantation town), King Kamehameha historic site, Mauna Kea observatory telescope, MacKenzie State Park (hiking, picnics, beach), Wood Valley Buddhist temple.

Getting Here *From Hilo.* By car, Rte. 11 to Keaau, Rte. 130 to Rte. 137 (45 mins). Rental car, limousine, taxi available.

Special Notes No smoking in bathhouse area. Remember to bring strong sunscreen, mosquito repellent, and flashlight.

The New Millennium Institute

Spiritual awareness

The Big Island of Hawaii Discovering a Frank Lloyd Wright house in ranch country on the Big Island of Hawaii may seem curious, as the New Millennium Institute wasn't planned here by the master architect. Constructed over a period of three years by craftsmen working from a 1950s Wright design that the architect himself did not use, the Institute opened in 1996 under the auspices of a nonprofit educational organization, Parker School. The organization specializes in weeklong retreats with some of today's most eminent visionaries.

Four guest rooms are available at the Institute; other participants stay at nearby bed-and-breakfast lodging or luxury hotels such as the Hilton Waikoloa Village. Retreats are limited to 20 participants, and reservations are required well in advance. A typical day includes optional morning yoga, 3 hours of classroom time, and a gourmet lunch. Afternoons are free for recreation and field trips. Excursions can include King Kamehameha's sacred site; hikes in a state park containing an ancient healing center; a rain forest; and a visit to the Pu'ukohola Heiau temple, the last major religious structure of the ancient Hawaiian culture.

Nestled into an earth berm, the hemicycle home seems to embody visionary ideas. Meetings are held in a cylindrical tower that arcs 120 degrees around the "suspended" second floor. The gardens include a rock-walled hot tub and walking labyrinth.

Looming on the horizon is the world's most active volcano, Kilauea. In winter, there is skiing on slopes of Mt. Mauna Kea, which attracts stargazers with the world's largest telescope at its 14,000-foot summit. Also in the area are an organic farm that supplies vegetables for meals at the institute, a renewable-energy wind generation plant, and other projects that promote a sustainable way of living.

The New Millennium Institute
Waimea, HI 96778
Office: 1170 Waimanu St., Honolulu, HI 96814
Tel. 808/593–2297
Fax 808/593–2640

Administration Parker School Community Education Program coordinator, Susanne Sims

Season Year-round during scheduled programs

Accommodations House has 1 bedroom with king-size bed, Jacuzzi bathtub, fireplace; 1 bedroom with queen-size bed and bathroom shower; 2 rooms with twin beds, bathroom. Furniture designed by Frank Lloyd Wright includes built-in wooden cabinets, lighting fixtures, Taliesin wing chairs, convex dining table, and wind chimes. Full kitchen with washer/dryer, 2 fireplaces, TV with VCR, stereo radio/CD, library, phone, fax, computer.

Rates $975 for 6-night program, including some meals. Shared room $65 per person daily. Private room with queen bed and bathroom, $125. No credit cards.

Meal Plans Lunch served daily during retreat program, 2 evening meals. Organically grown vegetarian buffet includes salads, fruit, and pasta.

Getting Here *From Honolulu.* Interisland commuter flights by Mahalo, Aloha, and Hawaiian airlines to Keahole Kona Airport; from San Francisco, direct flights by United Airlines. Complimentary pickup provided for scheduled retreats; taxi, rental car available. By car, Hwy. 109 via Waimea (45 mins).

Sheraton Hotel Hana-Maui

Nonprogram resort

Maui An aura of the Old West pervades the Hotel Hana-Maui, which is set on an isolated coast in the middle of a cattle ranch. Hawaiian cowboys, called *paniolos*, lead white-face Hereford cattle in from pasture as you hike down the rocky coastal trail to catch the sunset at Red Sand Beach; a session of yoga at the Wellness Center is a nice follow-up, topped off by a shiatsu massage.

Above all, Hana is a place of soothing seclusion. Lodging is in spacious one-story cottages with tropical furnishings and private lanais. During dinner in the Plantation Great House, talented members of the staff offer performances of Hawaiian music and dance in an authentic style not packaged for commercial shows.

The 66-acre complex has a small wellness center, where you can work out surrounded by panoramic views. The mirrored aerobics studio provides a varied schedule of classes: low-impact aerobics, aquacise, and yoga at $10 per class. A nature walk begins the day at 9:30 AM. The spa director's philosophy reflects an appreciation of the island's natural beauty rather than emphasizing pampering attentions. For serious hikers, there is a four-hour trek into the lush tropical forest, with a stop to swim under the cascades of a waterfall.

Secluded, almost monastic, the 50-year-old hotel is a stronghold of Hawaiian culture and nature. Hana's terrain slopes gently upward across green pastures, rising to rain forests and the Haleakala Crater. It is a wild and magical place.

Sheraton Hotel Hana-Maui
Box 8, Hana, Maui, HI 967
Tel. 808/248–8211 or 800/782–9488
Fax 808/528–7377

Administration General manager, Chip Bahouch

Season Year-round

Accommodations 97 cottages with wooden floors and walls, tropical furniture. 2 queen-size beds, modern bathroom, private lanai, air-conditioning, ceiling fans.

Rates Daily $395–$795 per suite for 1 or 2 persons. No meals included. Add tax. AE, DC, MC, V.

Meal Plans Dining à la carte. The dining room specializes in Asian-Pacific cuisine featuring seafood and organic ingredients.

Services and Facilities **Exercise Equipment:** 2 Precor bikes, 2 Precor stairclimbers, Precor rowing machine, NordicTrack cross-country ski unit, 5-station Paramount gym. **Services:** Swedish and therapeutic massage; facial with coconut, honey, aloe vera; nature walk, hiking, aerobics classes, aquacise. **Swimming Facilities:** Outdoor lap pool, 80′ × 40′; ocean beaches. **Recreation Facilities:** Horseback riding, baseball, hay ride, breakfast cookout. **Evening Programs:** Folklore performances.

In the Area Hana Museum and cultural center, Seven Sacred Pools, lava sand beaches, historic sites, boar hunts, rodeos.

Getting Here *From the U.S. mainland.* Direct flights by United, Delta, American, and Hawaiian Airlines to Kahului Airport. Transfers by van (1½ hrs) or Aloha Island Air (15 mins). *From Honolulu.* By interisland airlines and American Hawaii cruises. Rental car available.

Strong, Stretched & Centered

Holistic health
Life enhancement
Sports conditioning

Maui Working out with the instructors' instructor is a fitness buff's dream come true. Over 200 graduates of professional sports certification programs come here for six weeks of the body/mind training program originated here by Gloria Keeling.

This is not a quick-fix, so you should be in shape before joining Gloria's beach gang. The techniques used reflect several cultures and range from tai chi to aquacize. Weight-reduction methods employ the notion of muscle definition as well as the concept of *ki*, the centered self.

Based at Kihei, the program participants work out at a fully equipped Powerhouse Gym. The staff instructors and advisers from the Maui Holistic Health Center work with you individually. Training sites include spectacular Haleakala crater (the world's sixth largest dormant volcano) and the numerous white-sand beaches for which Maui is celebrated.

You'll learn "gestalt dance" and African jazz rhythms with your aerobics in this high-powered experience in interdisciplinary training, with people devoted to nurturing a balance of mind and body fitness. Professional certification is awarded upon completion.

Strong, Stretched & Centered
Box 758, Paia, Maui, HI 96779
Tel. 808/575–2178
Fax 808/575–2275

Administration Program director, Gloria Keeling

Season Scheduled sessions year-round

Accommodations Lanai-style apartments with 2–3 bedrooms shared by participants. Twin beds, modern bath, ocean-view balcony or terrace. Furnished informally, with white rattan seating, lots of big cotton pillows, tropical fabrics; color TV, completely equipped kitchen. Beach area has shaded Jacuzzi and swimming pool. No maid service; laundry unit in each apartment.

Rates 6-week program $5,500 per person, double occupancy; additional $1,200 for single room. $1,000 advance payment. No credit cards.

Meal Plans 3 meals served family-style weekdays. Mostly vegetarian menu includes enchiladas with beans, choice of vegetables or chicken, eggplant Parmesan casserole, baked mahimahi fish, Thai satay noodles with oyster sauce, vegetables, and peanuts. On weekends, guests prepare their own meals.

Services and Facilities **Exercise Equipment:** Universal Gym, free weights, treadmills, Lifecycles, StairMaster. **Services:** Sports conditioning, weight-lifting training, massage, video analysis, instructor certification. **Swimming Facilities:** Outdoor pool, ocean beach. **Recreation Facilities:** Water sports, hiking; nearby tennis courts, golf course, bike rental, horseback riding, scuba and water sports, all for extra fees. **Evening Programs:** Workshops on health and fitness.

In the Area Group outings for snorkeling, overnight hike in Hana State Park, sunrise hike on Haleakala crater. Interisland cruises, helicopter sightseeing, shopping and nightlife in Lahaina, sugarcane train ride, Grand Wailea Resort & Spa.

Getting Here Direct flights to Maui's airport from Chicago and West Coast on United Airlines. *From Kahului.* About 20 mins to Kihei by taxi or rental car. Rental car available for group use.

Special Notes Continuing education credits available.

The Westin Maui

Nonprogram resort

Hawaii
Maui Breathtaking waterfalls, meandering streams, and a health club are among the attractions of this mega resort. The Westin Maui is set on 12 oceanfront acres and is bordered by two golf courses and a tennis complex; it has all the pleasures of paradise and none of the pain.

Take the wildlife and garden tour offered by Guest Services and you will learn that more than 650,000 gallons of water sustain the resort's aquatic needs. The pool area alone features five free-form swimming pools, two water slides, and a swim-up Jacuzzi hidden away in a grotto. Swans, flamingos, and other charming characters roam freely, adding their individual personalities to the tropical atmosphere.

The coed health club offers weight-training and an exercise room where aerobics classes are held daily. Step and low-impact sessions are offered for a modest charge per class plus the daily admission fee ($15), which is waived for hotel guests. There is a steam room, sauna, and Jacuzzi for relaxing stiff, sore muscles. Massage therapy is available by appointment.

The Westin Maui
2365 Kaanapali Pkwy., Lahaina, HI 96761
Tel. 808/667–2525 or 800/228–3000
Fax 808/661–5764

Administration General manager, Mathen Hart

Season Year-round

Accommodations 761-room resort has 2 towers, each 11 floors. Luxury rooms and suites, including the exclusive Royal Beach Club. Air-conditioned, private lanais, king-size or double beds, views of ocean or golf course.

Rates $255–$425 single or double occupancy, Royal Beach Club rooms $475, suites $650–$800. Add taxes, gratuities. Deposit: 2 nights' advance payment or credit-card confirmation. AE, DC, MC, V.

Meal Plans No special dining plan. 3 restaurants, snacks to Continental fare. Best choice: Sound of the Falls.

Services and Facilities **Exercise Facilities:** 10 Sprint weight-training units, 2 Stair-Masters, 3 Lifecycles, Cybex Smithpress, treadmill, dumbbells (to 40 lbs). **Services:** Lomi-Lomi massage, Swedish massage, shiatsu, reflexology, acupressure; beauty salon for facial, hair, and nail care. **Swimming Facilities:** 5 outdoor pools, ocean beach. **Recreation Facilities:** 11 tennis courts (6 lighted), 2 18-hole golf courses, water sports. **Evening Programs:** Resort entertainment, Hawaiiana demonstrations.

In the Area Guided tours of the resort include art collection and gardens. Lahaina (old whaling capital) shops, bars, restaurants; Mt. Haleakala; up-country ranches and rodeos; Sugar Cane Train Ride; winery tour; Maui Tropical Plantation (botanic gardens).

Getting Here *From Kapalua-West Airport.* By car, Hwy. 30 (Honoapiilani Hwy.) via Lahaina (10 mins). Complimentary transfers at airport. Rental car, taxi, shuttle van available.

Special Notes 10 barrier-free rooms specially appointed for guests with disabilities. Children can enjoy Hawaiian arts and crafts classes and seasonal day camp (Easter, summer, Thanksgiving, Christmas). No smoking in designated areas of the dining room and in health club; 2 no-smoking floors in Ocean Tower. Spa open daily 7 AM–8 PM. Spa open to nonhotel guests; daily facility fee $15.

Canada

Scenic splendor is an essential part of the fitness vacation in many areas of Canada. Still, Canadian resorts offer state-of-the-art health clubs and treatment centers, Hungarian kur and glacial mud facials, in addition to outdoor hikes, trail rides, tennis, skiing, kayaking, and mountain biking.

Western Canada is endowed with a wide range of health-oriented resorts, from ranches to luxury hotels, as well as a number of hot springs. At the venerable Banff Springs Hotel in Alberta, guests combine sports and personal training with a visit to the historic thermal springs, and enjoy the most extensive selection of bodywork in Canada at the new Solace Spa. The first destination spa opened in 1983 at the Hills Health & Guest Ranch in cariboo country, the heart of British Columbia. Recently expanded and upgraded, the fitness facilities are the core of the sports training and weight management programs, while the trail rides and cross-country skiing provide a balanced, family-oriented activity year-round. The Hills' "Executive Renewal Week" even attracts Japanese businessmen. On the Pacific Coast, the Ocean Pointe Resort has a full fitness program plus walks in Victoria's historic harbor area and museums. Also on the islands are rustic Hollyhock Farm, where holistic programs and sea kayaking are offered from spring to fall, and naturopathic EcoMed Wellness Spa.

Ontario resort spas include the luxurious Inn at Manitou, the new Ste. Anne's spa, and the family-oriented Wheels Country Inn. Thalassotherapy is the specialty of small resorts along the Gaspé Peninsula of French-speaking Quebec, which also has the farmlike Eastman Health Centre. For a demanding yoga regimen, try the Sivananda Ashram amid ski resorts of Mont Tremblant Park, near Montreal.

Canadian spas combine outdoor adventure with luxury pampering, for a change of pace from the more programmed spas south of the border. And since the currency exchange rate enhances the value of the U.S. dollar, there are substantial savings. (As of summer 1996, $1U.S. was worth $1.35 in Canadian currency.) Remember to bring identification papers for Canadian Customs: a voter registration card with photo, birth certificate, or passport will get you over the border without a hassle. Persons from outside the USA wishing to enter the States from Canada should make arrangements before leaving their home country; those planning to re-enter the States should check that they can comply with U.S. regulations. Hotel rates in Canada will include a room tax as well as GST (Goods & Services Tax), refundable to visitors upon application on departure.

Banff Springs Hotel

Luxury pampering
Taking the waters

Alberta
Banff
Built in the grand era of railroading at the turn of the century to accommodate visitors taking the waters, Banff Springs Hotel remains a bastion of traditional hospitality under Canadian-Pacific management, and added the impressive Solace Spa in 1995. Complete with a high-tech health club, mineralized seawater pools, and private therapy rooms where you

have a choice of Swedish or shiatsu massage, the spa complements an outdoor program of hikes and sports, from golf to
skiing. Also open to visitors not staying at the hotel for a $30
daily membership fee, the spa offers day spa packages as well
as a four-day retreat.

The turreted property—the largest in Canada west of
Toronto— looks like a castle out of Camelot, and is equally majestic inside. Most of the rooms are uniquely decorated, and
many are historically furnished. But instead of English lords
and ladies, the baronial halls may be filled with Japanese tour
groups. For maximum privacy and luxury, reserve one of four
suites built into towers above the spa; views of the valley and
distant mountains are priceless.

The hotel has 14 restaurants plus the new spa café, where
healthy breakfasts and lunches are available every day. A
grand staircase or elevator takes you down from the main
lobby to the three-level Solace Spa. With an aerobics studio
and strength-training equipment room whose glass walls overlook the Bow River valley and majestic mountains, it's the best
of the Northwest. The next level down is devoted to Kirsten
Florian skin care and a beauty salon, and the pool is accessible via interior stairs from the men's and women's locker
rooms. Also here are lounges with fireplace, glass-walled
sauna, inhalation room, steambath, and whirlpool.

Swimmers can use the huge indoor pool and interconnected
heated outdoor pool for free if staying at the hotel, or with a
daily membership of $20–$30. The spa has a skylit soaking pool
with minerals added to the water, and outdoor terraces with
mineral whirlpool exclusively for guests getting treatments.
The daily admission fee is waived for hotel guests who book a
minimum 25-minute spa treatment. There are 16 treatment
rooms on the pool level (two specially designed for wet bodywork), and a cascade shower. Due to heavy demand for appointments, it is wise to book spa services in advance of your
arrival at the resort.

Despite all the pampering activities, golf and skiing are still
the main attractions here, but other summer opportunities
bring cyclists and horseback riders, backpackers and river
rafters. Before the railroad and hotel builders arrived in 1885,
the hot springs were sacred, shrouded in clouds of steam. Rebuilt by Parks Canada, the spring-fed pools on the mountainside are open to the public, worth a hike in the morning for an
inexpensive, meditative soak in misty sunlight amid the pine
trees. Take a guided tour at the original Cave & Basin springs;
the admission fee includes admission to a museum with exhibits on the pools' development.

The sulfur-rich water has been replaced in the pools at Banff
Springs Hotel with a mixture of mineral salts from the sea.
The Solace Spa is a fitness buff's dream, and the handsomely
refurbished hotel still runs with railroadlike efficiency.

Banff Springs Hotel
Box 960, Banff, Alberta T0L 0C0
Tel. 403/762–2211 or 800/268–9411
Spa reservations: 403/762–1772
Fax 403/762–5755 hotel; 403/762–1766 spa

Administration	General manager, Ted Kissane; spa manager, Gordon Tareta
Season	Year-round
Accommodations	867 rooms and suites in original hotel and annex, Banff Springs Manor. Suites in several sizes with nooks and antiques. 3-story VIP suite with private glass elevator, sauna, whirlpool, and

---

Canada

Alberta

Banff Springs Hotel, **8**

Mountain Escape at Lake Louise Inn, **7**

British Columbia

Chateau Whistler Resort, **2**

EcoMed Wellness Spa & Clinic, **3**

Fairmont Hot Springs Resort, **9**

Harrison Hot Springs Hotel, **5**

The Hills Health Ranch, **6**

Hollyhock, **1**

Mountain Trek Fitness Retreat & Health Spa, **10**

Ocean Pointe Resort, **4**

New Brunswick

Manan Island Spa, **19**

Ontario

The Inn at Manitou, **11**

Ste. Anne's Country Inn & Spa, **13**

Wheels Country Spa at Wheels Inn, **12**

Quebec

Aqua-Mer Center, **21**

Auberge du Parc Inn, **20**

Auberge Villa Bellevue, **14**

Center d'Santé d'Eastman, **18**

Gray Rocks Inn, **16**

Sivananda Ashram, **15**

Spa Concept at Le Château Bromont, **17**

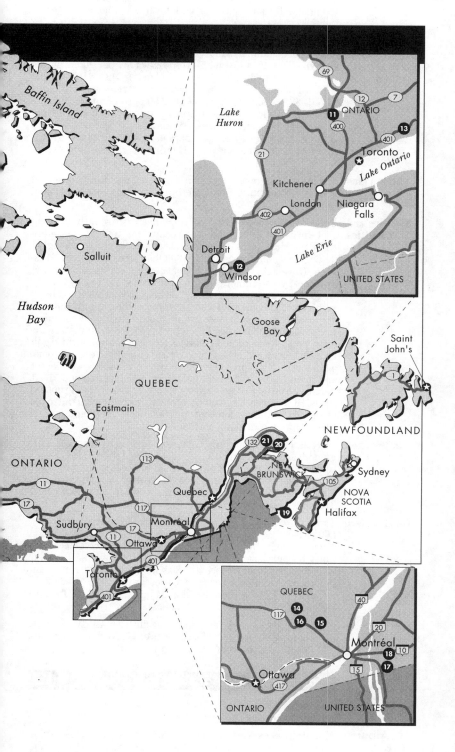

lap pool. All rooms have private bath, TV, phone, air-conditioning.

Rates May $160–$280 per room (C$) daily, single or double; suites $240–$595. Summer $180–$375 per room, suites $382–$644. Oct. 13—Dec. 22 and Jan. 2–Apr. $125–$187 per room, suites $205–$388. 2-bedroom suites (2–4 beds) $481–$1,024; VIP suite $1,500. 3-night/4-day Ultimate Retreat spa packages $1,551–$2,184 single, $1,236–$1,552.50 per person, double occupancy. Charlene Prickett Spa & Fitness Week (Oct.) from $1,530 per person, double occupancy. Day Spa package including lunch $145–$245 per person daily. Add taxes; gratuities included in spa packages. Confirm room with credit card. AE, MC, V.

Meal Plans Traditional à la carte menu in main dining room. Japanese and Italian restaurants. Spa Cafe open daily for breakfast and lunch.

Services and Facilities **Exercise Equipment:** 18-unit Bodymaster strength training system, 5 Trotter treadmills, 4 recumbent Tetrix bikes, 4 upright Tectrix bikes, 4 Climb Max steppers, Ivanko free weights (3–65 lbs), Smith machine (10–300 lbs plates). **Services:** Massage (Swedish, shiatsu, aromatherapy, therapeutic), hydrotherapy tub mineral and herbal baths, reflexology, body wraps (spirulina, moor mud, herbal, aromatherapy), body scrub, facials, AHA peel with spirulina; salon for hair, nail, and skin care, waxing; fitness training and nutritional consultation. **Swimming Facilities:** 32-meter indoor pool, 20-meter outdoor pool. **Recreation Facilities:** 27-hole championship golf course, bowling alley, 5 tennis courts (Plexi-Paved, outdoor), 5 ski areas: Mt. Norquay with 17 runs on 123 acres is closest and open till 9 PM Wed.–Sat. Sunshine Village has a 3,514-ft vertical drop and cross-country skiing on 20 miles of groomed trails. Bicycle rentals, white-water rafting in Banff. Trail maps at the park information center. Horseback riding and guided treks arranged through outfitters.

In the Area Cave and Basin Centennial Centre (interpretive displays, self-guided boardwalk trails). Columbia Icefield tours (May–Sept., weather permitting), Banff Festival of the Arts at the Banff Centre and School of Fine Arts (May–Aug.), art of the Canadian Rockies at the Whyte Museum in Banff, Olympic Park & Training Center near Calgary (bobsled ride).

Getting Here *From Calgary.* By bus, Brewster Transportation (tel. 800/661–1152) (2 hrs) or Greyhound. By car, Trans-Canada Hwy. to park entrances (2 hrs), where a 1-year vehicle pass must be purchased. By train, Rocky Mountaineer Railtour scheduled summer service (tel. 800/665–7245). Taxi, rental car, limousine available. Brewster Airporter (tel. 403/762–6700 or 800/661–1152) has scheduled shuttle bus service daily from/to Calgary International Airport (2 hrs).

Special Notes Hours for fitness, spa, and aquatic facilities 6 AM–10 PM daily. Minimum age in spa 18, in fitness center 16. No smoking in spa and designated areas of restaurants.

Mountain Escape at Lake Louise Inn

Holistic health
Luxury pampering

Alberta
Lake Louise Mountain hikes don't mean roughing it, nor do you have to give up morning coffee to get fit at this alpine resort. In the spring and fall the Lake Louise Inn features the Mountain Escape program, a health and lifestyle retreat with scheduled walks and exercise routines that take advantage of the invigorating

Rockies for inspiration. Lectures on healthy eating and fitness guidance from qualified staff members introduce you to the benefits of a healthy lifestyle.

From the sunrise eye-opener walk to an afternoon stretch-and-tone session, the emphasis is on personal development and learning how to set holistic health goals. A team of instructors works with you in small, compatible groups. Activities are geared to the general energy of the group rather than to peak performance, with one week dedicated to more challenging activities.

Breathtaking surrounding peaks come in view on walks around Lake Louise, and snow-covered Victoria Glacier is mirrored in the aqua-blue water. While one group does high-energy aerobics, another learns aquatic exercises in the pool. Two hour-long classes are scheduled each morning, and yoga is practiced before dinner. Massage and beauty services can be scheduled for an additional charge.

Mountain Escape at Lake Louise Inn

Box 209, Lake Louise, Alberta T0L 1E0
Tel. 403/522–3791 (800/661–9237 in western Canada)
Fax 403/522–2018

Administration General manager, Larry Hoskin; program director, Karen Samuels

Season 3 weeklong sessions per spring and fall seasons

Accommodations 91 motel-style rooms with double bed, private bath, and TV in a contemporary ski-lodge hotel complex.

Rates 6-day/6-night program $775–$995 (C$) single, $565–$675 per person, double occupancy. 4-day/4-night program $495 single, $425 double. Add 5% provincial tax, 7% service charge, GST. Deposit: $100 check with reservation. AE, MC, V.

Meal Plans 3 daily meals. Copies of spa cuisine recipes provided to guests on departure. Some vegetarian meals included in the 1,700-calorie-a-day diet plus between-meal refreshments. Nonalcoholic reception on Sunday evening.

Services and Facilities **Exercise Equipment:** Exercycles, Universal Gym Equipment. **Services:** Massage (Swedish, sports), facial; beauty salon for hair, nail, and skin care. **Swimming Facilities:** Heated indoor pool. **Spa Facilities:** Whirlpool, sauna. **Recreation Facilities:** Bicycle rental, 3 outdoor tennis courts; nearby horseback riding, downhill and cross-country skiing. **Evening Programs:** Lifestyle lectures.

In the Area Trail hiking, gondola rides at ski area, 2½-mi trail to Lake Agnes teahouse.

Getting Here *From Calgary.* By car, 110 mi on Trans-Canada Hwy. By bus, Greyhound and Brewster Transportation (tel. 800/661–1152).

Special Notes Bring hiking boots, warm clothing, gloves. Spa hours: daily 7 AM—10 PM.

Chateau Whistler Resort

Sports conditioning

British Columbia
Whistler/Blackcomb
Mountain

Any season is the right time to visit Whistler/Blackcomb. There's year-round skiing on the greatest vertical rise in North America, water sports in summer, and alpine hiking and horseback riding in summer, spring, and fall. And the Whistler/Blackcomb vacation area continues to expand its fitness and recreational facilities. Golfers can play four new courses in the area, including Chateau Whistler's 18-hole course designed by Robert Trent Jones, Jr. For information on golf packages, call 800/441–1414.

The baronial Chateau Whistler Resort, the largest hotel in Whistler Village, has a complete health club with a pre-ski stretch class, tennis instruction, and licensed therapists for sports massage. There are aerobics classes, a 30-foot indoor-outdoor pool, cardiovascular exercise equipment, coed sauna as well as separate sets of saunas and steam rooms for men and women. Only the somewhat undersized weight training room disappoints.

Designed around a pedestrian plaza, Whistler Village has dozens of boutiques and restaurants within a short walk from the hotel. The 12-story Chateau was built on a grand scale in 1990. The cathedral-ceiling lobby offers unobstructed views of Blackcomb Mountain's famed slopes, and guest rooms feature folk art and carpets inspired by Mennonite hooked rugs. Other decorative touches include Québec armoires, birdhouses, and baskets of apples. On an outdoor deck, a Jacuzzi beckons. A hydrotherapy sports-injury center in the village offers massage and a flotation tank.

Chateau Whistler Resort

4599 Chateau Blvd., Box 100, Whistler, British Columbia V0N 1B0
Tel. 604/938–8000 or 800/268–9411
Spa reservations: 604/938–2044
Fax 604/938–2055

Administration	General manager, David J. G. Roberts; health and tennis manager, Gary Winter
Season	Year-round
Accommodations	343-room high rise with standard rooms and deluxe suites, concierge club floor services. All with full bathroom and amenities, TV, telephone, radio, climate control.
Rates	$130–$195 (C$) daily in summer, single or double occupancy; winter rates $260–$295 daily, suites $350–$900. Add 7% GST, 10% tax. Deposit: 1 night's room and tax. AE, MC, V.
Meal Plans	Innovative menu in the Wildflower Restaurant with natural, organic ingredients from the area; fresh seafood, wild boar, venison in season. There is also a tapas bar and a lounge for light meals.
Services and Facilities	**Exercise Equipment:** 6-unit Keiser pneumatic weight-training circuit, 3 Climb Max stairclimbers, 2 Universal AerobiCycles, Universal treadmill, Concept 2 rowing ergometer, dumbbells. **Services:** Sports massage, 1-on-1 training, tennis lessons and camps. **Swimming Facilities:** Heated outdoor pool accessible from inside the health club. **Recreation Facilities:** Tennis courts and bike rental at the hotel; golf, canoeing, horseback riding nearby. 25 lifts and a gondola for downhill skiing; cross-country ski trails, glacier skiing (summer). Outdoor croquet court, fishing, paragliding school, ice skating, 2 18-hole golf courses. **Evening Programs:** Sleigh rides.
In the Area	Whistler Museum, ferry to Vancouver Island.
Getting Here	*From Vancouver.* By car, Hwy. 99 past Horseshoe Bay, Squamish, and Howe Sound (70 mi; 90 mins). By train, B.C. Rail (tel. 604/932–4003) daily at 7:30 AM (2½ hrs). By bus, Maverick Coach Lines (tel. 604/932–5031) from city terminal, Perimeter Airporter at 2 PM (tel. 604/261–2299). By air, AirBC Helijet Airways (tel. 604/938–1878) has scheduled flights on a

private plane to Pemberton Airport. Rental car, taxi, limousine available.

Special Notes Specially equipped guest rooms for people with disabilities. No smoking in therapy center and designated dining areas. 1 floor of no-smoking rooms. Spa hours: daily 6 AM–11 PM. No skiing first two weeks of June due to gondola maintenance.

EcoMed Wellness Spa & Clinic

Holistic health
Stress control

British Columbia
Nanoose Bay,
Vancouver Island

The seaside naturopathic program at EcoMed Wellness Spa & Clinic provides both therapies and testing for ailments ranging from allergies to cancer-related pain. Comprehensive diagnostic services and treatments include live blood cell analysis, acupuncture, oxygen therapies, stress management, nutritional counseling, and detoxification. Conditions treated include chronic fatigue syndrome, immune deficiencies, arthritis, diabetes.

Founded and directed by Stefan Kuprowsky, M.D., the spa and clinic are at Pacific Shores Nature Resort on the forested northern end of Vancouver Island. Set on one of British Columbia's warmest swimming bays, the resort offers a fitness center with ozonated swimming pool, indoor and outdoor hot tubs, beachfront nature trail, and bird sanctuary. Clusters of houses, rather than a hotel, provide accommodations for about a dozen guests.

Spa guests gather at the main house for meals, treatments, and consultation with Dr. Kuprowsky. Begun in 1994, the eco-spa concept attracts island residents for a day, as well as vacationers taking scheduled outings to a nearby nature reserve—Rathtrevor Park—and rain forest. Learning positive lifestyle habits and enjoying outdoor recreation, rather than exercise or diet, are the main focus of this informal health retreat.

Cleansing the body of toxins is the basis of healing retreats that range from one week to a month in length. Weekends and 7-day programs are devoted to health workshops, nature walks, and inner cleansing. Spa and esthetic services are on an à la carte basis or included in program packages. A hydrotherapy tub for herbal soaks, facials with natural products developed by Canadian skin care specialists, aromatherapy, and massage are available. Special workshops on organic gardening, natural fertility, and native spiritual traditions enhance the basic program of walks and treatments. Vegetarian meals, included in the daily program fee, feature fresh produce from nearby organic farms.

Vancouver Island provides outdoor adventure in abundance, from bathing in mountain streams to hot springs and ocean beaches, pleasant, small-town shopping, and busy ports for commercial fishing boats. Vast stands of old oaks, maple, and Douglas Fir trees cover the midsection and northern tip. On the island's more developed southern coast is Victoria, provincial capital and cultural center. Linked to the mainland and Vancouver by ferry and airline services, the island has excellent roads and a scenic railroad for day trips.

EcoMed Wellness Spa & Clinic
R.R. 1, Box 50, Nanoose Bay, British Columbia V0R 2R0
Tel. 604/468–7133
Fax 604/468–7135

Administration Owner/director, Stefan Kuprowsky, M.D.

Season Year-round

Accommodations 6 bedrooms, 6 suites in contemporary beachfront homes. All have bathroom, air-conditioning, TV, telephone, and local artwork. Furniture is West Coast modern, in light woods and fabrics. Choice of garden view or bayfront patio. Suites have full living room with fireplace, Jacuzzi bath, and kitchen.

Rates 2-night/3-day weekend retreat $495–$695 (C$) single, $395–$495 per person, double occupancy; Executive health assessment $1,595 single, $1,295 double; Inner Cleansing Weekend $1,095–$1,395 single, $995–$1,150 double. 7-day spa escape $1,495–$2,095 single, $1,095–$1,395 double. 1-week Healing Intensive $3,000–$3,600 single or double, companion rate $1,000. Add taxes and gratuities. Deposit: 50% of program cost. MC, V.

Meal Plans 3 meals daily included in program. Family-style, vegetarian meals include home-baked whole-grain bread, pasta, salads. Herbal tea, no coffee.

Services and Facilities **Exercise Equipment:** None. **Services:** Massage, hydrotherapy, acupuncture, aromatherapy, allergy and blood test. **Swimming Facilities:** Indoor ozonated pool, ocean beach. **Recreation Facilities:** Kayaking, canoeing, tennis; golf nearby.

In the Area Butchert Gardens, Chemainus (outdoor murals), Victoria (museums, shopping, galleries. performing arts), Hot Springs Cove.

Getting Here *From Vancouver.* By car, Hwy. 99 to BC Ferry terminal, scheduled service to Nanaimo, Hwy. 19 (Island Hwy.) north to Parksville Tourist Bureau, right to Beaver Creek Wharf Rd., left to Stroughler Rd., left to resort gate (3 hrs). By Air, commuter flights on AirBC to Nanaimo (20 mins). Rental car, taxi available.

Special Notes No smoking on premises. Bring medical records.

Fairmont Hot Springs Resort

Nonprogram resort
Taking the waters

British Columbia
Fairmont Hot Springs

Canada's largest hot mineral pools are an attraction of this family-oriented vacation complex in the Rocky Mountains. There's golf, skiing, and a deluxe Sports Center where spa treatments and exercise equipment make it possible to assemble your own spa program. The privately owned Fairmont Hot Springs Resort has large swimming pools for day visitors who come for sports and relaxation. The beautifully landscaped grounds are surrounded by mountain forests.

The recently completed esthetics department provides a wide range of skin care and beauty services, à la carte. Fitness facilities and a private pool are for guests in the lodge and villas. Two full-size racquetball courts, one squash court, coed saunas and whirlpool, and hydra-fitness exercise equipment are available. An optional spa-cuisine menu has been introduced to accompany fitness programs.

Fairmont Hot Springs Resort
Box 10, Fairmont Hot Springs, British Columbia V0B 1L0
Tel. 604/345–6311 or 800/663–4979
Telex 041–45108, Fax 604/345–6616

Administration General manager, Donald Bilodeau; therapist, Stephanie Clerk

Season Year-round

Accommodations 139 rooms with private baths in the main lodge. 5 cottages and 48 suites with cooking facilities. All with air-conditioning, TV, telephone, bath.

Rates $80–$200 (C$) daily per person, double occupancy. 2-night/2-day spa package, $189–$219 (C$) per person, double occupancy. Add 7% GST, 8% tax. Deposit: 1 night. AE, MC, V.

Meal Plans Health breakfast daily included in package. Breakfast buffet has fresh juices, bran muffins, yogurt, cottage cheese. Lunch menu is cold cucumber soup, salad of red cabbage and apple, pasta, curried chicken with yogurt dressing, fillet of sole with braised leeks. Dinner entrées include veal cutlet with wild mushrooms, breast of chicken stuffed with lobster, fillet of red snapper with curry sauce.

Services and Facilities **Exercise Equipment:** 9 Hydra weight-training units, stationary bike. **Services:** Swedish massage, fango, herbal wrap, loofah body scrub, salt-glow scrub, guided hikes, yoga, aerobics, aquacise classes. **Swimming Facilities:** Indoor and outdoor pools open year-round. **Spa Facilities:** Odorless mineral water for hot soaks and swimming pools, outdoor and indoor whirlpools. **Recreation Facilities:** 4 tennis courts, 2 racquetball courts, 1 squash court, 2 18-hole golf courses, water skiing, sailing, fishing, rafting, horseback riding, downhill and cross-country skiing, hiking.

In the Area Banff Springs National Park, Columbia Ice Field.

Getting Here *From Calgary.* By car, Hwy. 93, north of Cranbrook (3 hrs). By air, private airstrip. By bus, Greyhound (4 hrs). Spa open daily 8 AM–10 PM.

Harrison Hot Springs Hotel

Nonprogram resort
Taking the waters

British Columbia
Harrison Hot Springs

The large, modern hydrotherapy pavilion complements the new fitness facilities and refurbished guest rooms at the Harrison Hot Springs Hotel. The indoor-pool pavilion is constructed of wood and brick and decorated with native carvings, and looks onto the garden where an Olympic-size indoor swimming pool is filled with warm spring water year-round. The sulfurous, 104°F spring water provides effective if temporary relief for aching muscles. Future plans include adding mud baths, Jacuzzis, herbal wraps, and Oriental massage.

The pavilion has separate facilities for men and women, including private Roman baths with sunken seating. There's also an indoor tennis court and exercise room, where aerobics classes are scheduled; aquatic workouts are offered in the thermal pool. Joggers have the choice of running along the lake or on a Dynatrak paved circuit.

From the main road Lake Harrison looks scruffy: The strip of rocky, gray beach is lined with parked cars and RVs, but beyond the tourist bars and souvenir stands are wilderness tracks for hiking and quiet country roads. The hotel, long popular with honeymooners and conventioneers, is in the process of being upgraded and refurbished, but it's business as usual: afternoon tea is still served daily in front of the lobby fireplace.

Harrison Hot Springs Hotel
Harrison Hot Springs, British Columbia V0M 1K0
Tel. 604/796–2244 (800/663–2266 in the western United States and Canada), Telex 04–361551
Fax 604/796–9374

Administration	General manager, Gerald Hadway
Season	Year-round
Accommodations	300 motel-style rooms in main building, cottages in private garden area. Deluxe rooms in the new tower, some with lake view.
Rates	$124–$180 (C$) daily, double or single occupancy; 4-day/3-night midweek package $564–$485 per person, double occupancy, $289–$493 single. Add 7% GST, 8% tax. AE, D, MC, V.
Services and Facilities	**Exercise Equipment:** 5 Hydra-Fitness units, 18-station Universal Gym Equipment, 2 Lifecycles, 2 StairMasters. **Services:** Massage, 1-on-1 training. **Swimming Facilities:** Indoor pavilion pool open 24 hrs, outdoor pool 104°F for soaking, 94°F for swimming; lake. **Recreation Facilities:** Indoor and outdoor tennis courts, volleyball court; horseback riding, golf nearby; cross-country skiing, bicycle rental. **Evening Programs:** Dinner dancing in the Copper Room.
In the Area	Boat trips and fishing on the lake in summer. Minter Gardens showpieces in bloom Mar.–Oct.
Getting Here	*From Vancouver.* By car, Trans-Canada Hwy. (Rte. 1) east to exit for Rte. 9 at Minter Gardens; continue to Lake Harrison (2 hrs). By bus, Cascade Lines (tel. 604/662–7953) (3 hrs).
Special Notes	Some specially equipped rooms for people with disabilities. Indoor pool open 24 hrs, outdoor pool open 8–11.

The Hills Health Ranch

Luxury pampering
Nutrition and diet
Vibrant maturity
Weight management

British Columbia
108 Mile Ranch

Saddle up for a Western-style ranch workout replete with horse rides and line dancing at The Hills Health Ranch in cariboo country, in the heart of British Columbia. Facials, skin treatments, herbal wraps, and massages mix with hayrides and trail rides or, in winter, cross-country skiing, bringing together fun and fitness.

Woodsy A-frame chalets and a two-story inn fan out from the two-story, log-sided main lodge where the spa and indoor swimming pool are located. During winter the ranch is busy with skiers (several teams train here), but it's an all-season resort that offers special packages for weight management, beauty treatments, and an "Executive Renewal Week." Weekends and 11-day programs are available year-round; alternatively, you can schedule treatments and classes à la carte.

Opened in 1983, the ranch is the first Canadian Wellness Center to provide medically based programs in healthy living. Affiliation with the University of British Columbia has led to lifestyle research and special programs for rehabilitation after injury or surgery. There is special emphasis on the needs of the mature person, including maintaining a healthy heart through exercise and nutrition.

If you join the wellness program, you'll participate in exercise, nutrition, and stress management sessions, and receive body-work treatments. After an initial fitness evaluation you'll begin your scheduled activities: morning power walks, daily guided hikes, aerobics and step classes, line dancing, aquaerobics in the indoor pool, circuit and weight-training, and stretching/relaxation classes. A physician will address medical concerns and a kinesiologist, estheticians, massage therapist, and fitness instructor will work with you throughout the program. Guests have a choice of hearty fare or spa cuisine, as the staff caters to the whole person, providing a high level of personal service.

With 200 kilometers (130 miles) of hiking and riding trails, there are daily outings and weeklong wilderness adventure packages. A resident wrangler runs the stables, where you can join morning and afternoon horseback rides, which even novices and young riders enjoy. After a morning on the trail, lunch is served in a mountain meadow. At night, there are hayrides and a sing-along at Willy's Wigwam, an authentic Indian teepee.

Encompassing 20,000 acres of lakes, mountains, and forest, this privately owned and operated ranch provides western hospitality while helping you cope with weight problems and aging.

The Hills Health Ranch
C-26, 108 Mile Ranch, British Columbia V0K 2Z0
Tel. 604/791–5225
Fax 604/791–6384

Administration President, Patrick Corbett; program director, Juanita Corbett; fitness director, Tim Cooper

Season Year-round

Accommodations 20 private chalets with up to 3 bedrooms, kitchen, bath, TV, and balcony; alpine cottages for couples and singles. 10 deluxe rooms in the Ranch House have private bathroom, air-conditioning, telephone. 16 larger rooms, each with balcony, in 2-story Manor House inn.

Rates Weekend $259 (C$) per person, double occupancy, $349 single; 7-day Executive Renewal package $1,395 per person double, $1,649 single. 7-day Inches Off package $999 per person double, $1,249 single. Vital Maturity Week $1,545 single, $1,215 double. 10-night weight loss package $2,119 single, $1,669 double. Add 12% service charge, 7% GST. Deposit of $50 or 25% of total cost 2 weeks prior to arrival. Cancellations within 2 weeks of reservation not refundable. AE, MC, V.

Meal Plans 3 calorie-counted meals a day with health packages. 1,000–1,200 calories a day diet recommended for weight loss. Personalized low-fat menu served in private dining area.

Services and Facilities **Exercise Equipment:** 8-station Apex circuit, Alpine 2000 stepper, HRT preference stationary bicycles, Quinton treadmill, free weights. **Services:** Massage, reflexology, aromatherapy, paraffin hand and foot treatment, facial, herbal wrap, loofah scrub, full-body mud pack, manicure, pedicure. **Swimming Facilities:** Indoor swimming pool. **Spa Facilities:** 2 whirlpools, 2 saunas. **Recreation Facilities:** Stables, horseback riding (1- and 2-hr and overnight rides), cross-country skiing, hiking, curling, ice skating, tobogganing. Nearby tennis courts, golf course, mountain bike and canoe rental, lake fishing and swimming. **Evening Programs:** Western dancing with live local music, workshops on nutrition and wellness.

In the Area Williams Lake (art gallery, July 4th stampede), Gibraltar Gold Mine, Barker Village (gold rush era), Helmicken Falls.

Getting Here By air, Air Canada/AirBC (tel. 800/776–3000) daily flights to Williams Lake Airport. Transfers on arrival/departure. *From Vancouver.* By car, use main routes through the Rockies to the village of 100 Mile House, Hwy. 97. By train, BC Rail's (tel. 604/932–4000) Cariboo Dayliner operates 3 times weekly on scenic route to Williams Lake (5 hrs). Complimentary transfers on arrival/departure.

Special Notes Riding and skiing instruction and teepee parties for children. No smoking in dining room and spa. Bring warm clothing and 2 pairs of running shoes. Spa open daily 8 AM–10 PM.

Hollyhock

Holistic health
Life enhancement
Spiritual awareness

British Columbia
Cortes Island

Secluded on a Pacific coastal island, Hollyhock is an holistic community devoted to educational programs in healthy, natural living. Situated 100 miles north of Vancouver and accessible only by air or ferry, Hollyhock welcomes visitors for weekend getaways or for one of the more than 70 seminars and workshops offered here. Subjects range from health and healing to shamanism, a spiritual retreat for couples, and tai chi chuan training. Guests are free to enjoy the island retreat's guided nature walks, organic gardens, and beaches, and bodywork is available for a fee.

Since 1982, specialists in alternative therapies and spiritual health have drawn inspiration from each other in this island setting. The informal "campus," where group discussions are held, is made up of wood dormitories surrounded by the forest and beach. There's plenty of room to jog, swim, or find the solitude to meditate.

Mornings begin with yoga and meditation. You can arrange for bodywork including Swedish massage or skin care. Families camp or share rooms, and kids can enroll in kayaking or other special programs. For relaxation, there are forest trails and beaches, the water, and the hot tub.

Holiday packages, 2–7 nights, and daily rates allow visitors to enjoy the facilities, take a guided nature walk, do some birdwatching, and try bodywork and skin-care services.

Hollyhock
Box 127, Manson's Landing, Cortes Island,
British Columbia V0P 1K0
Tel. 604/935–6773 or 800/933–6339
Fax 604/935–6424

Administration Executive director, Brian Fryer

Season Mid-Mar.–Sept. 1

Accommodations Semiprivate or dormitory rooms (3–6 people per room). A few double and single rooms come with either shared or private bath. Heated buildings with communal showers and toilets. Tent sites without sleeping gear or tent can be reserved.

Rates Weekend Getaway (2 nights) $199–$289 (C$) single/shared bath, $219–$309 single/private bath; $169–$259 per person, double occupancy. Dormitory bedroom $149–$209 per person. Tenting site $119–$169. 7-night holiday package $589–$869 single, $484–$764 per person double occupancy; dormitory bed $414–$589; tenting $309–$449. Daily rate $84–$134 single, $69–$109 double, $59–$94 dormitory, $44–$64 tenting. $40–$65 per day for children 4–12. Add 8% BC room tax, 7% GST. Tuition for workshops and seminars is additional. Deposit: $250 for workshop and holiday package, $125 for short stays. MC, V.

Meal Plans 3 buffet meals daily included with accommodations. Mostly vegetarian, some seafood. Homemade breads and soups, and Friday evening barbecue oysters and salmon are favorites.

Services and Facilities **Services:** Swedish massage, reflexology, acupressure, deep tissue massage, Breema massage (clothed), body wrap, facial. **Swimming Facilities:** Private lake, ocean beaches. **Recreation Facilities:** Kayaks, canoes, rowboat, sailboats, hot tub, wilderness interpretation tour.

In the Area Vancouver Island: Hot Springs Cove (natural hot spring), Victoria, British Columbia capitol, provincial museum (native arts and history).

Getting Here *From Seattle and Vancouver.* By car and BC ferries (tel. 604/386–3431), via Vancouver Island. By air, scheduled commuter flights on Air Canada/AirBC (tel. 800/663–3721) from Seattle and Vancouver to Campbell River for nearest ferry connection. Direct flights to Cortes Island by scheduled seaplane service: Kenmore Air (tel. 206/486–8400) from Seattle, Coval Airlines (tel. 604/287–8871) from Vancouver. Complimentary transfers on arrival/departure at Manson's Landing for 11-mi trip to Hollyhock.

Special Notes No smoking indoors. Bring warm clothes, flashlight, rainwear, sturdy walking shoes, and footwear that slips on and off easily. Children's programs include sailing and kayaking expeditions for 12–15-year-olds, and kid's camp.

Mountain Trek Fitness Retreat & Health Spa

Holistic health

British Columbia
Ainsworth Hot Springs

Focused on hiking, snowshoeing, and fitness, Mountain Trek combines spa and wellness programs with outdoor adventure. On 34 acres of forest overlooking Kootenay Lake and the Purcell Mountains, the rustic cedar lodge is a comfortable base from which to explore high country trails, picnic in pristine meadows, and soak in the hot springs. Options include overnight camping in the mountains, and a combination of fasting and internal cleansing.

Hiking, the core activity of the program (there are six daily treks per week), begins with an orientation on Saturday afternoon. You'll learn some local lore, including information about the Whitewater Glacier Trail, one of the most accessible, that once attracted miners searching for gold and silver in the White Grizzly Wilderness (called Pic-ha-kee-lowna by indigenous people). You may see grizzlies, deer, mountain goats, and marmots as you explore alpine slopes, expansive flower meadows, and a variety of ecological zones with soapstone and serpentine in temperate forests. The lead-and-shepherd guide system allows everyone to go at their own pace.

Workouts in the main lodge are scheduled before and after hikes, and exercise clothing is provided daily. Yoga sessions are held in a wood-floor studio, with views of the mountains and lake. A separate weight-training room has a selection of Cybex equipment and free weights. Within a five-minute walk are natural thermal spring baths, and there is an outdoor hot tub next to the lodge's sauna.

The all-inclusive week lets you schedule three massages. Each participant or couple has a private bedroom and bathroom, equipped with robes and knapsacks. Optional fasting weeks are structured with daily educational lectures, colonics, massage, walks, and a diet of juices. The supervised cleansing program in cooperation with NaturesPath Center is based on the teachings of Dr. Bernard Jensen, with a daily regime of cleansing drinks and enhanced intestinal cleansing. Health checkups and lectures by a naturopathic physician are included with the minimum stay of six days.

Geared to beginner, intermediate, and advanced levels of hiking ability, over 20 trails are within an hour's drive of the lodge. The daily program begins with yoga or stretch class and finishes with massage and a soak at the hot springs. Awesome scenery is matched by the serenity of Kootenay mountain country. This is a place where you can safely challenge yourself in the company of a dozen like-minded souls and a caring staff.

Mountain Trek Fitness Retreat & Health Spa

Box 1352, Ainsworth Hot Springs, British Columbia
V0G 1A0
Tel. 604/229–5636 or 800/661–5161
Fax 604/229–5636

Administration Founder-director, Wendy Pope

Season Year-round scheduled weeks

Accommodations Cedar 2-story lodge with 6 single bedrooms, 4 double rooms with queen-size bed. All have private toilet with shower. No TV, phone, air-conditioning. Self-service laundry room.

Rates 6-night hiking program $1,725–$2,025 (C$). 2-week Fit 'n Fast program $2,465. Supervised NaturesPath program $200 per day. Snowshoeing 6-day/night package $1,725 per person. Add 7% GST, 8% BC tax, and 7% service charge. Deposit: $500 check. No credit cards.

Meal Plans 3 low-fat, high-carbohydrate meals and snacks daily, served buffet style. Breakfast can be cinnamon rice and raisin cereal, fresh fruit and juice, polenta cake with summer fruit sauce, or banana pancakes. Lunch on trail includes spicy tabouli, whole-wheat pita sandwich or millet burger, fruit, sweet potato muffin. Dinner entrée is spinach and mushroom lasagna, tofu sukiyaki with rice, angel-hair pasta with tomato and artichoke, or cashew/carrot curry with basmati rice. Fresh bread baked daily; steamed vegetables, soup, and salad served with dinner.

Services and Facilities **Exercise Equipment:** 8-unit Cybex weight-training gym, stair stepper, free weights. **Services:** Massage, colonic. **Swimming Facilities:** Nearby pool.

In the Area Nelson (pioneer settlement), hot springs, glacier-fed Kootenay Lake.

Getting Here *From Vancouver and Calgary.* By air, Air Canada/AirBC (tel. 800/776–3000) or Time Air (Canadian International Airlines, tel. 800/426–7000) scheduled flights (1 hr). Transfers provided from Castlegar Airport for Sat. arrival and Fri. morning departure. By car from Vancouver, Trans-Canada Hwy. to Hope, Hwy. 3 east to Nelson, Hwy. 3A east, Hwy. 31 to Ainsworth (8 hrs). By car from Calgary, Trans-Canada Hwy., Hwy. 93 north to Hwy. 95 past Cranbrook, Hwy. 3 to Creston, Hwy. 3A to Kootenay Bay (ferry), Hwy. 31 (7 hrs).

Special Notes Bring hiking boots. Tent, Sherpa snowshoes, sweatsuits provided for seasonal programs. Daily personal laundry service is complimentary.

Ocean Pointe Resort

Holistic health
Life enhancement
Luxury pampering

British Columbia
Victoria,
Vancouver Island

The Ocean Pointe Resort offers the best of two worlds: the charm and sophistication of Victoria, the capital of British Columbia, and the beauty and solitude of its location on the Inner Harbour. Opened in 1992, the spa brings sophisticated skin care and bodywork, and elegant spa cuisine. Open to all hotel guests free of charge, the fitness facilities are staffed by trainers with experience in exercise for senior citizens as well as young people. Scheduled classes in yoga and aquaerobics, plus a series of speakers on nutrition and lifestyle, round out the holistic program. A wide range of beauty and facial treatments are available à la carte, or with three- or five-day packages, including Thalgo's micronized seaweed products from France, Aveda's line of natural hair-care products, aromatherapy baths and massages, and an anticellulite program.

The combination of spa and hotel fitness center appeals to businesspeople as well as vacationers and local residents. Those on working holiday can take a premeeting morning jog along the waterfront or play a lunchtime game of squash or racquetball in the fitness center. Vacationers who have more free time can luxuriate in the glass-walled ozonated swimming pool (there's no chlorine), taking in panoramic views of the working harbor. Relaxation comes with balneotherapy—underwater massage—in a Somethy tub imported from France: air pressure jets swirl mineral salts, essential oils, or marine algae mixed for detoxification. The final touch is a full-hour massage.

Ocean Pointe also makes a convenient base from which to explore the Victorian byways of the city as well as the provincial park on the Pacific side of Vancouver Island. Take a scenic day trip on the E&N Railroad, departing from its terminal near the hotel. The mild climate enjoyed most of the year makes the island a mecca for golf, sailing, fishing, and scuba as well. Ocean Pointe Resort's concierge can schedule your tee-off time at the Olympic View golf course or court time on one of the hotel's two tennis courts. Seacoast Expeditions' 12-passenger Zodiacs depart from the resort dock to view marine mammal life, including whales (Apr.–Oct.), with wetgear included in the excursion price.

The property is comfortable and finely decorated, with original art and antiques in all the public rooms. Many of the guest rooms are oversized and feature alcoves or dormer windows with a view of the harbor and distant Olympic Mountains. Spa guests have the added advantage of dining in The Victorian Restaurant, where the menu lists percentages of calories from fat, and sodium content of all items. Dinner by candlelight is a bonus.

Ocean Pointe Resort
45 Songhee Rd., Victoria, British Columbia V9A 6T3
Tel. 604/360–2999 or 800/667–4677
Fax 604/360–1041

Administration General manager, Ulrich Stolle; spa manager, Jennifer Siemens

Season Year-round

Accommodations 250 rooms, including 34 suites, with king-size, 2 double, or twin beds. Choice rooms have Inner Harbour view. All with modern furnishings, private bathroom, TV, telephone with voice mail, desk, lighted closets. 17 junior suites have compact kitchens.

Rates $109–$290 (C$) single or double occupancy. 3-night Time-Out spa package $883–$921 per person, double occupancy, $1,090–$1,165 single; 5-night Rejuvenation package $1,518–$1,581 double, $1,862—$1,987 single. Day spa packages (no lodging) $120–$300. Add 7% GST, 7% provincial tax, and gratuities. AE, DC, MC, V.

Meal Plans Lunch and dinner included in spa packages. Menu choices in The Victorian Restaurant include Dungeness crab, fennel and cilantro bisque, medley of organic salad greens, or tea-smoked squab on cellophane noodles for starters; pan-seared arctic char and lobster, or grilled chicken breast with couscous and asparagus as entrées.

Services and Facilities **Exercise Equipment**: 11-station circuit training, 2 StairMasters, 2 Windracer bikes, rowing machine, ergometer, Startrac treadmill. **Services**: Massage (Swedish, reflexology, aromatherapy, relaxation), body wrap, paraffin back treatment, body peeling, thalassotherapy, facial, anti-age skin treatments. Beauty salon for hair, nails, and makeup. **Swimming Facilities**: Indoor pool. **Recreation Facilities**: 2 tennis courts, squash/racquetball court; 18-hole golf course, marina nearby.

Getting Here *From Seattle and Vancouver*. By air, AirBC/Air Canada (tel. 800/776—3000), Time Air (tel. 800/426–7000), Helijet Airways (tel. 604/938–1878). From Seattle to Inner Harbour, Kenmore Air (tel. 206/486–8400) seaplane (40 mins) or Victoria Clipper (tel. 800/888–2535) ferry (3 hrs). By car, B.C. Ferry (tel. 604/386–3431) from Seattle or Tsawwassen to Swartz Bay (3 hrs). By bus/ferry, Gray Line (tel. 206/624–5077; 4 hrs).

Special Notes 7 rooms specially equipped for people with wheelchairs and people with hearing disabilities. Spa open weekdays 8 AM–10 PM; weekends 9–5; Pool/fitness center 6:30 AM–10 PM daily.

Manan Island Spa

Luxury pampering

New Brunswick
Grand Manan
You won't find an organized spa program at this property, but that's one of Manan Island Spa's primary draws: Guests have the freedom to indulge in hydrotherapy baths and seaweed body wraps (using locally grown dulse, an edible seaweed), or explore the provincial parks, including Fundy National Park with its steep wooded hills, below which the world's highest tides surge upon the cliffs and beaches.

Manan Island, situated in Fundy bay, combines the flavors of New England, Scotland, and France in its heritage, and the design of the eight-bedroom Manon Island Spa reflects the influence: It looks like a New England summer cottage, particularly in the antiques-filled parlor and bedrooms. French thalassotherapy treatments are offered as well as walks in the highlands.

Naturalists have been coming here since James Audubon visited in 1832 and recorded more than 250 different species of birds, including the bald eagle, which still nests here. Whale watching, photography, painting, and rock collecting are popular pastimes. Willa Cather, a frequent visitor during the 1930s, wrote that the island was "tranquilizing to the spirit and seemed to open up great space for it to roam in."

Manan Island Spa

North Head, Grand Manan, New Brunswick E0G 2M0
Tel. 506/662–8624 or 216/562–9171
Fax 506/662–8392

Administration Director, Joanne Liuzzo; manager, Susan Wilcox

Season June–Sept.

Accommodations 8 bedrooms with private baths. Some king-size brass beds, up-stairs views.

Rates Daily B&B $59 (C$), single, $69 for 2 double. 3-day/3-night Sea Scape package $330 single, $525 for 2 double. Deposit: 50% advance payment. Cancellation charge for notification less than 48 hrs in advance of arrival date. AE, MC, V.

Meal Plans Continental breakfast included in rates.

Services and Facilities **Services:** Massage, body mask, body polish Dulse scrub, facial, bath (dulse, fango milk whey, seaweed). **Swimming Facilities:** Nearby ocean beaches and lakes (water tends to be cool). **Recreation Facilities:** Bikes available to guests at the inn; canoeing by arrangement. 17 nature trails along the shore to landmarks such as Hole-in-the-Wall cave at Whale Cove, where dulse is harvested.

In the Area Whale-watching expeditions; museum of over 300 island birds, local geological exhibits at Grand Harbour.

Getting Here *From mainland.* By Black Harbor ferry (tel. 506/662–3724), daily (2 hrs). Reserve space in advance. Ferry lands at Blacks Harbour on the coastal road (Rte. 1) from St. John and the airport. Short walk from ferry dock on island to inn. *From Maine.* By car, border crossing at Calais/St. Stephen to Rte. 1. Free parking at both ferry terminals.

Special Notes No smoking in the spa or dining room.

The Inn at Manitou

Life enhancement
Luxury pampering
Sports conditioning

Ontario
Lake
Manitouwabing
Nestled on the shores of Lake Manitouwabing near Parry Sound, The Inn is a popular retreat for guests seeking peace and seclusion. Tennis clinics have been a staple here since the early 1960s, but in the spring of 1990 The Inn at Manitou opened a full-service spa that provides cross-training as well as luxury pampering. Two regularly scheduled aerobics classes are held daily, morning and afternoon, either high- or low-impact, steps, or stretching. In the dining room, you choose from classic French cuisine or gourmet spa dining.

The elegant but tiny spa is in the same building as the indoor tennis court and exercise room, with a maple hardwood "Everflex" floating floor. Among the six private treatment rooms are two designed for wet therapies (mud masks, body wraps, and loofah scrubs) and furnished with a hydrotherapy tub with 47 underwater jets and a hand-operated hose. Personal trainers are on hand to provide one-on-one sessions, and the spa director does a fitness evaluation on request.

The menu of massage and mud treatments is extensive: Swedish, shiatsu, aromatherapy, reflexology and holistic massage, body wraps, and skin care. Premassage facials involve cleansing the skin with a special mud from the Rhine River, and mud is used in several treatments: for body wraps, enabling the minerals and other active ingredients to be absorbed by the body, or for mud baths in the hydrotherapy tub. Known as MoorMud, it was used by monks during the 14th and 15th centuries to cure everything from rheumatism to asthma and depression. The rediscovered, imported mud is said to contain 3,000 organic ingredients.

Fitness classes as well as a personal screening and consultation come with all spa packages. All guests are invited to join staff-led morning walks and are supplied with a pair of weighted gloves to add a little muscle toning. For inn guests there are spa packages, 3–7 days, which include a selection of personal services and consultation with the spa director to assure appointments do not conflict with your tennis schedule.

The Inn at Manitou

McKellar, Ontario P0G 1C0
Tel. 705/389–2171 or 800/571–8818
Fax 705/389–3818
Winter: 251 Davenport Rd., Toronto, Ontario M5R 1J9
Tel. 416/967–3466, Fax 416/967–6434

Administration Owners-managers, Sheila and Ben Wise

Season May–Oct.

Accommodations 33 chalet-style rooms, most lakefront, each with log-burning fireplace, modern bathroom; 11 suites with sunken living room, antique marble fireplace, dressing room, bathroom with whirlpool tub, private sauna, sundeck. Also 3-bedroom luxury country house.

Rates $165–$295 per person daily, full American plan, double occupancy. Single supplement $35–$95 per day. Private house $995 per day. 1-day spa sampler (no lodging) $160; Spa programs for inn guests 3-day $170, 4-day $220, 7-day $380. Add 7% GST, room tax, and 16% service charge. Deposit: $350 per person. DC, MC, V.

Meal Plans Choice of regular menu or spa cuisine. 3 meals daily, plus mid-morning and afternoon juice and fruit breaks. Spa menu is low in sodium, fat, and cholesterol. Breakfast can be a cold buffet of fresh fruit and juices, cereal, Muesli, granola, yogurt, muffins, brioche, croissants, plus individually cooked egg-white omelet with a ragout of shrimp and coriander tomato. Lunch may be warm white asparagus with blood orange sabayon, pizza with marinated goat cheese, soup of melon and strawberries, or buffet specialties. Dinner entrées include fillet of rabbit with sage and pesto sauce, grilled breast of guinea hen with sesame seeds, Georgian Bay trout paper-baked with peaches, Provini veal chop; desserts are poached pears in Beaujolais with vanilla sauce, cream caramel flavored with Grand Marnier, or floating island perfumed with vervan.

Services and Facilities **Exercise Equipment:** 2 Trotter 575 treadmills, 2 Lifecycles, 2 Monark bikes, StairMaster, Legflex, free weights. **Services:** Massage (Swedish, Trager, shiatsu), reflexology, aromatherapy, herbal wraps, mud wraps, Moor therapy (scalp massage, body polish, body mask), facial, seaweed or mineral bath, hand paraffin treatment, waxing, manicure, pedicure, nutrition and fitness consultation. **Swimming Facilities:** Outdoor heated pool 20´ × 40´. **Recreation Facilities:** 12 outdoor tennis courts (4 clay), 1 indoor tennis court, horseback riding English style, mountain hiking, water sports, fishing, billiards, mountain bikes, lake cruises.

Getting Here *From Toronto.* By car, Hwy. 400 north to Parry Sound, right on Hwy. 124 to McKellar, right on McKellar Center Rd. for 5 mi (2½ hrs). By plane, float-plane charter service ($513 each way); private planes land at Parry Sound District Airport. By limousine from Pearson International Airport ($275 each way). Taxi, rental car available.

Special Notes Men requested to wear jacket at dinner. Tennis camp for teenagers (July–Aug.).

Ste. Anne's Country Inn & Spa

Life enhancement
Luxury pampering

Ontario
Grafton

Morning aerobics at Ste. Anne's Country Inn & Spa provides a view of the 350-acre estate for a dozen early risers. The octagonal studio has a wide-planked pine floor, country-style window panes, and a fresh, invigorating feeling. Built as a farmhouse in 1857, embellished by later owners from Texas, the inn emerged from a four-year rejuvenation by the current owners in 1996 with a new 1,400-square-foot Fitness Centre, spa cuisine menu, and scheduled wellness week learning programs.

Daily yoga, meditation, and aerobics classes can be combined with a soak in hot mud or herbal body scrub to soothe aching muscles and cleanse toxins from the body. In the basement, a wet treatment area and coed steam room surround the hot tub set in its own skylit cedar cubicle. Here you sink into a bath filled with with a mixture of moor mud dug from a lake formed by Canadian glaciers, and Saskatchewan clay. This treatment is followed by either a sea salt scrub or an herbal body polish, then shower in a deluge of springwater with a high-pressure hose or the waterfall cabinet.

Redolent of herbs, woodsy fireplaces, and fresh flowers, the 12-room inn could be a castle in Scotland. Carved into a stone archway at the estate entrance is Ste. Anne's coat of arms, designed for the family of Samuel Massey who settled here to farm the rolling drumlins of the Northumberland Hills near Lake Ontario. The Latin phrase "Sol Lucet Omnibus" over the insignia translates as "Where the Sun Always Shines." But like Canadian politics in which Massey gained fame, the building has had ups and downs. The new spa built by the Corcoran family provides a sunny retreat despite the whims of weather. You can sink into a wing chair to read a book from an eclectic collection in the parlor, or repair to the Jacuzzi. The daily schedule often includes a cooking class in the kitchen.

The human touch comes in a stress-buster hour-long Swedish massage (said to provide the equivalent benefits of four hours of quality sleep), and in a wide range of body treatments. Personal trainers are on hand for one-on-one sessions, although the selection of exercise equipment is limited. Excursions organized by the innkeeper include a cruise up the Trent Severn Waterway on his classic 30-foot Searay Cruiser, bike rides along the lake, and antiques hunting in nearby small towns.

While day spa packages offer a sampler of treatments and classes, plus lunch and tea, you have the flexibility of staying for a few days rather than following a fixed regimen. Set in rambling, stone-walled wings, guest rooms are appointed with antiques, fireplace, and twin or king-size beds, sizes ranging from cozy to deluxe suites. Daily rates include all meals and afternoon tea. Additional accommodations nearby are available with use of the inn facilities.

Just east of Toronto and easily reached by train, the inn offers a healthful and picturesque retreat from town. Seasonal events include an introduction to massaging your partner, cooking with herbs, and painting watercolors. Also on the property are miles of trails through a cedar forest, a ranch for deer and elk, outdoor tennis courts, a spring-fed swimming pool, and an organic herb garden.

Ste. Anne's Country Inn & Spa
R.R. #1, Grafton, Ontario K0K 2G0
Tel. 905/349–2493 or 800/263–2663
Fax 905/349–3531

Administration	Innkeeper, Jim Corcoran
Season	Year-round
Accommodations	12 guest rooms in 2-story manor house and adjoining wings, all with fireplace, sitting area, private bathroom. Suites have cathedral ceiling, Jacuzzi tub. Furnished with antiques, four-poster bed or king-size and twins. TV, air-conditioning, telephone available on request. Bathrobes provided.
Rates	Day spa package $175 full day, $95 half day. Rooms $225–$280 single, $175–$205 per person, double occupancy. Add 12% service charge, plus taxes. Deposit: full payment of day spa package, one night for room. AE, MC, V.
Meal Plans	3 meals daily included in room rate. Country spa fare menu choices include breakfast of buttermilk pancakes, muesli, muffins, juices, coffee or herbal tea; lunch entrées can be venison tourtiére. Dinner starts with raw vegetables and mustard sauce, mandarin orange salad, choice of three main items like pork brochette with peppers or chicken Normandy, and a dessert of meringue or fruit cobbler. Vegetarian meals on request.
Services and Facilities	**Exercise Equipment:** Trotter Supertrainer treadmill, Weider bicycle, NordicTrack, Tunturi rower. **Swimming Facilities:** Outdoor 25-meter concrete unheated pool with spring water. **Recreation Facilities:** 3 Har-Tru tennis courts, mountain bikes (free); nearby golf courses, cross-country skiing, ice skating.
In the Area	Lake Ontario Waterfront Trail, Bay of Quinte, Presqu'ile Provincial Park, Rice Lake (fishing, ice skating), Algonquin Regional Park (wilderness trek, visitor center, fishing), Toronto.
Getting Here	*From Toronto.* By train, VIA Rail (tel. 800/361–1235) to Cobourg (1 hr). Complimentary transfers from Cobourg station. By car, Hwy. 401 east to Exit 487 (Grafton/Centreton), north on Aird St. for 1.5 km, Academy Hill Rd. to Massey Rd. (75 mins). Taxi, rental car, limousine available.
Special Notes	No smoking on premises. Minimum age 16. Ground-floor rooms for persons with disabilities. Minimum stay 2 days weekends and holidays.

Wheels Country Spa at Wheels Inn

Luxury pampering

Ontario
Chatham

Total fun and fitness is the concept of Wheels Inn, a motel that grew into an indoor resort with 7 acres of sports and spa facilities under one roof. Cavort with the kids in the outdoor-indoor swimming pool and water slide, or choose from 42 revitalizing services in the European-style Wheels Country Spa.

Taking a serious approach to shape-ups, staff members have credentials for cardiovascular and muscular testing. They do basic body measurements, a wellness profile, and one-on-one training in a well-equipped fitness center.

Runners and joggers can set courses passing the town's Victorian mansions and modern marina. There are 15 routes mapped out, ranging from 1.8 to 13.5 miles, and an indoor track where 22 laps equal 1 mile.

A wide variety of revitalizing body and skin treatments offered here is unique for Canada. Services are priced on an à la carte basis or on half-day or full-day packages. In this oasis of quiet luxury, stress melts away in the hands of certified masseurs and masseuses. There is also a fully equipped beauty salon. You can schedule a session of reflexology work on nerve centers or be cocooned in a fragrant herbal wrap. Therapeutic Swedish massage and invigorating body scrubs with a loofah sponge working sea salts and avocado oil into your skin are part of package offerings. There is a three-day deluxe spa program and a five-day "Super Tone-Up," which must be reserved in advance.

Aerobics classes, on a cushioned floor, are scheduled according to your fitness level, from beginner to high-impact for the super-advanced, and run throughout the day, from 9 AM to 7 PM. People who live nearby can join the club and use the facilities, so you'll never be at a loss for company.

All activities are coed, and you can join a group doing "aquabics" in the fitness pool, or the "renaissance" program for those with arthritis and circulatory problems. Then relax in the whirlpool and steam baths.

Meals are served in the hotel atrium and dining room, or specially prepared lunches can be served in the privacy of the spa lounge for guests who want to avoid temptation. For kids there's a supervised day-care center and "Wild Zone" on the premises.

Wheels Country Spa at Wheels Inn

Best Western Wheels Inn
Box 637, Chatham, Ontario N7M 5K8
Tel. 519/351-1100, 519/436-5500 (spa); 800/265-5265 (in Canada); 800/265-5257 (in U.S.)
Telex 64-7110

Administration President, Steven Bradley; spa director, Jeanette Tielemans

Season Year-round

Accommodations Spa program limited to 30 participants. The inn has 354 rooms, standard motel amenities, and "club class" rooms.

Rates 3-day package $676 (C$) per person, double occupancy, $771 single. Program includes daily massage, herbal wrap, exercise periods, 3 spa meals, other services. 1-day Pamper Yourself package $175, 2-day/1-night pamper package $280 single, $253 double. Add 7% GST; deposit $100. Refundable upon 5-day notice. Rooms-only reservations through Best Western. AE, MC, V.

Meal Plans 3 meals total 1,000 calories per day for spa program participants. Low in salt and fat; choices include meat, fish, salads.

Services and Facilities **Exercise Equipment:** 10 Nautilus weight-training units, 2 Windracer bikes, 2 StairMasters, Universal gym, 6 Schwinn Air Dyne bikes, 3 Concept 2 rowers, free weights (5–200 lbs), leg-lift benches. **Services:** Swedish massage, facial, loofah body scrub, herbal wrap, reflexology, relaxation body treatment; beauty salon for hair, nail, and skin care. **Swimming Facilities:** 4-lane lap pool in the Fitness and Racquet Club; Olympic-size pool with indoor and outdoor sections in the atrium. **Spa Facilities:** Saunas, whirlpools. **Recreation Facilities:** Indoor courts:

6 tennis, 9 racquetball, 4 squash; maps of area running and jogging trails; water slides; 24-lane bowling alley.

In the Area Walks through Colasanti's Greenhouses, acres of tropical plants; wine tastings in nearby Blenheim at the Charral Winery. The Guy Lombardo Museum in his hometown, London; Uncle Tom's Cabin, home of Rev. Josiah Henson in Dresden, used on the Underground Railroad.

Getting Here *From border crossing at Detroit/Windsor.* By car, Hwy. 401 to Exit 81 North, then turn right and left at traffic lights (1 hr). *From London, Ontario or Toronto.* By car, Hwy. 401. By train, VIA Rail (tel. 800/561–3949) serves Chatham from Toronto with 4 trains daily (5 on Thurs.). By air, Windsor/London airport, 1 hr from inn. Local taxi and bus available.

Special Notes Children's programs include day-care center and Kent Kiddie Kollege, with daily activities and special summer outings for children 6–12. No smoking in designated areas. Spa open Mon.–Thurs. 9–9, Fri 9–7, Sat. 9–5, Sun. 9–1.

Aqua-Mer Center

Taking the waters

Québec
Carleton
The complete marine cure at this seaside auberge uses natural elements—seawater, algae, mud—and a mild Atlantic climate charged with iodine and negative ions. A combination of European and American therapies revitalizes your body while you relax and enjoy the Gaspé food and scenery at Aqua-Mer Center.

The sequence of treatments prescribed for you after consultation with the professional staff involves bathing and exercising in the indoor swimming pool filled with comfortably heated seawater. There are no cold plunges into the ocean, but brisk walks along the beach and a massage under alternating showers of warm and cold water are encouraged. To stimulate blood circulation and lymph drainage you will be massaged in underwater-jet baths; this will enhance the effect of algae added to seawater that has been heated to a high temperature. Follow this with a toning shower that focuses high-powered jets on every muscle in your body for invigorating results.

Aqua-Mer has a full circuit of treatments with mud, sand, algae, and seawater. Additional complementary treatments include pressotherapy (with pressure cuffs on your legs to enhance circulation), lymphatic drainage massage, shiatsu, and negative ionization. Half of each day is reserved for personal activity, which can be guided mountain tours, excursions to area attractions, or simply relaxing in the quiet room as you enjoy the view.

Aqua-Mer Center

868 Boulevard Perron, Carleton, Québec G0C 1J0
In winter: 145 rue du Pacifique, Laval, Québec H7N 3X9
Tel. spring–fall, 418/364–7055 or 800/463–0867; in winter,
514/629–5591 or 800/363–2303
Fax spring–fall, 418/364–7351; in winter, 514/629–5591

Administration Director, Yolande Dubois

Season May 15–Nov. 1

Accommodations 27 rooms in 3-story auberge and adjoining building. Program participants also stay in the nearby 15-room Thermotel. All have private bath or shower, 2 single beds, bathrobes. No TV, telephone, air-conditioning. Day visitors accommodated on a space-available basis.

Rates	6-day/7-night marine cure $1,045–$1,245 (C$) per person, double occupancy, $1,195–$1,450 single. 5-day marine cure without accommodation includes 5 meals, $575–$625 per person. Add 7% GST; gratuities extra. 25% deposit; balance on arrival. Refunds with notification 30 days prior to reserved dates. AE, MC, V.
Meal Plans	3 meals a day in health café at the Marine Cure Center. Approximately 1,000 calories a day, including fish, chicken, fresh seasonal vegetables. Similar light cuisine at local inns.
Services and Facilities	**Services:** Hydromassage, rain massage, affusion shower, Swiss shower, body wraps, fango, facial, lymphatic massage, pressotherapy, shiatsu, Swedish massage, manicure, pedicure, negative ionization, vertebral board. **Swimming Facilities:** Indoor pool. **Recreation Facilities:** Nearby 9-hole golf course, 3 tennis courts, paddleboats.
In the Area	Mont Saint-Joseph, Miguasha (fossil site), Carleton shops and churches.
Getting Here	*From Montréal.* By bus, Chartered coach departs every Sun. morning, returns Sat. evening (5 hrs). By car, Hwy. 20 and 132 east via Mont Joli (4 hrs). By air, scheduled Air Canada (tel. 800/776–3000) commuter service to Charlo airport, NB. By train, VIA Rail (tel. 800/561–3949) to Carleton. Complimentary transfers on arrival/departure Sun. at Charlo airport and Carleton train station.
Special Notes	Bring bathing cap, slippers, 2 swimsuits, beach towel, workout clothing, walking shoes.

Auberge du Parc Inn

Luxury pampering

Québec *Paspebiac*	Settle in for a relaxing week of seawater soaks and gourmet meals at this quiet retreat on the Baie des Chaleurs. Thalassotherapy is the main attraction at this inn, with a touch of Brittany and a style of its own. You are treated with mud, algae, and mineral-rich water pumped directly from the bay. Massage is part of the daily routine for guests on the one-week package.

Group activity is kept to a minimum, but there are stretch-and-tone sessions, and in warm weather groups exercise in the outdoor swimming pool. But a large part of your day is occupied by treatments, a passive program that most of the men and women who come here regularly seem to prefer.

Small and self-contained, the 30-room inn books no more than 40 guests a week for treatments. French is spoken most of the time, though staff members are bilingual. Having some awareness of local customs helps, but with a sense of humor, you can solve any problems or miscommunications.

After a walk in the countryside, your appetite sharpened by the salty air, you'll be served low-calorie meals that are a pleasant alternative to typical French-Canadian cooking.

Auberge du Parc Inn
C.P. 40, Paspebiac, Québec G0C 2K0
Tel. 418/752–3355 (800/463–0890 in Québec)

Administration	Manager, Madame Arthur Le Marquand
Season	Year-round
Accommodations	30 modern bedrooms with private bath in a country manor house. Bathrooms are shared.

Rates   7-day package $1,205–$1,365 (C$) per person double occupancy, $1,375–$1,555 single. Add 6.5% room tax, 7% GST, and gratuities. Deposit: 10% advance payment on booking. MC, V.

Meal Plans   3 meals a day included in package. Seafood and fresh produce from local farms featured.

Services and Facilities   **Services:** Massage, pressotherapy, facial, algae body wrap, hydrotherapy. **Swimming Facilities:** Indoor and outdoor seawater pools; nearby beaches. **Recreation Facilities:** Hiking; golf, tennis, cross-country skiing nearby.

Getting Here   *From Québec City.* On the main approach to the Gaspé Peninsula, by car, Hwy. 20 to Rivière-du-Loup, then Hwy. 132 east via Mt. Jolie through Matapedia (5 hrs).

Special Notes   No smoking in spa. 2-day marine cure package available.

Auberge Villa Bellevue

Nonprogram resort

Québec
Mont Tremblant

Sports training and fitness classes are the specialty of Club Spa Santé at the Auberge Villa Bellevue. On a natural lake close to the provincial park, the resort is near one of eastern Canada's most popular vacation playgrounds. The indoor swimming pool, exercise room, whirlpool, and sauna are open for year-round use by guests at no extra charge, and are open to others for a daily fee (C$7.75). Aerobics classes and aquacise exercise in the pool are scheduled daily during the ski season.

Conditioning prior to skiing can begin with an evaluation of your physical fitness by a credentialed member of the club staff. A personal training program is developed in this hour-long consultation (C$65). Fitness instructors are on hand daily to help you get started on the program. An alpine ski school operates at the resort, and there is free transportation to the slopes of Mt. Tremblant every day. For cross-country skiing, the resort maintains trails and a heated hut where equipment can be rented.

There is tennis instruction with a resident professional, and four courts can be rented by the hour ($10). The resort has mountain bikes that can be rented by the hour ($8 C$) or for a half day ($18 C$). Guests are invited to join a guided bike outing every Tuesday at 2 PM, which includes use of equipment ($20 C$). Summer brings family-oriented programs, and children from age 3 to teens can join activity every afternoon.

The meal plans allow you to select heart-healthy cuisine among five items on the fixed menu. Planned by a local dietitian in consultation with the executive chef, the Menu Santé provides a balance of high-energy and low-calorie food.

Auberge Villa Bellevue
Chemin Principal, Mont Tremblant, Que. J0T 2H0
Tel. 819/425–2734 or 800/567–6763
Spa reservations 819/425–2737
Fax 819/425–9360

Administration   Owner-director, Serge DuBois

Season   Year-round

Accommodations   102 bedrooms including 14 deluxe rooms with king-size or 2 queen-size beds, air-conditioning, TV, phone, and screened windows. Also, 8 condominium apartments have fully equipped kitchen, 2–3 bedrooms and baths, furnished in contemporary style, with fireplace, TV, phone, balcony or patio.

Rates 5-night package $255–$365 US in lodge or pavilion room, per person double occupancy, $388–$510 single; apartment $365 per person. Daily rate $54–$79 per person double, $74–$113 single. Children stay free of charge with parents. Add 6.5% room tax, 7% GST. Rates include gratuities. AE, DC, MC, V.

Meal Plans Breakfast and dinner daily included in the 5-night package and daily rate. Menu Santé dinner selections include grilled salmon, roast skinless chicken, pasta, veal, seasonal salads. Special diets accommodated with advance request.

Services and Facilities **Exercise Equipment:** 8 Solaris weight training units, Sprint stepper, 2 Cateye stationary bikes, free weights. **Services:** Swedish massage. **Swimming Facilities:** Private beach on Lake Ouimet; heated indoor lap pool 20 meters (65´). **Recreation Facilities:** 4 Har-Tru clay tennis courts ($10 per hour), windsurfing and sailing on the lake, 7 mountain bicycles for rent, kayaks, canoes, paddleboats. Ski instruction, ski equipment, and ice skate rental.

In the Area Mont Tremblant Provincial Park, about 15 mi from the villa, with full range of winter and summer activities. Shopping and antiques hunting in St. Jovite. Musée de la Faune (natural history).

Getting Here *From Montréal and Québec.* By bus, Voyageur Lines (tel. 514/842–2281) from Montréal and Québec City. By car, from Montréal airports and train station, Rte. 130 (90 mins). Rental cars, taxi available.

Special Notes No smoking in designated areas. Spa hours: daily 7 AM–10 PM in ski season; summer hours vary.

Centre d'Santé d'Eastman/ Eastman Health Center

Life enhancement

Québec
Eastman

On a farm, nestled in the rolling countryside of the Eastern Townships (about an hour's drive southeast of Montréal), the Centre d'Santé d'Eastman is a low-key retreat for body and mind. The bucolic setting and up-to-date facilities are a unique and necessary blend for anyone looking for a relaxing, rejuvenating getaway. Hydrotherapy is the specialty, from algae body wraps to thalasso tub.

Seven buildings house the spa facilities and up to 35 guests. A barn is home to the kitchen and dining areas, and the stone farmhouse, complete with flared roof and jutting dormer windows, is the locale for the hospitality lounge. Exercise is optional and not strenuous. Three guided walks are held daily, and yoga and tai chi chuan sessions are scheduled. A series of treatments designed to rid the skin of impurities is also available. The spa package includes a daily massage, three meals, and a snack.

The oxygen bath is said to produce vitality and a long-lasting sense of well-being. Encased in what looks like an iron lung, you are bathed in 104°F water mixed with carbon dioxide and jets of essential oils, then you receive 10 minutes of oxygen inhalation. Another house specialty is an algae body wrap with seaweed imported from France.

Centre d'Santé d'Eastman

895 Chemin des Diligences, Eastman, Québec J0E 1P0
Tel. 514/297–3009; in Canada, 800/665–5272

Administration Director-owner, Jocelyna Dubuc; spa director, Jocelyne Veillette

Season Year-round

Accommodations 19 rooms in main house and cottages, with private or shared bath. No TV, telephone. Comfortably furnished country rooms, some a short walk from spa and dining.

Rates 2-day Health Stay package $275–$335 (C$) per person, double occupancy, $315–$395 single. 2-day Relaxation spa package $390–$450 double, $430–$510 single. Add 7% room tax, 7% GST and gratuities. AE, MC, V.

Meal Plans 3 meals a day served family style. Vegetarian menu includes eggs, dairy products, decaffeinated tea and coffee. Breakfast can be an omelet with toast, crepes with Québec maple syrup, cereal, yogurt, fruit, or herb power drink. Lunch is soup, plate of raw vegetables. Chinese stir-fry is a dinner specialty. The buffet typically includes vegetable soup, 3 salads (carrot, sprouts, lettuce), eggplant Parmesan, whole wheat fettucine, vegetable rolls, and French apple pie. At 3 PM tisanes (herbal tea) are set out with fruit, cakes, and cookies.

Services and Facilities **Swimming Facilities:** Outdoor pool, lake. **Services:** Massage, polarity, reflexology, body wrap, hydrotherapy tub, thalassotherapy, body scrub, facial, oxygen bath, aromatherapy, leg waxing. **Recreation Facilities:** Horseback riding. **Evening Programs:** Sleigh rides, cooking class, health lecture, tai chi chuan, yoga.

In the Area Québec City, Gaspé Peninsula, Theatre de la Marjolaine.

Getting Here *From Montréal.* By car, Autoroute 10 exit 106 to Eastman, Rte. 245 to Rte. 112, Chemin du Lac d'Argent (1 hr). By bus, Voyageur (tel. 514/842–2281) to Eastman; call for pickup. *From Vermont.* Hwy. 55.

Gray Rocks Inn

Sports conditioning

Québec
St. Jovite Gray Rocks was built in 1906 as a hunting lodge, and in the late 1930s it opened the area's first Austrian-style ski school. In 1987 the resort evolved into a sports resort with the addition of Le Spa, offering a full-service fitness program. Classes and personal services are provided à la carte, although guests aren't charged for using the exercise equipment, coed sauna, or whirlpools. Along with an active social schedule, there are lean cuisine options for dining, making the Gray Rocks vacation package one of the best values in this part of Canada.

If you start with a fitness appraisal to help establish your goals, staff members, including an exercise physiologist, will test your cardiovascular capacity, body composition, and muscle flexibility. A computerized model provides an in-depth analysis of factors that affect your overall wellness. The spa has gained certification for customized exercise programs on their equipment. There are also aerobic dance sessions, stretch classes, and water-supported exercise in the pool.

Gray Rocks Inn

Box 1000, St. Jovite, Québec J0T 2H0
Tel. 819/425–2771 or 800/567–6767
Fax 819/425–3474

Administration	General manager, Philip Robinson; spa director, Carol Keyes
Season	Year-round
Accommodations	180-bedroom ski-lodge with Spartan furnishings, private bathrooms. 24-room private, upscale "Le Chateau" a short distance around the lake. 56 apartments (1–3 bedrooms) in cottages.
Rates	Summer 6-night package with 3 meals daily, $990–$1,350 (C$) per person, double occupancy, $1,140–$1,650 single. Daily rates: summer from $130 per person double, winter from $99 per person double. Add 7% GST and local tax. AE, DC, MC, V.
Services and Facilities	**Exercise Equipment:** 4 Nautilus weight-training units, 3 Lifecycles, 2 ergometers, 2 Monark bikes, Liferower, free weights (5–50 lbs), leg-extension and leg-curl benches, 2 NordicTracks. **Services:** Massage. **Swimming Facilities:** Outdoor pools (not heated); lap pool in the spa. Private beach on Lake Ouimet. **Recreation Facilities:** 22 tennis courts, horseback riding, golf, jogging and hiking trails. Ski school mid-Nov.–Apr. **Evening Programs:** Dancing and theme parties.
In the Area	Sleigh rides, shopping in nearby villages. Mont Tremblant Provincial Park (15 mi) for hiking and skiing.
Getting Here	*From Montréal.* By train (2 hrs). By air, 4,200-ft landing strip for private aircraft. By bus, Voyageur (tel. 514/842–2281) service direct to inn. Local taxi and rental cars.
Special Notes	No smoking in spa. Spa open 7 AM–10 PM daily in summer, 8–8 in winter. Daily facility pass ($10) for nonresidents.

Sivananda Ashram

Kid fitness
Spiritual awareness

Québec *Val Morin*	Vacationers come here to relax the mind and revitalize the body by practicing yoga from dawn to sunset. Just an hour from Montréal, the yoga camp is an accessible oasis of peace and harmony. Yet there is time for skiing and family fun within the daily schedule of meditation and vegetarian diet that you are required to follow.

Aside from the bare essentials of lodging, campers revel in the natural beauty of 350 acres of unspoiled woodland. At dawn, you are called to meditation, followed by yogic exercise or *asanas* that stretch and invigorate the body. A first meal comes at mid-morning, peak energy time; supper follows the 4 PM *asana* session. In between, you are free to enjoy the recreational facilities, to hike, or to get a massage. Sunset meditation and a concert of Indian music and dance conclude most days.

Based on five principles for a long and healthy life prescribed by Swami Vishnu Devananda, the program teaches how to breathe and exercise and how to combine diet with positive thinking and meditation.

Rebuilt after a fire in 1995, the new guest lodge is an ecologically sound building constructed with straw bale walls supported by wooden post-and-pole beams. There are rooms for 60 persons, a dining room, and a kitchen.

Sivananda Ashram
Eighth Ave., Val Morin, Québec J0T 2R0
Tel. 819/322–3226 or 800/263–9642 in Canada
Fax 819/322–5876

Administration Founder, Swami Vishnu Devananda; director, Swami Kartikeyananda

Season Year-round

Accommodations 2-story lodge with private and dormitory rooms. Simply furnished with 60 beds, linens, chest of drawers. Some rooms with private bath. Tent space on grounds.

Rates Single-price all-inclusive policy $50 (US$) per person sharing room with private bath, $35–$40 without bath. Single room without bath $50. Tent space $30. Dormitory bed $35. Reservations by mail, with deposit for $50 per person. AE, MC, V.

Meal Plans 2 vegetarian buffets daily. No meat, fish, eggs, alcohol, or coffee. Brunch has fruit, hot grain cereal, baked casserole of seasonal vegetables, rice, salad, herbal tea.

Services and Facilities **Swimming Facilities:** Large outdoor pool, lake. **Spa Facilities:** Sauna, massage. **Recreation Facilities:** Hiking, biking, volleyball, downhill and cross-country skiing. **Evening programs:** Traditional music and dancing of India, bonfires, and silent walks.

Getting Here *From Montréal.* By car, Laurentian Autoroute (Rte. 15), Exit 76. By bus, chartered service for special weekends and peak periods from Centre Sivananda (tel. 514/279–3545); Voyageur lines (tel. 514/842–2281) to Val Morin daily. Taxi service available in Val Morin. Airport pickup arranged for $50 (C$).

Special Notes Kids' Yoga Camp, for ages 4–14, is a month-long combination of yogic exercises, swimming, and other activities. No smoking. Remember to bring an exercise mat or blanket, sandals or shoes that can be slipped on and off easily, and warm clothing.

Spa Concept at Le Château Bromont

Luxury pampering
Nutrition and diet

Québec
Bromont

Revitalization and beautification are the basis of the Spa Concept program at Château Bromont, 100 kilometers (60 miles) from Montréal and 20 minutes from the U.S. border.

Emphasizing serious shape-ups, the Château has a fully equipped gymnasium, indoor and outdoor swimming pools, and an aerobics studio. The daily schedule includes aquafitness Jazzercise, stretch and tone, and low-impact aerobics classes.

European-style treatments are a major attraction for cosmopolitan Montréalers, who make up the majority of the guests. Included in packages for one to seven nights are body peeling, herbal wraps, and an unusually wide choice of massages—from soothing Swedish to shiatsu, Trager, and reflexology. Special therapies include polarity, lymphatic drainage, and baths with mud, sea algae, or essential oils. There are indoor and outdoor whirlpools, and a sauna.

Health programs are based on an evaluation of your lifestyle and on an energy test. The spa directress may advise energy-balancing exercise and specific treatments if you are on a five-night program. Otherwise there is no minimum stay, and services can be booked à la carte.

Spa Concept at Le Château Bromont
90 rue Stanstead, Bromont, Québec J0E 1L0
Tel. 514/534–2717 or 800/567–7727
Fax 514/534–0599

Administration Owner-director, Yvette Pratte Marchessalt

Season Year-round

Accommodations 154 rooms in a country lodge with rustic furnishings. All rooms with air-conditioning, private bath.

Rates 5-night package $1,220 (C$) per person, double occupancy, $1,435 single; 1-night package $280 double, $340 single. 3-night package $735 double, $855 single. Add 7% GST and local tax. Deposit: 1 night's accommodation. MC, V.

Meal Plans 3 meals daily included in packages. Meals are nutritionally balanced, low in calories. Herbal teas available.

Services and Facilities **Services:** Massage (Swedish, Esalen, shiatsu, aromatherapy, reflexology), lymphatic drainage, electro-puncture, balneotherapy, colonic irrigation, exfoliation, polarity therapy, herbal wrap, body peel, facial, fango pack, algotherapy, pressotherapy; beauty salon for hair, nail, and skin care. **Swimming Facilities:** Indoor and outdoor swimming pools. **Recreation Facilities:** Tennis and squash courts, racquetball, shuffleboard, volleyball, horseshoes, mountain biking; nearby downhill and cross-country skiing, horseback riding, water slides.

Getting Here *From Montréal.* By car, Rte. 10E to Exit 78, right turn on Bromont Blvd. to ski-slope area (1 hr).

Mexico

T he concept of spas in Mexico can be traced back to the ancient Aztecs, who bathed and worshiped spirits at the country's steaming hot springs. Throughout Mexico today, these *balnearios* (mineral water baths) and *baños termales* (thermal hot-spring baths) are a bargain, offering mud baths, thermal waters, and warm hospitality. The largest and most luxurious of them is in Ixtapan de la Sal, two hours' drive southeast of Mexico City, but rustic Rio Caliente Spa, secluded in a national forest near Guadalajara, provides refreshing sweats at bargain prices.

A very different experience, and a success since it opened more than 50 years ago, is the Rancho La Puerta in Baja California, founded by Deborah Szekely and her late husband. This is the action-oriented counterpart to the Golden Door in California; its holistic health program, vegetarian meals, and the stress-free environment of the Sierra Madres blend into a seamless vacation experience.

The best equipped examples of the new resort-based spas are at Hotel Hacienda Cocoyoc in the state of Morelos near Mexico City, Avandaro Golf & Spa Resort, a mountain retreat also near the capital city, and on the Pacific coast, Paradise Village Beach Resort & Spa in Nuevo Vallarta, Nayarit state. On the Caribbean coast, Cancún now has a full-service facility at the Melia Cancun Resort & Spa, which packs a lot of pampering into its tiny beachfront perch.

Taking the waters at Aztec-inspired Ixtapan de la Sal in mountainous Mexico state is better than ever, thanks to recent refurbishment at Hotel Ixtapan. And the new temazcal bath at Spa Prehispanico in Oaxaca's Puerto Escondido takes you back to the ancient cleansing sweat lodge ceremony. While longtime favorite Hotel Balneario San José de Purúa is closed for major renovations, you can soak in radioactive waters at Hotel Agua Blanca.

Don't expect organized group programs; aside from Rancho La Puerta, these resort spas tailor your schedule on a personal, daily basis. Increasingly sophisticated treatments and spa cuisine appear, along with traditional food and fun, to make a healthy holiday one of Mexico's best buys.

Avandaro Golf & Spa Resort

Luxury pampering

Valle de Bravo Perhaps the last thing you'd expect to find 80 miles west of Mexico City is this miniature village, set in the pines beside a vast lake. The cooler temperatures can be attributed to the area's high altitude, 6,000 feet above sea level. The climate allows for some very unlikely south-of-the-border experiences: crackling fires in guest suites at night to fend off the chill and invigorating hikes over the hills to witness the annual migration of the monarch butterflies. Programs are customized, as there is no group activity.

The spa is housed in a tile-roof hacienda overlooking the golf course. The latest equipment for facials and anticellulite treatments is available in the salon on the lower level of the spa building, and separate facilities for men and women on the main level include Swiss showers and a set of plunge pools (hot and cold) equipped with a waterfall for an invigorating natural massage. Upstairs is a small aerobics studio used for scheduled classes or individual workouts led by video instructors. The daily fee for hotel guests, $95 (Mex$), includes classes, exercise clothing, and use of facilities. Paying for spa services à la carte with a credit card secures the best exchange rate.

Carved out of the pine forest, velvety-green lawns of Avandaro's 18-hole championship golf course spread beyond the spa building. Also on the grounds are seven tennis courts and two restaurants. Accommodations are in deluxe adobe villas, or standard rooms in motel-style cabins near the reception center.

Popular with upscale families from Mexico City who own homes or timeshare apartments at the resort, the spa gets lots of traffic on weekends. Plan an excursion to the lakeside village in the valley, Valle de Bravo, a 400-year-old pueblo that offers shopping for arts and crafts, sidewalk cafés, and boating.

Avandaro Golf & Spa Resort

Vega del Rio S/N-Rancho Avandaro
Valle de Bravo 51200
Reservations: 800/223–6510 in US
Canada, 800/424–5500, Hotel 52–726/60366
Fax 52–726/60122
Mexico City: Anatole France 139, Polanco C. P. 11560
Tel. 525/280–1532, Fax 525/282–0578

Administration	General manager, Alexandra Simon, spa director, Samantha Chain
Season	Year-round
Accommodations	100 suites and rooms in Spanish colonial–style adobe villas. All have wood-burning fireplace, TV, telephone, tiled modern bathroom; 60 junior suites with sitting area, dining table, balcony or terrace.
Rates	8-day/7-night Slim & Trim package $1,745–$2,187 (US$) for 2 persons, double occupancy, $1,120–$1,340 single. Daily rate without spa for 2 persons, double occupancy, in standard room $86, in suite $180. Tax and gratuities included. Deposit: 50% advance payment. AE, MC, V.
Meal Plans	3 meals daily from spa cuisine à la carte menu in Las Terrazas Restaurant included with spa packages. Weekend rate for suites includes breakfast only. Daily specials can be grilled mountain trout, pasta, seafood, chicken, and steaks. Vegetarian meals on request.
Services and Facilities	**Exercise Equipment:** 5 Paramount weight-training units, 2 Lifecycles, 2 Trotter 540 treadmills, 2 Lifesteps, Precor rower, Tunturi stretch unit, Premier barbell bench, dumbbells (3–50 lbs). **Services:** Massage (Swedish, sports, aromatherapy), shiatsu, reflexology, pressotherapy, loofah salt glow, facials, herbal wrap, electronic stimulation of facial and body liftings, anticellulite treatment, antistress biofeedback, nutritional analysis. Salon for hair, nail, and skin care. **Swimming Facilities:** Heated outdoor swimming pool. **Recreation Facilities:** 7 tennis courts, 18-hole golf course, hiking and nature trails, Ping-Pong; nearby horseback riding, water sports, hang gliding.
In the Area	Lake Avandaro, Valle de Bravo (colonial pueblo), Toluca (Friday market, botanical garden, Spanish colonial architecture), trout farm, La Gavia (16th-century hacienda), volcano hike.
Getting Here	*From Mexico City.* By car, Constituyendes Av. to Autopista (toll road) Rte. 15 via Toluca, Hwy. 134 through national

Mexico

Avandaro Golf & Spa Resort, **9**

Club Med–Huatulco, **11**

Hotel Balneario Comanjilla, **7**

Hotel Hacienda Cocoyoc, **8**

Hotel Ixtapan, **10**

Melia Cabo Real, **3**

Melia Cancun Resort & Spa, **12**

Paradise Village Beach Resort & Spa, **4**

Qualton Club & Spa Vallarta, **5**

Rancho La Puerta, **1**

Río Caliente Spa, **6**

Rosarito Beach Hotel & Casa Playa Spa, **2**

forest, Hwy. 86, Hwy. 8 to Valle de Bravo (3 hrs). Hotel provides complimentary round-trip transportation from Mexico City International Airport and hotels in Zona Rosa as part of spa packages, Sunday only. 1-way transfer other days $75.

Special Notes Ground-floor accommodations accessible for people with disabilities. Minimum age in spa is 16 for women, 18 for men. No smoking in spa. Spa open Mon.–Thurs. 8–7, Fri. and Sat. 8–9, Sun. 8–8.

Balnearios

Nonprogram resort
Taking the waters

A central belt cutting all the way to the Gulf of Mexico as well as the Pacific coast of Mexico comprises a vast volcanic zone. Hundreds of hot springs dot the region, and one entire state— Aguascalientes—has been named for the hot waters.

While most of the springs are not developed, some are popular with Mexican families, and within this volcanic area is Mexico's most beautiful mountain scenery. Here are some of the places where "taking the waters" can be enjoyed year-round.

Agua Blanca Hotel, Jungapeo, Michoacán
Carretera Zitacuaro, Cd. Hidalgo
Tel. 8 in Jungapeo

Set deep in a canyon is the 10-room Agua Blanca hotel, with three thermal pools fed by radioactive waters that flow over cascades at 30°C. Silence, manicured lawns, and luxuriant flower beds enhance this serene escape. Nearby are San Jose Purua and the sanctuary of Monarch butterflies.

Aqua Hedionda
Av. Progreso s/n, Cuautla, Morelos
Tel. 735/2–044

Sulfuric waters fill two public pools, wading pools, and eight private pools. Facilities include showers and dressing rooms, and the resort houses a restaurant with dancing on weekends. Located close to Cuernavaca.

El Almeal
Prolongacion Virginia Hernandez s/n. Cuautla, Morelos
Tel. 735/2–1751

Two spring-fed pools, wading pools, playing fields, and a restaurant enhance this public spa. Dressing rooms and lockers provided for daily admission fee. Scenic railroad excursion Thursday, Saturday, and Sunday. Hiking trails nearby to Popacatepti and Ixtaccihuatl.

Hotel Balneario Atzimba
Av. Lazaro Cardenas, 58930 Zinapecuaro, Michoacán
Tel. 435/5–0042
Fax 435/5–0050

Adjacent to a popular water park, this rustic 12-room hotel with thermal water baths is about 30 minutes from Morelia, capital of the state. There is a small restaurant and lots of space for unwinding.

Hotel Balneario Chignahuapan
Km. 5 Carretera de Chignahuapan, Puebla
Tel. 777/1–0599

At the edge of a canyon into which a cold-water stream plunges hundreds of feet and mixes with hot sulfur springs, the 37-room hotel has huge tiled bathing pools. All rooms with private bath, small balcony. Nearby are Tiaxcala, a colonial town noted for the Sanctuary of the Virgin of Ocotlan, and pre-Hispanic murals at the Cacaxtla archaeological site.

Hotel Balneario La Caldera

Km. 29 Libramiento, Carretera Abosolo, 36970,
Abasolo, Guanajuato
Tel. 456/3–0020 and 456/3–0021 (also fax line)

Private baths fed with thermal mineral water, an outdoor Jacuzzi, two swimming pools, two basketball courts, squash court, two tennis courts, soccer field, and extensive gardens are features of the 116-room La Caldera. All rooms have private bath, TV, air-conditioning. Located just west of Irapuato, Mexico's strawberry center.

Hotel Balneario Lourdes

Reservation office: Francisco Zarco 389, San Luis
Potosi, S.L.P.
Tel. 481/2–3232 or 481/3–8065

This spa, with 36 double rooms, a heated pool fed by mineral waters, horseback riding, squash and tennis courts, is 59 kilometers (37 miles) south of the picturesque colonial city of San Luis Potosi.

Hotel Tainul

Km. 15 Carretera Cd.
Valles-Tampico, Cd. Valles
Mailing Address: Box 87, Cd. Valles, S.L.P.
Tel. 91–138/2–0000
Fax 91–138/2–4414

Located 15 minutes from Ciudad Valles and 100 kilometers (62 miles) from Tampico, the three-star Hotel Tainul has 142 air-conditioned rooms and 16 suites. The thermal-water swimming pool, fed by sulfur springs, and a freshwater pool, are part of the spa complex. Services include facial, massage, manicure, and pedicure. Restaurant and tennis courts for hotel guests.

Las Estacas Nature Park

Tlaltizapán, Morelos
Tel. 91–734/50077, Fax 91–734/50159
Mailing Address: C.P. 62000, Cuernavaca, Mor.

Towering stands of bamboo, amate, and royal palm trees shade swift-flowing streams from a volcanic spring that pours 8,000 liters of water per second into the park's one-kilometer waterway. Clear and refreshingly cool, the river is popular with families who float in tubes, swim, and dive. Overnight accommodations (100 pesos) are in 10 nicely maintained cabins, with private bathroom, twin beds, porch. Visitors come for a day (30 pesos), relax in the palapas for lunch, and join volleyball, basketball, and soccer games. Children's wading pools adjoin a concrete swimming pool. Based near Cuernavaca, the park is developing educational programs about the ecology of the area, once a major sugar-growing center.

Oaxtepec Vacation Center

Reservation Center in Mexico City: Heriberto Frias 241,
Col. Navarte or C.P. 03020, Mexico, D.F.
Tel. 525–639/4200 or 525–639/0071
Resort 91–735/60101

This spa, 56 kilometers (35 miles) east of Cuernavaca, near Cuautla in the state of Morelos, has closed the thermal pool, a favorite retreat of Móctezuma, but has vast spring-fed swimming pools, athletic fields, and restaurants run by the Mexican Social Security Institute. Overnight accommodations available in cottages or guest rooms.

Spa Hispanico at Hotel Aldea del Bazar
Av. Benito Juarez Lote No. 7, Puerto Escondido, Oaxaca.
Tel. 91–958/20508

Set in a tropical garden by the sea, the temazcal bath is a 500-year-old sweat lodge for cleansing toxins from the body and attaining a spiritual state. Start with a body scrub and massage under the palm trees, then sit in the marble-walled temazcals (one for groups, one solo) as herbal water is poured on hot rocks. Try a facial with mud from volcanic ash. The new white-walled hotel's 47 deluxe rooms and two suites create a Moorish fantasy, complete with swimming pool. Nearby is a private beach club and restaurant. Also in Tehuacan, Puebla state, under same management.

Club Med-Huatulco

Sports conditioning

Oaxaca
Santa Cruz

The green hills and emerald waters of Club Med's Huatulco village are on the Pacific coast 525 kilometers (325 miles) south of Acapulco. The air-conditioned fitness center is equipped with a large selection of Paramount weight-training equipment, plus padded floor for aerobics classes.

Choose between sports and exercise to help work off the éclairs or chocolate mousse from last night's dinner. Sessions of low- and high-impact aerobics, and stretching (45–60 minutes), are offered throughout the day. You have unlimited 24-hour access to three air-conditioned squash courts, tennis on 12 courts, and a practice golf course. Water-sports activities are popular, but the challenge of flying on a circus trapeze is the big attraction. Instructors strap you to safety cables and demonstrate proper form between 4 and 6 every afternoon. Those who survive stage a show Friday evening.

Opened in 1988, Huatuclco is the largest Club Med in North America. It has its own water purification system, using reverse osmosis. On twin coves, casita-style lodgings are terraced on the hillsides. There are three large freshwater swimming pools (one is Olympic-size) and a choice of four ocean coves with gentle surf. Meals are served in five specialty dining rooms. The all-inclusive package, which is a Club Med tradition, takes the stress out of a week devoted to well-being.

Club Med-Huatulco
Bahia de Tangolunda, Santa Cruz, Oaxaca
Tel. 52–958/1–0033
Fax 52–958/1–0101
Reservations: 3 E. 54th St., New York, NY 10019
Tel. 212/977–2100 or 800/258–2633

Administration Rotating Club Med manager

Season Year-round

Accommodations 500 air-conditioned units furnished with twin beds, optional partition. Rattan furniture, local crafts and bedspreads, private sea-view terrace with hammock. Each casita has a bathroom and shower; electrical voltage is 110.

Rates All-inclusive weekly rate, $950–$1,200 per person, double occupancy; add 10% for single room. Payment of 25% deposit due within a week of reservation, plus club membership fee ($50 annual, $30 initiation). Airfare from gateway city included. AE, MC, V.

Meal Plans Buffets with unlimited choices for breakfast, lunch, and dinner. Choice of 5 restaurants serving Italian, Argentine, Moroccan, seafood, Club Med salads, grilled chicken, and tropical fruits. Milk, coffee, tea, and dinner wine included; bottled water available.

Services and Facilities **Exercise Equipment:** 15-unit Paramount weight-training circuit, 2 Precor 714 steppers, 2 Lifecycles, free weights (3–10 lbs), barbells (2½–45 lbs), 2 bench presses, incline benches. **Services:** Scheduled classes for aerobics, stretch, step, and water exercises; massage. **Swimming Facilities:** 3 outdoor pools, 4 ocean beaches. **Recreation Facilities:** Trapeze class, juggling, archery, sailing, kayaking, windsurfing, snorkeling, 12 tennis courts (7 lighted), 3 indoor squash courts, practice golf course, volleyball, basketball, softball, billiards, Ping-Pong. Nearby horseback riding, 9-hole golf course, fishing, scuba diving (extra charge). **Evening Programs:** Nightly entertainment and dancing.

In the Area Monte Alban (Zapotec archaeological ruins), Oaxaca (16th-century colonial architecture, Indian marketplace), Mitla, Monte Alban (Aztec ruins).

Getting Here *From Dallas.* Club Med charter flights on American Airlines every Sunday. Transfers to club provided. Taxi 1-way $25.

Special Notes Registered nurse in residence. Airport fee required with proof of U.S. citizenship. Children 6 and over accommodated with parents. Bring tennis racket and balls, exercise gloves.

Hotel Balneario Comanjilla

Taking the waters

Guanajuato In the heart of the fertile Bajío region, the pleasantly old-fash-
León ioned Hotel Balneario Comanjilla is a quiet, secluded resort convenient to the beautiful nearby colonial city of Guanajuato and industrial León (the leather capital of Mexico). Gardens surround the two-story guest buildings, one of which houses an aerobics studio and conference facilities.

Exercise programs are organized on request only, and massage ($15) appointments must be made well in advance. Medical and nutritional consultation is available to guests in Spanish only. Nevertheless, two swimming pools filled with warm thermal water, well-appointed guest rooms, tennis courts, and stables make the trip worthwhile for honeymooners, Texas snowbirds, and, perhaps, you, regardless of language barriers.

Hotel Balneario Comajilla
Carretera Panamericana 45, Km. 385
Apt. Postal 111, 37000 León, Gto.
Tel. 52–47/12–0091
Fax 52–47/12–0949

Administration Manager, Sr. Arturo Sainz

Season Year-round

Accommodations 120 rooms in 2-story Spanish-colonial buildings. All with tiled private bathroom, phone, TV, and air-conditioning. 4 suites have step-down Roman bath with thermal water. All with 2 king-size beds, balcony or patio, view of forest or pool.

Rates Daily rate includes 3 meals. 430 pesos for two persons in standard double room; 580 pesos for two persons in suite.

Meal Plan 3 meals daily included in daily room rate. An à la carte menu is offered in the hotel dining room.

Services and Facilities **Exercise Facilities:** 2 stationary bikes, free weights. **Services:** Massage, facial, medical evaluation. **Spa Facilities:** 2 outdoor pools. **Recreation Facilities:** 2 tennis courts, bicycles, horseback riding, billiards, Ping-Pong.

In the Area San Miguel de Allende, Guanajuato (museums, university, fall festival), León (leather shopping, particularly for shoes).

Getting Here *From León.* By car, Hwy. 45 to Silao, Km 385; follow rural road signs to hotel (40 mins). Taxi, rental car available at Bajio Regional Airport (20 mins).

Special Notes Ground-floor rooms are accessible for people with disabilities.

Hotel Hacienda Cocoyoc

Luxury pampering

Morelos
Cuautla

An hour's drive from Mexico City, Hotel Hacienda Cocoyoc captures the charm of a bygone era of sugar plantations. But beyond the ancient aquaduct and grand swimming pools is the most modern spa this side of the Sierra Madre. Opened in 1996, the spa building has separate wings for men and women, each with steam bath, sauna, showers (Swiss multijet), wet-treatment room, and private massage rooms. Sunlight streams into the lounges where you await treatments, or relax in a big whirlpool under a pyramid-shaped skylight. Locker room attendants hand you limewater refreshers (water comes from a well on the property) and provide robe and sandals. Amenities include hair dryer, grooming items. The daily facility fee added to your bill is $8 (US$).

Spa services can be combined with golf at the resort's sister club in a nearby residential development, or the 9-hole course adjoining the spa. And there are personal trainers for tennis and golf, as well as for workouts and water aerobics. The exercise room is small, but new Nautilus equipment is available without charge.

With a wide range of treatments à la carte, the spa concentrates on relaxation techniques, detoxifying, and revitalizing. For total escape, slip into the alpha jet capsule and see if you can generate relaxing alpha waves. The spa environment itself, all polished stone and wood in golden tones, sunlit but secluded, is conducive to a stress-free escape. Meals can be at the spa café or the main dining room, but informality is the rule.

Staying in one of the private casitas that border the gardens adds a romantic touch. Each unit comes with a walled garden where a pool big enough for two provides a refreshing dip in the morning and evening. In the bathroom, hand-painted tiles cover the walls and step-down shower. Accommodations are in several buildings, and the main hacienda provides two restaurants and conference facilities. Secluded from the outside world of noisy truck traffic and sugar cane farming, this is quintessential, old-fashioned Mexico.

Hotel Hacienda Cocoyoc

Box 300, Cuautla 622736, Morelos
Tel. 52/735–622–11 or 52/735–612–11
Fax 52/735–612–12
Reservations Office in Mexico City: 550–7331

Administration Managing director/owner, Paulino Rivera Tores; spa director, Gloria Reyes Gomez

Season Year-round

Accommodations 298 rooms in high-ceiling suites and private casitas. Superior garden units have walled patio pool, four-poster bed, sitting room, tiled bathroom, TV, telephone. No air-conditioning.

Rates Daily per room for two, $365–$495 (Mex$), suite with pool $650–$750. Add tax and gratuity. AE, MC, V.

Meal Plans No meal plan available. Two restaurants serve Mexican and Continental fare. Spa selections include egg-white omelet with mushrooms or cactus, breakfast granola; lunch and dinner entrées include grilled fish fillet with steamed vegetables, chicken breast stuffed with huichole corn mushroom, stuffed baby squid, fettucine, spinach crepe, salad. Dessert is homemade sorbet, fresh fruit, dietetic ice cream. Herbal tea, coffee served.

Services and Facilities **Exercise Equipment**: Nautilus Time Machine unit, 2 Nautilus steppers, 2 Nautilus bikes. **Services**: Massage (Swedish, sports, anti-stress), mineral mud wrap, thalasso wrap and hydromassage, reflexology, facials, passive pressotherapy, glycolic peel, loofah scrub, computerized body composition analysis. **Swimming Facilities**: 4 outdoor pools. **Recreation Facilities**: 9-hole executive golf course on site, nearby 18-hole course, 3 tennis courts, jogging trail. **Evening Programs**: Disco.

In the Area Archaeological sites (Tepoztlan, Xochicalo), Las Estacas nature park, Cuernavaca (Cortes palace museum and Diego Rivera mural, Borda gardens), Sunday market in Tepoztlan.

Getting Here *From Mexico City.* By car, Hwy. 95 to Autopista Acapulco, exit Cualtla di Teopoztlian, Hwy. 115 (2 hrs). By bus, Pulman de Morelos (tel. 18 91 99) from Terminal del Sur or Tasquena Metro station (2 hrs). Van service by hotel $100 round-trip. Taxi, rental car available.

Hotel Ixtapan

Luxury pampering
Taking the waters

Mexico
Ixtapan de la Sal
Hotel Ixtapan, the largest and most luxurious thermal springs health resort in Mexico, is in Ixtapan de la Sal, which has been a popular center for cures since the 16th-century Aztec emperor Móctezuma came to bathe. It is 119 kilometers (65 miles) southwest of Mexico City, easily accessible from the capital by car or limousine service.

Recently rejuvenated by the resident owners, the hotel's health and beauty programs feature fresh-fruit facials, calorie-controlled meal option, and bathing in thermal waters. Aquacise classes are held in a thermal-water pool, 20 meters by 8 meters, open to all guests.

New furniture in guest rooms, and a covered outdoor whirlpool, are among recent improvements to the hotel, which dates from 1942. A water treatment plant and a power plant maintain the hotel's safety and privacy. The spa and fitness centers are on separate floors for men and women. While facilities for aerobics classes and exercise are limited, the spa has a marble whirlpool centerpiece where you can relax while awaiting a facial or massage in private cubicles. On the top floor is a men's gym and solarium.

The thermal waters originate from an extinct volcano about an hour away and are piped into a huge lake in the Parque Acuatico adjoining the hotel grounds. An open-air swimming pool in the hotel gardens has plankton-heavy thermal water, but the new whirlpool features natural, filtered water. In a public bathhouse across from the gardens, you can have a private soak in 20 marble-walled Roman baths, which come with two beds where you rest and cool down. The sunken whirlpools are filled with warm mineral water, ideal for a late-afternoon soak or a Sunday indulgence when hotel masseuses have the day off.

Packages are an excellent value, including daily massage and treatments in four- and seven-day programs, but you must arrive on a Sunday. The rate includes accommodations, meals, and treatments. Treatments are gentle and relaxing, and exercises are not strenuous. The masseuses work muscles by hand and utilize electric vibrators as well. Optional diet plan and medical supervision are available with the spa packages.

Among recreational facilities at this 35-acre family resort are a 9-hole golf course, disco, bars, train rides, horse-drawn carriages, water slides, and a bowling alley. Avoid weekend crowds if possible.

Hotel Ixtapan
Ixtapan de la Sal, 51900 Mexico
Office: Tonala 177, Col. Roma, 06700, Mexico City, D.F.
Tel. 52–5/264–2613 for office in Mexico City
Fax 52–5/264–2529
U.S. Reservation Center
Tel. 210/341–8151 or 800/638–7950
Fax 210/342–9789

Administration Director, Roberto San Roman; program director, Carlos S. Tovak

Season Year-round

Accommodations 168 rooms plus 48 private villas; pre-Hispanic motifs, colorful native fabrics; rooms comfortable with king-size bed plus sofa bed standard; all suites with private baths and air-conditioning. Superior rooms with balcony face gardens.

Rates 7-day/6-night spa program (Sun.–Sat.), $784–$825 per person double occupancy, $945–$995 single. 4-day/4-night program (Sun.–Thurs. or Wed.–Sun.), $404–$425 double, $565–$650 single. Daily $135–$210 for 2 persons double, full American plan. Add 10% tax plus gratuities. Deposit: 50% at time of booking, plus $95 transfer ($85 return to Mexico City) if requested. No credit cards.

Meal Plans 3 meals daily included in spa packages and daily rate. Choice of full menu in main dining room, or spa room. 900-calorie diet menu has fruit or juice with either tea or coffee for breakfast; cream of carrot soup, fresh fruit, and either chicken with mushrooms or plain tuna fish for lunch; dinner choices include fresh rainbow trout, omelet, and cheese plate.

Services and Facilities **Exercise Equipment:** Multistation Universal weight-training unit, Lifefitness cycle, stepper, rower, treadmill, cross-country skier, free weights, benches. **Services:** Massage, reflexology, acupuncture, mud packs, facial; hair, skin, and nail treatments. **Bathing Facilities:** Indoor and outdoor pools, private whirlpools. **Swimming Facilities:** Outdoor pools. **Recreation**

Facilities: Tennis courts, 9-hole golf course, horseback riding, volleyball, badminton. **Evening Programs:** Resort entertainment, movies, folkloric ballet.

In the Area Taxco (artisan center), archaeological sites, El Salto (canyon, cascade), Caves of La Estrella.

Getting Here *From Mexico City.* By car, Hwy. 15 to toll road (Autopista) via Toluca, then Ixtapan de la Sal toll road (Cuota) to Hwy. 55 exit. (2 hrs). By bus from Observatorio terminal. Hotel provides transfers on arrival/departure at airport or downtown hotels $180 round-trip, including tolls and tax. Taxi, rental car available.

Special Notes Elevators and ground-floor rooms are accessible for people with disabilities. Minicamp and play areas for children. No smoking in baths. Electrical current is 60 cycles/120 volts.

Melia Cabo Real

Nonprogram resort

Baja California
San Jose del Cabo
Perched on the rugged tip of Baja California, where the Sea of Cortés meets the Pacific Ocean, the spa at the Melia Cabo Real resort is enjoyed by nature lovers and fitness buffs alike. Whale-watching in the Sea of Cortés is a popular pastime, as are desert cycling, mountain jogging, horseback riding, and a full range of water sports. Deep-sea fishing for marlin is also a major attraction.

The hotel is crowned by a unique glass-and-marble pyramid, and bordered by cactus gardens, flowering bougainvillea, and palms. A beachfront restaurant and two swimming pools are reached by cobblestone walkways. The health center's coed gym offers sessions of yoga and tai chi chuan, in addition to personalized exercise supervised by trained fitness instructors. Aquacise and weight-training classes are scheduled in the pool. For relaxation, each locker room has a sauna, steam room, and Jacuzzi. Exercise equipment is minimal, and bodywork is limited to massage and wraps with herbs or mineral salts. Beauty salon services are available as part of the Avanti spa package, or à la carte.

Melia Cabo Real
Carretera Cabo San Lucas, Sector 5, Km 19.5
Los Cabos, Baja California Sur 23400
Tel. 52–114/4–0000 or 800/336–3542
Fax 52–114/4–0101

Administration General manager, Cristobal Tortosa; spa director, Lucrecia M. Aguilar

Season Year-round

Accommodations 286 double rooms and 14 suites, all with oceanfront view, air-conditioning, satellite TV, telephone, marble-floor bathroom with 110-volt (U.S.) electricity outlets. Garden-level rooms have landscaped private terrace; all others have private balcony.

Rates 5-day/4-night Health, Beauty, and Pamper Package, including 3 meals daily, spa services, and airport transfers, $897 per person, double occupancy. 1-day spa package (no lodging) $260 per person. Tax included. Daily room rate $158–$293 single or double occupancy, suites $380–$700. Add 10% tax, plus 10% service charge. Deposit: guarantee by credit card. AE, DC, MC, V.

Meal Plans 3 meals daily included in spa package. The weight-loss menu for breakfast is egg-white omelet or granola with low-fat milk, peach melba, juices, coffee, tea, and toast. Lunch can be soup, steamed broccoli and cauliflower, chicken breast, tossed salad, or broiled fish, zucchini and tomato. Dessert is an apple or apricot. Dinner entrées include broiled beef, fish, or chicken; vegetarian plate with cottage cheese; or spinach salad.

Services and Facilities **Exercise Equipment:** 2 Universal weights units, 2 stationary bikes, EZ Stepper, free weights, slant board. **Services:** Massage, herbal wrap, mineral salt wraps, reflexology, 1-on-1 instruction; salon for hair, nail, and skin care. **Swimming Facilities:** 2 outdoor freshwater pools, ocean beach. **Recreation Facilities:** Water sports, scuba, beach volleyball, table tennis, 2 tennis courts (lighted, $9 per hr); 18-hole golf course nearby, horseback riding, boat tours. **Evening Programs:** Live music and dancing nightly.

Getting Here *From Cabo San Lucas International Airport.* By car, Hwy. 1 southwest (25 km), resort entrance at Km 19 (30 mins). Complimentary transfers included in 5-day spa package. Taxi, rental car available.

Special Notes Ground-floor rooms available for people with disabilities.

Melia Cancún Resort & Spa

Nonprogram resort

Quintana Roo
Cancún Amid the strip of high-rise hotels for which Cancún is renowned, is the boutique spa at the Melia Cancún Resort, notable because it's the only such beachfront facility in this popular resort town. Perched on a spectacular white sand beach, well-acclaimed Melia Hotel overlooks the turquoise waters of the Caribbean. Enjoying massages poolside is the prescription for relaxation, and outdoor treatment cabanas let you enjoy the sea air without sun. Aerobics classes are held on the pool terrace and in the pool. When you've had enough sun, the spa is a cool retreat, with fully equipped fitness room, and salon for facials and skin and hair treatments.

At day's end try the spa's aloe spritzer—a soothing tonic, involving a body shampoo followed by a cooling aloe body gel. Other specialties are the Mayan clay mask, sea-salt loofah scrub, and aromatherapy massage. For the ultimate relaxer, schedule an al fresco massage in the torchlit garden cabana.

Melia Cancún Resort & Spa
Blvd. Kukulkan, No. 23 Zona Hotelera
77500 Cancún, Quintana Roo
Tel. 52–988/5–1160 or 800/336–3542
Fax 52–988/5–1263

Administration Managing director, Ricardo Verdayes, spa manager Solorro Domingues

Season Year-round

Accommodations 413 deluxe rooms, 36 junior suites, 1 presidential suite. All have balcony with ocean or lagoon view, private bathroom, TV, telephone, air-conditioning.

Rates Daily per room (single or double occupancy) $195–$300, junior suites $255–$490. Spa packages from $297 per night. 3-night/4-day package $1,139–$1,289 single, $900–$975 per person, double occupancy. Add 10% tax and 15% service charge. AE, DC, MC, V.

Meal Plans Spa meals served in Spa Caribe room; daily meal plan available.

Services and Facilities	**Exercise Equipment:** Badger strength conditioning units, 3 Quinton treadmills, 2 Lifesteps, 3 Lifecycles, free weights. **Services:** Massage, aromatherapy, hydrating facial, clay mask, loofah body scrub, aloe body wrap; salon for hair, nail, and skin care. **Swimming Facilities:** 3 outdoor pools, ocean beach. **Recreation Facilities:** 3 tennis courts (lighted, hard surface), executive golf course, water sports. **Evening Programs:** Music, Ballet Folklorico.
In the Area	Mayan ruins, Cozumel (scuba).
Getting Here	*From Miami.* By air, United, Mexicana, American Airlines, and others have scheduled service. Taxi, rental car available.

Paradise Village Beach Resort

Luxury pampering

Nayarit *Nueva Vallarta*	On a peninsula between the beach and marina, the spa at Paradise Village Beach Resort is a modern Mayan temple of glass and marble devoted to health, fitness, and beauty. Inside this cool oasis are separate wings for men and women, equipped with private hydrotherapy tubs, Vichy shower, whirlpool, sauna, and steam room. The coed cardiovascular and weight training rooms have views of the water and TV while you work out on state-of-the-art equipment. Aerobics classes are scheduled throughout the day in a mirrored studio. And a snack bar offers refreshment.

Treatment selections are extensive, and the private rooms for massage, facials, and wraps have a calming effect. The spa also has a lap pool and beauty salon. Day packages can be booked, or your vacation plan will be custom-tailored.

Opened in 1993, accommodations in the beachfront tower are in condominium apartments, with two or three bedrooms, full kitchen, and living room, plus private terrace. The hotel features a lagoon-size swimming pool, complete with rocky grottoes, flowing waterfalls, and a Mayan-style temple. There is an 18-hole golf course at the resort, plus another nearby.

Paradise Village Beach Resort & Spa
Avenida de los Cocoteros 001, Nueva Vallarta, Nayarit 63731
Tel. 52–329/70–770 or 800/995–5714
Fax 52–329/70–920

Administration	Manager, Ricardo Orozco; spa director, Diana Mestre
Season	Year-round
Accommodations	265 apartments in 8-story tower. Modern furnishings, with king-size or twin beds, full kitchen with daily maid service, bathroom, air-conditioning, TV, telephone. Choice of one or two bedrooms.
Rates	3-night Renewal package $628–$754 (US$) single, $430–$493 per person, double occupancy; 7-night Stress Reducer $1,538–$1,832 single, $1,081–$1,228 double. Day Spa packages $74–$196. Add 15% tax, plus gratuities. AE, MC, V.
Meal Plans	3 meals daily included in spa packages. Choice of spa menu or regular restaurant, with $50 beverage credit per person.
Services and Facilities	**Exercise Equipment:** 12-unit Paramount weight-training circuit, 4 Trotter treadmills, 2 recumbent Lifecycles, 4 Lifecycle and Tectrix bikes, Olympic bench and bar, free weights and dumbbells. **Services:** Massage (aromatherapy, reflexology, shiatsu, relaxation, lymphatic drainage), facials, thalassotherapy bath, herbal wrap, loofah body scrub, paraffin body treatment,

fitness evaluation; salon for hair, nail, and skin care. **Swimming Facilities:** Outdoor pool, indoor lap pool, ocean beach. **Recreation Facilities:** 4 lighted tennis courts, 18-hole golf course, kayaks, windsurfing (fee), fishing excursion, horseback riding.

In the Area Puerto Vallarta (Old Town, beaches).

Getting Here *From Puerto Vallarta.* Taxi, rental car, limousine available (20 mins).

Qualton Club & Spa Vallarta

Luxury pampering

Jalisco
Puerto Vallarta

The steamy romance of Elizabeth Taylor and Richard Burton put Puerto Vallarta on the international tourist map, and the Qualton Club & Spa Vallarta will keep it there. In a seaside complex of high-rise hotels near the international airport, here's a budget-priced property for fitness buffs on a beach holiday. The club has a large fitness center where you can join yoga, step-aerobics, and water-aerobics classes daily, or use a full circuit of weight-training equipment in air-conditioned studios. The club's all-inclusive daily rate includes spa admission, meals, and refreshments. (A daily $10 spa pass is available to nonresidents.)

Supervised by certified aerobics instructors, activities are scheduled from 7AM to 7:30PM. At 7AM a tennis clinic starts the day, followed by low-impact aerobics, cross-training workout sessions, and yoga. There are also bodywork and beauty-salon services available daily at an additional charge. Fitness evaluations are conducted in specially equipped testing rooms. Staff members test your aerobic capacity, strength, flexibility, and blood pressure prior to starting you on a schedule of exercise.

A wide range of relaxing massages, herbal wraps, and facials are available, too, and guests are pampered with body and beauty treatments using natural extracts and herbs. Even the mud in fango treatments has a history: It comes from a volcanic source in Michoacán, where it is purified for exclusive use here.

Qualton Club & Spa Vallarta
Km 2.5 Av. Las Palmas, Puerto Vallarta, Jalisco, 48300
Reservations: 800/421-2134
Tel. 52-322/44-4446
Fax 52-322/44-4445

Administration General manager, Roland Bernard; spa manager, Silvia Elena Velasco Santana

Season Year-round

Accommodations 248 deluxe rooms with balcony in a 4-star resort with 2 5-story wings connected by a 14-story tower. Top floors have 26 deluxe rooms, 4 master suites, 2 presidential suites with private Jacuzzi and terrace. Club guests get all food and drinks in the room rates. All rooms are air-conditioned, with marble-floored bathroom, color TV, telephone.

Rates Daily rate $75 per person double, $105 single, $65 per person triple. Add 10% tax, plus gratuities. Deposit: 1 night's lodging. AE, DC, MC, V.

Meal Plans Breakfast choices include egg-white omelet with steamed vegetables, yogurt, whole-grain cereal, tropical fruit. Lunch can be vegetarian chili, grilled fish, or sautéed vegetables. Dinner choices (available in the Villa Linda restaurant) include skinless chicken fajitas, pasta primavera, baked snapper, broiled chicken breast Florentine with steamed vegetables over spinach, or fish fillet.

Services and Facilities

Exercise Equipment: 22-unit Paramount weight-training circuit, 3 Lifecycles, 2 Lifesteps, 2 Lifestride treadmills, Precor step machine, dumbbells, barbells (1¼ –45 lbs), benches. **Services:** Massage, herbal wrap, loofah body scrub, facial, fango, aromatherapy, computerized health and fitness evaluations, skin and nail care. **Spa Facilities:** Steam room, sauna, whirlpool. **Swimming Facilities:** Outdoor pool, ocean beach. **Recreation Facilities:** Tennis court (concrete surface, lighted) in spa, 8 courts nearby, water sports, Los Flamingos golf course (PGA par-72, designed by Percy Cliff), horseback riding on the beach.

In the Area

Gringo Gulch (celebrity homes), Mismaloya (John Huston's setting for *Night of the Iguana*), Villa Vallarta Mall (shopping), Yelapa (beach restaurants, freshwater lagoon), Playa Las Animas (natural beach), ferry to Baja California.

Getting Here

From Mexico City. By air, scheduled flights by Mexicana, Aeromexico, American (45 mins). Also direct service from Dallas by Continental. Taxi, rental car available.

Special Notes

Ground-floor accommodations, ramps, elevators for people with disabilities. Spa open Mon.–Sat. 7 AM–8:30 PM. Rubber-sole shoes required in workout rooms.

Rancho La Puerta

Life enhancement
Weight management

Baja California
Tecate

The Rancho La Puerta regimen can be easy or challenging. Hiking on sacred Mount Kuchumaa, a broad range of exercise classes (more than 60 daily), meatless meals spiced with Mexican specialties, and spa pampering are among your options.

The original formula for fitness has expanded since the resort opened 56 years ago, but the basic attractions endure: a nearly perfect year-round climate that's dry (an average of 341 sunny days) and pollen-free, the natural beauty of purple foothills ringed by impressive mountains, and the mostly vegetarian diet. The ranch has had a high percentage of repeaters, and newcomers quickly get into the swing of things.

Encouraged by instructors who use innovative techniques in workouts, and soothed by a massage or herbal wrap, you focus on recharging body and mind. Some classes are intense, others relaxing; counselors are on hand to help with your schedule. There is a beautiful new health center, offering meditation and back care as well as massage.

Rancho La Puerta is in the style of a Mexican village, with a central complex of swimming pools, men's and women's health centers (each with sauna, steam room, Jacuzzi), library, and lounges, linked by brick-paved walkways to casitas and villas that accommodate 150 guests. Gyms dot the landscape; some are open-air, others are enclosed for cool days. No sign-up is required for any of the numerous classes, including aerobic circuit training, back-care workshop, better breathing, body awareness, Hatha yoga, self-defense, and a progressive series of fitness and stretching sessions for men.

This flowering oasis, set amid 575 acres of seclusion, also gives you a taste of Mexican resort life. Accommodations vary from studiolike rancheras to luxury haciendas and villas decorated with native handmade furniture and rugs. Many feature tile floors, fireplaces, and kitchenettes. (Large units can be shared by single guests or families on request.)

After two or three days on a low-fat, high-carbohydrate diet, without distractions from TV, newspapers, or telephone, guests usually discover that their appetite for food has decreased remarkably, while they look and feel healthier. Some do go "over the hill" into town, tempted by Tecate's shops and burrito bars.

Rancho La Puerta

Tecate, Baja California
Tel. 52–6/654–1155
Reservations: Box 463057, Escondido, CA 92046
Tel. 619/744–4222 or 800/443–7565
Fax 619/744–5007

Administration Manager, Jose Manuel Jasso; fitness director, Phyllis Pilgrim

Season Year-round; special weeks for couples only during Mar. and Oct.

Accommodations Single-level ranchera rooms and deluxe studio suites (75) with bath in adobe haciendas and villas. Some large units with 2 bedrooms, 2 baths, southwestern-style beamed ceilings, fireplace, and dining-living area. The maximum number of guests is 150, cared for by a staff of more than 350. No air-conditioning, TV, telephone.

Rates The weeklong program, Sat.–Sat., includes use of all fitness facilities, 3 meals a day. Rate varies according to accommodation. Treatments and personal services charged on an individual basis. Single accommodations $1,950–$2,445, double $1,560–$1,837 per person, plus tax. Villa Studios have additional single bed; Villa Suites accommodate up to 4 persons. Gratuities optional. Minimum stay 1 week. Deposit: $250 per person within 14 days of request for accommodations; balance payable 30 days prior to arrival. MC, V.

Meal Plans The mostly vegetarian diet includes fish 2 times a week; wine on Fri. optional. Breakfast choices change daily: scrambled eggs and tofu with tortilla, hot and cold cereal, boiled egg, and fresh fruits are typically offered. The lunch buffet may include vegetable soup, tofu sandwiches, a vegetable platter, quesadillas of ricotta cheese and tofu, and garlic herbed pizza. Dinner entrées include lasagna, enchiladas, shrimp casserole, Thai spring roll, grilled swordfish, and steamed vegetables spiced with cilantro-based salsa. Fasting on liquified fruits fortified with fresh vegetables and nuts on Mon.

Services and Facilities **Exercise Equipment:** Supervised weight-training gym with 6 Startrac treadmills, 15 Cybex weight units, 6 StairMasters (4000 PT), 8 Monark bikes, PTS recumbent bike, 4 Bio-Health computerized bikes, dumbbells, incline benches, Smith machine. **Services:** Massage, herbal wraps; beauty salon for hair, nail, and skin care daily by appointment. Charges will be added to your account. Golden Door hypoallergenic cosmetics used exclusively. **Swimming Facilities:** 3 outdoor pools, 1 heated, used primarily for aquatic exercise classes. **Recreation Facilities:** Tennis on 6 lighted courts, a putting green, volleyball and basketball courts. Hiking ranges from "moderate" to a challenging climb up Mt. Kuchumaa. Outdoor running track. **Evening Programs:** Movie and lecture scheduled nightly. Recreation hall is open for Ping-Pong and other games.

In the Area Tecate is 5 km (3 mi) from the ranch; Tijuana, 40 km (25 mi) west, bustles with curio shops, a cultural center, and bullfights on summer Sun.

Getting Here *From San Diego airport.* Complimentary transfers on arrival/departure. By car, I-5 south to Hwy. 94, Tecate turnoff to Rte. 188, south to border crossing, right at 2nd light, onto Hwy. 2, 3 mi on right (1½ hrs). Taxi, rental car available.

Special Notes Most facilities are barrier-free and ground-level. Call for reservations. No smoking inside buildings. Treatment facilities open daily 7 AM–noon; 2–8 PM except Sat.

Río Caliente Spa

Life enhancement
Nutrition and diet
Taking the waters

Jalisco For thousands of years, Indians used the meandering river of
Guadalajara hot mineral water for curative purposes. Now the fertile valley around the tiny village of La Primavera is a national forest. And the Río Caliente Spa offers nature-oriented holidays, including vegetarian meals and convivial company.

The synthesis of therapies, diet, sun, and bathing is the key to enjoying this unique health resort. As you enter the bathhouse you'll encounter a 20-foot wall of volcanic rock, in front of which are wooden benches where guests relax while enjoying a sweat. A stream of hot thermal water snakes through the room, emitting puffs of steam. Welcome to the Aztec steam room.

Classes in yoga, tai chi, and aquatics are scheduled for all guests who want to participate. Spa services are provided by a well-trained staff.

Río Caliente Spa

Apdo. Postal 5-67 Colonia Chapalita, Guadalajara 43042, Jalisco
No telephone at spa
Reservations: Box 897, Millbrae, CA 94030
Tel. 415/615–9543
Fax 415/615–0601

Administration Director, Caroline Durston

Season Year-round

Accommodations 48 cabanas and rooms for 80 guests in the main buildings; handcrafted beds and chairs; colorful fabrics by local artisans; small and simple rooms, all with private bath or shower; no phones, TV, or air conditioning. Some have fireplace.

Rates Daily rate $66–$75 (US$) per person, double occupancy, $79–$90 single. 7-night program $560 single, $465 sharing. 10-night stress-buster package $800 single, $670 sharing. Rate includes vegetarian buffet meals, activity program, lodging. Personal services and trips range from $5 to $18. 10% discount for stays of 30 days or longer. Taxes and gratuities additional. $100 deposit. No credit cards.

Meal Plans Vegetarian meals served buffet style 3 times daily. Tropical foods in season include guavas, jícama, zapote, and guanabana. Organically grown raw greens, raw and cooked vegetables, soups and home-baked grain casseroles supplement vegetarian platters.

Services and **Services:** Massage, reflexology, facial, manicure, pedicure,
Facilities fango mud packs. **Bathing Facilities:** Separate walled plunge pools for men and women, swimming pool; waterfall for nude bathing. **Swimming Facilities:** Outdoor pool. **Recreation Facilities:** Hiking.

In the Area Group trips into Guadalajara (crafts market, Orozco murals), Tlaquepaque (colonial architecture, crafts center), Tequila (brewery). Other attractions include Lake Chapala, Cabanas Institute (center for arts), and Plaza of the Mariachis in Guadalajara.

Getting Here *From Guadalajara.* By car, Hwy. 80 to La Primavera (1 hr). Taxi, rental car available.

Special Notes Limited access for people with disabilities. No smoking indoors. Electrical voltage is 110 AC (compatible to U.S.).

Rosarito Beach Hotel & Casa Playa Spa

Luxury pampering

Baja California Built in the 1930s, when glamorous getaways were for Holly-
Rosarito Beach wood celebrities, the Rosarito Beach Hotel has an ornately decorated, Old Mexico ambience, combined with a modern hotel wing and the state-of-the-art Casa Playa Spa, housed in a former beach mansion. Programs are personalized by the director, and spa packages are customized.

As you enter the whitewashed, red-tiled archway, you'll discover a romantic garden, and the hotel lobby tiled and decorated with murals by Matias Santoyo. In the spa adjoining the hotel, you are offered an extensive list of bodywork and beauty-salon services. Sandals, a robe, towels, and a personal locker are issued daily. The coed Jacuzzi, sauna, steam room, and fitness gym are open to all hotel guests. A daily membership fee ($10) is charged for use of the facilities, exercise classes cost $5 each. Seaweed and fango treatments are the specialty here.

Rosarito Beach Hotel & Casa Playa Spa
Blvd. Benito Juarez #31, Plaza Rosarito
Baja California Norte 22710
Tel. 52–661/2–0144 or 800/343–8582

Administration General manager, Xavier Hinoko; spa director, Gilda Mayen

Season Year-round

Accommodations 280 oceanfront rooms and suites, including an 8-story addition built in 1994. All rooms air-conditioned, with balcony or patio, private bathroom, TV, phone.

Rates $49–$89 per room for 2. Day of Beauty $151 including spa lunch. 4-hour thalassotherapy package including spa lunch $136. Packages include tax. Add 10% VAT, plus gratuity to room rates. AE, MC, V.

Meal Plans All meals à la carte. Spa lunch can be steamed halibut, skinless roasted chicken with steamed vegetable and rice, or spinach salad. Dinner entrées include tequila-sautéed salmon with mushrooms, spinach pasta with tomato sauce, green gazpacho.

Services and **Exercise Equipment:** 2 multistation Universal gyms, 4 Nautilus
Facilities units, 12 Lifecycles, 4 Monark stationary bikes, 2 treadmills, StairMaster, 4 Nautilus units, free weights. **Services:** Swedish massage, reflexology, body wrap, salt-glow scrub, body polish, parafango heat pack, hydrotherapy bath, facial, aromatherapy; hair, nail, and skin care; cholesterol test, fitness profile, personal training. **Swimming Facilities:** 2 outdoor pools, children's pool. **Recreation Facilities:** Tennis, racquetball, volleyball, surfing, miniature golf. Nearby horseback riding. **Evening Programs:** Fri. and Sat. evening fiestas.

In the Area Tijuana (crafts market, Sun. bullfights), Los Cabos (fishing), Puerto Nuevo (lobster feast).

Getting Here *From San Diego.* By car, I–5 or I–805 to the U.S./Mexico border at Tijuana, follow signs to Hwy. 1-D "Rosarito-Ensenada Cuota" (toll road), south to 3rd Rosarito Beach exit (45 mins). By bus, Baja California Tours (tel. 619/454–7166). Rental car available.

Special Notes Spa open Mon.–Sat. 8:30–6:30, Sun. 8–5. Minimum age is 16. No smoking in spa, but other areas are unrestricted.

The Caribbean,
the Bahamas, Bermuda

The current trend in the Caribbean is to import European thalassotherapy and American fitness programs. On French St. Martin, Privilege Resort and Spa has sailing and tennis options. Spas on St. Lucia hark back to the time of King Louis XIV, who built baths in the 17th century for his troops at the hot springs. Today you can relax at the tony Jalousie Plantation or LeSport, the fitness buff's counterpart to Club Med, which has seawater treatments. For a structured course of treatments, Martinique has a dedicated thalassotherapy center.

Jamaica offers the widest range of options, from all-inclusive resorts like The Enchanted Garden, luxurious Sans Souci Lido, and Ciboney, to the rustic Milk River Bath Hotel. Negril's sports-oriented Swept Away and a new spa at the Half Moon Club expand the range of opportunities for combining a Caribbean holiday with a health regime.

Bermuda vacations may include French facials and bodywork at the Sonesta Beach Hotel or Cambridge Beaches, both with well-appointed spas operated by the Bersalon group. Cruise ship passengers are welcome to use the spa facilities. Hiking along the Railway Trail can complete your fitness regimen on the island.

Holistic island retreats are good healthy alternatives to resorts. The Bahamas have no-frills Sivananda Ashram on Paradise Beach in Nassau, as well as upscale Sandals Royal Bahamian Resort & Spa. St. John in the U.S. Virgin Islands is the winter outpost for the New York–based Omega Institute's programs. And in Puerto Rico, the rain forest and the ocean provide backdrops for bodywork at La Casa de Vida Natural.

Today the Caribbean spa experience is a mixture of fun and fitness. Don't expect a self-contained spa with structured programs; instead look for a resort within your budget that offers many options. You can go scuba diving at a Bonaire resort spa, take the waters on Guadeloupe at Ravine Chaude, or play golf at the Four Seasons Resort on Nevis or Hyatt Regency casino resorts on Aruba and Puerto Rico.

Although it is still illegal for U.S. citizens to travel from home to Cuba for vacation, Cuban spas may be of interest to our foreign readers. Wings Of the World, Inc. (tel. 800/465–8687, 416/482–1223 in Canada) has eight-day itineraries with flights via Mexico City and Cancún. Medical treatment spas and hot springs are managed by Cubanacán Corp. (tel. 537/33–9080, fax 537/33–6308) and the Gaviota Hotel Group (tel. 537/22–7670, fax 537/33–2780). The island remains off-limits to U.S. citizens.

Hyatt Regency Aruba

Nonprogram resort

Aruba
Palm Beach

Fifteen miles north of the northern coast of Venezuela, the 70-square-mile island of Aruba has a dry warmth cooled by the constant trade winds. Aruba is an autonomous state within the Netherlands fold, and it is one of the most stable, secure, and prosperous islands in the Caribbean. There are colorful

Dutch colonial villages like San Nicholas, and caves with hieroglyphics, as well as the glitzy casino hotels clustered on Palm Beach.

Set on a 12-acre strip of beach, 2 miles from the island's pastel-colored capital of Oranjestad, the Hyatt Regency Aruba resort focuses on water sports. Opened in 1990, the resort has an 8,000-square-foot three-level swimming pool with cascading waterfalls and tropical lagoons facing a powdery white sand beach. Canoe rentals, sailboats, and a 50-foot luxury catamaran for sunset cruises are all available, and two dive boats ferry guests to coral reefs and sunken shipwrecks.

The health and fitness facilities—including exercise room, coed sauna, steam room, outdoor whirlpool, and sundeck for aerobics classes—overlook the sea and are open to hotel guests without charge. For those who don't want to get wet or sweat, the gardens feature a 5,000-square-foot saltwater lagoon replete with native fish and wildlife; a poolside restaurant fashioned out of native coral stone is good for lounging.

Hike from the natural bridge (carved by the sea), on the rugged coast near Boca Prins, to Andicouri for a romantic picnic on a secluded beach surrounded by a coconut plantation. Aruba's volcanic origins are revealed at Casi Bari, a rock garden of giants, and at tall, unusual rock formations called *Ayo*. Hikers can enjoy panoramic, breezy views from paths cut into the rock. Arikok National Park, home to iguanas, hares, wild goats, and the rare wayacca tree, is getting new trails and an interpretive center.

Golfers gain a new perspective on the island's desert landscape of cacti, wind-shaped divi divi trees, and rock formations at the new Tierra Del Sol Golf & Country Club. Managed by Hyatt, the 18-hole, par-71 course designed by the Trent Jones Group is open to the public.

Hyatt Regency Aruba
85 J. E. Irausquin Blvd., Aruba
Tel. 297–83–1234 or 800/233–1234

Administration   General Manager, Hendrik Santos

Season   Year-round

Accommodations   360 rooms and suites in 9-story tower and 2 wings of 4 and 5 stories. Regency Club has 27 deluxe rooms, lounge, concierge service. All rooms are spacious, with balcony and full modern bath, queen-size beds, air-conditioning, TV, telephone, maid service.

Rates $185–$425 per room daily, single or double occupancy, suite $450–$700; Regency Club $305–$490. Credit-card confirmation. AE, DC, MC, V.

Meal Plans   Heart-healthy options on main dining room menu. No special meal plan is available. Vegetarian dishes, fruit salad, grilled fish among daily selections. Snack bar in health spa has herbal teas, protein drinks, fruit.

Services and Facilities   **Exercise Equipment:** Universal gym, StairMaster, Precor treadmill, Lifecycle, Concept 2 rowing machine, free weights. **Services:** Massage (Swedish, shiatsu, acupressure, reflexology). Beauty salon for hairstyling, manicure, pedicure. **Swimming Facilities:** Outdoor pool, ocean beach. **Recreation Facilities:** 2 tennis courts, water sports, cruiser and mountain bikes. **Evening Programs:** Carnival costume show and barbecue, casino.

Aruba
Hyatt Regency
Aruba Resort, **24**

The Bahamas
Sandals Royal Baha-
mian Resort & Spa, **3**
Sivananda Ashram
Yoga Retreat, **4**

Belize
Maruba Resort &
Jungle Spa, **25**

Bermuda
Cambridge Beaches, **2**
Sonesta Beach Hotel
& Spa, **1**

Bonaire
Harbour Village
Beach Resort, **23**

Dominican Republic
Renaissance Jaragua
Resort, **10**

Grenada
LaSource, **22**

Guadeloupe
Centre de
Thalassothérapie
Manioukani, **18**
Guadeloupe Thermal
Springs, **16**
Hotel Marissol, **17**

Jamaica
Ciboney, **8**
The Enchanted
Garden, **6**
Jamaican Mineral
Springs, **9**
The Sans Souci Lido, **7**
Swept Away, **5**

Martinique
Centre de Thalasso-
thérapie du Carbet, **19**

Nevis
Four Seasons
Resort, **15**

Puerto Rico
La Casa de
Vida Natural, **11**
Spa Caribe at the
Hyatt Resorts, **12**

St. Lucia
Jalousie Plantation, **20**
Le Sport, **21**

St. Maarten-St. Martin
Privilege Resort and
Spa, **14**

U.S. Virgin Islands
Omega Journeys at
Maho Bay, **13**

The Caribbean, the Bahamas,

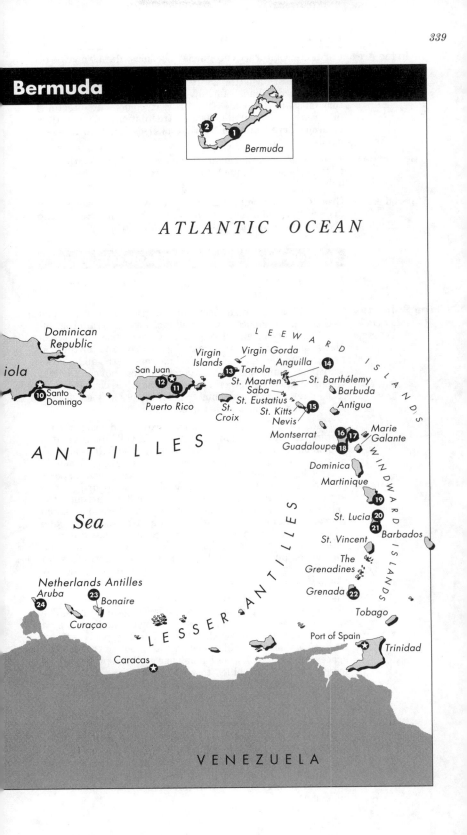

Bermuda

Bermuda

ATLANTIC OCEAN

Dominican
Republic

iola

Santo
Domingo

San Juan

Puerto Rico

Virgin
Islands

Virgin Gorda

Tortola

St. Maarten

Saba

St. Croix

St. Eustatius

St. Kitts

Nevis

Anguilla

St. Barthélemy

Barbuda

Antigua

LEEWARD ISLANDS

Montserrat

Guadaloupe

Marie
Galante

Dominica

Martinique

WINDWARD ISLANDS

St. Lucia

St. Vincent

Barbados

The
Grenadines

ANTILLES

Sea

Netherlands Antilles

Aruba

Bonaire

Curaçao

LESSER ANTILLES

Grenada

Tobago

Caracas

Port of Spain

Trinidad

VENEZUELA

In the Area Caribbean Cultural Center in San Nicholas. Marlab marine biology tour (3 hrs) booked through DePalm Tours. Trail riding at Rancho El Paso (tel. 23310). Boca Prins (sand dunes, secluded beach), Chapel of Alto Vista (1750), Fort Zoutman (history museum) and Olde School Straat (colonial architecture) in Oranjestad, DePalm Island (recreation), Santa Anna Church (carved altar) in Noord, Cas di Cultura (concerts, art exhibits).

Getting Here *From Aruba International Airport.* By car, L. G. Smith Blvd. to Palm Beach (20 mins). Bus, taxi, rental car, moped available.

Special Notes Ground-floor accommodations and elevators for people with disabilities. Children under 12 stay with parents free; Camp Hyatt features nature walks. No smoking in spa.

Sandals Royal Bahamian Resort and Spa

Luxury pampering   *Couples only*
Nonprogram resort

The Bahamas This new Sandals resort combines a grand manor, steeped
Cable Beach, in Colonial decadence, with an all-inclusive program that of-
Nassau fers workouts in an air-conditioned penthouse with ocean views, and water sports. Created as part of a major renovation in 1996, the spa facilities include mud baths and a large whirlpool, sauna and steam rooms, and cardiovascular and weight training equipment. Beachside aerobics classes are offered daily at no charge, but spa treatments and services at the Wellness Clinic are à la carte.

Spread over 13 acres of landscaped gardens and beach, the resort includes a sports complex with tennis, volleyball, croquet, and indoor games room. Opened in 1948 as the Balmoral Club, a private reserve for the rich and titled, the Manor House is on a modest strip of powdery sand beach where a water sports pavilion and dock offer SCUBA diving, windsurfing, and kayaking. Gardens abloom with bougainvillea surround the enlarged swimming pool and restaurants. There are sunken Roman columns, waterfalls, a water-mist spray and whirlpools, and open-air bar (no charge for drinks). Sun worshipers can retreat to a private offshore island and enjoy nature in the buff, a freshwater pool, and Jacuzzi. Golfers get complimentary greens fees and transportation to nearby Cable Beach Golf Club.

The six-story hotel offers spacious rooms with sweeping ocean views, plus 27 secluded honeymoon suites in garden villas. The spa can be reached by elevator in the main building or by a private entrance alongside the swimming pool terrace. Chrome and mirrors add a sleek, modern look to the smallish spaces where you can work out at leisure or book private treatments. Services are billed to your account, or payable with credit card. Aerobics classes are complimentary to all guests weekdays at 10:30 AM and 6:30 PM.

An introduction to total well-being is provided at the Wellness Clinic. This new concept, developed by a Florida-based consultant, offers counseling on stress management, diet and nutrition. Under the direction of a Spa Counselor, guests are given an overview of the facilities and treatments. "Spa Treatments for Two," where couples enjoy treatments together in the privacy of a softly lit spa room, are popular with honeymooners.

Unlimited, nonstop food and beverages are included in the daily rate. Six restaurants within the resort offer heart-healthy options, from Asian-Pacific, Italian, Cricketeers pub, and Cafe Goombay serving Bahamian fare, to gourmet cuisine in the Crystal Room, where white-glove dinner service must be reserved in advance. Fruit and juice bars as well as unlimited premium-brand alcoholic beverages come with the Sandals trademarked package, for couples only.

Sandals Royal Bahamian Resort and Spa
Box C.B. 13005, Cable Beach, Nassau, Bahamas
Tel. 809/327–6400 or 800/726–3257
Fax 809/327–6961

Administration General manager, Stephen Zaide

Season Year-round

Accommodations Beachfront main building has 196 rooms; villas and town houses offer 27 suites with king-size bed in pink buildings accented by white sculpture. Ocean-view rooms furnished with English antique reproductions, king-size bed, dressing room, bath with shower and bathtub. All have cable TV, clock radio, hair dryer, air-conditioning, bathrobes. Most rooms have balcony or garden patio.

Rates Daily from $580 per person, double occupancy; villa suite 7-night package $2,575 per person, double. Add 4% room tax, $15 departure tax. Gratuities and airport transfers included. Minimum stay 2 nights. First-night confirmation by credit card. AE, DC, MC, V.

Meal Plans 3 meals daily, plus unlimited snacks, fruit and juice, and alcoholic beverages. Buffet breakfast includes granola, egg-white omelet. Lunch can be conch fritters, seafood salad, or grilled grouper. Dinner offers innovative crossovers of Continental and island fare: Gâteau de Conch et coquilles Saint-Jacques au Safron is a mousse of Bahamian conch and scallops baked in delicate saffron sauce. Other specialties include grouper baked in pastry shell with sabayon sauce, sushi, and rack of lamb dusted with herbs, roasted and broiled.

Services and Facilities **Exercise Equipment:** Cybex weight training system (6 stations), 2 Lifecycles, 2 treadmills, 2 stairclimbers, free weights. **Services:** Swedish massage, aromatherapy, reflexology, herbal wrap, anti-cellulite treatment, mud bath; salon for hair, nail, and skin care, including rapid peel, facial, manicure, pedicure, waxing. **Swimming Facilities:** Outdoor freshwater pool, ocean beach. **Recreation Facilities:** 2 tennis courts (lighted), paddle boats, sailboats, canoes, kayaks, glass-bottom boat, windsurfing, snorkeling, lawn chess, volleyball, shuffleboard, croquet, karaoke, billiards/pool. Nearby bicycle rental, 18-hole golf course, indoor sports center. **Evening Programs:** Casino and theater nearby (complimentary transportation).

In the Area Seafloor Aquarium (performing dolphins and sea lions), Fort Charlotte (botanic garden), Adastra Gardens (performing flamingos), Junkanoo Art Gallery.

Getting Here *From Nassau International Airport.* By car, coastal road (10 mins). Transfers provided by Sandals. Jitney minibus for trips into town. Taxi, rental car available.

Special Notes Elevator to all floors of main building. No smoking in spa or designated dining areas. Spa open daily 9–7:30.

Sivananda Ashram Yoga Retreat

Spiritual awareness

The Bahamas
Paradise Island,
Nassau

A few steps from one of the best-known beaches in the Bahamas, secluded in a grove of pines and palm trees, is a unique combination of spiritual retreat and tropical holiday. Based on the teachings of Swami Vishnu Devananda, the yogic discipline and vegetarian diet at the Sivananda Yoga Vedata Retreat are identical to Sivananda ashrams in Canada, New York, and California, but the sunny climate and beach make this one of the best bargains anywhere. People come here to recuperate from job burnout or to heal after surgery.

The regimen is intensive; attendance at classes and meditations is mandatory for all guests. Mornings begin at 6 with a session of yogic exercises, or *asanas,* to stretch and invigorate the body. Chanting sessions are held twice daily, at 8 AM and 4 PM, although attendance is not strictly enforced. Brunch is served at 10, then you are free to enjoy the beach or a relaxing massage.

Although there are big luxury hotels and casinos a short walk away, the environment here is totally suffused with a mystical quality—partly due to the quaint appearance of the houseboats and the buildings perched on stilts. The main house, once the retreat of a wealthy family and leased since 1967 to the Sivananda group in appreciation for healing services, might have sunk into the sand long ago without the volunteer labor of the retreat members. Lodging is in small wooden cabins, furnished with bare essentials. Many guests prefer to bring their own tent and camp among the tropical shrubbery. You may arrive any day; average stay is two weeks.

Meals are a communal affair, with buffets of steamed vegetables, lentils, and salads—many of which are bland, as no spices, onion, or garlic are used. To provide the proper nutritional balance, there is an organic herb and vegetable garden. Coconuts come gratis from the palm trees that shelter the 4½-acre compound. For snacks and sweets, a canteen is tucked into a building near the communal laundry and shower facilities. After meals, guests wash their own plates and utensils and dry them on open-air racks. There's no air-conditioning at this retreat, but a filtration system provides plenty of cool, chemical-free drinking water.

On the northern tip of Paradise Island, the retreat is shaded by casuarina trees and palms. Harbor boats and a bridge provide access to the center of Nassau. Club Med is next door.

Sivananda Ashram Yoga Retreat
Box N7550, Paradise Island, Nassau, Bahamas
Tel. 809/363–2902 or 800/783–9642
Fax 809/363–3783

Administration Program director, Swami Swaroopanada

Season Year-round

Accommodations Wooden huts on the beach, dormitory rooms, and cottages provide 103 beds. Each room is furnished with 2–6 beds and table; linens and towels provided. Communal shower and toilet facilities, laundry equipment. Tent space: 50 sites.

Rates $45–$55 per person daily, in dormitory rooms shared by 2–6 persons. Single cabin $75–$85, semi-private room $50–$70 per person. Beachfront meditation huts are preferred location. Tent space $40–$50 per person, per night. $200 advance payment. MC, V.

Meal Plans The lacto-vegetarian diet includes midmorning meal of whole-grain cereal, fresh fruit, homemade yogurt, and wheat bread. Dinner dishes include stir-fried tofu and rice, steamed vegetables, green salad. No fish, meat, fowl, eggs, or coffee served.

Services and Facilities **Services:** Massage (shiatsu, reflexology), personal counseling. **Swimming Facilities:** Ocean beach. **Recreation Facilities:** Tennis court, volleyball, walks. **Evening Programs:** Workshops in Vedata culture, philosophy. Concerts.

In the Area Boat trips, botanical gardens, Colonial and Victorian architecture.

Getting Here *From Nassau International Airport.* Shared taxi van (fixed fee) to Mermaid Marina, Bay and Deveaux streets. Shuttle service by Ashram boat operates on daily schedule.

Special Notes Yoga training for children. No smoking on premises. Remember to bring blankets during winter months, and beach towel.

Maruba Resort & Jungle Spa

Holistic health
Luxury pampering

Belize
Maskall Village

Set amid 4,000 acres of rain forest, gardens, and orchards, the Maruba Resort & Jungle Spa is a relaxing, romantic, natural environment. Picking the treatments right off the trees, owner Franziska Nicholson and her brother Nicky brew medicinal tea or blend cream for skin care. That includes an anti-itch lotion, a mix of antiseptic allspice and bark from the gumbolimbo tree, to alleviate the pain of sunburn and insect bites. Sand scrubs, sea sulfur clay body packs, and a Mayan herbal wrap reduce stress and muscle fatigue while improving circulation and cleansing the skin.

Mornings are devoted to jungle safaris, by boat, bike, hiking, or on horseback. For the already fit, there is a 24-mile trek to Altun Ha, a Mayan archaeological site. Divers can take an excursion that includes use of SCUBA equipment at a nearby beach. Hiking with an experienced herbalist introduces you to medicinal uses of local indigenous plants.

A pre-breakfast walk and stretch pumps up your metabolism and gets the kinks out. Included in the daily program are scheduled exercise sessions set to jungle rhythms; punta rock low-impact cardiovascular workout, aquaerobics to hip hop and rock. One-on-one training is available for an additional fee.

The fusion of Mayan, Creole, and African designs is dramatic. Most rooms have thatched roofs, with palms or other plants growing inside, and vines winding around fixtures. Hammocks swing lazily amid the cabanas, and you can watch the birds or view the flora and fauna without disturbing their activities. From the Jungle Suite, set high above the trees, the view takes in pineapple fields and coconut palms surrounding the compound.

With temperatures between 80 and 90 degrees, working up a sweat is easy. The open-air spa provides a variety of packages, one to five nights; some include fishing and bird-watching, others focus on weight control and rejuvenation. Meal options are offered, with a choice of just room and breakfast, modified American plan (breakfast and dinner), and three meals daily. Notable are the five-course dinners, which include fresh seafood, ranging from conch to lobster, as well as game and vegetables raised right on the property.

After a day trekking in the rain forest, a soak in the rock-walled waterfall swimming pool is the preferred cool-down. At night, a Japanese hot tub makes stargazing an unforgettable experience. The forest comes alive with animal sounds—the rasp and hoot of howler monkeys, the endless percussion of insects—as you dine by candlelight.

Located 30 miles from the international airport at Belize City, the resort provides transfers three times daily for arriving and departing guests ($50 round-trip).

Maruba Resort & Jungle Spa

40 ½ Old Northern Hwy., Maskall Village,
Tel. 501/2–22199
Reservations: Box 300703, Houston, TX 77230
Tel. 713/799–2031 or 800/627–8227
Fax 713/795–8573

Administration   General manager, Franziska Nicholson; program director, Veronika Nicholson

Season   Year-round

Accommodations   15 rooms in cabanas constructed of indigenous materials, each with 2 twin beds, window screens, no TV or telephone. Air-conditioning ($10 daily charge) in 5 rooms. All have private bathroom.

Rates   Spa packages including meals, transfers: 1 night $310 single, $280 per person, double occupancy; 2-night Rejuvenation package $470 single, $410 double; 5-nights $1,300 single, $1,153 double; 26-day weight control program $4,147 single or double. Daily room rate $110–$156.50 single, $130–$223 for 2 persons, double. Suites $150–$280 per person, single or double. Day Spa package with lunch $125–$135. Add 15% VAT, 7% room tax, 15% service charge. Deposit: 1 night accommodation. AE, MC, V.

Meal Plans   3 meals daily included in spa packages. Breakfast is fresh tropical fruit, juices, choice of French toast, pancakes, omelet, eggs any style, herbal tea or coffee. Lunch offers lobster salad (in season), pasta salad, smoked chicken salad, wild game sandwich, or rice and beans with stewed chicken. Dinner begins with soup, salad, and appetizer; entrées can be sautéed red snapper, pasta with tomato-papaya sauce, grilled chicken with anise seed rice. Desserts include banana strudel, chocolate coconut pie, after-dinner drink. Vegetarian meals and special diets on request.

Services and Facilities   **Exercise Equipment:** None. **Services:** Massage (stress-reduction, aromatherapy), body wrap (herbal, seaweed), mineral bath, body pack (clay, sea sulfer, moor mud), body scrub, facial, manicure, pedicure, bee honey facial treatment. **Swimming Facilities:** Outdoor swimming pool. **Recreation Facilities:** Bicycles, boats, horseback riding.

In the Area   Blue Hole National Park (sink hole), Crooked Tree Wildlife Sanctuary (black howler monkeys, tropical birds), Ambergris Caye (diving, snorkeling), Mountain Pine Ridge Forest Reserve, Caracol (Mayan ruins), Cockscomb Sanctuary (jaguars, puma, deer).

Getting Here   *From Godson International Airport.* By car, Old Northern Hwy. to Maskall Village (45 mins). Taxi, rental car available. Resort van provides scheduled transfers (off-schedule transfers available on request).

Special Notes   English is the principal language. U.S. currency accepted. Bring passport.

Cambridge Beaches

Luxury pampering

Bermuda
Somerset

New in 1993, the Spa at Cambridge Beaches is set in a cottage colony that is more like a club than a resort. On a 25-acre peninsula, with private ocean beaches and bayside marina, the resort has suites facing the beach and croquet lawn, plus the spa building. A private retreat here can combine classic treatments with the latest in European therapies. Planned as a one-day package or in combination with Bermuda's golf courses, sailing, and heritage-home tours, this is an easy-paced escape.

Cathiodermie facials by Guinot of Paris incorporate gentle stimulation of skin tissue with electronic rollers that cause a tingling sensation. Using a thermal clay mask, the licensed esthetician dissolves impurities and toxins, leaving the tissue rehydrated and rejuvenated. Ionithermie treatments firm and tone slack skin, and help rid the body of cellulite. Using galvanic current, the Ionithermie machine is attached to your face, body, or bust. Treatments over a period of several days are said to shed inches. This can be combined with bodywraps using seaweed, plant extracts, and other natural ingredients.

A Cambridge Beaches "Classic Spa Day" might start with a consultation and computerized body-fat analysis, followed by exercise, sauna, and massage. Especially for men, half-day program includes massage, Cathiodermie facial for rough skin, Redken hair treatment. In the locker room are robes, toiletries, coed sauna, steam bath, and whirlpool. Both full-day and half-day packages include lunch on a bayside terrace.

The four-day winter escape package (mid-Nov.–Apr.) offers combinations of services for men and women. A personalized spa holiday program is developed to focus on your special needs and interests. Included are deluxe waterview accommodations as well as afternoon tea, full breakfast and dinner daily, with the option of having spa cuisine cooked to order. Evenings are dress-up occasions, with music and often dancing outdoors on a terrace that overlooks Cambridge's private marina on Somerset Long Bay. Casual elegance sets the style here, with an international mix of guests, many of whom return every year.

Somerset's shady lanes are ideal for walks, jogging, and hikes. A moped can be rented at Cambridge Beaches and taken aboard a ferry for a trip to St. George's at the eastern end of the island via Hamilton, where the best shops and pubs are located. A short hike from Cambridge Beaches along the Railway Trail brings you to Scaur Hill Fort, built in the 1870s to protect the Royal Naval Dockyard. Now it's a 22-acre park with breathtaking views of the Great Sound and its armada of sailboats. Spend a day at the restored Dockyard complex, a maritime museum and crafts center, with several pleasant places to dine. Hikers and bikers can use the Railway Trail, a secluded 18-mile track that runs toward Southampton along the route of the old Bermuda Railway, past beautiful estates, the Lantana Cottages (where you can dine on an exchange plan with Cambridge Beaches), and the Somerset Squire pub.

The 21-square-mile island is divided into nine geographical divisions, called parishes, served by public bus. With nearly 150 islands, Bermuda has numerous bridges, plus ferry services. The town of St. George, founded in 1612 on the eastern tip of the island, retains many quaint features of 17th-century community life. The city of Hamilton has been the capital of Bermuda since 1815. Competitive cricket matches are played every Sunday during the summer, and kite flying matches are held at Easter time. There are eight British-style golf courses—and British driving rules; if you rent a moped, remember to drive on the left side of the road.

Cambridge Beaches

30 Kings Point Rd., Sandys MA 02, Bermuda
Tel. 44/1234–0331 or 800/468–7300 (800/463–5990 in
Canada)
Bersalon spa reservations: Tel. 441/292–8570,
Fax 441/295–2506
Fax 441/234–3352

Administration General manager, Michael J. Winfield; spa director, Michael Ternant

Season Year-round

Accommodations 82 individually decorated cottage rooms and suites, all with private bathroom, some with whirlpool bath. Furnishings are traditional, with flowered chintz drapery, large closets. Air-conditioning, telephone, and screened windows. TV not included, but sets can be rented.

Rates Daily $335–$550 for 2 persons, double occupancy, plus 10% tax, $12.60 daily service charge, and gratuities. Half-day spa packages $140–$175, full-day $260. 4-day/3-night His N'Her Winter Getaway $775–$926 per person, double occupancy. Taxes and gratuities not included in package rates. Deposit: 2 nights payment. No credit cards.

Meal Plans Breakfast, dinner, and tea included in daily tariff and spa packages. Breakfast buffet has granola and health cereals, fresh fruit, juices. Eggs can be ordered. Dinner specialties include grilled fish with steamed vegetables, skinless breast of chicken with couscous, and vegetarian plate. Special diets accommodated. Room service in cottage. Exchange dining at six other hotels.

Services and Facilities **Exercise Equipment:** Multistation Universal gym, computerized FitStep climber, 2 AerobiCycles, Tredex treadmill, free weights. **Services:** Massage (Swedish, sports, reflexology, aromatherapy), paraffin body treatments and wraps, salt-glow polish, G-5 toning, peel, Ionithermie, Cathiodermie; salon for hair, nail, skin care. Fitness consultation, computerized bodyfat analysis, nutrition consultation. **Swimming Facilities:** Heated saltwater pool, 5 beaches. **Recreation Facilities:** Marina with power and sail boats, windsurfing, snorkeling equipment, canoes, kayaks. 3 tennis courts (1 lighted), croquet lawn, putting green. Golf courses nearby offer member privileges. Moped and cycle rental. **Evening Programs:** Nightly entertainment, special cruise, dancing.

In the Area Dockyard (maritime museum), Art Centre, Crafts Market, Heydon Trust Chapel, Gibb's Hill Lighthouse, St. George (colonial capital), Hamilton (City Hall art museum and theater, Parliament buildings, shopping), botanical garden, Bermuda Biological Station (ocean studies).

Getting Here *From the U.S. East Coast.* By air, USAir and Kiwi Airlines have scheduled service daily. By ship, summer sailings include Celebrity Cruises from New York, which docks in Somerset at King's Wharf; Majesty Cruise Lines' *Royal Majesty* on regular service from Boston to Old Town in St. George; and Cunard. By ferry from Hamilton, complimentary trip 3 times per week, with scheduled service to Watford Bridge (20 mins). By bus, frequent service on shore road to Somerset (45 mins). Taxi available, no rental car.

Sonesta Beach Hotel & Spa

Luxury pampering

Bermuda
Southampton

Workouts and relaxation are the program at the Sonesta Beach Hotel & Spa. You can drop in between business meetings or after a round of golf or plan a comprehensive schedule of treatments and exercise classes for three to seven days. Package plans can begin any day of the week.

Aerobics are moderate or vigorous, plotted over 30- or 40-minute periods, alternating active and passive exercise with relaxing stretches. You can select from early morning walks (moderate), circuit training (vigorous), workouts in the water, and yoga; morning yoga sessions are held on the lawn overlooking the sea. One of the special features of the resort's spa packages is a low rate for three persons sharing one of the big oceanfront bedrooms.

If you simply want to be pampered and left alone to swim or shop, there are four-day spa sampler packages, including the 100 program using aromatic oils from flowers and plants, fruits and herbs for facial and body treatments. If you wish to try many different activities and treatments, there are dance exercise routines and one-on-one sessions with a personal trainer. Daily walks on the beach and stretch class are included in a spa package, or you can simply pay a daily facility charge ($10) and use the whirlpool baths, Finnish sauna, Turkish steam bath, and Universal equipment room.

The larger brother of the spa at Cambridge Beaches, this hotel facility has 12 treatment rooms, an aerobics studio, a large weight-training room, and separate facilities for men and women. Leotard, warm-up suit, gym shorts, shirt, robe, and slippers provided daily.

Set on a 25-acre peninsula, the resort has three beaches with gentle surf, tennis courts, and water sports. For swimmers, the freshwater swimming pool has an all-weather glass dome enclosure. Renovations in guest rooms were completed in 1995.

Sonesta Beach Hotel & Spa
South Rd., Horseshoe Bay, Southampton
Tel. 441/238–8122 or 800/766–3782
Fax 441/238–8463

Bersalon Co. Ltd.
Box HM1044, Hamilton HM EX, Bermuda
Tel. 441/292–8570 or 441/238–1226
Fax 441/295–2506

Administration
General manager, David Boyd, spa director, Michael Ternent

Season
Year-round

Accommodations
6-story hotel and Bay Wing suites with 403 guest rooms, ocean or bay view, balcony or patio. Spacious split-level units have sitting area and dressing room, full bath, modern rattan furniture, floor-to-ceiling windows. Queen- or king-size beds, full carpeting, air-conditioning, color TV, telephone.

Rates
3-night Spa Sampler package $1,201.65–$1,393 per person, double occupancy; $1,669–$1,881 single, $1,078.65–$1,909.50 triple. 6-day/5-night Eurospa Classic package, $2,232.50 per person, double, $3,014 single, $2,027.67 triple. Taxes and gratuities included in spa packages. Daily tariff $250–$370 per room, plus 7.25% tax, $6.30–$14.20 daily service charge. Deposit: 2-night payment at booking. AE, DC, MC, V.

Meal Plans Breakfast and dinner daily included in 3–5 night packages. Breakfast may be a whole-grain cereal with fruit; lunch, a garden salad or cold seafood platter. Dinner entrées include grilled swordfish, vegetarian lasagna, and skewers of vegetables broiled with sea scallops. 2 juice breaks are included in the daily program.

Services and Facilities **Exercise Equipment:** Universal weight-training gym (5 stations), 2 AerobiCycles, Tredex computerized bicycle, recumbent bike, 2 stairclimbers, 2 treadmills, hand weights. **Services:** Massage (Swedish, aromatherapy, reflexology, G-5 mechanical), facials for men and women, loofah body scrub, herbal wrap, manicure, pedicure, Cathiodermie facial, aromatherapy scalp treatment, Ionithermie cellulite control treatments. Hairstyling and beauty-salon services, paraffin treatments for hands and feet, personal trainer. **Swimming Facilities:** Outdoor and indoor freshwater pools, 3 ocean beaches. **Recreation Facilities:** 6 lighted tennis courts, volleyball, badminton, croquet, shuffleboard, table tennis. Golf and bicycle rental nearby. Water sports include scuba diving and windsurfing. Horseback riding available at Spicelands Riding Centre, Warwick. **Evening Programs:** Resort entertainment.

In the Area St. George's (replica of colonists' ship *Deliverance*), Blue Grotto (dolphin show), Verdmont House (Georgian antiques), Hamilton (shopping, museums), Maritime Museum at the Dockyard.

Getting Here *From Bermuda International Airport.* By taxi, North Shore Rd. to South Rd. (45 mins). Public bus for trips to town. Frequent ferry service to points on the island. Moped available, no rental cars. Departure tax $20.

Special Notes Play area in gardens for children; those under 18 not permitted in spa. No smoking in spa or designated sections of the dining room. Bring proof of citizenship, or passport.

Harbour Village Beach Resort

Luxury pampering

Bonaire
Kralendjik

Designed to complement an active diving and snorkeling program, the spa at Harbour Village Resort is a cool and calm retreat from the beach scene. This is the best place to experience treatments with salt from the island's own flats, used for body polishing and baths. Water attractions include an outdoor Roman-style step-down pool for aerobics and toning classes, as well as a tranquil lounging pool into which cascades refreshing desalinated water.

Bonairian fitness programs begin with exercise on the beach and in the water. After a day of diving, you can retreat to the spa for a sports massage, body exfoliation, and the calming effects of breathing class. Relaxation techniques are taught by spa staff members, who also conduct sessions of tai chi. Mornings they lead nature hikes or a 4-mile bike ride along the island's rugged but beautiful coastline to cliffs called 1,000 steps. Welcome to Bonaire's natural StairMaster.

The two-story spa building has an aerobics studio with specially designed sprung floor, workout room with cardiovascular and weight-training equipment, and café. Treatments are in nine air-conditioned and windowed rooms, or outdoor in massage cabanas. Opened in 1995, the red-tile roofed facility fits into the Dutch-Caribbean style of the resort villas. On a quarter-mile stretch of white sand beach, Harbour Village has a 60-slip marina, tennis courts with night lighting, and full-service dive shop.

While the landscape is arid, underwater spectacle is the big draw. The coral reef, marine life, and more than 200 species of fish visible beneath the water's surface are endlessly fascinating. A structured snorkeling program introduced by the island government in cooperation with *Skin Diver* magazine provides in-depth looks at prime sites. Established in 1979 to safeguard these treasures, Bonaire National Park is much like a museum, with guides and information to round-out the experience as you float peacefully or explore with SCUBA equipment. The trails start right at the resort beach, and dive boat trips are scheduled daily.

Harbour Village Resort
Box 312, Kralendijk, Bonaire, Netherlands Antilles
Tel. 5997–7500, Fax 5997–7507
Reservations: Tel. 305/567–9509 or 800/424–0004
Fax 305/567–9659

Administration Spa director, Carol Upper

Season Year-round

Accommodations 72 rooms and suites in two-story villas clustered on courtyards and a private beach. Ground-floor lanai suites have veranda facing beach, entry from courtyard. Furnished with rattan seating, flowered drapes, and king- or queen-size bed, all are air-conditioned, have ceiling fans, white tile floor in bathroom. Amenities include hair dryer, robes, cable TV, direct-dial phone.

Rates Daily $265–$295 per room for one or two persons, suites $355–$725, 4-night/5-day spa package $1,520–$1,720 single, $1,130–$1,230 per person, double occupancy. 7-night program with Airlink services between Curaçao and Bonaire, $2,710–$3,060 single, $2,035–$2,210 double. Half-day spa program package $74–$155, including facility fee. Add taxes and service charge. AE, D, MC, V.

Meal Plans 3 meals daily included in packages. Seafood, vegetarian menu also has imported beef or chicken entrées. Tropical fruit and juices available throughout the day. Lunch can be seasonal mixed greens salad, turkey sandwich, or charbroiled catch of the day. Dinner includes choice of cold soup or salad, cannelloni, poached wahoo fish, braised chicken, grilled fruits.

Services and Facilities **Exercise Equipment:** Paramount multistation gym, 2 Lifecycle upright bikes, 2 Precor stairclimbers, 2 treadmills, 2 Concept 2 rowers. **Services:** Massage (stress-buster, sport), facial, hydrotherapy bath, sea salt exfoliation, body polish, after-sun treatments; salon for hair, nail, and skin care. **Swimming Facilities:** Outdoor freshwater pool, ocean beach. **Recreation Facilities:** 2 tennis courts (lighted), diving, snorkeling, deep-sea fishing, sailing. Nearby bike rental, horseback riding.

In the Area Lake Gotomeer (flamingo habitat), Washington/Slagbaii National Park (nature preserve, Arawak inscriptions), Fundashon Marcultura (marine research center), Klein Bonaire (reef).

Getting Here *From Miami.* By air, scheduled flights on ALM, Air Aruba, and American Airlines to Curaçao, continuing on Harbour Village Airlink. Rental car available.

Special Notes Spa open daily 7–7. Minimum age is 14. No smoking inside building.

Renaissance Jaragua Hotel

Luxury pampering

Dominican Republic
Santo Domingo

The Wellness Place at Jaragua Hotel provides an alternative to the flashy casino. On the oceanfront boulevard in the center of the hemisphere's oldest city, it's a few minutes' drive from the colonial capital founded by Bartholomew Columbus, the brother of the Discoverer. Vacationers can combine culture and fitness with casino action.

The new and the old meet on Avenida George Washington, a lively strip of hotels, restaurants, and shops fronting the ocean. There is no beach here, but spa goers hardly notice; with an oversize swimming pool surrounded by tropical gardens, Scandinavian saunas, Turkish steam bath, Roman whirlpool, and cold plunge, the Wellness Place is an ideal escape from the sun. The freestanding fitness facility, all marble and glass, is an oasis of aerobics and bodywork. You work out on exercise equipment or join a class in the aerobics studio. Aquacize class is scheduled in the Olympic-size swimming pool.

Pampering services come in several packages or à la carte. You can get an herbal wrap, a body scrub, a facial, or a massage. The daily entrance fee of $10 is waived when you book a massage. With this come robe, slippers, and snacks of fresh fruit and juices throughout the day.

Secluded on 14½ palm-fringed acres, the hotel has a tennis stadium with four clay courts and spectator seating. During the day this facility can be used by spa guests free of charge. From your room it's a pleasant walk or jog through the garden and alongside the lagoon to the spa. Not for a serious spa buff, this is a place to relax and join the merengue beat.

Renaissance Jaragua Hotel

367 George Washington Ave., Santo Domingo, Dominican Republic
Tel. 809/221–2222 or 800/484–7283
Fax 809/686–0528

Administration
General manager, Alvaro Soto; spa director, Haydee Polanco

Season
Year-round

Accommodations
10-story Jaragua Tower and an older 2-level wing of Garden Club rooms provide 300 luxury rooms. 6 suites with butler, marble baths. All rooms with modern rattan furniture, king or double beds, large bath with magnified makeup mirror, hair dryer. Air-conditioned, carpeted, 3 telephones with direct dial, color cable TV, decorative works by Dominican artists.

Rates
$150–$180 daily for 2 persons; 1- and 2-bedroom suites $400–$1,000 for 2 persons. Add 18% tax, 10% service charge. Day Spa packages at Wellness Place (no lodging) $112–$193, including tax. Deposit: 1 night's payment at time of booking. AE, DC, MC, V.

Meal Plans
Lunch included in Wellness Place packages, fruit plate, salad, or à la carte. Choice of heart-healthy options at 4 restaurants: Latin American Cafe for meats char-broiled, grilled, or cooked on a spit; Oriental Cafe for stir-fry specialties; fresh homemade pasta in the Italian Cafe; New York deli.

Services and Facilities
Exercise Equipment: Nautilus gym (10 stations), stationary bicycles, treadmills, rowing machine, free weights. **Services:** Swedish massage, reflexology, anti-cellulite treatment, saltglow loofah body scrub, herbal wrap, facial, depilation. Beauty salon for hair, nail, and skin care. **Swimming Facilities:** Olympic-size outdoor pool. **Recreation Facilities:** 4 lighted tennis courts.

Evening Programs: Casino theater; National Theater for concerts and opera.

In the Area Daily beach trip (complimentary), walking tour of the colonial area, Columbus lighthouse museum, Cathedral of Santa Maria la Menor (oldest in the Hemisphere, Columbus monument), Museum of the Royal Houses in the colonial quarter, Gallery of Modern Art and Natural History Museum downtown, National Botanical Gardens (train ride) in northern section of the city, Altos de Chavon (artisans, museum of Taino Indian artifacts) near La Romana, Baseball (Oct.–Feb.), Merengue Festival (July), Polo (Casa de Campo).

Getting Here *From Punta Caucedo Airport.* By taxi (45 mins). Public bus, rental car available.

Special Notes Elevators and ramps to all levels for people with disabilities. No smoking in the spa. Spa open weekdays 7 AM–9 PM, Sat. 9–7, Sun. 9–4.

LaSource

Luxury pampering

Grenada The fitness buff's alternative to Club Med, LaSource opened
Pink Gin Beach in late 1993 as an all-inclusive resort that offers the benefits of an active beach vacation combined with health and beauty treatments.

The body holiday package introduced at LeSport, its sister resort on St. Lucia, has been updated with a lighter menu, first-class accommodations, and a private nine-hole golf course. Once you arrive you can forget about money matters; even wine and bottled waters are included in the package, and tipping is not permitted.

The Oasis spa provides European-style services such as thalassotherapy in seaweed body wraps, and aromatherapy massage with essential oils of herbs and flowers. After an examination by the resort's nurse, you are programmed for complimentary treatments. (Additional services may be booked based on availability.) Aerobics classes (one hour) include step, stretch and tone, and floor exercise with reggae music. Daily sessions of yoga, meditation, and tai chi are scheduled, and a group jog takes place on the beach each morning. Join the optional daily hike at 7 AM to explore the island, then relax in the coed sauna and outdoor whirlpool.

The wooden cottages are designed in the fashion of a Victorian-era West Indian village, sitting amid 40 lush acres between two hills on Grenada's southwestern coast. The elegant colonial architecture features handcrafted wooden trellises and high-ceiling rooms, some of them beamed. Custom-carved four-poster beds, doors, and shutters enhance the rooms. Wood, including mahogany and teak imported from Venezuela, is used extensively in buildings on the grounds.

From a landscaped courtyard, you reach the broad expanse of Pink Gin Beach, where a free-form two-level swimming pool and oversize whirlpool beckon. The pool-terrace bar and restaurant serve buffet breakfast and lunch. Dinner is a sumptuous buffet two nights on the terrace, and served in the Great House restaurant and its veranda other nights.

On the island's southwestern coast, this self-contained beach resort provides the added value of restorative treatments. No spartan regimen here; spa director Bruce McDougall, an accredited massage therapist, teaches a honeymoon massage class for couples.

LaSource

Box 852, St. George's, Grenada, West Indies
Tel. 809/444-2556 or 800/544-2883
Fax 809/444-2561

Administration General manager, Gary Stevens; spa director, Bruce Mc-Dougall

Season Year-round

Accommodations 100 rooms, including 9 suites, in pastel-color low-rise buildings on a sloping hill. Guest rooms have marble floors, Bokhara rugs, chenille bedspreads. Slatted shutters and terra-cotta tile balconies frame beach and ocean views. All rooms have walk-in closets, air-conditioning, ceiling fans, clock radio, telephone. Bathrooms are oversize, with marble floor and walls, hair dryer, makeup mirror, and bathrobes. Suites come with bay window area and pullout sofa bed. No TV. Top-floor rooms have 18´ beamed ceilings.

Rates Daily package $220–$305 per person, double occupancy. Single supplement $40 per night. Taxes and gratuities included. AE, MC, V.

Meal Plans 3 meals and tea included in the daily tariff. Breakfast buffet includes eggs, hot and cold cereals, meats, breads and pastries, yogurt, tropical fruit, and juices. Lunch at the Terrace Restaurant is a buffet of hot and cold items, with salads, pasta, fish, and meat. Dinner entrées can be ordered from light cuisine menu including cabbage roll of risotto and local vegetables in callaloo puree, or from a menu of Great House specialties: callaloo soup, spicy crab cakes, cassoulet of duck and sausage with white haricot beans, Wiener schnitzel, char-grilled marlin with eggplant caviar. Desserts include tropical fruit, Spice Island meringue, and mango ice cream. Wine comes with lunch and dinner.

Services and Facilities **Exercise Equipment:** Paramount 9-unit weight-training circuit Precor stepper, 2 Tunturi Pro-Trainer bikes, 2 Bodyguard rowing units, incline and flat benches, free weights (3–25 lbs). **Services:** Massage (Swedish, aromatherapy), reflexology, body wrap, loofah salt rub, facial, scalp massage. Classes in couples massage, jazz warm-up, reggae, stress management. Beauty salon services (extra fee). **Swimming Facilities:** 2 freshwater pools, 2 ocean beaches. **Recreation Facilities:** 2 tennis courts (lighted), 9-hole golf course and putting green, archery, fencing, volleyball, table tennis, water sports, snorkeling equipment, scuba diving. **Evening Programs:** Dancing with live band music, barbecue.

In the Area St. George's (19th-century English colonial capital), Grenada National Museum (island history), Market Square, Fort George, spice-processing station near Gouyave, Grand Etang Forest National Park (hiking trails, lake).

Getting Here *From Point Salines International Airport.* Transfers provided (5 mins). Taxi, rental car available.

Special Notes Minimum age in spa is 15. Children sharing room with parents 50% discount, no treatments; under 6 years of age, $15 per night. Limited facilities for people with disabilities.

Guadeloupe Thermal Springs

Taking the waters

Guadeloupe Christopher Columbus saw the volcano La Soufrière erupting
Basse-Terre when he stepped ashore November 4, 1493, at Sainte-Marie, a fishing village along the road to Guadeloupe's principal city,

Pointe-à-Pitre. The native Caribs were not hospitable to the Discoverer. All that's left of that time are primitive drawings scratched into black rocks at Trois-Rivières, where the road branches toward La Soufrière, and you can join hiking trips with Friends of the Nature Park. The volcanic waters are now tapped for therapeutic use.

This butterfly-shaped island provides both thalassotherapy and thermal water therapies on a par with those available at resorts in Brittany and the French Riviera. However, the treatment centers have no hotel facility, and visitors must arrange lodging nearby. Among numerous hotels, from deluxe to inexpensive, the Novotel Marissol beach resort has fitness facilities and programs of "remise en forme" for beauty and health.

The medically oriented Centre Thermal Harry Hamousin provides French hydrotherapy equipment and therapists, treatments for rheumatism, asthma, and skin problems. The classic "cure" has come to the Caribbean.

Physical training to aid recovery from injuries includes exercise in shallow pools of mineral water and on special equipment in the gymnasium. Respiratory problems are treated with aerosol-like inhalations of mineral water. There are shower sprays with high-powered jets of water and sulfur baths. The thermal center is open every morning except Sunday and accepts reservations for one-time treatments. Serious problems require consultation with a doctor at the nearby clinic Les Eaux Vives. Arrangements can be made by your hotel or directly with the clinic, and medical records should be brought along for the interview with *le médecin thermal*. Several doctors speak English if your French isn't sufficient.

As an overseas department of France (not a colony or an independent country), Guadeloupe offers its citizens all the benefits of the mother country, including health insurance coverage for the cost of spa therapy. Thus the Centre Thermal Harry Hamousin, a private institution, enjoys a steady stream of visitors from Europe and other islands in the French Antilles. Opened in 1978 with state-of-the-art facilities, the center now welcomes any visitors needing massage or special therapy.

Newer and oriented less toward medical treatments is *Espace Santé de Ravine Chaude* at the Station Thermale René Toribio. Operated as a day spa, the facilities include baths and two swimming pools filled with thermal water, three restaurants (dietetic and gastronomic), and a solarium. A medical doctor is on staff to consult with visitors on treatments. Therapies for rheumatism and anti-stress are structured as a "cure" over several days. Postnatal care also is provided through underwater massage, aromatherapy, and pressotherapy. Open daily from 10 AM to 11 PM, the spa charges an admission fee of 25 francs, and treatments are priced individually or in a package from 500 FF including lunch; weekend with lodging and meals 1,405 FF.

Pointe-à-Pitre bustles with its busy port, shopping centers, and marinas. On market days the stalls are filled with herb sellers hawking natural seasonings and medicines: *matriquin*, Marie-Perrine, *zhébe-gras*, *fleupappilon*, *bois-de l'homme*, *bonnet-carré*, and the like. All the tastes and stimulations of the Creole flavorings and remedies are still on sale, alongside modern pharmacies and boutiques laden with Parisian fashions. In August it all comes together in honor of St. Laurent, patron saint of cooks, in La Fête de Cuisiniéres.

Centre Thermal Harry Hamousin
Matouba Papaye, 97120 Saint-Claude, Guadeloupe
Tel. 590/80–53–19
Fax 590/80–06–08

Administration Director, Harry Beaubois Espace Santé de Ravine Chaude
97129 Le Lamentin, Guadeloupe
Tel. 590/25–75–92
Fax 590/25–76–28

Administration Owner-director, Senator Mayor René Toribio

Special Notes No smoking in the center; bathers required to wear cap, slippers. Remember to bring passport and medical certificate.

Hotel Marissol

Luxury pampering

Guadeloupe French and American fitness regimens merge at Novotel's
Gosier large and popular Hotel Marissol beach resort. Set in a tropical garden perfumed by blossoms, the facilities include a "hammam" steam room and private rooms for massage and thalassotherapy. Light gymnastics on the beach and stretching exercises in the swimming pool are offered at no extra charge for all guests.

The Gym Tropic is open daily, except Sunday, 8–8. There is a coed steam room, aerobics studio, and hydrotherapy tubs but no exercise equipment. Workout clothing is provided daily.

European spa treatments are a plus: underwater massage, steam baths, a facial, and whirlpool treatment with seaweed and oils. Classes are scheduled for yoga, tai chi, and aerobics, all optional.

Hotel Marissol
Bas-du-Fort, 97190 Gosier, Guadeloupe
Tel. 590/90–84–44 or 800/221–4542
Fax 590/90–83–32

Administration Manager, M. Delahousse

Season Year-round

Accommodations 200 air-conditioned rooms (50 bungalows) with terrace or loggia. Modern furniture accented with island fabrics and prints. All rooms have private bath, radio, direct-dial telephone, color TV with satellite programs.

Rates Daily rate $125–$260 per room for 2; bungalow for 2, $135–$250. 25% payment at time of booking. MC, V.

Meal Plans Fitness package includes breakfast and dinner. Breakfast buffet includes yogurt, croissants, granola, fresh fruit. Selections from the dinner menu include steamed vegetables, fresh grilled fish, salads. Grilled specialties: veal scallops, entrecôte steak, seafood brochette.

Services and Facilities **Services:** Massage, body wrap with seaweed, underwater massage, whirlpool bath with seaweed, skin and nail care. **Swimming Facilities:** Outdoor freshwater pool, ocean beach. **Recreation Facilities:** Tennis, hiking, water sports.

In the Area Scuba, mountain hiking, thermal mineral-water treatments at Centre Harry Hamousin, Nature Park, La Soufrière (volcano), Manioukani thalassotherapy center.

Getting Here *From Le Raizet Airport.* Complimentary transfers on arrival and departure. Taxi, rental car available.

Special Notes No smoking in fitness center. Bring passport.

Centre de Thalassotherapie Manioukani

Preventive medicine
Taking the waters

Guadeloupe Centre de Thalassotherapy Manioukani uses fresh seawater
Gourbeyre for baths and an exercise pool where physical fitness classes
are held every morning. The heated seawater is said to improve circulation in your legs, and to help persons suffering
from rheumatism. Also offered are postnatal and slimming
programs.

Opened in 1995, this attractive building is owned by a couple
who are medical doctors; on staff are a physiologist, chiropractor, and dietitian. Facilities include hydromassage tubs,
nasal spray, and a steam room (hammam). Near a marina on
the Caribbean coast in Basse-Terre, Manioukani provides free
transportation for guests booking an overnight package at
Grande Anse Hotel, from 1,200 FF per person. Within walking distance is CGOSH resort, bungalows from 1,950 FF single with two dietetic meals daily. Or you can stay at Hotel
Marissol and book a one-day package.

Overnight packages, with or without meals and accommodation, are offered on weekends. Options include dietetic meals,
physical fitness training, and simply relaxation. Concentrated
programs (cures) for six days address rheumatism, circulatory
problems, skin care, and slimming.

Centre de Manioukani
Marina Riviere-Sens, 97113 Gourbeyre, Guadeloupe
Tel. 590/99–02–02

Administration Owner-director, Dr. Pierre Saint-Luce

Season Year-round

Rates 2-day weekend package (without meals and accommodation)
800 FF per person. 2-night/3-day weekend package with accommodation 1,200–4,900 FF single, 1,360–5,100 FF per person, double occupancy. 6-day dietetic program 4,200–6,600 FF
single, 4,500–5,100 FF per person, double. Deposit: 1,200 FF.
No credit cards.

Ciboney

Nonprogram resort

Jamaica Clustered on a hillside near Ocho Rios, the villas of Ciboney
Ocho Rios opened in 1990, providing a fresh approach to the all-inclusive
resort concept. Designed for privacy, the suites are ideal for
honeymoons and romantic escapes. Couples can have an entire villa with its own housekeeper, or share a four-apartment
villa.

The spa and fitness facilities are tucked into a rambling Great
House that serves as a social center and hotel. Recalling plantation days, the lobby staircase leads down to the Orchids
restaurant. Among seven dining options at the resort, Orchids
takes spa cuisine seriously. The dinner features are displayed
as you enter to help you make selections from the menu.

The airy Elysium Spa delights sybarites but is short on serious spa programs. You can be steamed, massaged, and exfoli-
ated from head to toe. The well-appointed exercise room is
air-conditioned, has three scheduled aerobics classes most

days, step or low-impact. Instructors are on hand in the exercise equipment room for circuit training. Otherwise, you're on your own. The beach club, reached by a short hike or van ride to the bottom of the hill, has water sports equipment and a restaurant.

Relaxing personal services are offered at the spa by appointment. If you stay a minimum of three nights, the 25-minute sessions of massage, reflexology, and nail care are complimentary. Treatments are provided in curtained cubicles or on a semireclined chair in a garden atrium, by locally trained masseuses who gently knead sore muscles. The spa salon provides a limited selection of facials, paraffin treatments, and hair styling for men and women at an additional charge. There are separate men's and women's saunas and steam rooms, a coed Jacuzzi with cold-water plunge pool, and a Swiss shower.

While a full-body massage can be booked for $50, the bodywork here may disappoint serious spa goers. On the positive side, the spa includes sports and fine dining in the package price. But the real attractions of this Radisson resort are the villas, with their own swimming pools, and the attentive staffers who do their utmost to make you feel at home.

Ciboney

Box 728, Main St., Ocho Rios, St. Ann, Jamaica
Tel. 809/974–1027 or 800/777–7800
Fax 809/974–5838

Administration	General manager, Robert Perrin
Season	Year-round
Accommodations	300 luxury units including 36 rooms in the Great House, 236 villa suites with 1–4 bedrooms, 14 single villas, and studios. Bedrooms have air-conditioning, ceiling fan, TV, VCR, radio, phone, private bathroom with hair dryer. Villa suites have kitchenette with stocked bar and snacks, living room, semi-private swimming pool. Modern island furniture, rattan seating.
Rates	Daily all-inclusive tariff for Great House room $392 for 2 persons, double occupancy; 1-bedroom villa suites $452–$532 per couple. Taxes and gratuities included. AE, DC, MC, V.
Meal Plans	3 meals and unlimited snacks, selected wines, and bar service included in daily tariff. Breakfast at the Market includes home-baked breads and pastry, eggs cooked to order, cereals, yogurt, tropical fruits, and juices. Lunch on the beach at Casa Nina can be pasta, salad, grilled fish. Orchids restaurant dinner menu has choice of appetizer such as jumbo shrimp in an island curry sauce, seafood terrine or lasagna, smoked chicken. Low-fat entrée selections are seared marlin with papaya salsa, breast of roast chicken marinated in Zinfandel, medallions of pork with warm cabbage salad. Dessert is tropical marinated fruits with sponge cake, breadfruit pudding, or orange Bavarian cream.
Services and Facilities	**Exercise Equipment:** 7-station Universal weight-training gym, 5 Lifecycles, 2 StairMaster PT4000, barbells (5–45 lbs), hand weights (4–10 lbs), slant boards. **Services:** Massage, reflexology, sea-salt scrub, mango facial, paraffin foot/hand treatment, waxing. Salon for hair, nail, and skin care. **Swimming Facilities:** 2 large free-form pools with Jacuzzi, 90 villa pools, small ocean beach. **Recreation Facilities:** 6 tennis courts (lighted, 4 with Har-Tru surface), 2 squash courts, racquetball court (air-conditioned), croquet, table tennis, basketball half-court, water-sports equipment, paddleboats, canoes. Nearby stables and 2

18-hole golf courses. **Evening Programs:** Music, barbecue, folkloric show.

In the Area Dunn's River Falls, Coyoba River Gardens and Museum (island personalities), 18th-century plantation great house museums, Firefly (Noel Coward home), Golden Eye (Ian Fleming wrote James Bond novels here).

Getting Here *From Montego Bay.* Transfers provided on arrival and departure.

Special Notes Minimum age at resort is 16. Facilities for people with disabilities are limited. Shuttle bus service to beach club.

The Enchanted Garden

Luxury pampering
Nonprogram resort

Jamaica Set amid 20 acres of rain forest, botanical gardens, waterfalls,
Ocho Rios and rolling lawns, this leafy retreat was designed as an alternative to the island's other, more active beach resorts. Here you can take a class in couples massage, float in a natural pool beneath a cascade, or bliss out in one of the private garden nooks where a masseuse awaits with aromatherapy.

The spa is a cheerful, air-conditioned hideaway. Emphasis is on all things natural, from facials with fresh-cut aloe plants to aromatherapy with jasmine oils straight from the garden. More than 50 essential oils are available, custom-mixed to suit your mood. The menu of services includes treatments with vegetable mud, rich in trace elements from the sea, and micronized seaweed.

A typical day may begin with a power walk through the exquisite botanical gardens on the hillside, climbing to the top of the falls. Lunch can be a beach picnic outing, or selected from the pasta bar at the pools. The all-inclusive package plan allows you to dine at several specialty restaurants in the gardens, selecting spa cuisine options that are low in fat, sodium, and calories.

Strolling to the spa, you can stop at the Seaquarium building to plan excursions, take tea, and learn about the island's flora and fauna. A soaring aviary provides a walk-through tour and some close-up bird-watching. The botanical gardens and aviary are open to visitors who come for lunch or dinner ($45–$55) or just for a tour ($10). Combined with a half-day package in the spa, this is a bargain escape for cruise ship passengers and guests at hotels in Ocho Rios.

The spa's scheduled classes in the aerobics studio are stretch and tone, body sculpting, dancercise, and yoga. The limited selection of exercise equipment may be a disappointment for fitness buffs, though the facilities do include a Turkish steam bath, Finnish sauna, outdoor whirlpools, and a Swiss shower with multiple heads. Robe and sandals are provided.

While there is a small beach club down the hill, you may want to rent a car and drive along the coastal route to Dunn's River waterfalls (a slippery challenge to climbers) and visit Port Antonio, a Victorian town made famous by movie star Errol Flynn and the banana boats (sing "hey Mr. Talleyman"). Shop for island produce and crafts at Musgrave Market; naseberry (known also as sapodilla), cho-cho, star apple, pimiento, and the tiny fig banana are heaped on stands. Nearby, Boston Beach is lined with smokey shacks selling jerk pork and chicken barbecued over a pimiento wood fire. If this brings out the naturalist in you, head inland through Fern Gulley to the town of Bath for a look at Jamaica's original spa gardens and mineral springs.

The Enchanted Garden

Box 204, Ocho Rios, St. Ann, Jamaica
Tel. 809/974–1400 or 800/554–2000
Fax 809/974–5823

Administration	General manager, Frederick March; spa director, Erica Martin
Season	Year-round
Accommodations	112 bedrooms and suites with 1–3 bedrooms terraced into hillside gardens. 40 deluxe, modern town houses include sunken living room, private patio with plunge pool, kitchen. TV with satellite channels, telephone, air-conditioning, maid and turn-down service.
Rates	Daily all-inclusive package: $125–$200 single, $90–$150 per person, double occupancy; 1-bedroom suite with living room $190–$215 per person double, $220–$240 single. Half-day packages $90–$180, full-day $100–$190. Taxes included; add gratuities. AE, MC, V.
Meal Plans	The all-inclusive daily rate covers 3 meals, snacks, afternoon tea, and open bar. Specialty restaurants feature pasta, Middle Eastern, and Far Eastern cuisine. New American menu choices at L'Eau Mirage are grilled marlin, fillet of mahimahi with papaya relish, cold poached scallops with tomato vinaigrette, pepper-crusted beef with white beans, warm curried crab and papaya salad. Breakfast can be egg-white omelet, cereal, tropical fruit, and homemade Jamaican bread. Vegetarian meals available on request.
Services and Facilities	**Exercise Equipment:** Precor treadmill, 3 Schwinn Air Dyne stationary bicycles, 2 rowing machines, NordicTrack cross-country ski machine, free weights. **Services:** Massage (Swedish, aromatherapy, shiatsu, reflexology, anti-cellulite), salt-glow body scrub, body wraps, hydrotherapy bath with essential oils, collagen body polish, waxing. **Swimming Facilities:** 3 outdoor swimming pools, nearby ocean beach. **Recreation Facilities:** 2 tennis courts (lighted), nearby golf and riding, water volleyball, reggae lessons. **Evening Programs:** Nightclub, Jamaican show and buffet dinner (Fri.).
Getting Here	*From Montego Bay airport.* Complimentary transfers. Taxi, rental car available.
Special Notes	Spa hours daily 9–6. Minimum age: 16. Juice bar in Seaquarium café above spa. Shuttle bus to beach.

Jamaican Mineral Springs

Taking the waters

Jamaica *Milk River and Bath*	Getting off the beaten track is easy, but you need a car to explore some of the most scenic areas of the hilly island of Jamaica. In addition to breathtaking vistas there are botanical gardens, a bird sanctuary, and two spas built around mineral springs that have been attracting cure seekers for nearly two centuries.

Legend holds that an African slave, wounded in an uprising, was healed by bathing in pools of water fed by hot springs located high in the lush valleys between Kingston and Port Antonio. English plantation owners seeking respite from the coastal heat spread the word. By the beginning of the 18th century there was a spa hotel, church, and botanical garden for cultivation of medicinal herbs in the town of Bath. What remains today is primitive, nothing like its Georgian namesake in England. The waters, however, still gush forth in a setting of tropical splendor enjoyed by hill people and an occasional visitor.

From the town, a narrow road cuts through fern gullies alongside the Sulphur River to reach Bath Fountain Hotel. Cut into rocks beneath the hotel are private chambers where you can soak in the sulfurous warm water. European spa experts have confirmed high levels of radioactivity.

The hotel's 10 guest rooms are airy and simply furnished; no air-conditioning. Meals are prepared to order in the public dining room (no credit cards). *Bath Fountain Hotel, Bath, St. Thomas Parish. Rooms cost $360 (J$) per night, without private bath; $450–$480 (J$) with bathroom, for 2 persons.*

West of Kingston's high-rise government center, past agricultural and industrial developments, is the former capital city, Spanish Town, and from there you can reach the Milk River mineral baths in about two hours. Stop to admire the main square, surrounded by Georgian buildings that date from 1762. One now houses the Jamaican People's Museum of Craft and Technology. A classical statue of Admiral George Rodney commemorates his 1792 naval victory over the French that saved the British colony.

Continuing westward on Route B12 past the market town of May Pen, you reach the Milk River near a crossroads called Toll Gate. Built on a hillside, the spa hotel has private cubicles hewn from stone that are filled directly from the springs. Here, too, an analysis of the water in 1952 confirmed a high degree of radioactivity and minerals, similar to that of the best European spa waters.

Although there are no special treatments or exercise equipment, the hotel has a large outdoor swimming pool filled with the cool mineral water. Ocean beaches and citrus groves are a few miles away. Trout Hall, which grows *ugli* fruit, can be visited on request.

Most of the guests at Milk River come to soak three times a day, reserving cubicles with the receptionist. Bottles of mineral water are on the tables in the dining room. The hotel has seen better days (and may again); the 22 guest rooms are simple, clean, and inexpensive, with breakfast and dinner included in the daily tariff. The mineral water swimming pool is open to day-only visitors for a small fee.

Milk River Bath and Hotel

Milk River Post Office, Clarendon, Jamaica
Tel. 809/924–9544

Administration   General manager, Gloria Cole

Rates   Double room with private bath $84 (US$) for 2 persons, single room with private bath $62. Tax and service included. MC, V.

The Sans Souci Lido

Luxury pampering
Taking the waters

Jamaica   Charlie's Spa at the Sans Souci Lido resort takes a fresh ap-
Ocho Rios   proach to island holidays. More hedonistic than health-oriented, the resort atmosphere up on the hill complements

vigorous workouts on the beach. It's a pleasant combination if you're interested in toning up or taking off a few pounds.

With the sea on one side and a cascade of mineral water on the other, the spa provides instant stress reduction. The waters, however, are not used for therapy or beauty treatments; you can soak or swim at leisure, and you may join an exercise class in the pool.

In 1993, SuperClubs management took over the luxurious hideaway at Sans Souci, revamping the facilities—and its image. The Sans Souci Lido is now an all-inclusive resort, including spa services, meals, drinks, golf, tennis, and water sports in the daily tariff. All guest rooms were upgraded with marble bathrooms, many of them with whirlpool tubs, and amenities such as hair dryers and robes. New suites in the beach wing are smaller and can be noisy at night because of the 24-hour bar below. The beach-level exercise equipment room is air-conditioned; aerobics classes are held in a sea view open-air pavilion. The result is a program that offers more than the sum of its parts.

Begin with a fast-paced walk through the terraced gardens and along the curve of beach where tennis courts and water sports await your pleasure. The sound of a violin or flute draws you to the beach restaurant, where a band of roving musicians entertains. Buffet breakfast and lunch here is a sampler of island fare, plus Continental and Japanese favorites.

Bodywork and facials at the spa require appointments. Check in early at the tiny spa office alongside a pool that's home to mascot Charlie, a huge sea turtle who thrives in the mineral water. The Hideaway is a charming gazebo on the rocks, just big enough for a private massage, limited to 30 minutes in the all-inclusive plan. Facials and other treatments are given inside tiny wooden cottages clinging to the rocks. Higher up are rock-walled wet-treatment rooms with an alfresco shower, called "The Ridge," where seaweed and mud wraps are scheduled. At the top is a beauty salon, where a complimentary manicure and pedicure are offered.

A beach-level grotto conceals a dry sauna and treatment area for skin exfoliation with sea salt, followed by a rubdown with cleansing oil and then a walk into the sea. The shallow water here is a mix of saltiness and refreshingly cool mineral water from the springs. It's ideal for washing off oils and salts used for body scrubs (depending on your skin type, the scrub will include aloe, peppermint, or coconut, plus cornmeal).

Sybarites can enjoy a secluded soak in a whirlpool tucked into the garden. A special treat is hidden in a beach grotto where the spring water seeps into a sand-bottom pool. For extra privacy, request an upper-level suite, or one of the penthouses, where you can sunbathe among the treetops.

Launched in late 1993, the Sans Souci Lido concept has attracted a younger guest than previously encountered here, many honeymoooners, some families with adult children, and single spa goers. Afternoon tea in the Great House is an opportunity to mix with guests and make plans for the gala beach party or tennis. Hostesses introduce single newcomers to one another. Be sure to make dinner reservations in the Great House dining room or on the terrace under the stars.

The Sans Souci Lido
Box 364, Ocho Rios, St. Ann, Jamaica
Tel. 809/974–2353 or 800/859–7873
Fax 809/974–2544

Administration General manager, Patrick Drake; spa director, Margaret Spencer

Season Year-round

Accommodations 111 suites and rooms in villa-style buildings overlooking gardens and the sea. Newer suites in 3-story beach wing. All have TV, telephone, private balcony, air-conditioning, but no window screens. Traditional furnishings, with sitting area, tea kettle, minibar stocked with complimentary wine, waters, beer. Main building houses the Casanova Restaurant and bar/lounge.

Rates 3 nights in deluxe ocean-view room $950–$1,120 per person, double occupancy; suite with Jacuzzi $1,170–$1,390; Penthouse $1,140–$1,710. 7 nights $1,750–$2,180 per person, double occupancy; Jacuzzi suite $2,300–$2,710; Penthouse $2,810–$3,330 per person double. Single supplement: $150 per day. Taxes and gratuities included. AE, DC, MC, V.

Meal Plans Breakfast, lunch, and dinner, snacks, and 24-hr room service included in tariff. Breakfast can be sliced pineapple, granola, or egg-white omelet with whole wheat toast. Lunch buffet has salads, grilled tuna sandwich, shrimp ceviche, pasta primavera, spinach and ricotta cannelloni. Dinner in Casanova restaurant includes seafood fettuccine, smoked marlin appetizer, broiled lobster, or vegetarian lasagna. Beach restaurant serves Continental menu at dinner.

Services and Facilities **Exercise Equipment:** 2 Schwinn bikes, Lifecycle 9100, Concept 2 rower, dumbbells (15–50 lbs), benches, free weights, 8-station Bodymaster multigym, Precor treadmill. **Services:** Massage, aromatherapy, reflexology, fango mud body and face treatment, paraffin wax hand and foot treatment, seaweed wrap, body scrub, facial; beauty salon for hair, nail, and skin care. **Swimming Facilities:** 2 pools and private beaches. **Spa Facilities:** Mineral springwater swimming and soaking pools, whirlpool, sauna. **Recreation Facilities:** Complimentary golf (18 or 9 holes) at nearby Runaway Bay, bike outing, shopping trip. Free use of water-sports equipment, including scuba trip, snorkeling gear. 3 tennis courts (lighted), croquet on beach. Nearby are St. Ann Polo Club; horseback riding at Chukka Cove. **Evening Programs:** Folkloric groups, combo for dancing on terrace.

In the Area Rose Hall and Greenwood Great House museums, Coyaba River Garden and Museum (pre-Columbian to Bob Marley), Ocho Rios craft market, Dunn's River Falls, Prospect Plantation (agricultural training center), Firefly (Noel Coward residence), Golden Eye (home of James Bond novelist Ian Fleming).

Getting Here *From Montego Bay Airport.* Transfers (about 2 hrs) are included in package plans. Air Jamaica and American Airlines have flights from U.S. cities and Canada. Taxi or limousine available at all times.

Special Notes Elevator connects guest rooms with spa facilities on the beach. (Hillside location of the hotel requires considerable stair climbing.) Minimum stay is 3 nights. Minimum age is 16.

Swept Away

Sports conditioning *Couples only*

Jamaica As a counterpoint to the laid-back pace of life on the beach at
Negril Jamaica's westernmost point, the Swept Away resort stresses a sports and fitness regimen within its 20-acre complex. Included in the rates are unlimited use of the island's first indoor

air-conditioned racquetball and squash courts, tennis lessons with resident professionals, and a fully equipped dive shop.

From the open-air reception area, paths lead to 26 two-story villas set rather close together in beachside gardens. The standard villa has four minisuites arranged on two levels around a plant-filled atrium. It is a quiet environment, far removed from the frenetic pace of most vacation villages, but plenty of action vibrates at the tennis complex and around the beach bar and pool. Most guests are young couples, some are honeymooners.

The sports center is set apart from the villas by the island's main road. At the reception desk you can book courts and massages, and check on scheduled classes in the aerobics pavilion. An Olympic-length lap pool is used for aquacise sessions. Joggers can check out a nine-station parcourse on the half-mile running track. Cool-down options include yoga, stress management class, and massage. A fitness evaluation is recommended prior to starting exercise.

Tennis buffs get workouts with pros at three daily clinics. There is a ball machine and racket-stringing equipment. If you haven't brought a racket, you can borrow one. Tournaments are held throughout the week.

Massage therapy is close at hand; two rooms are in a thatch-roofed pavilion in the center of the sports complex, complete with outdoor Jacuzzi. (Massage is not part of the all-inclusive package; charges go on your account.)

The weights room here is an open-air pavilion with high-tech German equipment. Instructors are on hand throughout the day to coach you on proper use of the equipment. Certified in aerobics by AFAA, the staff gives classes in Reebok step, abs and gluts, body sculpting, and stretch. A power-lifting competition is scheduled every Wednesday evening; the gym stays open till 11 PM.

In the clubhouse are men's and women's locker rooms with steam rooms and saunas. A sports-theme bar with big-screen TV opens at noon, and there is an open-air restaurant. Resort guests can dine here at no extra charge.

The resort offers unlimited use of water-sports equipment: Windsurfing, kayaking, sunfish sailing, paddle-boating, and waterskiing are all featured. Snorkeling gear is also provided, as are outings in a glass-bottom boat. For certified divers, SCUBA trips to nearby reefs depart three times daily in the resort's own dive boat. A certification course is available for an extra fee.

With the ambience of a private club, Swept Away allows you to set your own pace. Bicycles are available when you want to explore the area's more lively beaches at leisure. Relax on your veranda and enjoy the sunset. Room service delivers afternoon tea or Continental breakfast at your bidding while you soak up the romantic vista. In the two-level beachside dining pavilion, diversions range from billiards and a piano bar to a games room with a big-screen color TV that brings in stateside programs. Many guests seem content to simply lounge by the seaside freshwater pool; snacks are always available at the juice and veggie bar.

Swept Away
Box 77, Long Bay, Negril, Jamaica
Tel. 809/957–4061 or 800/545–7937
Fax 809/957–4060

Administration General manager, Jeremy Jones; spa manager, Nancy Machado

Season Year-round

Accommodations 134 suites housed in 2-story villas. Jamaican handwork adds to the tropical look of rooms with wooden louvered walls, furnished with rattan rocker and wicker chairs, and plush cushions. King-size beds have cedar headboard; warm colors and earth-tone materials include decorative clay masks, lamps, and floor tiles. Private veranda, air conditioner, ceiling fan, telephone.

Rates Choice of villa: garden, sea view, beachfront. Per-couple packages for 4 days/3 nights $1,245–$1,860; 8 days/7 nights $2,597–$3,990. Rates include all meals, use of sports equipment and fitness facilities with instruction, alcoholic beverages, gratuities, and hotel taxes. Airport transfers provided. Deposit: 1 night's payment. Minimum stay: 3 nights. AE, DC, MC, V.

Meal Plan Buffet breakfast and lunch; dinner served by candlelight. Spa cuisine options include egg-white omelet cooked to order, hot and cold cereals for breakfast. Lunch can be steamed vegetables, skinless chicken breast, baked fish. Dinner entrées include goat chops in phyllo dough, curried-goat stew, grilled fish in fruit sauce, homemade fish pâté, pasta. Jamaican buffet on Friday evening includes ackee and strudel made with native applelike vegetable. Beach bar serves pita sandwich with tuna fish or chicken, fruit, vegetables, juices, beer, and bottled water. Italian restaurant at sports complex open for lunch and dinner has calorie-controlled pizza and pasta.

Services and Facilities **Exercise Equipment:** 22-unit PROFI weight-training gym, free weights and dumbbells (5–100 lbs), 2 Lifecycles, 2 recumbent Lifecycles, NordicTrack cross-country skier, rowing ergometer, 2 StairMasters. **Services:** Swedish massage (extra charge), tennis clinics and private lessons, introduction to scuba. **Swimming Facilities:** 2 outdoor freshwater pools, lap pool, ocean beach, clothing-optional beach. **Recreation Facilities:** 10 tennis courts (lighted, 4 hard-surface, 5 clay), jogging track, basketball court, 2 racquetball courts, 2 squash courts; dive shop with 3 trips daily, sea kayaks, Windsurfers. **Evening Programs:** Nightly dancing, band and show weekends.

In the Area Paradise Park (18th-century plantation), Great Morass (bird sanctuary), Savanna-la-Mar (19th-century sugar port), Milk River Bath (geothermal springs).

Getting Here *From Montego Bay.* By car, round-trip transfers provided (1½ hrs). By air, scheduled Air Jamaica and American Airlines flights. Rental car, taxi available.

Special Notes Ground-floor accommodations for people with disabilities. No children. Fitness center open daily 7–7, till 11 Wed.

Centre de Thalassothérapie du Carbet

Life enhancement
Taking the waters

Martinique Seawater and kinesitherapy are the basis of an aquatic work-
Carbet out at the indoor pools of the Centre de Thalassothérapie near Fort-de-France, capital city of the island. Considered effective in the treatment of rheumatism, the four-step procedure takes about 2½ hours and costs 300 francs.

Beginning with a plunge into heated seawater (33°C), you may participate in group exercise or simply relax. The pool has built-in underwater jets to massage sore muscles. A more intense underwater massage is next, in a private tub with jets designed to effect lymphatic drainage. The third step is a *douche à affusion,* a full body massage under a continuous shower of seawater.

The massage therapist devotes special attention to relieving tension in the vertebrae of your spine. The water pressure helps relax muscles. The final douche is in a shower stall lined with high-pressure jets aimed at cellulite points, the abdomen, and the vertebrae.

Supplementary services available include electrotherapy to recondition muscles after injury, an algae body mask, and antiarthritis and antiaging treatments for the skin. Inhalation of seawater mist is advised for asthma sufferers, and negative ions are introduced to relieve nervous tension.

While the center is open to the public every day with the exception of Sunday, there is no fitness program in conjunction with a hotel. Nearby is the beachfront Hotel Marouba (tel. 596/78–12–88; fax 596/78–05–65), which has single rooms at 440F–620F, double rooms 680F–950F for 2 persons daily, including Continental breakfast. Also within a short walk is the 10-room Hotel Christophe Colomb (tel. 596/78–05–38) with single and double rooms 250F–300F daily.

Popular in France, this is spa therapy that sybarites can combine with a Caribbean holiday.

Centre de Thalassothérapie du Carbet
Grand'Anse
97221 Carbet, Martinique
Tel. 596/78–08–78

Administration General manager, Dr. Jacques-Joseph Louisia

Season Year-round; open weekdays 7–6, Sat. 7–1; closed Sun.

Getting Here *From Fort-de-France.* By car, coastal road toward St. Pierre, 16 mi (25 mins). Taxi, rental car available.

Special Notes Bring bathing cap, sandals, swimwear. Robe and towels provided.

Four Seasons Resort

Nonprogram resort

Nevis Pristine beaches, aquamarine seas, and tropical rain forests
Pinney's Beach set the scene for the Four Seasons Resort on tiny Nevis. Opened in 1991, this luxurious resort seemed at first to clash with the island culture. But today it has become a welcome part of the community. Visitors arrive aboard a private launch at the resort's dock after a VIP greeting in St. Kitts, Nevis's sister island, 2 miles and 30 minutes across the channel. Or private planes can land at the tiny Nevis airstrip. Guests set their own pace, choosing among a number of sports options.

The resort has a sports-vacation package, available year-round, which is an excellent value, including unlimited tennis and golf. The tennis complex has 10 courts supervised by Peter Burwash professionals who provide clinics and one-on-one training. The golf course is a major attraction at this resort. Joggers and walkers enjoy circuiting the links on a paved path that goes through lush forest and up into the foothills of Nevis Peak.

Swimmers gained a dedicated two-lane lap pool when facilities at the beach pavilion were expanded recently. Other water-sports opportunities incorporate sailboards, kayaks, and snorkeling equipment.

The Health Club, in the Sports Pavilion, has men's and ladies' saunas, a unisex hair salon, three massage rooms, and an air-conditioned workout room. Aerobics classes, including step, stretch-and-tone, and aquaerobics, and early morning walks and beach jogs are open to all guests, free of charge. Croquet, volleyball, and shuffleboard are also offered.

Details make the difference: iced facecloths in the weight-training room, along with pitchers of fresh fruit juices; morning coffee and muffins laid out at the health club; a library of feature films for your VCR viewing; and in-room massage at your convenience. Experienced massage therapists, a rare commodity in the islands, provide some of the best bodywork anywhere.

The Dining Room is reminiscent of a plantation great house, with a plank floor, a high ceiling with rafters, a cut-stone fireplace, ceiling fans, and a small dance floor. The alternative cuisine found at all Four Seasons hotels, is low in sodium and fat, easy on calorie count but full of fresh herbs and vegetables. Seafood naturally is the main attraction, but island fare also can be sampled among heart-healthy choices.

The 12 plantation-style guest lodges have screened porches on the second floor and private patios with screened doors for ground-floor rooms. Each building has about a dozen rooms and suites, provided with robes and slippers, TV and VCR, and minibar. Bathrooms are extra-large, with separate stall shower and toilet room. Also available are fully furnished and serviced private villas and estate homes.

The legacy of 300 years of British rule is still evident on the 36-square-mile island. Thanks to its sulfur bath and health spa, its 82 sugar estates, and the slave trade, the island once was known as the "Queen of the Caribbees." The Bath Hotel (circa 1778), now in disrepair and used as a police building, overlooks a wooden bathhouse where for $2 you can soak in hot mineral water.

There are several magnificent plantation homes to tour; ask the resort concierge for information. A perfect way to end your day is on Nevis Peak, where you can enjoy the spectacular sunset, and perhaps catch a glimpse of wild monkeys with 6-foot-long tails.

Four Seasons Resort
Box 565, Charlestown, Nevis, West Indies
Tel. 809/469–1111
Reservations: 800/332–3442 in U.S., 800/268–6282 in Canada
Fax 809/469–1112

Administration General manager, Mark Hellring; fitness/activities director, Juliette Borcher; tennis director, John Maycock

Season Year-round

Accommodations 196 rooms and suites in 2-story plantation-style lodges. Choice of king-size or 2 double beds, beach or golf view. Oversize marble-tiled bathroom with full amenities, hair dryer, lighted makeup mirror. All air-conditioned, with ceiling fans, TV and VCR, refrigerator, telephone. Self-service laundry facility (complimentary) in each lodge.

Rates $250–$625 daily per room, single and double; suites $450–$2,450 for 1-bedroom, $750–$3,075 for 2-bedroom. Villas $700–$2,150, homes $1,250–$3,800 daily. Rates are European

Plan (room only). Add 17% taxes and service charge. 7-night Romance in Paradise package, $3,900–$6,800 for 2 persons, includes massage, Modified American Plan (breakfast and dinner), unlimited golf and tennis. Sporting Spree package $550–$1,025 per night, per room for 2, with 2 meals. Tax and service charge included in packages. Deposit: 3 nights payment. AE, DC, MC, V.

Meal Plans Modified American Plan $80 for breakfast and dinner daily; included in some packages. The breakfast buffet features tropical fruits and juices in season, Grenadian spice muffins, omelets, meats, and grills. Alternative choices are homemade granola, West Indian frittata, and vegetarian burger. Lunch can be herbed smoked chicken with mixed seasonal greens, salad of Nevis tomato, cucumber, and sweet peppers with marinated Spanish onions; or selections from the Mediterranean appetizer buffet. Dinner choices include grilled Caribbean fish, seafood gumbo, Caesar salad, and rotisserie specialties such as local range hen and lamb. Alternative cuisine selections include blackened local red snapper with sautéed spaghetti squash, Asian seared salmon with warm bean-sprout salad, local yellow tomato with Maui onion and roast pepper vinaigrette, spinach salad with jerk chicken, paw paw. Vegetarian menu available.

Services and Facilities **Exercise Equipment:** 4 StairMasters, 4 Quinton treadmills, 2 Schwinn Air Dyne bicycles, Concept 2 rowing machine, Bodymaster multiunit, free weights (5–50 lbs), benches. **Services:** Massage (Swedish, aromatherapy, sports); salon for hair, nail, and skin care. **Swimming Facilities:** Freshwater swimming pool, 25-m lap pool, ocean beach. **Recreation Facilities:** 18-hole golf course, 10 tennis courts (6 composition courts, 4 red clay; 3 lighted), water sports, volleyball, croquet, scuba, fishing. Horseback riding nearby. **Evening Programs:** Dancing, folklore show, movie features (Mon. and Fri.), pub with 2 pool tables, darts, shuffleboard table.

In the Area Nevis Peak (wild monkeys), Charlestown (shopping, crafts, colonial architecture), St. Kitts (colonial architecture, Brimstone Hill Fortress [c. 1680]).

Getting Here *From San Juan.* American Eagle flights to St. Kitts, resort shuttle by car to 40-passenger launch (transfer $45 roundtrip). Also, scheduled flights from St. Martin and Antigua directly to Nevis.

Special Notes Ground-floor rooms accommodate people with disabilities. Complimentary daylong program for children ages 3–10. Nurse on duty daily. Passport and departure tax required. Dress code in Great House.

La Casa de Vida Natural

Holistic health
Preventive medicine

Puerto Rico
Luquillo Secluded in the foothills of the Caribbean National Forest, practically in the shadow of towering El Yunque, the highest peak on the island, La Casa de Vida Natural has carved out a 10-acre center for natural health, offering vegetarian meals; mud, herbal, and seaweed treatments; and psychological counseling. With one of the island's best ocean beaches just down the hill at Luquillo, and hiking trails leading into the lush rain forest of El Yunque, this low-key, informal getaway has scheduled sessions winter and summer. Accommodations consist of an old farmhouse and guest house, with space for a dozen guests and staff.

The health center offers nonintrusive diagnostic procedures as well as kinesiology and massage. Workshops on physical and mental health are scheduled periodically, and individual counseling is available by appointment. The focus may be on building a psychological immune system, love and hate in health, or organic farming. Specialists on staff include a naturopathic doctor and a certified acupuncturist.

Taking an integrated biological and psychological approach to prevention and cure of disease, the center's services are geared to serve a wide range of interests. Therapies such as cleansing the body with burial in sand and immersion in mud can be combined with colonics and urine analysis. Aerobics classes and Jazzercise are organized in an open-air pavilion.

The program developed by New York–based psychoanalyst Jane G. Goldberg was introduced in 1988. At present, only 16 guests can be accommodated, and plans are to keep the center small, emphasizing personal attention to each guest.

Surrounded by natural beauty, panoramic views of the ocean, and the mountains, the pristine air and water are in natural harmony with the earth. Luquillo Beach, once a thriving coconut plantation, is protected by barrier reefs. The crescent-shape, white-sand beach is perfect for swimming and picnics. El Yunque, protected by the U.S. National Park Service, encompasses 28,000 acres. Reaching an elevation of 3,526 feet, its rain forest includes 240 different tree species, as well as orchids and wildflowers. Brief tropical showers keep things lush, moist, and cool.

Hot sulfur springs, known to the earliest Taino Indians, are an hour's drive from the center. At the Parador Baños de Coamo you can bathe in the same pool where Franklin D. Roosevelt, Thomas Edison, Alexander Graham Bell, and Frank Lloyd Wright took the waters. Now a modern mountain inn, the Parador offers Puerto Rican meals as well as overnight lodging. (Rte. 856, tel. 809/825–2186).

La Casa de Vida Natural

Box 1919, Rio Grande, Luquillo, Puerto Rico 00745
Tel. 809/887–4359 or 212/260–5823

Administration Managers, Elizabeth and Russel Pentz

Season Year-round

Accommodations Renovated farmhouse and cottage have 7 guest rooms, simply furnished with 2 beds or queen-size bed; no air-conditioning; shared baths.

Rates 5-day workshop $595 single, $535 per person, double occupancy. Bed-and-Breakfast daily rate weekdays $75 single, $45 per person double; weekends $125 single, $100 per person double. Add 7% tax, 15% service charge. Advance payment $125 for workshops or 2 nights' lodging. Nonprogram lodging $100 per couple, without meals. MC, V.

Meal Plans 3 meals daily included in workshop fee. Vegetarian diet emphasizes raw fruits and vegetables grown on the property; whole-grain home-baked bread, sprouts, juices, salads. Special diets are accommodated.

Services and Facilities **Services:** Massage (full body, $50), colonics, mud pack, sand burial, polarity, herbal/seaweed wrap, facial. Holistic medical counseling, nutritional and psychological consultation. **Swimming Facilities:** Outdoor pool; ocean beaches nearby. **Spa Facilities:** Baños de Coamo (1 hr drive). **Recreation Facilities:** Hiking, river boating. **Evening Programs:** Informal workshops.

In the Area Fajardo (marina, ferry to Vieques and St. Thomas), National Park Service interpretive program at El Yunque.

Getting Here *From San Juan.* By car, Hwy. 3 east to Luquillo Beach, Carr. 186 to Rte. 9960, El Verde (1 hr). Rental car, taxi, public car (*publico*) available. Complimentary airport transfers.

Special Notes No smoking on property.

Spa Caribe at the Hyatt Resorts

Nonprogram resort

Puerto Rico Talking back to the exercise machines might improve your fit-
Dorado ness rating during a workout at the health clubs in Hyatt's sports-oriented resorts. Like a personal coach, the computerized system monitors your progress. Powercise machines converse not only with the users but with each other. Their composite rating is handed to you at the end of the exercise circuit, with suggestions for additional improvement. These high-tech shape-ups are featured at both the Hyatt Regency Cerromar Beach and the Hyatt Dorado Beach, sister resorts 2 miles apart, on the north shore of the island, 22 miles west of San Juan. In addition to computerized equipment, they offer aerobics classes and aquaerobics, jogging trails, sauna, and a parcourse. Plus, there's professional pampering.

Geared to serve large groups at conferences and conventions in the resort, the spa also caters to health club regulars. A full day of exercise and bodywork, with facial as well as computerized evaluation, is available with a $195 Spa Sampler package. Groups meeting at both resorts are offered corporate games, seminars, workshops, and spouse programs, all supervised by experts. Spa services are available daily, à la carte. In addition to the usual body and skin care, the specialties include neuromuscular therapy, sports massage, herbal wraps, and loofah body scrub. Peter Burwash–trained tennis pros offer a full agenda on 21 courts.

Spa Caribe at the Hyatt Resorts
Hyatt Resorts in Puerto Rico, Dorado, P.R. 00646
Tel. 809/796–1234 or 800/233–1234
Telex 3859758, Fax 809/796–4647

Administration Cerromar Beach Hotel, Carlos Cabrera; Dorado Beach Hotel, Michael Walsh; spa manager, Lizmari Santaliz

Season Year-round

Accommodations Low-rise construction, luxurious landscaping, and vast swimming pools are hallmarks of these resorts. Hyatt Regency Cerromar Beach has 506 rooms on 7 floors, the Dorado Beach has 300 rooms on 2 floors. Both hotels feature sleek new tropical looks: rattan furniture, pastel fabrics, island prints on bedcovers and window drapery; baths have marble-top counters, tile floors, contemporary lighting.

Rates At Cerromar Beach, $170–$420 daily, at Dorado Beach $165–$648 daily, single or double occupancy. Regency Club from $465 per room. Add 9% tax, 15% service charge. Guarantee by credit card. AE, MC, V.

Meal Plans Hyatt Cuisine Naturale menu of light fare, including fish and salads, available. Modified American Plan (breakfast and dinner) $60 per person for adults, $29 for children.

Services and **Exercise Equipment:** Powercise system (8 machines),
Facilities Lifestride treadmill, 4 Lifecycles, Liferower, Hydra-Fitness muscular and cardiovascular training units. Outdoor par-

course with Dynacourt equipment. **Services:** Massage (Swedish, reflexology, sports, neck and shoulder), herbal wrap, loofah body scrub, facial cleansing treatments, aromatherapy. Salon for hair, nail, and skin care. **Swimming Facilities:** Outdoor freshwater pools, ocean beaches. **Recreation Facilities:** 21 tennis courts, 6 golf courses, bicycling, volleyball, pool volleyball, water sports. **Evening Programs:** Resort entertainment, casino.

In the Area   Scuba, deep-sea fishing, sightseeing tours, Old San Juan (colonial architecture, art galleries, boutiques, museums), El Yunque rain forest, Camuy caves, Aricebo Observatory, San German (architecture, university).

Getting Here   *From San Juan.* By car, Hwy. 22 (De Diego Expwy.), Rte. 693 to Dorado (30 mins). By air, Dorado Airport. By public car (*publico*) from Old San Juan (1 hr). Airport transfers ($45) by Dorado Transport Van. Rental car, taxi available. Shuttle service between hotels.

Special Notes   Specially equipped rooms by advance request for people with disabilities. Elevators to all levels. Supervised Camp Hyatt (fee) for children June–Labor Day. No smoking in spa and designated dining areas; no-smoking rooms available. Daily spa admission: $6. Spa hours daily 7–7.

Jalousie Plantation

Luxury pampering
Taking the waters

St. Lucia   Nestled between the Piton Mountains and a 320-acre nature
Soufrière   preserve, Jalousie Plantation resort is an intimate hideaway for the rich and famous. In a startlingly scenic forest, the resort occupies the site of a 17th-century sugar plantation. Private cottages with private plunge pools terrace up the hill, and the old sugar mill has guest rooms as well as a restaurant. Under new ownership, the resort was closed for renovations in mid-1996. An expanded spa facility and program will be introduced in 1997.

Nearby are the thermal baths at Mt. Soufrière and Diamond Falls. A dormant volcano, with pits and open craters of boiling, sulferous mud, Soufrière has spring-fed pools of heated mineral water that have been used since French forces occupied the island during the 17th century. King Louis XVI had the baths built during this time. Cooler, sweeter-smelling water feeds the pools at Diamond Falls.

Jalousie Plantation
Box 251, Soufrière, St. Lucia
Tel. 809/459–7666
Fax 809/459–5007

Le Sport

Luxury pampering
Sports conditioning
Taking the waters

St. Lucia   Thalassotherapy came to the tiny nation of St. Lucia in a big
Cariblue Beach   way when the all-inclusive Le Sport resort opened in 1989. At the elegant Oasis bathhouse, you are massaged with seawater by jets in the hydrotherapy tub and relaxed with a seaweed wrap. Set on a hill overlooking the sea, the Oasis provides sophisticated European equipment for seawater therapy as part of Le Sport's vacation program called the "Body Holiday."

The food segment of the Body Holiday program is called "cuisine legère," which simply means that calories don't count. Emulating the renowned Michel Guerard, the chefs provide meals balanced in complex carbohydrates and low in sodium and sugar. The regular menu, however, also has interesting options (*see* Meal Plans, *below*). Wine is included with lunch and dinner, and an open bar is stocked with premium brand liquors, fresh fruit juices, and mineral waters.

A checkup with the staff nurse precedes any treatment. Stress-linked fatigue and muscle tension, poor circulation, and lymphatic drainage are noted, and measurements are taken for blood pressure, heart rate, and weight. A prescribed course of treatments can include the "hydrator," a bubbling bath with herbs and sea algae, in which underwater jets needle away at the fatty tissue found on the upper arms, thighs, and calves. Another pool fitted with underwater jets is for exercise in seawater, which is denser than fresh water and thus gives greater support for the body. And the therapeutic nutrients of seaweed act as catalysts to create changes in the skin as you are wrapped, cocoonlike, in a coating of algae and sea mud. The seawater spray with a jet hose, said to improve circulation, intimidates some guests. The scheduled treatments are included in the price of your holiday package; salon services can be booked à la carte.

Meditation, exercise sessions, and outings are scheduled daily at the Oasis. Designed in a Moorish style, the facility has private treatment rooms and a studio where yoga and tai chi classes are provided at no charge. You can join power walks and guided bike trips, classes including step, stretch-and-tone, low-impact, and water aerobics.

St. Lucia's natural resources also include sulfur baths. Twin volcanic peaks called Petit Piton and Gros Piton rise dramatically above the tiny village of Soufrière on the southwest coast where signs point to the Diamond Mineral Baths, constructed on order of Louis XVI during the 18th century for the benefit of French soldiers garrisoned in the West Indies. From bubbling, underground springs, the sulfurous water flows into natural pools near a seven-acre crater of boiling yellow-gray mud and hissing steam vents. Bathing here is said to cure whatever ails you.

A short jaunt up into the hills, across the ridge, brings you into the rain forest. Between Soufrière and Fond St. Jacques, it's a three-hour trek through a tropical wonderland of dense foliage, flowering plants, and colorful birds. Local guides can map out and supervise hikes for you, and serious hikers can trek to the top of Gros Piton (2,460 ft.) through four different vegetation zones, from dry coastal to thick cloud forest. At the top, you'll be rewarded with distant views of St. Vincent and the Grenadines, while closer at hand, frigate birds perform a delicate aerial ballet.

Le Sport's Oasis is a laissez-faire spa, not for those who want a regimented program. The eat-and-drink-all-you-want policy may particularly suit the less motivated spa goer. A new beauty salon, Clarins Institute de Beauté, provides head-to-toe services (packages $37–$100), from eyelash care to pedicure, and five kinds of facials, including one especially for men.

Le Sport

Box 437, Castries, St. Lucia
Tel. 809/450–8551
Telex LC 6330; Fax 809/450–0368

Administration Owner-director, Craig Bernard; manager, Michael Bryant; spa manager, Martha Willie

Season Year-round

Accommodations 102 rooms oceanfront or with garden view in pavilions linked to dining room and lounge. Rooms have tropical contemporary look, rattan furniture. Air-conditioning, private balcony or patio, full modern bath with hair dryer, robes; all rooms with telephone, radio.

Rates $225–$335 daily per person, double or triple occupancy; single supplement $75 daily. 3-bedroom Plantation House, daily $425–$460, single supplement $200. Credit-card guarantee for first night. Tax and gratuities included in rates. AE, MC, V.

Meal Plans 3 meals daily included in program price. Breakfast buffet: fresh fruits and juices, bran and Muesli cereals, omelets, smoked salmon, pastries, coffee, milk, tea. Lunch buffet selections include fresh salads, stuffed chicken legs in leek-and-cream sauce, boiled wild rice, julienne of carrots and zucchini. Dinner options may typically include broccoli soufflé, scallop of veal with champagne sabayon, fresh asparagus. Spa cuisine choices may be steamed kingfish with carrot and pimiento sauce, or sea scallops with a julienne of carrots and snow peas in a raspberry vinaigrette sauce.

Services and Facilities **Exercise Equipment:** 10-station Universal multitrainer, Lifecycle, Life treadmills, Life stepper, Life rowing machine, Universal ab crunch machine, thigh machine, fencing outfits, free weights (2–40 lbs). **Services:** Massage, hydrotherapy, facial, reflexology, aromatherapy, Scotch douche, body wrap, loofah scrub, scalp treatment. Clarins salon for hair, nail, and skin care. **Swimming Facilities:** 2 outdoor freshwater pools (one for laps, one for exercise), seawater pool, ocean beach. **Recreation Facilities:** 9-hole golf course, tennis court (lighted), croquet, golf school, bicycling, archery, volleyball, scuba diving, windsurfing, waterskiing. **Evening Programs:** Live entertainment nightly, disco.

In the Area Pigeon Island National Park (museum), Rodney Bay marina, Castries market (built 1894), Government House; Aqua Action Festival in early June.

Getting Here *From Castries.* By car, coastal road to Gros Ilet (20 mins). Complimentary transfers on arrival/departure at Hewanora Airport (90 mins). Taxi, rental car available.

Special Notes Minimum age in spa: 15. Children 6–15 sharing room with parents 50% discount. Daily charge for children up to 5 years: $15. Access for persons with disabilities is limited.

Privilege Resort and Spa

Luxury pampering
Sports conditioning
Taking the waters

St. Martin/St. Maarten
Anse Marcel
Panoramic views come with spa and sports workouts at the new Privilege Resort and Spa, which is perched on hills overlooking the beach and marina at Anse Marcel on the French side of bi-national St. Martin/St. Maarten. This unique hideaway provides European treatments to rejuvenate sun-damaged skin and aching muscles, as well as six-day "cures"— courses for slimming, anti-stress, or simply relaxing. For a sampler of French balneotherapy, try an underwater massage in the high-tech Doyer tub, or the Swiss shower temple, a multijet cabinet equipped with a control panel for cascades of

varying intensity. The sea-oriented treatments available feature purified marine algae and seaweed from Brittany.

Sailing and sports training can be combined with the spa program or arranged to fit your own schedule. Aerobics classes are held in the late afternoon or at 8:30 AM. One of the most popular sessions, open to all resort guests without charge, is "aquagym" in the outdoor swimming pool cantilevered between the spa and restaurant. Close by the pool is the sports complex with tennis, squash, and racquetball courts, and an open-air pavilion with exercise equipment. A trainer is available for body-building and a few rounds of boxing-bag technique.

Opened in 1992, both the hotel and spa at Privilege Resort provide privacy and old-world service not found in neighboring resorts. Creole-style cottages provide most of the guest rooms; some visitors are housed in ultra-privacy at the residence of the resort owner. Suites have two marble-walled bathrooms in addition to a large living room. While all lodging is air-conditioned, there is no screening to protect against mosquitoes if you prefer fresh air at night.

Programs for four to seven nights offer a wide variety of sports and spa options, plus a shopping excursion. On Sunday, when the spa is closed, guests sail to neighboring islands, with lunch on board, at no extra charge. A three-day sailing package is available for those desiring an extended cruise. Other seasonal packages take advantage of low summer rates. If you want to do it all, the eight-day Spa Trek package is a VIP adventure, complete with sightseeing and airport transfers by helicopter.

Privilege Resort and Spa

Anse Marcel, 97150 St. Martin, French West Indies
Tel. 590/87–3838; Fax 590/87–4412
Reservations: 800/874–8541

Administration	Owner-director, Robert David
Season	Year-round
Accommodations	80 spacious guest rooms, including 2 suites, with private terrace in 2-story hotel units or villa. Furnished in tropical style, bedrooms come with seating area and pullout sofa bed, king-size bed, minibar, room safe, full modern bathroom with hair dryer, separate toilet. All rooms have ceiling fan, air-conditioning with remote control, TV, telephone, terra-cotta tile floor.
Rates	7-night Spa Trek Program $1,795–$2,065 per person, double occupancy, $2,225–$2,695 single. 5-night Health Spa package $1,240–$1,745 double, $1,550–$2,375 single, suite $1,475–$2,245. Packages include treatments, airport transfers, meals, tax. Daily rate with Continental breakfast $189–$367 double for 2, $151–$294 single, suites $305–$556. Credit card guarantee for 1 night. AE, MC, V.
Meal Plans	Breakfast and dinner daily included in spa packages. Continental breakfast with fresh orange juice, croissant, and choice of eggs. No spa menu; dietetic cuisine can be green salad or grilled tuna steak with steamed vegetables. Gourmet dining terrace has Caribbean fish soup, salmon escalope in a Creole sauce, carpaccio of fish Tahitian style, snails in pastry with white wine and mushrooms, shrimp in a basil sauce, scallop ravioli with leek, duck breast with mango compote.
Services and Facilities	**Exercise Equipment:** Multigym, French air pressure weight-training units, free weights and benches, 2 stationary bikes, punching bags and gloves. **Services:** Swedish massage, shiatsu,

lymphatic drainage, seaweed or mud wraps, manicure, pedicure, hydrotub, underwater massage, cures (slimming, antistress, anti-cellulite). **Swimming Facilities**: 2 outdoor pools, ocean beach. **Recreation Facilities**: 6 tennis courts, 4 squash/2 racquetball courts (all lighted), water sports. Nearby golf (18 holes) at Mullet Bay, horseback riding. **Evening Programs**: Disco dancing, casinos.

In the Area   Marigot (shopping), Orient Beach (clothing-optional beach), St. Bart, Anguilla.

Getting Here   *From Princess Julianna Airport.* Taxi (30 mins); complimentary transfers included in packages. Rental car available at resort. Helicopter service.

Special Notes   Access to all facilities for people with disabilities, but terrain is hilly. Spa open Mon.–Sat. 8–8. Electrical current 220 V (converter plug in bathrooms). Passport or voter registration and photo ID required for customs clearance, plus $10 departure tax.

Omega Journeys at Maho Bay

Holistic health
Spiritual awareness

U.S. Virgin Islands
Maho Bay, St. John

Workshops in health, music, movement, and personal growth are mixed with fun in the sun during four weeklong programs planned by the New York–based Omega Institute. The annual migration to the sunny beaches of St. John is joined by faculty members who lead explorations into the body, mind, and spirit. Living close to nature in a tent village, the workshop participants experience many dimensions of natural healing.

Early birds can start the day with sunrise meditation, tai chi, or yoga. Workshops run two hours each morning and afternoon, allowing a choice of several subjects. Informal and experiential, the group sessions are devoted to bringing health, mindfulness, and peace into the many dimensions of contemporary life.

Drawn from a variety of professions, ages, and backgrounds, the participants find common ground in the open-minded, natural atmosphere. Maho Bay Camp Resort is a unique tent-cottage community dedicated to the concept of simple comforts and life in harmony with nature. Perched in thickly wooded hillsides, the canvas-walled cottages are set on plank decks that cantilever over the forest. The 16-by-16-foot units blend in so naturally that they seem to be part of the environment.

Within the Virgin Islands National Park, the campground has unrestricted access to miles of pristine beaches and well-marked hiking trails, where you may pursue both ecological and historical interests. The National Park Service conducts free tours and lectures on island flora, fauna, and marine biology, as well as on St. John's colorful history and culture.

Try to make time to drive over Bordeaux Mountain, with its rain forest and spectacular views, to Coral Bay and East End, where descendants of the Danish settlers still farm in the old style.

Omega Journeys at Maho Bay
Maho Bay, St. John
Reservations: Omega Institute, 260 Lake Dr.,
Rhinebeck, NY 12572
Tel. 914/266–4444 or 800/944–1001

Administration President, Stephan Rechtschaffen, M.D.

Season Jan.–mid-Feb.

Accommodations 96 tent/cottages tucked into foliage on 14 acres overlooking white-sand beach. Wooden floors, 2 beds, living/dining area (equipped with 2-burner propane stove), lounge chairs, sofa. Linens and bedding supplied, no maid service. Boardwalks connect to toilets, showers, dining pavilion, commissary.

Rates 1 week with workshops, lodging, meals, and round-trip airfare from New York, $1,475 per person, double occupancy. Lodging for single persons and children available. 50% payment at time of booking. MC, V.

Meal Plans Vegetarian meals 3 times daily. Omega's natural-food chefs prepare sumptuous buffets of vegetables and tropical fruits. Some fish and dairy products are available. Lunch includes salads, home-baked whole wheat bread. Dinner menus offer vegetarian lasagna, baked eggplant Parmesan, tofu casserole.

Services and Facilities **Services:** Personal consultation on nutrition, body movement, energy training, yoga instruction. **Swimming Facilities:** Ocean beaches. **Recreation Facilities:** Tennis, hiking, volleyball. **Evening Programs:** Informal workshops, concerts.

In the Area National Park Service interpretive tours, ferry to Tortola, catamaran trips, Annaberg Plantation (Danish-era ruins, special programs), Trunk Bay (underwater trail).

Getting Here *From Cruz Bay.* By bus, shuttle service from ferry landing or along Northshore Rd. (15 mins). Car rental, taxi, minimoke, bicycle rental available.

Special Notes No smoking indoors. Remember to bring flashlight, insect repellent, hiking shoes.

3 **Health &
Fitness
Cruises**

Staying fit at sea is no longer a matter of doing 10 laps around the promenade deck. Today's luxury liners feature fitness facilities and programs that are the equal of anything ashore. Seagoing spas were an innovation of the 1970s; many older ships are being phased out in 1997 under new safety laws, while a new wave of superliners is scheduled to arrive. Selecting a cruise that suits your schedule and budget requires research (see *Fodor's Worldwide Cruises and Ports of Call*) and the services of a knowledgable travel agent accredited by the Cruise Lines International Association (CLIA, tel. 212/921–0066).

Since water is the basic ingredient in many spa cures, it was argued, a spa on the high seas should only make the experience more enjoyable. With abundant fresh air and sunshine, pools filled with filtered seawater, and aerobics classes on deck, the cruise would be an invigorating escape from health club routines at home. For cruise connoisseurs, however, diet was a dirty word. And the gourmet meals and lavish buffets aboard ship have been the downfall of many calorie counters. Then came the American Heart Association's "Eating Away From Home" program adapted for shipboard dining by most cruise lines. Outstanding examples are Michel Roux's vegetarian menu for Celebrity Cruises' liners, the menu of spa cuisine aboard Cunard's *Queen Elizabeth 2*, the Holland America Line's "Light and Healthy" cuisine, and Carnival Cruises' Spa Nautica menu.

Advance planning is important for those on a special diet. Specific foods and general preferences should be discussed with a travel agent, who can then secure a confirmation of your meal plan from the cruise line. All the leading lines offer such services at no extra charge.

Smoke-free cruising is a new option. Introduced by the Majesty Cruise Line in cooperation with the Smoke Free Travel Council, cruises from Miami aboard the *Royal Majesty* offer no-smoking cabins as well as a totally smoke-free dining room. On the Norwegian Cruise Line's *S/S Norway* and *Seaward*, one entire dining room is no-smoking, and you can request a no-smoking cabin. Carnival Cruise Lines banned smoking in dining rooms on its entire fleet. Most ships now designate a no-smoking section in the dining room, so specify your preference when booking the cruise.

Norwegian Cruise Line has annual Fitness and Beauty cruises in October. Guest lecturers on nutrition, sports medicine, hairstyling, and makeup make the trip along with football, golf, and tennis stars. Basketball cruises, baseball cruises, and football cruises allow passengers to team up for fun and fitness aboard the *Seaward* and its sister ship the *Norway*. Taking spas to sea, Sheila Cluff (The Oaks at Ojai, Palms at Palm Springs, CA) leads programs aboard Caribbean, Alaska, and Mexican Riviera cruises (tel. 800/892–4995).

Shore excursions on these cruises offer more than shopping and sightseeing. Several lines, including Norwegian Cruise Line and the *Cunard Countess*, provide entrée to local racquet clubs, golf courses, and fitness centers. Some ships have access to private ports of call, islands where passengers may swim, snorkel, and sunbathe on their own "deserted island." Others have scheduled nature walks and bicycle tours.

While the Caribbean and the Bahamas account for 60% of all cruise destinations, a steadily growing fleet of ships sails from California and Canadian ports. Alaska, the Mexican Riviera, and the Hawaiian islands offer exciting variations on the cruise theme. The rates quoted here are published, and may be discounted at certain times of the year. In addition, some cruise lines offer discounts for early bookings, and for repeat passengers.

As a new wave of luxury liners comes on line, look for more adventure cruises exploring less-traveled ports and nature preserves. Small, specially designed expedition vessels are sailing to Alaska and along the Pacific coast for Clipper Adventure Cruises, Seaquest Cruises, and Windstar Cruises.

This chapter highlights the best spas at sea in North American waters. Cruise fares are given as a basis for planning, as of mid-1996, and options include cruise-only fares, without an airline flight to your port of embarkation, or an air/sea fare combination. Also, there are port taxes added to fares. For newcomers to fitness programs, the cruise may be a good way to inaugurate a personal fitness routine that can then be continued effectively at home. Staff instructors offer one-on-one workouts—perhaps the best bargain in fitness education. And there's a healthy bonus from mother nature: The bracing effect of the fresh air generated by sea water and sun may be just what the doctor ordered for our high-pressure society.

Carnival Cruise Lines

The 2,040-passenger megaships *Sensation, Ecstasy, Fascination, Fantasy, Inspiration,* and *Imagination* give Carnival Cruise Lines passengers access to spas that are bigger than the on-board casinos. Similar but with 2,642-passenger capacity are 101,000-ton sister ships *Carnival Destiny and Triumph.* Every cruise ship has a spa, where you can exercise with a view of the sea on a Keiser progressive resistance system, Nautilus equipment, rowing and stair-climbing machines, free weights, and stationary bicycles. On the two uppermost decks, with floor-to-ceiling windows, the spa has six whirlpools (also with a sea view), men's and women's saunas, steam rooms, showers, and locker rooms. The large glass-and-mirror-enclosed aerobics studio is busy all day. Classes include "Cardio-Funk" and "Cardio-Pump," step, and an hour-long advanced high-energy workout. You can join aquaerobics in the swimming pool or organized walks on the ships' upper decks. A ⅛-mile jogging track encircles the deck. Familiarizations with the equipment and talks by the spa staff are offered regularly throughout each cruise. On deck are swimming pools, and the *Carnival Destiny* has an impressive water slide.

A beauty salon and private massage rooms complete the enclosed portion of the 12,000-square-foot spa. Operated by London-based Steiner spa professionals, the services offered include a range of facials, massages, and beauty treatments in a spacious two-level spa. Among new "European-style" treatments are Ionithermie slimming through use of a cleansing algae concentrate, and "La Therapie" facial with essential oils and low-level electrical stimulation. Several rooms designed for seaweed treatments and herbal wraps have private showers, and one has a hydrotherapy bath. Appointments can be made immediately after embarkation, and services are available on days when the ship is in port.

Calorie-conscious passengers can take advantage of a Nautica Spa Selection on the menu at each meal. In addition, a circular salad bar in the grill area is open for lunch and dinner, and there is a pasta station with made-to-order selections.

While the spa has separate saunas for men and women, the coed whirlpools made of red-and-black ceramic tile allow passengers to bask in bubbling water while gazing up to the heavens through a skylight.

Carnival Cruise Lines. *3655 NW 87th Ave., Miami, FL 33178, tel. 305/599-2600 or 800/227-6482 (800/325-1214 in FL).* Commissioned in 1990–1996. Liberian registry, Italian officers, international staff. Ports: Caribbean, Mexico.

Fitness Facilities: 35 weight-training units, 3 Precor 825L bikes, 2 StairMaster PT4000, 2 Precor steppers, rower, free weights (2–25 lbs), Roman chairs, benches. **Services:** Massage, reflexology, loofah scrub, facial, cathiodermie facial, herbal pack, aromatherapy, pressotherapy (air bags), G5 weight loss massage, eucalyptus steam inhalation. **Sports:** 2 outdoor pools, trapshooting, table tennis, shuffleboard. Fares include airfare from major cities: $659–$1,339 for 4-day cruise to the Bahamas; $1,399–$2,439 for 7-day cruise.

Special Notes: No smoking in dining rooms. Children's playroom available on all ships. Some cabins equipped for people with disabilities.

Celebrity Cruises

With the debut of the Century and Galaxy in 1996, Celebrity Cruises laid claim to the largest spa at sea. These 1,750-passenger liners will be joined by a sister ship, 1,870–passenger Mercury, in the fall of 1997. The top-deck AquaSpa^{SM} has an indoor exercise pool with underwater jets. Workouts in the warm seawater enhance circulation, leaving you relaxed and refreshed. Nearby are a coed steam room and separate locker rooms with shower/sauna for men and women.

The 10,000-square-foot spas are operated by Steiner of London. Each has a window-walled weights room, providing panoramic views as you exercise. Classes are scheduled in a cushion-floored aerobics studio, and passengers relax in six outdoor whirlpools. For an Asian de-stressor, try Rasul, based on a cleansing ceremony that includes a seaweed-soap shower, medicinal mud pack, herbal steam bath, and massage. The Aquameditation bath, also new to the *Century* and the *Galaxy*, includes rotating shower heads in a pre-massage soak. The extensive selection of beauty services is provided by a professional staff, who also schedule fitness classes that range from cardio-funk low-impact aerobics to designer body conditioning and a 30-minute session of aquaerobics in the outdoor swimming pool. In addition to a dozen pieces of exercise equipment, there are ½-mile outdoor jogging tracks.

Dieters choose between a full vegetarian menu designed by London restaurateur Michel Roux and the regular menu with highlighted items that are low in sodium and cholesterol.

The 52 Sky Suites with marble-tiled baths and butler service are top of the line. Also 61 cabins with balconies.

Celebrity Cruises. *800 Blue Lagoon Dr., Miami, FL 33126, tel. 305/262-8322 or 800/437-3111.* Deluxe staterooms and outside cabins; most cabins are compact, all have private shower and toilet. Liberian registry, Greek officers, and European staff. Ports: Caribbean, Alaska, Bermuda.

Fitness Facilities: Universal 5-station gym, 2 Tredex treadmills, NordicTrack cross-country ski machine, 3 Aerobicycles, 2 rowing machines, free weights. 2 outdoor swimming pools, whirlpools, indoor thalassotherapy pool. **Services:** Massage, Cathiodermie revitalizing facial, Ionithermie slimming treatment, bodybrushing, personal fitness analysis, body-fat analysis, personal training; salon for hair, nail, and skin care.

Fares for 7-day cruise from $1,049 per person, double occupancy, not including airfare. Sails from Miami on Saturday and Sunday.

Special Notes Wheelchair access in 8 cabins for persons with disabilities.

Costa Cruises

Italian-accented cruising with the Costa fleet reached a peak in 1996 with the debut of the 1,950-passenger flagship M.V. Costa Victoria. Featuring spa treatments with the exclusive Terme di Saturnia cosmetics developed at one of Italy's leading spa resorts, the Pompeii Spa offers a variety of "ahh la carte"ᔆᴹ body therapies, including seaweed or algae, and moor mud. Workouts come with great views of the sea in a window-walled fitness center, which has weight-training equipment, stationary bicycles, and stairsteppers. Operated by Alders International, the spa is staffed with well-trained professionals who can develop a personalized exercise program for you. Services can be selected in packages from half-day to six days, pre-booked by your travel agent.

At the center of the Pompeii Spa is an indoor swimming pool surrounded by columns; certain lanes are dedicated to lap swimmers. The room itself has a large Italian mosaic covering the walls and the ceiling. Separate dressing rooms for men and women include Turkish bath, Finnish sauna, and showers. From the center of the spa, a 500-meter jogging track connects to the gymnasium and an aerobics studio on Traviata Deck (#6).

Built in Italy, this glamorous liner recalls the golden era of transatlantic ships. Mealtime resembles a Roman festival, but heart-healthy options are on the menu. And for exercise, there's a pizza dough throwing contest, tarantella dancing, and boccie ball games.

Costa Cruise Lines. *World Trade Center, 80 S.W. 8th St., Miami, FL 33130, tel. 305/358–7325 or 800/462–6782.* Deluxe outside staterooms and suites with whirlpool bath; standard cabins, with 2 lower beds that convert to a queen-size bed, shower and toilet. 20 staterooms equipped for persons with disabilities. Italian registry, Italian officers and dining room staff, European stewardesses.

Fitness Facilities: Strength-training exercise machines, cardiovascular equipment including treadmills, step machine, rower. **Services:** Massage, reflexology, body wrap, body scrub, thalassotherapy, hydrotherapy bath, deep-cleansing facial, rehydrating facial, personal training.

Cruises to the Eastern and Western Caribbean. Fares for a 7-day cruise from Ft. Lauderdale without airfare, reserved 90 days or more in advance, $795–$2,790 per person, double occupancy.

Crystal Harmony

This 960-passenger liner has a 3,000-square-foot ocean-view spa and fitness center that offers aerobic and Jazzercise instruction and treatments that include thalassotherapy, moortherapy, and aromatherapy. Passengers relax in men's and women's saunas and steam rooms, tee-off at a golf simulator, jog on a full promenade deck, play on paddle tennis or volleyball courts, swim in a lap pool, soak in Jacuzzis, or socialize in an indoor/outdoor swimming pool with built-in bar. A fitness trainer is aboard, and there are special slimming programs using the DeCleor program. Operated by Steiner of London, the pampering program includes facials, body wrap, and a French hand treatment. The spa also offers a salon for hair, nail, and skin care, and a men's barbershop.

All staterooms have bathroom with tub and shower, double vanity. Dinner is served at your choice of time in Italian or Chinese restaurants.

Crystal Cruises. *2121 Avenue of the Stars, Los Angeles, CA 90067, tel. 310/785-9300.* 8 passenger decks with 480 deluxe staterooms, including 62 penthouse suites. All outside accommodations except 19 inside cabins; many have private verandas; all have king- or queen-size beds. Bahamian registry, Norwegian and Japanese officers, Italian dining staff, international crew.

Fitness Facilities: 3 treadmills, 3 Lifecycles, 2 StairMasters, 2 rowing machines, 4 Lifecircuit weight training machines, free weights. **Services:** Massage, facials, body scrub, herbal wrap; foot, hand, and eye treatments; personal trainer; beauty salon.

Cruises from Acapulco, New Orleans, San Juan, Fort Lauderdale; fares including airfare for 11-day trans-Canal cruise $3,217–$9,930 per person, double occupancy.

Cunard Countess

Active vacationers aboard the *Cunard Countess* can take advantage of a state-of-the-art fitness center. The 2,000-square-foot exercise facility is packed with the latest in LifeFitness equipment. Trainers are on hand daily to assure proper form in your workout. Aerobics class, weight training seminars, and nutritional lectures are part of the program at no additional charge for all passengers. Country & Western entertainment is the ship's specialty, and you can join line dancing aerobics classes with the country sound.

When your workout is over, you can relax in one of two adjacent Jacuzzis, a European-style sauna, and an outdoor swimming pool. Ashore, you can enjoy beach facilities at Cunard resorts and sign up for water skiing, golf, tennis, horseback riding, 5K "fun runs," and hikes in remote jungles. (Shore excursions are booked aboard ship for an additional fee.)

Cunard Line. *555 Fifth Ave., New York, NY 10017, tel. 212/880-7304 or 800/221-4770.* Commissioned in 1976, refurbished 1986. 790 passengers. British registry and officers, international staff.

Fitness Facilities: Lido Deck fitness center with 12-station Paramount circuit, 2 LifeRowers, 5 Lifecycles, 2 Lifesteps, computerized weight training system, outdoor swimming pool, 2 whirlpools. **Services:** Massage, one-on-one training, barbershop/beauty salon. **Sports:** Golf driving range, basketball practice, paddle tennis court, table tennis, shuffleboard.

Cruises round-trip from San Juan every Saturday, alternating itineraries. Fares for a 7-day cruise $795–$2,225 per person double occupancy, not including airfare.

Holland America Line

With a Passport to Fitness program aboard every ship in its fleet, Holland America Line offers one of the best values in health and fitness cruises year-round. Passengers pick up a passport aboard the ship to earn stamps for fitness classes, team sports, and beauty treatments. Even ordering lunch and dinner from the Light and Healthy menu in the dining room earns a stamp (the menu includes such items as grilled seabass with warm tomato salad, or chicken breast salad). Prizes are awarded for 20–40 stamps. Aerobics classes and aquatic work-outs are available to all passengers. Tennis and golf programs and a scuba certification course are offered on shore excursions. The Ocean Spa has a gymnasium with exercise equipment and a small area for aerobics classes. Large windows provide ocean views while you're working out. In fair weather, exercise classes are held on the teak deck. There are locker rooms for men and women, with steam rooms and saunas, plus four massage rooms.

Immaculately maintained and decorated with an extensive collection of art and antiques, the Dutch fleet will expand with the 1,320-passenger, faster *Rotterdam VI* in 1997. These are true ocean liners, with services and amenities in the grand tradition of transatlantic travel.

The Ocean Spas aboard the 1,266-passenger sister ships *Maasdam, Statendam, Veendam,* and *Ryndam* have 4,126 square feet for an aerobics studio, strength training equipment, stationary bicycles, treadmills, stairclimbers, rowing machines, and free weights. Refresh at the juice bar, sets of saunas and steam rooms, and two outdoor whirlpools. The spa is operated by Steiner of London, and offers aromatherapy, body wraps, and massage, as well as hair salon services.

Holland America Line. *300 Elliott Ave. W, Seattle, WA 98119, tel. 206/281–3535 or 800/426–0327.* Netherlands Antilles registry, Dutch and British officers, Indonesian and Filipino staff.

Fitness Facilities: 10-unit Hydra-Fitness circuit, Lifecycles, 2 StairMasters, rowing machines, free and pully weights, slant boards, treadmills, 2 outdoor swimming pools (1 has whirlpool jets), 2 saunas. **Services:** Massage, facials, manicure, pedicure, hairstyling, makeup consultation. **Sports:** Tennis courts, shuffleboard, scuba instruction, volleyball.

Caribbean cruise fares start at $1,212, with 40%–45% savings possible through the advance-booking program. Fares for 7-day Alaska cruise from $1,100, with 25% savings for early bookings. Winter cruises from Ft. Lauderdale, Tampa, and New Orleans. Other cruises: New England and Eastern Canada, Panama Canal, Mexico, Hawaii.

Special Note: Four staterooms for people with disabilities.

SS Norway

The 14-room, 6,000-square-foot Roman Spa, which opened in 1990, aboard the SS *Norway* launched a new era of spa luxury at sea. Featuring the first hydrotherapy baths on a cruise ship, the spa employs European-trained specialists in thalassotherapy, shiatsu, reflexology, aromatherapy, thermal body wraps, and a wide range of beauty services. Services can be booked à la carte; five package programs are available for a complete spa vacation, ranging from a half-day introductory sampler for $124.50 to 10 hours of treatments for $493. The daily fee for use of the spa facility is waived if you book a treatment such as the $66 massage, plus 12% gratuity.

On Dolphin Deck, the new Roman Spa is a sybaritic enclave of 16 private treatment rooms (each equipped with shower), men's and women's saunas and steam rooms, a seawater aquacise pool and Jacuzzi, juice bar, and an exercise room with computerized cardiovascular equipment. The *Norway's* spa treatments incorporate ancient Roman philosophy and a sea theme with Phytomer marine algae and moor mud products by Remé Laure. For relaxation, try 30 minutes in the Nouveux Yu capsule. Advance appointments prior to sailing can be made by calling the spa operators, Steiner Group (tel. 800/275–5293, or in Florida 305/358–9002). The spa is open every day, 8–8 during the cruise.

For more active passengers there is a "In Motion on the Ocean" fitness program that awards prizes for participating in the various physical activities scheduled every day. The ship's Olympic Deck is dedicated to fitness: a glass-walled gymnasium with state-of-the-art exercise equipment, and a 360-degree jogging/walking track. Team games are organized in the "*Norway* Olympics," and snorkeling is offered at a beach party on NCL's private uninhabited island in the Bahamas. Added features during the Fitness and Beauty Cruise at the end of October include workshops on nutrition, sports medicine, and skin care; running clinics; and workouts with sports personalities. During the rest of the year, golf and tennis Pro-Am cruises have professionals aboard to help improve your game, and opportunities for play abound on shore. Fitness walks are organized in each port.

Norwegian Cruise Line. *95 Merrick Way, Coral Gables, FL 33134, tel. 305/447–9660 or 800/327–7030.* Entered service as the *France*, in 1962, refitted as the *Norway* in 1979, renovated and expanded in 1990, refurbished 1996. 2,032 passengers. Norwegian registry and officers, international staff.

Fitness Facilities: Gymnasium with Cybex weight training equipment, 2 Liferowers, 3 Lifecycles, 2 Lifesteps, free weights, Ivanko dumbells, Roman Spa with Bally cardiovascular equipment, 2 outdoor swimming pools, outdoor jogging track. **Services:** Massage, facials, hydrotherapy bath, bodywrap, makeup cleansing; hair, nail, and skin care. **Sports:** Racquetball, basketball, volleyball courts, golf putting and driving areas, skeet shooting.

Cruise-only fares $649–$3,789, not including airfare and transfers. Year-round 7-night cruises departing from Miami on Saturday.

Princess Cruises

After 30 years of "Love Boat" fame, Princess Cruise Lines introduced Grand Class^SM ships *Sun Princess* in 1995 and *Dawn Princess* in spring 1997, to be followed in 1998 by the world's largest cruise ship, *Grand Princess.* Built in Italy, the new sister ships each can carry 1,950 passengers.

Fourteen stories high and nearly three football fields in length, with five swimming pools, two restaurants tiered on three decks, and a computerized golf center, these floating resorts feature both intimate spaces and grand vistas. With over a dozen pieces of exercise equipment in the 3,250-square-foot fitness center, plus an outdoor ⅙-mile jogging track, the fitness facilities are part of the Cruisercise® program that awards prizes for participation in exercise activity. The fleetwide program was designed by Kathy Smith, fitness trainer for the Stars & Stripes U.S. sailing team. On all ships a daily schedule of classes includes walk-a-mile, stretch and tone, high-or low-impact aerobics, and aquacize.

High on the ship, with views overlooking the bow, The Riviera Spa wraps around a swimming pool and Jacuzzi on the Lido deck. The spacious beauty salon has 10 stations for hairstyling and eight treatment rooms, one with a hydrotherapy tub. Sign up for facials, massage, body wraps, and a hydrotherapy soak in seaweed or herbs.

The dining room menu offers heart-healthy items that are low in sodium and cholesterol, prepared according to American Heart Association guidelines. Dining options include a 24-hour food court in the Lido Cafe, and a pizzeria.

Recalling the days of the great ocean liners, the teak decks and decorative accents in brass, warm woods, and marble enhance spacious staterooms. More than 70% of the cabins have a private balcony.

Princess Cruises. *10100 Santa Monica Blvd., Los Angeles, CA 90067, tel. 310/553–1770 or 800/421–0522.* British registry and officers, Italian dining room staff, British stewards.

Fitness Facilities: Gymnasium with Hydra-fitness 11-station multipurpose weights unit, rowing machines, treadmill, Paramount Uniflex sports trainer, Lifecycles, slant boards, free weights; aerobics studio with classes at all levels scheduled daily; 5 outdoor swimming pools (with a 33' pool for laps), 6 whirlpools, sauna. **Services:** Massage, facials, moortherapy facial mask, leg and back treatment, throat and décolleté treatment, foot and hand treatment, body wrap, eye treatment. Salon for hair, nail, and skin care.

Cruises include Alaska, Trans-Panama Canal, Caribbean. Cruise-only fares for 7 days from Ft. Lauderdale, $1,200–$3,200 per person, double occupancy. 7-day Alaska cruise from Vancouver $1,750–$4,600 double, cruise only.

Special Notes: 19 cabins equipped for wheelchair users.

Queen Elizabeth 2

The Steiner spa aboard Cunard's majestic Queen Elizabeth 2 is a treat for body, mind, and spirit. Steiner, after all, holds royal warrants as hairdresser to the queen. But here the accent is on thalassotherapy, a French concept of seawater-based bodywork and exercise in fresh seawater. An indoor swimming pool is part of the fitness center (open to all passengers free of charge), which has a full line of Cybex equipment and computerized exercise bikes, as well as an aerobics studio. The spa is a separate enclave on the ship's lowest deck (7) with a unique hydrotherapy pool in which you follow a circuit of underwater jets. The effect is like getting your muscles massaged while you exercise or relax amid bubbling geysers. The London-trained therapists usher you into a private treatment room (there are 10) for a seaweed body mask, enveloping you in a mixture of Phytomer algae, followed by a full-hour massage to sounds of the sea. Other treatments on the spa's list provide the energizing and remineralizing effect of a hydrotub bath with freeze-dried seaweed, inhalations to clear your sinus problems, or a water blitz massage in which concentrated jets play across your body. Spacious and accented by teak and silver, the white-tile spa pool, coed steam room, and locker rooms with saunas can be used for a daily fee or as part of packages. The Steiner salon is on an upper deck (1) with four private rooms for Ionithermie anti-cellulite body-slimming treatments and Cathiodermie deep-cleansing facials.

Newly created spa cuisine is on the menu in all dining rooms, made to order in the Grill rooms. The benefits of British

Airways' "Well-Being in the Air" program are an added bonus, as your QE2 ticket includes one-way air transportation with the option of following a scientifically designed fitness and food plan during the flight.

On all voyages, including Caribbean and Bermuda cruises, passengers can participate in the fitness center's scheduled classes. One-on-one training is offered for a fee, as well as a nutritional assessment and fitness evaluation. Open from 7AM to 7PM, the indoor saltwater swimming pool can be reached by elevator. Additional swimming pools are on deck.

Following a major face-lift in 1994, the superliner reflects a distinctive lifestyle as well as the heritage and tradition of great ocean liners. Transformation of the Lido into an informal buffet-style restaurant for breakfast and lunch, new bathrooms in all cabins, an Observation Lounge with panoramic vistas, and a pub with dart board are among recent enhancements.

Cunard Line. *555 Fifth Ave., New York, NY 10017, tel. 212/880-7304 or 800/221-4770.* Launched in 1967, re-entered service 1987; major refurbishment 1994. 1,800 passengers. British registry, British and European officers.

Fitness Facilities: 7-unit Cybex weight training circuit, 2 Stair-Masters, 4 Lifecycles, 2 treadmills, free weights, aerobics studio with scheduled classes and personal trainer. **Services:** Massage, Ionithermie, Cathiodermie facial, Phytomer seaweed body mask, Elemis aromatherapy facial, thalassotherapy body scrub, Oligomer hydrotherapeutic bath. Salon for hair, nail, and skin care.

Cruises from New York to New England, Bermuda, Caribbean. 5-day cruise-only fares $1,000–$4,040, suites $13,110–$14,440 per person, double occupancy. Transatlantic air/sea fares (1996) $1,895–$9,330, suites $23,820–$39,080 per person, double.

SSC Radisson Diamond

The entire top deck of the SSC *Radisson Diamond* is devoted to a spa and jogging track, and there is a marina that descends into the sea. The twin-hull design accommodates 177 staterooms. New technology called SSC (Semi-Submersible Craft) minimizes engine and propeller noise and maximizes deck space. From the five-story atrium, you are whisked up a glass elevator to three decks of suites (there are 12 decks total) and a glass-walled dining room. All cabins are suite-size with private balcony, queen-size bed, TV, VCR, stereo, and a full bath with shower.

The Diamond Spa, on Deck 11, offers a selection of services by Steiner of London. Past the reception area are two skin-care rooms, four rooms for bodywork. There are separate saunas and steam rooms for men and women, and exercise equipment. Exercise classes, scheduled twice each morning and afternoon, are held in the main lounge or on deck. You can join stretch/walk at 7:30 AM, then a step class, water aerobics, or line dancing. The open-air swimming pool and Jacuzzi are tiny, but in port you can swim in a floating marina equipped for snorkeling, windsurfing, and water jet boats.

With an open-seating policy in the main dining room, you can order off the menu, request a special diet, or select from the "Simplicity" menu. Evening entertainment is limited to the casino and TV. The ship's rates do not cover personal services in the spa and salon.

Radisson Diamond Cruises. *600 Corporate Dr., Ft. Lauderdale, FL 33334, tel. 305/776-6123 or 800/333-3333.* Debut in 1992. 350 passengers. Finnish registry, international crew.

Fitness Facilities: Exercise room with 4 David cam weight machines, 2 Lifesteps, 2 Liferowers, 4 Lifecycles, free weights. **Services:** Massage, facials, body wraps, hand and foot treatment, aromatherapy. Salon for hair, nail, and skin care.

Cruises from San Juan and Fort Lauderdale on 4-, 5-, and 7-day itineraries. Fares approximately $600 per person, per day, double occupancy. Spa packages $140–$465.

Royal Caribbean Cruise Line

The 1995 introduction of the Royal Caribbean Cruise Line's 70,000-ton, 1,804-passenger *Legend of the Seas* marked the company's first design of a ship for destinations outside the Caribbean and Bahamas. Known for its *Song of Norway* and *Song of America* (which have no spa/exercise facility), and 2,354-passenger *Monarch of the Seas*, RCCL now cruises to Hawaii and Alaska, as well as offering Panama Canal, transatlantic, and European programs. With the arrival of sister ship *Splendour of the Seas* in 1996, the fleet gained a second megaship, and four more arrive through 1998.

From the Centrum, a dramatic, glass-walled atrium on these new liners, elevators whisk you to the Steiner of London spa high atop the ship. There is a fitness program called Ship-Shape, an 18-hole miniature golf course with real links, and heart-healthy cuisine in the restaurants.

On these French-built megaships, the spa is on Sun Deck just aft of the Solarium, an indoor/outdoor dining and entertainment area with swimming pool under a retractable glass canopy. Decorated with green plants, Roman columns, statues and artworks, it's a convenient place to unwind after exercise sessions. Reached from the central lobby, the spa contains a unisex hair salon with seven stations, two treatment rooms for facials and manicure/pedicure, five massage rooms, and changing rooms with saunas and steam baths. There is an aerobics area large enough for 35 participants during scheduled classes, and exercise equipment facing the glass-walled view of the sea.

Steiner offers a variety of packages during the cruise, and the spa remains open for treatments during port days.

Royal Caribbean Cruise Line, *1050 Caribbean Way, Miami, FL 33132, tel. 305/539-6572 or 800/327-6700.* Norwegian registry and officers, international staff.

Fitness Facilities: 10-unit strength training system, 6 recumbent bicycles, 4 step machines, 4 treadmills, 2 incline benches, free weights. **Services:** Massage, reflexology, herbal wrap; salon for hair, nail, and skin care.

Cruises from Miami, Acapulco, Honolulu, Vancouver, Los Angeles. Fares with early booking discount for 10- and 11-night Panama Canal cruise from $1,499 per person, double occupancy; 7-night Alaska or Caribbean cruise from $1,149.

Royal Majesty

The *Royal Majesty* debuted in 1992 as the first ship to ban smoking in the dining room. 132 of the cabins are also smoke-free.

A well-equipped sea-view spa managed by Steiner of London is situated high atop the ship, and healthful Regal Bodies spa cuisine is available in the dining room. The spa has an aerobics studio with wooden floor where aerobics and tai chi classes are scheduled daily. There are massage rooms, 2 saunas, a smallish outdoor swimming pool, and a pair of whirlpools.

Majesty Cruise Line. *Box 025420, Miami, FL 33132, tel. 305/530–8900 or 800/645–8111.* Commissioned in 1992. 1,056 passengers. Panamanian registry, Greek officers, international crew.

Fitness Facilities: Gymnasium with 2 StairMasters, Lifecycle, Fly, recumbent bike, 4 weight training machines, free weights, NordicTrack cross-country machine, rowing machine. **Services:** Massage, personal training; hair, nail, and skin salon.

Cruises from Miami. Fares for 3-night Bahamas cruise, including airfare, $489–$969 per person, double occupancy; 4-night cruise to Nassau, Key West, and private island, $599–$1,099 per person. Summer cruises to Bermuda from Boston, $1,099–$3,299.

Seaward

The *Seaward*, a Finnish-built addition to the Norwegian Cruise Line fleet, is a 42,000-ton beauty complete with cascading waterfall, cushioned running track, and basketball court. Although smaller than her big sister the *Norway*, she has a quarter-mile promenade deck that encircles the ship—a detail missing on many new liners. The top-deck spa/salon, operated by Steiner of London, all glass and gleaming chrome, affords panoramic views of the sea to those working out. Separate saunas and showers are provided for men and women, and massage is available. The accent is on sports: The ship's two swimming pools and adjacent whirlpools have splash areas surrounded by Astroturf, where a "dive-in" center offers snorkeling equipment and instruction. Excursions in port take in some of the finest golf courses and tennis courts in the islands. Pro-Am cruises team passengers with golf and tennis pros on designated weeks throughout the year. Racquet Club cruises and Tee-Up golf cruises offer clinics and workshops at sea and special games and matches ashore.

Dining alternatives include a choice of lighter meals at an informal café and an à la carte restaurant where meals are prepared to order.

Norwegian Cruise Line. *95 Merrick Way, Coral Gables, FL 33134, tel. 305/447–9660 or 800/327–7030.* Inaugurated in 1988. 1,534 passengers. Bahamian registry, Norwegian officers, international crew.

Fitness Facilities: Health spa with Cybex strength training equipment, Lifecycle stationary bicycles, Lifefitness cardiovascular exercise equipment, rowing machines, Ivanko free weight dumbbells, 2 outdoor swimming pools, whirlpools, sauna; no steam room. **Services:** Massage, facials, moortherapy facial mask, throat and decollete treatment; eye, foot, and hand treatments; exfoliation; herbal or thermal body wrap; salon for hair, nail, and skin care. **Sports:** Volleyball, snorkeling, skeet shooting, golf driving.

Cruises from San Juan. Cruise-only fare $689–$2,489 per person, double occupancy.

Seawind Crown

Sailing from Aruba, the classic *Seawind Crown* offers features not found on larger ships, such as squash and volleyball courts, as well as a fitness center. In addition to the coed sauna and cold plunge pool, there are two outdoor swimming pools (one heated) and a jogging track for deck exercise.

Seawind Cruise Line. *1750 Coral Way, Miami, FL 33145, tel. 305/285-9494 or 800/258-8006.* Commissioned as TSS *Vasco da Gama*, rebuilt 1989. Panamanian registry, Portuguese and Greek officers, European dining room staff, Portuguese cabin service. 624 passengers. Cabins have color TV, terry cloth robes, bathroom with hair dryer.

Fitness Facilities: StairMaster, 4-station Universal strength training machine, AerobiCycle, Universal free weights, 2 benches. **Services:** Massage; salon for hair, nail, and skin care.

Cruises from Aruba every Sunday. Fares $945–$2,395 per person, double occupancy, including airfare and early booking discount from U.S. cities. Accommodations for people with disabilities in 2 cabins.

Wind Spirit and Wind Star

A blend of modern technology and the romance of cruising under sail, the yachtlike *Wind Spirit* and *Wind Star* offer a tiny fitness center and a full program of water sports. While under sail, a computerized system raises the six sails automatically in less than two minutes. While anchored in secluded coves, away from the routes of the large cruise ships, the vessel's crew members organize waterskiing and snorkeling expeditions. There is SCUBA equipment aboard for certified divers. Shore excursions to golf and tennis resorts can be arranged through the ship's purser.

Spa services, managed by Allder International of London, feature the Italian-made Terme di Saturnia skin-care products developed at the famed thermal water spa in Tuscany.

Windstar Cruises. *300 Elliott Avenue West, Seattle, WA 98119, tel. 206/298-3057 or 800/258-7248 (Canada, 800/263-0844).* Commissioned in 1988. 148 passengers. Bahamian registry, international crew.

Fitness Facilities: Exercise room with 2 rowing machines, stationary bikes, outdoor swimming pool, sauna. **Services:** Massage, facial, hand, and foot treatment. **Sports:** Water sports program, shore excursions for golf and tennis.

Cruises the Windward and Leeward islands. Fares for 7-day cruise $3,395 per person, double occupancy, with advance reservation discount, $5,093 single. Suite $4,414–$6,790. Airfare not included.

WHEREVER YOU TRAVEL, *H*ELP IS NEVER FAR AWAY.

From planning your trip to

providing travel assistance along

the way, American Express®

Travel Service Offices are

always there to help.

For the office nearest you in the United States, call
1-800-AXP-3429.

Travel

http://www.americanexpress.com/travel